THE GERMAN FINANCIAL SYSTEM

The German Financial System

Edited by

JAN PIETER KRAHNEN
REINHARD H. SCHMIDT

OXFORD

UNIVERSITY PRESS

Great Clarendon Street, Oxford OX2 6DP

Oxford University Press is a department of the University of Oxford.
It furthers the University's objective of excellence in research, scholarship,
and education by publishing worldwide in

Oxford New York

Auckland Bangkok Buenos Aires Cape Town Chennai
Dar es Salaam Delhi Hong Kong Istanbul Karachi Kolkata
Kuala Lumpur Madrid Melbourne Mexico City Mumbai Nairobi
São Paulo Shanghai Taipei Tokyo Toronto

Oxford is a registered trade mark of Oxford University Press
in the UK and in certain other countries

Published in the United States
by Oxford University Press Inc., New York

© OUP 2004

The moral rights of the author have been asserted

Database right Oxford University Press (maker)

First published 2004

British Library Cataloguing in Publication Data

Data available

Library of Congress Cataloging in Publication Data

Data available

ISBN 0-19-925316-1

1 3 5 7 9 10 8 6 4 2

Typeset by Newgen Imaging Systems (P) Ltd., Chennai, India
Printed in Great Britain
on acid-free paper by
Biddles Ltd., King's Lynn, Norfolk

Preface

This book about the German financial system was written by a group of German academics with a genuine research interest in the topic and a certain sense of how complex reality can be. The book aspires to be comprehensive in its coverage, up to date in its information content, shaped by a unified set of questions and theoretical concepts, inspired by theoretical arguments about the role and structure of financial systems and based on genuine theoretical and empirical research. Last but not least, the book should also be accessible to those who do not read and speak German and who may not be trained economists.

The idea of writing and editing this book was born almost three years ago when, through our own work and through the interaction with fellow academics from other countries, we became aware of three facts.

First, there was, and still is, simply no book on the market which satisfies all of the requirements listed above. Even if we were to disregard the language requirement, there is still no book currently available about the German financial system which compares to the inspiring monographs that cover the British, French, and American financial systems. Thus there was, and in our view still is, a void to be filled.

Second, several colleagues and friends from other countries told us that they knew little about finance in Germany and that they would like to know more, especially since in both academic and popular literature Germany is regularly portrayed as a country with a bank-based financial system. These friends and acquaintances also told us that they would appreciate a book which undertook to look at the German financial system from the perspective of foreign readers and which would, therefore, highlight the special features of the German financial system, assuming of course that such features exist.

The third fact which encouraged us even more to embark on this project was that there are several propositions about the German financial system in recent academic and non-academic literature which cast doubt on what can be regarded as conventional wisdom with respect to Germany. These propositions concern, among others, the role of house banks in Germany, the role of banks as intermediaries, and the financing patterns of non-financial enterprises. For us, these statements are particularly challenging since they are not only contrary to what has been believed for years, but they are also contrary to some of our own recent empirical findings. This made us think that there may be other cases of recent statements about the German financial system which warrant and even require a closer look to be taken.

These three factors also shaped the way we organized the process which led to the present book. We tried to bring together authors who are themselves involved in research related to the German financial system and its specific features and peculiarities, whether these are true or only assumed peculiarities, or indeed mere myths. We asked our authors to take these peculiarities and myths as the starting point of the chapters which they would be contributing to the book, and finally, we discussed with the group of authors on several occasions the outline of all parts of the book.

We were extremely pleased to find a set of authors who were enthusiastic about our research questions and about the idea of pursuing this agenda in the form of a book addressed especially to foreign readers. The clear common focus on the true or assumed peculiarities of the German financial system is one of the features which distinguishes this book from others.

We were even more delighted to find excellent authors with the relevant research interests and backgrounds in our closest working environment, namely that of the University of Frankfurt. With only one exception, all of those who have contributed to this book are currently, or have been at some earlier point in time, teaching and doing research at the Johann Wolfgang Goethe University of Frankfurt and/or the Center for Financial Studies (CFS) which is affiliated to the University. This is a second distinguishing feature; in a way we are proud to call our book the Frankfurt book on the German financial system.

The third distinguishing feature of this book is that it places great emphasis on empirical research, which in recent years has been a major focus of finance-related studies in Germany in general, and in Frankfurt in particular.

We want to conclude this preface by expressing our gratitude to a number of people and institutions whose support has made this book project possible. First and foremost, we would like to thank our eighteen authors. They have done an excellent job, and they were willing to accept our general idea of what the focus of the book should be, and our criticism of various versions of their chapters. The book is in a sense the outcome of a joint learning process, and we are proud to have been a part of this process. Moreover, we are grateful to the authors as well as to other colleagues from our university and its Finance Group and from the Center for Financial Studies for their cooperation and sustained support, which ultimately made the project possible.

The concept of the book as a whole, as well as that of the individual chapters, was developed and discussed among all contributors, which transformed our endeavour on many occasions into an exciting group project. The discussions went on for more than a year and proved to be a stimulating experience. Karl-Hermann Fischer orchestrated this discussion process. To him, we owe a huge debt. Towards the end of the project, Michael Schmidt took over the role of coordinating the work on an operational level. If we have not drifted away too much from our time schedule, he takes the merit—and we are extremely grateful to him for this, while we bear the full and exclusive responsibility for the fact that the project took longer than we had originally anticipated.

We have also received support from a number of colleagues whom we had asked to serve as external referees for the individual chapters. Their critical and constructive suggestions have been carefully taken into account in the revision of the chapters. For their encouraging and useful comments we would like to thank Franklin Allen, Ekkehard Boehmer, Jean Dermine, Thierry Foucault, Wolfgang Gerke, Thomas Hellmann, Martin Hellwig, Christian Kirchner, Steven Ongena, Bernd Rudolph, Richard Stehle, Axel Weber, and Volker Wieland.

The staff at our chairs have done a very good job in helping us to bring the manuscript into a uniform format that is also in accordance with the publisher's guidelines, including the preparation of the index and the proof-reading of most of the chapters. We are very grateful to this entire group which includes Patrick Behr, Dennis Hänsel, Christian Hirsch, Andy Jobst, Samuel Lee, and Baris Serifsoy. We hope that readers will not find our English to be too 'Germanic' and are grateful to Diane Chatterton-Weber, the language consultant at CFS, as well as to Paul Keith and George McElheny, the professional translators from IPC, who have corrected our English draft versions with great diligence and patience. In this connection, we also thank the Center for Financial Studies and IPC for funding this essential part of the work. Finally, we would like to thank Dr Reckers, now on the Bundesbank's Board of Managing Directors and formerly the President of the Landeszentralbank Hessen-Thüringen, for the LZB's support for our project. Finally, we are grateful to the German Science Foundation (Deutsche Forschungsgemeinschaft), since the research which underlies the contribution of several authors of this book has been undertaken with DFG funding during recent years. Furthermore, one of the editors has greatly benefited from a DFG-funded sabbatical semester, much of which was devoted to the completion of the book.

Last but not least a word of thanks goes to Andrew Schuller, the editor responsible at Oxford University Press. He has not only been very supportive since the beginning of the project, but also duly impatient when the project came closer to its end without really being finished in time. Thank you, Andrew, for pushing us forward!

We would like to conclude with a personal remark. It was fun and a great source of inspiration and satisfaction to act as the editors of this book and as the initiators and coordinators of a great project during a time which was not always easy. What made it difficult was indeed the scarcity of time. It applied to all of the authors and to ourselves in particular. One of us had to cope with the additional task of being the Dean of the Faculty of Business and Economics of the Goethe-University, and as everybody who knows him no doubt realizes, the other one always has far too many commitments! However, it suffices to say that if we were given the opportunity, we would certainly be delighted to do this project again.

Frankfurt/Main, August 2003
Jan Pieter Krahnen
Reinhard H. Schmidt

Contents

Figures

Tables

Notes on Contributors

Ralf Elsas has been Assistant Professor of Finance at Goethe-Universität Frankfurt since 2001. He was visiting professor at the University of Florida, Gainesville in 2003. His research is focused on empirical corporate finance and banking. Recent publications have appeared in the *Journal of Financial Intermediation* and the *Journal of Banking and Finance*.

Karl-Hermann Fischer earned his doctoral degree from Goethe University in Frankfurt/Main. He has been a recipient of the Barclays Global Investors Best Paper Award at the 2000 Annual Meeting of the European Finance Association (EFA). His research interest is in the field of banking, corporate finance and industrial organization. He currently holds a position in the financial services industry.

Stefanie A. Franzke is a Ph.D. candidate in business administration at the J. W. Goethe-University Frankfurt, and has been a member of the academic staff at the Center for Financial Studies since 1998. Stefanie's thesis, under the supervision of Jan Pieter Krahnen, deals with 'venture capital in Germany'. Stefanie has presented her research at national and international conferences, including the Annual Meetings of the German Finance Association in Vienna and Mainz, CEPR/CEMFI-Meeting in Madrid, CMI conference in Toronto, and EIASM, Brussels. She has collaborated with researchers at LSE, London, exchanging ideas in the field of venture capital, while visiting there.

Since 2001, **Stefanie Grohs** has been Managing Director of the Verein für Socialpolitik (German Economic Association). She studied business administration at the Goethe-University Frankfurt, Germany, and was Assistant at the Chair of International Banking and Finance.

Andreas Hackethal received his degrees from Frankfurt University, Germany, and the University of Iowa, Iowa City. Currently, he is an Assistant Professor at Frankfurt University's finance department and Co-Director of Frankfurt University's E-Finance-Lab. His research interests include financial system architecture, corporate finance, and bank management. Andreas Hackethal was an internal auditor for a large German bank before joining a global consulting company as a Project Manager. On a part-time basis, he is advising clients from the automotive and financial services industry.

Since 1995, Dr. **Jan Pieter Krahnen** has held the Chair of Corporate Finance at Goethe-Universitaet in Frankfurt/Main, Germany. He is also Director of the

Center for Financial Studies, a non-profit research institution in Frankfurt, and a CEPR-Research Fellow in financial economics. Current research projects concentrate on risk management and debt markets. Dr. Krahnen has published extensively in the field of corporate finance and banking. The most recent publications have appeared in the *Journal of Financial Intermediation, Journal of Banking and Finance*, and the *Experimental Economics*. He is on the Editorial Board of the *Journal of Banking and Finance* and the *Journal of Financial Services Research*.

Since 2002, Dr. **Christian Laux** has held the Chair of Corporate Finance and Risk Management at the Goethe-University Frankfurt/Main, Germany. Current research projects include the relation between organization and finance, internal capital markets, and risk management. Dr. Laux has published in the field of corporate finance and contract theory. His publications appeared in the *RAND Journal of Economics; Journal of Law, Economics and Organization*; and the *Journal of Economic Behaviour and Organization*.

Christian Leuz is the Harold Stott Term Assistant Professor in Accounting at the Wharton School of the University of Pennsylvania. Prior to this position, he lectured at the Otto Beisheim Graduate School of Management, the University of Tübingen and the Goethe University Frankfurt, Germany. He was the Harry Reynolds International Visiting Professor at the Wharton School and a visiting doctoral fellow at the Simon School of Business, University of Rochester, NY. Professor Leuz earned his doctoral degree in 1996 at the Goethe University where he also received his 'Habilitation' in business administration in 2000. His most recent publications have appeared in the *Journal of Financial Economics* and the *Journal of Accounting Research*. He is an Associate Editor of the *European Accounting Review*.

Professor Dr. **Raimond Maurer** holds, since 2000, the Chair of Investment, Portfolio Management and Pension Finance J. W. Goethe-University Frankfurt/Main (Germany). He got his Diploma (1991), Doctorate (1995), and Habilitation (1999) in business administration all from Mannheim University. Dr. Maurer is Member of the German Society of Insurance and Financial Mathematics (DGVFM), the German A.F.I.R. Group (Actuarial Approach for Financial Risk), and Research Fellow of the Center for Financial Studies. His research interests and publications are in the fields of institutional investors, investment analysis, real estate, and pension finance. The most recent publications have appeared in the *ASTIN Bulletin, Journal of Real Estate Research, Journal of Pension Economics and Finance*, and *Financial Analysts Journal*.

Professor **Eric Nowak** joined the Faculty of Economics at the University of Lugano in May 2003. He was born in September 1970 in Bochum, Germany.

Following his final school-leaving examination at Salem College in Germany, he studied business economics (finance and accounting) at the University of St. Gallen, Switzerland, and at the Bocconi University in Milan, Italy. After working 2 years at the Swiss Institute of Banking and Finance, he completed his doctoral dissertation at the University of St. Gallen while being a Research Fellow of the Swiss National Science Foundation with Sherwin Rosen at the University of Chicago. Since November 1997 he was Assistant Professor of finance at the Johann Wolfgang-Goethe University Frankfurt/Main (Germany), where he received his *venia legendi* in June 2002. From October 2002 until April 2003, he was Visiting Professor of finance at the University of Hohenheim, Germany, and at the COPPEAD Graduate School of Business in Rio de Janeiro, Brazil. In his field of research, corporate finance and accounting, Eric has participated in prestigious conferences, such as the annual meeting of the European Finance Association (EFA), the annual conference of the European Financial Management Association (EFMA), or the European Accounting Association (EAA). In addition, he is a frequent publisher and referee for international journals, such as the *Journal of Applied Corporate Finance* or the *Journal of Small Business Management.*

Christian Pfeil studied economics at the University of Saarland, Germany and the University Michigan, Ann Arbor, MI from 1990 to 1995. After graduation, he joined the Chair of Professor J. Eichberger (mathematical economics) at the University of Saarland as a Ph.D. student in 1995. Upon finishing his dissertation in 1999, he visited the Department of Economics at the University of Melbourne, Australia. During this visit, he taught a course in organizational theory and contract theory. In February 2000, Christian Pfeil joined the Chair of Professor R. H. Schmidt (international banking and finance) in the Department of Finance at J. W. Goethe University, Frankfurt, Germany. Since January 2001, he is Head of Division, Financial and Federal Affairs, at Staatskanzlei of the Saarland, Germany.

After working for an insurance company for three years, Dr. **Oliver Rieckers**, LL.M. studied law at the Georg-August University in Göttingen and at the University of Chicago. Since 2001 he has been working as an assistant to Prof. Dr. Gerald Spindler in Göttingen. He has published in the field of German and U.S. Corporation and Securities Law. The most recent publications have appeared in the *European Business Law Review* and in *Recht der Internationalen Wirtschaft.*

Frank A. Schmid has been a Senior Economist at the Federal Reserve Bank of St. Louis, MO since 1997. He was previously affiliated with the Wharton Financial Institutions Center (1995–97), Free University Berlin (1994–95), and the University of Vienna, Austria (1991–94). He has taught at CERGE-EI, J. W. Goethe-University Frankfurt, Germany, University of Osnabrück,

Germany, and University of Vienna, among others. His list of publications includes papers in the *Journal of Financial Economics, Journal of Corporate Finance*, and the *Journal of Institutional and Theoretical Economics*. His current research interest is in financial markets, monetary policy, and banking.

Reinhard H. Schmidt was trained as an economist at the University of Frankfurt, Germany, and the Stanford GSB and held positions as a professor of finance and economics in the universities of Frankfurt, Göttingen, Trier, Germany, and Georgetown, Washington, DC, before taking his current position in Frankfurt in 1991. He is married and has one daughter. Reinhard H. Schmidt has published 16 books, about 40 articles in national and international academic journals, and over 50 chapters in books in the fields of capital markets, contract theory, and financial systems in industrialized and developing countries. Between 2001 and 2003, he was the Dean of the Frankfurt Faculty of Business Administration and Economics. He is a member of the European Shadow Financial Regulatory Committee and the Chairman of the Supervisory Board of an investment company which invests in micro-finance institutions.

Professor Dr. **Gerald Spindler** is the Head of the Chair of Civil Law, Commercial and Economic Law, Comparative Law, Multimedia Law, and Telecommunication Law at the University of Göttingen, Germany. This department is, among other topics, mainly occupied with legal questions regarding e-commerce, that is, Internet and telecommunication law.

Apart from teaching, various books, more than 90 articles in law reviews, as well as expert legal opinions are published by Professor Spindler. He is Editor of one of the most renowned German law reviews covering the whole area of cyberspace law and telecommunication law. Professor Spindler was the national and European reporter for e-commerce during the XVIth International Conference of the International Academy of Comparative Law in Brisbane/Australia, 2002. He also acted as a speaker at the IST-Conference of the EEC on new developments in Information Society in Nice, 2000.

Professor Spindler is Vice-Chairman of the German Society of Law and Information Science and has also advised the German as well as the European legislator regarding various questions concerning the information society.

Since 2000, Dr. **Erik Theissen** has held the Chair of Finance at Rheinische Friedrich-Wilhelms-Universitaet Bonn, Germany. Current research projects concentrate on market microstructure and experimental asset markets.

Professor Theissen has published extensively in renowned international journals. Recent publications have appeared in the *European Finance Review; Journal of International Financial Markets, Institutions and Money; Journal of Empirical Finance; Journal of Financial Intermediation*; and the *Journal of Financial Markets*.

Dr. **Marcel Tyrell** received his degrees from the University of Applied Sciences, Wiesbaden, Goethe-University in Frankfurt, and the Trier, Germany. Currently, he is a part-time lecturer at the last two universities. He is also involved as a researcher in projects of the Center of Financial Studies, a non-profit research in Frankfurt, and of the Deutsche Bundesbank in Frankfurt. His research interests include financial system architecture, the role of information in capital markets and banks, relationship lending, and macro finance. The publications appeared in the *Journal of Financial Intermediation, Journal of Institutional and Theoretical Economics*, and the *European Financial Management*.

Mark Wahrenburg hold the Chair of Bank Management at Goethe-University of Frankfurt, Germany, since 1999. He held prior positions at the universities of Witten/Herdecke and Cologne. His research interests focus on risk management of banks and venture captial finance. The results of his work have been published in recognized journals such as the European Financial Management Journal, Empirical Economics, Kredit und Kapital, and Zeitschrift für Betriebswirtschaft. Besides his academic background, Mark Wahrenburg has a long-standing consulting experience in the area of bank risk management from work at McKinsey and AMS Management Systems. He is also the founder of an Internet start-up company which he recently sold after three rounds of financing.

Andreas Worms is Deputy Head of the Money and Capital Markets Division of the Deutsche Bundesbank. He holds a Doctorate in economics of Goethe-Universitaet in Frankfurt/Main, Germany, where he also teaches monetary economics. Before Dr. Worms came to the Bundesbank in 1997, he was Research and Teaching Assistant at the Chair for Monetary Economics at Goethe-Universitaet and at the Institut für Kapitalmarktforschung (now Center for Financial Studies, CFS) in Frankfurt/Main. Current research projects focus on monetary policy rules, the monetary transmission process, and financial stability issues. Dr. Worms has published mainly in the field of Monetary Economics, recently, for example, in the *Journal of the European Economic Association, Oxford Review of Economic Policy*, and the *Journal of Applied Economics and Economic Policy*.

Since 2002, **Jens Wüstemann** has held the Chair for Accounting at the University of Mannheim, Germany. He is a board member of the National Research Center on Concepts of Rationality, Decision-Making, and Economic Modeling (SFB 504) at the same university and also leads a connected project. He has the position of an Academic Director of the joint Executive M.B.A. Program of Mannheim University and the ESSEC, Paris, France. His research interests and publications include institutional economics, the role of accounting information in financial systems, economic analysis of securities regulation, the design of enforcement mechanism in capital markets, and normative accounting theory.

PART I

INTRODUCTION AND OVERVIEW

1

The Purpose and Structure of the Book

JAN PIETER KRAHNEN AND REINHARD H. SCHMIDT

1.1. MOTIVATION

In both academic and non-academic writings, Germany is often cited as the most prominent example of a country with a bank-based financial system. In this respect it is typically grouped together with Japan, and compared to the United Kingdom and particularly the United States as the leading examples of market-oriented systems. From many conversations and interactions with colleagues and press reports from around the world we have come to the conclusion that there is surprisingly little knowledge about the true characteristics of Germany's financial system. While we have seen many innovations in the financial architecture of this country, these developments and substantial changes seem to have escaped the perception of fellow observers. This book aims to rectify this situation. It presents a survey of the economics of financial markets, institutions, and practices in Germany, structured in individual chapters that look at banking and insurance, capital markets, monetary transmission, financial regulation, corporate governance and investor protection, venture capital and M&A, competition, and accounting.

When we first began thinking about the concept of this book, we invited a group of fellow economists, mostly from our home institution, the Goethe Universität in Frankfurt, to an informal workshop with the intention of enumerating the myths surrounding various segments of Germany's financial architecture, and confronting these myths with what they and we knew about the functioning of financial markets and institutions in this country. This workshop turned out to be an exciting exercise, which convinced us to start work on this project seriously. Many of the participants at that initial workshop are now among the authors of the chapters in the book. All authors are or have been for the most part, at some point, associated with the Goethe Universität of Frankfurt or CFS, the Center for Financial Studies which is affiliated to the University. Again, all the authors have participated in several discussions on the structure and the central thread of this book, in the search for a unifying approach to all segments of the financial system. The reader will have to judge whether we have been successful in this respect. The completion of the book, and many of its chapters, has been a team effort—a tremendous, positive experience for which we are very grateful.

Our decision to write this book was reinforced by an academic conference in Frankfurt that was part of the EU-sponsored research network 'Understanding Financial Architecture', in April 2001.[1] At this conference, Luigi Zingales presented his paper with Ragu Rajan on the politics of financial development in the twentieth century (Rajan and Zingales 2003). These authors claim that political contexts, rather than legal traditions, are the most significant factors in explaining the course of financial development in an economy. This is in stark contrast to the widely shared view of the time, which attributed the basic structure of national financial systems to their legal tradition, in particular to whether this adheres to the common law or the civil law tradition. The former is believed to give rise to market-oriented systems, like the United States or the United Kingdom, while the latter purportedly encourages the development of bank-based systems, like in Germany or Japan (see La Porta *et al.* 1998).

The discussion about the merits of Rajan and Zingales' contribution during and after the conference suggested to us that there is a growing need for detailed empirical studies at the country level in order to facilitate the understanding of local financial architecture. Rajan and Zingales' and many other related contributions (to which we will turn below) have broken new ground in analysing international data sets, often comprising more than twenty countries and their financial architectures. This cross-sectional analysis is deemed necessary in order to be able to draw general conclusions about the structure and the dynamics of financial systems, and thus to derive policy recommendations relating, among others, to emerging economies too, such as the financial systems in Central Eastern Europe. However, in order to yield valid conclusions about the determinants of the development and performance of financial systems, a solid understanding of the local or national architecture, their different markets and institutions, and their interplay is required. The present book represents the attempt to write one such country study. The individual chapters of this book are, therefore, meant not only to provide information and analysis, but also to shed light on a number of myths surrounding the German financial system. Perhaps the most obvious myth about the German financial system is the controversy concerning relationship lending. Traditionally, it was assumed that now, almost as much as a century ago, relationship lending is a fact of life. One can regard this as a myth, since timely empirical evidence has, until quite recently, been more than scarce. This may be the reason why the most well-known book in English about the German financial system (Edwards and Fischer 1994) casts doubt on this alleged fact.

---

[1] The conference was organized jointly by the Centre of Economic Policy Research (CEPR) and the Center for Financial Studies (CFS) on behalf of the European Union's Research and Training Network 'Understanding Financial Architecture'.

As the Edwards and Fischer book is indeed, and for good reasons, well known, one could see the 'new myth' in their statement that relationship lending is merely a myth, as opposed to a reality. In one of the chapters, this issue is taken up and discussed on the basis of new data, with the notable result that one can indeed find hard empirical evidence for the continuing existence of relationship lending in Germany. The question, therefore, is which myth is true in substance and which one is merely a myth.

Looking into one of the role models of a bank-based financial system, namely Germany, also makes a contribution to the larger research efforts relating to financial system comparisons (see esp. Allen and Gale 2000). In the second chapter of this book, Schmidt and Tyrell will present a bird's-eye view of the local financial architecture, and in the concluding chapter we, as the editors, will ask ourselves whether the label 'bank-based' is still appropriate today. Evidently, this discussion is closely related to the current literature on financial system development, and it brings us back to the programmatic challenge posed in the course of the above-mentioned conference on 'Understanding financial architecture'.

1.2. QUESTIONS TO BE ASKED: WHAT CAN WE LEARN FROM THE MODERN LITERATURE ON FINANCIAL DEVELOPMENT?

The upsurge of studies on financial system design was heavily influenced by the financial sector reform activities of the IMF and the World Bank in the late 1980s and early 1990s. During this period, both institutions were engaged in extensive studies on the structure and performance of the financial systems of developing and transforming economies, as surveyed by the World Bank (1989) and Stiglitz (1993). These institutions suggested measures to improve the functioning of banking and financial markets in LDCs, and they used their influence to shape the regulatory framework in many countries.

An important study by King and Levine (1993), which provided a great stimulus to the empirical research in this area, investigated the extent to which the state of financial development of an economy contributes to income, wealth, and growth. In their cross-country regressions, King and Levine measured the state of financial development by proxies like deposits, the market value of stocks, long-term loans, and bank branches per million inhabitants, and related these measures to various measures of economic success and development. Whatever proxy was used, the state of financial development proved to be a good and consistently significant predictor of per capita income, wealth and growth. The findings of King and Levine strengthened the plea made by policy advisers to restructure the financial infrastructure of many countries.

The next logical step in analysing the finance–growth nexus was taken by studies published in the second half of the 1990s, again in collaboration with researchers from the World Bank.[2] La Porta, Lopez de Silanes, Shleifer, and Vishny (henceforth LLSV) tried to identify the driving factors behind observed national financial structures. In a series of papers LLSV identified what they called the legal tradition of the country as the major determinant of its current financial structure. The positive relationship between the presence of a common law tradition and the prevalence of capital market orientation was significant in a sample comprising more than fifty countries from around the world. The authors reasoned that the common law tradition, with its reliance on a constantly evolving stream of rules through court decisions, encourages financial markets' development by strengthening investor protection. In contrast, countries rooted in the civil law tradition, like those in continental Europe, including Germany, and also Japan, tend to have less stringent rules, particularly those relating to accounting, to protect investors, and less effective minority shareholder protection. On the other hand, these countries tend to offer superior protection for creditors and incumbent managers.

The studies and conclusions by LLSV have stimulated a new round of discussion about the causes of financial development. We will briefly touch on two aspects of this debate, as they are directly linked to the content of the present book, that is, the methodology of cross-country regressions, and the appropriateness of using bank-based and market-based financial systems as the basis of description. First, on the methodological side, in the LLSV cross-country regressions is an implicit understanding that 'more developed' means 'more similar to a market-based system', probably like the US system. Thus, the list of variables describing the state of financial development of any given country consists of indices that tend to take on high values for the United States and the United Kingdom. Regression results are therefore valid, if and only if a theoretical argument can be made that the development of the financial infrastructure is tantamount to developing an infrastructure similar to that of the United States. If such a theoretical argument cannot be made, the cross-country regressions are probably misspecified (Mankiw 1995).

The analysis by LLSV as well as that by most participants in the debate uses a concept of the financial system that distinguishes between two polar types of financial systems, the bank-based and the market-based system. This distinction is used by many observers of financial development, ranging from Goldsmith (1969) and Rybczynski (1984) to Roe (1994), Walter (1993), Pagano and Volpin (2001), Schmidt, Hackethal, and Tyrell (2002), and to Allen and Gale (1995, 2000). Prototypes of market-based systems are those of the United States and the United Kingdom, while those of Japan and Germany are considered to be archetypal bank-based systems. While this distinction seems intuitively plausible, and is in fact used a lot in the public discussion, it does not fully stand up to scrutiny. Recent research has looked into the details of this bipolar system description in a historical perspective and has found

---

[2] The World Bank research department was headed by Joseph Stiglitz during much of this time.

little evidence for stable and common patterns. Thus, Caroline Fohlin (2000) in a paper on the historical patterns of banking in an international comparison, concludes that few banking systems truly fit the proposed bipolar classification over time. Based on this finding, she doubts that the legal tradition of a country can really be the main determinant of the character of its financial system development. In a similar vein, Rajan and Zingales (2003) supplement the LLSV analysis with a historical perspective. Their four measures of financial development are similar to those used by LLSV. One captures the development of the banking sector (deposits/GDP), the other three capture the development of the stock market (equity issues/fixed capital formation, stock market capitalization/GDP, and number of traded companies/population). They find that financial system development is not monotone over time. There can be a conversion from a bank-based to a capital market-based system, and vice versa. In particular, the financial systems of several countries, including Germany, were strongly capital market-oriented before the First World War, then became bank-oriented, and reversed their change again only recently, in the 1980s and 1990s of last century (see also Tilly 1992 on Germany). Like Fohlin, these authors also conclude that this is evidence against the LLSV-explanation of financial development, because by definition the legal traditions remained stable throughout the entire period. Rajan and Zingales, and to some extent also Pagano and Volpin (2001), propose a different explanation that builds on the changes in the political context within nations, in particular the activities of interest groups that wish to secure rents for themselves. If these interest groups gain support, which tends to happen notably after large economic shocks, the level of competition and particularly the activities of markets are curtailed. This explains why financial system development is reversible, that is, markets may both gain and lose importance and disappear over time.

The literature just cited has demonstrated that, on closer inspection, the financial system cannot easily be subsumed under the bipolar typology of bank-based and market-based models. Rajan and Zingales show that Germany, the perceived role model of a bank-based system, once had the most developed stock market in Europe. Around the turn of the century—from the nineteenth to the twentieth century—there were more than 5,000 public firms in Germany, 30 per cent of which were listed and traded. In 1913, stock market capitalization relative to GDP was higher in Germany than in the United States, and it was as high as in Japan. At the same time, the 1913 ratio of deposits to GDP, an indicator of banking development, was lower in Germany than in the United States, and on par with the United Kingdom.

We consider this book to be a contribution to an investigation into the working of a financial system, which is typically classified as bank-based. This investigation consists of a number of partial views on different parts and aspects of the financial system, each one adding to our understanding, and supplementing the view of the entire system. Quite naturally, questions arise concerning the possibility of interdependence and complementarity between observed features. And questions also arise relating to the change of institutions and functional performance over time. While these questions surface in many chapters, a more integrated view is put forward only in the concluding chapter. Taking stock, we will then try to answer, from the perspective of the year 2003, whether the German financial system was, and still is, an example of what is commonly called a bank-based financial system. This will bring us full circle, back to the observation in the first sentence of the introduction, namely the citations of Germany as a role model of a bank-based system.

1.3. MYTHS, METHODS, AND MAJOR INSIGHTS

The book is divided into four parts. Part I comprises the introduction and the overview, Part II looks at the financial sector and corporate finance (7 chapters), Part III focuses on regulation and corporate governance (5 chapters), and finally Part IV takes stock and looks ahead to what might be in store. Except for the first and the last one, which also have the function of embracing the many details presented in the other chapters, and of tying them together, all chapters are able to stand alone. However, the sequence of the chapters is chosen to allow a smooth discourse. The next few pages will briefly visit each chapter, emphasizing their content. A more integrative view on all parts of this book must wait until the concluding chapter.

Chapter 2 by Schmidt and Tyrell '*What Constitutes a Financial System in General and the German Financial System in Particular?*' prepares the ground for later chapters. It starts by discussing what is generally understood by 'financial system', a key term of this book, and by showing why and in what respect the financial system of a country is important. The authors then go on to discuss what has to be done in order to arrive at an appropriate economic understanding of such a system. Relying on their earlier work on this issue, the authors stress the importance of analysing the systemic nature of a financial system. They refer to the interdependence between the institutional framework and the various segments that constitute a financial system, such as the banking industry, the capital markets, corporate governance, and risk sharing. Schmidt and Tyrell advocate an approach which emphasizes the ways in which the various elements of a financial system interact or, in other words, in what sense a financial system really is a system.

The second half of the chapter offers a general overview of the German financial system and provides a first indication of how the elements of the German financial system are indeed related to each other. Moreover, it at least partially compensates for the inevitable gaps which the remainder of the book leaves in this context.

Part II on the financial sector and corporate finance comprises seven chapters. It begins with three chapters analysing the structure of the major components of the financial sector, that is, banking, institutional investors (insurance and investment funds), and the stock markets. These chapters are followed by one on the way in which monetary policy functions under the influence of the specific features of the German financial sector. The remaining three chapters then look at different aspects of corporation finance in Germany, namely bank financing, venture capital, and M&A.

Chapter 3 by Andreas Hackethal on '*German Banks and Banking Structure*' gives a survey of the current structure of the banking system in Germany, focusing on its three pillars, that is, savings banks, cooperative banks, and private banks. The relative importance of these pillars has remained remarkably stable over the past decades. The importance, both absolute and relative, of markets in the channelling of funds from households to the corporate sector has not risen over the past decade, nor has the role of commercial banking shrunk during this period. Germany has a large number of active small banks, and even its big private banks are relatively small when measured by their domestic market shares. Another feature of the German banking system, which is not usually to be expected in an advanced industrial country like Germany, is that more than half of total bank assets are held by banks which are, by their legal and ownership structure, not strictly profit-oriented. The public savings bank sector is the largest part of the banking sector, and cooperative banking also plays a larger role than in most other countries. When it comes to retail and SME-banking, their provision of banking services to the German economy can hardly be overestimated.

In his contribution to this book, Andreas Hackethal pays special attention to two much debated features attributed to financial system development in Germany, namely disintermediation and the alleged 'death of commercial banking'. The author finds no supporting evidence for any of these claims. While the secular decline of conventional banking with its focus on deposit taking and lending is easily verified in the United States, the data provided by Hackethal suggest that this trend does not apply to Germany. Its banking system might very well maintain many of its peculiarities in the years to come.

Chapter 4 by Raimond Maurer on '*Institutional Investors in Germany: Insurance Companies and Investment Funds*' presents a rich survey of the role of insurance and investment companies in the German capital markets. In the direct insurance market, for instance, the author presents surprising evidence on the differences relating to the rate of growth (1980–99) of the ratio of gross premiums to GDP, the so-called penetration ratio between industrialized countries. Germany has fallen to the lower ranks, probably owing to the prevalence of its pay-as-you-go pension system. Another important aspect covered in this chapter refers to the asset management process in life insurance, with a special focus on return smoothing, a notable feature of insurance companies, and on the implications of guaranteed minimum returns, which are customary in the German market. Together with the absence of marking to market, the combined result of smoothing and minimum return on book values can actually lead to quite risky portfolio strategies, as evidenced by what seemed to some observers like a recent crisis in the life insurance industry in Germany in early 2003.

Maurer continues by surveying the investment fund industry, and finds signs of convergence in strategy and regulation in both fields. The reduction in tax-financed pension schemes which is expected before long, is likely to feed growth rates in both the life insurance and investment fund industries for many years to come.

In the chapter on '*Organized Equity Markets*', Erik Theissen analyses the macro- and the microstructure of the German stock market. He presents evidence on, among other things, market size, the distribution of stock owner-ship, and transactions costs. In the section on market microstructure, the functioning of the Xetra electronic platform is described in detail, as is the working of the more traditional floor trading. The author presents material allowing a direct comparison to be drawn between the two most prominent trading institutions, that is, the electronic platform and floor trading. His conclusions support the idea that a blending of both trading technologies may be desirable. Theissen also assesses the future development of the stock market in Germany, and sets it in a European perspective.

The discussion of the institutional side of the German financial sector concludes with a view from the angle of the monetary authority. It has always been assumed that the structure of the financial system at large might deter-mine the power and the reach of monetary policy in a country. Relying on recent material, Andreas Worms in the chapter on '*Monetary Policy Trans-mission and the Financial System in Germany*' evaluates the credit channel of monetary policy in Germany. Among the many findings he reports, one stands out in particular, namely that the effect of monetary policy on real variables, especially on corporate credit supply, is cushioned by specific features of the German banking system. This finding is in line with what would be expected in a system formed by relationship lending. Andreas Worms drills downs further and shows, using a new data set, that the three pillar structure creates opportunities for intra-pillar buffers which are able to explain the weak effect of monetary policy on the supply of loans to businesses.

The second half of Part II contains three chapters on various aspects of corporate finance in Germany. It starts with the chapter on '*Universal Banks and Relationships with Firms*' by Ralf Elsas and Jan Krahnen. This chapter aims at shedding new light on the issue of relationship lending, and the once prominent role of *Hausbanks*, which have recently been declared to be a myth rather than reality in Edwards and Fischer, 1994. The authors of the chapter in our book differentiate between the role of the bank as an (equity) investor of large stock companies, holding their shares, sitting on their boards, and using proxy votes as a means to exert control. Their assessment relies on various recent empirical studies which find a positive wealth effect (both book and market values) of equity ownership concentration and also of bank ownership in non-financial firms, and no effect of board seats and proxy voting.

Elsas and Krahnen then address banks as lenders and the nature of their relationships with firms. They start by clarifying what is meant by a *Hausbank* in empirical research. Building on a body of recent empirical work, they report a set of findings that confirm the hypothesis that there are indeed significant positive effects of relationships on firm performance in Germany. These effects concern the availability of credit in situations of a temporary liquidity shock and the ability of a company in distress to access fresh money and to undertake a serious workout effort, rather than being driven into liquidation right away. These findings underscore the importance of relationships in understanding the functioning of the German financial system, and thus carry over to several other chapters of this book. It is suggested that the alleged myth of relationship banking in Germany is itself probably a myth.

In Chapter 8 on '*Initial Public Offerings and Venture Capital in Germany*' Stefanie Franzke, Stefanie Grohs, and Christian Laux take great care in describing the market participants and issue costs in Germany, relying on a comprehensive data set. They then go on to discuss different explanations for the modest number of IPOs over the past decades. In keeping with the broader structure of a largely bank-based financial system in Germany, they address two determinants of the belated development of (public) equity markets in Germany. The two determinants are the dominance of universal banks and the economic significance of small to medium-sized closely held and typically family-owned firms in the German economy, the famous *Mittelstand*.

Franzke, Grohs, and Laux then discuss IPOs and the role and the development of venture capital in Germany. Observers of the German financial system have for a long time believed that it is part and parcel of the general bank-based character of this system that IPOs and VC are 'underdeveloped'. In the authors' view, these observers are right. Before the early 1980s, there was hardly any IPO and VC activity worth mentioning in Germany. For instance, the average number of IPOs per year between 1949 and 1982 was a mere 3.3. Even after 1982 the situation did not change a great deal. IPO and VC activities picked up, but only to reach a level (19.5), which is still quite low by international standards. Only in the second half of the 1990s, was there what might in retrospect be called a mini-revolution. With the huge IPO of Deutsche Telekom, the stock price bubble and the opening of the *Neuer Markt* in 1997, it seemed for a while that IPO and VC activity would reach the level observed in other comparably advanced countries. In particular the exit option offered by the *Neuer Markt* seemed to make venture capital financing much easier than it used to be. However, this was a short boom period, and it ended abruptly after stock prices started to fall on a general scale in 2000. Moreover, the boom was, with hindsight, also not as strong as it appeared to be at the time.

After providing extensive empirical material on IPOs and VC in Germany, the authors address the question about what might be behind the underdevelopment of these parts of the German financial system. As they write, 'understanding the reasons is an indispensable part of understanding the

German financial system'. In their view, it can be directly traced back to the interests and the influence of Germany's large private banks that IPOs and VC were grossly repressed before 1995 and that this situation has only partially changed since then.

The chapter by Frank Schmid and Mark Wahrenburg on '*Mergers and Acquisitions in Germany—Social Setting and Regulatory Framework*' concludes the part on corporate financing. They provide an illustrative account of fairly recent changes in what had been considered a no-go area for the German financial system, the market for corporate control. The very first successful hostile takeover among public companies dates back only a few years. In contrast, there has always been a considerable level of (friendly) M&A activity among SMEs. The authors then try to explain why there was so little relevant activity among larger corporations in the past. They stress the legal and social framework of the *Soziale Marktwirtschaft* (social market economy) as being a consumer-oriented, egalitarian economic approach adopted by the economic and political elites in Germany during the second half of the twentieth century. In keeping with this approach, there have been a number of legal impediments that effectively increase the cost of (hostile) takeovers considerably, among them codetermination (which gives workers and unions half of the seats in the supervisory board in large publicly held corporations), and specific voting restrictions (which have, after 50 years, only recently been ruled out).

Part III of the book gives an account of legal rules and business practices that determine financing decisions in Germany, including regulation of financial institutions, accounting, corporate governance, and competition in banking.

Chapter 10 by Karl-Hermann Fischer and Christian Pfeil sets the stage in addressing '*Regulation and Competition in German Banking*'. The authors embed their analysis of banking regulation in an IO framework, which allows them to assess the degree of competition in banking by drawing on regional rather than (simply) on aggregate data, thus leveraging the credibility of their findings. The history of German banking regulation since its initiation in 1931 makes clear that it also served to stabilize the structure of the entire banking system, evidenced by the fact that the mix of private, cooperative and savings banks was largely the same then as it was in the year 2000. The monetary authorities have as well contributed to this remarkable stability or, as it might also be called, rigidity.

Fischer and Pfeil also present new material on the assessment of concentration and competition, building on two concepts. First, they explicitly recognize a self-imposed 'regional principle' that prevents savings banks and cooperative banks from being active outside an allocated territory, and second, in calculating concentration ratios they are careful to distinguish between retail banking (where the relevant market is regional) and investment banking (where the relevant market is national or global). Their findings are highly original and relevant, cumulating in the statement that at the end of the 1990s the overall level of competition in German banking was high by international standards. There are many more facets to this chapter, filled with original empirical evidence. Among them are the reasons for the late introduction of money market funds in Germany, new measures concerning liquidity insurance provided by banks, and the official encouragement of groups of banks to maintain their own monitoring systems, bail-out mechanisms and deposit insurance schemes. A concluding section discusses the challenges for public banks in Germany stemming from the recent decision to phase out the state guarantee for state-owned universal banks.

Chapter 11 on '*Legal Aspects of Corporate Governance*' by Oliver Rieckers and Gerald Spindler explains the legal background of ownership, management and control in Germany to the outside observer. Rieckers and Spindler remind the reader of the fact that until recently German corporate governance was considered to be an export model. Only in the 1990s did the tide change, and since then Germany's stakeholder-oriented system has been looked upon more critically. Due to the rule-based legal tradition, the structure of corporate governance is quite inflexible. For instance, the separation of power and responsibility between the general meeting of shareholders, the supervisory board and the management board is largely defined by law, and leaves little room for shareholder activism. The degree of empowerment of shareholders in Germany turns out to be quite different from that in the Anglo-American systems. After succinctly specifying these fundamental differences, Rieckers and Spindler describe the corporate governance potential of share capital and outside debt, as well as the control by minority shareholders and creditors. In their concluding section, Rieckers and Spindler survey important issues currently in the lawmaker's workshop, and discuss their likely implication for financial markets.

Chapter 12 by Reinhard H. Schmidt looks at '*Corporate Governance in Germany (from) an Economic Perspective*'. His major theme is the alleged regime switch in Germany from a traditional, insider-controlled to a modern, outsider-controlled system, where the latter relies on market interaction and valuation rather than on relationships, and is one-sidedly shareholder-oriented rather than stakeholder-oriented. The chapter is composed of two parts. The first half argues that until the late 1990s, the German corporate governance system conformed to the model of an insider-controlled system, which corresponds neatly to the presumed character of the financial system as a whole, namely that of being bank-based. Schmidt argues that German corporate governance has been a consistent system of complementary elements.

In the second half of the chapter, Schmidt discusses recent developments and policy measures aimed at modernizing and strengthening corporate governance in Germany and asks whether these developments indicate a fundamental or structural change from an insider-controlled system based on relationships to an outsider-controlled system based on markets. Many of those who have supported the recent changes in German corporate governance have indeed argued that such a transition is needed, preferably as a rather gradual process. As it seems to the author, the public labelling of the recent changes may be misleading. Instead of indicating a step-by-step transition to a market-based system, he finds ample indications that the recent changes should rather be interpreted as—appropriate and necessary—measures to strengthen the system as it used to be, that is, as an insider-controlled pluralistic or stakeholder-oriented system. Thus, the transition may not be in the making. However, Schmidt argues that in the process of making the system simply better, its systemic consistency might be called into question, and if this is indeed the case the traditional governance system is not likely to function in the future. As a consequence, there is the definite possibility that Germany may rather soon change to having a market-based governance system, which will then be indistinguishable from those in the Anglo-American world.

Chapter 13 on '*Investor Protection and Capital Market Regulation in Germany*', written by Eric Nowak, contains a comprehensive overview of legal innovations since the early 1990s. This is a particularly interesting phase, because between 1991 and 2002 a series of financial market promotion acts reshaped the basis for corporate governance and outside ownership in this country. As the author lays out in detail, these acts have redefined, among other things, existing legislation on shareholder rights, market regulation, and accounting. These innovations call into question the widespread belief that in Germany shareholder rights are weak and unprotected, while those of creditors are strong and well defined. These recent developments have not yet found their way into academic research. However, Nowak suggests that a case for the development of a strong equity culture in Germany can now be made.

Chapter 14 concludes Part III on regulation and corporate governance by describing and analysing a second area of recent fundamental regulatory change, namely accounting. In their chapter on '*The Role of Accounting in the German Financial System*', Christian Leuz and Jens Wüstemann endeavour to develop an economic interpretation of the most basic principles of German accounting, both past and present. Their contribution will be surprising to most readers who have not grown up with the substance of a principles-oriented accounting system, based on the century-old *Handelsgesetzbuch* (HGB). Relying on the broad concept of the separation of ownership and control under asymmetric information, Leuz and Wüstemann argue that the traditional HGB-based accounting system was intended to create, and has indeed achieved, a high level of information transfer between the corporation and the small group of inside stakeholders, in particular large shareholders, large creditors, and worker representatives. Outside stakeholders, on the other hand, have remained poorly informed—in line with the minor role dispersed ownership has played in Germany to date. Leuz and Wüstemann describe the strong impact that the current European harmonization process has had on German accounting standards. They then go on to develop a set of propositions, based on their prior analysis, which are amenable to empirical testing.

Building on much recent work, to which Leuz was a main contributor, the authors are able to confirm several important implications of their theory, concerning in particular the opaqueness of accounting information, the high level of earnings management, and the importance of dividend restrictions in Germany, despite their absence from debt contracts. This evidence is compatible with the insider-oriented governance and ownership system described in the corporate governance chapters of this section.

The title '*Taking Stock and Looking Ahead*' clearly conveys the editors' intentions in the concluding chapter of the book. They would have preferred to have been able to derive a clear and unambiguous statement about the current status and the future development of the German financial system from the insights of the individual chapters. However, since the individual chapters only address parts or aspects of the financial system and as the developments reported there do not all point in the same direction, the concluding chapter must make an attempt to go further than merely summing up.

Only a few years ago, Germany arguably had a consistent bank-based financial system, quite distinct from a market-based system. Towards the end of the 1990s, Germany seemed to be rapidly making the conversion to a capital market-dominated system. However, whether this process has come to a standstill, now awaits to be seen.

The chapter concludes by juxtaposing three views of possible development paths for the entire system. One view, the market-takes-it-all position, holds that there is strong economic pressure to continue the current transition from an 'inferior' and outdated bank-based model to a 'superior' and more modern capital market-based financial system. The second view, the markets-or-banks position, also assumes that there is pressure to complete the transformation into a market-based system, but for a different reason. Rather than an increase in efficiency, this view emphasizes the consistency of all parts of the financial system, which, after the dramatic legal and institutional changes of the last couple of years do not allow the restoration of a bank-based system. Finally, the third view, the markets-and-banks position, departs from the traditional distinction between the two types of financial systems and argues that what we observe in Germany is the emergence of a new, hybrid type of financial system. In this hybrid model, financial intermediaries continue to develop and maintain relationships, while markets provide a major part of the required funding. Thus, according to this view, the distribution of roles between intermediaries and markets is redefined on the basis of the value-relevance of relationships in the economy. All three views lead to distinct predictions with respect to the future of banking and capital markets in Germany. The future might tell us which of the three views has come closest to predicting what will really have happened.

As we stated earlier on, in combining a number of micro studies on different segments of the German financial system, we hope to give a fuller picture of what may be associated with a bank-based financial system, which seems to be in a transition process to either a capital market-based system or to something which cannot be categorized using this conventional bipolar classification. This fuller picture will probably carry us away from an over-simplified market-based versus bank-based view of financial systems. We have tried to cover many important parts and aspects of the German financial system, but the picture we present is far from comprehensive. In particular, we have not covered two specific aspects, which demand further attention. The two topics missing here most are corporate financial decisions and the process of European integration. The first topic entails the typical reactions of capital markets to particular decisions taken at the level of the firm, such as the dividend policy, or the sources of finance for long-term investments, and the reliance on internal finance. The second topic would have to deal with the implications of European harmonization for financial system development. While the impact of European harmonization is addressed in several chapters of this book, for example, the chapters on investor protection, on corporate governance, or on accounting standards, we do not describe in any detail what is happening to Europe as a financial system. Rather, we have treated Germany as a self-contained financial system, with its own roots and development path. It would be worthwhile devoting a second book to the issue of the comparison and convergence of financial systems in Europe.

1.4. WHO SHOULD READ THIS BOOK?

There are several audiences who might want to look at the book as a whole or to certain chapters of it. First, practitioners in financial institutions and non-financial corporations will, it is hoped, take an interest in the survey-type presentations of how the various segments of the German financial system function, which regulations are relevant, and where future developments are likely to go. This profile should be relevant to corporate management and institutional investors from around the world.

Second, policy-makers and regulators, both at the national and at the European level, might be interested in the content of this book because it tries especially hard to tie together the loose ends emanating from the partial views in Chapters 3–14, and to come up with an assessment of the general properties of the German financial system at large. Regulators and policy-makers require an understanding of the mechanics of an existing financial system. In particular, they may want to anticipate possible side effects of specific regulatory innovations on the working of the financial system, be it the stock market, the IPO process, the bank lending process, or a specific financial law. An example, currently debated around the world, is the possible impact of a change in bank capital standards under Basle II on the credit supply for small and medium-sized enterprises. Clearly, such projections would presuppose an understanding of how banks allocate their funds to SMEs, and how risk adjusted loan rates would probably alter their portfolio decisions. The general case behind this example is that financial system engineering, an important policy topic in many countries nowadays, will have to build on a profound knowledge of the existing financial structure, as offered in this book for the case of Germany.

Last, but certainly not least, we hope that this book finds the attention of our fellow economists, be they general economists or financial economists and be they in academia or at commercial research institutions or departments. Of course, we would be particularly delighted to learn that our academic colleagues find it advisable to make their students consult our book.

We believe that, in particular, empirical minded economists may find it worthwhile to pursue detailed studies on this and other local financial architectures, like Italy, France, UK, and Japan. Cross-country comparative work would greatly benefit from such studies, both within an enlarged Europe and across continents. These studies would deliver information on the definition of reasonable variables or proxies to be used in cross-sectional regressions, and model specifications could be expected that are less prone to misspecification than those currently in use. Theoretical minded economists should also find many parts of this book rich in terms of presenting observable patterns of market activity that merit a profound theoretical analysis—and subsequently inspire a new round of empirical research, which could then be focused even on more forceful hypotheses.

References

Allen, F., and Gale, D. (1995). 'A welfare comparison of intermediaries and financial markets in Germany and the U.S.', *European Economic Review*, 39: 179–209.

——, and —— (2000). *Comparing Financial Systems*. MIT Press.

Edwards, J., and Fischer, K. (1994). *Banks, finance and investment in Germany*. Cambridge: Cambridge University Press.

Fohlin, C. (2000). 'Economic, Political, and Legal Factors in Financial System Development: International Patterns in Historical Perspective', Social Science Working Paper. No. 1089.

Goldsmith, R. W. (1969). *Financial Structure and Development*. New Haven and London: Yale University Press.

King, R., and Levine, R. (1993). 'Finance and Growth: Schumpeter Might be Right', *Quarterly Journal of Economics*, 108: 717–37.

La Porta, R., Lopez-de-Silanes, F., Shleifer, A., and Vishny, R. (1998). 'Law and Finance', *Journal of Political Economy*, 106: 1113–55.

Mankiw, N. G. (1995). 'The Growth of Nations', *Brookings Papers on Economic Activity*, 1995(1): 275–326.

Pagano, M., and Volpin, P. (2001). 'The Political Economy of Finance', *Oxford Review of Economic Policy*, 17(4): 502–19.

Rajan, R. G., and Zingales, L. (2003). 'The Great Reversals: Politics of Financial Development in the 20th Century', forthcoming in *Journal of Financial Economics*.

Roe, M. J. (1994). *Strong Managers, Weak Owners*. Princeton: Princeton University Press.

Rybczynski, T. (1984). 'Industrial Financial Systems in Europe, U.S. and Japan', *Journal of Economic Behaviour and Organization*, 5: 275–86.

Schmidt, R. H., Hackethal, A., and Tyrell, M. (2002). 'The Convergence of Financial Systems in Europe', in *German Financial Markets and Institutions: Selected Studies*, Special Issue 1–02 of Schmalenbach Business Review (2002), 7–53.

Stiglitz, J. (1993). 'The Role of the State in Financial Markets', in *Proceedings of the World Bank Conference on Development Economics 1993*. Washington DC: 19–52.

Tilly, R. (1992). 'An Overview on the Role of the Large German Banks up to 1914', in Y. Cassis (ed.), *Finance and Financiers in European History, 1880–1960*. Cambridge: Cambridge University Press, 93–112.

Walter, I. (1993). *The Battle of the Systems*. Kiel: Institut für Weltwirtschaft.

World Bank (1989). *World Development Report 1989, Financial Systems and Development*. Washington DC.

2

What Constitutes a Financial System in General and the German Financial System in Particular?

REINHARD H. SCHMIDT AND MARCEL TYRELL

2.1. THE PURPOSE AND STRUCTURE OF THIS CHAPTER

This chapter first discusses two issues that have a general bearing on the entire book, and then provides a broad overview of the German financial system. The first general issue is that of clarifying what we mean by the key term 'financial system' and, based on this definition, of showing why the financial system of a country is important and what it might be important for. Obviously, a definition of its subject matter and an explanation of its importance are required at the outset of any book. But it is all the more important in our case because the term 'financial system' is used in a number of very different ways, both in the academic literature and in non-academic discourse, and because the importance of the financial system is not generally acknowledged. As we will explain in Section 2.2, we use the term 'financial system' in a broad sense which sets it clearly apart from the narrower concept of the 'financial sector'.

The second general issue, which we will take up in Section 2.3, involves a discussion of how financial systems are described and analysed. This is a necessary step too, since there is no standard way of doing it. Obviously, the definition of the object of analysis and the method by which the object is to be analysed are closely related to one another. The overall structure of the present book reflects our broad definition of the term 'financial system': It deals not only with the German financial sector, but also with financial aspects of what happens in the real sectors of the German economy. As we will argue, we consider as the most useful approach to describing and analysing financial systems one which emphasizes the ways in which the various elements of a financial system are related to each other, and in which they interact. In other words, we wish to underscore the fact that a financial system really is *a system*, and to explain why this is so.

In Section 2.4 we will then provide a first general overview of the German financial system. In addition to putting the following chapters into perspective, this overview serves two purposes. It is intended to provide a first indication of how the elements of the German financial system are related to each other, and thus to support our claim that there is indeed some merit in emphasizing the systemic features of financial systems in general and of the German financial system in particular; and it is intended to at least partially compensate for the inevitable gaps in the material presented in the remainder of the book. The chapter concludes by briefly comparing the general characteristics of the German financial system with those of the financial systems of other advanced industrial countries, and taking a brief look at recent developments which, as will be argued at greater length in the concluding chapter of the book, might undermine the 'systemic' character of the German financial system, a crucial aspect which is emphasized in Section 2.5.2.

2.2. THE MEANING OF THE TERM 'FINANCIAL SYSTEM' AND THE IMPORTANCE OF FINANCIAL SYSTEMS

2.2.1. Defining Terms and Topics: 'Financial Sector' Versus 'Financial System'

What is a financial system, and what does the term 'financial system' properly refer to? The answer to these questions is not obvious, as one can easily see if one imagines the situation of a young World Bank economist who is instructed by her superiors to fly to some faraway country and come back with an overview of the 'financial system' of that country. What would she look at and what should she look at? What would those who sent her on the mission be interested in knowing?

She would certainly come back with information concerning the central bank and the monetary system of the country, its banks, and its stock market, if there is one. But this information may not be all that her superiors want to know. A policy-relevant analysis should put first things first. At least at a conceptual level, the analysis of any financial system should start with people and their business endeavours; it should examine their financial needs and their demand for financial services, and it should identify the ways in which these needs are satisfied and their demand is met. Accordingly, the underlying questions are:

1. How do people accumulate wealth and transfer income over time? Which options are available and how are they used?
2. How do businesses obtain financing if they, or their owners or managers, have attractive investment opportunities for which their own funds would not be sufficient?
3. How do people cope with risks?

Addressing these questions raises others, some of which may be more familiar: Are there institutions in that country which meet the demand for savings opportunities, credit facilities, and risk management or insurance services? And if they exist, what is the nature of those institutions, how do they function, who owns and governs them, how do they operate, and how are they designed and regulated? And most importantly, what role do those institutions play in helping real people to solve their financial problems? How important is external financing in comparison to internal financing? How important are real savings or real investment, as means of storing and transferring wealth over time, in comparison to financial savings? And how important is formal insurance relative to other methods of risk mitigation, that is, those which involve measures confined solely to the real sectors of the economy? How important are formal, that is, regulated and supervised financial institutions and organized markets in comparison to informal financial relationships, such as those that may exist between friends and family members? Are the financial institutions and the organized markets 'good' according to some suitable standard? And is the legal and regulatory system conducive to the provision of financial services and the establishment of financial institutions and their proper functioning?

These questions are equally important for all countries, irrespective of whether one looks at Indonesia, Poland, or Germany. As the young World Bank economist will hopefully have come to realize after a few days, the formal financial institutions may not be the most important part of the financial system of any of these countries. These considerations motivate our distinction between two concepts and their definitions.

1. The narrow concept is that of the *financial sector*. We define the financial sector as that part—or sector—of an economy which offers and provides financial services to the other sectors of the economy. It consists of the central bank, other banks, non-bank financial institutions, organized financial markets, and the relevant regulatory and supervisory institutions.
2. The broader concept is that of the *financial system*. It can be defined in general terms as the interaction between the supply of and the demand for the provision of capital and other finance-related services.

In addition to the supply side, that is, the financial sector and its activities, the concept of the financial system also includes the demand side, and thus the economic units which may demand financial services. The demand for these services comes from many economic units, but most importantly from households which accumulate wealth or simply carry income over from one time period to the next, and from firms which need capital for investing.

The widening of the focus is more than a change of definition, since the concept of the financial system also includes units in the non-financial sector in so far as they *do not* demand, or *do not succeed in obtaining*, services from the formal financial sector. Indeed, if we wish to understand the financial system of a country, we must also indicate the extent to which, and the forms in which, households and other surplus units undertake real investment merely in order to accumulate and transfer assets; how firms and other deficit units obtain financing directly from households and other surplus units or engage in self-financing; and how households and firms protect themselves against risks. The state is also a part of the financial system, not only because it too supplies and demands financial services, but also because it serves as the organizer and regulator of the financial sector.

There is a second dimension in which the concept of the financial system is broader than that of the financial sector. Financial flows are mirrored in flows of information and flows of potential and actual influence. From the perspective of new institutional economics, there are obvious reasons why this is so, and it is also obvious that financial flows, information flows, and flows of influence are interdependent: Each of the three types of relationship plays a key role in determining the nature of the other two types. Actual and potential flows of information and influence constitute the essence of 'the corporate governance system'. As finance without governance would scarcely be possible, the corporate governance system is therefore an integral part of the financial system of any country.[1]

2.2.2. The Importance of Having a Good Financial System

For a long time it has been common knowledge among economists that a well-functioning financial system is important for welfare and economic growth. Hilferding, for example, emphasized the role of the German banks in supporting the belated growth of industry in Germany. Schumpeter's view of the banker as the partner and supporter of the entrepreneur is well known, as is Gerschenkron's historical account of this role.[2] Practitioners in banking and business as well as politicians who are active in this area will typically share the view that 'finance matters'.

The conventional view of the financial system as a factor contributing to growth lost its prominence in academic circles at the time when the neoclassical theory of economic growth gained general acceptance, as the analytical structure of this theory does not accommodate banks or the financial sector in general. Moreover, while some economists continued to consider financial development as an engine of growth, others claimed that it was not a cause but

---

[1] Many authors make a distinction between the narrow and the broad concept which largely corresponds to our distinction between the financial sector and the financial system. But their terminology does not always reflect this distinction; the term 'financial system' is often used to denote merely the financial sector.

[2] See Hilferding (1910), Schumpeter (1934), and Gerschenkron (1962). The case studies in McKinnon (1973) provided some early evidence that finance matters. However, the importance of German banks in the late nineteenth and early twentieth centuries is questioned in more recent work by Fohlin (2000), Verdier (1999), and Rajan and Zingales (2003).

rather a consequence and a symptom of real economic development. For example, Hicks (1969) argued that the financial system of the United Kingdom played an important role in the Industrial Revolution, while Robinson (1952) questioned this view and suggested that the financial system developed as a result of economic growth, that is, that the causality went in the other direction.

The discussion about the role and importance of financial systems was revived around 1990. The World Development Report of 1989, which was specifically dedicated to this topic, provided the first econometric evidence that finance matters for growth and development; and it also suggested a causal link running from finance to growth. This strand of research culminated in the work of King and Levine. As the title of one of their influential papers indicates, they claim that 'Schumpeter might be right' (King and Levine 1993). More recent work, which is summarized in Levine (1997) and Winkler (2001), points in the same direction.

If one looks at this literature in detail one can easily recognize that, in its search for academic rigour, it does not, in fact, refer to the entire financial system in the broad sense introduced above, but more narrowly to the financial sector. However, the finding can easily be generalized using arguments such as those put forward in the work on 'law and finance' by La Porta *et al.*[3] Thus, at least at the current state of the debate, one can safely conclude that a good financial system seems to be conducive to economic welfare and growth and that, therefore, the topic of this book is indeed an important one. But this then raises the question of standards of assessment. We will address this question in the following section.

2.3. DIFFERENT APPROACHES TO ANALYSING FINANCIAL SYSTEMS

As there are many contexts in which the financial system is considered to be relevant, it is not surprising that there are also many different ways in which financial systems are described and analysed in the literature. Each of them reflects not only a different focus, but also a different concept of what is, and what is not, part of the financial system. However, there does not seem to exist a common view of how one should describe financial systems.[4]

In what follows, we shall briefly characterize four ways of describing and analysing financial systems. Let us refer to them as the 'institutional approach', the 'intermediation approach', the 'functional approach', and the 'systemic approach'. As will hopefully become clear, the four approaches are not mutually exclusive. Instead, they build on each other at least to a certain

---

[3] See, for instance, La Porta *et al.* (1998), Mayer and Sussman (2001), and Pagano and Volpin (2001) for surveys and Hellwig (2000) for a thorough discussion of the importance of a well-functioning financial system.

[4] Different ways of describing and analysing a financial system are discussed at length in Papenfuss (1999).

extent. We will conclude this section by indicating why we advocate using the most comprehensive approach, and by demonstrating in which sense it is in line with the broad concept of the financial system introduced above.

2.3.1. The Institutional Approach

As the term suggests, the institutional approach focuses on the existing institutions such as the banks, insurance companies, investment and pension funds, financial markets, and the central bank system. Descriptions and classifications of those institutions which in their totality make up the financial sector of a country are the dominant topic in the literature which follows this approach.[5] Thus, the institutional approach is narrow in its focus, and it is not analytical. This characterization of the institutional approach is not intended to be demeaning, since knowledge of the facts is a prerequisite for any attempt to dig deeper.

In addition to descriptions, classifications and statistical material, work which follows this approach can, and typically does, also offer comments and assessments pertaining to certain features of the various institutions within the financial sector or of the sector as a whole. For instance, it might be supplemented by an evaluation of the degree of competition in the banking sector, of its openness to foreign competitors and of the competition within and between different groups of financial intermediaries; or the transparency of price determination and investor protection in financial markets; or the quality of regulation and supervision.

2.3.2. The Intermediation Approach

Although, strictly speaking, no approach can be 'purely descriptive' in so far as any description involves the application of at least some analytical criteria which determine what to select and report, it is nonetheless true to say that the institutional approach is primarily descriptive in the sense that it is not explicitly shaped by theoretical considerations concerning, for example, the economic functions of the financial sector and its constituent institutions and their role in the national economy. Conventional economic approaches are different in this respect. One of these, which we do not wish to discuss at this point, is the monetary approach. It regards the financial sector, which is composed of the central bank and the commercial banking system, as the apparatus which supplies money to the real economy.[6]

---

[5] This type of description can be found in numerous textbooks and monographs. See Faugère and Voisin (1994) regarding the French financial system, Buckle and Thompson (1998) regarding the UK financial system, and various chapters in the manual compiled by Obst and Hintner (2000) on the German financial system.

[6] For the case of Germany, see Alexander and Bohl (2000) and various publications by the Deutsche Bundesbank, esp. Deutsche Bundesbank (1995). Chapter 6 in this volume contains elements of this approach.

There is another conventional economic approach which can be traced back to the work of Gurley and Shaw[7] and which emphasizes a different role of the financial sector, namely that of intermediation and transformation. In its original form, this approach, which we call the 'intermediation approach' for convenience, views the financial sector as composed of banks and other financial intermediaries. Intermediaries go between 'surplus spending units', which have more income in a given time period than they themselves want to spend on consumption and real investments during that period, and 'deficit spending units', which want to spend more than they have in terms of current income and income carried over from earlier time periods. In simple terms, the surplus units are savers, which is the characteristic role of households, and the deficit units are investors, the typical role of firms, and in many cases also of the state. Intermediaries substitute for direct finance by accepting some form of deposits from the savers and providing loans or equity to investors.

Intermediation helps to alleviate some of the problems which would make direct finance difficult. The main problem is that of divergent preferences and economic needs. Typically, savers prefer to have their funds available at short notice, to invest small amounts for relatively short terms, and to have their funds used for purposes which involve a low level of risk. Typical investors want exactly the opposite: They need funds without the threat of having them with-drawn unexpectedly; they want to have larger amounts for a longer period of time; and they want to be able to invest them in assets which may include some that entail a higher level of risk. In addition, there is a problem of information and incentives, or of adverse selection and moral hazard, which makes direct finance difficult. Being less informed and less capable of monitoring the use of their funds, savers might simply abstain from directly financing investors, or request compensations which make external financing unattractive for investors.

Intermediaries perform the following functions: They can provide liquidity; they can compensate for a certain mismatch of maturities and amounts, that is, perform what is referred to as term-to-maturity transformation and unit-size transformation; they can act as experts in assessing the economic potential of those who seek funding; and finally they serve as 'delegated monitors' (Diamond 1984, and the extensions in Diamond and Rajan 2001, and Tyrell 2003). In performing these functions, the financial sector can create value for the economy.

In an extended version, this approach also takes account of the economic role of financial markets and in particular secondary markets, and thus of the securitization of financial assets. Financial markets can also perform some of the transformation functions listed above. By doing so, they also mitigate the tensions which would stand in the way of transferring financial surplus from

---

[7] See Gurley and Shaw (1960) and with respect to developing countries Shaw (1973) and McKinnon (1973). For descriptions of financial systems in this tradition, see Bain (1992), Ferrandier and Koen (1994) and Kaufman (1997).

those who want to save to those who have good investment opportunities. Moreover, intermediation in the strict sense of on-balance-sheet intermediation can be combined with intermediation via markets in various ways. Allen and Santomero (2001), for example, show for the case of the United States how the role of banks has shifted from acting as financial intermediaries themselves to facilitating access to capital markets and to the transformation services that the capital markets provide to the economic units of the non-financial sectors of the economy.

This concept of what financial intermediaries and financial markets do suggests a way of describing and analysing a given financial system in terms of the extent and the effects of intermediation, transformation, and securitization. Evidently, such an approach is much more theory-based than the institutional approach. It not only covers the financial sector, but also includes, as an essential element, the non-financial sectors. Thus, it deals with the financial system as a whole. Moreover, it lends itself relatively well to measurement (see Hackethal and Schmidt 2000, 2003) and suggests a straightforward standard for evaluation: A financial system is 'better' if it provides more intermediation in the narrow and in the broad sense. However, the intermediation approach is quite selective in terms of what it takes into consideration, which indicates that one could usefully combine it with further extensions. The two approaches to which we turn now can be regarded as relevant extensions.

2.3.3. The Functional Approach

While the institutional approach is useful in its emphasis on the given institutional structure, it goes too far in this respect and has some serious weaknesses. As Merton argues, it cannot explain how and why the institutional structure of a financial system changes and how it could evolve over time. More generally, it lacks a deeper understanding of the functions a financial system should perform. While the intermediation approach does have a firm theoretical basis and emphasizes functions, it is not entirely satisfactory in so far as it only focuses on two functions of the financial sector, namely intermediation and transformation.

Robert C. Merton and various co-authors have developed an alternative to the institutional perspective and, one might add, a generalization of the intermediation approach.[8] What they call the functional approach focuses on *functions* rather than institutions *as given* and, therefore, as the conceptual point of departure. In this approach five functions are identified and distinguished from the primary or core function at a less abstract and aggregate level. A financial system provides

(1) a way to transfer economic resources through time and across regions and industries, which is singled out as the core function of any financial system;

---

[8] See Merton (1990 and 1995) and Merton and Bodie (1995) for an in-depth description of this approach, and Crane *et al.* (1995) for various applications.

(2) a payments system to facilitate the trade of goods, services, and financial claims;

(3) a mechanism for pooling resources and for subdividing shares in large-scale indivisible enterprises;

(4) a way to manage uncertainty and control risk;

(5) price information that can be useful in coordinating decentralized decision-making;

(6) a way to deal with asymmetric information and incentive problems.

As its advocates claim, the functional approach offers a useful frame of reference for analysing a country's entire financial system; it is more reliable and generates more insights than an institutional approach because the basic functions of a financial system are essentially the same in all economies and are more stable than the identity and structure of the institutions performing them. According to this approach, the analysis of a financial system starts by describing the functions performed by the different elements of a country's financial system and determining how the functions are currently being performed (see Merton and Bodie 1995: 17).

The functional approach has the virtue of abstracting from institutional detail and instead focusing on the underlying economics. However, it may also go too far. A strict application of this approach presupposes that functions are *separable*, and this assumption may be wrong: On the one side, an arrangement in which a particular type of institution performs multiple financial functions at the same time may be efficient,[9] and on the other side, specific configurations of institutions may be required to reduce frictions which would otherwise hamper the allocation of resources, and thus lower the performance of a financial system. This requirement, namely the complementarity between different elements (institutions) of a financial system, will be discussed in more detail in the next subsection. As a result, there are major trade-offs and interrelationships between the different functions described above and the different institutions performing those functions (see Allen and Gale 2000 for a thorough analysis of these trade-offs). In this respect different financial systems may have different strengths and weaknesses, which the functional perspective seems hardly capable of grasping.

2.3.4. The Systemic Approach

A systemic approach aspires to accomplish just that: It describes and analyses a financial system in terms of the interrelations between its elements and the impact which these interrelations have on the performance of the system as a whole. In a systemic perspective, a financial system is an ordered set of *complementary* and possibly *consistent* elements or subsystems.

---

[9] For instance, this can be the case for the institution 'bank', which can be understood as the specific combination of the functions of liquidity provision and relationship lending (Diamond and Rajan 2001). See Rajan (1996) for a similar critique of the functional approach with respect to the institution 'commercial bank'.

What is the meaning of 'complementarity'? Two (or more) elements of a system are complementary to each other

(1) if the positive effects of the values taken on by the elements mutually reinforce each other in terms of a relevant evaluation function, and the negative effects mutually mitigate each other; that is

(2) if a higher value for one element increases the benefit yielded by an isolated small increase in the value for the other element (and vice versa); and

(3) if, as a result, the 'quality' or the 'economic value' of a system depends on the values taken on by its (complementary) features being consistent with each other or, to put it simply, on the values 'fitting together'.[10]

Whether the elements or subsystems of a given system are complementary is determined by theoretical considerations. In the case of financial systems, such considerations would have to show that elements such as the role of banks in the financial sector, the financing patterns of corporations and the governance structure of big corporations, as well as the role of financial markets as compared to that of intermediaries, the structure of the pension system and certain parts of the legal system are complementary to each other. This can indeed be shown to be the case.[11] Thus, it is accurate to say that all financial systems are shaped by the complementarity of their main elements. Moreover, theoretical considerations allow the conclusion that there may not be more than a few or even only two 'efficient' types of financial systems, as is reflected in the well-known classification of financial systems into two groups, depending on whether they are perceived as being bank-based or capital market-based.

However, *complementarity* implies merely that a potential exists: Economic benefits may accrue, but only if the main elements of a (financial) system take on values which fit well together. This potential will not necessarily be realized. This is precisely the aspect covered by the concept of 'consistency'. We refer to a system made up of complementary elements as being consistent if the benefits of complementarity are exploited and if, therefore, a small change in the value taken on by an individual feature, or by several features, does not permit an improvement in terms of the objective function or the evaluation function. Whether or not a given financial system is consistent is an empirical question.

---

[10] There are much more formal ways of defining and characterizing the concept of complementarity, which use the mathematical apparatus of lattice theory; see Fudenberg and Tirole (1991), Topkis (1998), and Hackethal (2000). The concept has been popularized in the economic literature by the work of Milgrom and Roberts in the context of organizational design; see, for example, Milgrom and Roberts (1990, 1995*a*, *b*) but also Aoki (2001). For an application of the concept of complementarity to the field of financial systems see Aoki and Patrick (1994) and Schmidt *et al.* (2002).

[11] See Hackethal and Tyrell (1999), Hackethal and Schmidt (2000) and Tyrell and Schmidt (2001) for various combinations of the financial system elements listed here.

As a consequence, the financial system of a country can be characterized by determining which of the known types of financial systems (defined on the basis of their complementary elements) it conforms to—if any at all—and by investigating to what extent its elements are indeed consistent.

Of course, these definitions of complementarity and consistency presuppose that there is a standard of measurement with which systems can be evaluated—at least approximately—in terms of the benefits they offer, and that the values taken on by the elements can be measured at least in the weak form of an ordinal ranking and/or that it is possible to distinguish between 'polar' values. The standard for assessment might be a general level of economic welfare or the contribution which the financial system makes to economic growth; but it might also be the extent to which the functions of financial systems listed by Merton and his co-authors are performed, and also how well they are performed.

A consistent system of complementary elements is in a state of (static) equilibrium. Typically, the key elements of systems characterized by complementarity include multiple equilibria or local optima.[12] In most cases it is impossible for the individual actors operating in the system to judge whether a local optimum is also the global optimum. This feature has important implications for the development of financial systems and especially for the issue of the convergence of different financial systems over time. With respect to the German financial system this aspect will be taken up in the final chapter of this book.

The twin concepts of complementarity and consistency would seem to give a more precise meaning to what is colloquially called 'a real system', as it is highly plausible to assume that one's assessment of individual elements, and indeed of a specific change in one element, depends in a crucial way on the values which the other elements of the system take on. What are the implications of this insight for the task of describing and analysing a given financial system? Unfortunately, a formal proof of complementarity and consistency based on the mathematical theory which underlies the theory of complementarity cannot be performed in practice because it would require much more information than is available. However, one can attempt to describe a given financial system informally in such a way that complementarities which are *presumed* to exist become visible. If one can show that different key elements of the financial system in question fit together in a specific way, then this system is also likely to be consistent, and it can be classified as belonging to one of the two types of financial system distinguished above. Thus, this investigation should be a part of the characterization of any financial system.

---

[12] For this reason it is important to determine the *key* elements of a financial system. If a change in the value of an individual element would inevitably undermine the consistency of the whole system, we refer to this element as a key or core element. For instance, a fundamental change in the character of a country's pension system from a pay-as-you-go system to a capital-funded system would lead to an inconsistency if that country's financial system was bank-based. See Tyrell and Schmidt (2001) for more details.

2.3.5. Implications

All four approaches discussed above have their merits, and each of them is taken into account in the following chapters of the book as well as in the following section of the present chapter. However, as the systemic approach is the most comprehensive one, we will now attempt to outline the most important features of the German financial system using the concept of complementarity. We will argue that these features *together* constitute, or at least did constitute until quite recently, a system of complementary elements, each of which fits together with the others, thus making the others more effective than they would otherwise be.

2.4. THE GERMAN FINANCIAL SYSTEM: AN OVERVIEW OF ITS CHARACTERISTIC FEATURES

2.4.1. Introduction

We start our overview of the German financial system in Section 2.4.2 with a brief description of the financial sector, including the regulatory environment, using the institutional approach. In Section 2.4.3, we then look at the different functions which a financial system has to perform. We describe which part of the financial system fulfils which functions, and especially how resources are collected, allocated, and controlled in the German financial system. The main focus in this section will be on the role of banks as financial intermediaries, on the patterns of German corporate finance, and on corporate governance in Germany. However, this section also includes a brief characterization of the savings behaviour and portfolio choice of German households and of the German pension system, two topics which are not covered specifically by individual chapters in the present book. Thus, Section 2.4.3 applies both the narrower intermediation perspective and the broader functional perspective to the case of the German financial system.

In Section 2.4.4, we bring the different elements together and trace a picture of the overall financial system, identifying its peculiarities and especially its systemic character, as we perceive it. We will argue in this section that in the mid-to-late 1990s, that is, before the major stock market rally of the late 1990s and the ensuing downward spiral, the German financial system was indeed a consistent system. Since that time, however, the German financial system has undergone considerable changes, and these recent developments may have distorted the picture of complementarity and consistency. More precisely, they would appear to cast doubt on the *conceivable* proposition that the German financial system is still today a largely consistent one. However, we make no such proposition here. Whether the German financial system still is what it seems to have been only 7, or even only 5 years ago, or whether it has recently changed its character in a fundamental way is too complicated a question to be discussed seriously within the limited space of this section. In the concluding chapter of this book, the two editors will explain why both possibilities appear plausible—and why it is also too early to take a firm stand on this issue. The chapters that follow will present most of the material on which such an assessment might be based. Thus, the present chapter serves as a point of reference for the following chapters. To a certain extent, this section and especially Section 2.4.4 characterizes, not the German financial system as of the time of writing, but rather that of the mid-to-late 1990s. Through the use of present and past tense, as well as occasional footnotes and cross references, we indicate which of the features of the German financial system described in this section have changed substantially during the last half-decade.

2.4.2. The Institutional Perspective

The financial sector of a country encompasses the financial intermediaries, which can be subdivided into banks, non-bank financial intermediaries (NBFIs) and financial markets, and also the regulatory environment in which these institutions operate. It is in this sequence that we now consider each of these elements in turn.

2.4.2.1. *Banks*

In the mid-1990s the German banking system exhibited characteristics, especially its structural complexity and the power of its banks, that differentiated it from many other banking systems in industrialized countries.[13] A bank, in legal terms a 'credit institution', is defined in Article 1 of the Banking Act of 1961 as any enterprise which is professionally engaged in the activities of accepting deposits, making loans, discounting bills, providing securities brokerage services and trust (safe custody) services, factoring, financial guarantees, and funds transfer or payment (giro) services as well as providing other services which the relevant authorities might define as banking services. According to this broad definition, there were approximately 3,700 legally independent banks with more than 48,000 banking offices in Germany in 1995.[14] Thus, in terms of the large numbers of banks and banking offices, Germany was, and still is, one of the most heavily 'banked' economies in the world. The number of banks in Germany has declined in recent years, but is still large by international standards.

The vast majority of the banks are universal banks, which means that they are engaged, to a greater or lesser extent, in all of the activities listed above, plus typical investment banking services and the provision of insurance products through subsidiaries or closely connected insurance firms.

[13] For a detailed description of the German banking sector, see Büschgen (1993), Süchting and Paul (1998), and Hartmann-Wendels *et al.* (1998).

[14] See Deutsche Bundesbank (1996, 2002) for most of the data in the following description. Chapter 3 of the book explains the extent to which, and the reasons why, the number of banks has decreased since then.

Table 2.1. *Structural figures for the German banking sector*

Bank group	Balance sheet total, million	Percentage of balance sheet total (%)	Number of credit institutions	Domestic branches
1995	DM			
Private commercial banks	2,218,356	27.4	331	7305
Big banks	*978,322*	*12.1*	*3*	*3624*
Savings bank group	3,046,470	37.7	637	19,504
Credit cooperative group	1,149,666	14.2	2595	17,248
All other categories	1,675,208	20.7	221	4167
Total	8,089,700		3784	48,224
2001	Euro			
Private commercial banks	2,458,055	33.2	303	5576
Big banks	*1,648,863*	*22.3*	*4*	*2369*
Savings bank group	2,575,194	34.8	547	17,094
Credit cooperative group	783,972	10.6	1623	14,602
All other categories	1,577,028	21.3	222	3867
Total	7,394,249		2695	41139

Source: Deutsche Bundesbank (1996, 2002).

With respect to their ownership structure, the German universal banks can be subdivided into three categories: private commercial banks, savings banks, and cooperative banks. Only about 330 of Germany's banks, or roughly 10 per cent of the total number of banking institutions, were private commercial banks, and thus, at least based on their ownership structure and their legal status, profit-maximizing entities.[15] In 1995, the group of private commercial banks included the three major publicly listed banks Deutsche Bank, Dresdner Bank, and Commerzbank; the regional commercial banks with extensive branch networks; and the few remaining private banking outfits.[16]

Table 2.1 provides information on the fractions of the three major banking groups with respect to the number of legally independent institutions, total bank assets, and bank branches for both 1995 and 2001.

The private commercial banks dominate the securities trading and custody business and also play a dominant role as investment bankers on the IPO market. In addition, especially the big joint stock banks hold substantial

---

[15] In terms of the volume of bank assets under their control, this group represented 27 per cent of total German bank assets in 1995. The market share of the so-called big banks ('Grossbanken') amounted to only 12 per cent.

[16] Since the merger of the two large exchange-listed Bavarian banks in 1998 to form Hypo-Vereinsbank, the banking statistics of the Deutsche Bundesbank have included it as a fourth 'big bank'. In addition, the insurance company Allianz took over the Dresdner Bank in 2001, which is therefore no longer publicly listed.

interests in commercial enterprises and other financial institutions that provide specialized and mortgage banking services. Regional commercial banks have a strong local presence. Apart from being universal banks, they are in many cases strongly engaged in some specialized activity, for example, housing finance. Smaller private banks typically have the legal form of a partnership and specialize in the financing of a particular industrial sector or in the provision of selected banking services to wealthy customers, such as investment advisory and trustee services. In the mid-1990s, only about sixty subsidiaries, and branches of foreign commercial banks operated in Germany, representing only 2 per cent of total banking assets. One group of foreign banks mainly provided their services to German subsidiaries of foreign firms, while another group plays an important role in the various fields of investment banking.

In terms of total assets and banking offices, the savings banks group is the biggest group in the German banking sector. It comprises three layers of institutions, consisting of about 600 local savings banks, thirteen regional-level banks (called *Landesbanken* or *Landbanks*, 'Land' being the term given to each of the states that make up the Federal Republic) and one institution at the top of the system. With only a few exceptions, savings banks are owned by the public sector, that is, municipalities, districts, and federal states. This implies that the public sector bears liability if the savings banks run into financial difficulties and is also obliged to make sufficient capital available to them. For this reason and because of their legal mandate, savings banks are not strictly profit-maximizing entities.

Local savings banks operate only in their designated region, and thus they hardly compete with each other. They provide local customers with a wide range of banking services, excluding only those services that they cannot provide efficiently because of being too small, and those that are prohibited by the relevant savings banks law. This is where the *Landbanks* come into play. Moreover, the *Landbanks* serve as a clearing houses for the local savings banks as well as holding their excess liquidity reserves, and are typically also the *Hausbank* of the respective *Land*. They are fully fledged universal banks and wield enormous power based on the strong branch presence of the savings banks.

The third important group is the cooperative banking group, comprising a larger number of independent institutions than any of the other groups. In 1995, there were nearly 2,600 local cooperative banks with 17,000 branches. But typically these banks were rather small: The entire cooperative group represented only 14 per cent of total German banking assets. Cooperative banks are member-owned, and according to their by-laws their main function is to support the business of their member-owners. Thus, these institutions too are not standard profit-maximizing entities. In recent years, a wave of intra-sectoral mergers has greatly reduced the number of local cooperative banks, and the upper levels of the cooperative banking system have been restructured.

These three banking groups also shape the German payment system. In Germany credit transfers and direct debits are the predominant form of payment transactions. Nearly every bank belongs to one of the banking groups which in each case operate their own giro network to process retail payments.[17] The processing in these networks is usually carried out on a bilateral basis with settlements effected by one or more of the banking group's central institutions. This stands in sharp contrast to most other industrialized countries where because of other banking structures typically cheques are used in non-cash payments (see European Central Bank 2002 for more details).

Apart from these three main categories of (universal) banks, banks with a somewhat narrower scope also play an important role in Germany. There are about 200 non-universal public and private banking institutions representing more than 20 per cent of total German banking assets. One important subgroup here are the public and private mortgage banks. These institutions enjoy a special status and the privilege of being authorized to issue mortgage bonds ('Pfandbriefe'), that is, asset-backed securities with long maturities. Furthermore, the group of specialist banks includes various government-funded banks with special mandates to support economic development in Germany and in other countries; and also the Deutsche Postbank AG.

Let us briefly summarize the main characteristics of the German banking system as outlined above.[18]

1. It was—and still is—dominated by universal banks, almost all of which are genuine universal banks in the sense that they are not merely financial conglomerates, but rather accommodate almost all divisions within a single institution.

2. The majority of institutions are not bound to the principle of profit-maximization. Most banks provide the full range of financial services, but in fact—aside from a few exceptions, notably some of the so-called big banks—they concentrate on retail deposit-taking and lending. Not only urban but also rural populations enjoy good access to these banking services.

3. Competition is greater between the different groups of banks than within each group.

4. The clear predominance of banks is also reflected in the fact that the ratio of banking assets to GDP is relatively high, compared to other industrialized countries and compared to corresponding measures for the stock market.

5. In purely quantitative terms, the three (or four) big German banks do not seem to be as important as the biggest banks in most other countries. Yet,

[17] Deutsche Postbank AG is also a big player in the payment services market because it operates with more than 14,000 branches a big giro network.

[18] Banks and bank–client relations are discussed at greater length in Chapters 3 and 7 in this book.

this assessment is no longer strictly true if one takes account of the other roles they play, in addition to lending and deposit taking.

2.4.2.2. *Non-bank financial intermediaries*

By international and especially by Anglo-Saxon standards, non-bank financial intermediaries (NBFIs) or institutional investors[19] were still a relatively small segment of the financial sector in Germany in the mid-1990s.[20] This applies in particular to investment funds, which have considerably gained in importance since then, however.

NBFIs in Germany can be subdivided into two main groups: insurance companies and investment companies. Insurance companies are the largest group of NBFIs. Especially life insurance companies are of interest here because they are important institutional investors that manage savings on behalf of small investors.[21] In the mid-1990s, domestic insurance companies dominated the German life insurance market,[22] and 46 per cent of total premium volume was generated by the four biggest companies. Nevertheless, compared to other industrialized countries, the market concentration was still low (see also Albrecht and Schradin 1999).

The portfolio composition of the German life insurance industry shows some interesting peculiarities. Fifty-seven per cent of the funds were invested in loans and bonds—especially loans to banks, bank bonds and government bonds—but a mere 17 per cent in domestic equities and virtually nothing in foreign assets.[23] It is important to add here that there are close connections between the insurance and banking industries which manifest themselves in cross-holdings of equity and seats on the respective supervisory boards (see Böhmer 2001).

The investment industry was a latecomer to the German financial sector. With a mere 9 per cent of GDP, the volume of total assets under management in 1998 was far below the comparable figures in the United Kingdom, the United States, or France. There are two types of investment funds: the so-called special funds, which are administered only for institutional investors; and public funds, which are offered to the general public. In the late 1990s about two-thirds of the capital managed by the investment industry was held in special funds.[24]

---

[19] As Raimond Maurer does in Chapter 4 on institutional investors in Germany in this book, we follow Davis and Steil (2001) in using the term institutional investors as a synonym for NBFIs.

[20] See the figures in Davis and Steil (2001: 7–8) and Schmidt *et al.* (1999).

[21] In the mid-1990s, pension funds were virtually non-existent in Germany because of the structure of the German social security system. After the pension reform legislation of 2001 this is slowly changing.

[22] In 1997 international companies had a 13 per cent share of total premium volume. See Albrecht and Schradin (1999) for these and the following figures.

[23] See Davis and Steil (2001: 33). The fraction invested in shares had increased in the late 1990s, but never came close to the level attained in Great Britain, for example. For details, see Chapter 4 in this book.

[24] The insurance industry was by far the largest category of investors in special funds in 1999, followed by credit institutions (Laux and Päsler 2001).

In the context of the German investment business it is important to distinguish between two types of legal entity, namely the investment companies which manage funds, and the funds themselves. The investors who provide the capital which is administered by this type of institutional investor are share-holders in the fund, but not shareholders in the investment company. In the mid-1990s, and still today, the shareholders of the investment companies were and are mostly banks—in many cases a single bank or a single banking group—and these banks would also typically serve as marketing channels for the shares in their investment funds. The dual role of the sponsoring banks gives them a great deal of influence on the business decisions of the investment companies, and may create the basis for conflicts of interest between the banks as shareholders in the investment companies and the shareholders in the funds.[25]

The investment behaviour of German investment funds is, on average, rather conservative. In 1995 only about 25 per cent of the assets of all investment funds were invested in domestic or foreign equities, while the overwhelming proportion went into bank and government bonds or into liquid assets. It is surely not too far-fetched to assume that the investment policy of the invest-ment industry corresponded to the fundamental interest of the banks in maintaining their role as lenders and underwriters, and also reflected the influence which the banks have on other parts of the German financial sector.

2.4.2.3. *Financial markets*

In an institutional sense, financial markets comprise the primary and organ-ized secondary markets for securities and other tradable financial instruments, and also the money market. In what follows, we mainly focus on the organized markets for stocks and bonds.[26]

Although in terms of absolute capitalization the German stock market was the fourth largest equity market after the United States, Japan, and the United Kingdom in the mid-1990s, in comparison to the size of the German economy it was, and still is, relatively small.[27]

In 1995, only 678 domestic companies were listed on any of the German stock exchanges. IPO activity was virtually non-existent (for details, see Chapter 8 in this book). The number of listed German corporations had been declining for years. If a corporation did aspire to go public and be listed, then typically one of the big commercial banks accompanied this new issue as the investment bank and underwriter. Thus, all in all, as a source of funding and as an investment vehicle, the organized stock market was indeed 'underdeveloped'.

---

[25] The empirical results in Baums (1996), Baums and Theissen (1999) do not show that this potential conflict of interest has an adverse impact on the performance of the funds.

[26] Some aspects of the German money market are discussed in Chapter 6 on the monetary transmission mechanism in this book.

[27] See DAI-Factbook 2001 for most of the data used in this section. The market capitalization/ GDP ratio increased considerably in the stock market boom of the late 1990s but fell again in 2001/2002. See Chapter 5 in this book for more details.

Until the early 1990s, the limited importance of the stock market was reflected in its institutional structure. The main stock exchange was located in Frankfurt, but the overall German stock market was highly fragmented, consisting of a number of individual exchanges, which were overly regulated in certain respects—for example, in terms of their listing requirements—while investor protection was still in its infancy. A law prohibiting insider trading has been introduced as recently as 1994, and it was only then that an institution designed to implement this and other investor protection measures began to take shape.[28]

The German stock exchange system consisted of three market segments, the official market ('amtlicher Markt'), the semi-official market ('geregelter Markt') for small caps and the over-the-counter market ('Freiverkehr'). The *Neuer Markt* for young technology-oriented stocks was created only in 1997. In their role as the majority owner of the Deutsche Börse AG, which runs much of the German stock exchange system, the banks played, and in fact still play, a dominant role in determining the overall development and even the operational policies of the stock exchanges. In 2002, the system of market segments was revised. As a consequence of a series of failures and scandals, the *Neuer Markt*, which had attracted considerable attention and enjoyed great popularity for a time, has been closed down in the course of 2003.

In the mid-1990s, turnover on the German stock exchanges was also still low by international standards, and trading was heavily concentrated, focusing on just a few 'blue chips'. Liquidity was modest for various reasons. On average, the free float was, and still is, reduced by the fact that stock ownership is heavily concentrated and cross-holdings are pervasive with wealthy families, non-financial corporations, and banks and insurance companies as the biggest blockholders (see Franks and Mayer 1995; and Barca *et al.* 2001). The general public did not show any great interest in the stock market in the early to mid-1990s, as is evidenced by the fact that the share of the German population which owns stock directly or indirectly was much lower than in most comparable countries.

As Erik Theissen explains in his contribution to this book (Chapter 5), the German stock exchange seems to have improved greatly since the mid-1990s as far as its role and its institutional structure are concerned, whereas its role as an outlet for savings and as a source of funding seems to be limited to this day.

In terms of the value of outstanding securities the German bond market was and still is larger than the stock market. There are five main categories of bonds in the German markets, with almost all of the capital raised in the bond market flowing to banks and the public sector. Industrial bonds were virtually

---

[28] See Nowak (Chapter 13) for an account of how investor protection developed in the past decade in Germany. The author argues that since the turn of the millennium it has no longer been appropriate to speak of an underdeveloped stock market system as far as investor protection is concerned.

non-existent on the domestic market in the mid-1990s. DM bond issues on the Euromarket were larger but still small by international standards. The fact that banks did the underwriting of every new bond issue of the German government via a fixed consortium consisting of all bigger German banks is an additional indicator of the dominance of the banks over the entire financial sector.[29] With the advent of the Euro, the market for industrial bonds starts to become more lively now.

Besides the bond market there is an important market in *Schuldscheine*. *Schuldscheine* are not securities but negotiable promissory notes or loan certificates with variable terms and maturities of up to 15 years. They are issued in a private placement market but actively traded over the counter. As the minimum denomination has traditionally been DM 1 million, the main investors in this market have been institutions.

2.4.2.4. *The regulatory environment*

Until the end of the last millennium, financial regulation and supervision was fragmented, and there were substantial differences between the fields of banking, capital markets, and insurance.

Regulation of the banking sector is based primarily on the German Banking Act of 1961. As a consequence of various amendments to the Banking Act in the 1960s, the overall regime had been relatively liberal for quite some time. Earlier than in most other European countries, the establishment of banks and bank branches had been deregulated, and interest rates were fully liberalized as early as 1967. And apart from solvency-related provisions, there are also no restrictions on lending. Banks are free to invest in non-financial corporations and to engage in a broad spectrum of banking and bank-related activities, including almost all aspects of investment banking. Thus, the general regime provides the basis for true universal banking. Only insurance and mortgage banking activities have to be carried out via institutions with a separate legal identity. As far as the substance of regulatory practice is concerned, the emphasis has long been on capital adequacy and solvency regulation.

The overall responsibility for bank supervision rested with the Federal Banking Supervisory Authority (FBSA), an independent government authority under the auspices of the Ministry of Finance. In its practical work, the FBSA was expected to cooperate closely with the Bundesbank and its regional affiliates, the so-called *Landeszentralbanken*, which were responsible for on-site inspections. Overall, it seems fair to say that the German system of banking regulation and supervision was well developed and functioned well. It is indicative that between 1974 and 2001 there was no event in Germany which could be classified as a banking crisis.

---

[29] This federal bond consortium was abolished in 1998. Major federal securities are now auctioned through the 'Bund Issues Auction Group'. See Deutsche Bundesbank (1998) for further details.

In comparison to banking, the insurance industry was much more heavily regulated. In particular, the investment of funds by insurance companies was tightly restricted to assure solvency and liquidity at all times. As a result, most of the funds mobilized by the insurance companies were placed with banks and investment funds. In addition, activities associated with different insurance products, especially life insurance and property and liability insurance, have to be carried out through different legal entities. This is why German insurance companies tend to be complex groups with many subsidiaries.

Until the mid-1990s, regulation of the stock market was rather neglected. Rules favouring transparency and restricting insider trading were virtually non-existent, and the disclosure of price-sensitive information was rather weak. Not until then did the German authorities begin to transpose EU directives into national law. Thus, the stock market de- and reregulation was initiated by foreign rather than domestic interest groups.

The Deutsche Bundesbank opposed the deregulation of the money market, because it used this market as its primary means of controlling monetary growth. Consequently, commercial papers and money market mutual funds were only gradually introduced in the 1990s. Thus, in effect—and this may or may not have been intended—the Bundesbank protected the commercial banks against competition from other instruments and institutions. The Deutsche Bundesbank itself summarized its monetary policy design as follows: 'Owing to their pre-eminent position, credit institutions play a key part in the transmission of monetary stimuli, and provide the most important starting point for central bank policy measures' (Deutsche Bundesbank 1995: 43–4).

The institutional structure of financial regulation and supervision changed in 2002. Following the example of the British FSA, the German government created a new institution, the *Bundesaufsichtsamt für das Finanzwesen* (BAFin), integrating the traditional supervisory functions for the banking, insurance, and securities industries under one roof.

2.4.3. The Functional Perspective

The primary function of each financial system is to allow savings to be invested in wealth-creating projects, typically undertaken by firms. This process has many dimensions which should be taken into consideration when describing the German financial system. For instance, one should know how firms obtained funds and financed investments in Germany. Another perspective on how the German financial system operates can be obtained by looking at savings and the holding of financial and real assets by private households. In addition, one should ask what role different types of financial institutions (banks, non-bank financial intermediaries, and organized capital markets) play with respect to the functions of intermediation and transformation. These questions focus on the structure and the functions of the financial sector. Equally important are the risk-sharing mechanisms associated with the channelling of funds from units with surpluses to units with deficits and the way information is acquired and used in the process of allocating resources. In this section, these aspects of the financing process will be surveyed, applying both the narrower intermediation approach and the wider functional approach to describing and analysing a financial system.

2.4.3.1. *Intermediation and the distribution of roles in the financial sector*

In order to characterize the structure and the functions of the financial sector in Germany in quantitative terms, we will rely primarily on intermediation ratios.[30] This type of ratio is based on the notion of an economy as a collection of sectors which exchange real goods, services, and funds with each other. The implementation of transactions entailing financial resources implies that funds flow between the parties, the total amount of these flows being manifested in stocks of claims held by certain sectors which are matched by stocks of liabilities incurred by other sectors.

Intermediation ratios (IRs) are defined and calculated on the basis of the stocks accumulated over several periods. They measure the share of the claims— or liabilities—of a sector (or group of sectors) which are claims on—or liabilities to—the entire financial sector or, more specifically, on the banking sector as a percentage of the total claims—or liabilities—of the sector under consideration *vis-à-vis* all other economic sectors. Intermediation ratios provide an indication of how important the financial sector or, more specifically, the banking sector is in channelling funds from surplus to deficit units. As a time series, an intermediation ratio provides an indication of how this role develops.

Central banks or the respective national statistical offices compile records of the financial flows within an economy. These statistics provide an ideal source of data for the computation of the two types of ratios. Given that these figures distinguish between sectors rather than individual economic agents, the study of intermediation ratios can only deal with inter-sectoral stocks, but not with intra-sectoral stocks. In the official flow-of-funds statistics, the financial sector is typically subdivided into the banking sector on the one hand and the NBFI sector on the other hand. See Hackethal (2000), for a detailed discussion of the database.

In Figures 2.1 and 2.2, the most important intermediation ratios have been plotted for Germany covering the time period from 1982 to 1998. The General Asset Intermediation Ratio (abbreviation: Asset-IR and shown in Figure 2.1) and the General Liability Intermediation Ratio (which is by construction numerically almost indistinguishable from the Asset-IR and is therefore not

---

[30] The results presented in this section are an extension of those reported in Schmidt *et al.* (1999), where the financial sector structures of different industrialized countries in the 1980s and 1990s are compared. See this study for details concerning the data and the methodology.

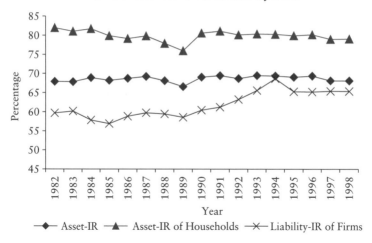

Figure 2.1. *General intermediation ratios.*
Source: Schmidt *et al.* (1999).

shown) reflect the highest degree of aggregation. The Asset-IR indicates what fraction of the total financial claims of all non-financial sectors is accounted for by claims on the entire financial sector. Correspondingly, the Liability-IR represents the fraction of all inter-sectoral liabilities of the non-financial sectors that are liabilities to the financial sector.[31]

The general IRs for all non-financial sectors can be disaggregated in three ways to yield partial ratios, and thus more detailed information. First, the investment and financing behaviour of individual non-financial sectors can be considered separately. For example, the Asset-IR of Households (Figure 2.1) shows which fraction of the total financial assets of households consists of claims on the financial sector. Correspondingly, the Liability-IR of Firms (Figure 2.1) shows which fraction of the inter-sectoral liabilities of firms is owed to financial intermediaries. Second, it is possible to address the question of how the claims on (liabilities to) the financial sector break down into claims on (liabilities to) banks on the one hand and NBFIs on the other. Thus, for example, the Asset-IR with Banks (Figure 2.2) indicates which portion of the total financial assets of the real sectors is invested with banks, and the Liability-IR to Banks shows the fraction of liabilities that is owed to the banking sector. Finally, these two forms of disaggregation can be combined to produce a third form which is even more detailed. The Asset-IR of Households with Banks (Figure 2.1) indicates the role played by banks in mobilizing the

---

[31] If the financial accounts of the financial sector were balanced—that is, if financial institutions had no real assets—then, following the logic of a flow-of-funds analysis, the financial assets of the non-financial sectors would necessarily be equal to the total value of their liabilities. In that case, the Asset-IR and the Liability-IR would have to be identical. In the case of Germany, the values of these two ratios are nearly identical.

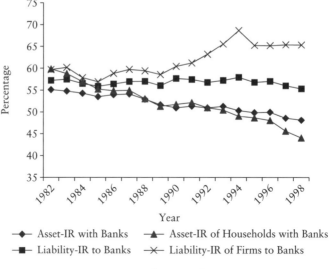

Figure 2.2. *Partial intermediation ratios.*

Source: Schmidt *et al.* (1999).

financial assets of households. In an analogous fashion, the Liability-IR of Firms to Banks provides a measure of the role of banks in enterprise financing.

Taken together, these ratios show that at least until the end of the 1990s banks were the dominant financial institutions in terms of their role in channelling funds from households to firms. Private households invested their funds mainly with banks, using traditional non-securitized financial instruments, and to the extent that firms financed themselves externally, they did so mainly by taking on bank credit. What may be most surprising is the stability of the intermediation ratios over time. Most importantly, with the exception of households' deposits with banks, intermediation in general and bank intermediation in particular has hardly changed over time. In an international comparison, the high level of bank intermediation, as measured by the Asset-IR and the Liability-IR *vis-à-vis* banks, stands out as a characteristic feature of the German financial system (see Schmidt *et al.* 1999; and Hackethal 2001 for more details).

An additional point emerges if we look at the intermediation ratios of the banking sector itself, which can be calculated in a manner analogous to that used to compute the IRs of the non-financial sectors if total inter-sectoral assets or total inter-sectoral liabilities are selected as the denominator. The Asset-IR of Banks shown in Figure 2.3 indicates the extent to which banks do *not* channel their funds directly to the real sectors, but rather provide them first to other financial intermediaries, which, by definition, are NBFIs. The Liability-IR of Banks in Figure 2.3 shows the fraction of banks' funding which they obtain from NBFIs. The higher the values for these two ratios are, the

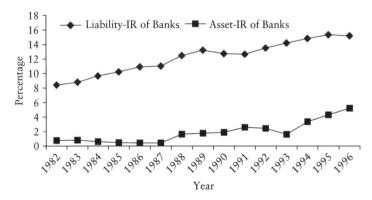

Figure 2.3. *Intermediation ratios of banks.*
Source: Schmidt *et al.* (1999).

longer is the chain of intermediation. In Germany, this chain of intermediation became longer in the course of the 1980s and 1990s. Since the early 1980s there has been a clear tendency on the part of banks in Germany to increase the proportion of their funding that they obtain from NBFIs. However, there has not been a corresponding change on the banks' asset side. As providers of loans the banks do not seem to have lost ground.

2.4.3.2. *The savings behaviour of households*
One weakness of studies based on flows of funds is the high level of aggregation of the underlying data, which corresponds to the fact that one can only differentiate between sectors and that therefore intra-sectoral financial relationships are not captured. Therefore, micro-based studies are of great value as a means of checking the robustness of the results. In the following, we report some results of studies by Börsch-Supan and co-authors[32] that describe the savings behaviour and portfolio choices of German households in the 1980s and the early 1990s based on a synthetic panel of four cross sections of the German Income and Expenditure Survey.

These studies show, first of all, that financial savings rates in Germany have been fairly high by international standards despite the fact that Germany has one of the most generous public pension and health insurance systems in the world. The authors call this the 'German savings puzzle'. Second, home

---

[32] See Börsch-Supan and Eymann (2002) and Börsch-Supan *et al.* (1999, 2000*a*, *b*) for details and further references. The source data are taken from the 'Einkommens- und Verbrauchsstichproben' (EVS) 1978, 1983, 1988, and 1993. A similar study, using national accounts data, was provided by the Deutsche Bundesbank (1999). Neither data set provides an unbiased estimate of households' asset holdings. The national accounts exclude the holding of foreign assets and the EVS the top 3 per cent of German households per income. Because both data sets reflect similar trends, the biases do not seem to be crucial.

ownership rates are low by international standards. Third, German private households are not highly indebted. Consumer credit levels are low compared to the Anglo-Saxon countries and it was only recently that debt financing of real estate increased to nearly two-thirds of the sales value of housing. Fourth, non-financial assets, that is, mainly real estate wealth, represent roughly two-thirds of the total wealth of households. In 1993, financial portfolios were still dominated by relatively safe assets, that is, checking and savings accounts and domestic bonds issued either by the government or by banks, and by illiquid assets, mainly life insurance policies. Only 12 per cent of the population of western Germany held stocks directly, whereas more than 60 per cent of the households held a life insurance policy and one third had domestic bonds in their portfolio. See Table 2.2 for some figures. Thus, in general these studies confirm the results of the study by Schmidt *et al.* (1999) based on flow-of-funds statistics, namely that conventional financial intermediaries and in particular banks played the dominant role as mobilizers of household savings. Especially, if one compares the portfolio structure of German households to the portfolio structure of households in the United States and in the United Kingdom—as was done in the recent book by Guiso *et al.* (2002)—then large differences will become apparent: Households in the Anglo-Saxon countries have higher direct and indirect stockholdings, and the fraction of total risky (financial) assets in their portfolios is usually higher (see the country chapters in Guiso *et al.* 2002).

2.4.3.3. *Financing patterns of non-financial firms*

The fact that private households, as surplus units, invest their funds mainly with banks and insurance companies and that banks use a large fraction of these funds for loans to business should be reflected in the financing patterns of firms. For Germany, one would expect to find that bank loans make up a large proportion of the financing of firms. However, in a series of influential papers, Mayer (1988, 1990) and Corbett and Jenkinson (1996, 1997) investigated how firms in a number of different industrialized countries obtained funds and financed investments. Their general finding was that in all countries covered in their studies external financing was unimportant and, moreover, that bank financing played a particularly unspectacular role in the case of Germany, a country which has always been regarded as having a bank-based financial system. The fraction of financing through bank loans was found to amount to only 11 per cent in Germany, as against 14 per cent in the United Kingdom, a country generally regarded as having a capital market-based financial system.

The Mayer and Corbett and Jenkinson studies have been replicated and essentially confirmed by a number of authors, including Edwards and Fischer (1994) for the case of Germany. Edwards and Fischer come to the conclusion that 'the lack of any evidence that the bank loans are more important in Germany (compared to other countries, especially to Anglo-Saxon countries)

Table 2.2. *Breakdown of portfolios held by German households*

	Asset shares according to survey data			Ownership rates			
	1983 (West)	1988 (West)	1993 (Unified)	1978 (West)	1983 (West)	1988 (West)	1993 (Unified)
Financial assets							
Checking and savings acc's	26.9	26.4	24.1	91.2	90.6	84.7	99.4
Government bonds	3.2	2.4	4.7	6.3	6.4	4.8	10.5
Other bonds	11.3	11.7	15.2	16.8	21.3	22.6	30.8
Stocks	3.8	4.7	4.3	10.0	9.7	11.4	10.0
Mutual funds and managed investment accounts	1.5	2.2	4.7	3.8	3.3	4.7	12.9
Life insurance contracts	36.3	39.1	29.1	69.9	67.2	64.6	n/a
Building society savings contracts	13.1	9.9	7.2	37.1	40.5	38.7	40.2
Other financial assets	4.0	3.5	10.7	n/a	5.8	5.3	21.8
Total financial assets	19.7	20.9	28.0	96.5	96.7	94.1	99.6
Fraction of 'clearly safe' financial assets	26.9	26.4	24.1	91.2	90.6	84.7	99.4
Fraction of 'fairly safe' financial assets	66.8	64.9	64.1	80.9	81.3	78.2	82.6
Fraction of 'risky' financial assets	6.3	8.8	11.8	14.1	13.7	17.9	25.1
Non-financial assets							
Total real estate	81.2	80.2	73.4	43.3	46.0	47.4	45.8
Total 'risky' assets	n/a	n/a	n/a	n/a	17.8	n/a	n/a
Debt							
Mortgage and real estate debt	92.4	91.4	90.2	24.1	26.2	25.0	23.5
Consumer credit	7.6	8.7	9.8	14.5	17.3	19.1	21.8
Consumer credit in % of total net wealth(used as correction term)	1.0	1.1	1.4				
Total debt	12.5	12.6	14.5	34.9	38.7	38.6	39.4

Source: Börsch-Supan/Eymann, 2002.

casts a great deal of doubt on one of the basic components of the conventional view of the German system of investment finance' (p. 69).

In fact, these results, including those published by Edwards and Fischer for Germany, appear to have become the new 'conventional view'. This finding, which is widely quoted in the literature, can only be regarded as a puzzle.[33] Which type of conventional wisdom seems more in line with reality? Hackethal and Schmidt (2003) attempt to resolve this puzzle by showing that the result

---

[33] A collection of references to the work of Mayer and Corbett and Jenkinson, including those whose authors call these findings a puzzle, can be found in Hackethal and Schmidt (2003).

obtained by Mayer, Corbett, Jenkinson, and others stems from a seemingly innocuous assumption in their methodology. Mayer and his followers assume that all financing that flows from one type of source, such as the funds flowing from the banking sector to the non-financial sector, are first used to fund the reverse flow of the same type, such as debt repayment from corporations to banks. By implication, it is assumed that only what remains after this netting is used for investment purposes. If computations are made on this basis, bank loans that are taken out by one company explicitly for the purpose of financing investments are offset by the debt repayments made by another company, which in preceding periods undertook investments that were financed with bank loans. In a hypothetical situation involving zero growth and in which investments are financed exclusively with bank loans, which must, of course, be paid back in subsequent periods, the method developed by Mayer and his collaborators shows that the contribution of bank financing equals 0 per cent. Since internally generated finance is the only source of funds for which there is no corresponding use of funds, this method suggests that internally generated funds are invariably used to finance investments. As a result, they seem to play an overwhelming, and de facto almost exclusive, role in financing corporate investment in every country.

With the same basic intention as Mayer and his followers, though without employing their problematic assumption, and using the same type of raw data, Hackethal and Schmidt (2003) developed an alternative design to measure the extent to which investment is financed with funds from different sources. Instead of arbitrarily allocating inflows of funds from individual sources to certain outflows and then offsetting the outflows against the seemingly corresponding inflows, they reconstruct gross financial flows, without specifying ex ante how any of the inflowing funds are used. Table 2.3 shows the results for Germany, Japan, and the United States.

The case of Germany, especially, is of interest here. The results reported in Table 2.3 show that German banks provide a far larger share of external corporate financing than American banks, whereas securities financing, which is behind NBFI financing, is virtually insignificant. In addition, Hackethal and Schmidt (2003) find that, in contrast to the 'new conventional wisdom', bank finance is nearly as important as internal finance in Germany, which is clearly not the case in the United States. The overall picture of financing patterns which emerges from their data is consistent with the results of various studies using balance sheet data to analyse and compare national financing patterns.[34] Moreover, it is also in line with the other findings reported in this chapter which indicate that banks played a strong role as providers of business finance at least until the mid-1990s.

---

[34] An overview of these studies is contained in Schmidt and Tyrell (1997). See also Sauvé and Scheuer (1999) for a detailed and comprehensive analysis of corporate finance in Germany and France based on balance sheet data from the Deutsche Bundesbank and the Banque de France.

Table 2.3. *Financing patterns of German, Japanese, and American companies*

Country	Sector	Percentages of the volume of long-term external corporate finance					
		1970–74	1975–79	1980–84	1985–89	1990–96	1970–96
US	Banks	0.51	0.49	0.49	0.46	0.36	0.44
	NBFIs	0.36	0.39	0.40	0.41	0.49	0.42
	Households	0.12	0.11	0.07	0.07	0.09	0.09
	Foreign countries/State	0.01	0.02	0.04	0.06	0.06	0.04
	Securities	0.42	0.42	0.41	0.45	0.48	0.45
Germany	Banks	0.80	0.82	0.84	0.82	0.83	0.82
	NBFIs	0.14	0.14	0.12	0.13	0.11	0.12
	Households	0.04	0.03	0.03	0.04	0.04	0.04
	Foreign countries/State	0.02	0.01	0.01	0.02	0.03	0.02
	Securities	0.12	0.09	0.08	0.11	0.13	0.12
Japan	Banks	0.95	0.95	0.95	0.91	0.92	0.93
	NBFIs	0.02	0.02	0.03	0.06	0.06	0.05
	Households	0.02	0.02	0.01	0.02	0.01	0.02
	Foreign countries/State	0.01	0.00	0.01	0.00	0.01	0.01
	Securities	0.10	0.10	0.10	0.15	0.16	0.13

Source: Hackethal/Schmidt (2000).

2.4.3.4. *Risk-sharing, risk allocation, and the German pension system*

An important function of every financial system is risk-sharing. It is often argued that financial markets are particularly well suited to perform this function, which Allen and Gale (1995, 1997) call cross-sectional or 'intra-temporal risk' sharing, that is, the diversification and efficient allocation of the risk to wealth or income at a given point in time. Risks associated with holding stocks, bonds, or other financial assets constitute an especially important type of risk that individuals face. However, as can be seen from their portfolio structures discussed above, German households were largely shielded from this risk, at least in the mid-1990s. Both the amount of financial assets and the proportions of risky financial assets among total financial assets held by German households were low in comparison to the United States and the United Kingdom.

But besides risks that exist at given points in time, there is another form of risk, which Allen and Gale call 'intertemporal risk'. This risk refers to the availability of economic resources at the level of the economy as a whole or to the aggregate value of all assets, and cannot be diversified at a given point of time through trading risky assets. However, it can be averaged over time in a way that reduces the impact on individual welfare. One means of achieving this objective is intergenerational risk-sharing, through which the risk associated with a given stock of assets is spread across generations at different positions in their life cycles. Another possibility is asset accumulation, which serves to reduce fluctuations in consumption over time.

In a series of papers, Allen and Gale (1995, 1997, 2000) show that in a bank-based financial system such as the German system, long-lived financial institutions, that is, banks and insurance companies, can achieve intertemporal risk smoothing through asset accumulation. They can accumulate reserves in good times and draw them down in bad times. But this mechanism only functions as long as the financial intermediaries are not subject to substantial competition from financial markets and are not under strong pressure to use relevant market options when they seem attractive. Competition from markets would unravel the intertemporal smoothing provided by financial institutions because in good times individuals as well as financial intermediaries would rather opt out of the banking system and its practice of accumulating reserves, and instead invest in the market to earn a higher return on their respective investment. The more attractive securities markets are as outlets for investment and the more banks are driven by the objective of maximizing profit, the more attractive it is for both sides to abandon a system which, de facto, offers protection against intertemporal risk.

The distinction between intertemporal and intratemporal risk reduction provides a framework for examining the role of risk management in the German financial system. It is helpful to recall our description of the German banking sector as one in which not strictly profit-oriented banks play an important role until this day, and in which even the private banks had for a long time been under relatively little pressure to maximize profit or market value; and also our description of Germany's 'underdeveloped' stock market system, and our account of household portfolio structures. Using the ideas of Allen and Gale, one can argue that in the bank-based German financial system of the 1980s and early to mid-1990s, risk management was mainly achieved through intertemporal risk smoothing performed by financial intermediaries and in particular by banks and savings banks. They were in a position to, and probably did, reduce intertemporal risk by accumulating assets and issuing low-risk liabilities to typical households as depositors. The reverse side of the coin was that cross-sectional risk sharing through markets was less developed, and had to be less developed in order to sustain the system. This may not have been such a high price to pay, since the demand from households for options to cope with intratemporal risk may have been low due to typical portfolio structures.

However, in addition to the risks associated with the holding of financial assets, people face many other risks, such as the risk of unemployment, illness, changes in the value of human capital, and changes in retirement income, to name but a few. In this context the German social security system and in particular its pension system are important.

Germany has a payroll tax-based PAYG system (see Börsch-Supan and Schnabel 1999 for details). It covers almost all employees and provides almost all retirement income within a single system with relatively transparent rules.

In 1993, the first pillar of the pension system, the public PAYG-financed pension system, provided on average 85 per cent of the total retirement income of a two-person household, and at 70 per cent the replacement rate of the public pension scheme was relatively high.

This design of the traditional German public pension system was consistent with the prevailing system of risk management in Germany. The pension system absorbed one very important class of risk through intergenerational risk-sharing. In addition it reduced the demand for cross-sectional or intra-temporal risk management in the economy and thus the need for having a highly developed stock market, which, if it existed, might have undermined the system of risk management through asset accumulation. Finally, given the relative generosity of the public pension system there was less of a need to develop institutional investors such as the British or American pension funds and also not much capital which would have flowed into the capital market through these intermediaries (see Tyrell and Schmidt 2001 for a detailed analysis of the interaction of financial systems and pension systems).

2.4.3.5. *Information production and dissemination*
Another function of a financial system is the production and dissemination of information, and therefore the type of information provision prevailing in the economy under consideration is yet another element by which a given financial system can be characterized.[35] In market-based financial systems, accounting and disclosure requirements are typically more geared to providing public information. Moreover, active stock markets and high levels of direct and indirect investment of household wealth in the capital market create incentives for private information production by investors, fund managers, and analysts whose information is indirectly made public through the impact of their trading behaviour on stock prices.

Generally speaking, the demand for public information is relatively low if capital market investment has only a limited importance for household savings and firm financing. In bank-based financial systems, only relatively few companies are listed and there are few institutional investors. Accordingly, there are also few analysts following individual stocks. This seems to have been the case in Germany until the late 1990s. Moreover, at least until that time German accounting and disclosure regulations were not primarily geared towards satisfying the information needs of investors (see Chapter 14 in this book for a characterization and assessment of German accounting and disclosure). One can, therefore, surmise that both the direct and the indirect provision and dissemination of public information was not well developed.

In contrast, in a bank-based financial system like Germany, banks as the main external providers of finance to firms need a high level of information, including proprietary information that would not be suitable for public

---

[35] On the following, see esp. Allen and Gale (2000) and Tyrell (2003).

disclosure. The greater prevalence of universal banking based on long-term and relatively close relationships between banks and borrowing firms in turn enables banks to acquire considerable amounts of information about the firms they lend to. Shareholdings by banks in large corporations and the specific forms of corporate governance that prevail in Germany provide additional information and opportunities for information acquisition. Therefore, both in terms of how it is generated and how it is used, information is mainly private rather than public in a bank-based financial system. As Elsas and Krahnen report in their contribution to this book (Chapter 7), there is not only ample anecdotal but also hard econometric evidence that this view of information production and dissemination fits the reality of the German financial system well.

2.4.3.6. *The control of capital: Corporate governance in Germany*
A financial system can perform its main function of channelling funds from savers to investors only if it offers sufficient assurance to the providers of the funds that they will reap the rewards which have been promised to them.[36] To the extent that this assurance is not provided by contracts alone, potential financiers will want to monitor and possibly influence managerial decisions. At least they will want to be sure that certain people—or certain mechanisms—have assumed this role of monitoring and influencing the activities of the firm and its management on their behalf. This is obviously the case for providers of equity, who have a genuine interest in the proper functioning of corporate governance. Therefore, corporate governance is an essential part of any financial system, as we explained in Section 2.2.1 above.

However, corporate governance encompasses more than investor protection. Considerations similar to those which stand behind the logical link between equity capital and governance also apply to other stakeholders who invest their resources in a firm and whose expectations of later receiving an appropriate return on their investment also depend on not easily contractible decisions at the level of the individual firm. Lenders, especially long-term lenders, are one such group of stakeholders who may also want to play a role in corporate governance; employees, especially those with high skill levels and firm-specific knowledge, are another.

At least by Anglo-Saxon standards, the German corporate governance system has for a long time appeared to be somewhat anomalous.[37] It has been shaped by a legal tradition that dates back to the 1920s and regards corporations as entities which act not only in the interest of their shareholders, but also have to serve a multitude of other interests. These views may sound

---

[36] This is the starting point for the influential series of papers by La Porta *et al.* See esp. their 1997 article on 'legal determinants of external finance'.

[37] The topic of corporate governance is dealt with extensively in Chapters 11 and 12 of this book. Chapter 11 takes a legal perspective, while Chapter 12 takes an economic perspective. Therefore, references are kept to a minimum in the present section.

somewhat outdated today, but they have left their traces. Shareholder value, in the strict or radical sense of an exclusive commitment on the part of management to shareholders' interests, is still not part of German business culture, nor is it in line with actual practice or with the legal system.

Thus, the German legislation governing joint stock corporations ('Aktiengesellschaften') distinguishes between three 'organs' of a corporation: the general shareholders' meeting, the supervisory board, and the management board. The Joint Stock Corporation Act ('Aktiengesetz') gives little power to the shareholders' meeting, moderate power to the supervisory board ('Aufsichtsrat') and considerable power to the management board ('Vorstand'). According to the letter of the law, the *legal* mandate of the management board is to 'manage the company under its own responsibility'. This wording is generally taken to mean that the management board must act not only in the interests of owners or shareholders, but also take into account the interests of other stakeholder groups. As Rieckers and Spindler, two legal scholars, explain in their contribution to this book (Chapter 11), the law also assigns to the management board, at least implicitly, the task of striking a balance between different interests.

The main function of the supervisory board consists in appointing and monitoring the management board. But the supervisory board does not merely represent shareholders. For the typical large joint stock corporations, the law requires 'codetermination' at the corporate level. Under this system, the supervisory board is composed of two almost equally powerful groups of members: on the one hand, those who are elected by the general shareholders' meeting and could at least formally be regarded as representing the shareholders; and on the other, the group of labour representatives. This composition of the supervisory board indicates that it would be wrong to assume that the management board were merely required to maximize shareholder value. In reality, the situation is even more complicated than the legal procedure for electing the 'capital bench' of the supervisory board and the composition of the supervisory board might suggest. In most cases, a majority of votes are cast by banks, exercising proxy voting rights on behalf of the actual shareholders. Accordingly, the majority of those supervisory board members who are elected by the shareholders' meeting can hardly be regarded as genuine representatives of 'pure' investors, that is, of persons or entities that have no relationship with the corporation other than having invested their money and hoping that the share price will appreciate and that dividends will be paid out. Quite apart from the effects of labour representation, the 'genuine shareholder representatives' are a minority on the board of almost every big German corporation. Instead, many board members represent shareholders with large blocks of shares, or they come from the management of other big corporations, or they are high-ranking bank employees, or they are former top managers of the same company.

In addition, in strictly legal terms, the supervisory board is not entitled to issue orders to the top management. Thus, the composition of the supervisory board and its limited scope for interfering with the actions of the management reflect the fact that the management board is indeed relatively independent, which is congruent with its legal mandate, as referred to above. On the other hand, these same features make it all the more difficult to strictly and effectively monitor the top managers, and moreover to ensure that they act in the interests of shareholders, given that the legal definition of the task of the management is ambiguous.

If one goes back one step further and looks at the ownership structure of German publicly traded corporations, one notices another peculiarity: In the vast majority of cases, there is at least one blockholder that holds 25 per cent or more of the shares, and thus has the right to veto important decisions at the shareholders' meeting. Most of these blocks are held by other big corporations, or by wealthy families. An elaborate network of interlocking participating interests makes the corporate governance system even more complicated.

This brief description of the system of corporate structures, corporate governance, and corporate ownership would be incomplete if we did not point out that in Germany there was, and still is, no *public* market for corporate control as a means of disciplining bad management. Public takeover bids have always been extremely rare, and in the few cases in which there has been a hostile takeover, notably the Mannesmann–Vodafone case of 1999/2000, the bids were not inspired by corporate governance considerations. However, this does not imply that there has been no market for control at all. The findings of Jenkinson and Ljungqvist (2001) suggest that this market takes the form of a market for blocks of shares. As they report, this market is active and at times quite hostile to incumbent management.

At first glance, it might appear as if the German corporate governance system were inimical to 'small' shareholders, and therefore simply bad by international standards.[38] This assessment is clearly accurate in the sense that shareholders of this type play no active role in the corporate governance system. Moreover, analysis of the German corporate governance system as a whole suggests that their interests may be an important constraint—that they are shareholders who cannot be treated too negligently—but there does not seem to be any mechanism which would ensure that their interests were the dominant concern of those who 'govern' the big corporations.

However, one should not throw the baby out with the bathwater. There is no reason to assume that in the past the 'purely investing' public fared badly in the normal course of affairs in Germany. The financial rewards for investing in shares of publicly traded corporations have been in line with those earned in other countries.[39] In addition, if one looks at the German corporate governance

---

[38] This is also the impression which the reader may gain from the statistics quoted in the papers by La Porta *et al.*

[39] It may be interesting to note that, in terms of long-term share price performance, the German stock market—despite 'structural underdevelopment'—did *not* under-perform other equity markets in the post-Second World War period, and therefore even small investors on the stock market

system as a whole, one can recognize that the system has been—or at least for a long time it was—quite well adjusted to the apparent requirements and also quite balanced and ultimately also effective. We discuss these attributes in the next section, which shows how the various elements of the German financial system are interrelated.

2.4.4. The Systemic Perspective: Complementarity and Consistency

In concluding this overview of the German financial system, we now use the information concerning its institutional and functional aspects to outline its systemic features. Through the 1970s and 1980s and well into the 1990s, the key elements of the German financial system could be characterized as follows:

1. Banks dominated the financial sector.
2. Capital markets were relatively unimportant.
3. The predominant forms of financing for non-financial firms were internal financing and bank financing.
4. Corporate governance was stakeholder-oriented and accorded a limited role to small equity investors.
5. Risk management via the stock market in the sense of dealing with intratemporal risk seems to have played less of a role than risk management in the sense of intertemporal risk-sharing and risk reduction.

As we hope to demonstrate in this section, the above configuration of elements is consistent, and given that the elements of a financial system are complementary to each other, this apparent consistency indicates that the German financial system as a whole possessed a certain degree of strength.

As we emphasized at the beginning of this section, the following arguments refer mainly to the German financial system as it was a few years ago, leaving aside for the moment the question of whether the systemic features have survived the developments of the past few years. Moreover, this section is intentionally one-sided, in the sense that it does not attempt to account for the many reservations and qualifications that could be expressed with regard to our main proposition. We will not qualify each sentence by noting whether the features which we describe as prevailing in the mid-to-late 1990s are still the same today. The following chapters of this book will provide these details and bring the analysis up to the present time; and they will show that at the beginning of the new millennium the overall picture is much less clear than it was 7 or even 5 years ago.

Five to seven years ago, most German banks and especially the important banks were organized and operated as truly universal banks; they provided a wide array of financial services to their clients, in particular to incorporated

were able to benefit from holding shares. See the comparative analysis of global stock markets by Jorion and Goetzmann (1999) which make the point that 'Germany experienced a steep run-up in prices, 6 per cent in real terms, over the period 1950–96' (p. 961).

and unincorporated business firms. Savings rates in Germany had been relatively high and stable, and bank deposits had, for a long time, remained the main vehicle for the accumulation of private financial savings as well as a stable and relatively cheap source of funds for the banking sector. The provision of banking services to the business community was integrated in the sense that internal flows of information seem to have been relatively easy and well developed. This enabled banks in their main capacity as lenders to benefit from the information they needed in order to entertain close relations with their customers. Bank–client relations conformed at least to a certain extent to the model of relationship lending and even of relationship banking. Banks performed various functions for their business clients, including investment banking services, and some banks also held a large number of equity participations in manufacturing, trade, and service companies. Nonetheless, the predominant role played by banks was that of a lender.

At that time, the stock market and financing via the capital market played only a minor role. In comparison to other countries, Germany's stock market was still largely underdeveloped as an investment opportunity for households as savers and as a source of funding for business. Thus, capital markets did not present a significant competitive challenge to banks in their role as collectors of deposits, providers of funding, and the dominant type of financial intermediary. Competition from foreign financial intermediaries was also limited, another factor which has contributed to the stable financial position of the German banking sector.

The high rate of intermediation in general and of bank intermediation in particular confirms the impression that the German financial system was clearly bank-dominated until the late 1990s. Apart from insurance companies, non-bank financial intermediaries were still of minor importance. There were, and still are, no pension funds in Germany, and almost all German unit trusts were organized and managed by bank-affiliated institutions. Just as the banks had been able to build up and maintain a strong position in the business of managing private investment, they also were the driving force in shaping the impressive institutional development of the German stock exchange system in its role as a secondary market.

The predominant financing patterns of non-financial companies reflect the strong role of banks. On average, German corporations are characterized by a relatively high level of internal financing and, to the extent that they use external funding, by a heavy dependence on bank loans. Accounting rules that emphasized creditor protection and restricted the distribution of economic profits seem to have contributed to the prevalence of internal financing and bank loan financing. A particularly interesting element of internal financing, and one that was also quite significant in quantitative terms, were pension reserves maintained within the big corporations.

So far, it appears that at least until the late 1990s, the overall structure of the German financial sector and the dominant patterns of firm financing seem to have been complementary and consistent. Strong banks, which are exposed to fairly limited competitive pressure and cushioned by an ample stock of cheap deposits, are in a relatively good position to act as 'partners' to their business clients. They can provide loans of a sufficient size and maturity, and offer a certain degree of liquidity insurance to their clients. They can even play an active role in supporting their customers if the latter get into financial difficulties. In turn, the fact that banks played a strong role in their relationships with their customers reinforced their dominance within the financial sector.

The overall impression of consistency is confirmed when we look again at the corporate governance system for large corporations. As was explained in the last section, this system seems to be biased against the typical small shareholders, and this might appear to be a serious shortcoming. Yet, there is also a positive side to this system: most importantly, the fact that it appears to be—or rather, have been—consistent with the aforementioned other features of the financial system. By law and in practice, power and influence in German corporations is distributed in a way which, at least in principle, is in line with the need to protect various types of claims. As we have seen, banks provide a large part of the external financing, and most bank lending is long term. This type of financing exposes banks to considerable risks, yet their strong position in the corporate governance system would appear to protect them, in their role as lenders, quite effectively, and thus reinforces and facilitates the prevailing form of external financing. Similar considerations apply to labour representation, even though the legalistic rigidities of the mandatory codetermination system would seem to be a serious deficiency of the German system. At least until quite recently, labour turnover has been lower in Germany than in other comparable countries (see Hackethal 2000 for empirical support). The employees' willingness to build up firm-specific human capital and to develop a relatively high degree of loyalty to a firm also exposes them to specific dangers and suggests that they would need protection (and might be willing to pay for it in appropriate forms). It would now seem to be generally accepted that the German system of corporate governance—with codetermination at shop floor and corporate levels, with former managers and managers of other firms holding seats on supervisory boards, and with management boards being legally committed to serving broader interests than merely those of the shareholders—has served to safeguard labour's interest in having stable and long-term employment, and thus to encourage employees to think of themselves as the 'partners' of their employers, and behave accordingly.

The German corporate governance system may also be balanced and quite effective. In this 'corporatist' system, power and influence are distributed among a relatively small group of active players, who are in a position to be relatively well informed, and can therefore monitor management well, at least in principle. The active and influential players represent big shareholders, big business, big management, big banks, and big labour. On the one hand, these influential players represent clearly divergent interests. As the balance of power between the powerful groups might occasionally shift, it is important that management is shielded from the direct influence of the supervisory board. The legal regime of the German joint stock corporation provides this isolation. On the other hand, in spite of their conflicts, the various influential players share a common task and common interests: they must be able to collectively monitor management, and they have a largely similar interest in assuring the stable development of 'their' corporations. Thus, monitoring and governing can function reasonably well—albeit, in a sense which is not necessarily in the best interests of the 'pure' shareholders.

Under relatively stable economic conditions, corporate governance designed along these lines might have been beneficial for the development and the implementation of long-term strategies and for the competitiveness of German corporations. Business success also tends to benefit investors. Therefore, the consistency of the corporate governance system may ultimately also be the reason why the interests of those shareholders who are not blockholders have not been violated to a large extent, even though the system gives them little opportunity to play an active role. But what may have mattered more, even for the small investors, is that German corporate governance was consistent with the financing patterns which have prevailed at least until quite recently, and thus also with the structure, the role and the functions of the German financial sector. This mutual compatibility may have been a source of strength for the entire system, since its individual elements tend to reinforce each other in the way in which they contribute to the functioning of the entire system.

An interesting and characteristic feature of the German financial system, in general, is that the role of the profit motive is somewhat limited, an assessment which applies to banks as well as to non-financial corporations. This state-ment does not mean that German banks and other German corporations are not profit-oriented; to claim any such thing would be to deny the obvious reality. But one can safely assume that strict profit maximization is not the dominant scheme of things in Germany. For the public sector savings banks group, this results from their legal mandate and structure. The same applies to the cooperative banking group. But it also applied to the big exchange listed corporations because of their internal governance system. In the case of large German corporations, the 'softening' of the profit orientation is an outgrowth of their governance structure and the strong role of stakeholder groups that are mainly interested in achieving stable growth rather than in maximizing profits.

From a systemic perspective, the moderate restrictions to pure profit orientation seem largely compatible with the relatively high level of debt financing and the focus of many German corporations on rather sophisticated technologies which require a high level of human capital in general and firm-specific human capital in particular. In order to attract long-term debt capital and specialized—and thus expropriable—human capital, firms need ways of assuring the providers of these resources that their interests are indeed safe-guarded to a certain extent. Thus, the financing patterns and the governance structure—and also the human capital endowments—have at least for a long time been well adjusted to one another (see Schmidt 2001; and Hackethal and Schmidt 2000 for more details).

The argument that the main elements of the financial system in Germany are not only complementary to each other, but have also long been consistent is not limited to the three key elements discussed at some length here, that is, the role of banks in the financial sector, the financing patterns of firms, and the corporate governance system. Indeed, it can easily be extended to other elements of the overall system.[40] For instance, it would also seem to apply to the way in which corporations accommodate the need to make important strategic changes; to the disclosure and accounting rules, which have traditionally favoured the interests of lenders, management, and staff by limiting the amount of financial surplus which is regarded as 'distributable profit'; to the basic structure of the bankruptcy law; and to the pension system.[41]

We can summarize this section by restating the two main propositions of the entire chapter. The first proposition is that the German financial system has for quite some time been a consistent system of complementary elements. We attempted to show that the values taken on by the various elements were such that the elements supported each other in their respective functions. The second proposition refers to the way in which, in our view, one should look at financial systems. We tried to demonstrate that it is indeed possible, and may offer important insights, to view a financial system not as a mere collection of elements, but also as a 'true' system composed of elements which strongly interact. But we would like to emphasize that complementarity and consistency are not directly observable features of a given financial system. Instead, they are the result of an economic interpretation of the observable facts. Moreover, we would certainly acknowledge that others may disagree on both counts: They might question our claim that the German system was largely consistent, and they may question our claim that complementarity and consistency are important features of a financial system.

2.5. A BRIEF INTERNATIONAL COMPARISON AND A SHORT OUTLOOK

2.5.1. Comparing Financial Systems

As the preceding overview has hopefully demonstrated, the common characterisation of the German financial system as being bank-dominated and as having an insider-control system of corporate governance seems justified—or at least was fully justified in the mid-to-late 1990s. From a systemic point of

[40] For a general account, see Hackethal and Schmidt (2000), and for a formal model Hackethal and Tyrell (1999).
[41] These extensions are discussed in Hackethal (2000: 296 ff.), Wüstemann (2002), Hackethal and Tyrell (1999), and Tyrell and Schmidt (2001), respectively.

view, this system is, or at least was, a consistent configuration of complementary elements. This prompts us to ask whether the financial systems of other large industrial countries are similar to or different from Germany's in this respect. We start with a brief look at large European economies[42] and then consider the situation in the United States and Japan.

The British financial system is the polar opposite to the German system. British banks play a relatively insignificant role as financial intermediaries and as providers of longer term financing to the business sector. For Britain, the intermediation ratios with respect to banks, which were shown for the case of Germany in Figures 2.1 and 2.2 above, are consistently lower both on the liability side (in particular, bank deposits by households) and even more so on the asset side of the banks' aggregate balance sheet (in particular, bank financing of non-financial firms). Bank deposits are not a widely used vehicle for household savings, and the level of firm financing by banks is moderate at best, and tends to be short term. Moreover, bank–customer relations are typically not close.

Compensating for the fact that banks play only a limited role as financial intermediaries, Britain's NBFIs, especially life insurance and pension funds, play a much stronger role than those in Germany. As British NBFIs tend to invest a large part of their mobilized funds in stocks, it is only to be expected that—in sharp contrast to the German situation—the stock market is also of great importance in the United Kingdom. The British stock market, both as a primary and as a secondary market, is well developed in institutional respects and in terms of its economic role. It even tends to play an important role in corporate governance, since hostile takeovers are frequent and can, at least in principle, be regarded as a device to force managers into adhering to shareholders' interests.

Thus, the British corporate governance system is in line with these features of the financial sector and with the prevailing mechanisms by which wealth is accumulated and held, and firms are financed. In the United Kingdom, it seems to be accepted without question that the overriding and indeed the only task of the management of a firm is to increase the wealth of the shareholders. Bank influence is absent from the governance of corporations, and various legal provisions ensure that banks refrain from getting involved in corporate governance and policies. But there is also no need for them to be active in boardrooms and workout groups, since the legal system and the short-term nature of their lending serves well enough to protect their interests as lenders. Similar considerations apply to employees. They are relatively well protected by a well-functioning labour market, meaning that they can walk away much more easily than their German counterparts, and therefore would, in economic

---

[42] We have developed this comparison in a series of papers which are summarized in Schmidt *et al.* (2002).

terms, be less willing to bid for the right to have an active role in corporate governance. Employees do not have such a role, and they would also not need to have it. But if they had it, this would be inconsistent with the entire system. This is why there is no reason to have a 'difficult' governance system, and it is understandable that the stock market plays such a big role in the financial system as it seems to in the United Kingdom.

While it is the polar opposite of the German financial system in terms of how it functions, it is similar to the German system in so far as it also seems to be largely consistent. Moreover, like the German financial system, it is also surprisingly stable in terms of how it operates.

Until the mid-1980s, the French financial system was strongly dependent on the state, and more specifically on the central government having and using a host of instruments which enabled it to actively influence the financial sector. Under the umbrella of strong government guidance, the financial system was extremely bank-dominated, and the French corporate governance system was a peculiar kind of an insider-control system. Until the mid-1980s, there had been a certain 'logique' to the French system, and its *modus operandi* was different from that of either Germany or the United Kingdom. In the course of the 1980s, the French system altered dramatically, and although it was again the French state which introduced these changes and pushed them through, the entire French financial system has become much more market-oriented than it had ever been. The role of banks as intermediaries has declined dramatically over the last 20 years, a development which is reflected in the financing patterns of firms, and of large corporations especially. In their place, the liberalized capital market has gained ground. Moreover, the banks have also suffered in their other roles. The financial sector institutions which have taken over much of the former role of the banks are the NBFIs, in particular various types of investment funds.

All in all, one can certainly say that the developments that have taken place in the French financial system have brought it closer to the Anglo-Saxon model of a capital market-oriented financial system. Thus, in stark contrast to both the German bank-based financial system and the British capital market-based system, the French financial system has not been stable. Moreover, although one might have the impression that a simple conversion from one type of financial system to the polar opposite type has occurred, if one looks at the details the situation becomes less clear-cut. In many respects, the French financial system has—at least for a long period—not been a consistent set of complementary elements. As two important examples of inconsistencies, we would point to the French corporate governance system and to the French system of old age pensions. For a very long time—and indeed, this may even still be the case today—these elements of the French system have remained largely similar to what they used to be under the old regime of state-controlled capitalism that prevailed in the 1970s. In other words, the elements of the newly emerging French financial system have also not been consistent, and possibly they are still not consistent today. The combination of far-reaching changes and a situation of not yet having settled into a new consistent configuration or a new type of equilibrium may be the reason why, in the recent past, French economists, bankers and politicians have talked so much about a crisis which accompanied the end of 'l'exception française'.

We would like to conclude this discussion with an even briefer look at other continents. At the turn of the millennium, when the worldwide stock market rally was coming to an end, the American financial system was arguably even more market-oriented than before. Banks had become even less important both in the financial sector and in the financial system at large. Their role as mobilizers of savings and as lenders has steadily decreased in the course of the last 20 years, as can be read off from the intermediation ratios (Hackethal 2001). However, there are also a number of features and events which would seem to contradict the proposition that the American financial system is becoming ever more market-oriented. One of these is the demise of the Glass–Steagall Act in 1999 and with it the acceptance of the universal banking model, which could, in our view, strengthen the role of banks. Another is the wave of state regulation and legislation which undermines the functioning of the market for corporate control by creating numerous obstacles to truly hostile takeovers. All in all, therefore, the evidence would seem to be mixed, although no major inconsistencies appear to have emerged.

The case of Japan is much less ambiguous in this respect. Not long ago, the Japanese financial system was in almost all respects even more bank-dominated than the German system. One piece of evidence to support this claim is the very high rate of intermediation in Japan (Hackethal 2001) during the last decades; another is the fact that banks contribute a high percentage of non-financial firms' external financing, as reported by Sussman (1994) and Hackethal and Schmidt (2000). Hoshi provides a lucid account of the systemic features and the high degree of consistency of the Japanese financial system of a few years ago, and of its corporate governance system in particular.[43] It may well be that this consistency of the economic and social system, which included many more elements than merely the financial system, was one of the reasons for Japan's enormous economic success in the 1970s and 1980s.

However, this was not to last, it seems. Since the end of the so-called bubble economy, the Japanese financial system has been in a deep and almost permanent crisis which dwarfs that of the French financial system. A series of changes, some of them rather half-hearted, have pushed the Japanese financial system in the direction of the American system, without, however, leading it to a new system which can by now be characterized as consistent, and thus as economically attractive.

---

[43] See Hoshi (1998). The same picture of systemic coherence is provided, from a somewhat more general perspective, in the insightful work of Dore, see, for example, Dore (2000).

2.5.2. Caveats and a Brief Look Ahead

At least in one respect the German financial system is not different from those of other industrialized countries: It has changed a great deal during the last half decade. Before that, it did, however, differ in a fundamental way from many other financial systems, especially from those of the Anglo-Saxon countries. As we pointed out in Section 2.4.4, the German financial system has at least until quite recently been a largely consistent bank-based system. This section is supposed to add caveats and a short look ahead. We begin with the caveats. Our proposition that the German financial system was largely consistent is an assessment which rests on interpretations and ultimately on the personal judgement of its authors. Consistency is not a feature which lends itself to easy measurement. However, our proposition is not purely speculative. Over the past years, we have, often in collaboration with Andreas Hackethal, tried out, modified and extended the ideas of complementarity, consistency, and bank-orientation, and we found it useful and in accordance with the facts. Moreover, we find support for our ideas in the work of Allen and Gale over an equally long time. So, in this limited sense, our proposition is 'tested and confirmed'. Nevertheless, it is not proven in a formal way, and it cannot be proven. This requires a strong caveat.

In classifying the German financial system as having been bank-based or bank-dominated, we use a distinction which also requires a caveat: Such a qualification is only meaningful if there is at least one other type of financial system and if financial systems can be qualified as conforming to one of these types. There is indeed an alternative, namely that of a capital market-based or capital market-dominated financial system. However, not all financial systems can be classified as belonging to one of these two types. These types are theoretical constructs, and countries' real financial systems conform to them more or less well. Many real financial systems can hardly be classified as being of either of these two types. This fact limits the usefulness of this classification.

What appears like a third caveat is merely a warning of a possible misunderstanding. The recent wave of empirical research into the relationship between financial systems and economic growth seems to suggest that any classification of financial systems should be linked to some operational standard of evaluation. For instance, one might expect 'more capital market orientation' or 'more bank-dominance' to go hand in hand with higher growth rates. Levine and others investigates this relationship empirically, and their results do not support this expectation.[44] However, we do not regard these findings as invalidating our classification and detracting from its relevance, since what we regard as an important determinant of growth or welfare is not whether a financial system is bank-based or capital market-based, but rather

---

[44] See Levine (1997) and Levine (2002) with further references.

whether it is consistent. This feature has so far not been tested in empirical studies.

We now turn to predictions, anticipating what will be presented in greater detail in the concluding chapter of this book. While half a decade ago the German financial system still was a largely consistent bank based system, this has changed recently. The worldwide stock market boom and the 'new economy bubble' of the late 1990s have also affected the German financial system. Towards the end of the last century, the German financial system seemed to change rapidly and in a fundamental way. It seemed to undergo a *Gestalt switch*, that is, to lose its traditional character of being bank-based and to become a capital market-based system. At least the beginnings of such a fundamental transformation were readily observable. However, this process had only started, and it did not continue after the bursting of the stock market bubble in early 2000. It is hard to say whether the process was merely delayed or definitely stopped or even reversed. This is again a matter of interpretation. There are theoretical and empirical arguments which speak for each of the three possibilities—delay, termination, or reversal. In our view, 'the facts' have not given a loud and clear answer to the question of what has happened since 2000. Even at the time at which this book goes to the publisher (May of 2003), this is an open question. All that seems clear to us is that the German financial system has lost its former consistency. As we said before, we assume that the consistency of a financial system, or a good fit of its main elements, creates economic benefits. The converse statement is that inconsistency causes economic problems. This seems to be born out these days. There are several instances of grave contradictions in the financial system, and one can find a number of equally important problems. The stock market has lost its attraction; the famous *Neuer Markt*, the premier symbol of the transition to the market-based system, is being closed down after losing its credibility. The big private German banks are in serious trouble, not least because they have lost enormous sums of money in their ventures to become truly modern investment banks. In the business year of 2002, most of them had to show losses for the first time in their history. And while it was a traditional strength of the German financial system that creditworthy businesses can be almost sure to get loans from their banks, there is now the danger of a credit crunch.

A financial system with grave inconsistency is under pressure to restore consistency. A longer period in which such a system fails to restore a proper fit of its elements can even lead to a financial crisis. We do not really expect this to happen. However, we think that something needs to be done quickly and with great resolve to restore consistency, and thus also efficiency. In principle, this could be a reversion to the 'good old times' of the bank-based system. But for reasons which we do not want to explain here, this option is not realistic (see Schmidt *et al.* 2002; and also Chapters 12 and 15, this volume). Instead, we expect the German financial system to return to its path of transition to a capital market-based system. But the path is going to be rough and long.

References

Albrecht, P., and Schradin, H. (1999). 'Struktur der Versicherungswirtschaft', Seminar für Versicherungslehre. University of Cologne. Mimeo.

Alexander, V., and Bohl, M. (2000). 'Das Finanzsystem in Deutschland', in J. von Hagen and J. H. von Stein (eds.), *Obst/Hintner Geld-, Bank- und Börsenwesen*, 40th edn. Stuttgart, 447–70.

Allen, F., and Gale, D. (1995). 'A Welfare Comparison of Intermediaries and Financial Markets', *European Economic Review*, 39: 179–209.

——, and —— (1997). 'Financial Markets, Intermediaries and Intertemporal Smoothing', *Journal of Political Economy*, 105: 523–46.

——, and —— (2000). *Comparing Financial Systems*. Cambridge, MA: MIT Press.

——, and Santomero, A. (2001). 'What Do Financial Intermediaries Do?', *Journal of Banking and Finance*, 25: 271–94.

Aoki, M., and Patrick, H. (1994). *The Japanese Main Bank System*. Oxford: Oxford University Press.

Aoki, M. (2001). *Toward a Comparative Institutional Analysis*. Cambridge, MA: MIT Press.

Bain, A. D. (1992). *The Economics of the Financial System*, 2nd edn. Oxford: Basil Blackwell.

Barca, F., and Becht, M. (2001). *The Control of Corporate Europe*. Oxford: Oxford University Press.

Baums, T. (1996). 'Universal Banks and Investment Companies in Germany', in A. Saunders and I. Walter (eds.), *Financial System Design: Universal Banking Considered*. Homewood: Irwin, 124–60.

Baums, T., and Theissen, E. (1999). 'Banken, bankeigene Kapitalanlagegesellschaften und Aktienemissionen', *Zeitschrift für Bankrecht und Bankwirtschaft*, 11(3): 125–34.

Böhmer, E. (2001). 'Corporate Governance in Germany: Institutional background and empirical results', in K. Gugler (ed.), *Corporate governance and economic performance*. Oxford: Oxford University Press, 96–120.

Börsch-Supan, A. and Eymann, A. (2002). 'Household Portfolios in Germany', in L. Guiso *et al.* (eds.), *Household Portfolios*. Cambridge: MIT Press, 291–340.

——, Reil-Held, A., Rodepeter, R., Schnabel, R., and Winter, J. (1999). 'Ersparnisbildung in Deutschland: Messkonzepte und Ergebnisse auf Basis der EVS', *Allgemeines Statistisches Archiv*, 83: 385–415.

——, ——, ——, ——, and —— (2000*a*). 'Household Savings in Germany', Beiträge zur angewandten Wirtschaftsforschung 577–00. University of Mannheim.

——, ——, ——, ——, and —— (2000*b*). 'The German Savings Puzzle', Beiträge zur angewandten Wirtschaftsforschung 594–00. University of Mannheim.

——, and Schnabel, R. (1999). 'Social Security and Retirement in Germany', in J. Gruber and D. Wise (eds.), *Social Security and Retirement around the World*. Chicago: The University of Chicago Press, 135–80.

Buckle, M., and Thompson, J. (1998). *The UK Financial System, Theory and Practice*, 3rd edn. Manchester: Manchester University Press.

Büschgen, H. E. (1993). *Bankbetriebslehre: Bankgeschäfte und Bankmanagement*, 4th edn. Wiesbaden: Gabler.

Corbett, J., and Jenkinson, T. (1996). 'The Financing of Industry, 1970–89: An International Comparison', *Journal of the Japanese and International Economies*, 10: 71–96.

——, and —— (1997). 'How is Investment Financed? A Study of Germany, Japan, the United Kingdom and the United States', *The Manchester School Supplement*, 63–93.

Crane, D. B., Froot, K. A., Mason, S. P., Bodie, Z., and Perold, A. F. (1995). *The Global Financial System: A Functional Perspective*. Boston: Harvard Business School Press.

Davis, E. P., and Steil, B. (2001). *Institutional Investors*. Cambridge, MA: MIT Press.

Deutsches Aktieninstitut (2001). *DAI-Factbook 2001*. Frankfurt/Main.

Diamond, D. (1984). 'Financial Intermediation and Delegated Monitoring', *Review of Economic Studies*, 51: 393–414.

Diamond, D., and Rajan, R. G. (2001). 'Liquidity Risk, Liquidity Creation and Financial Fragility', *Journal of Political Economy*, 109: 287–327.

Deutsche Bundesbank (1995). 'The Monetary Policy of the Bundesbank', *Special Publications*. Frankfurt/Main.

—— (1996). *Banking Statistics* (June). Frankfurt/Main.

—— (1998). 'Structural Change in the German Capital Market in the Run-up to European Monetary Union.' *Monthly Reports* (April). Frankfurt/Main, 55–69.

—— (1999). 'Changes in Households' Asset Situation Since the Beginning of the Nineties.' *Monthly Reports* (January). Frankfurt/Main, 33–50.

—— (2002). *Banking Statistics* (May). Frankfurt/Main.

Dore, R. (2000). *Stock Market Capitalism: Welfare Capitalism*. Oxford: Oxford University Press.

Edwards, J., and Fischer, K. (1994). *Banks, Finance and Investment in Germany*. Cambridge: Cambridge University Press.

European Central Bank (2002). 'Payment and Securities Settlement Systems in the European Union', *Blue Book*. Frankfurt/Main.

Faugère, J.-P., and Voisin, C. (1994). *Le système financier français*. Paris: Nathan.

Ferrandier, R., and Koen, V. (1994). *Marchés de capiteaux et Techniques Financières*, 3rd edn. Paris: Jouve.

Fohlin, C. (2000). 'Relationship Banking, Liquidity, and Investment in the German Industrialization', *Journal of Finance*, 53: 1737–58.

Franks, J., and Mayer, C. (1995). 'Ownership and Control', in H. Siebert (ed.), *Trends in Business Organization: Do Participation and Cooperation Increase Competitiveness?* Tübingen: Mohr, 171–95.

Fudenberg D., and Tirole, J. (1991). *Game Theory*. Cambridge, MA: MIT Press.

Gerschenkron, A. (1962). *Economic Backwardness in Historical Perspective*. Cambridge, MA: Harvard University Press.

Guiso, L., Haliassos, M., and Jappelli, T. (2002). *Household Portfolios*. Cambridge, MA: MIT Press.

Gurley, J., and Shaw, E. (1960). *Money in a Theory of Finance*. Washington DC: Brookings Institution.

Hackethal, A. (2000). *Banken, Unternehmensfinanzierung und Finanzsysteme*. Frankfurt/Main: Peter Lang.

—— (2001). 'How Unique are US-Banks?—The Role of Banks in Five Major Financial Systems', *Jahrbuch für Nationalökonomie und Statistik*, 221: 592–619.

——, and Schmidt, R. H. (2000). 'Komplementarität und Finanzsysteme', in *Kredit und Kapital*. Supplement 15.

——, and Schmidt, R. H. (2003). 'Financing Patterns: Measurement Concepts and Empirical Results', Working Paper Series: Finance and Accounting No. 33. University of Frankfurt, revised version.

——, and Tyrell, M. (1999). 'Complementarity and Financial Systems—A Theoretical Approach', Working Paper Series: Finance and Accounting No. 10. University of Frankfurt.

Harhoff, D., and Körting, T. (1999). 'Lending Relationships in Germany—Empirical Evidence from Survey Data', *Journal of Banking and Finance*, 22: 1317–53.

Hartmann-Wendels, T., Pfingsten, A., and Weber, M. (1998). *Bankbetriebslehre*. Berlin *et al.*: Springer.

Hellwig, M. (2000). 'Die volkswirtschaftliche Bedeutung des Finanzsystems', in J. von Hagen, and J. H. von Stein (eds.), *Obst/Hintner: Geld-, Bank- und Börsenwesen*, 40th edn. Stuttgart: 3–37.

Hicks, J. (1969). *A Theory of Economic History*. Oxford: Clarendon Press.

Hilferding, R. (1910). *Das Finanzkapital. Eine Studie über die jüngste Entwicklung des Kapitalismus*. Vienna: Wiener Volksbuchhandlung, reprinted Düsseldorf 2001.

Hoshi, T. (1998). 'Japanese Corporate Governance as a System', in K. Hopt, *et al.* (eds.), *Comparative Corporate Governance—The State of the Art and Emerging Research*. Oxford: Oxford University Press.

Jenkinson, T., and Ljungqvist, A. P. (2001). 'The Role of Hostile Stakes in German Corporate Control', *Journal of Corporate Finance*, 7(4): 397–446.

Jorion, P., and Goetzmann, W. (1999). 'Global Stock Markets in the Twentieth Century', *Journal of Finance*, 54: 953–80.

Kaufman, G. (1997). *The U.S. Financial System*, 6th edn. Englewood Cliffs, NJ: Prentice Hall.

King, R., and Levine, R. (1993). 'Finance and Growth: Schumpeter Might be Right', *Quarterly Journal of Economics*, 108: 717–37.

La Porta, R., Lopez-de-Silanes, F., Shleifer, A., and Vishny, R. (1997). 'Legal Determinants of External Finance'; *Journal of Finance*, 52: 1131–50.

——, ——, ——, and ——(1998). 'Law and Finance', *Journal of Political Economy*, 106: 1113–55.

Laux, M., and Päsler, R. (2001). *Die deutschen Spezialfonds*. Frankfurt/Main: Fritz Knapp.

Levine, R. (1997). 'Financial Development and Economic Growth: Views and Agenda', *Journal of Economic Literature*, 35: 688–726.

——(2002). 'Bank-Based or Market-Based Financial System: Which is Better?', Working Paper. University of Minnesota.

Mayer, C. (1988). 'New Issues in Corporate Finance', *European Economic Review*, 32: 1167–83.

Mayer, C. (1990). 'Financial Systems, Corporate Finance, and Economic Development', in G. Hubbard (ed.), *Asymmetric Information, Corporate Finance, and Investment*. Chicago: University of Chicago Press, 307–32.

Mayer, C., and Sussman, O. (2001). 'The Assessment: Finance, Law, and Growth', *Oxford Review of Economic Policy*, 17(4): 457–66.

McKinnon, R. (1973). *Money and Capital in Economic Development*. Washington, DC: Brookings Institutions.

Merton, R. C. (1990). 'The Financial System and Economic Performance', *Journal of Financial Services Research*, 4: 263–300.

——(1995). 'Financial Innovation and the Management and Regulation of Financial Institutions', *Journal of Banking and Finance*, 19: 461–82.

——, and Bodie, Z. (1995). 'A Conceptual Framework for Analyzing the Financial Environment', in D. B. Crane *et al.* (eds.), *The Global Financial System: A Functional Perspective*. Boston: Harvard Business School Press, 3–32.

Milgrom, P., and Roberts, J. (1990). 'The Economics of Modern Manufacturing: Technology, Strategy, and Organization', *American Economic Review*, 80: 511–28.

——, and——(1995a). 'Complementarities and Fit: Strategy, Structure, and Organizational Change in Manufacturing', *Journal of Accounting and Economics*, 19: 179–208.

——, and——(1995b). 'Continuous Adjustment and Fundamental Change in Business Strategy and Organization', in H. Siebert (ed.), *Trends in Business Organization: Do Participation and Cooperation Increase Competitiveness?* Tübingen: Mohr, 231–59.

Obst, G., and Hintner, O. (2000). In J. von Hagen, and J.H. von Stein (eds.), *Geld-, Bank- und Börsenwesen*. 40th edn. Stuttgart: Schäffer Poeschel.

Pagano, M., and Volpin, P. (2001). 'The Political Economy of Finance', *Oxford Review of Economic Policy*, 17(4): 502–19.

Papenfuss, H. (1999). *Beschreibungsmodi für Finanzsysteme*. Frankfurt/Main: Peter Lang.

Rajan, R. G. (1996). 'Why Banks Have a Future: Toward a New Theory of Commercial Banking', *Journal of Applied Corporate Finance*, 8: 114–35.

——, and Zingales, L. (2001). 'The Great Reversals: Politics of Financial Development in the 20th Century', forthcoming in *Journal of Financial Economics*.

Robinson, J. (1952). 'The Generalization of the General Theory', in *The Role of Interest and Other Essays*. London: Macmillan, 67–142.

Sauvé, A., and Scheuer, M. (1999). 'Corporate Finance in Germany and France', Deutsche Bundesbank: Frankfurt/Main.

Schmidt, R. H. (2001). 'Kontinuität und Wandel bei der Corporate Governance in Deutschland', *Schmalenbachs Zeitschrift für betriebswirtschaftliche Forschung*, Special Issue 47: 61–88.

——, Hackethal, A., and Tyrell, M. (1999). 'Disintermediation and the Role of Banks in Europe: An International Comparison', *Journal of Financial Intermediation*, 8: 36–67.

——, ——, and —— (2002). 'Convergence of Financial Systems in Europe', *Schmalenbach Business Review*, Special Issue 1–02: 7–54.

——, and Tyrell, M. (1997). 'Financial Systems, Corporate Finance and Corporate Governance', *European Financial Management*, 3: 159–87.

Schumpeter, J. (1934). *The Theory of Economic Development*. Cambridge, MA: Harvard University Press.

Shaw, E. S. (1973). *Financial Deepening in Economic Development*. New York: Oxford University Press.

Süchting, J., and Paul, S. (1998). *Bankmanagement*, 4th edn. Stuttgart: Schäffer-Poeschel.

Sussman, O. (1994). 'Investment and Banking: Some International Comparisons', *Oxford Review of Economic Policy*, 10(4): 79–93.

Topkis, D. M. (1998). *Supermodularity and Complementarity*. Princeton, NJ: Princeton University Press.

Tyrell, M. (2003). *Kapitalmärkte und Banken—Formen der Informationsverarbeitung als konstitutives Merkmal*. Wiesbaden: Gabler.

——, and Schmidt, R. H. (2001). 'Pension Systems and Financial Systems in Europe: A Comparison from the Point of View of Complementarity', *Ifo Studien*, 47: 469–503.

Verdier, D. (1999). 'The Origins of Universal Banking in 19th Century Europe, North America and Australasia', Working Paper. European University Institute. Florence.

Winkler, A. (2001). *Wirtschaftswachstum und Finanzsystementwicklung*. Mimeo.

World Bank (1989). *World Development Report 1989, Financial Systems and Development*. Washington DC.

Wüstemann, J. (2002). *Institutionenökonomik und internationale Rechnungslegungsordnungen*. Tübingen: Mohr.

PART II

FINANCIAL SECTORS AND CORPORATE FINANCE

3

German Banks and Banking Structure

ANDREAS HACKETHAL

3.1. INTRODUCTION—BANK DISINTERMEDIATION IN GERMANY?

In a recent speech, Bernd Fahrholz, the former CEO of Germany's third largest bank, acknowledged that 10 years ago the German banking market was still a cosy place and that, at that time, hardly anybody would have imagined that any disruptions could occur at all (Fahrholz 2001). He then went on to characterize the structures that had prevailed for most of the post Second World War era. The German financial system was one of many neatly delineated systems in Europe with its own currency and a banking sector that did not have to fear foreign competition. In Germany things were especially orderly, most banks were organized as universal banks and acted as *Hausbank*s to their customers.[1] Customers visited their local branch between 9 a.m. and 4 p.m. to deposit their surplus funds almost exclusively into savings accounts, and firms funded their investments primarily with bank loans. The public banking sector did business as usual and nobody disapproved of its state guarantees. According to Fahrholz, since then 'no stone has been left unturned'. Ever more efficient capital markets and specialized non-bank financial institutions have allegedly eroded the once strong role of traditional universal banks. Apparently, German banks are suffering the same fate as their peers around the world. This view is also held by many international commentators,[2] among them Franklin Edwards (1996: 41): 'Fundamental

---

[1] The relationship between a firm and its *Hausbank* is typically more information-intensive and longer-term oriented, and thus closer than any other of the firm's bank relationships. In the case of smaller firms, the *Hausbank* typically acts as the premier lender with a 'special responsibility', whereas in the case of larger corporations, the *Hausbank*—in addition to its role as an important lender—holds direct shareholdings in the company and is represented on the company's supervisory board (see Chapter 7 for a detailed discussion). Universal banks are commonly defined as banks that are active in both commercial banking and security underwriting and that hold equity stakes in their debtor firms. This organizational form of a bank is hence not only conducive, but almost a precondition for achieving *Hausbank* status for larger firms.

[2] See, for example, Becketti and Morris (1992), Boyd and Gertler (1993, 1995), Edwards and Mishkin (1995), Gorton and Rosen (1995), Greenbaum and Thakor (1995), Calomiris (1997),

forces not limited to the United States have caused a decline in the profitability of traditional banking throughout the world and have created an incentive for banks to expand into new activities and to take greater risks ... The decline of traditional banking is a global phenomenon'.

The sheer number of advocates subscribing to this view, as well as the firm conviction with which it is typically expressed, indicate that the banking industry is commonly believed to be in a process of profound structural change. As a consequence, universal banking and traditional commercial banking in particular, are supposedly in decline worldwide. There also seems to be a consensus on the reasons for this development. First, progress in communication and information technology combined with innovative financial instruments are believed to foster the efficiency of organized capital markets. Relevant information can be made available to all participants almost instantaneously and the participants' capacity to process this information has increased dramatically. In addition, new instruments allow for better customization to accommodate the specific needs of the participants. Because many services offered by commercial banks on the one hand and capital markets on the other can be regarded as substitutes, any efficiency gains realized by the markets could clearly be detrimental to the role of banks and would thus erode their 'uniqueness'[3] and, in turn, their share in the markets for financial services. Second, abandoning regulations that have historically shielded the banking industry from competition from non-bank financial intermediaries (NBFIs) and organized capital markets is regarded as fuelling this substitution process. This factor is assumed to be particularly strong in those cases in which the historically strong position of banks in a particular financial system may not have been based on their uniqueness, but

Litan and Rauch (1998) and Miller (1998). See also the collection of interviews with chief officers from the banking industry in Engler and Essinger (2000). For an opposing view, see, for example, Dermine (2002), who uses the ratio of total bank assets over GDP to measure the importance of banks. He finds that this ratio more than doubled in most European countries between 1981 and 2000 and argues that this expansion must have been due to the massive deregulation that took place in Europe during this period.

[3] James (1987) showed in his article 'Some Evidence on the Uniqueness of Bank Loans' that the announcement by an American corporation to take out a bank loan typically leads to an increase in the firm's market value. Based on the observation that entering a relationship with a bank creates value, James concludes that banks are unique with respect to the fulfilment of specific financial functions. For the sake of brevity we mention only some of the more recent contributions that investigate the uniqueness of the institution 'bank' (see Greenbaum and Thakor 1995; and Freixas and Rochet 1997 for two brilliant surveys on recent advances in the theory of financial intermediation). Because individual liquidity insurance à la Diamond and Dybvig (1983) is also being provided to some extent by money market mutual funds (Rajan 1996) and because thorough monitoring à la Diamond (1984) is also being conducted by finance and insurance companies, the uniqueness of banks must stem from the combination of these two functions under the roof of a single institution. Scope economies may result (a) from a more efficient use of liquidity reserves (Kashyap *et al.* 1999), (b) from a broader information base on debtors (Fama 1985; Lewis 1991), (c) from reduced incentive problems regarding the investment of deposited funds (Myers and Rajan 1998), and (d) from the improved ability to absorb systemic shocks (Allen and Gale 1997).

rather on the regulatory protection that they have enjoyed. Third, the trend towards globalization and, in the case of Europe, the monetary unification, is believed to intensify both forces—advances in technology and deregulation—as specialized non-bank financial intermediaries, for example, large credit card companies or reputable investment banks that are highly successful in their domestic financial system, seek to expand rapidly around the globe.

This chapter examines the current state and structure of the German banking market and its role within the German financial system. It thereby aims to answer the question whether the fundamental forces cited above have indeed dismantled the alleged uniqueness of German universal banks leading to similar developments and whether they will share the fate of their European and American peers leading to a structural convergence of national banking markets. In such a possible future scenario, banks are no longer clear substitutes for organized capital markets, but rather important complementary institutions. Instead of providing their customers with access to their own balance sheets, they will assist them in accessing increasingly complex capital markets and moving undesired risks off their balance sheet by means of financial innovations.

The next section describes the key characteristics of the major German banking groups. Section 3.3 analyses structural features and performance indicators of the German banking industry and compares them to those in other European countries and in the United States. It will become apparent that some trends like that of a declining number of banks, decreasing interest margins, and the increasing importance of fee-based business are discernible in all countries. However, this does not seem to be the entire story. In Section 3.4 we provide additional indicators which attempt to capture the role of the banks in several financial systems, and in Germany in particular. This evidence reveals that the simplistic convergence hypothesis might indeed be false. German commercial banks and especially savings and cooperative banks still seem to play a special role. Sections 3.5 and 3.6 conclude the chapter by discussing the outlook for private and public banks and by summarizing the main findings.

3.2. THE STRUCTURE OF THE BANKING MARKET

3.2.1. Banking Groups—an Overview

The German banking system is a universal banking system. Banks have been permitted to engage in all lines of banking businesses for a very long time and the few existing special banks have not emerged as a result of legal regulations. Rather, the laws governing these special banks have developed in response to their emergence and the perceived necessity to apply special regulations. Figure 3.1 shows that out of the roughly 3000 monetary financial institutions that existed at the end of 2000, 2,713 were universal banks and 218 were special institutions, including 141 entities that in our context should actually be classified as non-bank financial institutions (e.g. investment companies).

Monetary financial institutions 2931 (577)

Universal banks	2,713 (554)	Special institutions	218 (23
Commercial banks	354 (0)	Special banks	77 (22)
Big banks	4 (0)	Mortgage banks	31 (4)
Regional banks, other commercial		Building and loan associations	30 (11)
banks* and private bankers	255 (0)	Banks with special functions	16 (7)
Postbank	1 (0)	Other monetray financial	141 (1)
Branches of foreign banks	94 (0)	institutions	
Credit cooperatives	1,798 (0)	Investment companies	82 (1)
Primary cooperative institutions	1,795 (0)	Housing enterprises with savings	40 (0)
Regional cooperative central		facilities	
banks	3 (0)	Securities depositories and	
Savings banks	561 (554)	insitutions only conducting	
		guarantee business	28 (0)
Primary savings banks	548 (541)		
Landesbanks	13 (13)		

Figure 3.1. *German banking groups and number of banks (12/2000).*
Number of state-owned institutions in parantheses.
Note: *Included are banks majority-owned by foreign firms.
Source: Deutsche Bundesbank (2001).

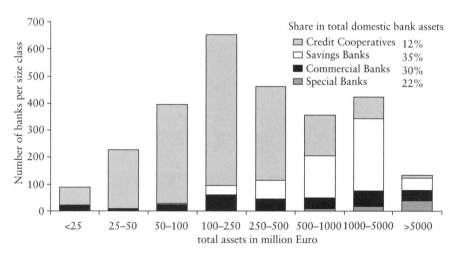

Figure 3.2. *Size distribution of banks from different groups (12/2000).*
Source: Deutsche Bundesbank (2000, 2001a).

About 20 per cent of all German banks belong to the public savings group and about 60 per cent belong to the cooperative banking sector. Hence, more than 80 per cent of all German banks are not strictly profit-maximizing entities. Figure 3.2 shows the size distribution of the banks from the four main bank groups. It reveals that most cooperative banks are indeed very small institutions. The majority had assets of less than 500 million Euro in 2000. In contrast, most savings banks and all *Landesbanks* had assets above this value. The private commercial banking group is quite heterogeneous with respect to size. Small private bankers as well as Germany's four largest banks belong to this group. Most special banks are among the largest German banks with total assets in excess of 5 billion Euro.

Appendix 3A.1 lists Germany's largest thirty banks by name, total domestic and international group assets, number of branches and employees and by bank group. These thirty banks amount to roughly 50 per cent of all German bank assets. This includes the four big private sector banks, which cover 16 per cent of German bank assets, ten of the thirteen public *Landesbanks* (19 per cent) and all three regional institutions of credit cooperatives (4 per cent). It is interesting to note that only thirteen of the thirty largest banks in Germany were strictly profit-maximizing entities. However, it has to be noted that the data in the top thirty list of the Association of German banks cannot be directly compared to the data of the Deutsche Bundesbank, which we refer to in most other tables and figures of this chapter. Whilst the former are based on the consolidated annual reports of banks, the Bundesbank data are based on monthly balance sheet statistics that cover only those parts of German banks which are located in Germany, that is, their headquarters and their domestic branches. Moreover, the top thirty list includes some double counting as the largest private mortgage banks appear on the list as part of Deutsche Bank, Dresdner Bank, and Commerzbank, respectively, as well as in their own right.

Because the combined market share in total domestic bank assets of the top five banks is lower than 20 per cent, the German banking system is often viewed as being very fragmented. As will be argued below, the savings bank group and the cooperative group might well be treated as if each were a single large entity. In this case, the top five market share jumps up to 59 per cent, which is close to the European average value of 57 per cent in 1999 (ECB 2000). We will now describe the four main banking groups in more detail.

3.2.2. Commercial Banks

The first German joint stock banks were established in the middle of the nineteenth century. At this time, private bankers were no longer able to satisfy the growing financing needs of mass-production industrial companies. A consolidation wave fuelled by the banking crisis of 1931/1932 led to the emergence of three dominant players, namely Dresdner Bank (founded in 1872), Deutsche Bank (1870), and Commerzbank (1870). After having been disbanded in the wake of the Second World War, all three reassembled between 1957 and 1958. Today, they still act as the *Hausbanks* to Germany's large industrial corporations and form the core of Germany's private commercial banking group. The Bayerische Hypo- und Vereinsbank (HVB), which resulted from a 1998 merger between two large Bavarian banks, joined the Deutsche Bundesbank category of big banks in 1999. Its retail business was traditionally located in the southern parts of Germany, but has been expanded to the rest of Germany, Austria, and Central and Eastern Europe during the recent past.

All four big banks are truly universal banks in that their retail and corporate banking businesses are complemented by growing investment banking activities. Deutsche Bank, which acquired the British investment bank Morgan Grenfell in 1989 and the US institution Bankers Trust in 1997, and Dresdner Bank, which followed suit by acquiring Kleinwort Benson in 1995 have been aggressively expanding their investment banking arms. In 1999, Deutsche ranked first, Dresdner second, and Commerzbank fourth among large European universal banks in terms of the portion of total capital that was allocated to wholesale and investment banking.[4] Moreover, the big banks' fully- or majority-owned mortgage banks,[5] their building and loan associations and their investment companies are among the largest in the German market. Their current bancassurance strategies, however, differ considerably. Whereas Deutsche Bank sold its insurance arm in 2001, Dresdner itself was bought by Allianz, Germany's largest insurance group, in the same year. Commerzbank is cooperating with Generali, Italy's largest insurance group, and HVB is cooperating with ERGO, Germany's second largest insurance company owned by Munich Re.

Although all four banks belong to the largest institutions in the world, their combined market share in deposits from German non-banks was lower than 14 per cent at the end of 2000. They operate 2873 branches compared to the 16,892 branches of the savings bank group and the 15,332 branches of the cooperative banking group. As a consequence of this discrepancy, the four big banks cooperate with regards to ATM usage; customers of one big bank can withdraw cash from an ATM of another big bank free of charge.

Regional and other commercial banks comprise of all German private second and third tier banks. The largest are Bankgesellschaft Berlin (rank 10 in 2000),[6] Postbank (rank 22), which is fully owned by the privatized German postal service, BHF-Bank (rank 27), which has been acquired by the Dutch ING Group in 1999, Deutsche Bank 24 (rank 31), which comprises the retail banking activities of Deutsche Bank Group, SEB (rank 34) which is fully owned by the Swedish Skandinaviska Enskilda Banken, Baden Württembergische Bank (rank 46), Deutsche Kreditbank (rank 51), Vereins- und Westbank (rank 52), Volkswagenbank, (rank 66), and Citibank Privatkunden (rank 73).

---

[4] In a joint study, Goldman Sachs and McKinsey estimate that German banks captured 23 per cent of total revenues in the European corporate banking market in 1999. However, British banks were still far ahead with a combined market share of 39 per cent (Leadem *et al.* 2001).

[5] Because of its status as a hybrid mortgage bank, HVB is the only German big bank that is exempted from the provision of the German mortgage act from 1899, which prohibits commercial banks from conducting mortgage banking business on their own behalf.

[6] Bankgesellschaft Berlin, a quoted holding company majority owned by the state of Berlin, was created from the merger of Landesbank Berlin and two commercial banks, Berliner Bank and Berlin Hyp in 1994. It represents the only case to date in Germany of a cross-sector consolidation. It continues to be the case that a private-sector bank cannot acquire a public-sector bank.

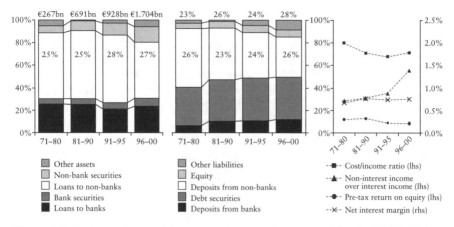

Figure 3.3. *Balance sheet and income statement of commercial banks (1971–2000).*

Note: Figures above asset-side columns show total domestic assets of all banks in the group at the end of 1980, 1990, 1995, and 2000. Percentage values indicate 5-year average market shares regarding total assets, loans to non-banks, and deposits from non-banks.

Source: Deutsche Bundesbank (1998, 2000, 2001a, b).

With the exception of some second tier banks such as BHF-Bank, SEB, and Citibank and the direct banks and brokerages like Volkswagenbank, Allgemeine Deutsche Direktbank (rank 96), Consors, and Comdirect most banks in this category focus on their regional retail or wholesale market.

Included in the group of commercial banks are also the private bankers. Some of them, like Joh. Berenberg, Gossler & Co. (founded in 1590 in Hamburg), B. Metzler Seel. Sohn & Co. KGaA (founded in Frankfurt in 1674) and Delbrück & Co. (founded in Cologne in 1712), are among the oldest banks still operating in Germany. Typically, they are controlled by owner–managers who are personally liable for the financial obligations of their banks. Their number has been declining; it went from 1406 institutions in 1925 to 491 in 1938 to only fifty at the end of 1998. Today their share in total assets of German banks' domestic operations is far below 1 per cent.

Roughly 2 per cent of the same asset base were under the control of the ninety (up from sixty-three in 1985) German branches of foreign banks that existed at the end of 2000. Adding up the assets of those fifty-six commercial and mortgage banks that were majority-owned by foreign banks—among them SEB and Citibank Privatkunden—yields the total share of German bank assets controlled by foreign banks or non-banks. This number was 8 per cent in 2000 and has remained fairly stable during the last 15 years.

Figure 3.3 depicts the aggregated balance sheet and three key performance indicators for German private commercial banks. Loans to non-banks as a portion of total assets have declined from roughly 60 per cent in the 1970s, 1980s, and early 1990s to 50 per cent during the late 1990s and have plummeted to 44 per cent in 2000. The portion of securities from non-banks, however, has increased from 7 per cent in 1971 to almost 15 per cent in 2000, indicating an increase in the importance of operations in close proximity to capital markets. The liability structure of commercial banks has changed even more dramatically. Although the banks in the group have managed to retain a market share of roughly 25 per cent over the last 30 years, the share of deposits from non-banks in total liabilities has dropped from over 52 per cent in the 1970s to 36 per cent in the late 1990s and was under 35 per cent in 2000. Deposits from banks and bank debentures now account for more than 50 per cent of total liabilities.

In line with these balance sheet developments, the ratio of non-interest income to interest income has increased steadily over the last 30 years and reached an all-time-high of 86 per cent in 2000 (59 per cent in 1999). During the same period the interest margin, defined as net interest revenue over total assets, has remained low at around 0.7 per cent. Pretax returns on equity have declined and reached an all-time-low of 6.6 per cent in 2000 (7.8 per cent in 1999). Partly because of the income squeeze, the cost–income ratio exceeded 75 per cent in 1999 and 2000 after commercial banks had managed to keep it below 70 per cent for most of the last decade.

3.2.3. The Savings Bank Group

The first German public savings bank was founded in 1801 in Göttingen after most existing private savings banks had suffered seriously from the Napoleonic wars. The Prussian savings bank act of 1838 ruled out the legal independency of all 234 Prussian savings banks and put them under the regime of the respective local governments. As a result of similar developments in all other German regions a total of 2700 public institutions existed at the beginning of the twentieth century. To avoid an excessive indebtedness of local governments in the wake of the great depression of 1929, savings banks were given autonomous legal status in 1931. Concurrently, the so-called *Gewährträgerhaftung* (guarantee obligation) was introduced, which makes the public founding entity liable without restriction in the event of default by their savings bank, and hence serves as a guarantee for third party lenders. In addition, the so called *Anstaltslast* (maintenance obligation) has since then placed with the founding entity the responsibility for ensuring that its savings bank is able to meet its financial obligations at all times, that is, providing a capital injection or liquidity support when the bank is threatened by insolvency. Because the maintenance obligation by itself virtually rules out a default of the savings bank, the guarantee obligation has been put into force in only a very few cases. Primarily owing to the constrained budgets of local governments and the avoidance of negative reputation effects, the maintenance obligation has also not been enforced very often. Mergers between banks susceptible to insolvency and healthy institutions have been preferred to bailouts.

Public savings banks are governed by the savings bank laws of the respective German states. These laws oblige the savings banks to serve the public interests of their region by fostering individual savings and by satisfying the credit needs of their local communities. They should thereby focus on the needs of employees, small and medium-sized enterprises—which are commonly referred to as the German *Mittelstand*—and their public authority. For example, public savings banks are obliged to open a transaction account for every applicant. Typically, the laws further require that although savings banks have to conduct their businesses according to sound economic principles, profit maximization must not be their primary business objective.[7] It also implies that the primary savings banks may typically not or only to a specified degree hold shares in enterprises outside the savings bank group, trade money market, equity or foreign exchange instruments on their own account or take part in an underwriting consortium. Moreover, to avoid competition between local savings banks, each institution is prohibited from operating outside its local area and encroaching upon its neighbours' territories.[8] In rural areas they typically compete with smaller cooperative banks, whereas in metropolitan areas they typically compete with the branches of the large private commercial banks.

Their governance structures are quite similar to those of private commercial banks. The executive board reports to a supervisory board called the *Verwaltungsrat*. Two-thirds of the seats of the supervisory board are typically determined by the founding entity as the owner of the bank, one-third is elected by the employees. A third body, the credit committee, consists of at least three members of the supervisory board and gives the founding entity the opportunity to exert influence on important credit decisions.

In addition to the 541 public savings banks there exist seven free savings banks, which are essentially self-controlled, and thus do not benefit from state guarantees but are otherwise more or less comparable to their public peers. One of them and at the same time the largest savings bank in Germany, the Hamburger Sparkasse (Haspa) acknowledged in its annual report for the year 2000 (p. 3) that it '[...]is unreservedly committed to the smaller business. The need to introduce an internal rating system (Basle II) will inevitably mean that lending terms will be tightened up to give more protection against lending risks. The smaller businesses will still get loans on attractive terms'. This statement is accompanied by the following: 'The profits we earn are ploughed back into Haspa. This sound footing has enabled us to adapt successfully to social and economic change throughout our 174-year history and to become a leading all-round financial institution for the local economic region.' This form of profit appropriation is indeed typical for most savings banks. According to Sinn (1996) the ratio of retained earnings to net income has on average been 50 per cent

---

[7] See, for example, section 3 (3) of the savings bank law of the State of Northrhine-Westfalia.

[8] Only when requested by a customer or after agreement by both the savings bank concerned and the regulator are they permitted to offer their services outside their defined market.

higher for savings banks than for private commercial banks in the period from 1980 to 1994. One obvious reason is of course that unlike their private competitors, public banks cannot raise external equity from third parties. Yet, critics often argue that the practice by founding entities of tolerating such low pay-out ratios in addition to the guarantees provided by the public owners via the maintenance and guarantee obligations unduly insulates public banks from the pressure typically exerted by private shareholders and thereby renders competitive advantages to the savings bank group as a whole and to the *Landesbanks* in particular. As a consequence, the group members would appear to be in a position to offer financial products to customers under favourable conditions which can hardly be matched by German and foreign private sector banks without squeezing margins to unattractive levels.[9]

Landesbanks and regional savings associations constitute the second tier of the savings bank group. The twelve *Landesbanks* have two primary functions. First, they serve as the *Hausbank* to their state(s) and as such provide cash management services and grant loans, which are mainly refinanced by means of public *Pfandbriefe*[10] (mortgage bonds) and public sector bonds. Second, they act as the central bank to the primary savings banks in their region and as such act as the clearing institution for interbank transfers and support the much smaller primary banks in providing complex, non-standard products and services to their customers. Moreover, they are truly universal banks in their own right providing commercial and investment banking services to larger domestic and foreign bank, non-bank, and public clients. They thus compete directly with the large private commercial banks.

Most *Landesbanks* are owned by the respective state, by other *Landesbanks*[11] and by the thirteen regional savings associations. The main function of these regional associations is to provide administrative services to their members, the regional savings banks. They run seven data centres that employ more than 5500 people, develop new financial products, conduct marketing campaigns and provide economic and market research insights, training, procurement and auditing services. As a link between savings banks and *Landesbanks* they also coordinate the activities between these two tiers of the group.

DGZ-Deka Bank is the central bank to all *Landesbanks* and together with the German Savings Bank Association (DSGV), in which all savings banks hold a stake, constitutes the third tier. Both the *Landesbanks* and the DSGV own 50 per cent of DGZ-Deka Bank. This institution fully controls the investment funds of the savings group, which had 136 billion Euro under management at the end of 2000, of which approximately 75 billion Euro were invested in retail funds resulting in a 20 per cent domestic market share.

---

[9] For a detailed presentation of this argument from the angle of private sector banks see, for example, Association of German Banks (2000: 6).

[10] See Section 2.5 for a discussion of the main features of *Pfandbriefe*.

[11] At the end of 2000, West LB, the largest *Landesbank*, for example owned 39.9 per cent of Landesbank Schleswig-Holstein which itself owned 49.5 per cent of Hamburgische Landesbank.

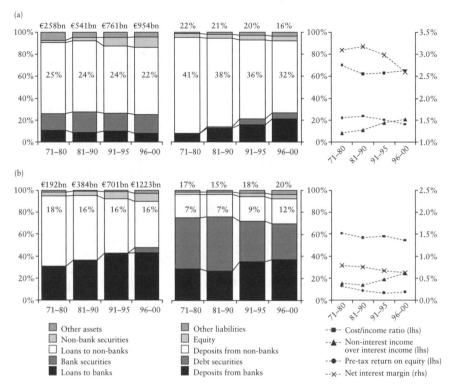

Figure 3.4. *Balance sheet and performance indicators of the savings bank group (1971–2000). (a) Primary savings banks (b) Landesbanks.*

Note: For notes and source please refer to Figure 6.3.

The savings bank group furthermore encompasses eleven regional public loan and building associations (market share in 2000: 34 per cent), eight leasing companies (21 per cent), two factoring companies (17 per cent), thirty-seven public insurance companies (life assurance: 10 per cent; composite insurance: 14 per cent) and seventy-five venture capital companies.

Except for the high degree of independence on the part of the primary savings banks granted by the 'federal corporatist' type of organization, the form of labour division within the savings bank group resembles the hierarchical structure of the big four universal private sector banks with their headquarters, regional centres, branches, and subsidiaries. Hence, the savings bank group could and maybe should be perceived as one large bancassurance entity. As such it constitutes the largest financial institution in the world with roughly 3000 billion Euro assets at the end of 2000.

Figure 3.4 shows the unconsolidated, domestic balance sheet and three performance indicators of the primary savings institutions and the *Landesbanks* for the past three decades. Because of their clear focus on traditional commercial banking, loans to non-banks represent the lion's share of the savings banks' domestic asset base. Their share has decreased only slightly from 65 per cent in the 1970s to around 60 per cent over the course of the 1990s and stood at 61 per cent in 2000. In stark contrast, the share of deposits from non-banks in total liabilities has sharply decreased from 87 to 69 per cent over the three decades and reached an all-time low of 62 per cent at the end of 2000. As a consequence of these disparate developments, the role of savings banks as providers of funds to other banks has eroded over time.

Instead, in their totality savings banks became net-borrowers in the inter-bank market. This development is mirrored on the asset side of the *Landesbanks*, which lent an increasing portion of their funds to primary savings banks in the form of long-term money for the matched funding of their mortgages. Traditionally, *Landesbanks* obtained these funds though either bank debentures sold to private and institutional investors or through deposits from other banks. It is partly because of the increasing importance for *Landesbanks* of wholesale banking that they overtook the primary savings banks in terms of total assets in the late 1990s and represented a fifth of total German domestic banking assets and 17 per cent of total loans to non-banks in 2000. The market share of savings banks in non-bank loans was only a little higher at 20 per cent. The combined market share of the savings bank group in non-bank loans fell slightly from 43 per cent in the seventies to below 40 per cent in the late 1990s.

The high interest margin of savings banks is certainly due to their strong focus on retail banking (i.e. offering savings products to households and loans to individuals and small and medium-size enterprises, SME) and in particular to the economic rents from an inert deposit base. Even though savers became more price sensitive during the 1990s and thereby caused margins to drop to 2.3 per cent in 2000, margins are still more than three times higher than those of private commercial banks with their stronger focus on the commercial banking business with larger clients. Not surprisingly, the ratio of non-interest income to interest income (slightly more than 20 per cent in 2000) of both savings banks and *Landesbanks* is much lower than it is for the private sector banks. What may come as a bit of a surprise, however, is the fact, that the cost/income ratio for the savings bank sector as a whole (60 per cent) was considerably lower in the late nineties than for the profit-maximizing private commercial banks (well over 70 per cent). Given that the savings banking sector is the undisputed market leader in German retail banking, this points to a lack of scale for private sector banks' retail banking operations.[12]

---

[12] Other indicators that underscore this view are risk-weighted assets per branch, loans per branch, and loans per employee. According to estimates by Morgan Stanley Dean Witter (2000), the values of all three ratios were far lower on average for the retail operations of the four big private sector banks than for the largest savings banks in 1998. Small market shares seem hence to translate into the inability of the private sector banks to generate sufficient retail business volume to cover the fixed costs of branch networks.

3.2.4. Cooperative Banking Group

In the early nineteenth century German craftsmen and farmers suffered from dire financial constraints because the existing private bankers were largely focusing on trade finance, private commercial banks were mainly granting loans to the manufacturing and transportation industry, and savings banks had to request collateral in exchange for credit. Starting in 1850, credit cooperatives were founded under the basic principles of self-aid, self-responsibility, and autonomous administration to mitigate these constraints. The savings of depositors were transferred to members with financing needs and once a year the profits of a credit cooperative were distributed among its members. Nowadays, profits are still paid out to members—whose number reached 15 million in 2000—but since 1974, non-members have also become eligible to receive loans. In 1972, all German credit cooperatives were united to form the German Association of *Volks-* and *Raiffeisenbanks*, which shares many structural features with the German Association of Saving Banks. The multi-tier structure comprises the primary credit cooperatives that provide mainly retail banking services to their local market. Their member individuals can exercise their control rights at members' meetings and via a supervisory board. Like the *Landesbanks*, the two central institutions of the cooperative banking group— the WGZ bank and the DZ-Bank[13]—provide a wide array of services to their primary institutions. They act as clearing institutions, provide access to national and international financial markets, provide asset liability management support and offer centralized back-office functions. In addition to their functions as the central body they compete with the larger private sector banks in the investment and commercial banking arena.

The cooperative banking group also includes two mortgage banks, one leasing company, one building and loan association, one insurance company and an investment company with approximately 60 billion Euro retail funds under management, and a 16 per cent market share at the end of 2000. The combined asset base of the group amounted to 920 billion Euro making it only slightly smaller than the entire Deutsche Bank Group. With its customer base of 30 million, it clearly exceeds Deutsche Bank's German 7.2 million customer base.

The small size of the primary institutions brings with it the competitive advantages of customer proximity and quick decision making. However, in combination with the legal restriction that equity can only be raised from the cooperative members, the small size in itself also curbs the loan business with larger enterprises and in effect precludes further profitable growth. The intense within-group M&A activity that has brought down the number of credit cooperatives from over 11,000 in 1970 to less than 1800 at the end of 2000 can be partly explained by this fact. Of course, in many cases the need to

---

[13] In 2001, DG Bank, the former apex institute of the cooperative banking group merged with GZ-Bank, one of two former regional cooperative central banks, to form DZ Bank.

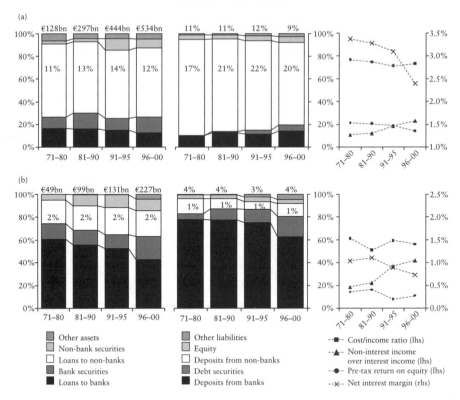

Figure 3.5. *Balance sheet and income statement of credit cooperatives (1971–2000). (a) Primary cooperative banks, (b) regional institutions and cooperative banks.*

Note: For notes and sources please refer to Figure 6.3.

exploit economies of scale, to better diversify the loan portfolio or to rescue weak peer institutions have also played an important role. However, as can be seen from Figures 3.4 and 3.5, the average cost/income ratio of the credit-cooperatives has hardly decreased during the last 30 years, and consequently is still higher than that of the savings banks.

With respect to balance sheet structure, the interest margin, the importance of non-interest income and pretax ROE, both levels and changes during the last decades are fairly comparable to those observed for the primary savings banks (see Figure 3.5); the drop in interest margins resulted in non-interest income exceeding 20 per cent of interest income and has caused pretax ROEs to fall below 20 per cent in recent years.

The balance sheet structure of the regional institutions of cooperative banks demonstrates their role as central banks for the primary institutions. More than 60 per cent of their assets and also more than 60 per cent of their liabilities are claims on other banks and funds owed to other banks, respectively. In the second half of the 1990s the three banks increasingly substituted bank loans and deposits by purchasing bank securities and issuing bearer bonds. Interest margins fell below 1 per cent and because of an increase in investment banking activities fee and trading income rose to over 40 per cent of interest income. At the end of 2000 the entire cooperative banking sector had a market share in total domestic banking assets of 13 per cent. Their market share in loans to non-banks and in deposits from non-banks has risen slightly over the course of the last 30 years.

3.2.5. Special Banks

Special banks accounted for 22 per cent of all German banking assets at the end of 2000. More than 15 per cent were controlled by thirty-one mortgage banks alone; among them four public mortgage banks, of which only the Westdeutsche Immobilienbank (rank 62) appears on the list of Germany's Top 100 banks. However, seven of the private mortgage banks rank among Germany's top thirty banks. In late 2001, the mortgage banking subsidiaries of Deutsche Bank (Eurohypo), Dresdner Bank (Deutsche Hypothekenbank) and Commerzbank (Rheinhyp) merged to create Germany's largest mortgage bank with a 25 per cent share in the German mortgage market and roughly Euro 240 billion in total assets, catapulting the new entity into Germany's top ten. The three big banks acknowledged their main motives to be to cut costs, to free up capital and to achieve the critical size for competing in the European market. According to the German mortgage bank law, mortgage banks are restricted in their business mix to granting loans, either backed by liens on property or by assets and tax income of public authorities, and to refinancing those loans by means of long-term deposits and bank debentures such as commercial and public *Pfandbriefe*. Commercial (public) *Pfandbriefe* are backed by a pool of residential or commercial mortgage loans (loans to and securities issued by public sector borrowers). Bond holders have a pari-passu first charge over the entire collateral pool and the mortgage bank remains liable if the assets in the pool turn out to be insufficient to meet any obligation arising from its *Pfandbriefe* outstanding. As a consequence of the strict legal framework provided by the German *Pfandbrief* law and the German mortgage bank law,[14] not a single *Pfandbrief* defaulted during the twentieth century. Especially since 1995, when so-called Jumbo-*Pfandbriefe* with a volume of over Euro 500 million per single issue were introduced, the German *Pfandbrief*-market has witnessed impressive growth. The volume of outstanding

---

[14] For example, the mortgage bank law requires that mortgages eligible as commercial *Pfandbrief* pool collateral must not exceed 60 per cent of a property's mortgageable value, that properties must be marketable and conservatively valued, and that total mortgages for financing building plots and uncompleted buildings not yielding income, as well as total mortgages against real estate in countries which do not accept preferential satisfaction of bondholders, must not exceed 10 per cent of the total mortgage pool each.

Pfandbriefe has almost doubled between the end of 1994 (Euro 420 billion) and the end of 2001 (Euro 820 billion), making German *Pfandbriefe* the largest segment in European bond markets.[15]

At the end of 2000, 62 per cent of German mortgage bank assets were loans to non-banks, 19 per cent were deposits with other banks, 8 per cent were non-bank securities and 7 per cent were bank securities. Sixty-seven per cent of total liabilities were in the form of bank debentures (mostly *Pfandbriefe*), 16 per cent were in the form of deposits from non-banks and 12 per cent were in the form of deposits from other banks. For the same year the cost–income ratio was 33 per cent and the pretax ROE reached an all-time low of 4.6 per cent after it had averaged 13 per cent over the nineties and 15 per cent over the 1980s.

The thirty German building and loan associations accounted for merely 2.5 per cent of total German bank assets at the end of 2000. However, 12 per cent of all time and savings deposits and 13 per cent of all mortgage loans to German individuals were deposits and loans, respectively, under savings and loan contracts. After signing such a contract with a building and loan association, the customer enters the savings phase during which he makes constant monthly payments. After the minimum savings amount has been accumulated (typically 40 per cent of the total contract sum) and subject to a customer-specific amount exceeding a threshold value, the customer is allotted the mortgage loan. During the second phase of the contract duration, the customer repays his loan and thereby replenishes the society's capital pool. After a sufficient number of periods this construction yields a closed system so that interest rates on deposits and on loans can remain almost constant across time.

The sixteen German banks with special functions have in common that they grant loans to individuals, enterprises, and projects that are deemed eligible for promotion by the German government. The private Industriekreditbank, for example, promotes SMEs that would otherwise not have access to capital markets. The private Liquiditäts-Konsortialbank, which is backed by all German universal banks, acts as a drawee for bills of exchanges drawn by banks that suffer from liquidity shortages. Also backed by other German banks, the AKA Ausfuhrkreditgesellschaft promotes German enterprises through export finance and direct loans to their foreign customers. The public-owned Kreditanstalt für Wiederaufbau (KfW) provides services in the areas of investment finance (e.g. structural investment programs in the eastern part of Germany), export and project finance and financial cooperation with developing countries. Its subsidiary DEG promotes private-sector initiatives in developing and reforming countries. The combined asset base of all banks with a special function amounted to 7.5 per cent of total domestic assets in 2000.

---

[15] See Maestroeni, O. (2001) for further details.

3.3. MAJOR TRENDS IN THE GERMAN BANKING MARKET

This section outlines some of the major trends in the German banking market and compares them to developments in other European countries and the United States. Based on the presented, and admittedly crude, evidence we attempt a preliminary assessment of whether German (and European) commercial banking is indeed in the middle of structural change and if so, whether it is in decline.

Figure 3.6 shows the development of the number of commercial, savings, and cooperative banks and their branches during the last 30 years. The total number of banks has decreased dramatically from more than 12,000 during the seventies to roughly 5,000 in the year 2000. This was mainly due to the consolidation within the cooperative sector. During the last 20 years, the total number of West German universal banks has been further halved to about 2,500. Again, the absorption of very small or stressed financial institutions by a sounder member of the cooperative or the savings banking group, respectively, was responsible for the lion's share of this reduction. In contrast, the number of branches (excluding those of the postal bank) increased considerably during the 1970s and 1980s reaching a peak of over 40,000 in the early 1990s. Even when Eastern German branches are excluded their number was still higher than it had been 10 years earlier. This has prompted many commentators to declare the German financial system to be over-banked.

Since 1990 the number of branches in the three major banking groups has come down to under 39,000, with the sharpest fall in the western parts of Germany, where about 5,400 branches were closed by 2000. Mainly

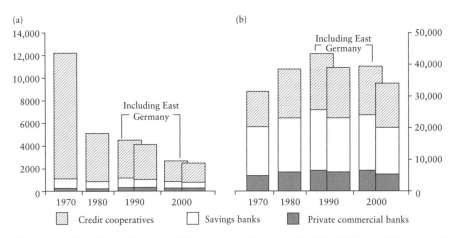

Figure 3.6. *Number of banks and branches in Germany (1970–2000). (a) Number of bank institutions in Germany, (b) number of bank branches in Germany.*

Source: Deutsche Bundesbank monthly report, various issues.

responsible for this decline were the savings banking and the cooperative banking groups, which trimmed down their branch network by 15 per cent and 13 per cent, respectively. Similar trends could be observed in the EU14 countries (excluding Luxembourg), in the United Kingdom and the United States for the period from 1985 to 1999.[16] Except for Greece, Ireland and the Netherlands, where less than 100 banks existed in 1985, the number of banks decreased in all these countries. For example, in Spain and France, the number of banks dropped by about 45 per cent, in the United States by almost 40 per cent and in Italy and the United Kingdom by slightly more than 25 per cent. As a result, the proportion of German banks in relation to the total number of European banks has remained more or less constant at almost 40 per cent during the last 20 years. The consolidation wave led to an increase in the market share in terms of assets of the five largest banks in the majority of European countries. As a result, the average ratio increased from 53 per cent in 1985 to 57 per cent in 1999, with Sweden (88 per cent), the Netherlands (82 per cent), Belgium (77 per cent), and Denmark (77 per cent) showing the highest values in 1999. Also with respect to branch network density, the German trend mirrors the general European trend. While the number of German branches per 1000 capita fell from 0.61 in 1985 to 0.54 in 1999, the European average has declined from 0.49 to 0.45. Germany now ranks fourth (1985: fifth) in terms of this ratio with higher values only for Spain (1.0), Belgium (0.68) and Austria (0.57) and hence might still be considered as over-banked by European and also by US[17] standards. The German banking association itself states in its 2002 banking survey (p. 70) that the number of bank branches exceeds that of gas stations by the factor 4 and quotes internal studies according to which the break-even point for retail operations lies below 0.25 branches per 1000 capita.

The following two figures encapsulate major trends in the profit and loss statements of European and US banks during the 15 years between 1985 and 1999. Interest margins deteriorated in all seven countries indicating an intensification of competition within the banking industries and/or from non-bank financial intermediaries and capital markets.[18] In 1999, only French interest margins were thinner than those in Germany. It might therefore be argued that the degree of competition among German banks is neither lower nor higher than in the other major countries (see Chapter 10). Declining interest margins have caused banks to seek alternative sources of income.

Consequently, and as can be observed from panel (b) in Figure 3.7, the relative importance of fee-based businesses like asset management, underwriting,

---

[16] The figures reported in this and the next paragraph are taken from ECB (2000).

[17] According to White (1998) the corresponding figure for the United States was 0.27 in 1996.

[18] Dermine (2002) shows that for many European countries this drop in net interest margins is primarily due to a squeeze in deposit margins, which in turn is also owed to lower general interest rate levels. Margins on consumer and corporate loans were found to have actually increased in many cases.

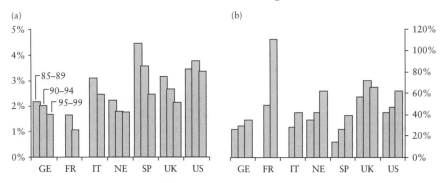

Figure 3.7. *Net interest margins and non-interest income contributions (1985–99). (a) Net interest income/total assets, (b) non-interest income/interest income.*

Note: Data for all banks in the case of GE (Germany), FR (France), IT (Italy), NE (Netherlands), SP (Spain), and for commercial banks only in the case of US and UK.

Source: OECD (1994, 2000).

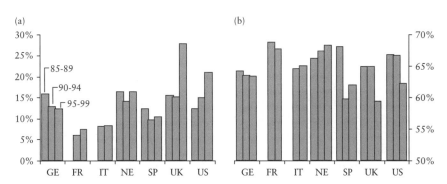

Figure 3.8. *Return on equity and cost/income ratios (1985–99). (a) Profit before tax/ equity, (b) operating expenses/gross income.*

Source: OECD (1994, 2000); for notes see Figure 6.7.

and advisory services as well as trading activities has risen in all countries. Not surprisingly, this trend has been the strongest in France, where margins were the lowest during the nineties. However, even in the United States, where banks enjoyed above-average interest margins during most of the observation period, the ratio increased considerably. These developments can be interpreted as general evidence of a global shift in the focus of banks from traditional commercial banking towards more capital market-oriented services. Although German banks have started to catch up, they still seem to be far behind in this regard.

Because of their successful efforts in cutting costs (see panel (b) in Figure 3.8) the Anglo-Saxon banks have managed to translate this shift into higher returns on equity. German banks have been less successful in reducing operating expenses and as a result have suffered from declining returns. In both respects they hold a middle position among their European peers.

Taken together the evidence presented so far seems to corroborate the common belief that traditional commercial banking is in decline all over the world and that German banks are no exception to this rule. Advocates of this view often cite as further evidence the shrinking share of banking assets in total financial sector assets. Allen and Santomero (2001) show for the United States that this share has halved from over 60 per cent in 1960 to below 30 per cent in 1998. Data from the German and British National Accounts Statistics reveal that the equivalent German figure declined from over 80 per cent to about 70 per cent and that the share for the United Kingdom declined from 65 per cent to below 50 per cent during the 1980s and 1990s of the last century. However, the empirical evidence that is presented in the next section casts crucial doubts on this view.

3.4. REPORTS OF THE DEATH OF COMMERCIAL BANKING MIGHT BE EXAGGERATED

In analysing the role of commercial banks in any given country it might indeed be misleading to only assess figures pertaining to the banking industry itself. Rather, the importance of banks for the other sectors of an economy should also be measured. Intermediation ratios and securitization ratios provide very helpful instruments for this purpose.[19] Their definition and measurement are based on the concept of an economy as a set of sectors that interchange goods, services and, most importantly for our context, financial funds. Accumulated over time these financial flows between economic sectors translate into financial claims of one sector and an offsetting liability item of another sector. Because this concept focuses on sectors and not on single economic units, only inter-sectoral, and not intra-sectoral, claims and liabilities, such as a loan from one bank to another bank, are considered. Intermediation ratios measure the proportion of sectors' total financial assets and liabilities, respectively, that

---

[19] The ratios are computed from National Account statistics, which the Deutsche Bundesbank describes as a unified data set which indicates from whom and to what extent funds of a specific type are channelled through a financial system, and what types of financial institutions are involved in this financial circuit (Deutsche Bundesbank 1995: 7). Structural differences in the data from different central banks and statistical offices with respect to subsector definition, degree of consolidation of items and general data reliability made data adjustments necessary. A discussion of adjustments and the estimated effects of remaining incongruencies can be found in Hackethal (2001). The ongoing process of standardizing compilation methods across countries will eliminate most methodological shortcomings. At the same time, however, historical comparisons will become more complicated as the changes imply structural breaks in the time series. For precisely this reason, it has not been possible to specify French and Japanese intermediation and securitization ratios for the years 1997/1998 and 1998, respectively. For data availability reasons, updating the UK ratios beyond 1995 was not possible, either. Please refer to Hackethal (2001) for a further discussion of the methodology and the data set and for a presentation of US and Japanese ratios prior to 1980.

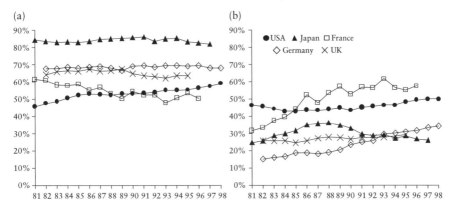

Figure 3.9. *General asset intermediation and securitization ratios (1981–98). (a) Asset-intermediation ratios of all sectors, (b) asset-securitization ratios of all sectors.*

Source: National Account Statistics.

constitute claims on financial institutions (asset intermediation ratios) or liabilities *vis-à-vis* financial institutions (liability intermediation ratios).

Securitization ratios take an instrumental perspective and measure the proportion of total claims and liabilities, respectively, that take the form of securities. In both cases ratios can be computed for different aggregation levels. The so-called general intermediation ratios indicate the importance of domestic financial intermediaries for all non-financial sectors, that is, households, enterprises, the non-financial public sector and all foreign entities. Partial intermediation ratios can be computed along three lines, that is, either by focusing on claims or liabilities of one non-financial sector *vis-à-vis* all financial intermediaries, by focusing on claims or liabilities of all non-financial sectors *vis-à-vis* one particular type of financial intermediary, or by employing a combination of these two approaches. Likewise, securitization ratios can be computed for all or a selection of non-financial sectors.

Figure 3.9, panel (a), shows the proportions of claims on the financial sector relative to the total claims of all non-financial sectors for the five largest economies in the world. Because financial assets of the entire financial sector must by definition roughly equal financial liabilities, these proportions must equal the respective proportions of liabilities *vis à vis* the financial sector in total liabilities. Except for France, where the ratio decreased from about 60 to 50 per cent, the role of financial intermediaries remained largely constant or—as has been the case in the United States—even increased during the 1980s and 1990s. Hence, financial and monetary integration, technological advances, and deregulation have certainly not led to a general trend of disintermediation. However, as can be seen from panel (b), these external factors have improved the sophistication of organized capital markets, and have thus resulted in a strong increase in the proportion of securities, that is, stocks, bonds, commercial paper, and investment certificates, in the portfolios of the non-financial sectors of three of the five countries. As securitization ratios are computed based on market values of securities, the burst of the bubble in Japanese equity markets led to a drop in the respective ratio in the early 1990s. It is interesting to note that the US ratio reached a level in 1998 which it had already had in 1970 and which in turn was still a long way away from the 60 per cent it had had in the early 1960s. As claims on pension funds and life assurance companies were counted as non-securitized claims, British securitization ratios are biased downward. Had they been counted as securitized claims, the British ratio would have reached a level comparable to that of the United States. Indeed, the liability securitization ratio of British non-financial sectors increased from 35 per cent at the beginning of the 1980s to almost 50 per cent in 1995, indicating the increasing role of these institutions as investors in corporate equity and government bonds. The corresponding ratios also rose sharply in France (from 31 to 65 per cent) and Germany (from 11 to 33 per cent) and to a lesser extent also in the United States (from 59 to 66 per cent) and Japan (from 25 to 26 per cent).

The two main observations concerning stable general intermediation ratios and increasing securitization ratios can be reconciled by taking into account the increasing role of non-bank financial institutions (NBFI) like insurance companies, pension and investment funds and the upward trend of stock markets in all countries except Japan during the nineties.

This becomes apparent in Figure 3.10, panel (a), which shows the proportion of household claims on banks to total household claims for the five countries. The downward trend is largely comparable to the trend for the asset intermediation ratios of all non-financial sectors *vis-à-vis* banks (see Hackethal 2001). It is more pronounced only because households constitute

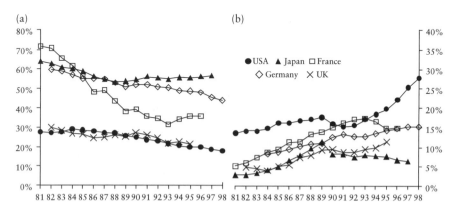

Figure 3.10. *Bank-intermediation ratios (1980–98). (a) Asset-intermediation ratios of households,* vis-à-vis *banks, (b) liability intermediation ratios of banks.*

Source: National Account Statistics.

the main surplus units in all countries.[20] Clearly, the role of banks as collectors of surplus capital from non-financial sectors declined in all five countries.

As total asset intermediation remained fairly constant, NBFIs must have gained market share at the expense of banks. Bank disintermediation on the asset side of households is, thus, a phenomenon that all observed financial systems share in common. It is important to note, however, that the level of bank intermediation still differs remarkably between those countries which have traditionally been deemed to be bank-based, namely Japan and Germany, on the one hand, and the capital market-based Anglo-Saxon countries, on the other hand (Rybczynski 1984). France is the exceptional case, in that its financial system seems to have evolved from being largely state-controlled and bank-based to a system in which marketable instruments have gained great importance to the detriment of intermediated instruments in the area of firm financing and, in particular, in the area of long-term saving.[21]

As the non-financial sectors restructured their portfolios by switching from bank deposits into insurance contracts, investment certificates and stocks, most banks had to seek alternative refinancing sources. Figure 3.10(b) reveals that as a consequence, the portion of funds from NBFI, whether in the form of deposits, money market instruments, bank debentures, or equity in total bank liabilities rose sharply in all five countries. In combining both insights from Figure 3.10 it can be concluded that asset-intermediation chains lengthened everywhere. NBFI moved in between surplus units and banks and in turn, invested part of the collected capital with banks. This certainly increased refinancing costs for banks leading to a fall in interest margins as shown in Figure 3.7. The effect on overall profitability, however, was probably smaller for German and French institutions than is indicated by Figure 3.8. Unlike their Anglo-Saxon peers, German and French banks own the dominant players in their domestic investment fund market so that decreasing net interest revenues were at least partially offset by increasing contributions from asset management operations, which, however, do not fully show up in the OECD-statistics.

In four of the five countries, bank intermediation also declined in importance from the debtors' perspective. Figure 3.11(a) shows an almost parallel development of the fraction of the inter-sectoral liabilities of British and US non-financial enterprises that are owed to banks. Bank loans, commercial paper, corporate bonds, and corporate equity held by banks constituted only

---

[20] Especially in the case of the United Kingdom, where many banks are heavily involved in inter-bank transactions with foreign banks, the sector 'Rest of the World', which itself encompasses all of these foreign counterparts, drives the general intermediation ratios. Partial ratios of households and enterprises are thus much more representative of UK banks' role within their domestic financial system.

[21] Refer to Schmidt *et al.* (1999, 2002) for a further discussion of the 'exception Française'. European Central Bank (2002) contains a discussion of recent developments in the French financial system and presents data for the year 2000.

about 10 per cent of enterprises' total inter-sectoral liabilities at the end of the observation period. Albeit from a higher level, bank finance in this wider sense has declined in France and Japan. A study by Morgan Stanley Dean Witter (2000: 81) indicates that the liability intermediation ratios *vis-à-vis* banks of Spanish and Italian enterprises also declined strongly during the nineties. In sharp contrast, German enterprises still rely heavily on banks as financiers. The ratio has remained roughly constant at 60 per cent.

A widely recognized series of studies initiated by Mayer (1988) led to a profound revision of academic thinking about the financing patterns of corporations in different countries. Using netted flow-of-funds data instead of balance sheet data, the studies found that internal financing is the dominant mode of financing in all countries, and that financial patterns do not differ very much between countries. Corbett and Jenkinson (1997: 85) conclude: 'The celebrated distinction between the market-based financial pattern of the United Kingdom and the United States and the bank-based pattern of Germany is inaccurate.' Hackethal and Schmidt (2002) demonstrate that the surprising empirical results found by Mayer et al. are mainly due to a hidden assumption underlying their methodology. Based on an alternative method that uses gross flows instead of net flows, Hackethal and Schmidt find that financial patterns are very much in line with the commonly held belief prior to Mayer's contribution and that gross-flow financial patterns can indeed be easily reconciled with the financial structures shown in Figure 3.11.

Figure 3.11(b) shows the results of a closely related study conducted by the Deutsche Bundesbank, which was based not on National Account Statistics but on detailed balance sheet data of about 20,000 German enterprises. Because of the inclusion of inter-sectoral liabilities and the fact that bank finance could only be extracted in the form of bank loans the levels of the

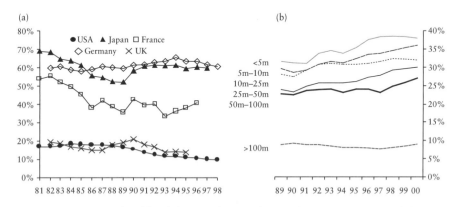

Figure 3.11. *Role of bank finance for non-financial enterprises. (a) Liability intermediation ratios of enterprises* vis-à-vis *banks (b) bank loans/total liabilities of German enterprises (DM-turnover classes).*

Source: National Account Statistics and Deutsche Bundesbank (2001*c*, 2002).

ratios are much lower than the corresponding liability intermediation ratios *vis-à-vis* banks in panel (a). The reported change in the ratio of bank loans to total liabilities for German enterprises from six different size classes is, however, of great help in explaining the extent to which German banks should still be considered unique. Whereas enterprises with annual sales exceeding DM 100 million have emancipated themselves slightly from bank loans, German SMEs have even increased their reliance on bank loans. Because the magnitude of information asymmetries is generally negatively correlated with firm size, this trend implies rising demand for the monitoring capabilities of German banks. This point is also stressed by Edwards (1996: 64): '[The] monitoring advantage is probably greatest with respect to small business borrowers, where problems of asymmetric information are particularly severe and where banks commonly provide those firms with unsecured credit.'

We can thus conclude that the predominant role of the *Mittelstand* for the German enterprise sector in conjunction with its preference for financing investments by means of bank loans is responsible for the fact that bank disintermediation cannot be observed on the asset side of the German banking sector as a whole. As mentioned in Section 3.2.2, the big commercial banks have traditionally been the *Hausbank*s to large corporations, whereas the savings banks have typically played the *Hausbank* role for SMEs. In conjunction with the observed increase in demand for loans by SMEs this might explain why the savings bank group was able to extend its market share in corporate loans from 30 per cent in 1990 to 39 per cent in 2000. According to a press clipping of the savings bank group from 15 March 2002, the savings bank group granted 86 per cent of all new loans to German enterprises and to the self-employed in 2001, and thereby increased its market share further to over 41 per cent. Its market share in loans to the German craft sector is estimated to be even higher at around 65 per cent (DSGV 2001). During the same period, the market share of private commercial banks dropped from 37 to 29 per cent,[22] whereas the market share of the cooperative sector remained almost constant at around 15 per cent. Apparently, the big universal banks have been withdrawing from traditional commercial loan business and attempting instead to refocus on commercial banking to larger corporations and corporate investment banking like underwriting, trading, and advisory. Retail banking is conducted mainly for synergy reasons, that is, to exercise control over a distribution channel for products originating and/or managed in other parts of the bank. In line with this strategy—which Deutsche Bank calls 'connectivity strategy'—the private commercial banks dominate the market

---

[22] This decrease is only to a very small part due to the growing success of asset-backed-securities (ABS) transactions. According to a 1999 survey among twelve large private sector banks, approximately 3 per cent of their total loans to German enterprises had been sold via ABS-transactions (Association of German Banks 2000: 17). Given that ABS-transactions are almost exclusively conducted by private sector banks, less than 1 per cent of all outstanding bank loans had been moved off banks' balance sheets at the end of 1999.

for security deposits, administering more than 40 per cent of the 34 million security deposits of German individuals in 2000. In terms of the market value of security deposit holdings, their market share was even higher at almost 60 per cent, indicating that the average wealth and propensity to invest in securities of their customers exceeds that of the customers of the other banking groups. Moreover, through their complete ownership of investment companies they controlled 42 per cent of the mutual investment fund market in Germany. Private commercial banks were also quicker to adopt new technologies. Their share in the 15 million German online accounts that existed at the end of 2000 amounted to 49 per cent. Of these online accounts 1.3 million were held with the four online brokerages of Germany's four big banks and another 530,000 with Consors, which had been founded by the small Nuremberg Schmidt bank and was bought by BNP Paribas in early 2002, making Germany the biggest online brokerage market in Europe by far.

These numbers stand in sharp contrast to the much smaller share of private commercial banks in demand deposits (30 per cent), and in savings deposits (15 per cent), in particular. In 2000, savings banks dominated these markets with market shares of 47 and 54 per cent, respectively, forcing private sector banks to rely on other, more costly refinancing sources (see Figure 3.3).

In the light of this clear dominance by savings banks in conventional retail banking to individuals and SMEs, the assessments of German big banks' CEOs, with which this chapter started out, seem indeed to be justified. Public banks' favourable refinancing conditions due to a strong core deposit base— and in the case of *Landesbanks* certainly also due to state guarantees—in conjunction with long-term and close customer relationships allow them to price corporate loans very aggressively. As a result, the big private sector banks suffer from razor-thin interest margins and possibly also from a lack of scale,[23] both of which preclude them from compensating for the high fixed costs of their still extensive branch network. Given the fact that their commercial banking operations no longer create sufficient value on a stand-alone basis, and given the increasing pressure from institutional investors to create value, they are seeking new business opportunities in areas where their international reach and their sheer size warrants competitive advantages, namely in capital market-oriented areas. This puts them in direct competition with other, primarily Anglo-Saxon bulge bracket banks, and thus implies a convergence in their market and resource-based strategies towards international standards. Viewed from this perspective, indeed no stone has been left unturned as far as large German private sector banks are concerned, and traditional commercial banking seems to be in decline like everywhere else.

---

[23] Equity analysts highlight the lack of scale by comparing large commercial banks and large savings banks along ratios such as loans per branch and loans per employees. They find that average ratios are much lower for the private sector banks and make lower market shares responsible for this observation (Morgan Stanley Dean Witter 2000: 48)

We would argue, however, that exogenous factors have not been the most important reason for this decline. Based on their dominant position in German commercial and retail banking, savings banks and *Landesbanks* have defended their large market shares against private sector banks. This has arguably put German large private sector banks under more competitive pressure than their European peers, prompting them to retreat from this low-margin business. For a concise assessment of the current role of banks in the German financial system it might, thus, be misleading to follow the majority of international observers in their primary focus on private sector banks. Instead, more attention should perhaps be devoted to the strong role of the savings banking and the cooperative banking group, as they seem to be more representative of the German banking system. As one telling piece of evidence, in an industry report on German banks analysts at JP Morgan view the large savings banks as sure candidates for the title of best bank in Germany (JP Morgan 1999). Their strategic focus on retail banking and relationship banking to SMEs, which ensure high market shares and cross-selling opportunities, together with the ongoing trend for bundling common activities at both a macro and a micro level, which leads to considerable cost reductions, enable them to effectively respond to current challenges in their business environment.[24] Viewed from this perspective and in the light of the trend by SMEs towards more bank financing, the German banking sector as a whole has apparently retained its importance for the German financial system and—in some specific areas—might even have become 'more unique' compared to other capital market-oriented financial systems.

This uniqueness is underscored by the fact that there has hardly been any foreign influx into the German retail market during the last decades. As noted before, the combined market share in terms of total assets of subsidiaries of foreign banks and German banks owned by foreign institutions has remained constant at around 4 per cent since 1985. Moreover, according to a study in the year 2000 by the European Central Bank, almost 90 per cent of all 946 mergers and acquisitions in which German credit institutions had been involved between 1995 and 1999 were purely domestic in nature. A study in 2001 by the Bank for International Settlements (BIS) reports a similar home bias. It is based on a data set produced by Thomson Financial Securities Services that allows a distinction to be drawn between the origin of the target

---

[24] La Porta *et al.* (2002) have in a recent study analysed the role of public banks in ninety-two countries by measuring the government-owned portion in the ten largest banks per country in 1970 and in 1995, respectively. Due to the large size of *Landesbanks*, the figures for Germany are well above the average for both years. Their results which '[...] are consistent with the political view of government ownership of firms, including banks, according to which such ownership politicizes the resource allocation and reduces efficiency' (p. 290) imply that the savings bank group exploits market power at the expense of competitors and, ultimately, clients or, alternatively, that the relationship does not hold for Germany. In this chapter, we argue in favour of the second explanation.

and the bidder bank. Between 1990 and 1999 the aggregated value of transactions in which a domestic bank was acquired by a foreign bank amounted to only 4 per cent of the value of deals in which both target and bidder had been German banks. The German experts interviewed for the BIS study view the fact that savings and cooperative banks cannot be acquired by non-group institutions as an important reason for the lack of cross-border M&A activity.

Another possible reason for the small number of cross border transactions is highlighted in Hackethal (2001). He compares the strategy profiles of more than 600 European commercial banks and finds substantial differences between banks from different countries. Based on two sets of variables that attempt to capture each bank's market position and each bank's endowment with resources he first clusters the sample banks into nine strategic groups.[25] Logit models are then applied to identify those attributes that are best suited to discriminate between the banks in different strategic groups. He finds that banks in different groups differ more strongly with respect to market position than with respect to resource endowment. More importantly, he finds that one particular group is almost exclusively populated by German commercial banks. The average bank in that group stands out as one with a lower return, a lower variance in returns, a lower equity ratio, a smaller role of non-interest income and a comparatively high asset growth rate. Most British banks were found to belong to a second group while most French, Spanish, and Italian banks all fell into a third category. Given that banks from the same strategic group can be assumed to be fairly homogenous with respect to their strategic profile but to differ substantially in that respect from banks in other groups, and based on the observation that the country of origin is particularly important in explaining group membership, it is conjectured that competition between similarly positioned domestic commercial banks is much more intense than competition between banks from different countries.

Moreover, Hackethal argues that strong path dependencies rooted in vast structural differences between European financial systems have caused second and third tier banks from different countries to react differently to identical changes in their business environment (e.g. regulatory harmonization and advances in technology) so that a convergence in terms of market–product combinations is not discernible. He concludes that these structural differences might at least partially explain the small number of instances in which foreign banks entered the German market. This line of reasoning implies that intensified competition from abroad is only to be expected if structural changes in the German banking market occur, that is, if the dominant position of savings and cooperative banks erode.

---

[25] The first set consists of variables such as growth rate in total assets, non-interest income over total income, loans to non-banks over assets, and variance in returns; variables in the second include cost–income ratio, fixed assets over total assets, personnel expense per employee and non-bank deposits over total assets.

3.5. OUTLOOK

There are at least four major issues besides technological advances and financial and monetary integration that carry the potential for eroding the dominant position of public banks and thus for changing the German banking landscape as it has been described above.

German private sector banks have, for many years, argued that state guarantees have endowed public banks with higher credit ratings than they would merit on a stand-alone basis. As a consequence, *Landesbanks* and large savings banks would have benefited from lower refinancing costs which would have unduly skewed the level playing field in Germany. In July 2001, the European Commission decided that all forms of public guarantees are to be regarded as state aid under European Union law and are therefore illegal. As a result, the guarantee obligation must be fully abolished by 2005 and the maintenance obligation must be adjusted in such a way that the financial relationship between the public owner and the public bank does not differ from a relationship under private law, that is, any subsidy must be reported to the Commission. There has been much speculation regarding the effect of such a ruling on the *Landesbanks*' competitive position. Based on the assessment that the ratings of *Landesbanks* would be lower on a stand alone basis than those of the big four commercial banks, some commentators reckon with a widening of the spreads of public banks' debentures by 25–50 basis points (Donges *et al.* 2001; Sinn 1996; and Morgan Stanley Dean Witter 2000). Others argue that only about one-fifth of these securities are not backed by pools of collateral so that the total effect on absolute refinancing cost is much smaller (Menkhoff 1997: 568). Because most funding of primary savings banks still comes from customer deposits that are fully secured by a deposit guarantee scheme, the removal of state guarantees will probably not have a big impact on their business model. The removal, however, may have an important side-effect in terms of ownership and governance structures as it may serve as a catalyst for the privatization of savings banks. This would, in turn, surely pave the way for a consolidation across banking groups, since teaming up with savings banks is the only way for private sector banks to achieve greater scale in their retail business.

A second issue relates directly to the core deposits as the most important source of funding, which some analysts estimate to contribute almost 30 per cent to the total net interest income of a savings bank (JP Morgan 1999: 10). Should the trend of disintermediation on the banks' liability sides continue, savings banks will probably lose a competitive advantage that has traditionally helped them, *inter alia*, to offer better loan rates to their SME clients than private sector banks. Another factor that some observers believe to be responsible for the low margins in the corporate loan business is the alleged failure of many smaller German banks to stipulate prices that fully reflect the default risk of the debtor.

The new capital adequacy regulation as a third issue which might affect the future landscape in German banking will require banks to choose a level of regulatory capital that corresponds closely to the credit risks inherent in their loan portfolios. It might be argued that this puts smaller banks which do not possess a sophisticated internal rating and risk management system at a disadvantage. However, as network-affiliated lenders, all savings banks and also all cooperative banks are currently in the process of jointly setting up rating and risk management systems that shall be certified by regulatory authorities for the entire group of member banks and not for each single bank. Moreover, as new drafts of the proposed new regulation take into account the concerns of continental European governments and banks alike, the foreseeable effect of new capital requirements on the German banking structure is becoming less obvious (Schmidt 2001).

In conclusion, we do not believe that the non-private sector banks are about to lose their dominant position in the German (retail) commercial banking market in the short or medium terms. It can be safely predicted that interest margins will further decrease due to an increasing price awareness of customers and an intensifying competition among all types of financial institutions. However, it seems equally safe to assume that both groups are in a position to react to increasing cost pressures by centralizing non-core functions and services and by conducting horizontal within-group mergers. Consequently, the opportunities to vertically disintegrate the industry value chain, which had been opened up by technological advances many years ago, will be finally seized by the banking industry, pushing back-office functions such as payment processing and custody outside the boundaries of many banks. It is even more likely that the consolidation trend in German banking will continue in the coming years. We will probably also witness an even stronger specialization of banks from different groups in terms of customers and products, that is, public and cooperative banks will continue to successfully focus on retail and SME clients and larger commercial banks will focus on capital market-oriented business with corporations, larger SMEs, institutions, and wealthy individuals.

3.6. CONCLUSION

In this chapter we have argued that great care has to be taken when generalizing structural trends from one financial system to another. Whilst conventional commercial banking is clearly in decline in the United States, it is far from clear whether the dominance of banks in the German financial system has been significantly eroded. We interpret the immense stability in intermediation ratios and financing patterns of firms between 1970 and 2000 as strong evidence for our view that the way in which and the extent to which German banks fulfil the central functions for the financial system[26] are still consistent with the overall logic of the financial system. Because of the observed stability and consistency we do not expect the German financial system and its banking industry as an integral part of this system to converge to the institutional arrangements typical for a market-oriented financial system.

However, in the light of recent developments in the German economy some words of caution are certainly warranted. In late 2002, when we were finalizing this chapter on German banks and banking structure record levels in insolvencies of German firms could be observed together with record levels of risk provisioning by German banks, historically low bank profitability levels, and massive layoffs of employees, especially in the area of corporate banking. The president of the German private banking association and chairman of Deutsche Bank's supervisory board, Rolf E. Breuer, declared that the state of the German banking industry has never been worse during the last 50 years. He expects that a third of all German banking branches will have to be closed soon.[27]

Many commentators argue that the dire business environment has finally uncovered a structural crisis in the banking industry that for many years was obscured by extraordinary effects: Reunification stimulated loan demand for much of the 1990s and the booming equity markets in combination with the rise of the internet economy propped up the banks' fee business. Not only have these positive effects vanished, but other costly effects such as the Year-2000- and the Euro-conversion as well as write-offs and follow-on costs of enormous internet technology investments have occurred in the recent past. It remains an open question to be answered in a subsequent edition of this book whether the majority of German banks will eventually be able to cope with the growing challenges by concentrating on core competencies, improving efficiency and possibly by inter-group cooperation and consolidation, or whether the German banking industry is indeed in a state of terminal decline.

---

[26] According to Bodie and Merton (1995) financial systems fulfil six basic functions, albeit by means of different institutional setups: (1) clearing and settlement of payments, (2) pooling of resources to undertake large-scale indivisible enterprise projects, (3) transferring economic resources through time and across geographic regions and industries, (4) managing risk and uncertainty, (5) providing price information, and (6) mitigating incentive problems.

[27] Börsenzeitung (2002).

Appendix 3A.1. *The thirty largest German banks by asset size (end 2000)*

Rank	Name	Total assets (€ mn)	Branches	Employees	Group
1	Deutsche Bank AG, Frankfurt/M.	940.033	2.287	98.311	Private
2	Bayerische Hypo- und Vereinsbank AG, München	716.514	2.421	72.867	Private
3	Dresdner Bank AG, Frankfurt/M.	483.498	1.360	51.459	Private
4	Commerzbank AG, Frankfurt/M.	459.662	1.064	39.044	Private
5	Westdeutsche Landesbank Girozentrale, Düsseldorf	400.040	20	11.390	Public
6	DZ Bank, Frankfurt/M.	342.123	19	14.195	Cooperative
7	Bayerische Landesbank Girozentrale, München	305.042	1	8.297	Public
8	Landesbank Baden-Württemberg, Stuttgart	292.624	256	9.886	Public
9	Kreditanstalt für Wiederaufbau, Frankfurt/M.	223.074	1	2.032	Public
10	Bankgesellschaft Berlin AG, Berlin	206.181	410	14.989	Private
11	Norddeutsche Landesbank Girozentrale, Hannover	186.331	160	7.886	Public
12	Depfa Deutsche Pfandbrief Bank AG, Wiesbaden	156.446	45	2.476	Private
13	Landesbank Hessen-Thüringen Girozentrale, Frankfurt/M.	130.900	14	2.133	Public
14	Landesbank Schleswig-Holstein Girozentrale, Kiel	128.085	2	2.361	Public
15	Landesbank Berlin Girozentrale, Berlin	96.983	200	5.781	Public
16	Deutsche Hypothekenbank Frankfurt-Hamburg AG, Frankfurt/M.	86.685	34	1.288	Private
17	Hamburgische Landesbank Girozentrale, Hamburg	80.725	9	2.132	Public
18	DGZ DekaBank, Frankfurt und Berlin	76.680	2	2.899	Public
19	Europäische Hypothekenbank der Deutschen Bank AG	73.477	40	879	Private
20	RHEINHYP Rheinische Hypothekenbank AG, Frankfurt/M.	72.624	29	860	Private
21	Deutsche Genossenschafts-Hypothekenbank AG, Hamburg	70.570	17	692	Cooperative
22	Postbank AG, Bonn	68.506	14.000	10.756	Private
23	Genossenschaftliche Zentralbank AG, Stuttgart	65.214	3	1.557	Cooperative
24	Landesbank Rheinland-Pfalz Girozentrale, Mainz	63.871	4	1.998	Public
25	Allgemeine Hypothekenbank AG, Frankfurt/M.	63.765	14	341	Private
26	Hypothekenbank in Essen AG, Essen	58.771	6	132	Private
27	Berliner Handels- und Frankfurter Bank AG, Frankfurt/M.	53.868	9	2.881	Private
28	WGZ Westdeutsche Genossenschafts-Zentralbank eG, Düsseldorf	51.794	5	1.410	Cooperative
29	Deutsche Ausgleichsbank, Bonn	51.600	1	793	Public
30	Landwirtschaftliche Rentenbank AG, Frankfurt/M.	51.447	1	192	Public

Source: Website of the German Banking Association (www.bdb.de).

References

Allen, F., and Gale, D. (1997). 'Financial Markets, Intermediaries and Intertemporal Smoothing', *Journal of Political Economy*, 105: 523–46.

——, and Santomero, A. M. (2001). 'What Do Financial Intermediaries Do?', *Journal of Banking and Finance*, 25(2): 271–94.

Association of German Banks (2000). *Daten, Fakten, Argumente—Private Banken, Partner des Mittelstandes*. Berlin (May).

Becketti, S., and Morris, C. S. (1992). 'Are Bank Loans Still Special?', *Federal Reserve Bank of Kansas Economic Review*, 77(3): 71–84.

Bodie, Z., and Merton, R. C. (1995). 'A conceptual framework for analyzing the financial environment', in D. B. Crane *et al.* (eds.), *The Global Financial System: A Functional Perspective*. Cambridge: Harvard Business School Press, 3–31.

Börsenzeitung (2002). 'Breuer erwartet Schließung jeder dritten Bankfiliale und weiteren Stellenabbau', (13 December): 1.

Boyd, J. H., and Gertler, M. (1993). 'U.S. Commercial Banking: Trends, Cycles, and Policy', in O. Blanchard and S. Fischer (eds.), *National Bureau of Economic Research Macroeconomics Review*, 319–68.

——, and —— (1995). 'Are Banks Dead? Or Are the Reports Greatly Exaggerated?' NBER Working Paper No. 5045.

Calomiris, C. W. (1997). 'On the Convergence of U.S. Banks to International Norms in Corporate Banking', 15th International Seminar on the New Institutional Economics, Wallerfangen/Germany (June), unpublished manuscript.

Corbett, J., and Jenkinson, J. (1997). 'How is Investment Financed? A Study of Germany, Japan, the United Kingdom and the United States', *The Manchester School Supplement*: 69–93

Dermine, J. (2002). 'European Banking: Past, Present and Future', Conference Paper for Second ECB Central Banking Conference on The Transformation of the European Financial System, Frankfurt am Main (24–25 October).

Deutsche Bundesbank (1995). 'Ergebnisse der gesamtwirtschaftlichen Finanzierungsrechnung für Deutschland 1990–1994', *Special Statistical Publication*, 4 (August).

—— (1998). '50 Jahre Deutsche Mark—Monetäre Statistiken 1948–1997 (CD-Rom)', Vahlen and C. H. Beck: Germany.

—— (2000). 'Banking Statistics 2000', *Statistical Supplement to the Monthly Report* (November).

—— (2001a). 'Banking Statistics 2001', *Statistical Supplement to the Monthly Report* (March).

—— (2001b). 'Die Ertragslage der deutschen Kreditinstitute im Jahr 2000', *Monthly Report* (September): 15–50.

—— (2001c). 'Bankbilanzen, Bankenwettbewerb und geldpolitische Transmission', *Monthly Report* (September): 51–70.

—— (2002). 'Zur Entwicklung der Bankkredite an den privaten Sektor', *Monthly Report* (October): 31–47.

Diamond, D. (1984). 'Financial Intermediation and Delegated Monitoring', *Review of Economic Studies*, 51: 393–414.

Diamond, D., and Dybvig, P. H. (1983). 'Bank Runs, Deposit Insurance, and Liquidity', *Journal of Political Economy*, 91: 401–19.

Donges, J. B., Eekhoff, J., Mösche, W., Neumann, M., and Sievert, O. (2001). 'Privatisierung von Landesbanken und Sparkassen', *Schriftenreihe Frankfurter Institut Stiftung Marktwirtschaft und Politik*, No. 38.

DSGV (2001). 'Markets 2000—Business Development, Trends, Analyses', condensed annual report.

European Central Bank (ECB) (2000). 'Mergers and Acquisitions Involving the EU Banking Industry—Facts and Implications', December, Frankfurt am Main.

——(2002). 'Report on Financial Structures', Frankfurt am Main.

Edwards, F. R. (1996). *The New Finance—Regulation & Financial Stability*. Washington, DC: The AEI Press.

——, and Mishkin, F. S. (1995). 'The Decline of Traditional Banking: Implications for Financial Stability and Regulatory Policy', *Economic Policy Review*, Federal Reserve Bank of New York, 1 (July): 27–45.

Engler, H., and Essinger, J. (2000). *The Future of Banking*. London: Financial Times/ Prentice Hall.

Fahrholz, B. (2001). 'Die Bank der Zukunft—Herausforderungen und Perspektiven', Lecture at Hohenheim University (20 June).

Fama, E. (1985). 'What's Different About Banks?', *Journal of Monetary Economics*, 15: 29–40.

Freixas, X., and Rochet, J.-C. (1997). *Microeconomics of Banking*. Cambridge, MA: MIT Press.

Gorton, G. B., and Rosen, R. (1995). 'Corporate Control, Portfolio Choice, and the Decline of Banking', *Journal of Finance*, 50: 1377–420.

Greenbaum, S. I., and Thakor, A. V. (1995). *Contemporary Financial Intermediation*. Fort Worth *et al.*: The Dryden Press.

Hackethal, A. (2001). 'How Unique are U.S. Banks?—The Role of Banks in Five Major Financial Systems', *Jahrbücher für Nationalökonomie und Statistik*, 221: 592–619.

——(2001a). 'Strategic Groups in European Commercial Banking', GEABA Discussion Paper No. 01-19.

——, and Schmidt, R. H. (2002). Financing Patterns—Measurement Concepts and Empirical Results (revised version)', Working Paper Series: Finance & Accounting, Goethe-University, Frankfurt am Main.

James, C. (1987). 'Some Evidence on the Uniqueness of Bank Loans', *Journal of Financial Economics*, 19: 217–35.

Kashyap, A. K., Rajan, R. G., and Stein, J. C. (1999). 'Banks as Liquidity Providers: An Explanation for the Co-Existence of Lending and Deposit-Taking', unpublished manuscript, University of Chicago, NBER and MIT Sloan School of Management.

La Porta, R., Lopez-de-Silanes, F., and Shleifer, A. (2002). 'Government Ownership of Banks', *Journal of Finance*, 57: 265–301.

Leadem, S. R., Chan, C. S., Enrico, C., Brinker, B., Heidegger, H., and Orlopp, B. (2001). 'The Future of Corporate Banking in Europe', Joint Study by Goldman Sachs and McKinsey & Company (January).

Lewis, M. K. (1991). 'Theory and Practice of the Banking Firm', in C. Green and D. T. Llewellyn (eds.), *Survey of Monetary Economics, Vol. 2*. London: Blackwell Press.

Litan, R. E., and Rauch, J. (1998). *American Finance for the 21st Century*. Washington, DC: The Brookings Institution.

Maestroeni, O. (2001). 'Pfandbrief-style products in Europe', *BIS Papers No. 5: The changing shape of fixed income markets: a collection of studies by central bank economists*, Bank for International Settlements (BIS), 44–66.

Mayer, C. (1988). 'New Issues in Corporate Finance', *European Economic Review*, 32: 1167–88.

Menkhoff, L. (1997). 'Öffentliche Banken—nutzlos und teuer?', *Ifo-Studien*, 43: 549–75.

Miller, G. P. (1998). 'On the Obsolescence of Commercial Banking', *Journal of Institutional and Theoretical Economics*, 154: 61–73.

Morgan, J. P. (1999). 'German Banks—Sparkassen', *Industry Update* (27 September).

Morgan Stanley Dean Witter (2000). 'German Banks', 19 January.

Myers, S. C., and Rajan, R. G. (1998). 'The Paradox of Liquidity', *Quarterly Journal of Economics*, 113: 733–71.

OECD (1994). 'Bank Profitability 1982–1992', Paris.

—— (2000). 'Bank Profitability 1990–1999', Paris.

Rajan, R. G. (1996). 'Is there a Future in Banking? Towards a New Theory of the Commercial Bank', mimeo.

Rybczynski, T. (1984). 'Industrial Financial Systems in Europe, U.S. and Japan', *Journal of Economic Behaviour and Organization*, 5: 275–86.

Schmidt, R. H. (2001). 'The Future of Banking in Europe', *Financial Markets and Portfolio Management*, 15(4): 429–49.

——, Hackethal, A., and Tyrell, M. (1999). 'Disintermediation and the Role of Banks in Europe: An International Comparison', *Journal of Financial Intermediation*, 8: 36–67.

——, ——, and —— (2002). 'The Convergence of Financial Systems in Europe', *Schmalenbach Business Review*, Special Issue 1/02: 7–53.

Sinn, H.-W. (1996). 'Der Staat im Bankwesen—zur Rolle der Landesbanken in Deutschland', Munich.

White, W. R. (1998). 'The Coming Transformation of European Banking?', BIS Working Paper No. 54.

4

Institutional Investors in Germany: Insurance Companies and Investment Funds

RAIMOND MAURER

4.1. INTRODUCTION

This chapter focuses on institutional investors as the most important non-bank financial intermediaries in the German financial sector. In line with Davis and Steil (2001: 12) and based on their financial function of pooling funds, we define institutional investors as specialized financial intermediaries who collect and manage assets on behalf of small investors toward specific objectives regarding the risk, return, and maturity of the involved claims.

Some general features are common to all institutional investors. From a macroeconomic perspective, these institutions provide a large volume of funds for the capital market which are used by both companies and the state. From a microeconomic perspective institutional investors provide households with a kind of risk and funds pooling, thus affording them a better trade-off between risk and reward than is generally possible through direct holdings. The pooling of funds allows institutional investors on the asset side to transact in large volumes. This enables them to invest in large-scale indivisible investments (e.g. real estate or partnerships), to achieve economies of scale (e.g. lower commission charges and advisory fees), and to cover the cost of a professional asset management. Institutional investors typically use investment vehicles like stocks, bonds, and money market instruments, which are available on large and liquid capital markets, both nationally and internationally. Only a relatively small part of their assets is invested in less liquid assets, such as properties or undisclosed partnerships, which are not listed on the stock exchange. The process by which assets collected by institutional investors are invested in the capital markets (i.e. the asset management process) is administered by professional external or internal fund managers, who develop and implement special investment and asset liability strategies. In terms of maturity, most institutional investors match assets and liabilities that are different from conventional debt instruments (e.g. bonds). Finally, the business of institutional investors is subject to a comprehensive financial regulation.

Despite these common features, however, institutional investors differ with respect to their businesses and regulation. The two major types of institutional investors in the German financial sector are *insurance companies* and *investment funds*. The main differences stem from the kind of uncertainty regarding the amount and timing of their financial liabilities, that is, the cash outlay made at a certain point in time to meet the contractual terms of an obligation issued by an institutional investor. Insurance contracts are typically designed with certain guarantees, that is, the insurance company functions as a risk bearer. Important risk management tools for an insurance company are the organization of risk pools, the generation of reserves, and solvency capital. In contrast to this, investment funds usually do not act as risk bearers and operate strictly on an individual basis. However, if investment companies offer their investment products within tax-supported individual pension accounts, they must by law (as any other providers) offer a so-called 'money back guarantee' in accordance with the regulatory solvency requirements.

It should be noted that Anglo-American type pension funds for externally funded occupational pension schemes are still of minor importance as institutional investment schemes in Germany. The reason for the lack of development of such schemes is twofold. In general, voluntary funded 'second pillar' occupational pension schemes do not play such an important role as they do in the United States or United Kingdom. This is due to the still quite generous benefits from and high contributions to 'first pillar' social security, which is financed on a pay-as-you-go system. Additionally, the most common method of organizing occupational pension schemes in Germany is still that of direct confirmation without resorting to an external institution. Hereby, the employer sets aside profit-reducing reserves (i.e. book reserves) during the working lifespan of the employee, and has to pay pension benefits directly to him or her during the post-retirement phase. About 60 per cent of the €330 billion allocated in German occupational pension schemes during the year 2000 comprised pension liabilities held on the balance sheets of sponsoring companies. Although more Anglo-American type pension funds were introduced in Germany with the Retirement Savings Act 2001 ('Altersvermögensgesetz'[1]), our analysis will largely neglect this type of institutional investor because of its currently minor significance. In the remainder of this chapter we will examine insurance and investment management companies, the nature of their businesses, their size and role in the financial sector, and the size and composition of the assets under their management. Furthermore, we will look at the regulations which influence investment decisions in this sector.

---

[1] Introduced by the former German Minister of Labour, Walter Riester, who was responsible for the reform of the pension system in the year 2001. This Act is also known as the 'Riester Reform'.

4.2. INSURANCE COMPANIES

4.2.1. Nature of their Business

With an insurance contract,[2] an individual pays a small sum (the insurance premium) to an insurance company and the company, in turn, guarantees to pay the policyholder specified sums, given that some determined future loss event occurs. Hence, insurance companies function as risk bearers, that is, the individual partially transfers negative financial consequences of the insured risk to the insurance company, at the expense of a fixed premium.

If the insurance contract is accepted by the insurance company, it becomes an asset for the policyholder and a (contingent) liability for the insurance company. Behind the insurance business lies the basic economic idea of pooling many individual risk exposures to loss in such a way that a risk reduction effect is produced.[3] This risk reduction effect allows insurance companies to offer insurance protection for low premiums (i.e. not much higher than the expected loss) in conjunction with a high level of credibility (i.e. the risk that the insurance company cannot meet its obligations is perceived to be sufficiently low. See Albrecht and Maurer 2000.).

From the viewpoint of financial economics, insurance companies can be viewed as leveraged financial institutions holding assets to back up liabilities, which are raised by issuing insurance contracts. In this sense, the insurance firm is holding two major portfolios: a portfolio of insurance contracts resulting in underwriting profits and a portfolio of financial assets resulting in investment income. The profits of the two portfolios are neither certain nor independent. The uncertainty of the underwriting profits results from the stochastic nature of the timing and the amount of future payments for insurance coverage. The uncertainty of the investment income is due to the fact that the returns of most financial assets are, in general, random. However, raising debt by issuing insurance policies is different from conventional debt instruments, such as bonds. While bonds generally have fixed coupon payments at fixed maturity dates, the timing and/or the payment amount of insurance policies are stochastic in nature. In addition, in contrast to fixed income financial instruments, no active secondary markets exist where the (uncertain) cash flows from insurance obligations are traded. Therefore, insurance leverage is not the same as financial leverage.[4]

---

[2] The legal structure of insurance contracts is extensively regulated and laid down in a special law on insurance contracts ('*Gesetz über den Versicherungsvertrag*' 30 May 1908).

[3] See Albrecht (1992) for a rigorous analysis of the effect of risk pooling for insurance coverage.

[4] See McCabe and Witt (1980) and Albrecht (1986). Especially with respect to life insurance policies, some attempts towards the establishment of a secondary market could be observed in the last decade. However, the current market volume for such products is of minor importance.

Insurance companies are important institutional investors because issuing insurance policies generates substantial investable funds. The total fund disposal for financial investments is derived from shareholder-supplied capital and from policyholder-supplied funds, which are referred to as liability reserves (see Fairley 1979; and MacCabe and Witt 1980). The reservoir of investable funds which is raised by issuing insurance policies results from a time lag between collecting the premiums and paying the losses. While the premiums are generally paid at the beginning of the insurance period, payments for loss events are made during and/or after the insurance period. To bridge this time lag between premium receipts and (uncertain) claim payments, the insurance company has to build up liability reserves (i.e. unearned premium and loss reserves). The assets backing these liabilities constitute the investable funds obtained by writing insurance policies.

4.2.2. Products, Size, and Role in the Financial Sector

4.2.2.1. *General market overview*

Measured in terms of gross premiums written by 1999, the German insurance industry is the fourth largest insurance market in the world after the United States, Japan, and Great Britain. Approximately 6 per cent of the world's premium volume was written in the German insurance market. At the end of 1980, however, this ratio had been around 9.25 per cent, that is, Germany has since lost substantial parts of its global market share. The insurance penetration ratio of 6.52 per cent is measured by the gross premiums of the direct insurance business in proportion to gross domestic product and is substantially lower than in other developed countries. Among the G7 countries, only Canada exhibits a slightly lower rate of 6.49 per cent. Moreover, the insurance density of US$1675.7, which measures the average insurance premium per capita, lies below the G7 average as well. This relative decline can be explained by the fact that insurance products have increasingly been shifted away from the public social security and pension systems to private contracting in the United States of America and in the United Kingdom. In contrast to this, the German public social security system is still continuing to provide generous benefits, requiring substantial contributions which are levied more and more by taxes than by insurance premiums. Table 4.1 summarizes important figures on the German insurance market in comparison to other G7 member countries for the years 1980 and 1999.

As in other developed countries, insurance companies operating in the German market offer a wide array of products in different insurance lines. The most important lines are property casualty insurance, life insurance, private health insurance, and re-insurance. With respect to the legal structure the suppliers of insurance coverage are organized as corporations, mutual or public insurance companies. Table 4.2 provides information about the market structure of the German insurance industry by the end of 2000.

Table 4.1. *The German market for direct insurance compared with other G7 countries*

	Global market share (in %)[a]		Penetration ratio[b] (in %)		Insurance density[c] (in USD)	
	1980	1999	1980	1999	1980	1999
Canada	2.86	1.80	5.11	6.49	520.4	1375.3
Germany	9.25	5.97	5.29	6.52	653.9	1675.7
France	5.20	5.30	3.69	8.52	419.2	2080.9
Italy	1.67	2.87	2.00	5.68	127.1	1152.7
Japan	13.61	21.29	5.12	11.17	506.9	3908.9
UK	7.14	8.82	5.78	13.35	554.7	3244.3
USA	43.63	34.22	7.23	8.55	833.7	2921.1

[a] Gross premiums as percentage of total world premium volume.
[b] Gross premiums in direct insurance business in proportion to gross domestic product.
[c] Gross premiums in direct insurance lines including pension funds per capita.

Source: Statistical Yearbook of Gesamtverband der Deutschen Versicherungswirtschaft 2001 and own calculations.

With respect to premiums written, life insurance companies, which enjoy a market share of 37.5 per cent are the most important line in the German market. Table 4.3 shows that most German insurance companies are organized as stock corporations, and as such cover about 70 per cent of the total premium volume. Yet, only about 15 per cent are listed on the stock exchange. This is due to the fact that current insurance regulations prohibit life (private health) insurance companies from providing insurance coverage in other lines. The intention of this mandatory specialization is to protect policyholders from financial problems of non-life insurance (non-private health) lines. In order to offer a wider range of insurance products, it is thus common to create holding structures, whereby only the head of the group is listed on the stock exchange. Re-insurance companies in particular have substantial participation in direct insurers. While re-insurance companies are generally organized as stock corporations, mutuals still play an important role with respect to both the number of companies and the premium volume in the direct insurance business. For instance, in the private health insurance line, 48.1 per cent of the total premium volume was written by mutuals. The importance of public insurers is minor. In addition, the German insurance market is dominated by domestic insurance companies; only 1.5 per cent of total premiums are written by foreign insurers.

Table 4.4 gives an overview of the volume of assets under management (measured as book values) and the portfolio composition among the main investment vehicles for the different insurance lines.

With more than €860 billion worth of assets under management (in 2000), German insurance companies are the most important institutional investors in

Table 4.2. *Market structure of the German insurance industry in 2000*

Number of German Insurance Companies (total)	622
Insurance lines	
Life insurance[a]	262 (123)[b]
Private health insurance	50
Re-insurance	39
Legal structure	
Corporations	340
Mutuals	249
Public	18
Foreign	15
Total premiums (in bill. €)	167,607
Insurance lines	
Property casualty	28.9%
Life insurance	37.5%
Private health insurance	12.4%
Re-insurance	21.2%
Legal structure	
Corporations	69.3%
Mutuals	22.0%
Public	7.2%
Foreign	1.5%

[a] Including Pensionskassen.
[b] Number in parentheses without Pensionskassen.

Source: Statistical Yearbook of Gesamtverband der Deutschen Versicherungswirtschaft 2001, Yearbook of the Bundesaufsichtsamt für das Versicherungswesen 2000, and own calculations.

Germany. Among them, life insurance companies, with a share of more than €600 billion, cover about 70 per cent of total assets under management. With respect to asset allocation, that is, the disposition of the overall portfolio among the main investment sectors, significant differences between the insurance lines can be observed. This is due to the differences in the nature of their liabilities, that is, the kind of uncertainty about future cash outflows. For instance, the uncertainty about the timing and amount of future liabilities in the P&C or re-insurance lines is much higher than in life insurance lines. Hence, in order to understand why and how insurance companies differ in their investment behaviour, it is necessary to discuss the designs of the different insurance products in more detail.

4.2.2.2. Life insurance

Life insurance companies provide insurance coverage for dependents against the financial risk of death. In addition, they are important vehicles for

Table 4.3. *Legal structure of direct insurance companies in Germany*

	Corporations	Mutuals	Public	Foreign	Total
Property casualty insurance companies					
Number	186	66	8	11	271
Market share[a] (%)	73.7	15.8	8.6	1.9	100
Life insurance companies					
Number	86	162	10	4	262
Market share[a] (%)	69.3	19.5	8.2	3.0	100
Private health insurance					
Number	29	21	0	0	50
Market share[a] (%)	51.9	48.1	0.0	0.0	100

[a] Premium volume in proportion to total premiums written (1999).

Source: Statistical Yearbook of Gesamtverband der Deutschen Versicherungswirtschaft 2001, Yearbook of the Bundesaufsichtsamt für das Versicherungswesen 2000 Part B, and own calculations.

Table 4.4. *Assets under management for German insurance companies 2000*

	Life-insurance[a]		Private health insurance		Property liability insurance		Re-insurance		Total	
	Bill. €	%	Bill. €	%	Bill. €	%	Bill. €	%	Bill. €	%
Real estate	19,014	3.2	1,787	2.5	4,421	4.6	1,933	2.1	27,155	3.1
Listed stocks	22,804	3.7	2,573	3.5	5,190	5.4	2,669	2.9	33,236	3.8
Special funds	139,632	22.9	15,438	21.2	22,781	23.7	15,830	17.2	193,681	22.3
Participations	23,171	3.8	3,023	4.2	14,515	15.1	50,341	54.7	91,050	10.4
Fixed income	404,361	66.4	49,865	68.6	49,215	51.2	21,259	23.1	524,700	60.3
Total	608,982	100	72,686	100	96,123	100	92,032	100	869,821	100

[a] Including Pensionskassen.

Source: Statistical Yearbook of Gesamtverband der Deutschen Versicherungswirtschaft 2001, Yearbook of the Bundesaufsichtsamt für das Versicherungswesen 2000 Part B, Deutsche Bundesbank, and own calculations.

long-term savings and drawn down accumulated savings for pension payments in the post retirement phase of the life cycle. In Germany, 262 life insurance companies with a premium volume (in 2000) of about €63 billion currently exist in the market. About 123 of the companies offer life insurance coverage to the general public. The other 139 companies are so called *Pensionskassen*, which constitute a special sort of (life-)insurance company (usually organized as a mutual) that is legally independent from the sponsoring employer (typically a company, public corporation, or industry group) and provides occupational retirement provision for employees. Because this type of occupational pension scheme is usually designed with insurance features (e.g. mortality and disability coverage) and substantial, defined benefit elements, the regulation of *Pensionskassen* is largely the same as for life insurance companies. With a market share of about 3 per cent of total premium written in the German life insurance market (in 2000) and with a share of about 10 per cent of total assets under management, *Pensionskassen* currently play only a minor role.

Life insurance companies typically offer three types of policies:

- term life insurance
- policies that build up a cash value (endowment policies)
- annuities.

With a *term life insurance*, the company must pay a certain amount (the face value of the policy) in exchange for a fixed premium if the policyholder dies within the insurance period, and must pay nothing if the insured person survives. The market share of term insurance with respect to the total premium volume is about 6 per cent. Usually term life insurance contracts have a relatively short maturity (e.g. 1–5 years), and (if the pool of insured risk is sufficiently high) low uncertainty about the timing and the amount of future claim payments. In general, for pure term life policies, it is not necessary to generate substantial liability reserves or the consequent funds for making investments.

Life insurance policies that build up a *cash value* (so called endowment policies) are the most important products in the German market. About 70 per cent of the total premium volume in the year 2000 was written for these vehicles for long-term savings. Such policies are designed with two characteristic features: an insurance protection component that provides death benefits (determined by the policy's face value) for a specified period of time (i.e. the insurance period, which is on average about 28 years), and an investment component that accumulates value over time. The investment feature creates a cash surrender value which the insurance company must pay at the end of the insurance period, or if the contract is terminated. To back the cash value, the life insurance company must generate reserves (so called 'Deckungsrückstellung'). The assets covering the liabilities have to be kept in a special fund ('Deckungsstock'), which must be managed separately from other insurance company assets. In addition, the assets in these funds are recorded in a register ('Deckungsstockverzeichnis') and cannot be disposed of without the permission of a trustee ('Treuhänder') confirmed by the supervision authority. Usually life policies in the German market are designed with a series of fixed premiums (the so-called contractual plans), which are determined primarily by the insured person's age at the time of issue, their gender as well as the face value and the duration of the contract. The life insurance company uses a certain part of the total insurance premium (based on a mortality table) to cover the mortality cost for death claims, a second part is used to cover acquisition and management expenses, and a third part is to be invested in specific assets to back the investment component.[5] The German cost system in life insurance traditionally uses front-end loads as a percentage of the policy's face value to cover marketing costs (about 4 per cent) and a fixed percentage of the gross single premium per year to cover management expenses (the average expense ratio in 2000 was about 3.53 per cent). Owing to the front-end load, for the first several years that a policy is in force, the cash value is usually significantly less than the premium paid by the policyholder, or even zero. Life insurance policies with an investment component have a number of income tax advantages for the policyholder and the beneficiary. First, life insurance proceeds paid by reason of the insured person's death are usually received free of income tax. In addition, if (unlimited) contributions into a cash-value life policy are paid from taxed income, the insurance period is at least 12 years, and the premium is not paid as a lump sum, then the periodic increases in the policy's cash value are currently not taxed as income. Finally, within the ('second pillar') occupational pension system, workers have the option to pay part of their income, up to a certain limit (currently €1,752), into a life insurance policy (so called 'Direktversicherung') with substantial tax privileges. This form of occupational pension is used particularly by small and medium-sized companies. In the year 2000, the sum of approximately €42.8 billion, which is about 13 per cent of total occupational pension schemes, was allocated to direct life insurance policies.

The most important endowment policies in the German life insurance market are

- index-linked policies
- unit-linked policies
- with-profits endowment policies.

With *index* or *unit-linked life policies*, the investment components are typically backed by an equity and/or bond portfolio represented by an appropriate index or a specific investment fund account which the policy-holder chooses. Therefore, the cash-value of the policy (and sometimes in part the death benefits as well) depend on the investment performance of the assets to which the policyholder wishes to allocate the investment component. Usually the cash-value of an index linked policy is designed with a guaranteed minimum return, while unit-linked life insurance policies are not. Only 10 per cent of the total premium volume for cash-value life policies was written for these types of products. The most important product in the German life insurance market is the traditional *participating cash-value policy* (i.e. with-profits endowment policy). The investment component of the policy is designed with a guaranteed yearly minimum return and a variable, not guaranteed surplus. The guaranteed return is set when the policy is issued and

---

[5] Because the different cost elements are not shown separately to the policyholder, these policies may be referred to as bundled contracts. See also Hallman and Rosenbloom (2000: 50).

remains fixed until the contract is terminated, that is, the cash value of the policy increases according to a present value schedule contained in the policy. The maximum interest rate that life insurers can use to calculate the guaranteed part return is limited by regulation. In general it should not exceed 60 per cent of the interest rate on long-term government bonds; in 1994 it was set at 4.00 per cent p.a. and in 2000 it was lowered to 3.25 per cent p.a. The policyholder's return that is in excess of the guaranteed return depends on the insurance company's experience with mortality, expenses and investment return. By regulation, the German life insurance companies must distribute at least 90 per cent of their annual profits, if positive, to policyholders.[6] Because of the competition for new business, however, the profit sharing rate is much higher. Technically, the surplus is paid out to those insured by an annual bonus, as well as a terminal bonus paid at the end of the contract.

The most important part of the surplus stems from the performance of the life insurance investment portfolio. Note that the guaranteed return is, at least at the start of the contract, lower than the current market interest rate level. Hence, it can be expected that a life insurance policy may generate a positive surplus from its investment portfolio in the first year of the contract, even if it is invested mostly in bonds. Despite the fact that the surplus is not guaranteed, German life insurance companies have a strong interest in keeping surplus rates stable over time. This is achieved via several smoothing vehicles (see Albrecht and Maurer 2002). To determine the with-profits bonus allocation to policyholders, the assets held by the insurance company are evaluated on the basis of book rather than market values. Therefore, it is possible to smooth the investment returns over time by accumulating explicit or hidden asset reserves in 'good' years (i.e. years in which the return on invested assets is above average) and using these reserves to preserve a bonus in the years when the insurance company earns less from its investments. This practice of 'smoothing over' is a central part of the profit sharing philosophy of German life insurers.[7]

To illustrate the effect of return smoothing, we collected—following Albrecht and Maurer (2002)—the annual net investment log returns on the basis of book values ('Nettoverzinsung') reported in the accounting statements of the thirty largest German life insurers (which represented about 75 per cent of the German life insurance market measured by premium volume) covering the years 1980–2000. For each of the thirty time series the average log return, the volatilities and the first order sample autocorrelations were calculated. Table 4.5 reports the statistics for those companies with the lowest, average and highest mean return over this time period.

---

[6] For a more technical description of surplus distribution in life insurance cf. for example, Ramlau-Hansen (1991).

[7] Cf. Fitch (2002). Since the accounting year 1997, the total hidden reserves on assets have to be disclosed in the insurance balance sheets.

Table 4.5. *Descriptive statistics for the investment returns of German life insurers*

	Insurance company with the … mean return (1980–2000)		
	Lowest	Median	Highest
Mean return (% p.a.)	6.88	7.24	7.51
Volatility (% p.a.)	0.60	0.66	0.41
Autocorrelation	0.37*	0.47*	0.56*

First-order sample autocorrelations marked with an asterisk (*) are statistically significant at the 5% level according to the Q-statistic of *Ljung/Box* (1979).

Looking at the mean returns, it can be observed that the market is characterized by a very high degree of homogeneity. Among the thirty largest German life-insurers, the one with the lowest (highest) average return over this time-period showed a value of 6.88 per cent (7.51 per cent). Moreover, the investment returns in the German life insurance market are very stable over time. The volatility of investment returns ranges from 0.37 to 0.56 per cent p.a. for the company with the lowest/highest mean return in the sample. In addition, the first order sample autocorrelation of the yearly returns to German life insurance companies is high and statistically different from zero. It is well known that return series with these statistical properties, that is, low volatilities and a high level of serial correlation, are due to temporal smoothing. Note that because of expense loading, front-end loads and exit penalties, the range of average returns between 6.88 to 7.51 per cent p.a. is not the same as the range of expected returns for a potential investor willing to buy life insurance contracts over a short investment horizon.

Besides the generation of hidden reserves arising when market values are higher than book values, insurers also have (under certain conditions) the chance to use temporary 'hidden losses' to smooth their investment returns. This is because insurers may deviate in certain circumstances from the strict lowest-value principle when evaluating financial assets in their balance sheet. This principle means that an asset must be written down to the market value if at the cut-off date the market value falls below the acquisition cost. Prominent examples are the so called *Schuldscheindarlehen*, which are special non-marketable fixed coupon bonds. In general, these bonds are issued at par according to the current interest rate level of traded government bonds with comparable duration. According to current German accounting rules, the book value of *Schuldscheindarlehen* may not be written down to a lower market value because of an increasing interest rate level. Therefore, from an accounting point of view (which is the basis for calculating the policyholder's bonus) as long as these bonds are held to maturity, they are protected from the price risk resulting from fluctuations in the term structure of interest rates. Since late 2001, regulators have also allowed insurance companies to deviate from the strict lowest-value principle for equity investments. According to § 341b HGB (German Commercial Code), if at the cut-off date the insurance company can argue that an individual equity will be kept and price fluctuations are only temporary, then owing to the high volatility in capital markets it is not necessary to write down the asset to its lower market value on the cut-off date, but instead to an average value over the year. For example (see Fitch 2003: 2), in the view of the auditors, it seems to be justifiable to use an average 12 months market value plus a 10 per cent loading, when preparing the 2002 balance sheets. By assuming an average value of 4191.85 points for the major German equity index (i.e. the DAX) in 2002, with a year end value of 2892.63 points, insurers must only write down if the acquisitions cost of this index-portfolio exceeds 4611.03 points. Note that this opportunity to generate 'hidden losses' (to support return smoothing) in a balance sheet is inconsistent with current International Accounting Standards (IAS).

Annuities sold by life insurance companies are a traditional and common vehicle for drawing down accumulated assets during the post-retirement phase. In exchange for a non-refundable premium paid as a lump-sum at the date of purchase, or as a fixed series of premium payments during a specified accumulation phase, the insurance company promises to make a series of periodic payments to the annuitant contingent on he or she surviving. The typical annuity product which is sold in the German market offers pension payments that have a guaranteed and a non-guaranteed part. Within the guaranteed part the insurance company promises life pension payments in fixed nominal terms (fixed annuity) or rising at a pre-specified fixed nominal escalation rate (grade annuity). As is the case for traditional cash-value life policies, the maximum interest rate insurers can use to calculate the guaranteed part of the annuity is restricted by regulation, and is currently at 3.25 per cent per annum. In addition, the life insurance company must apply with respect to the guaranteed part mortality tables valid on the date the contract was signed. The non-guaranteed part depends—in the same way as traditional cash-value life policies—on the insurance company's experience with mortality, investment returns and expenses (participating annuity).[8] In contrast to other important annuity markets, for example, the United Kingdom or United States, annuities which are explicitly indexed to inflation (real annuity) are currently uncommon in the German market. Like for other countries, the German market for private annuities is smaller than predictions from economic theory would suggest. While life annuities provide invaluable longevity insurance that cannot be replicated by pure investment vehicles, there are also disadvantages associated with annuitization. First, there is a serious loss of liquidity because (in general) assets cannot be recovered after purchase of the annuity, irrespective of any special needs. Second, in its simplest form where

---

[8] For a more detailed discussion of the German annuity market see Albrecht and Maurer (2002).

income payments are contingent on an individual's survival there is no chance of leaving out money for the heirs even in the event of an early death of the annuitant. Third, and probably the most important explanation for this phenomenon is the crowding out caused by the relative generosity of the German public defined benefit pension system. From a purely financial point of view, payments from state pensions can be characterized as annuities. For example, the total payments from commercial life insurance to annuitants in 2000 was about €2,457 million, which is only about 1.4 per cent of the payments from the public pension system. Additional demand for private annuities is anticipated because of the ongoing reductions of public pay-as-you-go pensions in favour of an extension of private funded pension plans. For example, the 'Riester' pension reform from 2001 requires that a certain fraction of the accumulated assets in tax-shielded individual retirement accounts must be annuitized not later than at the age of eighty five. However, such programmed new business is not without risk. A key factor to covering the financial aspects of longevity risk by organizing risk pools is to develop appropriate mortality tables for annuitants (see Mitchell and McCarthy 2001).

4.2.2.3. *Non-life insurance*
Property casualty insurance (also called non-life insurance) companies are offering insurance coverage for a wide variety of occurrences, that is, loss, damage, destruction of property, loss or impairment of income-producing ability, claims for damages by third parties from alleged negligence, and loss resulting from injury or death from occupational accidents (see Fabozzi 1998: 126). In the German insurance market 271 P&C companies are offering insurance protection in all important personal and commercial lines, for example, fire insurance, general liability insurance, private accident insurance, and automobile insurance. The market share of the P&C lines with respect to the total premium volume written in direct insurance lines is 29.2 per cent or €48,371 million. The most important line is automobile coverage with a market share of about 42 per cent and premiums written in all P&C lines.

Private Health Insurance protects people and their families against two types of losses: disability income losses and medical care expenses. In Germany, the main sources that provide health benefits are the state social security program and individual private health insurance. In general, employees and their non-employed dependents are compulsory members of the German state health programme, which provides substantial but highly regulated health benefits. Based on the *principle of solidarity*, premiums must be paid as a percentage of the current working income while the coverage provided is (at least for medical expenses) equal for all members of the state health insurance. High income workers earning more than the social security ceiling (currently about €5,000/month) can opt to leave the state health program and insure themselves against disability and/or medical expense risk via an individual policy offered by a commercial health insurance company (so called substitutive private health insurance). Additional demand for individual private health policies is generated from those who are not (e.g. the self-employed) or only in part (e.g. civil servants) compulsory members of the state health programme. Compared to the social security programme, private health insurance policies are much more flexible with their coverage. The premiums are calculated according to individual risk characteristics, for example, defined health benefits, age, and gender. To appreciate fully the important role of private health companies as institutional investors, it is necessary to know about some special features of this insurance that are the result of regulation. If a private health insurance company has accepted a risk, it may not terminate the contract. Additionally, the company may not raise premiums because of the increasing age of the policyholder. Hence, private health contracts are generally life-long policies, usually with a monthly fixed premium. Based on an actuarial table about mortality and morbidity of the individual, the company must calculate at the time the policy is issued an average premium over the total lifetime of the contract.[9] Thus, if the individual is young, the differences between the required premium and the yearly expected claim payments (plus expense loadings) are positive, while this difference becomes negative if the policyholder is old. Therefore, in order to smooth the premiums over time, the company reserves part of the premiums as long as the policyholder is young and uses this *ageing reserve* to finance negative excess premiums when he or she is old. This *ageing reserve* is an important reservoir for private health companies towards generating investable funds. Comparable to the mathematical reserves for life insurance companies, the (registered) asset backing of the ageing reserve must be separated from other assets, and dispositions are only possible with the approval of an appointed trustee.

Re-insurance is a financial arrangement between a re-insurance and an insurance company, whereby the re-insurer agrees, against payment of the re-insurance premium, to reimburse part of the uncertain payments for losses that the ceding insurer is called upon to pay the original policyholder.[10] In this sense, re-insurance may be defined as the direct insurer's insurance. From an economic standpoint, the rationale of writing re-insurance is to improve the probability distribution of the uncertain return on stockholders' equity in conjunction with a sufficient level of solvency on the part of the ceding insurance company. In general, the thirty-nine re-insurance companies operating (usually as corporations) in the German market offer proportional and non-proportional protection in all insurance lines. With respect to the €36 billion of total premium volume written during the year 2000, the most important re-insurance lines were life insurance with 21.4 per cent, followed by automobile insurance with 19 per cent of total premium payments for

---

[9] However, the company can increase (or decrease) premiums if the underlying actuarial assumptions change.   [10] See Loubergé (1981, 1983).

re-insurance coverage. While historically re-insurance was signed mostly on a facultative basis, re-insurance coverage today occurs mostly on a treaty basis. In the first case each arrangement refers to a specific insurance contract written by the direct insurer, which has to be separately negotiated between the re-insurer and the ceding insurer for each contract. In contrast to these case-by-case re-insurance trades, a treaty concerns a whole set of insurance contracts written by the direct insurer, typically in a particular insurance line (fire, homeowners) during a specific period of time. The primary writer has to cede and the re-insurance company is obligated to accept all contracts for which the treaty has been signed.

4.2.3. Regulation

Insurance companies are in business to provide financial protection, that is, to reimburse an individual in case the insured event occurs. Thus, the individual transfers the insured risk to the company. However, because the financial results of underwriting and investment activities are stochastic in nature, the company may become insolvent, and therefore be unable to pay. Kahneman and Tversky (1979) and Wakker *et al.* (1997) introduced the term probabilistic insurance to point out that most insurance is, in fact, only pseudo-certain.

The core of state regulation for German insurance companies is to bind this default risk by controlling the financial stability of an insurance company. The Insurance Supervision Act ('Versicherungsaufsichtsgesetz', VAG) which is exercised by the Federal Financial Supervisory Authority (BaFin) subjects German insurance companies to substantial legal provisions. Like pension funds or investment management companies, before an insurance company is allowed to operate, it must obtain a license from the BaFin (see §§ 5 ff. VAG). Permanent federal supervision of its financial stability (§ 81 I VAG) imposes additional constraints on a direct insurance company's business operations. However, since the deregulation of the Insurance Law in 1994, the insurance products offered by the companies are no longer subject to prior approval by the supervisory authority. The main focus of insurance supervision is clearly on solvency control. Besides requirements with respect to liability reserves, permanent state regulation of German insurers imposes at least two other important constraints relating to financial ratios:

- solvency requirements
- restrictions on financial investments.[11]

Solvency requirements The centrepiece of the solvency requirements in the property-liability-lines is intended to limit the exposure of the underwriting

---

[11] Re-insurance companies are excluded from solvency requirements and investment restrictions.

risk with respect to a certain level of equity (solvency) capital.[12] More formally, the minimum solvency requirements can be expressed by an upper bound χ on the insurance leverage, that is, the sum of premium proceeds (minus operation costs) over all lines in proportion to the regulatory capital of the insurance company. A reasonable rule of thumb[13] in the property-liability-lines is that the maximum insurance leverage is restricted to about $\chi < 1/0.18$ if re-insurance coverage is neglected. Note, that in addition to the stated equity capital, subordinated debt and hybrid assets (less intangible assets and 50 per cent of capital not paid up) are also part of the regulatory solvency capital of an insurance company.

The solvency requirements for the life insurance lines differ substantially from the property-liability-lines. In general, the required solvency capital depends on the mortality risk covered by term life contracts. Moreover, life insurance contracts that build up a cash value in conjunction with a minimum return guarantee that the required solvency capital depends on the mathematical reserves and the company's surplus strength. The minimum level of solvency capital is determined as follows:

- 4 per cent of technical reserves for endowment and annuity policies
- 1 per cent of technical reserves for unit-linked policies
- 0.3 per cent of sums insured for term insurance.

Reinsurance can reduce the required minimum solvency capital up to certain limits. Apart from the equity capital as discussed above, the regulatory solvency capital of a life insurance company also includes subordinated debt, hybrid capital (so called solvency capital A), the terminal bonus reserves, the non-committed bonus reserves (so called solvency capital B), with the approval of the *BaFin*, hidden reserves and estimated future profits (so called solvency capital C). In its annual report 2000, the *BaFin* reports that for about 10 per cent of life insurers, the supervisory authority allows the use of estimated future profits to cover the minimum solvency margin.

Investment restrictions The regulation of financial investments specifies the types of investment vehicles permissible for insurance companies to back their liability reserves as well as some general investment principles. In addition, the investment decisions are restricted by quantitative investment restrictions. For example, it is generally not permitted to invest more than 5 per cent of total assets backing liability reserves in a specific asset. In addition, important quantitative investment limits exist regarding the composition of the insurance

---

[12] In reality, the solvency capital of an insurance company is neither equal to the book, nor to the market value of the equity capital.

[13] This is due to the so called 'Beitragsindex' codified in §§ 1, 2 of KapitalausstattungsVO and Rundschreiben des BAV R 3/88, VerBAV, 1988, pp. 195 ff. for property liability insurers, cf. Maurer (2000), p. 215. Note, that the solvency requirements for life and health insurance companies are quite different.

company's asset allocation and the potential use of financial derivatives. For example, short sales are excluded, non-matched open currency positions are usually not allowed, financial derivatives like options, futures, and swaps can only be used for hedging, and for certain risky assets maximum investment weights (with respect to liability reserves) are established:[14]

(1) maximum investment weight of 35 per cent for listed stocks;
(2) maximum investment weight of 25 per cent for real estate;
(3) maximum investment weight of 10 per cent for non listed participation;
(4) maximum investment weight of 10 per cent for stocks outside the EU;
(5) maximum 20 per cent non-matched currency position.

However, these numbers are based on accounting data, that is, the book value of stocks should not exceed 35 per cent of the book value of the investable funds which back the liability reserves of the insurance company. The option to generate hidden valuation reserves (when the stock values are increasing), allows the maximal investment weight for stocks with respect to the market value of the total investable fund to be higher.

4.2.4. Outlook and Current Developments

In this final section we provide an outlook on some important developments in the German insurance industry. A fundamental reconception of the current system can be expected, with respect to the legal provisions for asset management and solvency requirements. For life insurers especially, the current solvency system is quite untransparent and not compatible with modern concepts of risk management and portfolio optimization. Most importantly, the replacement of the quantitative investment restrictions by a system relying on risk-based capital is being discussed (solvency II), as is the harmonization of solvency requirements at the European level. An important development was the introduction of a guarantee pool (a so called 'protector') for insolvent life insurance companies in 2002. In the past, such a pool solution was rejected by the insurance industry on the grounds of moral hazard and the alleged safety net provided by the regulated environment. However, due to the dramatic deterioration of equity values in conjunction with an inaccurate investment strategy (i.e. with equity exposures that are too high with respect to a short guarantee period of only one year) in 2001 and 2002 some life insurers ran into serious solvency problems. Thus, to keep the reputation of life insurance as a safe pension product with substantial return guarantees, the industry itself took up the initiative for such a pool solution. The practice of return smoothing, which is a central part of the bonus participation system in the German life insurance industry, should not be criticized *per se*. It provides a kind of risk sharing (similar but not identical to a pay-as-you-go system)

---

[14] Unit- or index-linked cash-value life policies are excluded from these restrictions.

between different generations of individuals using life insurance policies for long-term saving. However, the current way in which such a system is implemented is difficult to understand and not transparent.

The establishment of alternative risk transfer (ART) products as a substitute and/or supplement for re-insurance appears to be a growing business. In addition, some important implications regarding the current reform of the social security systems in Germany can be observed. The German Retirement Savings Act ('Altersvermögensgesetz'), which passed the German legislative body in May 2001, instituted a new funded system of supplementary pensions coupled with a general reduction in the level of state pay-as-you-age pensions. To compensate for the cut in state pension payouts, individuals will be able to invest, with some tax benefits, a part of their income in 'third pillar' individual and 'second pillar' occupational pension accounts which are offered by regulated financial institutions such as commercial banks, investment management companies, and life insurance companies. In order to qualify for the tax credit, the design of pension products has to satisfy a number of criteria stipulated in special laws. Pension products designed by life insurance companies are usually in line with these provisions. For example, in the case of 'second pillar' pension products, participating cash-value life policies are in line with the law on occupational pensions ('Betriebsrentengesetz'). For 'third pillar' pensions accounts, the law relating to the certification of individual pension products ('Altersvorsorge-Zertifizierungsgesetz') requires in its current version that, when the age of retirement is reached, a certain fraction of the accumulated assets must be drawn in the form of a lifelong annuity or a capital withdrawal plan with deferred annuitization not later than at the age of eighty five. In summary, on account of these legal requirements it can be expected that the life insurance industry will generate substantial new business in funded pensions.

4.3. INVESTMENT FUNDS

4.3.1. The Nature of their Business

The business idea of an investment fund is to enable investors from all classes of society to participate in and benefit from the profits of productive capital as well as real estate. In a more general perspective, the 'investment fund philosophy' is based on the principle of equal opportunities for all investors in all markets. To this end investment funds pool money by selling shares to many investors and invest the proceeds in a portfolio of securities and/or income-producing properties or both.

Investment funds can be classified as open-end and closed-end funds.[15] Open-end investment funds, also referred to as mutual funds, do not have a

---

[15] Cf. Hallman and Rosenbloom (2000), chapter five and Fabozzi (1998), chapter eight.

fixed number of outstanding units. Instead, the number of shares is changing as the funds continually stand ready to both sell new shares to all kinds of investors without limitations, and to redeem old shares on demand from them. This type of investment fund, which can issue and sell additional units at any time, is the most common type of investment fund in Germany. The price for purchase or redemption is based on the net asset value per share, which is usually computed daily. The net asset value is found by taking the actual market value of all assets held by the mutual fund, less any fund liability, and dividing by the number of outstanding units. In general, mutual funds do not leverage their position by issuing financial debt and they invest their capital according to the principles of risk diversification. Furthermore, mutual funds are regulated by a comprehensive legal framework (i.e. the Investment Companies Act) designed to protect investor rights. These are subject to state supervision. In the German market, mutual funds may be managed only by an investment management fund company ('Kapitalanlagegesellschaft', subsequently referred to as KAG) which is a specialized bank in the asset management field. A German KAG may be operated only in the legal form of a joint stock corporation or a limited liability company and usually manages the assets of many different mutual funds. Its shareholders are not the investors in the funds, but typically banks or insurance companies. From a legal point of view, the mutual fund itself is a special asset ('Sondervermögen') pool funded by the investors' capital contributions and must be strictly separated from the investment company's own assets. The unit certificates held by the investors are not comparable to equities, but are special securities representing a contractual claim of the unit-holder against the investment fund. The fund is managed on the basis of a management contract by the investment management company and the unit-holders (see Ernst and Young 2001).

In many respects, the closed-end investment company is similar to a typical cooperative. It issues a fixed number of shares and can also issue bonds to leverage the position of the common shareholders. Investors, who are simultaneously shareholders of the investment company, do not have the right to redeem their shares to the fund-company. Instead, shareholders must sell them on a secondary market, for example, on the stock exchange if it is an exchange-traded closed-end fund or, if the fund is not listed, in the over-the-counter market. Hence, the price of a closed-end share is determined by supply and demand and can fall below, or rise above, the net present value per share. In contrast to mutual funds, closed-end funds are often not subject to a special financial regulation and need not follow the principle of diversification. The bulk of closed-end funds existing in the German market are of this type.[16]

---

[16] An exception is the investment stock corporation ('Investmentaktiengesellschaft'). Like mutual funds, they have (since 1998) been regulated in accordance with the German Investment Law and are subject to state supervision. The shares of investment stock corporation must be traded on the stock exchange.

They mostly invest in special (not diversified) real estate projects, leverage the position of the common shareholder—driven by tax reasons—by issuing debt instruments, and operate (in contrast to mutual funds) without any special regulation or federal supervision concerning investor protection. In the remainder of this section we will focus on open-end investment funds only.

Investors gain a number of advantages by buying shares in a mutual fund.[17] First, smaller investors are able to enjoy a degree of diversification for a low investment budget, which they could not otherwise achieve on their own. Second, investment companies may offer experienced professional asset management to select and manage securities and properties in which the fund's capital will be invested. Third, investment companies may provide investors with economies of scale on transaction and management costs by pooling the assets of many individuals. Fourth, investment units are liquid insofar as unit-holders can ask for the redemption of their holdings to net-asset value prices at any point in time (in the case of mutual funds). Because of the open-end principle and the possibility of daily redemption, investors are highly flexible with respect to investing or withdrawing money from mutual funds, for example, by lump-sum payments or accumulation and withdrawal plans.

As with any other financial intermediary, there are costs associated with investing through investment funds. The fund management charges an investment management fee, usually as a percentage of the fund's average assets. Sometimes the fund management charges an extra performance fee if the return of the fund units is above a certain benchmark. Other costs of administrating a fund include expenses for providing investors with financial statements, the depository bank fee, and the costs of employing custodial and accounting services. To cover the distribution and sales costs, the investor pays either a front-end load when purchasing or a back-end load when selling a fund unit. Moreover, sales charges on reinvested distributions and an exchange fee for the option to switch from one fund to another within a family of mutual funds are possible. Further transaction costs arise in connection with the purchase and the sale of securities and properties to implement (start-up costs) and to update (turnover costs) the fund's portfolio strategy.

4.3.2. Products, Size, and Role in the Financial Sector

4.3.2.1. *General market overview*
With respect to assets under management by 2000, the German mutual funds industry is within the G7 countries the fifth largest behind the United States, Japan, France, and Italy. About €420 billion were invested in German mutual funds. At the end of 1980, this number had stood at €16 billion, that is, over the past 20 years the German investment industry has increased assets under management substantially. However, in terms of market share within the G7

---

[17] Cf. Hallman and Rosenbloom (2000), chapter five.

Table 4.6. *The German market for mutual funds compared with other G7 countries*

	Assets under management[a]		World market share (%)[b]		Assets per household[c]	
	1980	2000	1980	2000	1980	2000
Canada	5,274	297,069	2.20	2.89	221	9804
Germany	16,773	423,630	7.01	4.13	272	5154
France	40,182	766,100	16.79	7.46	323	13,029
Italy	n/a	449,930	n/a	4.38	n/a	7811
Japan	29,968	460,746	12.53	4.49	257	3645
UK	14,006	412,557	5.85	4.02	251	6981
USA	133,062	7,452,097	55.62	72.62	584	27,570
Total/Average	239,265	10,262,129	100.0	100.0	318	10,571

[a] In € million (including foreign funds of German provenance).

[b] Assets under management as percentage of total volume of G7 countries.

[c] Mutual fund units per capita in Euros (including foreign funds of German provenance).

Source: Statistical Yearbooks of Bundesverband Deutscher Investment- und Vermögensverwaltungsgesellschaften 1981, 2001, and own calculations.

countries, German mutual funds fell behind, from 7 per cent in 1980 to 4.1 per cent in 2000. In addition, the average amount of assets a household invested in mutual funds is €5154, a figure which is substantially lower than the average (i.e. €10,571) within the G7 countries. Only Japan exhibits a lower rate with €3645. One reason for this development of increasing absolute but decreasing relative importance of mutual funds might be that in contrast to many other G7 countries, in Germany there are no tax benefits for long-term savings with mutual funds.

Table 4.6 summarizes important figures on the German mutual fund market in comparison to other G7 countries for the years 1980 and 2000.

By the end of the year 2000, investors could choose between 1,119 different mutual funds, which were managed by eighty-one investment management companies (KAG) registered in Germany. Most of them are owned by commercial banks. The savings banks ('Sparkassen'), the credit cooperatives ('Genossenschaften') and the four large universal banks (Commerzbank, Deutsche Bank, Dresdner Bank, HypoVereinsbank) accounted for about 80 per cent of managed assets. Driven by recent mergers (e.g. Allianz and Dresdner Bank), insurance companies have begun to play an increasing role in the asset management industry.

The most important distribution channel for mutual funds are banks and their network of branches throughout Germany.[18] Around 63 per cent of all mutual fund sales in Germany during the year 2000 were brokered by banks.

---

[18] Cf. in the following PricewaterhouseCoopers (2002: 15–16).

The banks typically offer the mutual fund products of their 'own' investment management companies. Despite the fact that bank branches still remain the dominant distribution channel, the importance of other distribution platforms such as independent financial advisors (14 per cent in 2000), sales through internet banking, that is, direct banks and discount brokers (12 per cent in 2000), or insurance companies (5 per cent in 2000) has grown, both for customers and fund managers. Furthermore, a trend could be observed for offers not only of their own funds products, but also a large number of third party funds, similar to fund warehouses.

Aside from mutual funds ('Publikumsfonds') there is another important type of open-end investment funds, the so-called special funds ('Spezialfonds') which are also regulated in the Investment Companies Act. In contrast to mutual funds, which sell units to all private investors without limitation, a special fund is defined as an investment fund with no more than ten investors (often only one investor), who must be a legal entity. This type of fund was specifically developed for institutional investors as a way to outsource the management of their assets within a regulated framework. A special fund is subject to most of the provisions of German investment regulation and may invest in the same types of assets as mutual funds. In the following sections, we will provide a market overview for these types of investment funds and describe the most important features arising from regulation.

4.3.2.2. *Mutual funds*

With regard to the investment objectives and policies which must be described in a fund's prospectus, there are mutual funds available in the German market to meet just about any investment goal. An important (and traditional) criterion by which the various types of mutual funds can be classified is the asset class in which the unit's capital is invested. However, even within an asset class, fund managers present different investment styles (e.g. growth, value, small cap, large cap). Still, other funds are neither defined by a special asset class, nor by its investment style, but rather by a special investment objective such as retirement. In line with the definitions provided in the Investment Companies Act,[19] six different types of mutual funds exist in the German market:

- security funds
- real estate funds
- money market funds
- mixed security and real estate funds
- AS-funds
- funds-of-funds.

[19] In addition to the reported mutual fund types, participation funds ('Beteiligungs-Sondervermögen'), which are permitted to invest in securities and silent partnership interests, are also legally allowed within the Investment Company Act. However, no-participation fund has yet to be launched as a mutual fund in Germany.

Table 4.7. *Classification of German mutual funds by investment objective*

Type of fund	Number	Asset (mill. €)	Asset (% of total assets)
Security funds	915	225,952	73.60
Equity funds	420	141,628	46.14
Bond funds	288	59,887	19.51
Balanced funds	207	24,437	7.96
Real estate funds	20	48,931	15.94
Money market funds	39	20,196	6.58
Mixed funds	3	4,237	1.38
AS-funds	44	2,817	0.92
Fund-of-funds	97	4,852	1.58
Sum	1119	306,985	100

Source: Deutsche Bundesbank Kapitalmarktstatistik December 2001, p. 53.

Security and real estate funds are the traditional types of mutual funds. They have operated for more than three decades in the German market. The other mutual funds only came into force more recently, especially within the amendments of the Investment Company Act in 1994 and 1998. Table 4.7 provides an overview of the number and the total amount of assets under management from the different mutual fund types in the German market.

Security-funds ('Wertpapier-Sondervermögen') are the most important type of mutual fund in Germany. Measured by assets under management in 2000, the 915 security-based funds had a market share of more than 60 per cent of all mutual funds. Among these funds, an investor can choose between equity-based, bond-based, and balanced funds, as well as a variety of different investment styles.

Real estate funds ('Grundstücks-Sondervermögen') may invest in properties, certain types of participations in real estate companies, and in fixed income instruments (e.g. bonds and money markets). This type of fund is very popular among small investors, for example, as a hedge against inflation. By the end of 2000, the twenty real estate funds had a 15.94 per cent share of the total mutual funds assets in Germany. In contrast to the Real Estate Investment Trusts (REITs) in the United States of America or the real estate fund in Switzerland, open-ended real estate funds in Germany are not quoted on the stock exchange; investors can, however, ask for redemption of their fund units at any time based on the net asset value of the fund. While financial assets are valued according to their current market prices, the value of each property is based on appraisals by independent experts. To maintain the open-end principle, the German real estate funds continuously offer new shares to the public. The issue prices are calculated similarly on the basis of the net asset value, plus an offering charge which is usually 5 per cent. From an economic point of view, the offering premiums are not only raised to cover sales costs, but also to build an effective barrier which makes frequent transactions with the fund units unattractive (see Maurer and Sebastian 2002 for this point). It is essential for open-end real estate funds to avoid frequent changes in the capital volume because—in contrast to security funds—real estate funds cannot continuously buy and sell their properties. In order to be able to meet the repurchase guarantee to unit holders at any time, and to be able to invest money for a short term, German real estate funds typically hold about 25–50 per cent of their assets in fixed-income securities.

Money market funds ('Geldmarkt-Sondervermögen') have been legally permitted in Germany since 1994 and invest in cash or special money market instruments. In 2000, the thirty-nine money market funds in the mutual funds sector achieved a market share of 6.58 per cent of all mutual funds.

Fund-of-funds ('Investmentfondsanteil-Sondervermögen'), in compliance with the third Financial Market Improvement Act, may invest their assets in units of other German mutual funds as well as in units of foreign investment funds registered for public distribution in Germany. In general, German fund-of-funds are allowed to invest in all types of mutual funds, except other fund-of-funds, closed-end funds or special funds. In 2000, their market share was 1.58 per cent.

Mixed Security and Real Estate Funds ('Gemischte Wertpapier- und Grundstückssondervermögen') are a combination of real-estate and security-based funds. Thus, a mixed fund can invest in securities, properties, real estate funds, and participations in real estate companies. In the mutual funds sector, the market share of the three mixed funds was 1.38 per cent of all assets under management in 2000.

AS-funds ('Altersvorsorge-Sondervermögen') were introduced with the third Financial Market Improvement Act in April 1998 into the German Investment Companies Act. In contrast to other types of investment funds, AS funds are not defined by the underlying asset (e.g. bonds, equity, real estate) and the investment style (e.g. growth, value) followed by fund managers, but rather by the special objective of pension provision. Therefore, the legal structure of these funds is designed to offer private investors a means by which to improve their retirement provision on the basis of a defined contribution scheme. During the accumulation phase, AS-funds are designed as long-term savings plans with a minimum term of 18 years. Income (e.g. dividends, coupons) is reinvested, and there is an option to switch the accumulated wealth from the AS-fund to another fund of the same investment management company at no transaction cost. To ensure risk diversification by investing in different asset classes, AS-funds must comply (by law) with special minimum and maximum investment limits. For example, at least 51 per cent of the fund's assets must be invested in equities and real estate. Moreover, no more than 75 per cent may be invested in equities, up to 30 per cent in real estate, dormant holdings and/or units of participation funds must not exceed 10 per cent, foreign exchange exposures are limited to 30 per cent, and, finally, financial

Table 4.8. *Descriptive statistics for the investment returns of German mutual funds 1980–2002*

	Mean (% p.a.)	Std (% p.a.)	AR(1)	Correlation		
				Equities	Bonds	Real estate
Funds with highest average return						
Equities	9.97	15.79	− 0.02	1		
Bonds	7.52	5.60	0.06	0.54	1	
Real estate	6.46	1.59	0.66*	− 0.02	0.40	1
Funds with median average return						
Equities	8.20	25.66	0.03	1		
Bonds	6.99	4.64	− 0.02	0.12	1	
Real estate	6.18	1.81	0.80*	0.11	0.42	1
Funds with minimum average return						
Equities	5.23	26.05	0.07	1		
Bonds	6.13	6.34	− 0.30	0.40	1	
Real estate	5.58	2.13	0.81*	0.22	0.53	1

First-order sample autocorrelations AR(1) marked with an asterisk are statistically significant at the 5% level, according to the Q-statistic of *Ljung/Box* (1979).

derivatives can only be used for hedging. In contrast to Anglo-American type pension funds, AS-funds do not include insurance (e.g. mortality or disability) nor any kind of defined benefit elements (such as the provision of a minimum return guarantee). No special tax benefits are given to contributions to this type of mutual fund. The market share of the forty-four AS-funds by the end of 2000 was about 0.92 per cent of total assets under management.

In Table 4.8, we provide an overview of the historical risk and return profiles of German mutual funds within the main asset classes, that is, equities, bonds, and real estate. We thereby use the historical investment returns (including capital gains and dividends) for German mutual funds over the period 1980–2002. Three classes of well diversified funds have been studied: stocks, bonds, and real estate funds concentrating their assets mainly within the German capital and real estate market. Proceeding from a sample of seventeen stock funds, twenty-three bond funds and seven real estate funds we chose those funds which, for the average return over the period 1980–2002, took the highest, median, and lowest positions. The yearly time series returns offer the following estimates for the mean log return, volatility, first-order autocorrelation, and the correlation coefficients.

Mean returns, standard deviations, and sample autocorrelations presented in Table 4.8 differ among the different types of mutual funds, while equities are the most volatile asset class, and real estate funds exhibit the lowest volatility. This kind of cross-sectional homogeneity exists also for the mean return within the bond and real estate sector. The spread between the maximum and minimum bond fund is 1.39 per cent; and for real estate funds it is 0.88 per cent. However, the mean returns between the different equity funds are much more heterogeneous. The spread between the maximum and minimum funds is 4.39 per cent. For the maximum and minimum equity funds the mean returns are higher than those of bonds and real estate, that is, they provide investors with a (historically) positive risk premium to cover the higher volatility of this asset class. However, the risk premium for the equity funds with the lowest mean return, is negative.

Looking at the sample autocorrelations, it is interesting to note that the returns of German real estate funds show smoothing features similar to the investment yields of life insurers. The first order sample autocorrelation of the yearly returns of German real estate funds is large and statistically distinguishable from zero. As reported in the literature (Barkham and Geltner 1994 among others), real estate return series with such typical statistical properties, that is, low volatilities and a high level of serial correlation, are due to appraisal smoothing. The same is true for the German real estate funds because the unit values are based on annual expert appraisals of the properties held by the funds. It is well documented in real estate literature that appraisals are due to the asynchronous and temporally aggregated processing of relevant information, resulting in smoothed short-term returns (see among others Geltner 1993; or Maurer and Sebastian 2002). In contrast to this, equity and bond fund returns are determined on an exchange market that adjusts rapidly to changes in information and expectations. However, the smoothed prices of the German real estate funds represent the amount by which the fund must redeem units at each point in time. Therefore, despite the fact that the risk level of real estate mutual fund units is probably artificially low, for unit holders the smoothed return is the actual holding period return which they receive. Note that because of purchase transaction costs of about 5 per cent of the initial unit price, the reported average return is not the expected return for a potential investor who is willing to buy units of real estate funds.

4.3.2.3. *Special funds*
The number of special funds is about four times higher than the number of mutual funds. The assets under management of special funds are about 50 per cent higher than for mutual funds. Within the special funds sector, the balanced equity/bond funds play the most important role, with a market share of 59.37 per cent of total assets under management. The following Table 4.9 provides an overview of the number and the total amount of assets under management of the different types of special funds.

Table 4.10 provides an overview of the shareholders of special funds. Measured in terms of assets under management, the most important institutional investors are insurance companies with a market share of about 50 per cent. It is interesting to note that among them, life insurance companies are the

Table 4.9. *Classification of German special funds by investment objective*

Type of fund	Number	Asset (mill. €)	Asset (% of total assets)
Money market funds	5	613	0.12
Security-based funds	5,491	483,113	98.15
Equity funds	371	48,697	9.89
Bond funds	1,517	142,219	28.89
Balanced funds	3,603	292,197	59.37
Real estate funds	45	7,914	1.61
Fund-of-funds	41	579	0.12
Total	5,582	492,219	100.00

Source: Deutsche Bundesbank Kapitalmarktstatistik December 2001, p. 53.

Table 4.10. *Investors and assets under management for special funds*

Investor	Number of funds	Asset under management	
		in mill. €	in %
Domestic	5,534	488,678	99.28
Banks	1,954	125,826	25.56
Insurance companies	1,643	241,065	48.99
Other companies	1,261	84,832	17.23
Social security institutions	219	12,222	2.48
Non profit organizations	457	24,734	5.02
Foreign	48	3,541	0.72
Total	5,582	492,219	100.00

Source: Deutsche Bundesbank Kapitalmarktstatistik December 2001, p. 60.

most important users of special funds with €139,632 million worth of assets under management. Therefore, in the retail market for savings and pension products, life insurance companies who offer life policies with a cash value, and investment management companies who offer mutual funds products compete intensively with one another. In the market for special funds, however, they cooperate closely. In addition to insurance companies, commercial banks (25.56 per cent of assets under management) and industrial companies (17.23 per cent) are also important users of special funds. Social security institutions, non-profit organizations (churches, political parties, or unions), and foreign investors play a minor role.

4.3.3. Regulation

Investment management companies which offer mutual and special funds are regulated by a comprehensive legal framework, primarily by the Investment

Company Act ('Gesetz über Kapitalanlagegesellschaften', subsequently KAGG). The KAGG is a special law designed to provide investor protection and it is the statutory basis for the German investment fund market. It regulates a number of legal aspects such as licensing requirements, the organizational structure, the possible funds operated by the investment management company, the function and purpose of custodians, permitted investments, investment restrictions, valuation, accounting, auditing, and publication requirements, and the taxation of the fund. The state supervision of the rules laid down in the Investment Company Act is exercised by *BaFin*, providing legal compliance supervision. The supervisory authority is not allowed to intervene with the business decisions of an investment management company, as long as these comply with the existing laws and regulations (see for that point Laux and Siebel 1999: 67). Since its implementation in 1957, the KAGG was (de lege ferenda) subject to a number of important amendments which in general extended the investment opportunities for investment funds. The latest amendment was the fourth Financial Market Improvement Act in 2002 which made it easier for real estate funds to invest internationally.

A special feature of the governance structure is that an investment management company requires a supervisory board irrespective of its legal form. By law, the duty of a supervisory board is to ensure the interests of the investment fund's unit holders. In addition, a German investment management company must appoint one depositary bank for each of its investment funds. The depositary bank must be licensed to act as a depositary bank and is subject to state supervision. In performing its functions, the depositary bank must act independently of the investment management company. The selection, as well as all subsequent changes of the depositary bank, must be approved by the *BaFin*. An important function of such a custodian is to safeguard the assets of the investment fund. The assets of the investment fund are kept in segregated bank or security accounts at the depositary bank. Dispositions in the fund assets by the investment management company are subject to approval by the depositary bank. Thus, the involvement of the depositary bank prevents the investment management company from using the assets of the investment funds for its own account. Another important function of the depositary bank is to determine the net asset value and to act as a transfer agent with respect to the issue and redemption of fund units.

In addition to the Investment Company Act, investment funds are also subject to a number of other laws. For example, the promotion of foreign investment funds in Germany stems from the German Foreign Investment Act ('Auslandsinvestmentgesetz'). This law was introduced in 1969 in response to the collapse of the Investors Overseas Services (IOS), where thousands of investors lost their money. According to this law, the public marketing of foreign investment funds in Germany requires notification of the *BaFin*. With respect to the notification process, a distinction must be made between foreign funds situated in EU Member States or states that are part of the European

Economic Area, which set up the Directive 85/611/EEC (UCITS-funds) and other foreign funds (non UCITS-funds). While UCITS funds are subject to a simplified notification procedure, all other foreign funds publicly marketed in Germany must comply with more rigorous requirements in order to obtain permission to sell investment funds in Germany. UCITS-funds must invest in bonds and/or equities that are quoted on the stock exchange. Hence, within the different mutual fund types of the KAGG, only security based funds are currently consistent with the UCITS-directive.

Since the German Banking Law ('Gesetz über das Kreditwesen') treats investment management companies as special banks, they are, like commercial banks, also subject to the general provisions of the KWG. However, because of the special provisions ('lex specialis') in the Investment Company Act, there are important differences between the regulation of commercial banks and that of investment management companies. The most important difference is in the case of solvency requirements. Usually, commercial banks (like insurance companies) are risk bearers in their business. Therefore, they are subject to comprehensive risk-based solvency requirements.

In contrast, an investment management company usually assumes no obligation other than that of investing the funds, in a reasonable and prudent manner, in the interest of the investors. It provides no guarantees of the rate of investment return. Hence, the investor bears all the capital market risk and receives the full reward of the financial asset that backs the mutual fund units. Because of the balance sheets, investment management companies are not exposed to fluctuations in the capital market and are usually excluded from the risk-based solvency requirements set out in the German Banking Law. According to the German Investment Company Act, the minimum equity capital for investment fund management companies (i.e. the provider of the pension products) is €2.5 million, independent of assets under management and the number or type of funds. However, an important development accompanied the introduction of Individual Pension Accounts (IPA) within the Retirement Saving Act in May 2001. In order to qualify for a tax credit, the IPA products have to satisfy a number of criteria. These conditions are stipulated in a special law concerning the certification of individual pension products ('Altersvorsorge-Zertifizierungsgesetz') and are supervised by a special authority ('Zertifizierungsstelle') belonging to the German Federal Financial Supervisory Authority. An essential condition, which was the core of an intense and controversial debate during the social security reform in Germany, is the so-called 'money-back-guarantee'. This means that each provider of an IPA must promise the plan participant that the contract cash value at retirement is at least equal to the contributions paid into the IPA. If at retirement the market value of the assets in the IPA does not cover the money back guarantee, the provider must fill the gap with its own equity capital. Hence, if the provider of an IPA is an investment management company which uses its own mutual funds, the supervisory authority requires solvency capital.

The model for determining the regulatory solvency capital for investment management company is designed as follows (see Maurer and Schlag 2003). Let M denote the market current value of the IPA, B be the sum of the contributions paid into the account and let i_T be the continuously compounded yield on a zero coupon bond maturing in T months (i.e. the planned age of retirement), taken from the current term structure of German interest rates. Furthermore, let σ be the monthly volatility of returns of the mutual fund units backing the pension account.[20] For each IPA, the investment management company must build solvency capital equal to 8 per cent of the total contributions (i.e. $0.08B$), only if the market value of the pension account is lower than the risk-adjusted present value of the contribution.

$$M \leq \frac{B}{e^{i_T \cdot (T-1) - 2.33\sigma}} \Leftrightarrow$$

$$\frac{M}{B} \leq \frac{1}{e^{i_T \cdot (T-1) - 2.33\sigma}}$$

To calculate the present value of the guarantee a risk-adjusted discount factor is applied. The economic rationale behind this inequality suggests that at every point in time the investment management company has the chance to hedge all its shortfall risk by investing the present value of the contributions (i.e. $B/\exp(i_T \cdot T)$ into default-free zero bonds. Following this strategy ensures that, at the end of the accumulation period, the proceeds will equal the participant's contributions during the accumulation phase. If the provider does not use zero bonds, but instead employs mutual funds with higher volatility, nothing happens as long as the cash value of the policy is 'substantially' higher than the present value of the contributions. 'Substantially higher' means that, given a current cash value, there is a probability of only 1 per cent (note 2.33 is the 99 per cent quantile of the standard normal distribution) that the uncertain cash value of the IPA one month later will be lower than the present value of the contributions. This explains the risk adjustment aspect in the discount factor. The solvency test according to the inequality must be applied for each IPA. Therefore, the total solvency requirement of an investment management company is given by the sum of all IPA under management. The result of the solvency test must be reported to the supervision authority at the end of each month.

Hence, a temporary funding level defined as the ratio of market value of the IPA divided by the sum of contributions of lower than one (i.e. $M/B < 1$) is possible, without capital requirements. The extent to which such an underfunding is allowed depends on the volatility of the pension assets and the time

---

[20] The volatility must be estimated from historical time series returns of the fund unit prices, using a window between 2 and 5 years. If the IPA consists of more than one type of mutual fund, σ is computed as the weighted sum of the individual fund volatilities, according to the current asset allocation of the policy (i.e. diversification due to non-perfect correlation is neglected).

Table 4.11. *Critical funding level (as per cent of contributions)*

	Volatility (% per month)							
Months to go	0.29	0.58	0.87	1.15	1.44	2.89	5.77	7.22
240	45.4	45.8	46.1	46.4	46.7	48.3	51.6	53.4
120	67.8	68.2	68.7	69.1	69.6	72.0	77.0	79.6
60	82.7	83.3	83.8	84.4	85.0	87.9	94.0	97.2
12	97.1	97.7	98.4	99.0	99.7	103.1	110.3	114.1

remaining to the end of the accumulation period. For example (see Table 4.11), if the monthly returns of the pension assets have a volatility of 5.77 per cent per month, the risk-free interest rate is 4 per cent p.a., and the remaining accumulation period is 20 years, then the critical funding level (i.e. M/B) is 51.6 per cent. If the time to retirement is only 10 years, the minimum funding level increases to 77.0 per cent. However, the provider has the chance to reduce the volatility of the IPA and, in line with this, also the minimum funding level by investing more of the IPA assets in low volatility mutual funds.

To summarize, with an appropriate asset allocation, it is possible for the provider of a mutual fund-based IPA to avoid solvency requirements for the principal guarantee with a high probability.[21] However, the burden of such a conditional solvency system is the implementation of an efficient risk monitoring system for each IPA.

4.3.4. Outlook and Current Developments

The investment fund industry in Germany has experienced impressive growth during the last decade. Since 1995, the key driver of the industry's growth has been the huge increase in special funds. Along with an extension of funded pensions it can be expected that this type of product will maintain its attractiveness as a vehicle for outsourcing the asset management of corporate investors. However, more competition could emerge from asset management companies and/or repackaged debt, equity, or hybrid instruments offered outside the legal environment of the Investment Company Act. The primary reason for the huge development in the mutual funds sector was the increasing importance of equity funds at the end of the last decade. With the downturn of the equity markets around the world in 2001 and 2002 this trend has been stopped and substantial volumes have been shifted into 'safe haven products' like money market and real estate funds. The key driver for future growth in the retail sector for investment funds is without doubt the extension of funded pension schemes. However, this requires a legal framework which provides

---

[21] Further results for different hedging strategies can be found in Maurer and Schlag (2003).

households with the same tax incentives for investing in mutual funds as other long-term saving vehicles, especially those offered by the insurance industry. Traditionally, the German legislative body endows pension products in the second and third pillar with tax incentives only if it provides a certain level of return guarantee to private households. A tax-supported, purely defined contribution scheme, for example, like the 401(k) plan in the United States of America, does not exist in the German pension system. It is open to question, whether in the near future, such a product will be incorporated in the legal environment. Thus, in order to profit from the increasing importance of (tax-supported) private pensions within the current legal environment it will be necessary for investment management companies to be able to offer accumulation as well as decumulation pension products with return guarantees. Because the credibility of return guarantees given by any regulated institutional investor must be controlled by the supervisory authority, it is necessary to design appropriate solvency systems. One example of such a development is the design of accumulation products endowed with a money back guarantee and the corresponding solvency requirements for mutual-fund based 'Riester' pension products. In addition, it will be necessary for the investment industry to design products to offer individuals a reasonable alternative to annuities for the post-retirement phase.

References

Albrecht, P. (1992). *Zur Risikotransformationstheorie der Versicherung: Grundlagen und ökonomische Konsequenzen*. Karlsruhe.

——(1986). 'Zur Analyse des versicherungsspezifischen Leverage-Effekts sowie des finanzwirtschaftlichen Leverage-Effekts bei Risiko', *Zeitschrift für betriebswirtschaftliche Forschung*, 38: 575–85.

——, and Maurer, R. (2002). 'Self-Annuitization, Consumption Shortfall in Retirement and Asset Allocation: The Annuity Benchmark', in *Journal of Pension Economics and Finance*, 1: 269–88.

Barkham, R., and Geltner, D. (1994). 'Unsmoothing British Valuation-Based Returns Without Assuming an Efficient Market', *Journal of Property Research*, 11: 81–95.

Cummins, J. D. (1991). 'Statistical and Financial Models of Insurance Pricing and the Insurance Firm', *Journal of Risk and Insurance*, 58: 261–302.

Davis, P. E., and Steil, B. (2001). *Institutional Investors*. Cambridge, MA, London: MIT Press.

Ernst and Young (2001). *Investment Funds Market in Germany*. Frankfurt/Main.

Fabozzi, F. (1998). *Investment Management*, 2nd edn. New Jersey.

Fairley, W. (1979). 'Investment Income and Profit Margins in Property Liability Insurance: Theory and Empirical Results', *Bell Journal of Economics*, 10: 192–210.

Fitch Ratings (2002). *Special Report on German Life Insurers: Financing the Future*, 11. London.

——(2003). *Special Report on German Life Insurers: Insurers may be forced to write off billions*, 03. London.

Geltner, D. M. (1993). 'Estimating Market Values from Appraised Values without Assuming an Efficient Market', *Journal of Real Estate Economics*, 8: 325–46.

Hallman, G. V., and Rosenbloom, J. S. (2000). *Personal Financial Planning*. New York.

Kahneman, D., and Tversky, A. (1979). 'Prospect Theory: An Analysis of Decisions Under Risk', *Econometrica*, 47: 263–91.

Laux, M., and Siebel, R. (1999). The HS-Fund: A Modern Pension for Everyone, Frankfurt.

Loubergé, H. (1981). *Èconomie et finance de l'assurance et de la réassurance*. Genève.

Loubergé, H. (1983). 'A Portfolio Model of International Reinsurance Operations', *Journal of Risk and Insurance*, 50: 44–60.

Maurer, R. (2000). *Integrierte Erfolgssteuerung in der Schadenversicherung auf der Basis von Risiko-Wert-Modellen*. Karlsruhe.

——, and Sebastian, S. (2002). 'Inflation Risk Analysis of European Real Estate Securities', *Journal of Real Estate Research*, 24: 47–77.

——, and Schlag, C. (2003). 'Money-Back Guarantees in Individual Pension Accounts: Evidence from the German Pension Reform', in O. S. Mitchell and K. Smetters (eds.), *The Pension Challenge: Risk Transfers and Retirement Income Security*. Oxford: Oxford University Press.

McCabe, G., and Witt, R. C. (1980). 'Insurance Pricing and Regulation Under Uncertainty: A Chance-Constrained Approach', *Journal of Risk and Insurance*, 47: 607–35.

Mitchell, O., and McCarthy, D. (2001). 'Assessing the Impact of Mortality Assumptions on Annuity Valuation: Cross Country Evidence', Pension Research Council Working Paper 2001–3. The Wharton School. University of Pennsylvania.

PricewaterhouseCoopers (2002). *Investment Management Industry Profile Germany*. Frankfurt/Main.

Ramlau-Hansen, H. (1991). 'Distribution of surplus in life insurance', *ASTIN Bulletin*, 21: 57–71.

Wakker, P. P., Thaler, R. H., and Tversky, A. (1997). 'Probabilistic Insurance', *Journal of Risk and Uncertainty*, 15: 7–28.

5

Organized Equity Markets

ERIK THEISSEN

5.1. INTRODUCTION

The German financial system is the archetype of a bank-dominated system. This implies that organized capital markets are, in some sense, under-developed. Underdevelopment can, however, mean different things. In the present case two interpretations are potentially relevant:

1. A capital market may be underdeveloped in terms of volume. In a bank-dominated financial system one would expect the market for equity and corporate bonds to be smaller than they would be under a market-oriented system.
2. A capital market may be underdeveloped in terms of the organization of trading, of its operational efficiency and, as a result, in terms of liquidity and transaction costs.

The objective of this chapter is to take a closer look at the German capital market. The focus of attention is limited to the equity markets. In accordance with the two interpretations given above we address two specific questions. First, we present evidence on the volume of the German equity markets. Second, we describe the organization of the German equity markets, paying special attention to recent developments. We further present empirical evidence on the operational efficiency and liquidity of the German equity market.

This chapter is organized as follows. In Section 5.2 we present empirical evidence relating to the volume of the German equity markets and, in particular, to changes in the recent past. Section 5.3 describes the microstructure of the German equity markets and presents evidence on their liquidity. Section 5.4 concludes and discusses the implications of our findings for the organization of equity markets in Germany.

5.2. THE GERMAN EQUITY MARKET

It is to be expected in a bank-dominated financial system that internal financing and bank loans will be the dominant sources of funds, whereas

Table 5.1. *Market volume*

	1990	1995	2002
Corporate bonds, face value, € Mio	1,331	1,404	36,646
Outstanding equity, nominal value, € Mio	73,977	108,001	168,716
Outstanding equity, market value, € Mio	286,938	422,523	647,492
Market value of equity as a percentage of GDP	23.1%	23.5%	30.7%
Number of domestic listed companies	649	678	867

Note: The figures for corporate bonds exclude bonds issued by banks. GDP is for West Germany only.

Source: Deutsche Bundesbank, Monatsberichte, Deutsche Börse AG, Historical Statistics Cash Markets.

equity and bond issues are likely to play a much lesser role. The empirical results of Hackethal and Schmidt (2000) clearly support this view. They find that securitized funds account for 12 per cent of the volume of physical investment in Germany as compared to 48 per cent in the United States.[1] Rajan and Zingales (1995), using data from 1991, analyse the capital structure of non-financial exchange-listed companies in seven countries. The ratio of book equity to total capital is lowest in Germany, amounting to 28 per cent. Figures for non-listed companies are even lower than that. In 2000, the average ratio (over all companies) of book equity to total capital was a mere 17 per cent (DAI Factbook 2002, relying on data from Deutsche Bundesbank).

It is obvious that these financing patterns have implications for the volume of the securities markets. This conjecture is corroborated by the figures in Table 5.1. The corporate bond market is, despite an almost thirty-fold increase in volume since 1995, still negligible. The market value of exchange-listed equity has more than doubled in the last decade and now amounts to €647.5 billion (year end 2001). This increase is not due to the bull market of the nineties as is illustrated by the fact that the nominal value of equity[2] increased at about the same rate.

In spite of this increase the market capitalization of listed German firms is low in comparison to other countries. Table 5.2 presents figures on market capitalization as a percentage of the gross domestic product (GDP). The figures for Germany are way below the figures for the United Kingdom or the United States (archetypal market-dominated financial systems). They are even lower than the average for the Euro countries. The increase in the market capitalization

---

[1] Note that this result stands in contrast to the findings by Mayer (1988). Hackethal and Schmidt (2000) argue that this is due to implicit assumptions in his methodology. See their paper for a detailed discussion of this issue.

[2] The nominal value of the equity is a part of the book equity shown on the balance sheet. It is equivalent to the nominal capital ('gezeichnetes Kapital') of the firm defined in the corporate charter.

Table 5.2. *Market capitalization: international comparison*

	1990	1995	2001
Germany	25.0	23.9	58.1
€ countries	27.4	28.8	70.7
UK	88.2	121.6	152.0
US	48.7	95.2	136.3
Japan	98.6	71.4	55.4

Note: The table shows the market capitalization as a percentage of GDP.

Source: Deutsches Aktieninstitut: DAI Factbook 2002.

Table 5.3. *Share ownership*

	1992	1997	2001
Percentage of population over 14 with shareholdings	6.4	6.2	8.9
Percentage of population with mutual fund holdings	n/a	3.6	15.2
Percentage of population with mutual fund and/or share holdings	n/a	8.9	20.0
Private shareholdings			
€ billion	124.2	293.7	347.3
In % of total monetary wealth	5.69	9.53	9.47
Private mutual fund holdings			
€ billion	108.8	243.7	429.4
In % of total monetary wealth	4.99	7.91	11.71

Source: Deutsches Aktieninstitut: DAI Factbook 2002.

documented in Table 5.1 has not led to a convergence because market capitalization in the other countries has increased at about the same rate.

The low market capitalization does, of course, have implications for the portfolios of German households. Table 5.3 documents that less than 10 per cent of the population over 14 own shares. In 2001, share holdings and mutual fund holdings together amounted to slightly more than 20 per cent of the financial assets. When interpreting this figure, note that total financial assets do not include the value of pension claims against the state-run social security system.

The majority of financial assets are made up of bank deposits, bonds,[3] and life insurance contracts (see Börsch-Supan and Eymann 2000 for a more

---

[3] This statement does not contradict the low volume of the corporate bond market. There are large markets for government bonds and bonds issued by banks. The latter market comprises, among others, mortgage-backed bonds ('Pfandbriefe').

detailed analysis). Despite a recent increase in private share ownership, figures for Germany are, again, lower than those for the United States and the United Kingdom. For example, in 1998, 33.8 per cent of individuals in the United States owned shares directly, 48.5 per cent owned shares and / or mutual funds (New York Stock Exchange 2000).

Since households only invest a small percentage of their wealth in the stock market, the fraction of households in total shareholdings is low. Figure 5.1 shows the distribution of shareholdings. Households directly hold 15.3 per cent of the shares (compared to 39.1 per cent for households and non-profit organizations in the United States). An additional 14.0 per cent (US: 19.3 per cent) is held by mutual funds which, in turn, are at least partially held by households. Non-financial firms own 32.5 per cent of the shares. Banks and insurance companies hold 13.0 per cent and 9.7 per cent, respectively (US: 1.9 per cent and 6.5 per cent, respectively). Shareholdings of the state are negligible.

The analysis of market capitalization and the structure of household portfolios leads to a picture that is consistent with what one would expect to find in a bank-oriented financial system. The corporate bond market is close to non-existent, equity market capitalization is low, and only a small fraction of physical investment is financed by securitized funds. Household portfolios are tilted towards bank deposits, (government and bank-issued) bonds and insurance contracts. The conclusion, thus, is that the German equity market is indeed underdeveloped in terms of volume.

There is a second dimension in which the German capital market has been underdeveloped (at least by comparison to US standards): the legal dimension. The degree of shareholder protection is low in Germany, as is evidenced by the international survey in La Porta *et al.* (1998). Things are beginning to change,

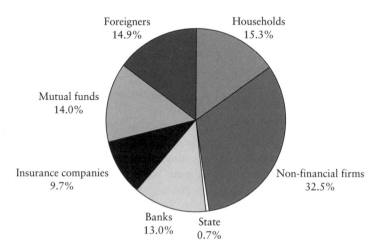

Figure 5.1. *Shareholdings (% of total shareholdings, year end 2000).*
Source: Deutsches Aktieninstitut: DAI Factbook 2002.

however.[4] For example, non-voting preferred stock is losing favour, disclosure requirements have been increased and a takeover law has been in effect since 2002. Also in 2002, the fourth Financial Market Promotion Act ('Finanz-marktförderungsgesetz') was passed. It comprised changes to the Exchange Law ('Börsengesetz') and to the Securities Trading Act ('Wertpapierhandelsgesetz'), aiming at more flexibility for the organization of exchanges, higher transparency and more stringent insider trading regulation. Furthermore, a new law (fifth Financial Market Promotion Act) is in preparation. One of its main objectives is to strengthen shareholder rights.

Insider trading was not prohibited until the mid-1990s. The Securities Trading Act ('Wertpapierhandelsgesetz') was passed in 1994 (at least in part as a response to international pressure). Among the 'developed countries' listed in table 1 of Bhattacharya and Daouk (2002), Germany was, together with Spain, the last country to pass insider trading laws. The Securities Trading Act prohibited from then on insider trading and established the securities supervisory unit ('Bundesaufsichtsamt für den Wertpapierhandel'), based in Frankfurt. In 2002 the securities supervisory unit was merged with the banking supervisory unit ('Bundesaufsichtsamt für das Kreditwesen') and the insurance supervisory unit ('Bundesaufsichtsamt für das Versicher-ungswesen') to form the Federal Financial Supervisory Authority ('Bunde-sanstalt für Finanzdienstleistungsaufsicht—BaFin'), located in Bonn and Frankfurt. The number of investigations in 2001 [2000] was fifty-five [fifty-one]. Twenty-five [twenty-two] cases were handed over to the court.[5]

The recent increase in market capitalization, the number of listed companies and private share ownership together with changes in legislation may be an indication of the convergence of the German equity market towards a more market-oriented system. The increase in market volume is, however, not markedly different from the growth in other countries and it may, therefore, be premature to conclude that the financing patterns of German corporations are really changing on a broad basis.

5.3. THE (MICRO)STRUCTURE OF THE GERMAN EQUITY MARKET

5.3.1. Trading Venues

Stock trading in Germany is fragmented both vertically and horizontally. In the vertical dimension there have traditionally been three market segments. The most liquid stocks are listed in the Official Market ('amtlicher Markt').[6] The Regulated Market ('geregelter Markt'), created in the mid-1980s, is a segment for mid- and

---

[4] See Nowak (2001) for a detailed description and interpretation of recent legal changes.

[5] The figures are taken from Bundesaufsichtsamt für den Wertpapierhandel (2002).

[6] 'Most liquid' is a euphemism because a considerable number of these stocks are rather illiquid in terms of market capitalization and trading volume.

small-caps. Finally, the Unofficial Market ('Freiverkehr') is the least regulated segment. In 1997 Deutsche Börse AG created the *Neuer Markt*, a segment for growth stocks that has attracted approximately 350 companies since its inception. Listing requirements in the *Neuer Markt* were stricter than in other segments. Inspired by the initial success of the Neuer Markt, Deutsche Börse AG created an additional segment called SMAX. This was a segment for small caps in more traditional ('old economy') industries. Listing requirements were lower than in the *Neuer Markt* but higher than in the Regulated Market.

Following the slump of 'new economy' share prices, the large number of bankruptcies of *Neuer Markt* firms and several cases of fraud, investors lost confidence in the growth segment. Consequently, Deutsche Börse AG closed both the *Neuer Markt* and the SMAX. At the same time, the market segments were re-organized. This was facilitated by a change in law that gave the exchange more discretion in setting the listing requirements. Besides the unregulated Unofficial Market, there are two segments:[7] *General standard* is the basis category. It is designed for smaller companies with a domestic focus. Listing requirements are low, and are not tailored to the needs of international investors. The *Prime standard* is designed for companies aiming at international visibility.

Listing requirements include

- application of international accounting standards (IFRS or US-GAAP)[8]
- quarterly reporting
- publication of a 'financial calendar' listing the most important corporate events (shareholders' meeting, analyst conferences etc.)
- regular analysts' conferences (minimum one per year)
- current reporting and *ad hoc* disclosure in English.

A prime standard listing is required for a stock to be included in one of the indices calculated and published by Deutsche Börse AG.[9] Figure 5.2 shows the most important members of the index 'family'. At the very top there is the DAX,

---

[7] Strictly speaking there are four segments. The Official Market and the Regulated Market are defined by law (German Stock Exchange Law, Listing Application Regulation). Any company seeking a listing may choose either of the two. In both cases, the company may opt for a 'general standard' or a 'prime standard' listing. This results in a total of four segments. However, the differences between the Official Market and the Regulated Market *within* either the general standard or the prime standard category are immaterial. Note that the Official Market and the Regulated Market segments, since they are defined by law, exist at all German exchanges. The categories general standard and prime standard are specific to the markets operated by Deutsche Börse AG, that is, to the Frankfurt Stock Exchange and Xetra.

[8] Leuz and Verrecchia (2000) present evidence that switching from the German to an international reporting regime is associated with lower bid–ask spreads and higher trading volume.

[9] An exception is the CDAX, a broad index that includes all listed companies, that is, those with a prime standard listing as well as those with a general standard listing. Even before the inception of the new segmentation Deutsche Börse AG used its discretion in the composition of its indices to exert pressure on companies. This pressure aimed at increased information disclosure and compliance with certain codes of conduct. For example, in order to be included in the DAX or MDAX

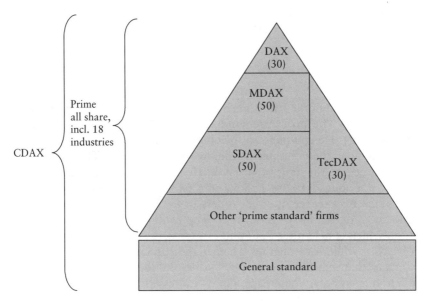

Figure 5.2. *Equity indices.*

Note: The 18 industries include Automobile, Banks, Basic Resources, Chemicals, Construction, Consumer, Financial Services, Food & Beverages, Industrial, Insurance, Media, Pharma & Healthcare, Retail, Software, Technology, Telecommunication, Transport & Logistics, Utilities.

a blue chip index comprising the thirty most liquid forms. The MDAX contains the following fifty 'old economy' firms. The SDAX includes an additional fifty 'old economy' firms. The TecDAX contains the thirty most liquid high tech ('new economy') firms. All firms listed in the prime standard segment are contained in the prime all share index, which is subdivided into eighteen industry indices. All indices are calculated as performance indices.[10] Besides these stock indices, Deutsche Börse AG publishes the VDAX, a volatility index calculated from implied volatilities inferred from equity option prices.

With regard to the horizontal dimension, trading is fragmented between seven exchanges and the electronic trading system Xetra. The most liquid stocks are traded on all markets. Among the eight exchanges the Frankfurt stock exchange is by far the largest.[11] We, therefore, restrict the description of

a company had to publish quarterly reports. In 2001, the car manufacturer Porsche AG was excluded from the MDAX because the company refused to comply with this requirement. As Porsche still refuses to publish quarterly reports, Deutsche Börse AG has declined a prime standard listing.

[10] For details on the indices published by Deutsche Börse AG, see Deutsche Börse AG (2003).

[11] Regional exchanges exist in Berlin, Bremen, Düsseldorf, Hamburg, Hannover, Stuttgart, and Munich. Some of them have specialized in specific financial instruments. The Stuttgart Stock Exchange, for example, operates the warrant market EUWAX, the world's largest derivatives exchange in terms of listed instruments.

the trading protocol to the Frankfurt Stock Exchange (FSE) and Xetra. Both markets are run by Deutsche Börse AG[12] which, since February 2001, is itself a listed company.

5.3.2. Floor Trading

The trading system of the FSE bears many similarities to that of the New York Stock Exchange. The stocks are handled by a specialist ('Skontroführer', formerly 'Makler'). He conducts an opening call auction at 9:00 a.m. After the opening auction, the continuous trading session starts.[13] The specialist has exclusive access to the limit order book. He is allowed (but, unlike the NYSE specialist, not obliged) to trade on his own account. He announces bid and ask prices which may represent either orders in the limit order book or his willingness to trade for his own account. The trading day ends with a closing auction, which is held after 7:30 p.m.

It is worthwhile investigating whether the specialist system offers specific advantages that may explain its survival despite the competition of the electronic trading system. Some papers have addressed this issue and analyse the floor-based trading system of the FSE in detail.

Kehr *et al.* (2001) analyse the role of the specialist in the call auctions on the floor. They find that specialist participation reduces return volatility. They further document that the specialists, on average, do not earn profits on the trades they make on their own accounts. Their income thus appears to be restricted to the commissions they receive. A similar result for the continuous trading session is found by Freihube *et al.* (1999). Their results also suggest that the specialist is the dominant supplier of liquidity on the floor of the FSE. The quoted spread is narrower than the spread obtained from the orders in the limit order book maintained by the specialist in more than 55 per cent of the cases.[14] In these cases the spread represents the willingness of the specialist to trade on his own account rather than on behalf of a customer. Further, more than 46 per cent of the transactions occur at prices inside the quoted spread. In many of these cases the specialist is trading on his own account. In fact, Freihube *et al.* (1999) find that the specialist participates in more than 80 per cent of the transactions and accounts for more than 40 per cent of the trading volume. These figures are higher than the comparable figures for the NYSE reported by Madhavan and Sofianos (1998).

---

[12] The fact that Deutsche Börse AG operates a floor-based and an electronic market is, at least in part, due to the legal nature of the FSE. See Section 5.2 for details.

[13] For a large number of less liquid stocks there is only one daily call auction and no continuous trading session. The same applies for Xetra.

[14] Chung *et al.* (1999) report a comparable figure for the NYSE. There, the quoted spread is narrower than the spread calculated from the best bid and offer in the limit order book in only 29.3 per cent of the cases.

These results lead to the question of whether there is any advantage in having one dominant supplier of liquidity. A starting point for answering that question is the observation that specialist systems like those of the NYSE and the FSE are not anonymous. The non-anonymity may allow the specialist to identify informed traders *ex ante* or *ex post*.[15] *Ex-ante* identification may be based on observed trader behaviour and enables the specialist to offer less favourable prices to those traders that he considers to be informed. *Ex-post* identification of informed traders allows reputation building. The specialist will offer less favourable prices in future transactions to traders that have traded on private information in the past.[16] The specialist's sanctioning power may induce traders to trade less aggressively on their information in order to retain their reputation, and thus receive favourable prices in future transactions. This, in turn, decreases the degree of adverse information and may lead to a lower adverse selection component in effective bid–ask spreads. To fully exploit the information inferred (or, at least, inferable) from trader identities, it is advantageous to centralize the order flow. In a decentralized dealer market (like, for example, NASDAQ) each dealer only knows the identities of a subset of those who have traded. In the more centralized specialist system, on the other hand, the information is centralized at the specialist's desk.[17]

If the specialist is to make use of his information he must be able to price-discriminate. This is, however, easily achieved. The specialist may quote a large spread and offer price improvement to counter parties deemed uninformed (i.e. he executes transactions initiated by these traders at prices inside the quoted spread). Price improvement is thus explained by lower adverse selection costs. This has two testable implications:

1. Granting price improvement does not reduce the specialist's profits.
2. Since price improvement is offered because the adverse selection risk is lower, price-improved transactions contain less information about the future price of the stock. Consequently, there is less need to adjust the quoted prices after the transaction.

---

[15] Note that it is not required that the specialist is able to identify informed traders with certainty. It is sufficient if he is able to correctly assign to some traders a higher probability of trading on private information.

[16] See Benveniste *et al.* (1992), Chan and Weinstein (1993), and Desgranges and Foucault (2002) for a detailed theoretical analysis. The first two papers take into account the fact that traders on the floor are often brokers who represent customer orders.

[17] The empirical results in Garfinkel and Nimalendran (2003) are consistent with this interpretation. They analyse spreads on insider trading days, defined as days on which officers or directors have traded in shares of their company. They find that, in response to the higher degree of informational asymmetry, spreads increase both on the NYSE and in Nasdaq, but that the increase is more pronounced on the NYSE. The order flow is more centralized on the NYSE than in NASDAQ. This may enable the specialist to better exploit the potential benefits of non-anonymity.

Theissen (2003) uses data from the FSE to test these hypotheses empirically. He first documents that price improvement is frequently granted. On average, more than 40 per cent of the transactions are price-improved. Average effective spreads are 30 per cent lower than average quoted spreads. He then decomposes the spread into two components. The realized spread measures the revenue of the specialist, whereas the adverse selection component measures the amount lost to informed traders.

The results are fully consistent with the first implication. The realized spread on price-improved transactions is not smaller than the corresponding figure for non price-improved trades. A regression analysis including several control variables also yields the conclusion that there is no systematic relation between price improvement and specialist revenue. The second implication is tested by relating the adjustment of the quote midpoint after a transaction to the price improvement. It is found that the quote adjustment is significantly larger after transactions at a price equalling the bid or ask quote than after price-improved transactions. Again, the result is confirmed by a regression analysis which includes control variables.

The empirical work, thus, suggests that the specialist function is beneficial and may help to reduce adverse selection costs.

5.3.3. Screen Trading

In 1991 the electronic trading system, IBIS, was introduced. IBIS was an anonymous electronic open limit order book, organized as a 'hit-and-take' system in the terminology of Domowitz (1992).[18] In November 1997, IBIS was replaced by Xetra (Exchange Electronic Trading). Xetra is also used by the Austrian Stock Exchange and the Irish Stock Exchange. It is an anonymous electronic open limit order book with embedded call auctions. All stocks that are listed on the FSE are also traded in Xetra. Further, there are specific segments for foreign stocks (Xetra Stars). Table 5.4 presents a detailed description of the trading protocol.

Trading starts at 8:50 a.m. with an opening call auction. A second and a third call auction are held between 1:00 and 1:15 p.m. and at the close of trading (5.30 p.m.). Between the call auctions, continuous trading takes place. The trading session is organized as a continuous auction where investors can place limit orders or accept orders which were submitted by others. Trading is completely anonymous.

Since October 1998 there are designated sponsors for many stocks outside the DAX. In the (now defunct) market segments *Neuer Markt* and SMAX, each listed company was required to have at least one (SMAX) or two (*Neuer Markt*) sponsors. Since March 2003, firms are sorted into two categories according to their liquidity. Those in the low-liquidity category are only traded

---

[18] For a detailed description of IBIS see Schmidt and Iversen (1992).

Table 5.4. *Equity trading in Xetra*

Nature of trading system	• Electronic open limit order book
Trading mechanism by stock groups	• Liquid stocks: call auctions (open, intradaily, close) and continuous trading • Illiquid stocks: call auction
Call auctions	• Pre-trading phase with closed book, allows entry and modification of orders • Indicative prices are disseminated • Order imbalance information provided for DAX stocks and stocks with designated sponsors (see below) • Price determination based on volume maximization/order imbalance/reference price • Random price determination time
Admissible order types	• Market, limit, market-to-limit, stop orders • Additional execution conditions admissible: immediate-or-cancel, fill-or-kill • Validity constraints: good-for-day, good-till-date, good-till-cancelled (maximum validity 90 days) • Admissible trading restrictions, for example, auction only, opening only • Iceberg orders: specify overall volume and peak volume; iceberg orders are not identified in the book; time stamp equal to time at which peak appears on the screen
Trading hours	• 8.50 a.m. (beginning of opening auction) to 5.35 p.m. (end of closing auction) • Stocks traded by call auction only: 1.20–1.25 p.m. • Xetra XXL (block trading facility): crossings each 15 min from 9.30 a.m. to 6.00 p.m.
Priority rules	• Price, time (except hidden parts of iceberg orders)
Transparency in continuous trading session	• Open book • Exception 1: hidden parts of iceberg orders • Exception 2: liquidity provided by designated sponsors upon quote request
Anonymity	• Anonymous • Exception: Designated sponsors know identity of quote requesting party
Clearing and settlement	• Settlement two workdays after transaction • Central counterparty to be introduced in 2003
Minimum tick size	• €0.01 • €0.001 for instruments with prices below €0.1

Table 5.4. *Continued*

Minimum order size	• 1 share
Designated sponsors/liquidity providers	• Mandatory for 'low liquidity' stocks that are to be traded continuously (Stocks are categorized as high or low liquidity stocks according to execution costs and trading volume) • Must participate in auctions and volatility interruptions • Minimum quote quantities, maximum spreads (differentiated according to liquidity) and maximum response time specified • Regular performance measurement, published quarterly • Privileges: reduced fees, designated sponsors learn identity of quote-requesting trader
Domestic parallel trading venues	• Floor trading on the FSE and seven regional exchanges; • OTC trading • Internalization of orders through XetraBest, PIP
Circuit breakers	• Volatility interruption if potential price outside pre-defined range around reference price 1 (the last determined price) or reference price 2 (last auction price) • The width of the ranges are not disclosed to market participants and are adapted to market conditions • Market order interruption: when market orders exist that are not executable • Trading resumes with call auction • Exchange can suspend trading in case of information events; orders in the system are deleted
Handling of block trades	• Specific block trading segment (Xetra XXL) • Matching of orders at the Xetra quote midpoint (i.e. Xetra XXL itself does not contribute to price discovery) • Anonymous, closed order book

continuously when they have at least one designated sponsor. The institution of the sponsor has been introduced in order to increase market liquidity. The sponsor has to quote bid and ask prices and participate in the call auctions. There are minimum requirements, differentiated by stock liquidity, for the spreads, the quoted depths and the participation frequencies in the call auctions. The sponsors are regularly rated by the exchange. The ratings are made public.

The coexistence of floor and screen trading raises the question of whether one of the systems is generally superior. The German market offers almost ideal conditions to compare floor and screen trading. Since both markets are liquid, operate in parallel, and are based in the same country,[19] many of the ambiguities present in other studies are absent.[20] Empirical research has addressed two issues, liquidity and informational efficiency.

Screen-based trading systems are likely to offer higher operational efficiency. The possibility of remote access to the system may increase the number of market participants and, thereby, liquidity. On the other hand, a floor-based specialist system may (as argued in the preceding section) be better suited to cope with adverse selection problems. When comparing floor and screen trading systems we should, therefore, expect

(1) to see a larger fraction of informed traders in the electronic trading system than on the floor;
(2) to find a larger adverse selection component of the bid–ask spread in the electronic trading system;
(3) to find that floor trading is particularly advantageous for stocks with high adverse selection risk.

Empirical research into these issues has been (and, to a certain extent, still is) complicated by the non-availability of comprehensive data sets including quote data from the floor. Schmidt *et al.* (1993, 1996) compare floor and screen trading for German stocks. They relate transaction prices from the floor to spreads from the screen trading system and find that transaction prices from the floor tend to lie inside this spread. This allows conclusions about the relative magnitude of the spreads in the two trading systems, but it does not allows to decompose the spreads into its components.[21]

Grammig *et al.* (2001*b*) have access to a more comprehensive data set. They extend the method developed by Easley *et al.* (1996) to compare the probability of informed trading on the floor of the FSE and in IBIS (the predecessor

---

[19] Quite a number of papers (see Breedon and Holland 1998 for a survey) analyse the parallel trading of German Bund futures on the (floor-based) LIFFE and Eurex (formerly Deutsche Terminbörse). These studies are potentially affected by the facts that, first, Germany is the home market of the contract (although the contract has been 'invented' by the LIFFE) and, second, the market shares of the two markets have differed substantially in almost every sample period.

[20] One limitation remains, however. Results of comparisons between two markets which exist in parallel do not necessarily carry over to a situation in which a floor-based or an electronic exchange operates in isolation.

[21] Besides that, there is a potential bias in the methodology. Observations are recorded conditional on a transaction occurring on the floor. If transactions on the floor occur when the floor spread is low, this may bias the results in favour of the floor.

of Xetra, in operation from 1991 through 1997). They find that, first, the probability of informed trading is significantly lower on the floor and, second, both the size of the spread and the adverse selection component are positively related to the estimated probabilities of information-based trading.

Theissen (2002*a*) uses the same data set to analyse the bid–ask spreads in the two trading systems directly. He confirms the hypothesis that the adverse selection component is larger in IBIS than on the floor. The effective spreads tend to be larger on the floor for large stocks and larger in IBIS for small stocks. To the extent that firm size is a valid proxy for adverse selection risk (an assumption substantiated by, among others, the results of Easley *et al.* (1996) who show that the probability of informed trading is negatively related to firm size) this confirms the conjecture that floor trading is better suited to stocks with high adverse selection risk. This conclusion is corroborated by an analysis of market shares. The market share of the electronic trading system is negatively related to the total trading volume of the stock and is at least partially negatively related to return volatility. Finally, it is documented that spreads in the electronic trading system respond more heavily to changes in return volatility.

What do these results imply for price discovery in floor and screen trading systems? As documented by Grammig and Schiereck and Theissen (2001), the anonymous electronic trading system attracts a higher fraction of informed traders than the floor. This entails the prediction that the electronic trading system will incorporate new information faster into prices. Three further arguments corroborate this prediction. Orders can be entered faster into an electronic system and the execution of an order is immediate. Further, it is easier to disseminate market information, thereby increasing the transparency of the market and the information available to the traders. Finally, greater pre-trade transparency allows the price impact of a trade to be more accurately estimated.

The magnitude of the transaction costs determines whether a trader can profitably trade on a given piece of information. Given the results on the relation between spreads and firm size described above, one should therefore expect the share of the electronic trading system in the price discovery process to be positively related to firm size.

Grünbichler *et al.* (1994) were the first to analyse price discovery in floor and screen trading systems using data from the German market. They compare prices of the DAX index calculated from stock prices on the floor to the prices of the DAX futures contract which is traded electronically. They find that the screen-traded future leads the stock market. The Bund futures contract, traded on the floor of the LIFFE and in the electronic DTB (now EUREX), has been analysed in several papers (Breedon and Holland 1998; Fraser-Jenkins 1998; Kofman and Moser 1997; Martens 1998; Shyy and Lee 1995). Although the conclusions reached in these papers differ (partly due to different sample periods), the results on balance indicate that the electronic market leads the floor. It should be noted, however, that the electronic market is the home market. Therefore, it may be the price-leader for reasons other than the trading mechanism.

The German stock market with its unique feature of parallel floor and screen trading has also been subject to empirical investigation. Kirchner and Schlag (1998) document that the prices in the electronic trading system adjust to the price established in the opening auction on the floor. Both Kempf and Korn (1998) and Freihube and Theissen (2001) compare the two markets using stock index data. Kempf and Korn (1998) find that the integration between the electronic trading system and the (equally electronic) futures market is higher than the degree of integration between the floor and the futures market. Freihube and Theissen (2001) document that the screen-based XETRA system contributes more to the price discovery process than the floor for the blue-chip index DAX. The reverse is true, however, for the mid-cap index MDAX.

Stock-level analyses are provided by Bühler *et al.* (1995), Kehr (1997), Kirchner (1999), and Theissen (2002*b*). The results do not support the hypothesis that one of the markets is the leader in the price discovery process. The latter paper provides evidence that the contribution of the electronic trading system to the price discovery process is positively related to firm size.[22]

Taken together, the empirical results support the hypothesis that floor trading has specific advantages that are most evident for stocks with high adverse selection risk. This does not necessarily yield the conclusion that floor trading should be retained. This is unlikely to be an efficient solution because it would entrench the coexistence of two trading systems for the same stocks. The results may, however, yield insights into the appropriate design of electronic trading systems. What appears to be important is that the anonymity of the trading system should be reduced. It may also be worthwhile considering the introduction of a specialist into the system, at least for less liquid stocks.

5.3.4. Governance Structure of the Exchange

We restrict the description to Deutsche Börse AG. Deutsche Börse AG operates the FSE, the electronic trading system Xetra and has a 50 per cent stake in the Zürich-based EUREX, the world's largest derivatives exchange. It is thus by far the most important exchange in Germany.

The roots of the FSE go back to the 16th century. The exchange was governed by public law and was, until 1991, run by the Frankfurt Chamber of

---

[22] Grammig *et al.* (2001*a*) analyse price discovery of dually listed stocks in Xetra and on the NYSE (which is organized in a way similar to the FSE). They find that Xetra dominates the price discovery process. The authors point out that this result is, at least in part, due to the fact that Germany is the home market.

Commerce and Industry ('Industrie- und Handelskammer'). Deutsche Börse AG was founded in 1990 as Frankfurter Wertpapierbörse AG and renamed Deutsche Börse AG in 1992. It took over the operation of the FSE and also operates the electronic trading system Xetra. Besides its stake in EUREX, Deutsche Börse AG owns a number of subsidiaries and holds stakes in a variety of companies, the most important being its 100 per cent stake in Clearstream International.

Deutsche Börse AG is owned by banks and other financial institutions. Until early 2001, banks owned 81.9 per cent of the capital. The regional exchanges held another 10.1 per cent and the specialists owned 5.3 per cent. In February 2001 Deutsche Börse AG went public. Approximately 25 per cent of the capital was offered to the public. This reduced, but did not eliminate, the majority control exerted by banks. The stake of the four largest German banks was reduced from 35.2 per cent to 25.1 per cent. According to German corporate law, a 25+ per cent stake ('Sperrminorität') is sufficient to block important decisions like changes in the corporate charter or seasoned equity offerings. In October 2002, Deutsche Bank AG sold its 9.3 per cent stake to institutional investors.[23] Therefore, banks are losing their role as the dominant owner group. However, the supervisory board of Deutsche Börse AG is still dominated by banks. It consists of twenty-one members, seven of which are employee representatives. The remaining fourteen members are appointed by the shareholders' meeting. At year end 2002, twelve of them were members or former members of the executive board of a bank or a bank subsidiary.

Although Deutsche Börse AG is a privately owned company, it is not completely free in the strategic decisions it takes. This is due to the ambiguous legal status of the FSE. Deutsche Börse AG clearly favours electronic trading and would probably dispense with the trading floor. There is, however, a legal debate about whether Deutsche Börse AG is allowed to do so. The FSE is governed by public law and is only operated (but not owned) by Deutsche Börse AG. Some authors argue that the allowance to operate the exchange entails the obligation to do so, and thus prevents a closure of the floor. Therefore, legal action may be required in order to promote some of the necessary changes in the structure of the German equity markets.

5.3.5. The Liquidity of the German Equity Market: International Comparison

In this section we present descriptive statistics on the liquidity of the German Stock Market using both trading volume and execution costs as measures of liquidity. Table 5.5 compares the trading volume (in US-$ million) and the

---

[23] When the transaction became known, Deutsche Bank stated that the transaction would not impair the good relation to Deutsche Börse AG. Only some days later, however, Deutsche Bank announced that it would introduce a system to introduce inhouse internalization of customer orders.

Table 5.5. *Turnover (trading volume in per cent of market capitalization):*
international comparison

	Germany	France (year 2000)	Japan (Tokyo)	US (NYSE)
Volume in 2001 (million US$)	1439.9	1064.9	1656.7	10,388.9
Turnover in 2001 (%)	118.3	71.9	60.0	86.9

Note: We only include countries for which volume figures according to the Trading System View (as opposed to the Regulated Environment View) were given. Figures for France are for 2000.

Source: DAI Factbook 2002, original source of data: F.I.B.V.

turnover (the ratio of trading volume to market capitalization) for four major exchanges. The figures indicate that turnover is higher in Germany than in other countries. It should be noted, however, that volume figures are known to be unreliable and should, therefore, be interpreted with caution.

Booth *et al.* (1999) compare quoted spreads for the thirty most liquid stocks from Germany's IBIS system (which, in 1997, was replaced by Xetra) to those from the 30 most liquid Nasdaq stocks. Spreads in IBIS are lower (0.83% as compared to 1.07%). Part of this difference is likely to be due to the fact that the German stocks are more liquid (in terms of volume) than their Nasdaq counterparts. In addition, the data used is from 1991. Using data from 1996, Ellul (2002) compares transaction costs in IBIS with those in the French CAC system and in SEAQ. Again, transaction costs turn out to be lowest in IBIS.

Jain (2001) collected data from Bloomberg for fifty-one exchanges. Table 5.6 summarizes some of his results on transaction costs. The German market is characterized by high turnover (defined as the ratio of trading volume to market capitalization). Transaction costs are measured by quoted and effective bid–ask spreads. Both measures indicate that transaction costs in Germany are lower than in the United Kingdom but higher than in the United States (and, particularly, at the NYSE) and in Japan.[24]

The Plexus Group (2000) also conducted an international comparison of execution costs based on the company's database. Table 5.7 is based on data which the Plexus Group, Inc., generously provided. The table reports transaction costs, measured in basis points, for large, mid, and small cap stocks. Negative figures correspond to positive transaction costs.[25] Figures are differentiated with respect to the relative order size (order size in relation to

[24] London Economics (2002) also compared transaction costs in different markets. Their approach does, however, suffer from methodological problems. To give just one example, the authors claim to have calculated effective spreads for far more German and French stocks than are continuously traded in these markets. We have therefore disregarded their results.

[25] The data is based on the costs of institutional trades reported to the Plexus Group, Inc., by its clients. A positive number indicates that the transaction costs were negative. This may happen if the institutions acted as suppliers of liquidity, thereby earning, rather than paying, the spread.

Table 5.6. *Liquidity: international comparison I*

	Volatility	Turnover	Quoted spread all stocks	Quoted spread top 15 stocks (%)	Effective spread top 15 stocks (%)
Germany	0.11%	2.38	3.65	0.86	0.73
UK	0.12%	0.42	5.21	1.46	1.25
US—NYSE	0.12%	0.65	0.74	0.20	0.09
US—NASDAQ	0.42%	0.61	2.67	0.52	1.02
Japan	0.10%	0.39	2.13	0.80	0.72

Source: Jain (2001: table 2).

the average daily volume of the stock in question). This differentiation results in a more detailed picture. The results indicate that trading midcaps in Germany is expensive. Execution costs for small and medium-sized orders in both large and small caps are similar to those in the United States. Large orders (where 'large' means orders exceeding 50 per cent of the average daily trading volume) are associated with high execution costs.

We do not have an explanation for the high transaction costs associated with trading mid caps. The high costs for large trades lead to the conclusion that Germany is in need of a cost-efficient market for block trades.

5.3.6. Recent Developments

Recently, the stock exchange came under pressure from different sides. Institutional investors throughout Europe began pushing towards a unified equity market at least for blue chips. They are aiming at a decrease in transaction costs, most notably clearing and settlement costs. Deutsche Börse AG has reacted to this pressure by attempting to merge with the London Stock Exchange (LSE) and by acquiring the 50 per cent of Clearstream it did not already own. After the failure of the merger with the LSE there has been room for speculation about future developments. Whether Deutsche Börse AG, which, as it stands, is isolated, can manage to prevent potential competitors from successfully entering the market is an open question. In a publication on behalf of Deutsche Börse AG, dated December 1999 (Dornau 1999), it is argued that Xetra is the cost leader and, therefore, the potential for new entrants is limited. This conclusion stands in contrast to the claim by some institutional investors that clearing and settlement costs are much higher in Germany (and Europe in general) than in the United States.

On the retail end of the market, some of the regional exchanges (most notably Stuttgart) as well as a number of broker–dealers are competing for the retail order flow. The Stuttgart Stock Exchange has taken several measures to increase its attractiveness for private investors. The exchange extended the

Table 5.7. *Liquidity: international comparison II*

Trade size	Small caps				Mid caps				Large caps				US very large
	Ger	US	UK	Jap	Ger	US	UK	Jap	Ger	US	UK	Jap	
Smallest	n/a	1.19	−39.61	n/a	−44.77	−10.20	−13.70	42.32	−13.21	−2.84	−0.47	−3.98	−1.02
2	−26.42	−31.59	−12.76	n/a	−54.50	−9.05	−9.89	−1.11	−7.00	−2.26	−15.32	6.30	−3.49
3	−33.76	−26.35	−42.88	n/a	−35.77	−8.34	−5.37	−28.98	−4.88	−9.50	0.13	−39.87	−10.36
4	−90.27	−18.84	−76.05	n/a	−31.79	−14.97	−19.05	−18.11	−24.83	−4.51	−12.89	−41.14	−15.12
5	−55.24	−25.88	−29.91	−73.00	−63.00	−20.13	−8.84	−23.49	−50.90	−13.22	−24.84	−47.21	−24.45
Largest	−180.00	−119.55	−55.20	−196.00	−162.88	−92.53	−35.52	−152.78	−117.11	−84.30	−61.52	−170.02	−51.00

Notes: The figures represent trading costs in basis points. For Germany (Ger), UK, and Japan (Jap), small caps are defined as companies with market capitalization less then US$1 billion, mid caps have market capitalization between US$1 and 10 billion and large caps have market capitalization of more than US$10 billion. For the US, the respective figures are (in billion US$) less than 1, between 1 and 5, and between 5 and 25. Very large US stocks are those with market capitalization in excess of US$25 billion.

Trade size is defined relative to the average daily trading volume. The six groups are defined as less than 10 per cent, between 10 and 25 per cent, between 25 and 50 per cent, between 50 and 100 per cent, between 100 and 250 per cent, and more than 250 per cent of the average daily volume.

Source: The data was generously provided by the Plexus Group, Inc.

trading hours, abolished minimum trade size requirements and guaranteed execution at a price no worse than the prevailing Xetra quotes. As a consequence, the Stuttgart Stock Exchange has substantially increased its market share and has forced Deutsche Börse AG to take similar measures. Very recently, NASDAQ has joined with the regional exchanges in Berlin and Bremen and three banks (Dresdner Bank, Commerzbank, and comdirect, a subsidiary of Commerzbank) to form NASDAQ Deutschland. Since 21 March 2003, NASDAQ Deutschland has been operating an electronic auction market with additional liquidity supply through mandatory market making. However, the new trading system did not attract sufficient order flow and was closed only five months after its inception.

Some broker–dealers, in conjunction with direct brokers, offer OTC trading for retail customers, mainly in blue chips. As there is no such thing as the US intermarket trading system, best execution is not legally enforced (but may be guaranteed by the broker–dealer). It appears that the economics behind this OTC trading are not dissimilar to the economics underlying the payment for order flow arrangements in the United States. Retail orders are less affected by adverse selection problems and are, therefore, profitable. It may thus pay to improve the service for retail investors in order to attract and execute their orders.

Large banks (most notably Deutsche Bank AG) have been striving towards the inhouse execution of orders. Inhouse execution may mean the crossing of customer orders or execution of customer orders against the book of the bank (i.e. the bank acts as a market maker). Apparently, Deutsche Börse AG considered this to be a serious threat to its position. In September 2002, Deutsche Börse AG, therefore, introduced a system called Xetra Best that enables participating 'best executors' to internalize customer order flow (or purchased order flow) and execute the orders in Xetra. The customer is guaranteed a price that improves by at least one cent over the price the order would have received had it been routed to the Xetra order book. By creating this system, Deutsche Börse AG supports the diversion of order flow from its own trading platforms, but participates, through royalties, in the profits generated by inhouse execution.[26]

However, the inception of Xetra Best came too late to prevent Deutsche Bank from introducing its own system, called the Price Improvement System (PIP).

Internalization, if performed on a large scale, potentially impairs overall market quality by cream-skimming uninformed order flow. Liquidity providers in the main market face higher adverse selection risks and may respond with higher spreads. These spreads, in turn, determine the prices at which the internalized orders will be executed. It is, thus, possible that internalization may lead to a general increase in transaction costs. The US experience with

---

[26] For a detailed account of Xetra Best (though in German) see Theissen (2002c).

purchased order flow has, however, shown that this is not a necessary consequence. Therefore, empirical studies are required before the economic consequences of internalization can be assessed.

5.4. CONCLUSION

The purpose of this chapter was to describe the German equity market and to analyse whether it is underdeveloped in terms of volume or operational efficiency and liquidity. The German equity market is, in relation to the size of the economy, small. This is a natural consequence of a bank-dominated financial system.

The microstructure of the German equity market exhibits a number of peculiarities that make it a worthwhile object of empirical investigation. In particular, the coexistence of floor trading and electronic trading is a unique feature. Empirical research, briefly surveyed in Section 5.2, supports the conclusion that floor trading has specific advantages that are most evident for stocks with high adverse selection risk. These results yield insights into the appropriate design of electronic trading systems. They should be interpreted as a guideline towards the improvement of electronic trading systems rather than as a defence of floor trading.

An international comparison of execution costs leads to the conclusion that trading mid-caps and executing large orders is expensive on the German market. We do not have a good explanation for the first result. The second result, however, points to a deficiency of the German market, namely, the non-existence of a cost-efficient market for block trades.

An analysis of recent trends yields a somewhat diffuse picture. On the one hand, there is a trend towards an international consolidation of markets in Europe, as attested, for example, by the creation of Euronext. On the other hand, proprietary trading systems and internalization lead to a fragmentation at least at the retail end of the market. In light of this the creation of an intermarket trading system that serves as a verifiable benchmark for best execution for customer orders should be considered.

Some of the recent developments in Germany bear many similarities to the evolution of trading systems in the United States. Much of the research devoted to the US market (dealing, for example, with payment for order flow), may thus ultimately become highly relevant for the German market and may provide useful guidelines for future development.

References

Benveniste, L., Marcus, A., and Wilhelm, W. (1992). 'What's Special About the Specialist?', *Journal of Financial Economics*, 32: 61–86.

Bhattacharya, U., and Daouk, H. (2002). 'The World Price of Insider Trading', *Journal of Finance*, 57: 75–108.

Boersch-Supan, A. and Eymann, E. (2000). 'Household Portfolios in Germany', University of Mannheim. Working Paper (July).

Booth, G., Iversen, P., Sarkar, S., Schmidt, H., and Young, A. (1999). 'Market Structure and Bid–Ask Spreads: IBIS vs Nasdaq', *European Journal of Finance*, 5: 51–71.

Breedon, F., and Holland, A. (1998). 'Electronic versus Open Outcry Markets: The Case of the Bund Futures Contract', Bank of England. Working Paper No. 76 (January).

Bühler, A., Grünbichler, A., and Schmidt, H. (1995). 'Parkett und Computer im Preisfindungsprozeß', *Zeitschrift für Bankrecht und Bankwirtschaft*, 7: 234–43.

Bundesaufsichtsamt für den Wertpapierhandel (2002). *Jahresbericht 2001* (Download: http://www.bafin.de).

Chan, Y. S., and Weinstein, M. (1993). 'Reputation, Bid–Ask Spread and Market Structure', *Financial Analysts Journal* (July/August): 57–62.

Chung, K., Van Ness, B., and Van Ness, R. (1999). 'Limit Orders and the Bid–Ask Spread', *Journal of Financial Economics*, 53: 255–87.

Desgranges, G., and Foucault, T. (2002). 'Reputation-Based Pricing and Price Improvements in Dealership Markets', Université de Cergy and Groupe HEC. Working Paper (January).

Deutsche Börse AG (2003). *Guideline to the Equity Indices of Deutschen Börse.* Version 5.1. March.

Deutsche Bundesbank. *Monatsberichte* monthly reports, various issues.

Deutsches Aktieninstitut. (2002). *DAI Factbook.*

Domowitz, I. (1992). 'Automating the Price Discovery Process: Some International Comparisons and Regulatory Implications', *Journal of Financial Services Research*, 6: 305–26.

Dornau, R. (1999). *Alternative Handelssysteme in den USA und in Europa.* Deutsche Börse AG (December).

Easley, D., Kiefer, N., O'Hara, M., and Paperman, J. (1996). 'Liquidity, Information, and Infrequently Traded Stocks', *Journal of Finance*, 51: 1405–36.

Ellul, A. (2002). 'The Dominance of Hybrid Trading Systems: An Analysis of Execution Costs, Market Depth and Competition', Indiana University. Working Paper (October).

Fraser-Jenkins, I. (1998). 'Open Outcry versus Electronic Screen Trading: A Comparison of Trading on LIFFE and the DTB between 1995 and 1998', Bank of England. Working Paper.

Freihube, Th., and Theissen, E. (2001). 'An Index Is an Index Is an Index?', University of Frankfurt. Working Paper (February).

——, Kehr, C.-H., Krahnen, J., and Theissen, E. (1999). 'Was leisten die Kursmakler? Eine empirische Untersuchung am Beispiel der Frankfurter Wertpapierbörse', *Kredit und Kapital*, 32: 426–60.

Garfinkel, J. and Nimalendran, M. (2003). 'Market Structure and Trader Anonymity: An Analysis of Insider Trading', *Journal of Financial and Quantitative Analysis*, 38: 591–660.

Grammig, J., Melvin, M., and Schlag, C. (2001a). 'Price Discovery in International Equity Trading', CORE at Catholic University of Louvain, University of Arizona and University of Frankfurt. Working Paper (February).

——, Schiereck, D., and Theissen, E. (2001b). 'Knowing Me, Knowing You: Trader Anonymity and Informed Trading in Parallel Markets', *Journal of Financial Markets*, 4: 385–412.

Grünbichler, A., Longstaff, F., and Schwartz, E. (1994). 'Electronic Screen Trading and the Transmission of Information: An Empirical Examination', *Journal of Financial Intermediation*, 3: 166–87.

Hackethal, A., and Schmidt, R. (2000). 'Financing Patterns: Measurement Concepts and Empirical Results', University of Frankfurt. Working Paper (May).

Jain, P. (2001). 'Institutional Design and Liquidity on Stock Exchanges', Indiana University. Working Paper (April).

Kehr, C.-H. (1997). *Preisfindung bei verteilter Börsenstruktur*. Wiesbaden: Gabler-Verlag.

Kehr, C.-H., Krahnen, J., and Theissen, E. (2001). 'The Anatomy of a Call Market', *Journal of Financial Intermediation*, 10: 249–70.

Kempf, A., and Korn, O. (1998). 'Trading System and Market Integration', *Journal of Financial Intermediation*, 7: 220–39.

Kirchner, T. (1999). *Segmentierte Aktienmärkte*. Wiesbaden: Gabler-Verlag.

——, and Schlag, Ch. (1998). 'An Explorative Investigation of Intraday Trading on the German Stock Market', *Finanzmarkt und Portfolio Management*, 12: 13–31.

Kofman, P., and Moser, J. (1997). 'Spreads, Information Flows and Transparency Across Trading Systems', *Applied Financial Economics*, 7: 281–94.

La Porta, R., Lopez-de-Silanes, F., Shleifer, A., and Vishny, A. (1998). 'Law and Finance', *Journal of Political Economy*, 106: 1113–55.

Leuz, Ch., and Verrecchia, R. (2000). 'The Economic Consequences of Increased Disclosure', *Journal of Accounting Research*, 38 (Suppl.): 91–124.

London Economics (2002). *Quantification of the Macro-Economic Impact of Integration of EU Financial Markets*. Final Report to the European Commission (November).

Madhavan, A., and Sofianos, G. (1998). 'An Empirical Analysis of NYSE Specialist Trading', *Journal of Financial Economics*, 48: 189–210.

Martens, M. (1998). 'Price Discovery in High and Low Volatility Periods: Open Outcry versus Electronic Trading', *Journal of International Financial Markets, Institutions and Money*, 8: 243–60.

Mayer, C. (1988). 'New Issues in Corporate Finance', *European Economic Review*, 32: 1167–88.

New York Stock Exchange (2000). *Shareownership 2000*. https://www.nyse.com/marketinfo/shareownersurvey.html

Nowak, E. (2001). 'Recent Developments in German Capital Markets and Corporate Governance', *Journal of Applied Corporate Finance*, 14: 35–48.

Plexus Group (2000). *The Cost of International Liquidity*. Commentary 61 (April).

Rajan, R., and Zingales, L. (1995). 'What Do We Know about Capital Structure? Some Evidence from International Data', *Journal of Finance*, 50: 1421–60.

Schmidt, H., and Iversen, P. (1992). 'Automating German Equity Trading: Bid–Ask Spreads on Competing Systems', *Journal of Financial Services Research*, 6: 373–97.

——, Iversen, P., and Treske, K. (1993). 'Parkett oder Computer?', *Zeitschrift für Bankrecht und Bankwirtschaft*, 5: 209–21.

——, Oesterhelweg, O., and Treske, K. (1996). 'Deutsche Börsen im Leistungsvergleich: IBIS und BOSS-CUBE', *Kredit und Kapital*, 29: 90–122.

Shyy, G., and Lee, J.-H. (1995). 'Price Transmission and Information Asymmetry in Bund Futures Markets: LIFFE vs. DTB', *Journal of Futures Markets*, 15: 87–99.

Erik Theissen

Theissen, E. (2002*a*). 'Floor versus Screen Trading: Evidence from the German Stock Market', *Journal of Institutional and Theoretical Economics*, 158: 32–54.

——(2002*b*). 'Price Discovery in Floor and Screen Trading Systems', *Journal of Empirical Finance*, 9: 455–74.

——(2002*c*). 'Internalisierung und Marktqualität: Was bringt Xetra Best?', *Kredit und Kapital*, 35: 550–71.

——(2003). 'Trader Anonymity, Price Formation and Liquidity', *European Finance Review*, 7: 1–26.

6

Monetary Policy Transmission and the Financial System in Germany

ANDREAS WORMS

6.1. INTRODUCTION

The monetary transmission process consists of the channels through which monetary policy ultimately affects output and prices. There are several ways in which a better understanding of it is beneficial for the conduct of monetary policy. For example, it may enhance the quality of judgements regarding the timing and the extent of interest rate decisions, it is helpful when assessing the extent to which previous policy decisions have yet to produce their full effect and it can be a useful guide when selecting adequate indicators for the stance of monetary policy.

Clear knowledge of the structure and functioning of the financial system is crucial to a better understanding of the monetary transmission process in Germany and in the euro area as a whole. One reason is that the monetary policy instruments of the European Central Bank (and before 1999 those of the Deutsche Bundesbank) are directly connected to banks. Banks, therefore, are the starting point of the transmission process. Hence, when analysing how monetary policy affects the euro-area economy, it seems only natural to look more closely at banks and at how possible effects of monetary policy are spread over the economy.

A second reason is that banks play a key role in the euro-area as a whole and specifically in Germany. As of 1999, the ratio of banks' total assets to GDP is approximately twice as high in the euro-area and in Germany as in the United States of America (Ehrmann *et al.* 2001: table 1). Moreover, the ratio of bank loans to GDP is more than three times higher in the euro-area and in Germany than in the United States of America. Of course, the other side of the coin is that debt securities issued by the corporate sector and stock market capitalization are only of minor importance compared with the situation in the United States of America.

This chapter expresses the author's personal opinions and does not necessarily reflect the views of the Deutsche Bundesbank.

It is for these reasons that this chapter concentrates specifically on the banks' behaviour in monetary transmission. More precisely, it addresses the question of whether the loan *supply* of banks plays an active role in monetary transmission or whether loans adapt only passively to monetary-policy-induced changes in loan *demand*. The answer to this question may, on the one hand, help to assess whether certain economic agents are more strongly affected by monetary policy actions than others. On the other, it may provide important insights for the assessment of possible asymmetric effects of monetary policy across the euro-area countries (Guiso *et al.* 1999). Furthermore, it could be of assistance in assessing how possible changes in the financial structure might influence the transmission process.

After presenting results on the overall effects of monetary policy on output and prices in Germany in Section 6.2, a short overview of the most important transmission channels is given in Section 6.3. Section 6.4 focuses specifically on the role played by banks in monetary transmission in Germany. The first part of this section supplies the reader with some information on the structure of the German financial system. The second part contains a short discussion of the existing empirical literature and the third part presents empirical evidence on the existence of a credit channel. This transmission channel is analysed in greater detail because it is of specific relevance for mainly two reasons. One is that it closely links the structure of the financial system to the way monetary policy is transmitted to output and prices; the other is that its relevance is currently intensively discussed. Section 6.5 concludes.

The overall results are compatible with the notion that there exist close *Hausbank* relationships between banks and their loan customers. One feature of such a relationship would appear to be an implicit insurance against shocks such as restrictive monetary policy actions. In this case, small and medium-sized banks, in particular, draw on their liquid assets—mainly on their short-term interbank deposits—to shield their loan portfolio. This is facilitated (or is actually being rendered possible) by the institutional structure of the German banking system, which is characterized by two banking networks (the savings banks' sector and the cooperative sector) within which funds can be easily transferred from large to small and medium-sized banks.

6.2. THE EFFECTS OF MONETARY POLICY ON OUTPUT AND INFLATION IN GERMANY

Large sections of the macroeconomic literature view the monetary transmission process as little more than a 'black box'. In order, for example, to assess the strength and the dynamic pattern of the effects of monetary policy on output and inflation, it would seem to be largely unimportant *how* these effects come about; in other words, which variables actually transmit changes in monetary policy instruments to the final variables may be irrelevant.

In the literature, the question of how strongly monetary policy affects output and inflation over time is very often answered by applying vector-autoregressive (VAR) methods to a small set of macroeconomic variables of interest. Generally, a VAR captures the joint dynamic behaviour of the considered variables. The first step of this research strategy consists of estimating an equation for every endogenous variable of the system. This equation 'explains' the behaviour of the respective endogenous variable by its own history and the movements of all other included variables. The result of this first step can be interpreted as describing the equilibrium of the whole system. In the second step, these estimations can be used to run simulations in order to obtain the reaction of all endogenous variables to a shock that disturbs this equilibrium. In the case of a 'monetary policy shock', for example, the error term in the equation of the monetary policy variable— which is typically the short-term interest rate—is (temporarily) set to a value different from zero. This would correspond to an *exogenous* change in the short-term interest rate. The effects of such a disturbance can be displayed by 'impulse-response functions' (IRFs) which show the simulated reaction over time of each of the included endogenous variables to the (exogenous) monetary policy move.

Figure 6.1, for instance, shows four such IRFs resulting from an exercise of this kind. They are based on quarterly German data which are broadly in line with the 'stylized facts' obtained and analysed in many related studies, also for other countries.[1] These IRFs are based on the estimation of a VAR over the period 1970–98 that contains, as endogenous variables, the three-month interest rate, the real effective exchange rate, real GDP and consumer prices, and, as exogenous variables, a world commodity price index, US real GDP and the US short-term nominal interest rate.

The upper-left IRF (see (a) in Figure 6.1) shows the behaviour of the 3-month interest rate after an exogenous increase of this rate by one standard deviation of the interest rate shock (which amounts to an increase by approximately 0.44 percentage points). After this exogenous monetary policy action, the short-term interest rate declines steadily and falls significantly below its initial level after about one year. It returns to its initial level after approximately 18 quarters. The exchange rate reacts immediately to the interest rate increase by showing an appreciation, subsequently falling back steadily (Figure 6.1b). It reaches its initial value again after about 12 quarters. Real GDP falls significantly below its initial value after approximately 2–3 quarters (Figure 6.1c). The maximum reaction of real GDP is reached after about 6–7 quarters. It attains its initial value again after 18 quarters. No significant price reaction can be observed until 6 quarters after the shock

---

[1] The VAR has been estimated by Mojon and Peersman, whom I would like to thank for allowing me to use their results (Mojon and Peersman 2001). For a comparable exercise, see also Mihov (2001).

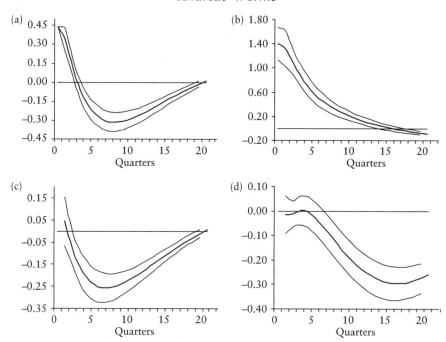

Figure 6.1. *IRFs of the money market rate (a), the exchange rate (b), real output (c), and consumer prices (d) to a positive interest rate shock.*

Notes: Interest rate increase by one standard deviation of the interest rate shocks, 90 per cent confidence bands. The underlying VAR consists of two blocks: **X** contains the exogenous variables (world commodity price index, US real GDP, US short-term interest rate), **Y** the endogenous variables (German 3-month interest rate, German real GDP, German consumer prices, real effective DM exchange rate). **X** influences **Y** (also contemporaneously) but there is no feedback. The analysis is carried out in levels to allow for implicit cointegrating relationships in the data. The data are seasonally adjusted logs, except the interest rates which are in levels. The VAR allows for a contemporary interaction between the interest rate and the exchange rate. The identification problem resulting from this is tackled by estimating the reaction coefficient on the exchange rate using the spread between the French and the German long-term interest rates and US$/Yen exchange rate as instruments.

Source: Mojon and Peersman (2001).

(Figure 6.1d). Afterwards, prices decline steadily, reaching a maximum effect after approximately 16 quarters.

As already mentioned, these results for Germany are broadly in line with those given in the relevant literature for other countries and other sample periods. An unexpected, temporary rise in the short-term interest rate tends to be followed by a temporary fall in output (of course, the strength of this effect depends on the size of the assumed shock). Prices are far more sluggish and start to decrease significantly only after a longer period of time.

6.3. THE CHANNELS OF MONETARY POLICY TRANSMISSION

While this VAR evidence helps to assess the timing and the overall effects of monetary policy on output and inflation, it cannot answer the question of how these effects come about, that is, through which transmission channels this outcome is created. Within such an analysis, therefore, monetary transmission remains a 'black box'. In order to shed some light in the darkness, it is necessary to go beyond such an analysis and to look more closely at those variables through which monetary policy actions may be transmitted.

While in reality the details of the transmission process of monetary policy are still insufficiently understood, economic theory distinguishes between and discusses several different monetary transmission channels (e.g. Mishkin 1996; Berk 1998). A simplified outline of the most important of these channels is given in Figure 6.2.[2] The starting point is a change in the central bank's monetary policy instruments (such as the official lending rates). Typically, this quickly leads to changes in money market interest rates (see (a) in Figure 6.2). Based on the expectation theory of the term structure of interest rates, according to which long-term rates depend on actual and expected future short-term rates (cf. Modigliani and Shiller 1973), this tends also to affect longer-term interest rates (Figure 6.2b). The strength and timing of this 'yield-curve

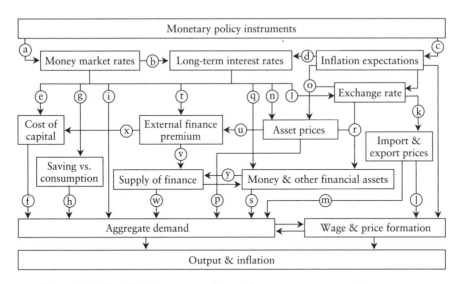

Figure 6.2. *Simplified representation of the monetary transmission process.*

---

[2] Figure 6.2 is certainly not exhaustive. Moreover, the effects of monetary-policy-induced changes in expectations are only roughly indicated (by 'inflation expectations'). Furthermore, Figure 6.2 does not contain feedback effects.

reaction' depends—among other things—on the extent to which the monetary-policy-induced change in the short-term interest rate is perceived as lasting. It is, therefore, closely connected to the issue of monetary policy credibility. Furthermore, it also depends on the effect that monetary policy has on inflation expectations (Figure 6.2c) because the latter influence market interest rates through the 'Fisher equation' (Figure 6.2d), according to which the nominal interest rate is approximately equal to the sum of the real interest rate and the expected rate of inflation.

These monetary-policy-induced changes in the sphere of market interest rates may affect aggregate output and inflation through a variety of different and intertwined transmission channels. Given this intertwining, it is difficult to clearly separate and structure the different transmission channels. Nevertheless, for present purposes, it may be useful to classify the transmission channels into those which crucially depend on the existence of imperfections in financial markets and those which can operate even if such imperfections are completely absent.[3] In line with large parts of the literature, the latter are referred to below as 'traditional transmission channels' (Bernanke 1983; Bernanke and Blinder 1992).

6.3.1. Traditional Channels

The interest rate channel comprises the more or less direct effects of interest rate changes on aggregate spending. It consists of several subchannels, one of which is the cost-of-capital channel, often believed to be one of the strongest in terms of the overall effect on GDP (McAdam and Morgan 2001): Owing to the existence of price rigidities,[4] a monetary-policy-induced increase in nominal interest rates implies an increase in real interest rates and eventually in the cost of capital (see (e) in Figure 6.2). This increases the cost to firms of holding inventories or of investing in equipment, machinery and real estate, which makes investment less profitable. If consumption is also (partly) financed by loans or mortgages, an increase in the cost of capital may also reduce consumption. This reduction in consumption and in investment leads to an overall reduction in aggregate demand (f).

The other side of this argument is that an increase in real interest rates also tends to increase the return on savings, making saving more attractive than consumption (g): private households tend to save a greater share of their

---

[3] Nevertheless, defining different transmission channels is always more or less arbitrary.

[4] Typically, three models of rigidities are distinguished: sticky wages, sticky prices, and limited participation models (Christiano *et al.* 1997). Sticky price and wage models are based on the assumption that price and wage changes are costly, so that a continuously changing pattern of prices and wages in reaction to shocks may be suboptimal. Limited participation models assume that nominal rigidities are due to the inability of households to quickly adjust their cash balances to changes in the environment; because households have only limited access to financial markets, they have to choose a portfolio structure for a comparatively long period of time.

disposable income in the light of monetary-policy-induced interest rates increases, which leads to a decline in aggregate demand (h).

Furthermore, a monetary-policy-induced rise in interest rates tends to bring about a direct increase in the disposable income of net lenders and worsens the cash flows of net borrowers (i) (van Els *et al.* 2001). In the literature, this effect is usually assumed to be fairly small because in case of an interest rate increase, lenders, on the one hand, tend to increase their spending, while borrowers, on the other, tend to reduce it. The overall effect is therefore unclear *a priori*. Since this channel leads to a redistribution of income among net borrowers and net lenders, its overall net effect depends crucially on the relative propensity of net lenders and net borrowers to spend. If net borrowers (mainly firms) have a higher marginal propensity to spend than net lenders (mainly private households), this channel leads to a reduction in aggregate demand in case of a restrictive monetary policy.[5]

The overall strength of the interest rate channel depends on the overall interest elasticity of aggregate demand—which itself relies heavily on the relative importance of the highly interest-sensitive components of aggregate demand in the economy (Issing 2001). With regard to the investment demand of firms, it is, for example, typically assumed that more capital-intensive production sectors, such as construction and manufacturing, are more interest-sensitive than less capital-intensive sectors, so that in countries in which these sectors are comparatively important, monetary policy should have strong effects through the interest rate channel.[6]

Moreover, the strength and the dynamic pattern with which monetary policy may affect GDP and prices through the interest rate channel depend on the existing financial structure. For example, interest rates tend to adjust faster in securities markets than in bank loan markets, so that it is typically assumed that, for instance, the cost-of-capital-channel needs more time to exert its effects on output and prices in a bank-based financial system than in a more market-based system. In addition, the degree of competition in various financial markets and the scope for arbitrage across these markets determine— among other things—the responsiveness of interest rates on new loan contracts (BIS 1995: esp. pp. ii–iv).

A further point is that both the adjustability of interest rates and the maturity structure crucially determine the speed at which monetary policy

---

[5] For a recent empirical analysis of the effects of interest rate changes on the income of German private households, see Westerheide (2001). Based on microdata on households, he finds only small income effects of interest rate changes. See also Hansen (1996), who analyses the impact of interest rates on private consumption in Germany. He finds a significant temporary increase in private consumption after a positive interest-rate shock which is due to the income effect. (Nevertheless, the overall effect of an interest rate increase on private consumption is negative.)

[6] See, for example, Hayo and Uhlenbrock (2000) and Carlino and De Fina (2000). Owing to the fact that the share of construction and manufacturing in GDP is relatively high in Germany and Spain (compared to the other euro-area countries), the latter study expects the interest rate channel to be particularly strong in these two countries.

actions are reflected in the relevant interest rates. For example, the larger the share of variable rate financing, the more important the income effects associated with monetary policy tend to be. Unfortunately, information on the degree of adjustability of interest rates is very limited (Borio 1995). However, in comparison with the United States of America and with many other European countries, characteristic of Germany would appear to be a small proportion of long-term loans at variable interest rates. This, combined with the fact that only a relatively small proportion of loans are short term (Borio 1996; Ehrmann *et al.* 2001: esp. table 3), would imply a comparatively slow (and possibly weak) response of firms' interest burdens to changes in short-term interest rates (Kneeshaw 1995: esp. 6).

The exchange rate channel stresses the fact that, in an economy with flexible exchange rates, monetary policy also works through changes in the exchange rate. According to the uncovered interest parity (UIP) condition, the nominal exchange rate is linked to the nominal interest rate differential between the respective countries by the market participants' arbitrage behaviour.[7] This typically implies that a monetary-policy-induced increase in short-term interest rates tends, ceteris paribus, to lead to an appreciation of the domestic currency *vis-à-vis* foreign currencies (see (j) in Figure 6.2). All other things being equal, such an appreciation increases the prices of domestic goods and services in foreign currency terms and, similarly, lowers the prices of foreign goods and services in terms of the domestic currency (k). This directly reduces consumer price inflation through its effect on import prices (l). Depending on the extent to which imported goods are used as input in the production process, this also tends to dampen domestic producer prices. Furthermore, by making exported products and services more expensive and imported products cheaper, the appreciation also has an impact on trade: in general, it leads to a lower volume of exports and an increase in imports, thus reducing real aggregate demand for domestic goods and services (m).

As regards the overall effect, the more open the economy, the more important the exchange rate channel should be for monetary transmission. The start of the third stage of European Monetary Union (EMU) has probably reduced its overall importance for the participating countries, due to the fact that the euro-area as whole is a relatively closed economy (Angeloni 2001; Issing 2001).

One of the most remarkable features of the exchange rate channel is that it may lead to rapid responses in some of the macroeconomic variables of interest. First, the exchange rate reacts rather quickly to monetary-policy-induced interest rate increases because there is only limited friction in financial markets (see the immediate reaction of the exchange rate in (b) of Figure 6.1).

---

[7] Typically, considerable deviations from UIP can be observed, especially in the short run. In this connection Taylor (1995) states that no single explanation for deviations from interest rate parity has yet been accepted.

Second, some empirical evidence indicates that changes in the exchange rate may quickly bring about corresponding changes in import prices, which, in turn, tend to affect the domestic price level accordingly.[8] Of course, the strength of this effect depends—at least in part—on the weight import prices have in the consumer price index.[9] On the basis of this argument, the frequent suspicion is that immediate reactions of inflation to monetary policy are mainly due to the exchange rate channel. Only afterwards do other channels, such as the interest rate channel, start to exert their effects on prices.

The way in which net exports are affected by changes in the exchange rate in the short run is not clear. It is possible that exchange-rate induced movements in the trade balance are characterized by an initial anomalous behaviour ('J-curve effect'). This could be the case if import and export prices react quickly compared to import and export volumes. An appreciation of the domestic currency in reaction to a restrictive monetary policy may, therefore, lead to a short-run *increase* in net exports.[10]

Monetary policy may also work through an *asset price channel* by affecting the value of financial assets, such as equities and bonds, and of real assets, such as property. This may be achieved, on the one hand, by changing the rate that is applied to discount future payments and, on the other, by affecting these payments themselves (see (n) in Figure 6.2). (Of course, monetary policy can also induce changes in asset prices through its effects on inflation expectations or on the exchange rate (o).) The wealth channel assumes that net wealth is a direct determinant of aggregate consumption, which therefore leads directly to a change in aggregate demand (p). If consumer spending is determined by the lifetime resources of consumers (human capital, real capital, and financial wealth), then a reduction in asset prices may put a downward pressure on consumption (Modigliani 1971; Mishkin 1996). Moreover, a monetary-policy-induced reduction in equity prices may also reduce the relative advantage of newly created capital over existing capital, rendering the creation of new capital less attractive, and thereby reducing aggregate spending (Tobin 1969; Meltzer 2001).

The *real balance effect* assumes a direct link between the volume of (real) money and aggregate spending. According to the conventional theory of money demand, a restrictive monetary policy reduces the amount of money

---

[8] Nevertheless, there is also evidence that points to the opposite. For example, in a summary of the results of almost fifty empirical studies, Menon states that the pass-through from exchange rate changes to prices is generally incomplete (Menon 1995). In a recent survey, Engel (2002) finds that consumer prices do not seem to be very responsive to exchange rate changes.

[9] Another important factor is the degree of competitiveness in the markets for import and export goods. For the estimation period 1975–95, Clostermann (1996) finds that—in the case of Germany—importers fully pass exchange rate fluctuations to their selling prices, whereas export prices remain largely unchanged when invoiced in domestic currency.

[10] Clostermann (1996) finds this initial 'perverse' balance of trade reaction to be present in Germany.

held,[11] since non-banks adapt their portfolios by switching to alternative types of (financial) assets in the wake of an interest rate increase (see (q) in Figure 6.2). Of course, a reduction in money can also be caused by other key variables such as changes in the exchange rate or in asset prices (r). If financial and real assets are substitutes in portfolios, then this will lead more or less directly to changes in these portfolios that cause a reduction in aggregate demand (s).[12]

6.3.2. Channels Based on Informationally Imperfect Financial Markets

All the aforementioned transmission channels work even in the case of perfect financial markets. For example, a monetary-policy-induced increase in the cost of capital—among other things—renders investment less attractive and thereby reduces the *demand* for funds. Accordingly, the volume of funds does not play an *active* role in these traditional transmission channels but rather adapts passively to changes in other key variables (Bernanke 1983; Bernanke and Blinder 1992; Cecchetti 2001).

However, there is an ongoing intensive debate as to whether monetary policy may also affect aggregate demand by changing the *supply* of funds. The 'credit-channel' argues that this is indeed the case by stressing the existence of informational imperfections in financial markets. The basic assumption is that a demander of funds is likely to have more information about his motives, the prospects of the success of a financing project and other circumstances relevant to the provision of the funds than a potential supplier ('asymmetric information'). Moreover, after the funds have been transferred, the supplier usually cannot monitor and control the actions of the demander completely. That may be tantamount to giving the latter an incentive to withhold disadvantageous information and to act in a way that is of benefit to him but detrimental to the supplier ('moral hazard').

The supplier tries to keep these risks as low as possible, for instance by increasing the amount of information (as far as possible) or by introducing certain contractual provisions, such as a demand for collateral. As a rule, however, such adjustment, monitoring, or incentive mechanisms increase the costs of the provision of funds; they result, for example, in more time-consuming procedures, constraints on the use of funds, or inflexibilities in the deployment of the assets used as collateral. Since that is detrimental to the demander of funds (as well), it is in his interests to keep the associated efficiency losses as low as possible.

Given such informationally imperfect financial markets, monetary-policy-induced changes in the supply of funds can—according to the credit channel

---

[11] For evidence relating to Germany, see, for example, Scharnagl (1998).

[12] See Meltzer (2001) and Koenig (1990). According to Woodford (2001), the 'real balance effect' is quantitatively trivial in practice.

theory—be due to two closely related sub-channels: the balance sheet channel, which stresses the differences between internal and external finance, and the bank lending channel, which stresses the differences between bank loans and other means of (external) finance.

6.3.2.1. *The balance sheet channel*

According to the cost-of-capital channel, a monetary-policy-induced increase in the real interest rate may render investment projects unattractive, leading to a reduction in aggregate demand (see (e) and (f) in Figure 6.2). The underlying concept can be expressed as a reduction of the (net) present value of the expected *future* payments caused by the interest-rate increase, which is either due to an increase of the discount rate that is applied to future payments and/ or to a reduction of these expected payments themselves. Hence, the argument is based on information about the present value of the expected return from the respective investment project (relative to the cost of capital), and therefore independent of information about the actual or former (balance sheet) situation of the borrower.

This independence no longer holds if financial markets are characterized by asymmetric information and moral hazard. In this case, external funding entails 'agency costs' which can be avoided by the investor as long as he is able to raise funds internally. The difference between the price of a unit of internal finance and a unit of external finance, the 'external finance premium', is dependent on several factors. For example, it is typically assumed to increase in line with the share of external financing in a borrower's total financing. Moreover, the external finance premium should decrease in line with a borrower's net worth (defined usually as the sum of the borrower's liquid assets and market collateral): The greater a potential borrower's level of net worth, the less the expected agency costs implied by the optimal financial contract will be, because a higher net worth enables the borrower to reduce his potential conflict of interest with the lender, either by self-financing a greater share or by offering more collateral to guarantee his liabilities (Bernanke and Gertler 1995).

This negative relationship between borrowers' net worth and the external finance premium has two important macroeconomic implications (Bernanke and Gertler 1989). First, the fact that net worth is likely to be procyclical, as borrowers are more solvent during good times, will generate a rise in agency costs, and therefore in the external finance premium in recessions and a decline in booms. This may lead to an exacerbation of business cycle fluctuations ('financial accelerator hypothesis').

Second, shocks to borrowers' net worth may alter the external finance premium and thereby cause real fluctuations. Such a shock could in principle be a monetary policy action. For example, higher interest rates caused by a restrictive monetary policy tend to increase the interest to be paid for outstanding debt. Ceteris paribus, this tends to lower borrowers' ability to generate funds internally, and therefore worsens their ratio of self-finance to overall finance.

This, in turn, tends to increase the external finance premium (see (t) in Figure 6.2). Moreover, a monetary-policy-induced interest rate increase tends to lower asset prices (n and o) which may reduce borrowers' net worth. While the wealth channel assumes the existence of a direct link between wealth and aggregate spending (p), the balance sheet channel stresses that monetary-policy-induced interest rate increases lower the value of those assets that can be used as collateral, which banks and other financiers request as a screening device and/or in order to create certain incentives. This may worsen the risk characteristics of potential borrowers, leading to an increase in the external finance premium (u). This tends to reduce the supply of funds (v) and/or to increase external financing costs (x). Both effects tend to dampen aggregate spending (f and w).

The 'pecking order hypothesis', which is closely linked to the credit channel theory through the assumption of information imperfections in financial markets, states that firms first use up their internally generated funds before asking for external funding in order to avoid—as far as possible—higher external finance premia (Myers and Majluf 1984; Fazzari *et al.* 1988; Myers 2001: esp. 91–5). Since an (unexpected) interest rate increase brought about by monetary policy may lead to an (unexpected) increase in the interest costs faced by firms—where the size and time patterns of this effect depend on the maturity structure of outstanding debt and the degree of diffusion of interest-rate-related derivatives—their net cash flow, and hence their ability to raise funds internally will, all things being equal, decrease as a result (Gertler and Gilchrist 1994: esp. 311; Gilchrist and Himmelberg 1995). Of course, the ability to raise funds internally can also be affected through other transmission channels. For example, monetary policy may reduce firms' (net) cash flows through the exchange rate or the interest rate channel by lowering their sales and turnover.

Ceteris paribus, that is, given constant expenditures, the reduction in internal funding will force firms to expand external funding. A *restrictive* monetary policy may, thus, have a *positive* effect on the *demand* for external finance— and thereby *increase* lending. This 'perverse' effect is fostered by existing loan commitments and lines of credit on which firms can draw quickly. In principle, however, this effect should become less important over time since credit lines will be used up and/or expenditures can then be adapted, resulting in a lower demand for external funds (cf. Worms 2001). This dependence of the demand for external funds on internal funds is sometimes labelled as the 'cash flow effect'. It is the most convincing explanation for the often found positive initial reaction of loans to restrictive monetary policy actions.[13]

---

[13] See, for example, Müller and Worms (1995) for descriptive evidence. Impulse responses with such an initial positive reaction of loans to a restrictive monetary policy shock can be found, for example, in Worms (1998) and Hülsewig *et al.* (2004) for Germany and in Bernanke and Gertler (1995) for the United States of America.

6.3.2.2. *The bank lending channel*

While the balance sheet channel refers to all types of finance, the bank lending channel concentrates specifically on bank loans. According to conventional money-demand theory, an interest-rate increase introduced by the central bank tends to reduce the demand for money because non-banks adapt their portfolios by switching to alternative types of financial assets (see (q) and (r) in Figure 6.2). While the real balance effect assumes a direct link between non-banks' deposits (i.e. money) and aggregate spending (s), this link is only indirect in the case of the bank lending channel. Here, the reduction in deposits leads to a decrease in banks' liabilities and to a corresponding decline in banks' assets. This may force banks to reduce their loan supply (y), which tends to dampen aggregate expenditure (x) unless the reduction in lending is accompanied by a corresponding expansion of alternative types of financing. Therefore, for the bank lending channel to have an effect on aggregate spending, non-banks should be unable to completely offset the reduction in bank loans by accordingly increasing other types of finance (e.g. trade credit).[14]

However, a bank's loan supply may, in principle, remain unaffected despite the monetary-policy-induced reduction in deposits (in this case, (y) in Figure 6.2 would be weak), if

(1) the bank is able to raise sufficient additional funds by, for example, issuing bank bonds (Romer and Romer 1990); and/or
(2) the bank can draw sufficiently on asset holdings other than loans by, for example, reducing securities holdings or deposits held with other banks.

With regard to (1) above, it is sufficient for the existence of a bank lending channel that banks do not face a perfectly elastic demand for their non-deposit liabilities. In this case, a monetary-policy-induced reduction in deposits will not be completely offset by an increase in other liabilities since it increases banks' (relative) cost of funds (Kashyap and Stein 1994). There are several good reasons why it can be assumed that the demand for non-deposit liabilities is not perfectly elastic (Bernanke and Gertler 1995). One is that they are not (completely) protected by deposit insurance. Another is that raising funds by issuing securities probably creates relatively high (fixed) transaction costs so that this financing instrument cannot be flexibly used by all banks.

As concerns case (2) above, banks will completely offset a reduction in their liabilities by reducing assets other than bank loans only if bank loans and those assets are completely substituted. In this case, a bank would be indifferent to the ratio of loans to other assets. However, perfect substitutability is not a realistic assumption. Loans and other assets may even be complementary

---

[14] The literature considers this assumption to be somewhat less controversial. See Freixas and Rochet (1997: 165).

to each other to a certain degree.[15] Different assets have different earnings, risk, and liquidity characteristics and banks may want to hold a certain combination of these different assets (including loans) in order to diversify risks and manage their liquidity.[16]

Nevertheless, if banks maintain close and long-term relationships with their loan customers, it may well be that they hold certain asset positions precisely in order to buffer shocks that would otherwise hit the loan portfolio. Such close customer relationships are valuable for the bank because they may help to reduce the costs that are due to informational imperfections in financial markets: A long-term relationship which may be characterized by repeated contracts between the bank and a loan customer, permits, on the one hand, the building of confidence and reputation. On the other, it allows the multiple use of information already obtained and of experience previously gained (Petersen and Rajan 1994). Compared, for instance, with market-based types of financing, bank loans facilitate the realisation of these advantages because they tie the contracting parties to one another, and enable individual provisions to be worked out.

6.4. IS THERE A CREDIT CHANNEL IN GERMANY?

The existence of a credit channel has several important implications for monetary policy. First, marginal cost and earning considerations are not the sole factors relevant to investment and funding decisions; the availability of funds must also be taken into account.[17] Second, the overall effect of monetary policy on aggregate expenditure can no longer be completely characterised by a vector of price variables. It depends on additional factors, such as the propensity to supply funds, the average degree of substitution between different forms of funding, and the distribution of these substitution rates among economic agents. Moreover, since the credit channel increases the restrictive impact of monetary policy compared with traditional transmission channels, the more strongly declining income tends, ceteris paribus, to put a downward pressure on interest rates. The net effect of a restrictive monetary policy on the level of interest rates may thus be unclear *a priori*. As a result, the interest rate level alone may be an insufficient indicator for the effects of monetary policy (Bernanke and Blinder 1988).

---

[15] The empirical results based on German banks in Upper and Worms (2002) are compatible with imperfect substitutability between bank loans and other assets.

[16] In principle, the earnings, risk, and liquidity characteristics of a given asset portfolio can be arbitrarily changed by combining it with a certain combination of financial derivatives. However, this implies additional costs.

[17] This implies, for example, that a restrictive monetary policy may also hit investment projects that are still productive—in contrast to the cost-of-capital channel. This furthermore implies that the allocation of a possible monetary-policy-induced decline in output may be socially inefficient (Cecchetti 2001; van Els *et al.* 2001).

Third, the credit channel implies that the transmission process of monetary policy is dependent on the structure of the financial system. This means that structural changes in the financial area may affect monetary transmission. Moreover, this dependence implies that monetary policy may affect economic agents asymmetrically, depending on the degree to which they suffer from the relevant financial market imperfections.[18] Given the differences in the financial systems across the euro-area countries, this dependence may also imply that the monetary policy in the euro-area affects some countries more strongly than others (BIS 1995; Favero *et al.* 1999; Dornbusch *et al.* 1998; Ramaswamy and Sloek 1998; Guiso *et al.* 1999). In this sense, the question of whether a credit channel exists in the euro-area is also of specific importance for the monetary policy of the Eurosystem.

From the viewpoint of this chapter, this dependence between the financial system and the monetary transmission process generates specific interest in the credit channel. Furthermore, the question of whether a credit channel exists (and how important it is) is intensively discussed in the economics literature. Therefore, the rest of this chapter concentrates on the issue of whether there is a credit channel in Germany. Given that Germany is the largest economy in the euro-area, the answer to this question has some relevance also for the euro-area as a whole.

6.4.1. Key Characteristics of the German Financial System

6.4.1.1. *The importance of bank loans*

Some specific structural features of the German financial system may be important when analysing the credit channel. One is that the volume of bank loans to domestic firms and households relative to nominal GDP is high compared with other countries (Ehrmann *et al.* 2001: table 1) and increased steadily during the 1990s (see rows 1 and 2 in Table 6.1). Starting from 54 per cent for firms and 29 per cent for households (including non-profit organizations) in 1991, these ratios respectively reached 63 per cent and 45 per cent in 2000.[19] This indicates, ceteris paribus, a high and growing potential for a credit channel that operates through bank loans.

Another key feature is that bank loans are very important as a means of obtaining finance. Households raise funds solely in the form of loans, with bank loans making up nearly 94 per cent of total borrowing as at the end of 1998 (Deutsche Bundesbank 2000: 34). Moreover, the share of bank loans in firms' total liabilities amounted to around 46 per cent at the end of 1998

---

[18] Such asymmetric effects may also exist at the national level, for example, with respect to regions (see Carlino and DeFina (2000) and Samolyk (1994), which both relate to the United States) or sectors (see Hayo and Uhlenbrock (2000) for Germany, Ganley and Salmon (1996) for the United Kingdom, and Dedola and Lippi (2000) for Germany, France, Italy, the United Kingdom, and the United States).

[19] See Supplement 1 to the Monthly Report of the Deutsche Bundesbank, table I.7.

Andreas Worms

Table 6.1. *Bank loans to domestic firms and private households in Germany, 1991–2000*

Bank loans		1991	1995	1998	2000
To domestic firms/GDP (in %)[a]	1	54	56	63	63
To domestic households/GDP (in %)[b]	2	29	34	39	45
As % of total liabilities of firms[c]	3	51	47	46	37
As % of balance sheet total:					
Large firms[d]	4	9	8	8	8
Smaller firms[d]	5	26	27	29	27
As % of total bank assets:					
All banks[e]	6	42	41	37	35
Small banks[f]	7	53	57	59	60
Medium-sized banks[f]	8	49	47	46	44
Large banks[f]	9	37	33	27	24

[a] Stock of loans to domestic enterprises and self-employed persons (end of year) divided by nominal GDP. Based on bank balance sheet statistics of the Deutsche Bundesbank.

[b] Stock of loans to domestic employed and other individuals and to non-profit organizations (end of year), divided by nominal GDP. Based on bank balance sheet statistics of the Deutsche Bundesbank.

[c] Self-employed persons excluded. Based on financial accounts data which is related to nominal values for securities. A computation at market rates for securities would make the shares of bank loans in external financing turn out much lower, in part owing to the marked rise in share prices.

[d] Based on data of a cylindered sample of enterprises from the production sector, wholesale and retail trade and transportation. 'Small': enterprises with an annual turnover of less than DM 100 million resp. €50 million (for 2000), 'large': enterprises with an annual turnover of DM 100 million resp. €50 million (for 2000) and more.

[e] The sum of loans to domestic private non-banks across all banks, divided by the sum of the balance sheet total across all banks (end-of-year data). Based on bank balance sheet statistics of the Deutsche Bundesbank.

[f] 'Small' banks: below 75th percentile of the distribution of total assets across all banks in t, 'large' banks: top percentile (all other banks are 'medium sized'). 1991 refers to January 1992, in all other cases, end of respective year. Based on bank balance sheet statistics of the Deutsche Bundesbank.

Source: Deutsche Bundesbank.

(Deutsche Bundesbank 2001c: 62). However, as shown in Table 6.1 (row 3), this percentage share has decreased over time: from an average of 51 per cent in 1991 to 37 per cent in 2000.

This overall declining trend is the result of an ongoing securitization process (Deutsche Bundesbank 2000). However, it is caused almost solely by the behaviour of very large firms. Table 6.1 shows that the ratio of bank loans to the balance sheet total[20] decreased for large firms (row 4) from 9 per cent in 1991 to 8 per cent in 2000 (row 4), while it increased slightly for small

---

[20] Note that the (levels of the) figures in row 3 cannot be directly compared with those in rows 4 and 5. The reason is mainly that row 4 is based on aggregate flow of funds data, while rows 4 and 5 are based on microdata from a sample of firms which is biased towards larger firms. Typically, those larger firms are on average characterized by lower loan-to-asset ratios. Nevertheless, the movements of those ratios over time should be representative and only those are interpreted above.

and medium-sized firms (row 5) from 26 per cent to 27 per cent (Deutsche Bundesbank 2001*c*; Friderichs *et al.* 1999). This indicates that the importance of bank loans as a means of obtaining external finance has not decreased for the large majority of small and medium-sized German firms, which are therefore of special interest in terms of the credit channel. This is compatible with the results presented in Hackethal (2001), who finds that in Germany the importance of banks as financiers of small and medium-sized enterprises increased during the 1990s.

6.4.1.2. *The structure of the banking system*

Table 6.2 presents some key figures on the structure of the German banking system. The upper part shows that credit cooperatives make up 70 per cent of all the institutions, whereas the savings banks make up about 18 per cent (column 1). The 'other banks' represent only around 12 per cent. This latter group is very heterogeneous and contains, for example, the four big banks ('Grossbanken'), the thirteen head institutions of the savings banks' sector and the four cooperative central banks (which are the head institutions of the cooperative sector),[21] foreign banks, private banks, and banks with special functions. Despite the comparatively small number of institutions, this latter group accounts for almost three quarters of all bank assets, while the many credit cooperatives together hold only 10 per cent (column 3). In terms of importance with respect to loans, the differences are not quite so striking, but still noteworthy (column 5).

Given that bank size plays an important role in the recent empirical literature on the credit channel, Table 6.2 also contains information on the size structure of the German banking system. The size groups are based on the distribution of total assets across all banks. Of the credit cooperatives, 93 per cent are 'small' (i.e. belong to the bottom three quartiles), while the majority (74 per cent) of the savings banks are of 'medium size'. The 'large' banks (defined as the top percentile, that is, the largest thirty-two banks in terms of total assets) consist only of 'other banks', that is, this group contains neither savings banks nor credit cooperatives (but eleven of the thirteen head institutions of the savings banks' sector and two of the four head institutions of the cooperative sector). These thirty-two large banks alone comprise more than half (55 per cent) of the total assets of all banks (column 3), the average bank size being about EUR 87.6 billion (column 7). This is very large compared with the average size of the 'smaller' (i.e. the small and medium-sized) banks, where the corresponding figure is only EUR 0.73 billion.

It is interesting, however, that the large banks' share of loans in total assets, at an average of 27 per cent, is far lower than that of the small and medium-sized banks (column 6). More generally, the lending business to domestic private non-banks seems to be of far greater importance for the smaller banks,

---

[21] Since October 2001, the number of cooperative central banks amounts to only two.

Table 6.2. *Structure of the German banking system (December 1998)*[a]

	No. of banks	Sum of total assets (EUR billion)	in %	Loans to domestic firms and individuals (EUR billion)	in %	Loans to total assets (4/2) in %	Total assets per bank Mean (EUR billion)	Total assets per bank Standard deviation (EUR billion)
Column	1	2	3	4	5	6	7	8
Total:	3228	4138	100	1886	100	37	1.6	10.6
savings banks	594	910	18	510	27	56	1.5	2.2
credit coops	2256	520	10	306	16	59	0.3	0.5
'other banks'[b]	378	3708	72	1070	57	29	9.8	29.5
Size groups based on distribution of total assets across all banks								
'Small' (bottom 75%)	2421	390	8	229	12	59	0.2	0.2
savings banks	157	54	1	31	2	58	0.4	0.2
credit coops	2087	303	6	185	10	61	0.2	0.1
'other banks'[b]	177	33	1	13	1	38	0.2	0.2
'Medium-sized' (75–99%)	775	1943	38	893	47	46	2.5	3.9
savings banks	437	856	17	478	25	56	1.9	2.5
credit coops	169	217	4	122	6	56	1.3	1.5
'other banks'[b]	169	870	17	293	16	34	5.2	6.6
'Large' (top percentile) (only 'other banks')	32	2805	55	764	41	27	87.6	58.7

[a] Based on the bank balance sheet statistics of the Deutsche Bundesbank. Some figures differ slightly from the data published in the Supplement to the Bundesbank Monthly Report (Banking Statistics) because a small number of banks were excluded in a data screening process.
[b] The head institutions of the savings banks' sector and the cooperative sector are assigned to the 'other banks'. For more detailed information on the size structure, see Worms, A. (2001).

that is, for credit cooperatives and savings banks, than for the large banks: On average, almost 60 per cent of the total assets of the small banks are loans to domestic private non-banks. This share amounts to 46 per cent in the case of the medium-sized banks (column 6). Moreover, Table 6.1 (rows 7 and 8) shows that the high share in the case of the small banks is the result of a steady increase during the 1990s, while it decreased for the medium-sized and the large banks in the same period.

Unfortunately, it is not possible to determine exactly the variation of loan customer size across banks, because detailed information on the individual borrowers of individual banks is not available. However, based on the breakdown of loans into certain borrower groups—as available from the *Bundesbank*'s quarterly borrower statistics—savings banks and credit cooperatives appear to give a greater share of their assets in the form of loans to those borrowers that may be assumed to be small or medium-sized on average. For example, at the end of 1998 more than 42 per cent of the loans of the saving banks and more than 47 per cent of the loans of the credit cooperatives were granted to individuals, compared with less than 14 per cent and 11 per cent respectively to domestic enterprises. By contrast, the 'other banks' on average hold 15 per cent of their loans *vis-à-vis* domestic enterprises but only about 14 per cent *vis-à-vis* domestic individuals.

6.4.1.3. *Close interbank ties within banking networks*
Overall, this picture is consistent with the idea that small and medium-sized firms and households are more likely to obtain loans from savings banks and credit cooperatives than from 'other banks' (see Hubbard 2000 for the United States). For that reason, they are of particular interest with regard to the credit channel.[22]

The savings bank sector and the cooperative sector can both be described as 'two-tier' systems consisting of a few large head institutions, which are the *Landesbanken* in the case of the savings banks and the cooperative central banks in the case of the cooperatives, and a large number of smaller affiliated institutions (Upper and Worms 2004: tables 2a and 2b; Ehrmann and Worms 2001). As for their interbank relationships, the cooperative banks and—to a lesser degree—the savings banks transact mainly with the head institutions of their own system:

1. On average, a savings bank holds almost two-thirds of its interbank *deposits vis-à-vis* the head institutions of its sector (see Table 6.3). In the case of the credit cooperatives, this share amounts to as much as 90 per cent. Most of these interbank deposits held with the head institutions have a maturity of up to one year only: 58 per cent in the case of the savings banks and 67 per cent in the case of the credit cooperatives.

---

[22] The large volumes of loans of the large banks (see rows 4 and 5 in Table 6.2) are probably mainly due to the fact that those banks give major individual loans to large enterprises which, however, have a number of other financing instruments available to them as an alternative to bank loans and are therefore of less interest to the credit channel.

Table 6.3. *Savings banks' and cooperative banks' book claims on, and book liabilities to their head institutions (as a percentage of their book claims on, or book liabilities to, all banks[a] in December 2000)*

	Savings banks	Cooperative banks
Deposits held with head institutions		
Short-term[b]	58	67
Medium-term[c]	3	19
Long-term[d]	4	4
Loans received from head institutions		
Short-term[b]	5	3
Medium-term[c]	0	0
Long-term[d]	54	70

[a] Unweighted average of the shares of the individual banks.
[b] Up to and including one year.
[c] More than one year but not more than 5 years.
[d] More than 5 years.

Source: Deutsche Bundesbank (2001c).

2. Fifty-nine per cent of the interbank *loans* of the average savings bank and 73 per cent of those of the average cooperative bank were granted by the head institutions of their respective system. While savings banks and credit cooperatives, therefore, hold mainly short-term deposits with their head institutions, they obtain mainly long-term loans from these bodies. This illustrates the strong maturity transformation that takes place within these two networks.

As a mirror image of these strong intra-sectoral links, savings banks and credit cooperatives hold only a small share of their interbank assets *vis-à-vis* banks outside their own system. By comparison, the links of the head institutions to banks outside their own system are stronger: they hold about 54 per cent (*Landesbanken*) and about 42 per cent (cooperative central banks) of their interbank claims *vis-à-vis* domestic banks that do not belong to their own system. Both systems, therefore, incorporate a kind of 'internal interbank market', with the head institutions providing the external links of their respective system.

6.4.2. Existing Evidence

In the preceding section bank loans were shown to be of specific importance for the financing of private non-banks in Germany. For a bank-based financial system of this kind, the question of whether a credit channel exists largely boils down to investigating whether there is an *active* role for banks, that is, for the *supply* of bank loans in monetary transmission.

One of the earliest studies that looked for a credit channel in Germany is Tsatsaronis (1995). On the basis of a VAR with macroeconomic time series, he finds the IRFs of money and bank loans to a monetary tightening to be inconsistent with the hypothesis that the resulting slowdown in economic activity is caused by a reduction in bank loan supply. He therefore concludes that the bank lending channel is irrelevant for Germany.

Based on a five-variable VAR, Guender and Moersch (1997) cannot find a significant reaction of aggregate bank loans to a restrictive monetary policy shock. Instead, loans react positively to a positive output shock. The authors interpret this as evidence to support the hypothesis that bank loans are driven solely by developments in the real economy and not by monetary policy. Therefore, they conclude that monetary policy does not work through the credit channel in Germany.

In a SVAR-analysis, Worms (1998) finds that a restrictive monetary policy shock leads initially to a significant increase in aggregate loans and only afterwards to a significant reduction. While the drop in loans is compatible with both the credit channel and traditional transmission channels, the initial increase is difficult to explain on the basis of the latter. He interprets this result as evidence in favour of the existence of a 'pecking order', according to which a restrictive monetary policy action reduces—by increasing interest rates— firms' ability to finance themselves internally. Given frictions in their expenditures, firms may then be forced to increase external finance, thereby increasing bank loans. The initial loan increase can therefore be interpreted in favour of both the existence of financial market imperfections (on which the 'pecking order hypothesis' as well as the credit channel theory are based) and the importance of close relationships between loan customers and their banks. The latter factor is the reason for banks' readiness to satisfy the initial increase in loan demand. However, the analysis is not able to assess the extent to which the resulting drop in bank loans is due to bank loan supply or demand factors.

All these studies are in the tradition of the early empirical analyses relating to the credit channel which mainly concentrated on the United States of America and looked at the timing of macroeconomic variables, such as money stock and real GDP. Basically, these studies test whether aggregate deposits (i.e. monetary aggregates) or aggregate bank loans can better forecast future income. They are based on the assumption that, given that the supply of bank loans plays an active role in monetary policy transmission, their volume should react immediately following a monetary policy action and (deposits and) GDP would move only thereafter. By contrast, if changes in the volume of bank loans are due mainly to demand effects (the volume of deposits and) GDP should react initially, with bank loans reacting only subsequently (King 1986; Romer and Romer 1989; Ramey 1993).

Nevertheless, the finding that deposits have a higher predictive power for future GDP than loans is also compatible with an active role of bank loan supply in monetary transmission: frictions such as contractual commitments and/or credit lines imply that the supply of bank loans cannot react as quickly to monetary policy as the volume of deposits. Even if there were no causal dependence between deposits (i.e. the money stock) and GDP, but merely between the supply of bank loans and GDP, one would naturally expect the predictive power of deposits to be higher than that of bank loans solely on account of the lead time of the former (Bernanke 1993; Gertler and Gilchrist 1994).

The literature on this subject has shown that the general problem of the analyses based on macroeconomic data is that movements in the *aggregate* volume of loans may essentially be interpreted as being induced similarly by loan supply as well as by loan demand: 'It is not possible using reduced-form estimates based on aggregate data alone, to identify whether bank balance sheet contractions are caused by shifts in loan supply or loan demand' (Cecchetti 1995: 92).

One way of tackling this identification problem is to give more structure to the estimations. Hülsewig *et al.* (2004), for example, try to cope with the supply-demand identification problem using a Vector Error Correction Model (VECM) that allows structural long-run loan demand and supply functions to be estimated. They find that a restrictive monetary policy shock affects both long-run loan demand and supply. The latter result is interpreted by the authors as evidence in favour of the credit channel. The major drawback of their methodology is that the supply–demand identification is only possible for long-run relationships. Therefore, the authors are not able to assess the extent to which short-run movements of the loan volume are due to demand or supply effects.

Another way to tackle the supply–demand identification problem is to exploit the heterogeneity across different (groups of) agents by analysing microdata—for example, balance sheet data of individual banks and/or firms—or data that were aggregated merely up to the level of certain groups of economic agents (Cecchetti 2001). This research strategy is based on the idea that if the theoretical foundations of the credit channel are valid, certain economic agents should react more strongly to monetary policy than others. In this connection, it is typically assumed that potential suppliers of finance see large firms as representing less pronounced information and incentive problems than small firms, possibly because they are more closely observed and controlled by the general public or because their overall business is less risky.

One should, therefore, expect restrictive monetary policy to have more marked effects on small than on large firms. Following this line of argument in his descriptive–statistical analysis, Stöss (1996) was unable to find any indication of banks discriminating against smaller enterprises in the wake of a restrictive monetary policy stance. Applying panel-econometric techniques to a sample of German manufacturing firms, von Kalckreuth (2001) finds that a firm's rating (which is used as an indicator of its financial health) significantly influences its investment decisions. The author interprets this as evidence in support of the credit channel, but stresses that this influence is very weak, so that this channel is of only minor importance. A similar conclusion is reached by Ehrmann (2000), who studies the response of firms' business conditions to monetary policy. He finds evidence that small firms are affected more strongly than large firms, and that these effects are somewhat reinforced during recessions.

The strategy of tackling the identification problem by exploiting hetero-geneity can be applied to banks, too. The idea that banks also face information and incentive problems when raising funds gives rise to the assumption that external finance premia also differ from one bank to another (Kashyap and Stein 2000). In parallel to the firms' case it is assumed that the external finance premium (and its monetary-policy-induced increase) is dependent on certain characteristics of the bank. If banks react differently to monetary policy because of a factor that is related to loan supply and not to loan demand, this differential loan reaction indicates a loan supply effect of monetary policy (Kashyap *et al.* 1993; Gertler and Gilchrist 1994). Typically, as for firms, size is used as the identifying variable. The idea is based on the assumption that bank size can serve as an indicator of the degree to which banks—as demanders of funds—suffer from informational imperfections in financial markets. For instance, large banks are rated much more intensively and are possibly far better diversified than small banks. This would imply that small banks encounter greater difficulties than large banks in attracting funds. Therefore, it should follow that small banks are forced to reduce their supply of loans more sharply than large banks in response to a restrictive monetary policy.

Following this argument, Küppers (2001) uses data that are disaggregated to the level of bank groups which differ with respect to the size of the average bank (savings banks, cooperative banks, and others). The point estimates of the resulting impulse responses show some differences across these bank groups in the way their loans react to monetary policy; these differences are consistent with an active role of banks in monetary transmission. However, his IRFs show large confidence intervals and a test for statistical significance of the differences between them—which has not been conducted—would prob-ably not lead to significant results. Kakes and Sturm (2001) also use data on different banking groups to estimate IRFs of their loan reaction to monetary policy. They also find evidence for a differential reaction of these banking groups to monetary policy, but their analysis suffers from the same problem of the significance of these differences being hard to assess.

Favero *et al.* (1999) and DeBondt (1999*b*) use microdata on a sample of banks to look for evidence of the credit channel. The first study looks at a short episode in 1992 when monetary conditions were tightened throughout Europe. The authors analyse four European countries but do not find evidence of a significant response of bank loans to the monetary tightening in any of them, including Germany. They interpret this as evidence that the credit channel does not exist. DeBondt's analysis is also based on a sample of banks' balance sheets but he runs panel estimations of a reduced form equation for a longer sample period. In the case of Germany, he finds evidence for a differential reaction of loans across banks which is interpreted as indicating the existence of the credit channel.

6.4.3. Results from Estimations Based on all German Banks

The bank-related studies listed above have some drawbacks. They are either based on grouped data (e.g. Küppers 2001) or cover only a sample of banks that is typically biased towards large banks (e.g. DeBondt 1999*b*).[23] Moreover, they do not allow for bank–individual changes in loan demand. Worms (2003) tries to overcome these shortcomings by (i) using a quarterly dataset covering the entire banking population in Germany on an individual basis, (ii) by explicitly taking into account bank–individual seasonal patterns and (iii) by using bank-specific income and risk variables to improve the control for *differential* loan demand effects.

6.4.3.1. *A first approach*

Worms (2003) tests the hypothesis that a bank's reaction to monetary policy depends on its size by estimating an equation of the following type:

$$\alpha(L)\Delta \log C_{n,t} = \beta_n + \gamma(L)[\Delta i_t \cdot \text{size}_n] + \Phi(L)\Delta X_{n,t} + d_t + \varepsilon_{n,t}. \tag{1}$$

(1) can be interpreted as the reduced form of a simple loan market model (Ehrmann *et al.* 2001). $C_{n,t}$ is the stock of loans to domestic private non-banks of bank n in quarter t (Δ indicates first differences, L is a lag operator), i_t is the short-term interest rate which serves as the indicator of monetary policy[24] and $\varepsilon_{n,t}$ is the error term. (1) allows for a bank-specific fixed effect β_n, that is, a bank-specific constant. size_n is the size of bank n, defined as the sum of total assets taken as a logarithm. Since the hypothesis test consists of looking for *differences* in the loan reaction across banks, the influence of pure time series (e.g. aggregate income and Δi_t) on loan growth is completely eliminated by including a set of time dummies d_t.[25]

A bank's loan reaction to monetary policy Δi_t is assumed to depend linearly on the bank's size. This is captured by the interaction term $[\Delta i_t \cdot \text{size}_n]$. Its

---

[23] The reason for this is that microdata on all German banks is not available to the general public. For the coverage of the publicly available and widely used database BankScope relative to the overall population of banks, see Ehrmann *et al.* (2001).

[24] For a discussion of different indicators of monetary policy, see Worms (2001) and the literature cited there.

[25] While this has the drawback of the (average) level effect of monetary policy also being captured by these dummies, that is, that i_t cannot be included as such, it guarantees a perfect control for the time effect on the endogenous variable and thereby enhances the power of the hypothesis test. Comparable estimations including time series (such as i_t) instead of a set of dummies are presented in Worms (2001) and Ehrmann *et al.* (2001).

long-run coefficient γ can be used to test for loan supply effects of monetary policy if loan movements caused by (i) loan demand or (ii) by loan supply factors other than monetary policy are adequately captured by the bank–individual control variables contained in $\mathbf{X}_{n,t}$ (and the time dummies). These are (the logarithm of) an income variable, $y_{n,t}$, and (the logarithm of) a default risk measure, $\mathrm{risk}_{n,t}$. The income of bank n's loan customers y_n is approximated by an average of sectoral real incomes (of nine production sectors and private households), with sector j's real income y^j being weighted by this sector's share in bank n's loan portfolio. $\mathrm{risk}_{n,t}$ is a sectoral average of the number of insolvencies. Sector j's insolvencies ins^j are weighted by this sector's share in bank n's loan portfolio.[26]

Equation (1) is estimated by applying GMM panel-estimation techniques as described in Arellano and Bond (1991). The database consists of quarterly data taken from the Bundesbank's bank balance sheet statistics covering the whole German banking population.[27] The sample period spans 1992–98. All bank-specific variables are seasonally adjusted on a bank-individual basis in order to allow for bank-specific seasonality. The main results are as follows.

1. The long-run coefficients of the control variables have the expected signs and are significant: a bank's loans increase with income and decrease with risk.
2. The long-run coefficient of the interaction term is insignificant: a bank's reaction to monetary policy does not (directly) depend on its size. This is contrary to what the credit channel theory would predict and also contrasts with the results of the existing empirical literature on the United States of America and on many other countries (cf. table 6.1; DeBondt 1999*a*).

6.4.3.2. *Interbank lending and monetary transmission*
Given the close interbank links of savings banks and cooperative banks to their head institutions (see Section 6.4.1.3), it may well be that in case of a restrictive monetary policy action, funds are channelled from the head institutions to their affiliated smaller institutions, thus counteracting potential funding problems otherwise faced by these small banks.

This has been analysed by Ehrmann and Worms (2001) within a VAR containing a short-term interest rate i, an inflation variable p and a variable for real output y. In their study, all banks are categorized into size groups based on the distribution of total assets across all banks (the bottom three

---

[26] size_n is also included in $\mathbf{X}_{n,t}$ in a non-interacted fashion in order to prevent that possible direct effects of this variable on loan growth are captured by the γ-coefficients.

[27] Due to the fact that the bank–individual variables are based on balance sheet data, a specific endogeneity problem emerges: if bank loans and other balance sheet positions are strongly correlated, it is not clear *a priori* which position drives the other. The following regressions cope with this problem in two ways: First, based on the Arellano and Bond procedure, all right-hand variables are instrumentalized by their lagged levels (GMM instruments). Second, the right-hand variables do not enter the regression contemporaneously.

quartiles: 'small'; as from and including the 95th percentile: 'large'; all others: 'medium-sized'). To be able to assess the response of various interbank variables to a monetary shock, the model also contains a net interbank variable l (interbank claims less interbank liabilities), for example, the net interbank claims of large banks *vis-à-vis* banks within the sectors, l_L (the large banks' 'intra-sectoral net interbank claims').

Monetary policy shocks are identified by two assumptions: (i) in the long run, all variables return to their initial value and (ii) interest rate shocks do not affect inflation and output as early as the same month. Figure 6.3 presents four IRFs to an exogenous increase in the short-term interest rate. Figure 6.3(a) shows that, after the shock, the net claims of large banks on banks outside their own sector drop significantly. This implies that large banks raise loans from other banks and/or reduce the balances they hold with other banks. A more detailed analysis shows that these funds come primarily from foreign banks.

In the case of small banks, no significant response of net claims on banks outside their own sector can be discerned (Figure 6.3b). However, their intrasectoral net interbank claims decrease immediately (Figure 6.3d). A more detailed analysis shows that this is mainly because small banks run down their short-term balances held with the large institutions in their own sector. As a mirror image, that reduction is accompanied by a rise in the intra-sectoral net interbank claims of large banks, mainly because their interbank liabilities decrease correspondingly (Figure 6.3c).

6.4.3.3. *The key role of short-term interbank deposits*
After a restrictive monetary policy shock funds, therefore, flow from the head institutions to the smaller banks of their respective system (Ehrmann and Worms 2001). These flows are mainly reductions of short-term deposits held by the small banks with the large banks. This is compatible with the notion that small banks reduce their short-term interbank deposits in order to cushion the effect of a restrictive monetary policy on their loans to private non-banks. Behaviour of this kind may be the reason why bank size did not emerge as a significant determinant of a bank's reaction to monetary policy.

Nevertheless, it is not clear whether the monetary-policy-induced interbank flows shown in Figure 6.3 are sufficient to offset possible bank-size-related effects completely. In order to test whether size effects are present once we check for the role played by short-term interbank deposits, the percentage share of interbank deposits with a maturity of up to three months in total assets, *ibk*, is additionally included.[28] The results can then be summarized as follows:

1. Like in the previous regression, the long-run coefficients of the control variables are significant and show the expected signs.

---

[28] Equation (1) is enhanced to include two interaction terms, $[\Delta i \cdot size]$ and $[\Delta i \cdot ibk]$. Moreover, the respective 'double interaction term' $[\Delta i \cdot size \cdot ibk]$ is also included to allow for possible second order effects (furthermore, size, *ibk* and size $\cdot$ *ibk* are also included in a non-interacted fashion).

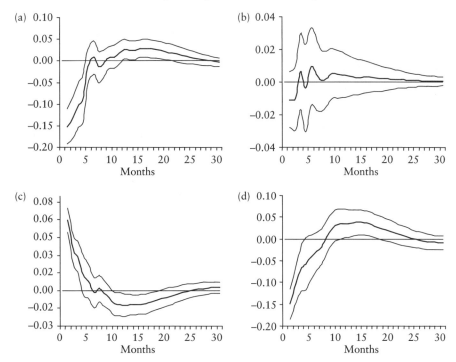

Figure 6.3. *IRFs of an interest rate shock to different interbank variables.*
Net interbank claims on banks outside a bank's own sector: (a) Large banks and
(b) Small banks. Net interbank claims on banks in a bank's own sector:
(c) Large banks and (d) Small banks.

Notes: Interest rate shock amounting to 2.5 basis points, which is equivalent to one standard deviation of the interest rate shocks; confidence interval: 90 per cent. The estimates are based on monthly data from 1992 to 1998 (from 1999, new definitions in the banking statistics). The vector of the variables is $X = [i, p, y, l_L, l]$: $i = 3$-month interest rate, $p =$ annualised monthly producer price inflation (is less subject to distortions due to German reunification than, say, consumer price inflation), $y =$ logarithmed index of industrial output (because of monthly recurrence), $l_L =$ net intra-sectoral interbank claims of large banks, $l =$ other net interbank claims of interest. If l_L is the interbank variable of interest, X consists only of $i, p, y,$ and l_L, (there are, correspondingly, only three cointegration vectors). The net interbank claims l and l_L are expressed here as a percentage of the corresponding total net assets.

Source: Ehrmann and Worms (2001).

2. The long-run coefficient of the interaction of *ibk* with Δi is significantly positive: A bank reduces its loans in response to an increase in the interest rate the less, the higher the share of short-term interbank deposits in total assets held by this bank.

3. The coefficient of the interaction of *size* with Δi is now significantly positive. Therefore, when controlling for the influence of short-term interbank deposits on a bank's reaction to monetary policy, a positive

size dependence can be found: ceteris paribus, the larger a bank is, the less it restricts its loans in response to a monetary-policy-induced interest rate increase.

This latter result is in line with the *credit channel* theory. However, the fact that such a positive coefficient of the size-interaction term does not show up in the first regression indicates that the effect of size is overruled by the influence exerted by short-term interbank deposits: The interbank flows between small and large banks that can be observed in reaction to a monetary policy action according to Ehrmann and Worms (2001) seem to be strong enough to dominate an existing differential behaviour with respect to bank size. The credit channel exists, but seems to be weak owing to the liquidity management of banks.

Result (2) implies that, ceteris paribus, a (potential) loan customer from a bank with a high share of short-term interbank deposits tends on average to suffer less from a monetary-policy-induced interest rate increase than does a loan customer of a bank with a small share. Therefore, banks that seek to shield their loan customers from a restrictive monetary policy—for example, because they maintain close *Hausbank* relationships with their loan customers (e.g. Elsas and Krahnen 1998)—would appear to hold comparatively large amounts of short-term interbank deposits in order to be able to draw on these in case of a squeeze in liquidity. This is fairly common practice among the smaller banks which are mainly savings banks and credit cooperatives. Moreover, given their local representation, these banks are especially designed in such a way as to ensure close (and ongoing) relationships with their loan customers.

All in all, the evidence presented in this chapter indicates that a credit channel does exist, i.e. monetary policy does have loan supply effects in Germany, but that owing to the specific structure of the German banking system, these effects are comparatively weak. On the one hand, smaller banks entertain local *Hausbank* relationships,[29] and therefore have an incentive to shield their loan portfolio from a restrictive monetary policy. On the other, the close interbank links that exist within the savings banks' sector and the cooperative sector enable smaller banks to quickly adapt their assets holdings so that this shielding actually becomes feasible.

6.5. SUMMARY AND CONCLUSIONS

After discussing some macroeconomic evidence on the overall effects of monetary policy on output and inflation, this chapter presented a brief overview of different transmission theories that stress various channels through which these effects may come about. However, despite considerable efforts in empirical research, the monetary transmission process still remains something of a 'black box'.

---

[29] See Berger *et al.* (2002) for recent evidence on the role of small banks in relationship lending in the United States.

Recently, a rapidly growing theoretical and empirical literature has been stressing the role of financial factors in the transmission of monetary policy. There are good reasons to believe that such factors, especially the structure of the banking system, are important for a better understanding of the monetary transmission process in Germany, too. On the one hand, the monetary policy instruments of the ECB are directly connected to banks; on the other, bank loans are a major means of raising external finance in Germany, especially for small and medium-sized firms and households.

A key feature of the German banking system is the existence of two close banking networks, the savings banks' sector and the cooperative sector. Both sectors consist, on the one hand, of a large number of small and medium-sized banks. On the other, they contain large banks which serve as head institutions to their respective network. The small and medium-sized banks hold comparatively large amounts of short-term deposits with the head institutions of their respective system, while at the same time the head institutions lend long-term to their affiliated smaller institutions. Hence, this 'internal interbank market' is characterized by close intra-sectoral links and a considerable degree of maturity transformation. This enables the smaller banks to draw on their liquid interbank assets easily and quickly in case of a monetary-policy-induced liquidity squeeze.

On the basis of this institutional structure, small and medium-sized German banks are better able than their US counterparts, for instance, to shield their loan portfolio against monetary policy. This is in line with the notion that smaller German banks, in particular, often serve as *Hausbank*s to their customers and that an implicit insurance against restrictive monetary policy shocks may be part of such a close lending relationship. Moreover, the structure of the German banking system supports this undertaking. On the one hand, since they are large in number, the cooperative and savings banks are well represented locally. This fosters their role as *Hausbank*s because it facilitates direct monitoring and close (personal) ties with the loan customers. On the other hand, within the two networks, the smaller banks are closely linked to large banks so that these *Hausbank*s are able to adjust their liquid assets quickly in the light of monetary policy shocks.

References

Angeloni, I. (2001). 'Discussion of Legal Structure, Financial Structure and the Monetary Transmission Mechanism', in Deutsche Bundesbank (ed.), *The Monetary Transmission Process—Recent Developments and Lessons for Europe*. Houndmills: Palgrave, 201–7.

Arellano, M., and Bond, S. (1991). 'Some tests of specification for panel data: Monte Carlo evidence and an application to employment equations', *The Review of Economic Studies*, 58: 277–97.

Berger, A. N., Miller, N. H., Petersen, M. A., Rajan, R. G., and Stein, J. C. (2002). 'Does function follow organizational form? Evidence from the lending practices of large and small banks', NBER Working Paper No. 8752 (February).

Berk, J. M. (1998). 'Monetary transmission: What do we know and how can we use it?', *Banca Nationale del Lavoro Quarterly Review*, 205: 145–70 (June).

Bernanke, B. S. (1983). 'Nonmonetary Effects of the Financial Crisis in the Propagation of the Great Depression', *American Economic Review*, 73: 257–76 (June).

——(1993). 'How important is the credit channel in the transmission of monetary policy—A comment', *Carnegie-Rochester Conference Series on Public Policy*, 39: 47–52.

——, and Blinder, A.S. (1988). 'Credit, Money, and Aggregate Demand', *American Economic Review*, 78(2): 435–9 (May).

——, and ——(1992). 'The Federal Funds Rate and the Channels of Monetary Transmission', *American Economic Review*, 82: 901–21 (September).

——, and Gertler, M. (1989). 'Agency costs, net worth, and business fluctuations', *American Economic Review*, 79(1): 14–31.

——, and ——(1995). 'Inside the Black Box: The *Credit Channel* of Monetary Policy Transmission', *Journal of Economic Perspectives*, 9(4): 27–48.

——, ——, and Gilchrist, S. (1996). 'The Financial Accelerator and the Flight to Quality', *Review of Economic Studies*, 78: 1–15.

Bank for International Settlements (BIS) (1995). 'Financial Structure and the Monetary Policy Transmission Mechanism', BIS—Monetary and Economic Department, C.B. 394 (March).

Borio, C. E. V. (1995). 'The structure of credit to the non-government sector and the transmission mechanism of monetary policy: a cross country comparison', in BIS (ed.), *Financial Structure and the Monetary Policy Transmission Mechanism*. BIS—Monetary and Economic Department, C.B. 394: 59–105 (March).

——(1996). 'Credit characteristics and the monetary policy transmission mechanism in fourteen industrial countries: facts, conjectures and some econometric evidence', in K. Alders *et al.* (eds.), *Monetary Policy in a Converging Europe*. Dordrecht: Kluwer, 77–115.

Carlino, G. A., and DeFina, R. H. (2000). 'Monetary Policy and the U.S. States and Regions: Some Implications for European Monetary Union', in J. v. Hagen and C. Waller (eds.), *Regional Aspects of Monetary Policy in Europe*. Boston: Kluwer, 45–67.

Cecchetti, S. G. (1995). 'Distinguishing Theories of the Monetary Transmission Mechanism', *Federal Reserve Bank of St. Louis Review*, 83–100 (May/June).

——(2001). 'Legal Structure, Financial Structure and the Monetary Transmission Mechanism', in Deutsche Bundesbank (ed.), *The Monetary Transmission Process—Recent Developments and Lessons for Europe*. Houndmills: Palgrave, 171–94.

Christiano, L. J., Eichenbaum, M., and Evans, C. L. (1997). 'Sticky Price and Limited Participation Models of Money: A Comparison', *European Economic Review*, 41: 1201–49.

Clostermann, J. (1996). 'The impact of the exchange rate on Germany's balance of trade', Deutsche Bundesbank Discussion Paper No. 7/96 (August).

DeBondt, G. J. (1999a). '*Credit channel*s in Europe: cross-country investigation', Nederlandsche Bank Research Memorandum No. 569 (February).

DeBondt, G. J. (1999*b*). *Financial Structure and Monetary Transmission in Europe—A Cross-Country Study*. Doctoral Dissertation, Universiteit van Amsterdam.

Dedola, L., and Lippi, F. (2000). 'The Monetary Transmission Mechanism: Evidence from the Industry Data of Five OECD Countries', Banca d'Italia. Mimeo.

Deutsche Bundesbank (1999). 'Taylor-Rate and Monetary Conditions Index', *Monthly Report* (April): 47–63.

——(2000). 'The relationship between bank lending and the bond market in Germany', *Monthly Report* (January): 33–47.

——(2001*a*). 'Overall financial flows in 2000', *Monthly Report* (June): 15–38.

——(2001*b*). 'Monetary developments in the euro area since the beginning of monetary union', *Monthly Report* (June): 39–55.

——(2001*c*). 'Bank balance sheets, bank competition and monetary policy transmission', *Monthly Report* (September).

Dornbusch, R., Favero, C. A., and Giavazzi, F. (1998). 'Immediate Challenges for the ECB: Issues in Formulating a Single Monetary Policy', *Economic Policy*, 26: 15–64.

Ehrmann, M. (2000). 'Firm size and monetary policy transmission: evidence from German business survey data', European Central Bank Working Paper No. 21 (May).

——, and Worms, A. (2001). 'Interbank lending and monetary policy transmission: Evidence for Germany', European Central Bank Working Paper No. 73 (July).

——, Gambacorta, L., Martinez-Pages, J., Sevestre, P., and Worms, A. (2001). 'Financial systems and the role of banks in monetary policy transmission in the euro area', European Central Bank Working Paper No. 105 (December).

Elsas, R., and Krahnen, J. P. (1998). 'Is relationship-lending special? Evidence from credit-file data in Germany', *Journal of Banking and Finance*, 22: 1283–316.

Engel, C. (2002). 'The responsiveness of consumer prices to exchange rate and the implications for exchange-rate policy: a survey of a few recent new open-economy macro models', NBER Working Paper No. 8725 (January).

European Central Bank. (2000). *Mergers and aquisitions involving the EU banking industry—facts and implications* (December).

Favero, C. A., Giavazzi, F., and Flabbi, L. (1999). 'The Transmission Mechanism of Monetary Policy in Europe: Evidence from Bank's Balance Sheets', NBER Working Paper No. 7231.

Fazzari, S. M., Hubbard, R. G., and Petersen, B. C. (1988). 'Financing Constraints and Corporate Investment', *Brookings Papers on Economic Activity*, 1: 141–95.

Freixas, X., and Rochet, J. C. (1997). *Microeconomics of Banking*. Cambridge: MIT Press.

Friderichs, H., Paranque, B., and Sauvé, A. (1999). 'Structures of corporate finance in Germany and France: a comparative analysis for west German and French incorporated enterprises with special reference to institutional factors', in A. Sauvé *et al.* *Corporate Finance in Germany and France*. Deutsche Bundesbank and Banque de France, 63–137.

Ganley, J., and Salmon, C. (1996). 'The industrial impact of monetary policy', *Bank of England Quarterly Bulletin* (August): 288–98.

Gertler, M., and Gilchrist, S. (1994). 'Monetary Policy, Business Cycles, and the Behavior of Small Manufacturing Firms', *Quarterly Journal of Economics*, 109 (May): 309–40.

Gilchrist, S., and Himmelberg, C. P. (1995). 'Evidence on the Role of Cash Flow for Investment', *Journal of Monetary Economics*, 541–72.

Guender, A., and Moersch, M. (1997). 'On the Existence of a *Credit channel* of Monetary Policy in Germany', *Kredit und Kapital*, 30: 173–85.

Guiso, L., Kashyap, A. K., Panetta, F., and Terlizzese, D. (1999). 'Will a common European monetary policy have asymmetric effects?', Federal Reserve Bank of Chicago. *Economic Perspectives*, 23: 56–75.

Hackethal, A. (2001). 'How unique are US-banks? The role of banks in five major financial systems', *Jahrbücher für Nationalökonomie und Statistik*, 221 (5/6): 592–619.

Hansen, H. J. (1996). 'The impact of interest rates on private consumption in Germany', Deutsche Bundesbank Discussion Paper No. 3/96.

Hayo, B., and Uhlenbrock, B. (2000). 'Industry effects of monetary policy in Germany', in J. von Hagen and C.J. Waller (eds.), *Regional Aspects of Monetary Policy in Europe*. Boston: Kluwer, 127–58.

Hsiao, C. (1992). *Analysis of panel data*. Econometric Society Monographs No. 11. Cambridge University Press.

Hubbard, H. G. (2000). 'Capital-market imperfections, investment, and the monetary transmission mechanism', Paper presented at the Bundesbank spring conference 'Investing Today for the World of Tomorrow', 28–9 April 2000.

Hülsewig, O., Winker, P., and Worms, A. (2004). 'Bank lending in the transmission of monetary policy: A VECM analysis for Germany', Jahrbücher für National Ökonomie und Statistik, forthcoming.

Issing, O. (2001). 'The Monetary Transmission Process: Concluding Remarks', in Deutsche Bundesbank (ed.), *The Monetary Transmission Process—Recent Developments and Lessons for Europe*. Houndmills: Palgrave, 283–93.

Kakes, J., and Sturm, J. E. (2001). 'Monetary policy and bank lending—Evidence from German banking groups', De Nederlandsche Bank, Mimeo (2001).

Kashyap, A. K., and Stein, J. C. (1994). 'Monetary policy and bank lending', in N. G. Mankiw (ed.), *Monetary Policy*. Chicago: University of Chicago Press, 221–56.

——, and —— (1995). 'The Impact of Monetary Policy on Bank Balance Sheets', *Carnegie-Rochester Conference Series on Public Policy*, 42 (June): 151–95.

——, and —— (2000). 'What Do a Million Observations on Banks Say About the Transmission of Monetary Policy?', *American Economic Review*, 90(3): 407–28.

——, ——, and Wilcox, D. W. (1993). 'Monetary Policy and Credit Conditions: Evidence from the Composition of External Finance', *American Economic Review*, 82: 78–98.

King, S. R. (1986). 'Monetary Transmission: Through Bank Loans, or Bank Liabilities?', *Journal of Money, Credit, and Banking*, 18(3): 290–303.

Kneeshaw, J. T. (1995). 'Non-financial sector balance sheets in the monetary transmission mechanism', in BIS (ed.), *Financial Structure and the Monetary Policy Transmission Mechanism*. BIS—Monetary and Economic Department, C.B. 394 (March): 1–58.

Koenig, E. F. (1990). 'Real Money Balances and the Timing of Consumption', *Quarterly Journal of Economics* (May): 399–425.

Küppers, M. (2001). 'Curtailing the black box: German banking groups in the transmission of monetary policy', *European Economic Review*, 45: 1907–30.

McAdam, P., and Morgan, J. (2001). 'The Monetary Transmission Mechanism at the Euro-Area Level: Issues and Results using Structural Macroeconomic Models', European Central Bank Working Paper No. 94 (December).

Meltzer, A. H. (2001). 'The Transmission Process', in Deutsche Bundesbank (ed.), *The Monetary Transmission Process—Recent Developments and Lessons for Europe*. Houndmills: Palgrave, 112–30.

Menon, J. (1995). 'Exchange rate pass-through', *Journal of Economic Surveys*, 9(2): 197–231.

Mihov, I. (2001). 'Monetary policy implementation and the transmission in the European Monetary Union', *Economic Policy*, 33: 371–406.

Mishkin, F. (1996). 'The Channels of Monetary Transmission: Lessons for Monetary Policy', *Banque de France Bulletin Digest*, 27: 33–44.

Modigliani, F. (1971). 'Monetary Policy and Consumption', in Federal Reserve Bank of Boston (ed.) *Consumer Spending and Monetary Policy*. Boston: The Linkages, 9–84.

——, and Shiller, R. (1973). 'Inflation, rational expectations and the term structure of interest rates', *Economica*, 40: 12–43.

Mojon, B., and Peersman, G. (2001). 'A VAR description of the effects of monetary policy in the individual countries of the euro area?', European Central Bank Working Paper No. 92 (December).

Müller, M., and Worms, A. (1995). 'Targeting Monetary Aggregates, Interest Rate Movements, and Credit Demand', Geld-Währung-Kapitalmarkt Working Paper No. 38. University of Frankfurt (February).

Myers, S. C. (2001). 'Capital Structure', *Journal of Economic Perspectives*, 15(2): 81–102.

——, and Majluf, N. S. (1984). 'Corporate Financing and Investment Decisions when Firms have Information that Investors do not have', *Journal of Financial Economics*, 13: 187–221.

Petersen, M. A., and Rajan, R. G. (1994). 'The benefits of lending relationships: evidence from small business data', *Journal of Finance*, 44: 3–37.

Ramaswamy, R., and Sloek, T. (1998). 'The Real Effects of Monetary Policy in the European Union: What are the differences?', *IMF Staff Paper*, 45(2): 374–91 (June).

Ramey, V. (1993). 'How important is the *credit channel* in the transmission of monetary policy?', *Carnegie-Rochester Conference Series on Public Policy*, 39: 1–45.

Romer, C. D., and Romer, D. H. (1989). 'Does monetary policy matter? A new test in the spirit of Friedman and Schwartz', NBER Macroeconomics Annual, 121–70.

——, and —— (1990). 'New Evidence on the Monetary Transmission Mechanism', *Brookings Papers on Economic Activity*, 1: 149–213.

Samolyk, K. A. (1994). 'Banking conditions and regional economic performance—Evidence of a regional *credit channel*', *Journal of Monetary Economics*, 34: 259–78.

Scharnagl, M. (1998). 'The stability of German money demand: not just a myth', *Empirical Economics*, 23(3): 355–86.

Stöss, E. (1996). 'Enterprises' financial structure and their response to monetary policy stimuli—An analysis based on the Deutsche Bundesbank's corporate balance sheet statistics', Deutsche Bundesbank Discussion Paper No. 9/96.

Taylor, J. B. (1995). 'The monetary transmission mechanism: An empirical framework', *The Journal of Economic Perspectives*, 9(4): 11–26.

Tobin, J. (1969). 'A General Equilibrium Approach to Monetary Theory', *Journal of Money, Credit, and Banking*, 1: 15–29.

Tsatsaronis, C. (1995). 'Is there a credit channel in the transmission of monetary policy? Evidence from four countries', in BIS (ed.), *Financial Structure and the Monetary Policy Transmission Mechanism*. BIS—Monetary and Economic Department, C.B. 394: 154–87.

Upper, C., and Worms, A. (2002). 'Banken als Bindeglied zwischen Geld- und Kapitalmarkt in Deutschland', in B. Schefold (ed.), *Exogenität und Endogenität— Die Geldmenge in der Geschichte des ökonomischen Denkens und in der modernen Politik*. Marburg: Metropolis, 93–132.

——, and —— (2004). 'Estimating bilateral exposures in the German interbank market: is there a danger of contagion?', *European Economic Review*, forthcoming.

van Els, P., Locarno, A., Morgan, J., and Vitelle, J. P. (2001). 'Monetary policy transmission in the euro area: what do aggregate and national structural models tell us?', European Central Bank Working Paper No. 95 (December).

von Kalckreuth, U. (2001). 'Monetary transmission in Germany: New perspectives on financial constraints and investment spending', Deutsche Bundesbank Discussion Paper No. 19/01 (December).

Westerheide, P. (2001). 'Einkommens- und Nachfrageeffekte von Zinsänderungen', *Kredit und Kapital*, 34: 303–26.

Woodford, M. (2001). 'Monetary policy in the information economy', NBER Working Paper No. 8674.

Worms, A. (1998). *Bankkredite an Unternehmen und ihre Rolle in der geldpolitischen Transmission in Deutschland*. Reihe Europäische Hochschulschriften, Reihe V: Volks- und Betriebswirtschaft, No. 2244. Frankfurt: Peter Lang.

—— (2001). 'Monetary policy effects on bank loans in Germany: A panel-econometric analysis', Deutsche Bundesbank Discussion Paper No. 17/01 (December).

—— (2003). 'Interbank relationships and the credit channel in Germany', *Empirica* 30/2: 179–98.

7

Universal Banks and Relationships with Firms

RALF ELSAS AND JAN PIETER KRAHNEN

7.1. MYTH AND MOTIVATION

[T]here are good reasons to choose the German rather than the British style of capital markets...In practice, the effectiveness of German banks as monitors of company performance...makes the German system unambigously superior.   Crafts (1992: 409)

The commonly-held view of the merits of the German system of finance for investment, in terms of the supply of external finance to firms and corporate control, receives no support from the analysis of available evidence.   Edwards/Fischer (1994: 240)

Some of the most widely expressed myths about the German financial system are concerned with the close ties and intensive interaction between banks and firms. Observers have stressed that bank–firm relationships in Germany are not only characterized by long-term debt financing commitments but also by a multitude of links. These include direct shareholdings, board representation, and proxy voting and are particularly significant for corporate governance. Specifically, it is often argued that bank involvement in the supply of capital and in corporate governance may be economically beneficial for two reasons. First, close ties between banks and borrowers are perceived to promote investment and improve the performance of firms. Second, owing to direct equity holdings, board representation, and proxy-voting rights, German universal banks are believed to play a special role as large and informed investors (shareholders). However, it is for the very same reasons that German universal banks are frequently accused of abusing their influence on firms, thereby exploiting rents and sustaining the entrenchment of firms against efficient transfers of firm control.

In order to understand the financial system in Germany properly, a distinction has to be made between the relatively small group of large, publicly traded corporations on the one hand, and the small and medium-sized companies on the other. The vast majority of corporate Germany, both in terms of numbers and sales, has no public equity. Banks play no role as shareholders, nor as proxy voters or board members, but usually just as lenders. However, for these firms, bank debt is the single most important source of outside financing, which in turn implies a major role for banks.

In this chapter we will discuss the role of banks for both groups of corporations, focusing on the information-intensive long-term relationships between banks and firms, often referred to as *Hausbank* financing. Within such *Hausbank* relationships, banks are said to be the primary financier, being equipped with more relevant, and more timely information than any other external investor (like, for example, an outside bank). Moreover, *Hausbanks* are deemed to accept a special responsibility in the event that borrowers should face financial distress. It is this *Hausbank* notion which implicitly underlies the supposed merits of bank–firm relationships mentioned above, and it is often used to describe the role of banks for all segments of firms. However, as indicated by the above statements of Crafts (1992) and Edwards and Fischer (1994), these merits are controversial.

The objective of this chapter is to present and discuss recent evidence to provide a clearer picture of the economic role of *Hausbanks*. Section 7.2 will start to look at the role of German banks for large and exchange-listed firms, abstracting from lending for a moment. Banks are seen as investors, with a role in corporate control and governance. This section will discuss recent evidence on the effect of bank influence on firms (or firm management), focussing on financing constraints and corporate performance.

The implications of banks for corporate governance in Section 7.2 apply to an exclusive circle of large, mostly public firms only, and they can by no means be generalized to apply to all of corporate Germany. Therefore, the subsequent sections turn to the lending business with regard to small and medium-sized firms. In Section 7.3, a brief outline of the theoretical notion of relationship lending will be provided. The next sections present the available evidence. In Section 7.4, the idea of intertemporal smoothing as an essential characteristic of implicit long-term contracts between firms and banks will be analysed. In Section 7.5, the decision-making process of banks when their borrowers face financial distress is addressed. We will briefly describe the present legal practice concerning financial distress in Germany, including a short description of the insolvency code. The role of *Hausbanks* and the institution of bank pools will be analysed by discussing recent studies using unique data on medium-sized corporate borrowers. Section 7.6 summarizes and concludes.

7.2. UNIVERSAL BANKS AS FINANCIERS OF LARGE COMPANIES: EQUITY STAKES AND PROXY VOTING

7.2.1. Overview

In early works by Hilferding (1909), and later Schumpeter (1939) and Gerschenkron (1962), the interaction between industrial firms and universal banks was presumed to have been of great importance for the industrialization of Germany in the nineteenth century, and only recently the economics of financial system architecture have once more become an active field of research (see Tilly 1992; La Porta *et al.* 1997, 1998; Rajan and Zingales 2001). In this context a distinction is generally made between two polar cases of financial architecture emphasizing market-based financial systems, such as the United States or United Kingdom, on the one hand and bank-based systems, like Japan and Germany, on the other.

This section explores the benefits of banking relationships for large publicly traded firms in Germany. The German financial system differs from US-type financial architecture in that German universal banks are allowed to take direct equity stakes, are often represented on the supervisory board of industrial firms and possess additional influence via proxy-voting rights. All of these characteristics are thought to be significant in terms of their potential to influence the decision making at the company level. Hence, corporate governance in Germany is said to be bank-dominated (Emmons and Schmid 1998: 20 and Chapter 12, this volume), and the question whether this is beneficial or detrimental in terms of overall social welfare is subject to debate. Cable (1985: 130), for example, on the basis of his empirical analysis concludes: 'it is clear from the results, that the relationship between industrial banking and firm performance has more to it than the provision of credit alone; it is bank control as well as bank lending which raises profitability'. In contrast, Fohlin (1998: 1755) concludes as a result of her analysis that 'the results undermine widely held beliefs about the benefits of universal banking'.

The conflicting empirical evidence on the role of banks for large firms can be attributed to the two approaches taken. Both approaches address the core question of corporate finance: Does the financing choice of firms affect investment, and therefore have real consequences? The first approach is concerned with bank influence and its impact on the performance of firms. In this class of studies, a measure of firm performance, for example the return on assets, is statistically related to a measure of bank dependence.

The second approach relates firm investment expenditures to a measure of internal and external financing (and future investment opportunities). The basic idea is that the existence of financing constraints leads firms to choose among financing sources according to a specific preference ranking. In particular, capital market imperfections lead to a preference for internal over external financing (see Fazzari *et al.* 1988; Kaplan and Zingales 1997). Furthermore, it is postulated that firms subject to tighter financing constraints will exhibit greater cash-flow sensitivity with respect to investments. Under this hypothesis, a certain degree of bank dependence on the part of a firm should mitigate financing constraints, since, in theory, banks reduce information asymmetries and have proper incentives for management control (see e.g. Houston and James 2001).

We provide some descriptive evidence on the long-term relationship between large, listed firms and universal banks in Germany in the next subsection.

7.2.2. Descriptive Evidence on Equity Holdings, Supervisory Board Representation, and the Proxy-Voting Rights of Banks

It is useful to start with a brief description of the governing bodies of a German listed corporation ('Aktiengesellschaft'—AG). The listed corporation has three governing bodies: the annual general meeting ('Hauptversammlung'), a supervisory board ('Aufsichtsrat') and a managing board ('Vorstand'). The supervisory board and the managing board have no membership overlap. The supervisory board must have a pre-specified number of employee representatives as members (codetermination, 'Mitbestimmung'). It is quite common for boards of affiliated firms to share several members. Typically some managers of the parent company are also members of a subsidiary's supervisory board.[1] The supervisory board often includes representatives of one or more of the firm's banks, which then typically have been providing debt for a long time, and which even may have equity stakes in the firm. Shareholders elect half of the members of the supervisory board. Their control rights are effectively confined to the general meeting (see Chapter 11, this volume).

Unlike in the United States, it is quite common in Germany for there to be significant blockholdings. Franks and Mayer (2001) and Boehmer (2001) provide evidence that for all listed firms over the period 1985–97 roughly 85 per cent of the firms had a blockholder with a stake above 25 per cent, whilst 57 per cent had one with a stake above 50 per cent. In some cases these blockholders are from the financial sector, but more often they are firms from the same or related industries, and wealthy families.

It is also relevant in a discussion of bank-firm relationships to note that until quite recently (see Chapter 13, this volume) deviations from share ownership and voting rights (i.e. control) occurred quite easily under German law. The German proxy-voting system allows shareholders to deposit their shares with banks, and grants them general power of attorney. The resulting additional voting power for the banks is presumed to be significant. For example, Baums and Fraune (1995) provide evidence on the situation regarding large German firms with a dispersed ownership structure in 1992. In their sample, banks held on average 13 per cent of effective voting rights at the general meeting due to direct equity holdings, and 61 per cent due to proxy-voting rights. Hence, if banks have mutual interest and coordinate their actions, their influence on management is potentially very strong. However, evidence on

---

[1] See Boehmer (1999) for a more detailed overview and references.

Table 7.1. *Measures of bank influence rights*

	Mean (%)	= 0%	≥ 25%	≥ 50%	Number of observations
Share of bank debt in total firm financing	17.1	n/a	25.0	n/a	144
Supervisory board representation by banks (dummy)	70.1	29.9	—	—	144
Share of bank representatives in board members representing capital	—	29.9	41.6	9.7	144
Firms with direct equity holdings by banks	24.3	75.7	8.3	2.1	144
Proxy-voting rights of banks at general meetings	29.5	n/a	41.5	20.0	65
Total bank voting rights at general meetings	37.9	n/a	49.2	35.4	65

Notes: The underlying sample consists of 144 large, listed German firms from manufacturing industries. Information on proxy-votes were collected from mandatory minutes of general meetings in 1990 and were available for a subsample of 65 firms.

Source: Own calculations based on numbers reported by Seger (1997): tables 25–39.

proxy-voting rights by banks is scarce since the data is not centrally (or even electronically) accessible.[2]

For the descriptive purposes of this subsection, Table 7.1 presents statistics on bank influence rights reported by Seger (1997). However, some caution is due since it is widely believed that bank influence rights have decreased in importance since 1990.

The first point to note is that the numbers shown in Table 7.1 are in line with the general pattern described above. Some interesting additional insights should be mentioned:

Supervisory Board 70 per cent of all sample firms have a bank representative as a member of the supervisory board, and in 41.6 per cent of all cases, bank representatives constitute more than 25 per cent of board members representing capital (i.e. excluding co-determination).[3]

---

[2] Exercised proxy-voting rights are documented publicly. However, there does not exist a centralized register or an electronic database for assessing this information, see Boehmer (1999). To this end, one has to ask the district court at the registered seat of the firms to examine the mandatory minutes of the general meetings.

[3] Note that German legislation requires a mandatory share of representatives of employees in the supervisory board ('Mitbestimmung'). Depending on firm size, this amounts to up to 50 per cent of all members.

Direct Equity Holdings The numbers in Table 7.1 imply that to some extent the relevance of direct equity holdings is exaggerated in the public debate, since banks actually hold such stakes in approximately only 25 per cent of all cases. Nevertheless, for 8 per cent of the sample firms these stakes are equal to or higher than 25 per cent of capital (i.e. a blocking minority, 'Sperrminorität'), enabling the respective bank to block all fundamental votes at the general meeting (i.e. those that change a firm's statutes).

Proxy-Voting Rights The sample mean of proxy-votes at general meetings is in excess of a blocking minority with roughly 30 per cent, and in 41.5 per cent of all cases the (aggregate) proxy-votes of all banks exceed 25 per cent. Adding proxy-votes and direct equity stakes shows that banks had a majority of votes at 35.4 per cent of general meetings.

Although these numbers would appear to provide strong support for the idea of close ties between large industrial firms and banks in Germany, some words of caution are due. It has to be kept in mind that these numbers are aggregated over all banks for a given firm. However, to effectively block, for example, a change in a firm's statutes, all banks have to agree on a mutual strategy and coordinate their actions. It is very likely that coordination failures and free-rider problems will reduce the effective power of banks significantly. Thus, a qualitative comparison to a situation where just one bank (or investor) may exercise the same nominal magnitude of influence rights is almost impossible. This appears to be particularly important for proxy-votes, where it is often the case that several banks are present at the general meeting.

7.2.3. Universal Banks and Firm Performance: Empirical Findings

Having established that German universal banks may exert significant influence on the management of large German firms, the question arises whether this is economically beneficial or detrimental. One way of addressing this issue is to test whether bank dependence of a firm systematically affects firm performance. Cable (1985) provided the first paper to report such a test with German company data. Since the results of Cable were based on a rather small cross section of firms, subsequent studies have extended the analysis, using larger data sets, and more sophisticated methodologies (see Gorton and Schmid 2000; Seger 1997).

There are at least two important issues which cause such an approach to be quite complex. First, the analysis of firm performance is a dynamic issue. However, company panel data covering a time-period of 10 or more years are difficult to collect, especially if data on voting rights of banks are needed. Second, and more importantly, there is no unambiguous theoretical hypothesis relating bank influence rights to firm performance. On the one hand, bank dependence may simply be seen as synonymous for the bargaining power of banks, allowing them to extract rents. This would imply a negative impact on firm performance.[4] On the other hand, bank dependence may be interpreted as resolving problems of informational asymmetries and incomplete contracting. This second view supports the hypothesis that firms which exhibit greater bank dependence will perform better (see Gorton and Schmid 2000).

Under both hypotheses, however, it is hard to explain why some firms rely on bank debt and some do not. If, for example, bank dependence is beneficial, why do some firms prefer not to have such close bank relationships? Following Demsetz and Lehn (1985), one answer to that question might be that firms choose that financing structure which is optimal to their individual needs. This would imply that firms in need of bank monitoring are bank dependent, and those that are not are independent. Hence, empirically, an equilibrium situation is observed where we do not expect to find any systematic differences in firm performance, since firms relying on banks are as profitable as those without bank dependence, just *because* they have already chosen to allow for bank monitoring.

Therefore, empirical analyses of the relation between bank dependence and firm performance suffer from problems of data availability and ambiguity in theoretical guidance. Nevertheless, an inductive approach may still be helpful in identifying any dominant patterns.

Table 7.2 summarizes a selection of recent studies addressing the relation between bank dependence and firm performance.[5] The table provides information on the structure and size of the underlying firm sample of all studies. In addition, the measures used for bank dependence and firm performance are provided, as well as a summary of the results.

The table shows some heterogeneity in these studies in terms of the underlying firm samples and available information. Nevertheless, the results are broadly consistent across studies.

We first turn to the relation between direct equity holdings by banks and firm performance. Gorton and Schmid (2000) consider two measures of bank influence: direct shareholdings, and proxy-voting rights. Their empirical model further tests for codetermination of employees, and overall shareholder concentration. Performance is measured either as the market-to-book value of equity, or as the return on equity. It turns out that bank control has a positive impact on firm performance, similar to the effect of blockholdings by non-financial investors. By controlling for both issues simultaneously, the authors find that direct shareholdings by banks improve firm performance beyond the level achieved by non-bank blockholders. The authors suggest that this superior control effect of banks is owing to better information and superior expertise, and or because of the additional threat to cut-off debt financing if the management refuses to comply with bank interests.

---

[4] See, for example, Weinstein and Yafeh (1998) for a corresponding model and empirical analysis with respect to Japanese firms, where firms and (main) banks constitute a so-called *keiretsu*.

[5] For ease of exposition, we refrain from giving a complete overview. Our selection comprises the most recent and comprehensive studies.

Table 7.2. *Studies on bank dependence, firm investment, and profitability for large German listed firms*

Study	Seger (1997)	Lehmann and Weigand (2000)	Gorton and Schmid (2000)	Elston (1998)	Fohlin (1998)
Panel I: General characteristics					
Observation period	1990–92	1992–96	1975/1986	1973–84	1903–13
Sample size	144	361	283/280	139	75
Industry affiliation	Non-financial, manufacturing	Manufacturing	Manufacturing	Manufacturing	Non-financial
Performance-measure	ROA, ROE, and others	ROA	Market-to-book value of equity, ROE	(Cash-flow sensitivity of investment)	(Cash-flow sensitivity of investment)
Measure of bank dependence	Debt share, equity stakes, supervisory board, proxy voting	Equity stake	Equity stakes, proxy voting	Direct bank equity stake	Cross directorate membership
Information on proxy-votes	Yes, sub-sample of firms	No	Yes, sub-sample of firms	No	—
Panel II: Impact of bank dependence measure on firm performance					
Bank debt financing	Negative	—	—	—	—
Equity control rights	Positive	Positive	Positive	—	—
Supervisory board representation	Insignificant	Insignificant	—	—	—
Panel III: Impact of bank dependence measure on investment/cash-flow correlation					
Supervisory board	—	—	—	—	Unstable/insignificant
Equity control rights	—	—	—	Negative	—

Note: ROE and ROA denote return on equity and return on assets, respectively.

These results are consistent with the findings by Lehmann and Weigand (2000) and Seger (1997), who report superior firm performance for highly concentrated ownership structures, and for equity holdings by banks. Note that the data of Lehmann and Weigand (2000) are more recent.

With regard to the impact of proxy-voting rights on firm performance, Gorton and Schmid (2000), Seger (1997) find no evidence that these are used to exert management control. Gorton and Schmid (2000) suggest this result to be due to the fact that proxy-voting rights merely reflect the degree of dispersion of shareholdings. That is, the lower the shareholder concentration, the higher will be the level of proxy-votes, since these arise from the delegation of voting rights to banks by small and non-pivotal investors. This characteristic feature of proxy-votes is consistant with high coordination costs associated with the exercising of such votes.

The relation between supervisory board representation by banks and firm performance is addressed in all three studies. Seger (1997) and Lehmann and Weigand (2000) consistently find no impact of board representation on firm performance. One possible explanation is provided by Gorton and Schmid (2000). They argue that membership of a supervisory board is derived from equity control rights. Their conjecture is supported by a regression analysis, indicating that board membership is systematically determined by equity holdings.

To summarize, recent studies suggest a beneficial role of direct equity stakes held by banks. Hence, there is some support for the conjecture that banks play a special role in the process of corporate governance in Germany. With respect to alternative means to exerting management control, that is, proxy-voting rights and supervisory board representation, the evidence supports the irrelevance of these factors. This is somewhat surprising in view of the common perception that proxy votes provide banks with a significant and frequently criticized degree of influence (e.g. Jürgens *et al.* 2000). However, when the coordination problems inherent in a strategic exercise of proxy-votes are taken into account, the irrelevancy result appears quite reasonable.

7.2.4. Banks, Liquidity, and Financing Constraints

The second approach to analysing the economic consequences of close ties between banks and large industrial firms is concerned with the ability of banks to mitigate firm financing constraints.

In a seminal study, Fazzari *et al.* (1988) argued that capital market imperfections lead to firm preferences for internal over external sources of financing, and that this can be analysed by regressing firm investment expenditures on a measure of internal financing and investment opportunities.[6] In a perfect

---

[6] Usually, a proxy for Tobin's Q is used as the measure for future investment opportunities.

Modigliani/Miller world, all investment projects with positive net present value will be financed, thus rendering the choice of funding irrelevant. In such a world, firm expenditures should not depend on the availability of internally generated funds. Hence, a regression of investment expenditures on cash flow should yield no systematic relation, having controlled for future investment opportunities. According to Fazzari *et al.* (1988), however, if capital market imperfections are present there should be a positive correlation between firm investment and cash flow, which would indicate the severity of financing constraints.[7]

Under the assumption that banks are able to mitigate financing constraints because of their role as active monitors of firm management, a negative impact of firms' bank dependence on the cash-flow correlation of investments is to be expected (Fohlin 1998; Houston and James 2001). This holds in particular for an analysis of German firms, as highlighted by the statement of Fohlin (1998: 1737): '[German universal banks] are thought to foster long-term relationships with industrial firms, promoting more efficient and stronger investment.'

International evidence consistently reports a strong (positive) correlation between cash flow and investment. This also holds for Germany as, for example, recently reported by Plötscher (2001). We are aware of only two corresponding studies which take into account bank dependence of German firms.

The study by Elston (1998) investigates the impact of bank dependence on firm investment expenditures by analysing a sample of 139 German manufacturing firms (see Table 7.2). She estimates cash-flow sensitivities over the period from 1973–84 for two subsamples: One consisting of twenty-six firms where banks had a high direct equity stake in the firms, and one where no equity stakes were reported.[8] The estimation results indicate that bank dependence mitigates financing constraints. The reported coefficients of cash-flow sensitivities are positive and significant, and they are significantly lower for the sub-sample of firms classified as bank dependent.

The study by Fohlin (1998) analyses a sample of firms over the period 1903–13, shifting the focus to Germany's late period of industrialization. The general characteristics of this study and its results are reported in Table 7.2. Fohlin (1998) measures bank dependence by cross-directorates between firms and banks, that is, cases where the bank is represented in either the executive

---

[7] Kaplan and Zingales (1997) show that observing a positive investment-cash flow correlation is not a sufficient condition for the existence of financing constraints. The same correlation pattern may be induced by managerial risk aversion or other types of agency problems in the spirit of Jensen's 'free cash flow' problem. See also the more general discussion of financing constraint research in Hubbard (1998).

[8] There were only weak disclosure rules regarding equity holdings by banks in place during this period, so that the classification of firms as having no bank relationship is noisy.

or supervisory board of the firm, or the firm is represented in the bank's executive or supervisory board. The results from different model specifications suggest that bank dependence systematically affects neither firm investments in terms of its level, nor investment correlation with cash flow.

This finding may be due to Fohlin's (1998) specific measure for bank dependence (cross-directorates), which questions its validity as a proxy for dependence. However, since the preceding section showed supervisory board representation revealed to be systematically correlated with direct equity stakes (and proxy-votes), Fohlin's results do indeed cast some doubt on a special role of banks for corporate governance in Germany. It could be expected that a mitigating effect of bank dependence on financial constraints would be most pronounced for the early stage of industrialization.

The empirical findings reported so far are inconclusive. Studies concerned with the impact of a firm's bank dependence on performance consistently find a positive impact of direct equity holdings by banks. In contrast, proxy-voting rights and supervisory board representation by banks appear to be irrelevant for management control.[9] Studies on the ability of banks to mitigate financing constraints of firms yield conflicting results, which may be attributed to differences in the underlying observation periods, or the definition of bank dependence. All studies reported so far have focused on large, exchange-listed companies. Note that firms in this size segment differ considerably from the vast majority of firms in Germany's industrial sector. Small and medium-sized firms, representing the majority of companies in terms of number and GDP-contribution, are subject to less stringent disclosure rules, are not followed by financial analysts, and are less likely to possess a publicly observable track record. Therefore, for SME companies, problems of informational asymmetries, and incomplete contracting tend to be more important, thus lending more weight to the effect of relationships between banks and firms. We will discuss the value of relationships in the remaining sections of this chapter, emphasizing in particular the notions of the *Hausbank* and relationship lending.

7.3. BANKS AS FINANCIERS OF SMALL AND MEDIUM ENTERPRISES: LENDING RELATIONSHIPS

7.3.1. The *Hausbank* Concept and Relationship Lending

In turning to small and medium-sized firms there is a shift in focus to the key economic function of banks, that is, their role as providers of external debt. Although we largely ignored debt provision in the preceding section, it is a stylized fact that bank debt is the single most important source of external funding

---

[9] This does not, of course, imply that supervisory board membership cannot provide valuable information for banks. The argument is that all benefits are primarily *caused* by equity holdings.

for corporations in Germany, as well as in many other countries (see Hackethal 2003, Chapter 3, this volume; Fischer and Pfeil 2003, Chapter 10, this volume). When non-listed firms are taken into consideration, the relevance of bank debt as a financing source becomes even greater, whereas the role of bank debt as a means of bank influence via direct equity holdings, supervisory board representation, and proxy-voting rights can easily be ignored. The reason is that these latter aspects are irrelevant for small and medium-sized enterprises, given to their legal form and the complete absence of public equity.[10]

As outlined above, the German notion of the *Hausbank* serves as a prime example of close ties between bank and firms, in particular if the lending function of banks is addressed. The *Hausbank* is regarded as the premier lender of a firm with more intensive and more timely information than a comparable arm's length bank (see e.g. Edwards and Fischer 1994; Elsas and Krahnen 1998). The *Hausbank* is further said to bear a 'special responsibility' in the event that its borrowers face financial distress.

At first glance, the economic rationale for 'a special responsibility' of a bank would appear unclear. The theoretical concept of relationship lending, however, provides such a rationale. Relationship lending is defined as a long-term implicit contract between a bank and its debtor.[11] Due to information acquisition and repeated interaction with the borrower over time, the *Hausbank* accumulates private information. This information privilege commits both parties to one another, establishing close ties between the bank and the borrower. The definition of Petersen and Rajan (1995) highlights the similarities between relationship lending and the *Hausbank* notion: 'By close and continued interaction, a firm may provide a lender with sufficient information about, and a voice in, a firm's affairs so as to lower the cost of and increase the availability of credit.'[12]

Following Boot (2000), three major potential benefits attributed to relationship lending can be distinguished:[13]

Information   A close relationship to its bank might induce a borrower to reveal more information than in arm's length financing (see Bhattacharya and

---

[10] Note that in terms of contribution to GDP, German firms predominantly have the legal form of a limited liability company ('GmbH') or a limited partnership ('KG'). For the latter, a GmbH is usually the limited partner ('GmbH & Co KG'), thereby resembling incorporation of the firm. Based on the German tax income report, incorporated enterprises and partnerships (including the GmbH & Co KG) constitute approximately one third of all firms in terms of numbers, while two thirds are sole proprietorships. See Deutsche Bundesbank (2001).

[11] For recent surveys on the theoretical concept of relationship lending and the respective international evidence, see Ongena and Smith (2000) and Boot (2000).

[12] Petersen and Rajan (1995: 6).

[13] Note that event studies based on US data confirm that established relationships are of value. James (1987), Lummer and McConnell (1989), and Billett *et al.* (1995) provide evidence on abnormal returns of bank loan announcements to firms. Slovin *et al.* (1993) complement this evidence showing that firm market value decreases if a lending bank goes bankrupt, that is, when the accumulated information capital of the bank is destroyed.

Chiesa 1995; Yosha 1995). In turn, a relationship lender might have stronger incentives for information acquisition, and may learn from the repeated interaction with the borrower (see Greenbaum and Thakor 1995; Caminal and Matutes 1997; Hackethal 2000).

Renegotiation Relationship lending is an implicit contract, allowing for contractual flexibility through the renegotiation of terms (see Boot *et al.* 1993).

Intertemporal interaction Commitment between the borrower and the bank allows for intertemporal transfers because it introduces a long-term perspective for the bank. If the borrower cannot switch to another financier easily, then the bank can expect to earn rents in future periods. These rents may in turn offset losses at other stages of the business (see e.g. Sharpe 1990; Petersen and Rajan 1995; Allen and Gale 1999).

All of these benefits have implications for two crucial issues: credit availability in general, and credit availability when borrowers face financial distress (i.e. credit availability in a narrow sense). As emphasized by Petersen and Rajan (1995) and Fischer (1990), the possibility of subsidizing firms in the beginning of a relationship may mitigate problems of moral hazard and which would have prohibited loan provision from arm's-length lenders.[14] Hence, relationship lending may increase credit availability.

Financial distress is related to credit availability and of particular importance for our analysis of German *Hausbanks*, since these are described as bearing 'a special responsibility' *vis-a-vis* their distressed borrowers. Financial distress characterizes a situation where firms are not able to meet current obligations and need liquidity at short notice. In such a situation, the long-term perspective of the relationship lender, its information privilege and the switching cost of financing will positively influence decisions by banks with respect denial (i.e. termination) or continuation of debt provision.

If a bank has private and presumably better information on a borrower's current and future economic prospects it will, in general, make different decisions in times when the borrower faces financial distress. In this situation, lenders have to decide whether to continue debt provision (or even increase their loan supply to bail the borrower out of the crises) or to terminate the credit relationship (which often terminates firm operations as well). To this end, lenders must assess whether the crisis is temporary or permanent, that is, whether the underlying investment projects of the borrowing firm are efficient, and whether default is strategic (Bolton and Scharfstein 1996). If the borrower still has investments with a positive net present value, the efficient decision is a workout and, thus, a continuation of the relationship. If the borrower's projects are of poor quality, however, termination will be

---

[14] See Berlin and Mester (1999) for an analysis of intertemporal transfers in loan pricing.

efficient. Of course, efficiency does not necessarily predict actual lender behaviour. But, if relationship lenders have better (e.g. in the sense of more precise) information on the borrowing firm, they will make efficient decisions more often, that is, be more likely to terminate if the borrower is bad and more likely to continue financing if the borrower is good. This can be interpreted as a kind of distress insurance, where the borrower chooses relationship lending *ex ante* as a form of financing that provides for more efficient bank decision-making in financial distress.

It is important to stress the point that such an insurance does not automatically lead to loan continuation. Rather, it can be expected *Hausbanks* they will more often decide in favour of the efficient alternative. In fact, economically, relationship lending can be interpreted as a commitment device for the borrower, ensuring *ex ante* that he will be liquidated if distress occurs. This commitment is credible, because the *ex ante* decision restricts his later actions in a desirable way (see Rajan 1992 who analyzes this point formally).

Our discussion of the empirical evidence on *Hausbank* relationships in Germany places special emphasis on such types of insurance provided by relationship lenders. But before turning to the evidence, the 'down side' of relationship lending (i.e. its costs) must be mentioned. First of all, relationship lending does not dominate other types of financing, since it is inevitably associated with costs. A potential source of costs for bank financing is related to monitoring (see e.g. Gale and Hellwig 1985; Diamond 1991). There are also switching costs involved in relationship lending in the sense of Sharpe (1990) and Rajan (1992). In their models, the information privilege of banks induces bargaining power, giving rise to a hold-up problem. Hence (additional or exclusive) borrowing from arm's length lenders may be used to limit rents which would otherwise would be exploited by informed lenders. Finally, the possibility of contract renegotiation may lead to a kind of 'soft-budget constraint' for borrowers, where relationship lenders perform the insurance function inefficiently. This in turn may adversely affect the incentives of the borrower to avoid bad outcomes *ex ante* (see Dewatripont and Maskin 1995).

To conclude, our brief discussion of the theory of relationship lending illustrates the complexity of this financial arrangement. Using relationship lending, or *Hausbanks*, for corporate financing can benefit firms, but relationship lending has negative aspects as well. This highlights the necessity of looking at empirical evidence in order to learn more about universal banks in Germany and their relationship with firms. Evidence on the existence of *Hausbanks* also directly addresses the question whether the *Hausbank* institution exists in the first place. Only recently, Edwards and Fischer (1994) have argued that *Hausbanks* in Germany are a myth (see the quotation at the beginning of this chapter). We will show in this subsection that their claim is mistaken, and we will show in the following sections that the existence of *Hausbank*s does, in fact, have real effects on firm financing patterns.

7.3.2. Characteristics of a *Hausbank*

Although the notion of the *Hausbank* is generally well known in Germany, in the exact characteristics of this institution have remained vague. A recent study by Elsas (2003) can shed some light on this issue.

The author provides an empirical analysis of the determinants of the *Hausbank* status of five German universal banks with respect to a given sample of corporate borrowers. The analysis is based on an exogenous criterion for a bank's *Hausbank* status, sampled in 1997, that is the self-assessment of banks regarding their own status. For the underlying firm sample, relevant credit officers at the banks were asked to assess and comply with the following: (i) *Is your bank the housebank of the given customer, yes or no?* and (ii) *Please provide a written explanation of your assessment.* The firm sample itself consists of 200 borrowers randomly drawn from the population of all corporate borrowers of the banks, meeting specific selection criteria with respect to size, debt structure, and the location of their headquarters.[15] The banks from which the firm observations originate are Deutsche Bank, Dresdner Bank, Bayerische Vereinsbank (now HypoVereinsbank), DG Bank (now DZ-Bank), and WestLB. All of these banks are universal banks with corporate credit business and belong to the top ten banks in Germany with respect to size and market share. The first three banks are for-profit private banks, while DG-Bank is the apex institution of the cooperatives sector. WestLB is the largest apex bank of the public savings banks sector. Hence the sample of banks represents all relevant sectors of the German banking system.

Table 7.3 shows the major results of the analysis of written responses by the banks with respect to their *Hausbank* status. In column 1, the table contains a definition of categories used to classify the written responses. For example, the second category is attributed to all responses indicating that the bank has a large share in the payment transactions of its borrower. Judged by the frequency with which a given factor is mentioned, it turns out that banks explained the incidence (or absence) of their *Hausbank* status primarily using nine factors. If a bank (i) has a high share in debt financing, (ii) has a high share in payment transactions, (iii), (iv) has a high share in either long-term or short-term financing, (v), (vi), (vii) undertakes special, exclusive or intense business with the firm, (viii) the duration of the bank–borrower relationship is

---

[15] Note that the response rate of the survey was 97.5 per cent (i.e. 195 observations), which is extremely high. This is due to the fact that the survey was conducted within a large-scale joint research project of the banks and five academic research teams, where an analysis of credit-management processes in Germany was conducted. See Elsas *et al.* (1998) for details.

Table 7.3. *Categories of responses on the housebank status of banks*

Factor definition ('the bank has ... ')	Mentioning frequencies		
	If the bank viewed itself *not* as *Hausbank*	If the bank viewed itself as *Hausbank*	Total (out of 195 observations)
High share debt financing	38	48	86
High share payment transactions	28	38	66
High share short-term financing	11	22	33
High share long-term financing	7	23	30
High business intensity	15	14	29
Exclusive business	11	18	29
Provides special services	11	14	25
Long duration	6	18	24
Influence on the management	1	21	22

Source: Elsas (2003: table 1, p. 10).

long, or (ix) has influence on the firm's management, then a *Hausbank* relationship is more likely to be observed.

By relating the banks' self-assessments to observed loan contract and borrower characteristics, the author further shows the following.

1. Relationship lending is systematically associated with a larger share of banks in total financing of the borrower.
2. Firms within a *Hausbank* relationship maintain a significantly lower number of bank relationships.
3. In keeping with the theoretical concept, relationship lending serves as a financing instrument intended to create bargaining power for the bank involved, thereby leading to a commitment between the two contracting parties.

The first two results can be illustrated by some descriptive statistics. Based on the same data set, Elsas and Krahnen (1998) report descriptive statistics for *Hausbank* and arm's length borrowers related to contractual and borrower characteristics. A selection is shown in Table 7.4.

To conclude, on the basis of the SME-sample used in Elsas and Krahnen (1998) and Elsas (2003), the observed characteristics of *Hausbank* relationships are consistent with the theory of relationship lending.

Table 7.4. *Descriptive statistics of borrowers with and without a housebank relationship*

Variable	Hausbank	Not Hausbank
Number of bank relationships	4.8	8.5
Duration of bank–borrower relationship (years)	23.1	25.3
Share in debt financing held by reporting bank (%)	46.0	26.0
Bank internal rating	2.8	3.3
Limited liability (% of all borrowers)	84.0	78.0
Size (sales in million Euro)	84.5	104.5
Number of observations	32	23

Notes: Calculations are based on observations from 1996. The *Hausbank* attribution is based on the self-assessments of loan officers combined with evidence from the credit files. Bank internal ratings are measured on a scale of 1–6, where category 1 indicates highest loan quality (lowest default probability) and 6 indicates worst loan quality, typically in default.

Source: Elsas and Krahnen (1998: p. 1296, table 3).

7.4. BANKS AS FINANCIERS OF SMALL AND MEDIUM ENTERPRISES: INTERTEMPORAL SMOOTHING, LIQUIDITY INSURANCE, AND CREDIT AVAILABILITY

7.4.1. Overview

As outlined above, a commitment between two contracting parties introduces monopoly power into the credit relationship. The most obvious benefit is to facilitate intertemporal transfers. For example, if the borrower is tied to the bank, the bank may charge interest rates on loans below the competitive level at the beginning of the relationship, knowing that it will be able to extract rents at a later stage (i.e. the bank will then be able to charge interest rates higher than the competitive level).

This section discusses some evidence on three specific issues associated with intertemporal contracting by relationship lenders. The first is concerned with the actual adjustment of interest rates on lines of credit to those corporate borrowers who are classified as either a *Hausbank* or non-*Hausbank* customer. The second issue addresses the potential insurance function of relationship lenders by discussing liquidity insurance provided by *Hausbank*s. The third issue is concerned with Petersen and Rajan's (1995) conjecture that intertemporal contracting due to relationship lending may increase the availability of credit to borrowers.

7.4.2. Evidence on Loan Pricing

Using the same data as in the previous section, Elsas and Krahnen (1998) and Elsas (2001) analyse the loan pricing of banks between *Hausbank* and arm's length relationships. The authors postulate that there will be differences in pricing patterns for two reasons: first, because relationship lenders conduct interest rate smoothing for their borrowers, as suggested by Berlin and Mester (1999), and second because of remuneration of *Hausbank*-specific services (like information production, distress insurance etc.) or monopoly rents which increase observed prices.

Elsas and Krahnen (1998) investigate the spreads charged by banks on lines of credit. Following the literature (see e.g. Berger and Udell 1995), it is appropriate to look at the pricing of lines of credit since, in general, banks have considerable freedom in price setting for these types of loan. Lines of credit serve as a means for providing firms with liquidity at short notice. Lines of credit (typically) do not have a fixed maturity or a linkage to some specific investment project.[16] Moreover, in Germany, lines of credit provide banks with the possibility to set interest rates almost at their discretion. Most of the loans are not linked to a reference rate (like e.g. the LIBOR), and no fixed spread is contractually pre-specified. Hence the pricing of lines of credit seems particularly interesting with respect to the price setting behaviour of banks.[17]

In terms of methodology, cross-sectional regressions of the interest rate spread on a set of explanatory variables are used.[18] The empirical model consists of control variables (like firm size, legal status), and a dummy variable indicating whether the borrower is involved in a *Hausbank* relationship. The dummy variable proxying for the *Hausbank* status of a particular lender captures the extent to which the *Hausbank* status shifts the regression function for *Hausbank* borrowers. This shift is positive if *Hausbank*s charge on average a positive premium, and negative if they price on average below the competitive level relevant for the non-*Hausbank* borrowers.

As can be seen from Table 7.5, interest rates charged on lines of credit are significantly sensitive to borrower default risk. However, the magnitude of the risk premium is quite small. Evaluated at the sample mean, it amounts to ninety-four basis points (above the reference rate, FIBOR).[19] The comparative

---

[16] In Germany, lines of credit are usually provided in conjunction with checking accounts and therefore resemble overdraft facilities.

[17] This is the standard approach in the literature, see, for example, Petersen and Rajan (1994, 1995), Berger and Udell (1995) for the United States, Degryse and van Cayseele (2000) for Belgian, and Harhoff and Körting (1998) for German firms (and a sample with small-scale industry).

[18] The spread on the amount outstanding is defined as the interest rate charged by the bank minus the 3-month FIBOR (Frankfurt Interbank Offered Rate).

[19] These numbers have to be interpreted with care. First, the corporate bond market in Germany 1996 was quite small, by American standards. Second, the calibration of internal ratings and external ratings is guess work here. We interpreted an internal rating of 1 and 2, the benchmark, as an A, and a rating of 5 as a B. This is a conservative estimate in the sense that it almost surely underestimates the differences in default probabilities among these internal rating classes. Even if we recall the small size of our sample, the observed price differential between bond market and loan market is disturbing, as a spread of ninety-four basis points can hardly be reconciled with earning positive profits in the loan business.

Table 7.5. *Determinants of interest rates charged on
lines of credit*

Regressors	Dependant: Interest rate spread on lines of credit 1996
Constant	6.96 (0.00)***
Firm size	− 0.24 (0.01)***
Rating 3 (medium default risk)	0.40 (0.06)*
Rating 4	0.60 (0.01)***
Rating 5 (high default risk)	0.94 (0.06)*
HB	− 0.28 (0.15)
No. of observations	83
adj. R^2	0.32

**** indicates significance at the 1/10 per cent level.

Notes: All observations are from 1996. HB is a dummy variable, taking the value of one if, according to the lender, it is a housebank relationship. Rating classes 1 and 2 are taken together and serve as the benchmark. *P*-values are in parentheses.

Source: Summary of results as reported in Elsas and Krahnen (1998: p. 1302, table 5).

spread on the market for corporate bonds in 1996 was probably considerably higher. Even more interestingly, the coefficient of the *Hausbank* dummy turns out to be insignificant. This suggests that on average there is no difference in price setting between *Hausbank* and arm's length customers. This observation is at variance with some of the literature (see e.g. Berger and Udell 1995; Degryse and van Cayseele 2000). There are at least three rational explanations for this result: (i) *Hausbank*s do not provide services any more valuable than those of arm's length banks, (ii) different patterns of intertemporal transfers cancel out in the cross section of borrowers, and (iii) adjusting interest rates is not the only way to remunerate *Hausbank* services, that is, the analysis ignores the cross-selling issue and other nonspread income components. Unfortunately, it is a unifying feature (or caveat) of all existing empirical studies on relationship lending and loan pricing that lack of data prevents from differentiating empirically between these explanations.

Elsas (2001) augments this analysis by using the same data within a panel framework, including the interest rate level, and an interaction term between the interest rate level and the *Hausbank* dummy. The interest rate level is included because interest rate adjustments by banks are known to be sticky in general and dependent on the interest rate level (see e.g. Berger and Udell 1992 for the US; Deutsche Bundesbank 1996 for Germany). The interaction term is the actual measure of a different pattern of intertemporal smoothing by *Hausbanks*. It turns out that spreads on lines of credit systematically vary in magnitude with the aggregate level of interest rates. However, the coefficient for the interaction term is insignificant, suggesting that *Hausbanks* do not differ from arm's length banks with respect to their degree of interest rate smoothing.

7.4.3. Liquidity Insurance

Elsas and Krahnen (1998) also look at whether *Hausbanks* provide liquidity insurance for borrowers. They analyse loan contract adjustments as a function of changes in borrower quality. An insurance function of relationship lenders implies that the lending behaviour of *Hausbanks* will differ systematically from that of arm's-length lenders. This should be particularly apparent in the case of a quality deterioration.

The main hypothesis states that owing to the properties of relationship lending, *Hausbanks* will increase (or at least not reduce) their loan supply if borrower quality deteriorates. Arm's length banks, in contrast, will reduce funding under these circumstances. The supporting role of *Hausbanks* in the event of a quality deterioration can be interpreted as a liquidity insurance. To test the hypothesis, Elsas and Krahnen (1998) regress changes in credit volume on contemporaneous changes of internal ratings, that is, the banks' assessment of borrower quality. The adjustment rate of loan supply is further differentiated by the *Hausbank* status. The results reported in Elsas and Krahnen (1998) support the claim that the availability of credit to firms in financial trouble is improved by relationship lending. To be specific, given a one-rating-notch deterioration of borrower quality, *Hausbanks* increase their loan supply, while arm's length lenders do not. Thus *Hausbanks* offer liquidity insurance to their clients. The insurance offered is not unconditional, however, as it is shown to depend on the magnitude of the change in quality. If the increase in default probability is large, implying a deterioration by two or more notches, all banks will decrease their financial commitment, irrespective of the *Hausbank* status. Elsas and Krahnen (1998) argue that liquidity insurance is an important real effect of relationship lending because its anticipation by firms is likely to have an impact on the entire financing structure of these firms. We, therefore, believe that liquidity insurance is an important attribute of a *Hausbank* system. Furthermore, the identification of liquidity insurance as a common outcome of close bank–firm relations suggests that *Hausbank*ing is indeed economically relevant and not merely a myth.

7.4.4. Credit Rationing

Credit rationing is an economic phenomenon typically associated with problems of information asymmetries or incomplete contracting in debt markets.

According to Baltensperger (1978) and Keeton (1979), equilibrium credit rationing occurs if a borrower's demand for credit is denied, even though this borrower is willing to pay all the price and non-price elements of a loan contract (see also Freixas and Rochet 1997: 137). Obviously, this definition includes the interest rate charged on the loan, and contract features such as collateralization or covenants.

Relationship lending may have an impact on credit rationing. Again, the basic idea is that relying on a relationship lender may enhance credit availability since this lender (i) already has better (private) information, (ii) may have better incentives to engage in costly information production, and (iii) may expect to extract rents from the relationship with the borrower in the future.

Fischer's study (2000) provides empirical insight in the role of information accumulation by banks (the essential feature of relationship lending) and credit rationing. It is concerned with the incentives encouraging banks to engage in costly information production and the role played by competition among banks in this context. Relying on a questionnaire, Fischer (2000) analyses information flows from the borrowers to banks during a loan application process.[20]

In a first step, the author analyses the impact of bank competition in local debt markets on the degree of information acquisition by banks. It turns out that banks in more concentrated local debt markets engage significantly more often in information acquisition than banks in more competitive environments. Since relationship lending can be interpreted as being based on information accumulation and being rationally intended for the creation of monopoly power within credit relationships (see Elsas 2003), these results carry over directly to the *Hausbank* case.

The next step considers firm behaviour with respect to taking discounts offered by suppliers, in other words, trade credit. The frequency of missing out on supplier discounts serves as a proxy for credit rationing since it is presumed to be the most expensive source of financing for firms.[21] The effect of relationship lending on credit availability can be tested by the impact of bank concentration in local debt markets on the frequency of firms taking discounts. The underlying idea is that the exogenous monopoly power of banks in credit relationships (i.e. bank concentration) has a similar effect on firm financing restrictions as the endogenous monopoly power arising from relationship lending (see Petersen and Rajan 1995). Since Fischer's results imply that banks in more concentrated markets do indeed invest more in information production and monitoring, it can be expected that firms located in those markets will be less financially constrained.

---

[20] The data set was provided by the Ifo-Institute (Institute for Economic Research), a leading policy research institution in Germany. The Ifo Institute conducted a survey on Corporate Finance in 1997, by sending a questionnaire to all firms that regularly participate in their yearly survey of firm investments.

[21] It is argued that not taking discounts offered by suppliers indicates financial constraints because of the high implicit price of doing so (see e.g. Petersen and Rajan 1995).

The analysis is conducted in the following way. The ordinal variable 'frequency of taking discounts', indicating the ordered items 'never/rarely/frequently/always', is regressed on a set of explanatory variables. These consist of control variables for firm heterogeneity such as firm size, profitability, financial leverage, and so forth.

The coefficient of the main variable of interest, a Herfindahl-index of bank concentration in local debt markets,[22] is positive and significantly different from zero. Hence, the higher the bank concentration in local debt markets, the more often firms will make use of discounts offered by suppliers. In other words, the higher (local) bank concentration, the less often will firms rely on expensive trade credit. Fischer's evidence is consistent with the notion of relationship lending as a means to increase credit availability. This finding is related to the results of Petersen and Rajan (1995) for US firms, albeit that Fischer (2000) offers a different explanation for this pattern, namely the value of accumulated private information.

However, it is questionable whether the frequency of taking supplier discounts is indeed a good proxy for the existence of credit rationing, since the opportunity costs decrease with the term of delayed settlement (see Petersen and Rajan 1997 for an extensive discussion of trade credit). However, a study by Plötscher (2001), using the same data underlying Fischer's results, finds that firms which use trade credit less frequently were indeed denied credit by their bank more often.[23]

To conclude, the previous results constitute evidence that *Hausbank* relationships do in fact confer economic benefits consistent with the theoretical concept of relationship lending. Elsas' (2003) findings indicate that the building block of relationship lending (or *Hausbank* relations) is the deliberate creation of monopoly power in credit relationships. Fischer (2000) shows that monopoly power indeed affects incentives to engage in costly monitoring and information production, with intuitively plausible consequences for credit availability.

The analysis by Elsas and Krahnen (1998) is closely related to intertemporal smoothing and the issue of credit availability. As already described in more detail, their findings suggest an important role for relationship lending in the provision of liquidity insurance. The following section will discuss complementary evidence on the special role of *Hausbanks* when their client firms actually are in financial distress.

---

[22] The Herfindahl-index is a common measure of concentration and defined as the sum of squared market shares of each individual economic entity present in the market. It accounts for the number of market participants as well as asymmetry between their individual market shares.

[23] Another caveat concerning trade credit goes back to Wilner (2000), who argues that customer relations between firms and suppliers exhibit characteristics similar to relationship lending if there is some commitment between the two (e.g. owing to the specificity of the suppliers' products). Hence, if the remuneration of supply also reflects premia for insurance-like services, it is difficult to evaluate intertemporal smoothing just by looking at interest rates in the cross section.

7.5. BANKS AS FINANCIERS OF SMALL AND MEDIUM ENTERPRISES: BORROWER DISTRESS, REORGANIZATION, AND LIQUIDATION

7.5.1. Introduction

So far we have seen that *Hausbank*s provide financial insurance in the case of single notch rating migrations, which are interpreted as a temporary, or mild deterioration of borrower quality. We will now turn to the case of migrations to junk ratings, that is a serious deterioration of borrower quality. In these cases borrowers are considered to be in financial distress, and banks prepare themselves for workout, liquidation, or court action. Administrative responsibilities within the banks typically shift to specialized workout departments.

The involvement of banks in the reorganization of distressed borrowers is greatly facilitated by the structure of the German insolvency code. This is true for the old code, the *Konkurs- und Vergleichsordnung* which was effective between 1877 and 1999, and it is still true for the new code, the *Insolvenzordnung*, albeit to a lesser degree. The new code was motivated largely by an alleged liquidation bias of the old code. Despite this criticism, advocated mostly by legal scholars, there is little empirical evidence available to support this claim. The frequently cited 0.5 per cent of all cases which enter the court-supervised reorganization proceedings ('Vergleichsverfahren'), while the remaining 99.5 per cent enter into bankruptcy proceedings ('Konkursverfahren'),[24] do not support the claim because these numbers abstract from all those instances in which an attempt is made to reorganize a distressed firm *prior* to court intervention.[25] In a statistical sense, the analysis of all cases that enter the court-supervised process, be it for bankruptcy or reorganization proceedings, rather than all cases that reach a certain level of default probability, provokes a sampling bias. The bias stems from the exclusion of all firms that have a significant default probability, that is, are near-insolvent, but are nevertheless privately restructured. Clearly, conclusions drawn from a biased sample cannot be generalized to the population.

Figure 7.1 is a sketch of the procedural logic of the former German insolvency code, the *Konkurs- und Vergleichsordnung* (in effect until 31 December 1998). The shaded area in Figure 7.1 refers to those cases that enter court proceedings, defining the biased sample referred to above. Clearly, this area captures only a subset of all distress cases.[26]

---

[24] ('Konkursverfahren') is sometimes translated as *compulsory liquidation* even though liquidation is not mandatory. For reasons of clarity we will adhere to the following terminology: ('Vergleichsordnung') as *reorganization proceedings* and ('Konkursordnung') as *bankruptcy proceedings*.

[25] See for these numbers Friderichs *et al.* (1999: 76). The same authors provide a survey of the old German insolvency code.

[26] Note further that 70 per cent of all cases entering bankruptcy proceedings were dismissed for lack of assets, see Friderichs *et al.* (1999: 76).

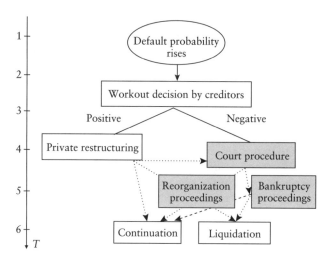

Figure 7.1. *Procedural logic of the German insolvency code inforce until end 1998.*

To evaluate the merits of the old and the new German insolvency code it is instructive to recall the timing of decisions by firm management, creditors, and the court in a typical distress situation. Figure 7.1 presents such a sequence, starting from an unexpected event that causes financial distress, followed by an upward adjustment of default expectation by the lender (T_1), and a decision by the lenders concerning a possible private reorganization $(T_{2,3})$. If this decision is negative, court proceedings will be started, leading either to reorganization proceedings or bankruptcy proceedings $(T_{4,5})$. If the decision is positive and if the private reorganization involving creditors is successful, the firm will reappear as a healthy business unit (continuation T_6). On the other hand, if the reorganization is not successful, the company will enter formal court proceedings (T_4).

The outcome of this consideration is that in order to measure the impact of a given insolvency code on the decision to liquidate or to reorganize a company, the corresponding efforts of creditors prior to court proceedings must also be taken into account. Working with a sample of 124 medium-sized German distressed borrowers, Brunner and Krahnen (2002) report that of the eighteen firms entering court proceedings, none emerged as a healthy entity, 50 per cent were liquidated, and the remaining 50 per cent were still pending. However, the vast majority of all cases, 85 per cent (106 cases), were in fact reorganized. Sixteen per cent (eighteen cases) were successfully reorganized, eighty-eight cases were still pending due to the long duration of the workouts.[27] Attempts to reorganize distressed borrowers are, therefore, very common in German financial markets as far as medium-sized industry is concerned.

---

[27] The underlying data set is an extension of the one used by Elsas and Krahnen (1998) and Elsas (2003), see Section 7.4 of this chapter.

In order to better understand why lending institutions are willing to become involved in out-of-court restructurings, we will delineate the German insolvency code in the next Section 7.5.2, before presenting some evidence on the role of *Hausbanks* in workout decision-making in Section 7.5.3. Section 7.5.4 will deal with multiple lending and the inherent risk of inefficient and premature liquidations. We will ask how the risk of a run on firm assets is mitigated. Our analysis centres on an effective institution in the German banking world, the so-called bank pool. This institution appears to be fairly successful in organizing collaborative action between several banks at the onset of financial distress.

7.5.2. German Insolvency Code: Old and New

The current German insolvency code was enacted on 1 January 1999.[28] It was intended to improve the old code by allowing an early commencement of court proceedings and by providing incentives for timely reorganization. To this end, imminent illiquidity has been defined as a new bankruptcy trigger. The new code supplements the two provisions of the old code relating to factual illiquidity and overindebtedness (i.e. when asset value is smaller than debt value). Thus, the borrower can ask for protection under the new bankruptcy code if he expects illiquidity to materialize. For a period of 3 months there will be an automatic stay with respect to all secured claims. The borrower or the insolvency administrator must present an insolvency plan to the court. This plan must be supported by a majority of lenders (by heads and by amounts) in the creditors committee, and a distinction must be made for each class of claims (secured, unsecured, unsecured junior, employees, and small/trade creditors).

Under specified circumstances, the court can overrule the voting of the creditor classes, in order to minimize the risk of strategic voting. Small creditors are protected by a Pareto principle, that is, minority creditors must not receive less than they would if there were no insolvency plan in the first place. The law does not impose details on the restructuring effort, but rather invites innovations in the reorganization efforts. Pre-insolvency claims, in particular collateral rights, are respected under the insolvency plan. In addition, secured creditors have special information rights during the insolvency proceedings, and they have a right of pre-emption for secured assets sold.

Overall, the new insolvency code is a blend between the old, creditor-friendly legislation and a US-style, debtor-oriented code. It allows for considerable flexibility with regard to possible arrangements among creditors. Until 1998, the old insolvency code allowed only factual illiquidity and overindebtedness as commencement facts for court-supervised bankruptcy

---

[28] See Kaiser (1996), Franks *et al.* (1996), Drukarczyk 1999, and Schmidt (1980) for additional details on the institutional features presented in this section.

Table 7.6. *Key characteristics of the old and new German insolvency code*

Characteristics of code	New code (since 1 Jan. 1999)	Old code (until 31 Dec. 1998)
Bankruptcy commencement (court proceedings) due to	• Overindebtedness • Factual insolvency • Imminent insolvency (only debtor)	• Overindebtedness • Factual insolvency
Insolvency plan?	Yes, consent by majority of all claimholder classes required	Not required outside formal bankruptcy proceedings
Automatic stay?	Yes, if protection under bankruptcy law is sought	No
Minority creditor protection?	Yes, insolvency plan must Pareto improve on current situation	No
Collateral rights?	Are respected throughout	Are respected throughout
Seniority of new funds provided within the scope of the insolvency procedure?	No fixed rule, negotiable within the limits of the insolvency plan	No

proceedings. Again, these proceedings could take one of two routes: bankruptcy proceedings and reorganization proceedings. In both cases, control was shifted from the (owner–) manager to an official trustee who was empowered and supervised by the courts. There was no general automatic stay, since secured creditors were free to take legal action individually in order to secure their claim.[29] Table 7.6 summarizes the key characteristics of the old and the new codes.

7.5.3. Workout Involvement by *Hausbanks*

We now turn to the decision of creditors to support workout activities prior to any court supervised formal bankruptcy proceedings. We shall try to shed light on two aspects of bank behaviour, that is, the involvement of lenders in pre-bankruptcy restructuring of distressed firms, and the role of *Hausbanks* in these situations.

The first question to be asked is whether banks get involved in the restructuring of firms to whom they have lent money and who they judge to be in distress? Using the credit-file data already introduced in Section 7.4, Elsas

---

[29] The strong creditor position in bankruptcy proceedings under the old code was facilitated in particular by the secured lenders' rights of separation ('Absonderung') and, in some cases, the right of sorting out of collateral (Aussonderung).

and Krahnen (2002) analyse a sample of sixty-two potentially distressed lending relationships, 21 per cent of which involve *Hausbanks*, while the rest relate to arm's length banks.[30]

Remarkably, only 6.5 per cent of all cases go straight into bankruptcy proceedings, either compulsory liquidation or composition proceedings. 37 per cent of all cases report a serious attempt of reorganization with bank participation. If such a workout occurs, bank participation includes the provision of fresh money, the initiation of management consulting and, in some cases, direct management involvement. The remaining 56.5 per cent experience no special workout treatment. Thus, formal insolvency proceedings (the lower right hand section of Figure 7.1) with respect to the sample of medium-sized German companies capture only a minor portion of all bank involvement in distressed firms. The prominence of lender involvement in pre-bankruptcy reorganization and restructuring is quite considerable by comparison with that of other countries, such as the United Kingdom (see Franks and Sussman 2000) or the US (see Gilson *et al.* 1990).

When attempting to predict the role of *Hausbanks* in a situation of borrower financial distress, it is useful to view the decision of a bank to participate in a workout as being a fundamental investment decision. In many cases restructuring will not be possible unless additional funds are provided. The outcome thus depends on whether an additional investment is seen as a positive net present value project. Each bank among the company's creditors will have to evaluate the present value of an extended financial commitment *vis-à-vis* the company. If this present value is positive, the required workout can be undertaken, otherwise the bank will not be willing to extend additional loans, or to take any other supportive action. Instead it will tend to pull back and, perhaps, trigger the liquidation of the company. However, strategic interaction between lenders as well as between lenders and the borrower may lead to violations of this NPV-based efficiency rule.

Ceteris paribus, supportive actions by a particular lender are more likely (i) the higher the seniority of his claims is over the claims of other creditors, (ii) the lower his bargaining costs are expected to be relative to other creditors, and (iii) the lower his uncertainty in the assessment of the real economic value of a debtor's assets. The first two conditions refer to the free-riding problem that emerges in a borrower distress situation with multiple lenders (Wruck 1990; Gilson *et al.* 1990). Relationship lending and the accumulation of collateral can be seen as being complementary in view of solving this free-riding problem. Relationship lending is associated with an instrumental role of the bank in total firm financing, which provides bargaining power against other lenders and against the borrower. Since collateral affects the seniority of

---

[30] The firms in this sample are a random draw of medium-sized (West-) German companies with at least one negative (junk) internal rating during the observation window 1992–96.

lenders,[31] the allocation of collateral determines bargaining power within the group of all lenders as well. That collateral thereby reduces conflicts among lenders in distress situations, is a hypothesis developed by Longhofer and Santos (2000) and Welch (1997).[32] Therefore, it is conclusive to note that according to Elsas and Krahnen (2002), *Hausbank*s are systematically more collateralized (more senior) than other banks.

The third condition regarding information on the borrower's business is especially true for those lenders with private information. Hence, all three conditions are met by relationship lenders, and it is therefore to be expected that these institutions will engage more frequently in workouts than normal lenders.

A closer look at the workout-decision-by-creditors node in Figure 7.1 is therefore justified in order to understand the determinants of bank involvement in corporate restructuring. To test this hypothesis Elsas and Krahnen (2002) run a probit regression where the binary dependent variable takes the value of one if any workout activity by a sample bank (such as providing fresh money, developing a restructuring plan, or pressing the board to replace management) is observed, and otherwise zero. The estimation identifies two primary significant explanatory variables which are robust across a variety of models. The first is the proportion of collateralized loans of total loans. The coefficient is positive, indicating that ceteris paribus more collateral (here: a higher seniority) increases the likelihood of active workout involvement by the banks.

The second significant variable is the *Hausbank* dummy variable, which takes the value of one if a particular bank is the *Hausbank* or the relationship lender of the company, and zero otherwise. The *Hausbank* dummy has a positive coefficient in the regression which is again robust across different model specifications. The interpretation here is that during a period of distress *Hausbank*s are more willing than arm's length banks to engage in workout activities. Taken together, these results support the hypothesis that *Hausbank*s play an active role in pre-bankruptcy corporate reorganization.

The above findings suggest that relationship lenders are typically major and senior lenders, presumably equipped with information privileges and, therefore, bargaining power against other lenders and the borrower. This combination increases their willingness to engage in a costly workout.

Since multiple lending is common in Germany, workouts and out-of-court reorganizations face problems of coordination among lenders, and of free-rider incentives. The next section reports how these problems can be overcome.

---

[31] According to the study by Elsas and Krahnen (2002), the majority of all collateral rights contractually agreed upon in the loan contracts of their sample correspond to inside collateral, that is, collateral that reallocates the seniority of lenders claims rather than extending the aggregate adhesive wealth liable for all lenders (outside collateral).

[32] In the German literature, this conflict reducing role of collateral has been discussed since 1980, see for example Schmidt (1980) and Rudolph (1984).

7.5.4. Multiple Lending and Pre-bankruptcy Workouts: How to Overcome Free-rider Incentives

The non-shaded area in Figure 7.1 describes an aspect of lending relationships that is frequently disregarded when corporate distress and the insolvency code are discussed. The pre-bankruptcy involvement of banks in corporate reorganizations seems to be a common phenomenon in Germany, however. *Hausbanks*, in particular, are prepared to take action in distress times, that is, to provide fresh money, request the advice of outside consultants, increase pressure by frequent monitoring etc., in order to support firm workout activities. In light of the typical debt structure of firms in Germany, that is, in most cases bank debt with multiple lenders, questions arise about how pre-bankruptcy involvement by banks can be sustained and the risk of a corporate run (a pre-emptive loan cancellation) be avoided.

Brunner and Krahnen (2002) have studied these issues. Their data set is an augmented version of the one used by Elsas and Krahnen (2002), containing detailed information on bank activities in corporate distress for 124 relationships over a 5–7 year period (observation period 1992–99).

Their major finding relates to an institution that for a long time was overlooked by financial economists when studying the German financial system, namely the bank pool. These pools play an instrumental role in explaining both the success of bank involvement in pre-bankruptcy corporate workouts and the apparent absence of bank involvement in formal bankruptcy proceedings.

For the sample analysed by Brunner and Krahnen (2002), in 47 per cent of all cases a bank pool was formed, typically at or shortly before the onset of borrower distress. The formation of a bank pool is more likely if the distress event is considered to be serious. For firms with a serious distress rating,[33] 70 per cent will turn to a bank pool, while for the less serious distress rating this number is only 42 per cent.

The institutional details of these pools follow a common contractual structure, which is intended to align the incentives of creditors and to hinder unilateral debt enforcement (which is always possible under the German law, particularly for secured creditors). Furthermore, bank pools coordinate lender involvement by nominating one pool leader as a trustee. Pools are typically formed when illiquidity of the borrower is expected by one lender. A formal pool agreement is signed that includes all banks and, in exceptional cases, trade creditors as well. The agreement covers the outstanding non-collateralized debt of each bank, for which the pool then seeks collateral coverage. Thus, most pool member banks have additional collateral outside the pool, which

---

[33] Again, bank internal ratings are measured on a six category scale, where categories 5 and 6 (highest default risks or actual default) are interpreted as expected or actual distress, see Brunner and Krahnen (2002).

was signed before pool formation. A stand-still agreement between all member banks guarantees that they will liquidate their collateral only with the consent of the pool. The shares of non-collateralized debt are the basis for determining individual pool-quotas. The bank with the largest quota becomes the pool leader. Of course, this is not necessarily the bank with the largest loan outstanding. Future in- and outflows of cash are then shared among pool members according to their quotas. Decision-making within the pool must be unanimous; members can leave the pool, but the contract makes it unattractive to do so.

What effect has pool formation on the success probability of a workout? To answer this question Brunner and Krahnen (2002) define workout success as a significant lowering of the default probability, proxied by an improvement of internal ratings from junk to investment grade. Workout success is then regressed on a number of explanatory variables. It turns out that the existence of a bank pool increases the probability of success (presumably because of its interest alignment function), while the number of bank relations, given that a pool exists, has a negative impact on this probability. The latter finding suggests that even bank pools are not able to completely resolve the coordination problems inherent in financial distress. These determinants of workout success are robust under various specifications of the basic model. A further test concerns the determinants of pool formation. The regression analysis reveals that for a particular firm in distress, pool formation is more likely when the number of banks involved is not too large, and when the loans outstanding have approximately the same size among all lenders (are not too unequal among lenders).

Referring once again to Figure 7.1, the evidence suggests that bank involvement in corporate restructuring in Germany is particularly strong in the periods preceding formal bankruptcy proceedings. *Hausbanks* play a special role in these times as they tend to accumulate collateral and emerge as the major monitor. They are typically not fully collateralized, so proper monitoring and workout incentives are upheld. Bank pools are an effective workout device, much in use among medium-sized distressed borrowers. As was argued above, this may be due to the fact that the German insolvency code (both the old and the new) respects creditor rights in its proceedings.

7.6. THE *HAUSBANK*: MYTH, REALITY, AND THE FUTURE

This chapter has reviewed recent evidence on the role of relationship lending in Germany. As a first step, we analysed close ties between banks and large industrial firms. This involved all the features usually regarded as instruments used by banks for influencing the management decisions of firms, that is, debt provision, direct equity stakes, proxy-voting rights, and supervisory board representation. The evidence reviewed shows that there is some support for a role of banks in corporate control exercised via equity held in their own right. The evidence further indicates that supervisory board representation appears to be caused by equity holdings, rather than constituting a control mechanism on its own. Finally, contrary to the common presumption in the literature, the available evidence does not suggest that banks use proxy-voting rights in a systematic way to influence management decisions. This might be due to the fact that the exercise of proxy-voting rights is complex because of inherent free-rider and coordination problems.

We then turned to the major firm segment of small and medium-sized firms. Here, bank–firm relationships mainly result from the provision of debt, a structure analysed theoretically under the notion of relationship lending. In particular, we found support for the idea that *Hausbanks* develop an informationally intense relationship with their customers, and that these special relationships are common among mid-sized firms. *Hausbank* relationships have real consequences. They provide access to funds after rating downgrades, when normal banks tend to reduce their loans. Furthermore, in distress situations *Hausbanks* are more likely to become involved in workout activities. Thus, in the light of the results reported on liquidity insurance and workout involvement, some earlier assessments in the literature (e.g. by Edwards and Fischer 1994) were not confirmed.

Typically, workouts are engineered prior to any court involvement, while hopeless cases are handed over to formal bankruptcy proceedings. This explains why court proceedings almost never lead to workout activities—a fact that some observers have erroneously interpreted as a sign of inefficiency of the insolvency code (see Kaiser 1996; or Franks *et al.* 1996: 86). In fact, pre-bankruptcy workout activities are common. In case of multiple banking, workouts are frequently made possible by forming a bank pool, which is an explicit contractual arrangement between all bank lenders. These pools align lender incentives and allow negotiations to be conducted in a coordinated manner.

Obviously, the available evidence is not sufficient to provide a comprehensive assessment of the pros and cons of bank–firm relationships in Germany. In our view, at least two avenues of future research are needed: First, it is still unclear whether the distinct behaviour observed for relationship lenders in borrower distress improves efficiency. To answer this question, more studies on bank behaviour in borrower distress are needed, using data which also cover the period after firm reorganization. Second, most of the theory on financial intermediation suggests that one bank lender is the optimal number of creditors. But then, why do we observe multiple bank relationships as a general pattern, in conjunction with relationship lending? What does this imply for the concept of relationship lending, which builds on information monopolies by banks? Currently, theory has not much to say about the sustainability of information monopolies under multiple banking. Further, it is unclear whether relationship lending may have some merits, *especially* in the context of multiple bank lending by firms. However, we believe that future investigation of German *Hausbank* relationships can provide interesting insights into these questions.

Thus, the overall evidence presented in this chapter clearly supports the hypothesis that relationship lending in Germany is a fact rather than a myth and, more importantly, that it has real economic effects on the financing of corporations. From an economic perspective, the evidence corroborates the existence long-term relationship investments of banks and their customers. This may well be seen as a valuable asset, particularly in the SME-sector. What will happen to this asset in the future? The German financial system has entered a transformation phase, driven by growing competitive pressure from financial markets. This pressure threatens to undermine the acceptance and the viability of financial relationships, both in commercial and investment banking. Therefore, in our opinion, the emerging central topic in the finance arena in Germany will be the confrontation between established private relationships and emerging public markets for financial services. Whatever the outcome of this encounter[34]—one should reckon with considerable tenacity of the former.

References

Allen, F., and Gale, D. (1999). 'Innovations in financial services, relationships, and risk sharing', *Financial Management*, 45: 1239–53.

Baltensperger, E. (1978). 'Credit rationing: Issues and questions', *Journal of Money, Credit, and Banking*, 10: 170–83.

Baums, T., and Fraune, C. (1995). 'Institutionelle Anleger und Publikumsgesellschaften: Eine empirische Untersuchung', *Die Aktiengesellschaft*, 40: 97–112.

Berger, A. N., and Udell, G. F. (1992). 'Some evidence on the empirical significance of credit rationing', *Journal of Political Economy*, 100: 1047–77.

——, and —— (1995). 'Relationship lending and lines of credit in small firm finance', *Journal of Business*, 68: 351–81.

Berlin, M., and Mester, L. (1999). 'Deposits and relationship lending', *Review of Financial Studies*, 12: 579–607.

Bhattacharya, S., and Chiesa, G. (1995). 'Proprietary information, financial intermediation, and research incentives', *Journal of Financial Intermediation*, 4: 328–57.

Billett, M. T., Flannery, M. J., and Garfinkel, J. A. (1995). 'The effect of lender identity on a borrowing firm's equity return', *Journal of Finance*, 50: 699–718.

Boehmer, E. (1999). 'Corporate Governance in Germany. Institutional Background and Empirical Results', Working Paper No. 78. Humboldt University Berlin, Berlin.

——(2001). 'Business groups, large shareholders, and bank control: An analysis of German takeovers', *Journal of Financial Intermediation*, 9: 117–48.

Bolton, P., and Scharfstein, D. (1996). 'Optimal debt structure and the number of creditors', *Journal of Political Economy*, 104: 1–25.

---

[34] This line of thought is taken up at greater length in the concluding chapter of this volume.

Boot, A. (2000). 'Relationship Banking: What do we know?', *Journal of Financial Intermediation*, 9: 7–25.

Boot, A., Greenbaum, S. I., and Thakor, A. V. (1993). 'Reputation and discretion in financial contracting', *American Economic Review*, 83: 1165–83.

Brunner, A., and Krahnen, J. P. (2002). 'Corporate debt restructuring: Evidence on lender coordination in financial distress', Goethe-Universität Frankfurt. Working Paper.

Cable, J. (1985). 'Capital market information and industrial performance: The role of West German banks', *Economic Journal*, 95: 118–32.

Caminal, R., and Matutes, C. (1997). 'Can competition in the credit market be excessive?', CEPR Discussion Paper No 1725.

Crafts, N. (1992). 'Productivity growth reconsidered', *Economic Policy*, 15: 387–414.

Degryse, H., and van Cayseele, P. (2000). 'Relationship lending within a bank-based system: Evidence from European small business data', *Journal of Financial Intermediation*, 9: 90–109.

Demsetz, H., and Lehn, K. (1985). 'The structure of corporate ownership: causes and consequences', *Journal of Political Economy*, 93: 1155–77.

Deutsche Bundesbank (1996). 'Reaktionen der Geldmarkt- und kurzfristigen Bankzinsen auf Änderungen der Notenbanksätze', *Monthly Report* (October): 33–48.

——(2001). 'Erträge und Finanzierungsverhältnisse deutscher Unternehmen nach Rechtsformen', *Monthly Report* (December): 45–77.

Dewatripont, M., and Maskin, E. (1995). 'Credit and efficiency in centralized versus decentralized markets', *Review of Economic Studies*, 62: 541–56.

Diamond, D. W. (1991). 'Monitoring and reputation: The choice between bank loans and privately placed debt', *Journal of Political Economy*, 99: 688–721.

Drukarczyk, J. (1999). *Finanzierung*, 8th edn. Stuttgart: Lucius und Lucius.

Edwards, J., and Fischer, K. (1994). *Banks, finance, and investment in Germany*. Cambridge. Cambridge University Press.

Elsas, R. (2001). *Die Bedeutung der Hausbank: Eine ökonomische Analyse*. Wiesbaden: Deutscher Universitätsverlag.

——(2003). 'Empirical determinants of relationship lending', *Journal of Financial Intermediation*, forthcoming. Universität Frankfurt. Working Paper.

——, and Krahnen, J. P. (1998). 'Is relationship lending special? Evidence from credit-file data in Germany', *Journal of Banking and Finance*, 22: 1283–316.

——, and —— (2002). 'Collateral, relationship lending, and financial distress: An empirical study on financial contracting', Goethe-Universität Frankfurt. Working Paper.

——, Henke, S., Machauer, A., Rott, R., and Schenk, G. (1998). 'Empirical analysis of credit relationships in small firms financing: Sampling design and descriptive statistics', Center for Financial Studies, Frankfurt. Working Paper 98/14.

Elston, J. A. (1998). 'Investment, liquidity constraints, and bank relationships: Evidence from German manufacturing firms', in S.W. Black and M. Moersch (eds.) *Competition and convergence in financial markets*. Amsterdam: North-Holland/ Elsevier Science.

Emmons, W. R., and Schmid, F. A. (1998). 'Universal banking, allocation of control rights, and corporate finance in Germany', *Federal Reserve Bank of St. Louis Review*. July/August: 19–42.

Fazzari, S., Hubbard, R. G., and Peterson, B. (1988). 'Investment and finance reconsidered', *Brookings Papers on Economic Activity*, 114–95.

Fischer, K.-H. (2000). 'Acquisition of information in loan markets and bank market power—An empirical investigation', Goethe-Universität Frankfurt. Working Paper.

Fischer, K. (1990). 'Hausbankbeziehungen als Instrument der Bindung zwischen Banken und Unternehmen: Eine theoretische und empirische Analyse', Unpublished PhD thesis. University of Bonn.

Fohlin, C. (1998). 'Relationship Banking, Liquidity, and Investment in the German Industrialization', *Journal of Finance*, 53: 1737–58.

Franks, J., and Mayer, C. (2001). 'The ownership and control of German corporations', *Review of Financial Studies*, 14: 943–77.

Franks, J., Nyborg, K. G., and Tourous, W. N. (1996). 'A comparison of US, UK, and German insolvency codes', *Financial Management*, 25: 86–101.

Freixas, X., and Rochet, J.-C. (1997). *Microeconomics of banking*. Cambridge, London: MIT Press.

Gale, D., and Hellwig, M. (1985). 'Incentive compatible debt contracts: The one period problem', *Review of Economic Studies*, 52: 647–63.

Gerschenkron, A. (1962). *Economic backwardness in historical perspective*. Harvard University Press.

Gilson, S. C., John, K., and Lang, L. (1990). 'Troubled debt restructurings—An empirical study of private reorganization of firms in default', *Journal of Financial Economics*, 27: 315–53.

Gorton, G., and Schmid, F. A. (2000). 'Universal banking and the performance of German firms', *Journal of Financial Economics*, 58: 29–80.

Greenbaum, S. I., and Thakor, A. V. (1995). *Contemporary financial intermediation*. Fort Worth: Dryden Press.

Hackethal, A. (2000). *Banken, Unternehmensfinanzierung, und Finanzsystem*. Frankfurt: Peter Lang Verlag.

Harhoff, D., and Körting, T. (1998). 'Lending relationships in Germany—Empirical evidence from survey data', *Journal of Banking and Finance*, 22: 1317–53.

Hilferding, R. (1909). *Das Finanzkapital*, vol. I, 1st edn reprinted in (1974). Frankfurt: Europäische Verlagsanstalt.

Houston, J. F., and James, C. (2001). 'Do relationships have limits? Banking relationships, financial constraints and investment', *Journal of Business*, 74: 347–74.

Hubbard, R. G. (1998). 'Capital-market imperfections and investment', *Journal of Economic Literature*, 36: 193–225.

James, C. M. (1987). 'Some evidence on the uniqueness of bank loans', *Journal of Financial Economics*, 19: 217–35.

Jürgens, U., Rupp, J., and Vitols, K. (2000). 'Corporate Governance and Shareholder Value in Deutschland', Wissenschaftszentrum Berlin, Berlin. Discussionpaper FS II 00–202.

Kaiser, K. (1996). 'European bankruptcy laws: Implications for corporations facing financial distress', *Financial Management*, 25: 67–85.

Kaplan, S. N., and Zingales, L. (1997). 'Do investment cash-flow sensitivities provide useful measures of financing constraints?', *Quarterly Journal of Economics*, 112: 168–215.

Keeton, W. (1979). *Equilibrium credit rationing*. New York: Garland Press.

La Porta, R., Lopez de Silanes, F., Shleifer, A., and Vishny, R. (1997). 'The legal determinants of external finance', *Journal of Finance*, 52: 1131–50.

——, ——, ——, and —— (1998). 'Law and Finance', *Journal of Political Economy*, 106: 1113–55.

Lehmann, E., and Weigand, J. (2000). 'Does the governed corporation perform better? Governance structures and corporate performance in Germany', *European Finance Review*, 4: 157–95.

Lummer, S. L., and McConnell, J. J. (1989). 'Further evidence on the bank lending process and capital market response to bank loan agreements', *Journal of Financial Economics*, 25: 99–122.

Ongena, S., and Smith, D. C. (2000). 'Bank relationships: A review', in P. Harker and A. Zenios (eds.). *The performance of financial institutions*. Cambridge: Cambridge University Press.

Petersen, M. A., and Rajan, R. G. (1994). 'The benefits of lending relationships: Evidence from small business data', *Journal of Finance*, 49: 3–37.

——, and —— (1995). 'The effect of credit market competition on lending relationships', *Quarterly Journal of Economics*, 110: 407–43.

——, and —— (1997). 'Trade credit: Some theories and evidence', *Review of Financial Studies*, 10: 661–92.

Plötscher, C. (2001). *Finanzierungsrestriktionen bei Unternehmen*. Wiesbaden: Deutscher Universitätsverlag.

Rajan, R. G. (1992). 'Insiders and outsiders: The choice between informed and arm's-length debt', *Journal of Finance*, 47: 1367–1400.

——, and Zingales, L. (2001). 'The great reversals: The politics of financial development in the 20th century', forthcoming in *Journal of Financial Economics*.

Rudolph, B. (1984). 'Kreditsicherheiten als Instrument zur Umverteilung und Begrenzung von Kreditrisiken', *Zeitschrift für Betriebswirtschaftliche Forschung*, 36: 16–43.

Schmidt, R. H. (1980). *Ökonomische Analyse des Insolvenzrechts*. Wiesbaden: Gabler-Verlag.

——, Hackethal, A., and Tyrell, M. (1999). 'Disintermediation and the role of banks in Europe: An international comparison', *Journal of Financial Intermediation*, 9: 36–69.

Seger, F. (1997). *Banken, Erfolg und Finanzierung*. Wiesbaden: Deutscher Universitätsverlag.

Sharpe, S. A. (1990). 'Asymmetric information, bank lending, and implicit contracts: A stylized model of customer relationships', *Journal of Finance*, 45: 1069–87.

Sheard, P. (1994). 'Main banks and the governance of financial distress', in M. Aoki and P. Hugh (eds.). *The Japanese main bank system*. Oxford.

Slovin, M. B., Sushka, M. E., and Polonchek, J. A. (1993). 'The value of bank durability: Borrowers as bank stakeholders', *Journal of Finance*, 48: 247–66.

Weinstein, D. E., and Yafeh, Y. (1998). 'On the costs of a bank-centered financial system: Evidence from the changing main bank relations in Japan', *Journal of Finance*, 53: 635–672.

Welch, J. (1997). 'Why is bank debt senior? A theory of asymmetry and claim priority based on the influence costs', *Review of Financial Studies*, 10(4): 1203–36.

Wilner, B. S. (2000). 'The exploitation of relationships in financial distress: The case of trade credit', *Journal of Finance*, 55: 153–78.

Wruck, K. (1990). 'Financial distress, reorganization, and organizational efficiency', *Journal of Financial Economics*, 27: 419–44.

Yosha, O. (1995). 'Information disclosure costs and the choice of financing source', *Journal of Financial Intermediation*, 4: 3–20.

8

Initial Public Offerings and Venture Capital in Germany*

STEFANIE FRANZKE, STEFANIE GROHS, AND
CHRISTIAN LAUX

8.1. INTRODUCTION

We present a survey on the role of initial public offerings (IPOs) and venture capital (VC) in Germany after the Second World War. Between 1945 and 1983 IPOs hardly played a role at all and only a minor role thereafter.[1] In addition, companies that chose an IPO were much older and larger than the average companies going public for the first time in the United States or the United Kingdom. The level of IPO underpricing in Germany, in contrast, has not been fundamentally different from that in other countries. The picture for venture capital financing is not much different from that provided by IPOs in Germany. For a long time venture capital financing was hardly significant, particularly as a source of early stage financing.

The unprecedented boom on the *Neuer Markt* between 1997 and 2000, when many small venture capital financed firms entered the market, provides a striking contrast to the preceding era. However, by US standards, the levels of both IPO and venture capital activities remained rather low even in this boom phase. The extent to which recent developments will have a lasting impact on the financing of German firms, the level of IPO activity, and venture capital financing, remains to be seen. At the time of writing, activity has come to a near standstill and the *Neuer Markt* has just been dissolved.

The low number of IPOs and the fairly low volume of VC financing in Germany before the introduction of the *Neuer Markt* are a striking and much

* We would like to thank Thomas Hellmann, Christian Leuz, Franz-Josef Leven, Giovanna Nicodano, Richard Stehle, and the editors of this volume for very valuable comments. We also thank seminar participants at the Goethe-University Frankfurt, University of Mannheim, and the 2001 FMG and ESF Workshop "Strategic Interactions in Relationship Finance: Bank Lending and Venture Capital".

[1] This was not always the case. Tilly (1992: 103–4) finds that both the volume of total market issues and the proportion of issuance consisting of equity were greater in Germany at the beginning of the twentieth century than they were in the United Kingdom. See also Fohlin (2000*a*), Rajan and Zingales (2003), and Schlag and Wodrich (2000).

debated phenomenon. Understanding the reasons for these apparent peculiarities is vital to understand the German financial system. The potential explanations that have been put forward range from differences in mentality to legal and institutional impediments and the availability of alternative sources of financing. Moreover, the recent literature discusses how interest groups may have benefited and influenced the situation. These groups include politicians, unions/workers, managers/controlling owners of established firms as well as banks.

The chapter is organized as follows: In Section 8.2 we illustrate the history and the recent increase of initial public offerings in Germany. Section 8.3 describes the development and the current status of the German venture capital market and compares it with the United States, United Kingdom, and France. In Section 8.4 we discuss why there are so few IPOs and so little VC financing activity in Germany. Section 8.5 concludes.

8.2. INITIAL PUBLIC OFFERINGS

8.2.1. Development of Initial Public Offerings and Firm Characteristics

For many observers the story of German IPOs (after the Second World War) starts in 1983 (Schürmann and Körfgen 1997: 23). Taking the IPOs listed in the DAI-Factbook, the average number of IPOs between 1949 and 1982, was only 3.3 per year. Even though this list only includes, for the years between 1949 and 1976, IPOs of firms that were still listed in 1994, it nevertheless shows that IPOs were rare events. (The yearly average for the years 1977–82 is 4.) Only the 1960s were associated with marked numbers of IPOs, most of them occurring in the context of the (partial) privatization of state-owned firms such as Veba, Preussag, VEW, Lufthansa, and Volkswagen. The low number of IPOs can be seen as evidence for the secondary role that the stock market played in Germany. Indeed, after the Second World War the number of listed German stock corporations decreased from 686 in 1956 to a minimum of 442 in 1983 (DAI Factbook 2003).

In 1983, the number of IPOs started to increase, reaching an annual average of 19.5 between 1984 and 1996. (See Table 8.1.) However, compared to the United States and the United Kingdom, IPO activity still remained rather low. For example, in the years between 1988 and 1995 a total of 151 IPOs were carried out in Germany, compared to more than 1000 in the United Kingdom and nearly 2500 new listings on the NYSE and the American Stock Exchanges and 3000 at Nasdaq (Schuster 1996: 5).

Starting in 1997, however, Germany witnessed an unprecedented increase in IPO activities. In the year 1999 alone, more IPOs were carried out than in the 10 years from 1988 to 1997. Of course, the worldwide stock market downturn after 2000 also resulted in a rather sudden end of the IPO boom in Germany. Whether IPO activity will resume again when stock market conditions

Table 8.1. *Number of Domestic IPOs in Germany*[a]

	1983	1984	1985	1986	1987	1988	1989	1990	1991	1992
Amtlicher Handel	6	11	8	17	9	3	10	11	9	2
Geregelter Markt[c]	1	10	4	11	10	12	16	20	10	7
Freiverkehr	4	2	1	1	0	0	2	3	0	0
Neuer Markt										
Total	11	23	13	29	19	15	28	34	19	9
	1993	1994	1995	1996	1997	1998	1999	2000	2001	2002[b]
Amtlicher Handel	6	3	12	6	10	15	30	13	5	1
Geregelter Markt[c]	3	8	8	6	4	14	10	11	7	3
Freiverkehr	2	4	0	2	9	8	22	3	3	2
Neuer Markt	.				13	42	113	115	11	1
Total	11	15	20	14	36	79	175	142	26	7

[a] The numbers are taken from the DAI-Factbook 2003.
[b] Until November 2002.
[c] The *Geregelter Markt* was introduced in 1987; data until 1987 refer to *Geregelter Freiverkehr*.

improve, or whether we have indeed observed a temporary and one-time IPO wave in Germany, remains to be seen.

As a first step in trying to understand the 'IPO waves' occurring in Germany it is interesting to note that the level of IPO activities is highly correlated with the conditions in the stock market. The first 'IPO wave' in Germany starting at the beginning of the 1980s and the second one in the late 1990s took place at times when stock prices were soaring in the United States of America as well as in Germany, while the interruptions in 1987, 1991, and 2000 occurred when the stock market crashed. This is in line with the observations in other countries that IPO activity is highly cyclical. But apart from increasing stock prices, two other events draw attention in the late 1990s: in 1996 the IPO of Deutsche Telekom with a volume of nearly €10,000 million was carried out, and in 1997 the *Neuer Markt* was opened at the Frankfurt stock exchange.

The introduction of the *Neuer Markt* was celebrated as a major innovation for the German equity market, which consists of two tiers, with two segments in each of the two tiers (see Chapter 5). The first tier comprises the *Amtlicher Handel* and the *Geregelter Markt*. The *Amtlicher Handel* is the main stock market segment in which all DAX companies are traded (which is comparable to the Official List in the United Kingdom). The *Geregelter Markt* was introduced in 1987 as a segment for small firms, with a lower market capitalization and a lower trade volume.[2] The second tier consists of the *Neuer Markt* and the *Freiverkehr*. The *Neuer Markt* was introduced for young innovative high-tech (growth) firms. The main differences between the

[2] The *Geregelter Markt* absorbed most of the firms that were listed on the *Geregelter Freiverkehr*.

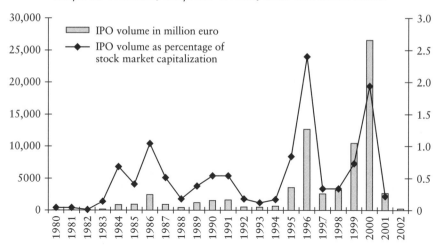

Figure 8.1. *IPO volume.*

different segments are the stringency of the listing, reporting, and disclosure requirements, with the *Neuer Markt* being more demanding.

As can be seen in Table 8.1, the huge increase in the number of IPOs, starting in 1997, stems mainly from new firms that were listed in the new market segment. The other segments do not show a similar increase in the number of IPOs.[3]

The Deutsche Telekom IPO and the IPO wave on the *Neuer Markt* are, of course, also reflected in the yearly total IPO volumes. However, the magnitude of the increase in IPO volume looks less dramatic if it is related to the market capitalization. Figure 8.1 reveals the extraordinary position of the Deutsche Telekom IPO in 1996 (DAI Factbook 2003). It is striking that the IPO volume as percentage of stock market capitalization raised through IPOs in 1986 exceeds that of 1998 or 1999, while the high relative IPO volume in 2000 is primarily due to the downturn in the stock market in the second half of 2000.

In addition to the low number of IPOs in Germany before the IPO boom on the *Neuer Markt*, the average age at the time of the listing as well as the average IPO volume are also worth noting.

In Germany the average age of a firm that carried out an IPO between 1975 and 1984 was 53 years. While the average IPO volume during the 1980s was nearly €40.5 million, this average increased to about €102 million (€83 million excluding Deutsche Telekom) between 1990 and 2000.[4] This contrasts with an average age of about 10 years and an average IPO volume of

---

[3] The number of IPOs on the *Geregelter Markt* declined as most companies opted for the *Neuer Markt*.

[4] DAI-Factbook. Of the 144 public offerings in the United Kingdom in 1985, 46 per cent had a volume of less than €5 million and 14.5 per cent had a volume of less than €2.5 million. (Investor's Chronicle 17 January 1986: 37–41, as quoted in Weichert 1987: 146.)

approximately €64 million (excluding T-online) for firms that listed at the *Neuer Markt* between 1997 and 2001. Moreover, firms going public at the *Neuer Markt* were significantly smaller, had higher sales growth, and higher market-to-book ratios compared with the IPOs on the established segments (Kukies 2000). Given the different aims of the different segments, this is reassuring. However, the difference in characteristics is striking in international comparison. In the 1980s, the average listed German firm was almost four times older at the time of listing than the average UK firm, and it raised on average three times more new equity than a UK firm. This marked difference is not reflected in the listings at the *Neuer Markt*, when compared to Nasdaq, where firms on average were about 7 years old and raised equity of about €148 million in the year 2000.

Indeed, before the *Neuer Markt* came into being the typical firm that carried out an IPO in Germany was a rather well-established firm in a mature industry. This result is puzzling as raising equity is arguably of less importance for these firms than for young and growing firms.

8.2.2. Costs of Initial Public Offerings

As will be discussed in greater detail in Section 8.4, the market for lead underwriters is highly concentrated in Germany. It was dominated by Deutsche Bank from 1959 to 1998 as the lead underwriter in 30 per cent of all IPOs, making more than 30 per cent of the total gross proceeds (Langemann 2000: 29). Moreover, between 1990 and 1996, the lead underwriter was one of the five major banks (Deutsche Bank, Dresdner Bank, Commerzbank, BHF-Bank, and DG Bank) in 73 per cent of all IPOs.

Even though firms were free to choose the method of going public, until 1994 issuers used only the fixed price method, in which banks perform the intermediary role, with all applications for IPOs being routed through the banks that make up the underwriting syndicate. The syndicate buys the stock at a fixed price and sells it to the market. Since 1995 book building has become the common method. It was first used on a larger scale for the Deutsche Telekom IPO in 1996.

The costs of going public comprise direct and indirect components. Examples of the first type are the underwriting and the listing fees. The average direct costs are between 5 and 10 per cent of the IPO volume, depending on the size of the IPO, the risks involved, and the complexity of the chosen IPO mechanism (Schürmann and Körfgen 1997: 180; Kaserer and Kraft 2003). The direct costs for listing at the different segments vary, but the differences hardly influence the choice of segment, and they are not much higher in Germany than in other countries so that they should not impede IPO activity (Fischer 2000).

From the perspective of the former owners, underpricing or initial returns constitute the indirect costs of going public. Initial returns are generally defined as the percentage increase, accruing to investors in IPOs of common stock, from the offer price to a closing market price shortly after public trading begins.[5]

The level of underpricing in Germany is comparable to that in other countries. The average underpricing in the years 1960–95 was between 10 and 32 per cent, depending on the market segments, the time period, and the sample size:[6] The average initial return decreased over time (Stehle and Erhardt 1999: 1399) and the number of cases in which the initial return was negative increased.[7] In addition, higher initial returns are observed in hot markets (Jenkinson and Ljungqvist 1996: 33).

When looking at the single market segments it becomes apparent that the average underpricing of firms in the *Amtlicher Handel* was lower than for other segments. Between 1987 and 1995 it was about 8 per cent (Stehle *et al.* 2000: table 1). Thus, the average initial return at the *Amtlicher Handel* was— if anything—lower than comparable measures in other industrialized countries (for surveys see, e.g. Ritter 1991; Loughran *et al.* 1994; Jenkinson and Ljungqvist 1996). This is in line with the argument that initial returns stem from asymmetric information about the quality of the firm to be listed: The age of firms and their successful business history at the time of their listing in Germany arguably result in a lower level of asymmetric information, and therefore in a lower initial return. Higher initial returns often stemmed from smaller and rather unknown companies, which went public on the *Geregelter Markt* or the *Freiverkehr* during the 1980s.

The average initial return for IPOs on the *Neuer Markt* between March 1997 and December 2001 was 49.81 per cent (Franzke and Schlag 2002; Kiss and Stehle 2002). This level seems to be very high. But while the average underpricing between 1991 and 1995 at Nasdaq was only 13.8 per cent (Habib and Ljungqvist 2001), the average underpricing in the US increased to 65 per cent during the internet bubble in 1999 and 2000 (Ritter and Welch 2002). According to Loughran and Ritter (2002) some of the increase can be explained by changes in the risk characteristics of the firms going public in this period. But they attribute much greater importance to the possibility of allocating proceeds from IPO underpricing to friends and families when book building is used.

---

[5] In the literature, the definition of initial return varies with respect to the methods of measurement, but of course they all deal with the difference between the issuing price and the stock price in the secondary market. The length of this period varies from study to study, with one day to several weeks being the usual time frame.

[6] Some studies, for example, exclude the ten firms for which the Portfolio Management GmbH was the underwriter in the mid of the 80s. (The Portfolio Management GmbH is discussed in more detail in Section 8.4.) The average initial return of these IPOs was 67 per cent. Seven of these companies failed after only a few years. Excluding these companies reduces the average underpricing by 10 to 15 per cent. See Stehle and Ehrhardt (1999) for a survey on IPO-underpricing studies in Germany, which includes Schmidt and Tyrell (1988), Uhlir (1989), and Ljungqvist (1997) among others.

[7] During the period from 1983 until 1988 only 13 per cent of the IPOs were overpriced. In the years from 1988 until 1992 this number rose to 21 per cent (Kaserer and Kempf 1995: 55).

The evidence indicates that the level of underpricing in Germany is not particularly high. This is surprising as one might have expected the small number of IPOs, and thus the banks' limited IPO experience as well as the high concentration in the market for lead underwriters to have resulted in a higher level of underpricing than in other countries. Hence, the low level of IPOs in Germany is unlikely to stem from higher direct or indirect costs of listings. Other potential reasons for the low number of IPOs in Germany are discussed in Section 8.4.

8.3. VENTURE CAPITAL FINANCING IN GERMANY

8.3.1. Development of the German Venture Capital Market

Before turning to the development of the German Venture Capital market it is important to note that in Germany the use of the term 'venture capital' differs from that in the Anglo-American literature. Whereas in the Anglo-American literature 'venture capital' is typically used in the sense of early-stage and expansion financing, the German understanding of 'venture capital' is more comprehensive and also includes the financing of buy-outs and buy-ins and later-stage financing operations of more mature, small to medium-sized companies. The term 'venture capital' as used in Germany is, therefore, more in keeping with the American notion of private equity (Black and Gilson 1998).

In much the same way as IPO activity, a German VC market did not really exist before the early 1980s. This was the case despite early and repeated attempts by the German government to stimulate the availability of equity financing for small to medium-sized companies.

In the 1960s (first phase), the founding of equity investment companies ('Kapitalbeteiligungsgesellschaften'—KBGs) was suggested as a solution to the perceived problem of an equity shortage in Germany (Persé 1962; Arbeitsgemeinschaft selbständiger Unternehmer 1965).[8] Like investment funds, KBGs should collect the capital of various financiers and invest it in a portfolio of companies. Preferably, such investments were to be in the form of a silent partnership,[9] and ideally the entrepreneur should buy back the KBGs' share after 5–10 years. In 1965 the first KBGs were founded, many of them as subsidiaries of banks (Nevermann and Falk 1986; Leopold and Frommann

---

[8] The following description of the development of VC in Germany is based in parts on Leopold and Frommann (1998) and Lessat *et al.* (1999).

[9] Silent partnerships are debt-like, as such they are supposed to have a finite life and leave as much autonomy of decision making to the general management as possible. They were and still are the dominant financial instrument used by KBGs and their portfolio companies. (For a detailed analysis of the financial contracting behaviour of German venture capitalists, see Bascha and Walz 2000.)

1998).[10] KBGs invested primarily in established, medium-sized companies and the total number of investments was rather low.

The second phase of VC in Germany started about 1970/71. To encourage KBGs to increase their investments in small to medium-sized businesses and new ventures, the German government in 1971 started to offer financial support through the European Recovery Programme (ERP).[11] However, KBGs made only little use of this programme since it implied severe restrictions. The law limited investors' return on investment to an average of 11 per cent p.a. (nowadays 12 per cent p.a.) over the contracted life span, which basically implied a cap on potential profits. As a consequence, KGBs did not invest in 'highly risky' projects (see, for instance, the report of the Bundesministerium für Wirtschaft 1995). Moreover, there was a maturity cap of 10 years for all investments, and the contractual arrangement between KBGs and portfolio companies was clearly biased in favour of the latter: portfolio companies had the opportunity to repay the financial intermediary prematurely. Thus, KBGs were often left with poor investments. Furthermore, suppliers of equity were not allowed to influence the daily business of the management. As a consequence of the lack of attention the European Recovery Programme received in these times, individual German Federal States ('Länder') supported the establishment of so-called equity finance companies for small and medium-sized firms ('Mittelständische Beteiligungsgesellschaften'—MBGs). Apart from the Länder, the owners of such MBGs consisted of the banking community including regional banks and often the respective regional Chambers of Industry and Commerce. Accordingly, publicly subsidized equity for investment purposes became relatively more important.

Schlegelmilch (1976) reports that in late 1975 the major part of capital was provided by private banks (about 42 per cent), savings banks (about 36 per cent) and MBGs (about 10 per cent). The financing of new ventures was rather an exception. All in all, during the second phase the market for direct-investment capital was essentially stagnant, both with regard to the number of companies offering equity and to the total volume invested.[12] The latter

---

[10] For the sake of comparison, in the United Kingdom about 20 years earlier, that is, in 1945, the *Industrial and Commercial Finance Corporation Ltd.*, today known as *3i*, was established at the initiative of the Bank of England and in cooperation with major banks. Also, in the United States the first professional VC company named *American Research and Development Corporation* was founded as early as 1949.

[11] See German Federal Ministry of Economics ('Bundesministerium für Wirtschaft' 1970). The financial support included the opportunity to refinance up to 75 per cent of investments at a preferential interest rate of 5 per cent p.a. and a coverage of potential losses of up to 70 per cent of total investment.

[12] In 1972 (1982) the number of venture companies amounts to thirty-three (twenty-six). Among them was *Deutsche Wagnisfinanzierungsgesellschaft* (WFG), which has attracted some attention in the literature. (See, for instance, Becker and Hellmann 2002.) In 1975 this venture capital fund was set up as a joint company between major German banks, partially guaranteed by the government. Although it 'was an outright failure' (Becker and Hellmann 2002: 6), from today's point of view, WFG was important for the further development of the German venture capital industry.

amounted to approximately €385 million by the end of 1982 compared to a credit volume of about €409 billion used by the corporate and self-employed sector (Gerke 1983).

In 1983 (beginning of third phase) for the first time the German venture capital market could be said to be expanding. The growth and changes in activities were triggered by a positive investment climate in Germany and euphoric reports on the success of the US venture capital market. Several equity investment companies were founded. Although banks continued to play the major role as founders and investors in such companies, the importance of private persons, insurance companies, and commercial enterprises as sponsors of VC companies grew considerably. Also, foreign venture capitalists started to establish subsidiaries in Germany, and MBGs, which had experienced little deal flow during the 1970s, became active again. Moreover, in order to offer non-institutional, especially retail, investors an indirect investment opportunity in the equity of non-listed small to medium-sized companies, the German parliament in 1987 enacted the law on equity finance companies ('Unternehmens-beteiligungsgesellschaften'—UBGs). Among other things, this law determined that UBGs, that is, such regulated VC companies, had to be stock corporations ('Aktiengesellschaften'—AGs), had to strive for a listing at the stock exchange and should invest in the equity of non-listed German companies.[13] In order to provide incentives for entrepreneurs to make use of UBGs, the government granted considerable tax advantages. For example, UBGs were exempted from trade tax and the capital gains tax. However, UBGs play a minor role in the German VC market. From 1996 to 1998, the number of VC companies that were organized as UBGs decreased from sixteen to nine.

All in all, the range of VC activities became broader; a movement towards the successful strategy of American venture capitalists was noticeable (Nevermann and Falk 1986; Schmidt 1988). On the one hand newly founded venture capitalists started to specialize in technology companies that demanded early-stage financing.[14] On the other, VC companies started to focus on management buy-outs and buy-ins. Buy-backs by entrepreneurs, which used to be the dominant exit strategy, were increasingly replaced by trade sales and some IPOs.[15] In summary, the German VC market developed considerably from 1983 to 1990, both with regard to professionalism as well as to size. As illustrated in Figure 8.2, the total

---

[13] These regulations have first been relaxed in 1994 and later on by the changes of the 3rd *Finanzmarktförderungsgesetz* in April 1998.

[14] However, since investments in these growth companies experienced considerable losses, the focus was shifted back to expansion financing of more mature businesses only a few years later.

[15] Between 1983 and 1990 Leopold and Frommann (1998) identify eight companies going public on the German market that were venture-backed. To compare, for the same time period Black and Gilson (1998) report more than 500 venture-backed IPOs in the United States.

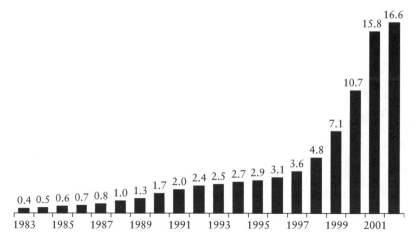

Figure 8.2. *Total portfolio volume held by members of the BVK (in € billion).*

Source: These numbers are taken from the BVK Statistik (2002).

invested VC volume quadrupled from approximately €0.4 billion in 1983 to €1.7 billion in 1990.[16]

After German reunification in October 1990 the number of newly established businesses increased.[17] Once again, the government offered special funds to foster start-ups and early-stage investments and now also to encourage investment in the newly formed German states.[18] In addition changes in legislation, with regard, for instance, to the law of UBGs, were carried through.[19] VC became an attractive proposition for investors in the German economy. A continuous, almost linear growth of the German VC industry could be observed during the fourth phase from 1991 to 1996. In 1996, the volume of the total VC portfolio exceeded €3 billion.

In 1997, as the *Neuer Markt* was launched offering a further exit facility to venture capitalists, the German VC industry entered into a unique boom period. Although buy backs and trade sales were still the preferred exit mechanisms for venture capitalists, the opportunity to exit the portfolio by means of an IPO

---

[16] Numbers on the German VC market given here and in the following are those of members of the German Venture Capital Association ('Bundesverband Deutscher Kapitalbeteiligungsgesellschaften'—BVK), which account (according to the BVK) for 90 per cent of the volume of the German VC market.

[17] Numbers are offered by the Institut für Mittelstandsforschung (IFM): http://www.ifm-bonn.de/dienste/gruend.htm.

[18] Details on the programmes are listed on the internet page of the Bundesministerium für Wirtschaft und Technologie: http://www.bmwi.de.

[19] The regulation of UBGs has been relaxed by the 3rd *Finanzmarktförderungsgesetz* of 1998. Among other things the changes implied that UBGs had no more aspirations towards a listing at a stock exchange. Nowadays the financing of small to medium-sized companies is the first and foremost aim. Moreover, the requirement to form a stock corporation was withdrawn. For more details see Vollmer (1998).

became a feasible option. While in 1996 about 6.7 per cent of the divested volume was sold by means of an IPO, this fraction rose to more than 12.5 per cent in 1998 and 1999. On average, the *Neuer Markt* covered about 75 per cent of the IPOs backed by VC between 1998 and 2000.[20] This fifth phase saw the peak of the remarkable development of the German VC industry, not only in terms of volume, but also in terms of the distribution among financing stages and industrial sectors. Between 1996 and 2000, about €10.8 billion in total were newly invested in 6300 companies, which is 68 per cent of total new VC investments and 47 per cent of all VC financed companies over the last 30 years (BVK Yearbook 2001). This highlights the insignificance of the German VC industry until the mid 1990s.[21] With regard to the distribution among financing stages, a strong movement towards early-stage financing can be discerned. While in 1996 only about 14 per cent of gross investments were in early-stage companies, this share reached about 36 per cent in 2000. No other European country achieved this degree of growth. The corresponding volume figure increased by a factor of 18 between these two years. About one-fifth of the early-stage investments were refinanced through public programmes implemented by KfW, Germany's main development bank.

While it had been criticized in the past that in Germany investments were mainly directed towards old industries (Leopold and Frommann 1998), the investment patterns during the boom phase became much more similar to those of the United States, which reflects the importance of the (new) high-tech sector. Computer, information technology, communications, and biotechnology, which had received around 19 per cent of new VC funds in 1996, accounted for more than 48 per cent of gross investments in 2000.[22] However, this overall remarkable development came to an abrupt halt in the second half of 2000 when the German VC market entered a period of consolidation, which is still enduring.

8.3.2. Current Status of the German Venture Capital Market and Its Comparison to the United States, United Kingdom, and France

Currently about 200–250 VC companies form the core of the institutional VC market in Germany.[23] As for the informal segment of this market, a study by

---

[20] The remaining 25 per cent can be split equally into IPOs on other German stock exchanges and on foreign stock exchanges such as the NASDAQ. For an in-depth study on venture-backed IPOs at *Neuer Markt*, see Franzke (2001).

[21] Whereas the volume of gross investments per deal has risen from €0.94 million in 1996 to €2.04 million per company in 2000, these numbers seem to be small compared with those of the United States ($19.1 million investments per company in 2000).

[22] However, the share of high-tech sectors in gross investments is even higher in the United States, while in the United Kingdom it is comparatively low running up to 24 per cent in 2000 (EVCA Yearbook 2001).

[23] See for instance BVK Statistik (2001) and Deutsche Bundesbank (2000). To compare, the National Venture Capital Association (NVCA) counts over 470 venture capital and private equity organizations as members (see www.nvca.org), representing merely a lower limit of active venture capital and private equity companies in the United States.

Lessat *et al.* (1999) estimates that roughly 27,000 business angels actively invest in growth companies and that a further pool of 219,000 business angels could be tapped.[24]

In absolute terms (with respect to the VC portfolio or new funds raised) the German VC market is still about 10–15 times smaller than the US market.[25] However, within Europe, the German VC market in 2001 ranked third with respect to the volume of the VC portfolio (€15.8 billion)[26] behind the United Kingdom (€39.8 billion) and France (€17.4 billion). The same holds true for the volume of new funds raised (see Table 8.2).[27]

Although the banking sector is still an important supplier of new capital, contributing about 32 per cent in 2001, the relative role of banks has decreased over time and is being taken over by insurance companies (21 per cent), private investments (8 per cent) and (foreign) pension funds (3 per cent). In Germany (foreign) pension funds as providers of VC were irrelevant until recently. They first appeared as a separate category in the statistics of BVK in 1995.[28] In sharp contrast to this, pension funds are, and have been for quite some time now, the main suppliers of VC in the United States and in the United Kingdom. In both countries pension funds contributed more or less 40 per cent to the funds raised in 2001. It is worth noting that the public sector plays a significant role as source of VC funds only in Germany.

With regard to the exit mechanism, the deteriorating climate for new issues due to a bear-market from March 2000 onwards is clearly reflected in the statistics. The volume divested by means of an IPO dropped from 19 per cent in 1999 to 8 per cent in 2001. Similar but more pronounced findings can be reported for the UK and the US market (see Table 8.2). Moreover, 36 per cent of all portfolio companies had to be written off in 2001. Silent partnerships, used particularly in later-stage operations, had a share of 16 per cent of the divested volume in 2001. However, compared to former times this has dropped dramatically (1996: 57 per cent).

In 2001 Germany followed the trend of the United States and United Kingdom where a tendency towards bigger funds with less early-stage and

---

[24] Estimates regarding their potential investment volume run up to €6.4 billion per year, including the investment volume of active business angels, which amounts to approximately €0.7 billion per year.

[25] To compare, Germany was about 3.4 times smaller than the United States with regard to inhabitants and about 1.3 times smaller with regard to GDP per inhabitants in 2001.

[26] According to the BVK Statistik (2002) the total portfolio volume held by members of the BVK increased to €16.6 billion in 2002 (see Figure 8.2). On average, foreign investors have held a stake of about 30 per cent of the VC funds in Germany during the period 1996–2001 (own estimations based on data of BVK Yearbooks 1996–2001).

[27] The ranking for these three countries is the same on the basis of VC investments as a proportion of the GDP in 2001: 0.646 per cent in the United Kingdom, 0.225 per cent in France and 0.215 per cent in Germany (see EVCA Yearbook 2002).

[28] Before 1995, the share of pension funds was so small, that it was counted under the category 'other'. See Leopold and Frommann (1998).

Table 8.2. *Comparative VC figures for Germany, France, United Kingdom, and the United States in 2001/1999*[a]

	Germany	France	United Kingdom	United States
Portfolio at cost (for the United States: capital under management) in billion[b]	€15.8/7.9	€17.4/5.3	€39.8/28.0	US$254.3/145.9
New funds raised in billion	€3.7/3.8	€5.5/4.3	€20.5/9.9	US$37.9/62.8
Type of investors offering new funds in per cent				
Banks	32/40	40/25	10/26	Banks + Insurance companies 25/16
Insurance companies	21/11	11/15	15/14	
Pension funds	3/9	6/9	40/31	42/44
Private investments	8/12	11/4	6/4	1/10
Public sector	16/14	4/3	4/2	0/0
Divestments by type of exit vehicle in per cent				No detailed information available: mainly trade sales and IPOs (climax in 1996: 262 VC-backed IPOs; the numbers for 2001/1999 are 35/244)
Trade sale	20/25	54/58	29/22	
IPO	8/19	17/16	8/26	
Write-off	36/21	9/3	23/5	
Repayment of preference shares/loans	2/7 Repayment of silent partnerships 16/14	4/2	24/32	
Stage distribution of investments in per cent				
Early-stage	26/32	17/18	13/2	24/22
Expansion	35/50	22/38	25/20	57/56
Buy-out	36/15	59/38	56/76	Later stage/ buy-out 18/16

[a] Numbers for Germany, the United Kingdom, and France are taken from the Yearbooks (2000, 2002) of the European Venture Capital Association (EVCA) and those for the United States from the Yearbook (2003) of the National Venture Capital Association (NVCA).
[b] The NVCA only gives figures for the capital under management of VC funds. The capital under management is defined as the accumulated VC managed by funds net the VC of funds, which have been liquidated or matured at the end of their life cycle (after 8 years). Capital under management, therefore, differs from the European definition of the VC portfolio.

more later-stage financing has been discernible for quite a few years. In line with this, buy-out activity, which is also particularly pronounced in France and the United Kingdom, has become more important in Germany and increased to a level of about 36 per cent (in terms of volume) in 2001.

While US venture capitalists report returns on investment (see for an overview Bygrave *et al.* 1999), to date no comparable data on the performance of the German VC market are available. There merely exist surveys on what venture capitalists expect to receive as return on their initial investment. According to Feinendegen *et al.* (2001) venture capitalists operating on the German market demanded an annual minimum rate of return ranging from 24.7 per cent p.a. (buy-out specialists) to 32 per cent p.a. (venture capitalists focusing on early-stage) in 2000. Comparing these numbers with those recently reported by Venture Economics (2002) for a sample of European VC funds, there is a considerable gap, at least for early-stage investments, between demand and reality. For 2001 Venture Economics reports an annualized pooled IRR for buy-out investments amounting to 18.5 per cent and early-stage investments amounting to 9.2 per cent.[29]

Summarizing the development of the German VC industry since 1965, we must emphasize the roles played by the government on the one hand and by banks on the other. The numerous government initiatives of the 1960s, 1970s, and early 1980s were fruitful in the sense that, by putting the equity financing of small to medium-sized companies on the agenda, they started and actively supported a movement towards a noticeable VC industry. Moreover banks, which served as founders of most KBGs in the 1960s and 1970s by providing the major share of the investment funds, have formed the basis for VC investments in an institutional framework that has been, and seems to have remained, clearly distinct from that of the United Kingdom or the United States.

8.4. WHY ARE THERE SO FEW IPOs AND SO LITTLE VC IN GERMANY?

8.4.1. Potential Reasons

The low number of IPOs and the fairly low volume of VC financing in Germany, in particular before the *Neuer Markt* boom, are striking when compared to the United States or United Kingdom. The reasons are much debated.

Before we proceed with a discussion of the potential reasons, it is important to note that IPOs and VC financing are complements, since IPOs are an important exit mechanism for VC financiers. Black and Gilson (1998) argue that a well-functioning stock market with an active IPO market is a prerequisite for an active VC market. In this case what needs to be analysed can be reduced to the question why there are so few IPOs. But the reverse causality

---

[29] The IRR of each fund of the analysed sample is measured from its interception to 31 December 2001. Moreover, Venture Economics (2002) recently reported that the private equity industry in Europe showed a long-term 10-year return of 16.5 per cent, a medium-term 5-year return of 20.4 per cent and a short-term 1-year return of −2.3 per cent.

may also be relevant: It could well be that there are few IPOs because VC financing plays such a modest role. However, the lack of VC financing cannot explain why so few non-venture backed or established firms want to go public and seek a listing on the stock market.

The potential answers to the question posed in this section's headline are manifold; they range from differences in mentality to differences in the legal and institutional system.

Mentality: The limited use of stock markets and venture capital as a source of financing is often attributed to national peculiarities in mentality. The argument could be developed along the following lines: US-style venture capital is *not needed* in Germany because of a lack of entrepreneurial initiative, and it is *not provided* because entrepreneurs are not willing to give up control, investors are too risk averse and Germany lacks qualified entrepreneurs and venture capitalists. Similar arguments could hold for IPOs and the stock market: There may be a 'lack of equity culture' because Germans are too risk averse and owners and managers fear a loss of control and higher disclosure requirements (Gerke *et al.* 1995).

Differences in mentality may well play a role. But it is important to distinguish between differences in mentality as such and differences in behaviour stemming from adaptations to the legal and institutional environment.[30]

Legal and institutional impediments: To the extent that private contracts cannot substitute for legal rules, the limited use of the stock market may be the result of insufficient legal rules (La Porta *et al.* 1997, 1998). Weak disclosure requirements, lack of transparency as well as missing or unenforceable minority protection and insider regulation may increase the costs of using the stock market due to information and incentive problems faced by outsiders.[31] Owners may view the costs of disclosure and transparency as an obstacle to listing their firm because they are not strict enough to overcome these problems. Germany has only recently adopted some stricter rules—similar to those in the United Kingdom and the United States—in the course of EU

---

[30] For example, Becker and Hellmann (2002), argue that one of the key problems that the venture capital industry faced in Germany was the lack of high quality entrepreneurs. However, high quality people go to where the money is. It is exactly the prospect of earning huge profits through a successful IPO that motivates talented people in the United States to start their own business, seeking venture financing. In addition, as argued in Becker and Hellmann (2002), in the 1970s and 1980s, public opinion towards entrepreneurs was rather hostile in Germany.

[31] Bhattacharya and Daouk (2002) find that the costs of equity are lower if insider-trading laws are enforced. Leuz and Verrecchia (2000) document a significant relationship between the choice of accounting standard (and therefore the level of disclosure) and a firm's cost of capital.

harmonization. For example, the second Financial Market Promotion Act of 1995 banned insider trading and introduced tighter disclosure rules.[32]

In addition, with eight stock exchanges under the supervision of the individual states and no central clearance and settlement system the German stock market was rather fragmented until the 1990s (Story and Walter 1997: 176). All these features of the German stock exchange system reduced the advantage of a listing because they reduce liquidity and increase the costs of trading. Centralized coordination of trading activities only started with the foundation of the Deutsche Börse AG in January 1993.

The literature also puts forward the German Stock Corporation Act ('Aktiengesetz') as an additional impediment to the wider use of the stock market. If firms want to list on the stock market, they have to become a public limited company (Aktiengesellschaft—AG). However, most firms, which are not listed, choose to conduct business as a limited liability company ('Gesellschaft mit beschränkter Haftung'—GmbH). It is argued that the legal requirements for an AG are too rigid and not suited to small corporations.[33] A case in point is, for example, codetermination and the dual board structure. But this argument cannot explain the low number of IPOs of large corporations. The Codetermination Law ('Mitbestimmungsgesetz') of 1976 also applies to GmbHs with more than 2,000 employees so that large GmbHs are also subject to codetermination and also have to implement a dual board structure.

To the extent that legal impediments reduce the use of the stock market as a source of financing, and therefore also reduce the availability of venture capital, the question arises why this situation has not been changed earlier. One possible reason is that there was no need for change because alternative sources of financing (and investment) were available.

Alternative sources of financing: Arguably long-term close relationships between banks and firms reduce the agency costs of external debt financing, and therefore increase the use of debt (bank) financing (Elsas and Krahnen 1998: chapter 7). Savings banks may also have boosted the use of debt financing. In addition, the German pension system, which allows employees' pension assets to be retained on the companies' books as capital, and enables hidden reserves to be built up, reduces the need to approach the capital market. Hence, the optimal level of debt is higher and (external) equity is less important in Germany, which is also reflected in the stock market. However, this mainly holds true for established firms for which debt and internal funds

---

[32] See Chapters 11–14 on legal and accounting issues as well as recent regulatory developments.

[33] The number of AGs in contrast to GmbHs is small and steadily decreasing. Moreover, only about one-fifth to one-sixth of all AGs are listed, most others are subsidiaries rather than independent firms (Kübler 1999: 161). With the introduction of the *kleine AG* some of the legal requirements were reduced to make the AG more attractive for small firms. But the relaxations do not apply if a firm is listed.

are possible sources of financing. They are not real alternatives for risky start-ups seeking external financing.

The ease of retaining funds and the German pension system resulted in a situation whereby large amounts of financial resources were allocated inside the firm rather than in the financial market. Hence, it is conceivable that large corporations that carried out innovations internally crowded out, at least in part, the external financing of new ventures.[34]

Listings at foreign stock exchanges may be viewed as an alternative to a listing in Germany. This alternative emerged in the 1990s when several venture-backed companies chose this option. It played no role before the 1990s.

The role of banks: It is certainly no exaggeration to say that the stock market in Germany was controlled by the large (universal) banks. They dominated the different committees and bodies of the exchange, including the committee that has to approve all listing decisions (for further discussion see Monopolkommission 1998: 99–101). In addition, the German Stock Exchange Listing Act ('Börsenzulassungsverordnung') required that the request for listing at the *Amtlicher Handel* had to be made by a bank in its function as underwriter. Moreover, banks de facto controlled the distribution channel through which stocks were sold and advised firms on their financing decision. Clearly banks had a dominant position in the IPO market. It is, therefore, interesting to note that the Advisory Council to the Federal Ministry of Economics ('Wissenschaftlicher Beirat des Bundesministeriums für Wirtschaft') and the monopolies commission ('Monopolkommission') argue that the reluctance of banks to list companies was a major reason for the small number of IPOs that we observed in Germany.

The firms that went public in Germany were much older and larger than demanded by the listing requirements. Observers conclude that banks tended to set very restrictive standards for meeting the requirements for a listing, which exceeded the formal listing requirements and in general could not be met by young companies (Schürmann 1980; Büschgen 1996; Wissenschaftlicher Beirat 1998; Monopolkommission 1998). The question, of course, is why was this the case. Some observers argue that the restrictive listing requirements were an outgrowth of (excessive) investor protection. This may sound surprising from today's perspective as today we make the lack of investor protection responsible for the low use of stock markets. At that time, however, investor protection seems to have implied investor protection against business risk rather than against the risk of fraud and misinformation.

---

[34] The German pension system may have another detrimental effect on stock markets. Strong pension funds as capital market participants may potentially be beneficial for other market participants as well.

Another possible reason why banks were reluctant to promote IPOs is that this line of business conflicted with the savings and loan business, which was certainly by far the most important line of business for German universal banks. To the extent that issuing equity and taking on loans are substitutes, the opportunity costs of an engagement in the issue business are higher for a universal bank than for an investment bank.[35] This is true in particular when the medium to long-run effects of equity are considered: firms that are financed for the most part by equity gain financial independence from banks through profit retention. Banks made this experience in Nazi Germany when, according to Hardach (1995), the banks lost much of their corporate business and were forced into a passive role because of the 'financial autarky' of industry resulting from retained profits, which in turn resulted from lucrative government contracts, low wages, and a limit on dividends.

Moreover, it is likely that there was a conflict of interest within banks between the two lines of businesses. An increased importance of the issuing business would have reduced the profits of the credit business as well as the value of the human capital of those who were active in the credit business. Those who were active in the credit business were, therefore, likely to oppose an increased involvement in the issuing business. But at the same time they were the main advisers to firms seeking financing.

Hence, mere profitability considerations as well as internal politicking may also have played a role when large universal banks did not oppose the myth that in order to protect investors, only the stocks of safe firms should be issued.

It is important to note in this context that the German Banking Act tightly regulates the entry of investment banks and was relaxed only recently. In addition, the German Stock Exchange Listing Act as well as the dominance of banks in the committees of the stock exchange and the distribution of stocks made entry in the market rather difficult (Giersch and Schmidt 1986; Gerke 1988). Until quite recently there were, therefore, hardly any independent investment banks in Germany that could have assumed the position as promoters of an active IPO and VC market.

It is interesting to take a closer look at the early 1980s when a small Munich-based asset management firm, Portfolio Management (PM), initiated several IPOs at the *Freiverkehr*, where at that time a listing was possible without having a bank as an underwriter. Of the fourteen IPOs in the years 1981–83, eight were led by PM (with an average volume of €4 million) and five by Deutsche Bank (with an average volume of €25 million). Even though most of the firms that were brought to the market by PM failed relatively soon, the activities of PM seem to have influenced the development of IPO activities in Germany. For example Schürmann and Körfgen (1987) argue that PM

---

[35] The concern that this is an important reason for the banks' limited engagement in the issue business is, for example, expressed by Deutsche Bundesbank (1984: 16), Schürmann and Körfgen (1987), Weichert (1987), Baums (1997: 1944), and Monopolkommission (1998: 60, 101).

undermined the mythology of 'conventional wisdom' about the required age and size of companies that would be eligible for an IPO and also helped to overcome banks' opposition against non-voting preferred stocks.[36] IPOs that were led by PM were characterized by a commitment of initial owners to hold a minimum fraction of the firm's stock (typically 50 per cent) for at least 5 years. PM was also innovative in increasing the fee volume by being the first to choose the IPO price rather than the face value of the stock as the basis for commission (leaving, of course, the percentage unchanged or even slightly increasing it).[37]

Banks reacted to PM's activities by making it more difficult to enter the market, justifying this with the failure of firms that were brought to the market by PM. While it was always required to have a bank as an underwriter to be accepted for the *Amtlicher Handel*, it then also became necessary de facto for the *Geregelter Markt* and the *Freiverkehr* (Deutsche Bundesbank 1997: 35).

Nevertheless, starting in 1983 an increase in the number of IPOs in Germany can be observed. Initially the number of banks that were involved in the issuing business was quite low (Gerke 1988: 224–5). In 1986 there were 4500 financial institutions in Germany, about 240 of which were members of the exchange. In twenty-nine out of the fifty-one IPOs that were carried out by banks (not PM) between 1975 and 1985, Deutsche Bank was the lead underwriter (Giersch and Schmidt 1986: 71, 74). This picture slowly changed. While between 1990 and 1996 it was still the case that in 73 per cent of the IPOs the lead underwriter was one of five banks (Deutsche Bank, Dresdner Bank, Commerzbank, BHF-Bank, and DG Bank), this fraction fell to only 41 per cent between 1997 and 2000 (DG Bank, Deutsche Bank, Commerzbank, Dresdner Bank, and West LB).

The banks' attitude towards IPOs was probably also influenced by the changing environment for banks. One major result of the process of liberalization, deregulation, and the emergence of new technologies has been a considerable intensification of competition in the financial sector. As a result the margins in the savings and loans business decreased, the legal entry barriers for investment banks were reduced, and listings abroad became a viable alternative for German firms.[38] As a consequence, banks started to expand the fee-based business with securities, insurance, investment funds in general and in investment banking for large banks in particular.[39] Interestingly, a similar

---

[36] Until four of five firms whose IPO was led by PM in the beginning of the 1980s used non-voting preferred stock, there was strong resistance by German banks to this form of financing (Schürmann and Körfgen 1987: 28). In the following years non-voting preferred stock was used in 41 per cent of the IPOs. Among them Porsche, Nixdorf, Henkel, VDO, and Massa.

[37] Large universal banks followed this practice and, interestingly, the myth disappeared that the IPO price of stocks with a face value of DM50 (€25) must not exceed DM200 (€100).

[38] In 1995 and 1996 more than 90 per cent of the VC-backed IPOs took place at a foreign stock exchange (the absolute number is 28). The percentage decreased to about 20 per cent after the introduction of the *Neuer Markt*, 1997–2002 (BVK Statistik 2001 and 2002).

[39] See, for example, Deutsche Bundesbank (1998: 43).

development could be observed in the United States in the 1920s when the commercial banks, concerned about 'disintermediation' due to the loss of some of their traditional lending business to the public market, expanded their investment banking activities (White 1984; Kroszner and Rajan 1994).

Banks' incentives are important because they play a major role as an intermediary in the equity market: They advise firms as well as investors and organize the institutional framework. Nevertheless, several other factors certainly also influenced the increase in IPO activities in Germany after 1980. We shall only mention the most important ones here: a new tax regulation which permitted the deduction of IPO expenses as business expenses in 1983; the introduction of the *Geregelter Markt* with its more transparent pricing process in 1987; increasing stock prices at the beginning of the 1980s; the successful IPO of Deutsche Telekom with an unprecedented marketing campaign; increasing stock prices in the 1990s; the introduction of the *Neuer Markt* with its new listing requirements and improved transparency aimed to attract firms for which there was general hype based on new technologies and business opportunities.

8.4.2. Discussion

The preceding subsection discussed potential reasons for why there were so few IPOs in Germany. One may ask which is the most important reason. However, discriminating between different factors is difficult. In fact, they are mutually reinforcing and complement each other. As an example, take the last argument about banks' interests. It may be asked whether the banks really had sufficient power to pursue their interests in such a potentially important and far reaching issue, and why was there no opposition? It seems that the interest of banks could only have an effect because legal impediments reduced participants' interest in the stock market, established firms had alternative sources of financing, legal rules restricted entry into investment banking, and incumbents benefited from reduced competition and did not strive for change.

Interests of incumbents: There are several reasons why the legal and institutional impediments for a stronger stock market (with more IPOs and venture capital financing) were not overcome—irrespective of whether this would have been optimal. First, there may have been ideological reasons. German politicians are quite proud of the social market economy ('soziale Marktwirtschaft') and may be reluctant to implement changes that are considered to be socially unjust (e.g. giving up codetermination, admitting hostile takeovers, giving external financiers more rights). Second, politicians may have benefited from not changing the system: Extracting rents from state-owned corporations or private firms (such as lucrative jobs for politicians and support for political projects) is easier if there is less competition (profits are higher and it is easier to deal with a few large private firms) and if the rights of minority shareholders are weak. Third, politicians, with a view to their re-election chances may try to avoid negative publicity from pressure groups. In addition, there are several ways in which incumbents may have benefited from a system where (i) it is difficult for new firms to receive financing for risky projects, (ii) transparency and disclosure are low, and (iii) cross holdings make hostile takeovers difficult (Rajan and Zingales 2003). All three effects reduce competition and external pressure for structural change: Unions, acting in the interest of members (i.e. employees), benefit by extracting higher wages as well as social benefits and protecting the jobs of current employees; managers and owners of existing firms may benefit from being able to extract higher private benefits of control. Of course, interests of the different incumbents are not always aligned. Nevertheless, they may form coalitions against those who would benefit from changing the system, for example, outside shareholders, entrepreneurs seeking funding or the unemployed. For example, managers and controlling shareholders may prefer less influence by the unions, but both are natural allies against external investors and the potential threat of a takeover (Hellwig 2000). Pagano and Volpin (2000) developed a model in which the controlling shareholders want low investor protection to extract larger benefits of control and to gain political support from workers by granting them more job security. If social benefits and job security are important, workers' benefits are tightly linked to the well-being of the firm. Perotti and von Thadden (2002) argue that workers and creditors prefer less risk and form coalitions to support bank over equity financing and benefit from low transparency.

A thorough discussion of the interests of the different groups and their influence on the political decision-making process in Germany is beyond the scope of this chapter. The idea that legal impediments in Germany may be the result of coalitions of interest groups is expressed most clearly in Wenger (1996). He argues that politicians insulate managers of large corporations from capital market pressure in exchange for corporate contributions to satisfy certain voting groups and provides examples of the expropriation of minority shareholders by coalitions of politicians, judges, and managers. Less pronounced are the following examples, which highlight some specific problems. For example, winning acceptance for Frankfurt as the location for the German Stock Exchange prior to opening the Deutsche Börse AG in Frankfurt in 1993 'required two years of negotiation with the state supervisors, brokers and governments as well as strong support from the Finance Ministry and Chancellor Kohl' (Story and Walter 1997: 181). While Frankfurt banks supported a strong central stock exchange in Frankfurt, they certainly did not favour all changes that would have strengthened the use of the stock market as a source of financing. According to Story and Walter 'banks feared handing power to a federal authority—such as the United States SEC—and were reluctant to strengthen in-house rules against insider trading' (Story and Walter 1997: 182) and therefore opposed the EU insider-trading directive.

Another example are the government's attempts to increase the amount of risk capital available for small firms. Becker and Hellmann (2002) trace the failure of the *Deutsche Wagnisfinanzierungsgesellschaft*, an early German venture capital firm, back to 'inappropriate contracting and governance structures'. They argue that one problem was misguided financing criteria that 'suited those banks that feared competition...in their core business' (Becker and Hellmann 2002: 23). But another important aspect was certainly that the government's programmes were biased towards entrepreneurs, as discussed in Section 8.3. The unwillingness to give more rights to financiers shows that the fear of outside intervention by investors was a widespread phenomenon in Germany. It was shared by politicians, press, and workers and was not only the concern of families and entrepreneurs. Indeed, when the management of a stock corporation is required by law to act in the 'common/public welfare of the nation', it is only consistent to restrict outside investors' ability to inter-fere.[40] Another example is the second Financial Market Promotion Act, which transferred an EU directive into German law and was viewed by politicians as an important step towards a more active stock market. However, as Story and Walter (1997: 183) argue, the law had a number of important deficiencies and 'political support for an open market in corporate assets was minimal'. Story and Walter conclude: 'The firm intention of German political, business or labour leaders was to ensure that capitalism in Germany would remain a national brand of its European variant' (Story and Walter 1997: 185). The examples above illustrate the strong role of path dependence for the devel-opment of a financial system as emphasized by Bebchuk and Roe (1999).

Reconsidering mentality: While it is conceivable that German investors may be more risk averse than those in other countries because they incurred huge losses as a consequence of the Second World War, it may also be the case that (small) investors did not fear business risk *per se* but rather information and incentive problems, which may be larger in Germany than in the United States or the United Kingdom. Moreover, the German economic miracle and the strength of the German middle class ('Mittelstand'), which runs the vast majority of firms on the basis of sole proprietorship, would hardly have been possible without entrepreneurial initiative. However, as Fiedler and Hellmann (2001) argue, this type of entrepreneurial spirit was quite different from the one needed for venture capital financing: 'The concept of sharing equity with outsiders was foreign to these entrepreneurs. They viewed their family busi-ness with pride and put great emphasis on retaining control' (Fiedler and Hellmann 2001: 34). This view is confirmed by Ehrhardt and Nowak (2001) who find that reputation benefits that families derive from controlling a

---

[40] The public welfare clause ('Gemeinwohlklausel') was introduced in § 70 of the stock cor-poration act of 1937. It was not included in the revision of 1965 but only because—as reasoned in the government draft—it goes without saying. (For details see Schmidt and Spindler 1997.)

business in a small town is an important source of private benefits of control, which are not transferable. Families protect these benefits in an IPO by retaining a large equity block and issuing dual class shares. This and the large fraction of sole proprietorships suggest that owners may indeed fear a loss of control. If it is not believed that German entrepreneurs value control more than entrepreneurs in the United States or in the United Kingdom, then differences must be sought in the legal and institutional setting. For example, Burkart *et al.* (2003) present a model that predicts that the founder's family will retain control through concentrated ownership and may continue to manage the firm if legal protection of minority shareholders is low, which is the case in Germany.[41] As a consequence, the benefits of issuing shares, in particular, seeking diversification, are lower. This effect is reinforced by the presence of alternative sources of financing. Also, the argument that one of the potential reasons for the initial success of the *Neuer Markt* was stricter disclosure rules (Johnson 1999; Kukies 2000; Bottazzi and Da Rin 2002) at least challenges the perception that disclosure requirements deterred owners in Germany.

8.5. CONCLUSION

The evidence of the low number of IPOs is particularly surprising in light of the active stock market that Germany witnessed before the two world wars (see footnote 1). Moreover, universal banks in Germany were very active in securities underwriting at that time (Fohlin 1999, 2000*b*). Understanding the reasons for this difference is important. Rajan and Zingales (2003) argue that the level of openness of markets (cross-border trade and capital flows) influences 'interest groups'' incentives to oppose the development of the financial sector. Their empirical evidence supports this argument and, indeed, after reunification Germany became a net importer of capital and there was a dramatic increase in capital flows. (See Leuz and Wüstemann in this volume) This suggests that the phenomenon of the *Neuer Markt* may not only be an episode but is the result of an increased openness of the market as measured by the level of cross-border trade and capital flows, which reduces the incumbent's benefits from resistance.

The argument that the low number of IPOs and venture capital financing in Germany might be the result of incumbents protecting their interests may lead to the conclusion that it hindered economic development in Germany. This conclusion may, however, be too hasty. Wurgler (2000) provides evidence that the German financial system did not prevent an efficient allocation of capital in the years 1964–92. Covering sixty-five countries and twenty-eight

---

[41] Another reason may be that German owners are particularly sensitive to a further loss of control because their rights are already restricted by codetermination and the strong position of German trade unions (Gerke 1998: 617).

industries, he finds Germany to have the highest elasticity of industry investment to value added, with United Kingdom and United States ranked 10th and 13th, respectively. Indeed there were times when the Anglo-American world looked jealously at the German house bank system as a system that allows for long-term investments and interpreted it as a source of stability. The low number of IPOs and the lack of competition from outsiders (in particular independent investment banks and new firms) may have protected this system and made it possible to value implicit contracts.[42] In other words, the 'backwardness' of the stock market may have been an integral part of the German financial system, which was advantageous in times of relative stability (see Chapter 2). However, a system that preserves implicit contracts, may hamper structural change in times of technological change (Hellwig 2000, 2001).

References

Arbeitsgemeinschaft Selbständiger Unternehmer (ASU) (1965). 'Die Aussprache', Special Edition. (October).

Bascha, A., and Walz, U. (2000). 'Financing Practices in the German Venture Capital Industry—An Empirical Assessment', mimeo.

Baums, T. (1997). 'Aktienmarkt und Finanzierung kleiner Unternehmen', *Zeitschrift für Wirtschaftsrecht*, 44: 1942–48.

Bebchuk, L., and Roe, M. (1999). 'A Theory of Path Dependence in Corporate Governance and Ownership', *Stanford Law Review*, 52: 127–70.

Becker, R., and Hellmann, T. (2002). 'The Genesis of Venture Capital—Lessons from the German Experience', Working Paper. Stanford University, in C. Keuschnigg and V. Kanniainen (eds.), *Venture Capital, Entrepreneurship, and Public Policy*. Cambridge: MIT Press, forthcoming.

Bhattacharya, U., and Daouk, H. (2002). 'The World Price of Insider Trading', *Journal of Finance*, 57: 75–108.

Black, B. S., and Gilson, R. J. (1998). 'Venture Capital and the Structure of Capital Markets: Banks versus Stock Markets', *Journal of Financial Economics*, 47: 243–77.

Bottazzi, L., and Da Rin, M. (2002). 'Europe's 'New' Stock Markets', mimeo.

Büschgen, H. E. (1996). 'Diskussion in Meinungsspiegel zu Going Public', *Betriebswirtschaftliche Forschung und Praxis*, 2: 208–32.

Bundesministerium für Wirtschaft (1970). 'Grundsätze für die Förderung der Beteiligungsfinanzierung bei kleinen und mittleren Unternehmen', I c 2 - 680840/7.

——(1995). 'Risikokapital für Existenzgründer und mittelständische Unternehmen', I A 6 - 70 50 25/9.

Bundesverband deutscher Kapitalbeteiligungsgesellschaften e.V. (BVK). BVK Yearbook 1996–2001. Berlin.

——BVK Statistik 2001 and 2002.

---

[42] For example, Petersen and Rajan (1995) provide evidence that strong credit market competition is detrimental to lending relationships and may tighten the capital constraint of small businesses.

Burkart, M., Fausto, P., and Shleifer, A. (2003). 'Family Firms', *Journal of Finance*, 58: 2167–201.

Bygrave, W. D., Hay, M., and Peeters, J. B. (1999). *The Venture Capital Handbook*. Financial Times Prentice Hall, London *et al*.

Deutsche Bundesbank (1984). 'Der Aktienmarkt in der Bundesrepublik Deutschland und seine Entwicklungsmöglichkeiten', *Monatsberichte der Deutschen Bundesbank* (April): 12–21.

——(1997). 'Die Aktie als Finanzierungs- und Anlageinstrument', *Monatsberichte der Deutschen Bundesbank* (January): 27–41.

——(1998). 'Entwicklung des Bankensektors und Marktstellung der Kreditinstituts-gruppen seit Anfang der neunziger Jahre', *Monatsberichte der Deutschen Bundesbank* (March): 33–64.

——(2000). 'Der Markt für Wagniskapital in Deutschland', *Monatsberichte der Deutschen Bundesbank* (October): 15–29.

Deutsches Aktieninstitut (DAI) (2003). Factbook 2003.

Ehrhardt, O., and Nowak, E. (2001). 'Private Benefits and Minority Shareholder Expropriation—Empirical Evidence from IPOs of German Family-Owned Firms', CFS Working Paper 2001/10.

Elsas, R., and Krahnen, J. P. (1998). 'Is Relationship Lending Special? Evidence from Credit File Data in Germany', *Journal of Banking and Finance*, 22: 1283–316.

European Private Equity and Venture Capital Association (EVCA): EVCA Yearbook 2000–02.

Feinendegen, S., Hommel, U., and Wright, M. (2001). 'Stand der Beteiligungskapi-talfinanzierung in Deutschland', *Finanz Betrieb*, 10: 569–77.

Fiedler, M.-O., and Hellmann, T. (2001). 'Against all Odds: The Late but Rapid Development of the German Venture Capital Industry', *Journal of Private Equity*, 4: 31–45.

Fischer, C. (2000). 'Why Do Companies Go Public? Empirical Evidence from Germany's Neuer Markt', mimeo.

Fohlin, C. (1999). 'Banking Industry Structure, Competition, and Performance: Germany, The U.S., and Britain in the Pre-War Era', California Institute of Technology. Social Science WP 1078.

——(2000*a*). 'IPO Underpricing in Two Universes: Berlin 1882–1892, and New York, 1998–2000', California Institute of Technology. Social Science WP 1088.

——(2000*b*). 'Corporate Capital Structure and the Influence of Universal Banks in Pre-War Germany', California Institute of Technology. Social Science WP 1030R.

Franzke, S. (2001). 'Underpricing of Venture-Backed and Non Venture-Backed IPOs: Germany's Neuer Markt', CFS Working Paper 2001/01.

——, and Schlag, C. (2002). 'Over-Allotment Options in IPOs on Germany's Neuer Markt—An Empirical Investigation', CFS Working Paper 2002/16.

Gerke, W. (1983). *Die Rolle der Kapitalbeteiligungsgesellschaften und Kreditinstitute bei der Technologiefinanzierung–Innovationsbörse Berlin, Venture Capital für junge Technologieunternehmen*. Berlin, 25–34.

——(1988). 'Hemmnisse für die Börsenneueinführung innovativer Mittel-standsunternehmen durch Beschränkung der Gewerbefreiheit für Investmentbanken', in W. Gerke (ed.), *Bankrisiken und Bankrecht*. Wiesbaden: Festschrift für Fritz Philipp, 213–28.

Gerke, W., Bank, M., Neukirchen, D., Rasch, S., Schröder, M., Spengel, C., Steiger, M., and Westerheide, P. (1995). *Probleme deutscher Mittelständischer Unternehmen beim Zugang zum Kapitalmarkt*. Schriftenreihe des ZEW 7. Baden-Baden: Nomos Verlagsgesellschaft.

——(1998). 'Market Failure in Venture Capital Markets for New Medium and Small Enterprises', in K. J. Hopt *et al.* (eds.), *Comparative Corporate Governance—The State of the Art and Emerging Research*. Oxford: Clarendon Press, 607–35.

Giersch, H., and Schmidt, H. (1986). *Offene Märkte für Beteiligungskapital: USA-Großbritannien-Bundesrepublik Deutschland*. Studie anlässlich des 125jährigen Jubiläums der Baden-Württembergischen Wertpapierbörse zu Stuttgart.

Habib, M. A., and Ljungqvist, A. P. (2001). 'Underpricing and Entrepreneurial Wealth Losses in IPOs: Theory and Evidence', *Review of Financial Studies*, 14: 433–58.

Hardach, G. (1995). 'Banking in Germany, 1918–1939', in Charles H. Feinstein (ed.), *Banking, Currency, and Finance in Europe Between the Wars*. Oxford: Clarendon Press, 269–95.

Hellwig, M. (2000). 'On the Economics and Politics of Corporate Finance and Corporate Control', in X. Vives (ed.), *Corporate Governance*. Cambridge: Cambridge University Press, 95–134.

——(2001). 'Corporate Governance and the Financing of Investment for Structural Change', in Deutsche Bundesbank (ed.), *Investing Today for the World of Tomorrow: Studies on the Investment Process in Europe*. Berlin *et al.*: Springer Verlag, 203–23.

Jenkinson, T., and Ljungqvist, A. P. (1996). *Going Public: The Theory and Evidence on how Companies Raise Equity Finance*. Oxford: Oxford University Press.

Johnson, S. (1999). 'Does Investor Protection Matter? Evidence from Germany's Neuer Markt', Working Paper. MIT.

Kaserer, C., and Kempf, V. (1995). 'Das Underpricing-Phänomen am deutschen Kapitalmarkt und seine Ursachen', *Zeitschrift für Bankrecht und Bankwirtschaft*, 7: 45–68.

——, and Kraft, M. (2003). 'How Issue Size, Risk, and Complexity are Influencing External Financing Costs: German IPOs Analyzed from an Economies of Scale Perspective', *Journal of Business Finance and Accounting*, 30: 479–512.

Kiss, I., and Stehle, R. (2002). 'Underpricing and Long-Term Performance of Initial Public Offerings at Germany's Neuer Markt, 1997–2001', Working Paper. Humboldt University Berlin.

Kroszner, R. S., and Rajan, R. G. (1994). 'Is the Glass-Steagall Act Justified? A Study of the U.S. Experience with Universal Banking before 1933', *American Economic Review*, 84: 810–32.

Kübler, F. (1999). *Gesellschaftsrecht*, 5th edn. Heidelberg: UTB Verlag.

Kukies, J. (2000). 'The Effects of Introducing a New Stock Exchange on the IPO process', mimeo.

Langemann, A. (2000). *Ökonomische Vorteile eines Börsengangs: Theoretische Begründbarkeit und empirische Evidenz*. Frankfurt am Main.

La Porta, R., Lopez-de-Silanes, F., Shleifer A., and Vishny, R. (1997). 'Legal Determinants of External Finance', *Journal of Finance*, 52: 1131–50.

——, ——, ——, and ——(1998). 'Law and Finance', *Journal of Political Economy*, 106: 1113–55.

Leopold, G. and Frommann, H. (1998). *Eigenkapital für den Mittelstand: Venture Capital im In und Ausland*. München: C. H. Beck.

Lessat, V., Hemer, J., and Tobias, H. (1999). *Beteiligungskapital und technologieorientierte Unternehmensgründung: Markt—Finanzierung—Rahmenbedingungen*. Wiesbaden: Gabler Verlag.

Leuz, C., and Verrecchia, R. (2000). 'The Economic Consequences of Increased Disclosure', *Journal of Accounting Research*, 38 (Suppl.): 91–124.

Ljungqvist, A. P. (1997). 'Pricing Initial Public Offerings: Further Evidence from Germany', *European Economic Review*, 41: 1309–20.

Loughran, T., and Ritter, J. R. (2002). 'Why Has IPO Underpricing Changed Over Time?', mimeo.

——, ——, and Rydqvist, K. (1994). 'Initial Public Offerings: International Insights', *Pacific-Basin Finance Journal*, 2: 165–99.

Monopolkommission (1998). *Ordnungspolitische Leitlinien für ein funktionsfähiges Finanzsystem: Sondergutachten der Monopolkommission*. Baden-Baden.

National Venture Capital Association (NVCA): NVCA Yearbook 2003.

Nevermann, H., and Falk, D. (1986). *Venture Capital—Ein betriebswirtschaftlicher und steuerlicher Vergleich zwischen den USA und der Bundesrepublik Deutschland*. Baden-Baden: NOMOS Verlagsgesellschaft.

Pagano, M., and Volpin, P. (2000). 'The Political Economy of Corporate Governance', CEPR Discussion Paper No. 2682.

Perotti, E., and von Thadden, E.-L. (2002). 'The Political Economy of Bank- and Market Dominance', mimeo. University of Lausanne (October).

Persé, H. J. (1962). *Die Partner-Investmentgesellschaft: Die Eigenfinanzierung von Einzelunternehmen und Personengesellschaften durch Investmentgesellschaften*. Wiesbaden: Gabler Verlag.

Petersen, M. A., and Rajan, R. G. (1995). 'The Effect of Credit Market Competition on Lending Relationships', *Quarterly Journal of Economics*, 110: 407–43.

Rajan, R. G., and Zingales, L. (2003). 'The Great Reversals: The Politics of Financial Development in the 20th Century', *Journal of Financial Economics*, 69: 5–50.

Ritter, J. (1991). 'The Long-Run Performance of Initial Public Offerings', *Journal of Finance*, 46: 3–27.

——, and Welch, I. (2002). 'A Review of IPO Activity, Pricing, and Allocations', *Journal of Finance*, 57: 1795–828.

Schlag, C., and Wodrich, A. (2000). 'Has There Always Been Underpricing and Long-Run Underperformance?—IPOs in Germany Before World War I', CFS Working Paper 12/2000.

Schlegelmilch, K. (1976). 'Die Kapitalbeteiligungsgesellschaften in der Bundesrepublik Deutschland', in K. Schlegelmilch und K. Juncker (eds.), *Die Kapitalbeteiligungsgesellschaft in Theorie und Praxis*. Festschrift für H. Joachim Krahnen. Frankfurt: Fritz Knapp Verlag, 35–48.

Schmidt, R. H. (1988). 'Venture Capital in Deutschland: ein Problem der Qualität', *Die Bank*, 4: 184–7.

——, and Tyrell, M. (1988). 'Underpricing bei Deutschen Erstemissionen 1984/85', *Zeitschrift für Betriebswirtschaft*, 58: 1193–203.

Schmidt, R. H., and Spindler, G. (1997). 'Shareholder-Value zwischen Ökonomie und Recht', in H. D. Assmann *et al.* (eds.), *Wirtschafts- und Medienrecht in der offenen Demokratie*. Heidelberg: C. F. Müller-Verlag, 515–55.

Schürmann, W. (1980). *Familienunternehmen und Börse: emittieren—warum und wie?* Wiesbaden: Gabler.

——, and Körfgen, K. (1987). *Familienunternehmen auf dem Weg zur Börse*, 2nd edn. München: C. H. Beck.

——, and —— (1997). *Familienunternehmen auf dem Weg zur Börse*, 3rd edn. München: C. H. Beck.

Schuster, J. (1996). 'Underpricing and Crisis—IPO Performance in Germany', Discussion Paper No. 252.

Stehle, R., and Erhardt, O. (1999). 'Renditen bei Börseneinführungen am deutschen Kapitalmarkt', *Zeitschrift für Betriebswirtschaft*, 69: 1395–422.

——, ——, and Przyborowsky, R. (2000). 'Long-run Stock Performance of German Initial Public Offerings and Seasoned Equity Issues', *European Financial Management Journal*, 6: 149–72.

Story, J., and Walter, I. (1997). *Political Economy of Financial Integration in Europe: The Battle of the Systems*. Boston: MIT Press.

Tilly, R. (1992). 'An Overview on the Role of the Large German Banks up to 1914', in Y. Cassis (ed.), *Finance and Financiers in European History, 1880–1960*. Cambridge: Cambridge University Press, 93–112.

Uhlir, H. (1989). 'Der Gang an die Börse und das Underpricing Phänomen', *Zeitschrift für Bankrecht und Bankwirtschaft*, 1: 2–16.

Venture Economics (2002). '2001 European Private Equity Short-term Performance Reflects Uncertain Economic Environment'.

Vollmer, L. (1998). 'Die Unternehmensbeteiligungsgesellschaften nach der Reform der UBGG', *Zeitschrift für Bankrecht und Bankwirtschaft*, 10: 221–76.

Weichert, R. (1987). *Probleme des Risikokapitalmarktes in der Bundesrepublik*. Tübingen: Mohr-Siebeck.

Wenger, E. (1996). 'Kapitalmarktrecht als Resultat deformierter Anreizstrukturen', in D. Sadowski *et al.* (eds.), *Regulierung und Unternehmenspolitik*. Wiesbaden: Gabler Verlag, 419–58.

White, E. (1984). 'Banking Innovation in the 1920's: The Growth of National Banks', *Financial Services, Business and Economic History*.

Wissenschaftlicher Beirat beim Bundesministerium für Wirtschaft (1998). 'Wagniskapital', Gutachten vom 25/26 April 1997. *Sammelband der Gutachten von 1987– 1997*. Stuttgart, 1897–1927.

Wurgler, J. (2000). 'Financial Markets and the Allocation of Capital', *Journal of Financial Economics*, 58: 187–214.

Internet-Pages:

http://www.bmwi.de (Internet page of the Federal Ministry of Economics and Technology)

http://www.ifm-bonn.de/dienste/gruend.htm

http://www.nvca.org (Internet page of the National Venture Capital Association (NVCA))

http://www.ventureeconomics.com (Internet page of Venture Economics)

9

Mergers and Acquisitions in Germany: Social Setting and Regulatory Framework

FRANK A. SCHMID AND MARK WAHRENBURG

9.1. INTRODUCTION

On 5 July 2001, the European parliament threw out the proposed European takeover directive after more than 12 years of negotiations. The defeat of the directive means that, for the foreseeable future, individual country law remains pre-eminent in both domestic and cross-border business combinations in Europe.

German members of the European parliament were pivotal in the vote on the takeover directive. The German government, along with opposition parties, business organizations, and organized labour all welcomed the decision. German chancellor Gerhard Schröder expressed satisfaction about the demise of the European takeover directive, stating 'Now Germany can do what I'd proposed all along' (*Financial Times* 2001*a*). The Schröder administration quickly drafted a national takeover law.

The Takeover Act, which entered into force on 1 January 2002, replaced the Takeover Code, which had been introduced in 1995 in a failed effort of self-regulation. Most significantly, the Takeover Act allows management to take defensive actions against unsolicited takeover bids on the condition that these actions are in the corporation's best interest. The law explicitly states that management may solicit competing bids in search of a 'white knight'. Also, the law gives shareholders the power to pre-approve defensive measures, which management may take at its own discretion within 18 months of such a shareholder resolution.

In the interim, the European Commission entrusted a group of experts with reviving the project of harmonizing takeover rules within the European Union.

The views expressed in this chapter are solely those of the authors and do not necessarily reflect official positions of the Federal Reserve Bank of St. Louis or the Federal Reserve System. The article was written while Schmid was visiting Johann Wolfgang Goethe-University Frankfurt.

The *Report of the High Level Group of Company Law Experts on Issues Related to Takeover Bids*, dubbed 'Winter Report' after the name of its chairman, Jaap Winter, was submitted to the Commission on 10 January 2002. The Winter group had two mandates. One mandate was to provide suggestions for creating a level playing field for cross-border mergers and acquisitions in Europe. The other mandate was to come forth with recommendations for modernizing corporate law and corporate governance in Europe. As this chapter was being written, the discussion of the report in academia and among policy-makers was still underway. Much of the criticism has zeroed in on the proposed 'one share, one vote' principle in takeover decisions and, related to that, the suggested breakthrough rule (Bebchuk and Hart 2002; Berklof and Burkhart 2002). Under the breakthrough rule, upon acquiring 75 per cent of the residual cash flow rights ('risk capital') of a corporation, a bidder would be able to gain full control over the corporation— regardless of the voting power this equity stake confers. The breakthrough rule would foil efforts of wealth-constrained founding families to retain control while their corporations expand—a subject to be discussed below.

National differences in corporate governance practices in Europe, such as board structures, shareholder structures, and labour participation rights, make it difficult to operate in the European cross-border mergers and acquisitions environment. Particularly thorny issues are 'golden shares' and labour participation in corporate decision-making. Golden shares are equity stakes held by government authorities, mostly in industries that are of national interest, such as utilities (energy, telecom, water) and defence. Frequently, golden shares date back to the time when the companies in question were privatized. Although golden shares might not fully insulate companies from takeover attempts, they render the government pivotal to the outcome. Not surprisingly, governments tend to favour 'domestic solutions' over cross-border takeovers—an uneven playing field. What's more, companies that have issued golden shares tend to acquire aggressively, be it at home or abroad. First, the government stake expands the company's borrowing capacity through the implicit government guarantee on its debt as demonstrated by the steep borrowing of privatized European telecom providers in the late 1990s. Second, the diminished takeover threat lessens the penalty for squandering financial resources on over-expansion—the European telecom industry, again, being a case in point.

The widespread use of golden shares among its European neighbours was critical for Germany in causing the collapse of the proposed takeover directive in the European parliament—a proposal that had been mute on this issue. In the meantime, the European Court of Justice on 4 June 2002, dealt a blow to the way the French and Portuguese governments at the time used golden shares to retain control over privatized companies, forcing these governments to rethink their practices. On the other hand, the court permitted a more restrained golden shares practice employed by the Belgium government, as reported by the *Financial Times* (2002*b*). Then, in a second verdict on 13 May 2003, the court ruled that golden shares practices in the United Kingdom and Spain violated the EU treaty by restricting the free movement of capital. The new ruling makes it clear that golden shares are only permissible where they maintain a measure of control over essential public services and keep the government's role to a minimum (*Financial Times* 2003*b*).

Another area in which the harmonization efforts of the European Union were struggling is labour participation in company decisions. On 8 October 2001, after 31 years of negotiation, the European Union gave birth to the *Societas Europea*, or SE. The legislation, which will go into effect in 2004, allows companies that operate in more than one state of the European Union to establish as a single company under EU law. The *Financial Times* (2001*b*) quotes Frits Bolkestein, the internal market commissioner, saying that the SE would 'enable companies to expand and restructure their cross-border operations without the costly and time-consuming red tape of having to set up a network of subsidiaries'.

European harmonization efforts notwithstanding, to date, individual country law dominates in both domestic and cross-border mergers and acquisitions in Europe. This chapter reviews the social setting and the regulatory framework for mergers and acquisitions or, more generally, for the transfer of cash flow rights on complex assets in Germany. We also provide a survey on takeover barriers. We stay clear of issues in flux, such as the current discussion of the Winter report. Descriptive statistical information we provide only to the degree necessary for characterizing critical attributes of the merger and acquisition activity in Germany. The interested reader may find extensive statistical data at < http://www.mergers-and-acquisitions.de/ > .

9.2. THE SOCIAL SETTING

For understanding the merger and acquisition activity in Germany, both in the opportunities they offer and the limits they are subject to, it is important to be familiar with the German way of doing business. Germany pursues a strongly consensus-oriented, egalitarian economic approach called *Soziale Marktwirtschaft*— a principle anchored in the country's constitution and shared by all quarters of society. This consensus-oriented business approach, which has been dubbed 'Rhineland capitalism' in the financial press (*Financial Times* 2002*d*), makes transactions in the market for corporate control particularly intricate. In mergers and acquisitions, third parties are at risk of being expropriated of unenforceable claims—be they pecuniary or non-pecuniary. Most importantly, transfers of residual cash flow rights might adversely affect labour if workers' claims are not fully protected by law—a prospect where contracts are incomplete (Gorton and Schmid 2002). A bidder who disregards the deeply ingrained preferences of German society for consensus, risks the takeover attempt being frustrated by resistance from organized labour or overt opposition from the government.

Two case studies may serve to exemplify the idiosyncratic characteristics of the German social environment for transfers of residual cash flow rights on complex assets.[1] The first case relates the acquisitions of Hoesch (1991/92) and Thyssen (1997/98) by Krupp. The second case recounts the takeover of Mannesmann by Vodafone of the United Kingdom (1999/2000). In particular the Thyssen and Mannesmann takeovers left their marks, profoundly and possibly irreversibly changing the way the German takeover market functions.

The first episode bears the trademark of Gerhard Cromme, then CEO of the privately held company Friedr. Krupp GmbH, a venerable German steel and engineering company. In 1991, Cromme announced that Krupp controlled a 24.9 per cent equity interest in Hoesch AG, a publicly traded competitor. At the time, in Germany the disclosure threshold for equity stakes was 25 per cent—a rule that allowed Krupp's share accumulation to go unnoticed. Cromme's move embarrassed Deutsche Bank, a financial behemoth that, by tradition, has had close ties (inclusive of equity stakes and non-executive director positions) to the German steel industry. Most significantly, Deutsche Bank orchestrated a rescue effort when Krupp went into financial distress in 1966. In utter disrespect, Cromme commissioned Credit Suisse for the secret share accumulation. Also, Cromme wittingly frustrated Deutsche Bank's restructuring efforts at Hoesch AG where Deutsche Bank—Hoesch's *Hausbank*—had just installed Karl Joseph Neukirchen as CEO. Initially Neukirchen resisted the idea of Hoesch being folded into Krupp, but succumbed. In December 1992, Krupp and Hoesch were merged into Fried. Krupp AG Hoesch-Krupp, a newly established publicly traded corporation.

The takeover succeeded despite a clause in Hoesch's articles of association that limited to 15 per cent the fraction of votes that a block holder could cast at Hoesch shareholder meetings. Of course, the anecdote does not prove that voting restrictions or the far-reaching powers of German universal banks do not pose takeover barriers. At a minimum, the fact that the merger went through indicates that these two particularities of the German takeover market are not necessarily prohibitive—a finding consistent with Jenkinson and Ljungqvist (2001).

Even more daring than Cromme's assault on Hoesch AG was his 1997 takeover bid for Thyssen AG—a German steel and engineering group considerably larger than Fried. Krupp AG Hoesch-Krupp. According to the *Financial Times* (1998), at the time, Thyssen was the 149th largest company in Europe while Krupp ranked 273rd—as measured by market capitalization. After Thyssen had rebuffed friendly advances in years past, Cromme enlisted

---

[1] Emmons and Schmid (1998) offer a systematic description of the social environment in Germany for reallocation of claims on residual cash flow.

Deutsche Bank for a hostile bid. Goldman Sachs of the United States devised the takeover plan under the telling code name *Hammer und Thor*. Deutsche Morgan Grenfell and Dresdner Kleinwort Benson, London-based investment banking subsidiaries of the respective German universal banks, arranged financing.

On 18 March 1997, the day after rumours of an imminent takeover attempt started circulating in the stock market, Krupp announced an unsolicited bid for Thyssen. Dieter Vogel, Thyssen's CEO, immediately denounced the offer. Possibly to the surprise of Krupp and Deutsche Bank, the German public was aghast. Soon Krupp and Deutsche Bank were to feel the wrath of the public, the political establishment, and organized labour.

Chancellor Helmut Kohl, whose administration rested on a coalition of the conservative Christian Democrats (CDU/CSU) and the moderately libertarian Free Democrats (FDP), on 19 March expressed his 'deep concern' over the matter. Kohl appealed to Krupp and Thyssen to 'live up to their social responsibilities' (*Die Welt* 1997). Johannes Rau, prime minister of a Social Democrat (SPD)-led administration in North Rhine-Westfalia—home state of both Krupp and Thyssen—moved quickly to broker talks between the two parties. Wolfgang Clement, the generally pro-business economics minister in the Rau administration, in addressing the state parliament, said he expected the talks to be conducted 'with the will to end the confrontation and reach a co-operative solution' (*Financial Times* 1997). As the pressure mounted, Krupp put the bid on hold, agreeing to an 8-day truce during which the parties were to negotiate a merger of their steel subsidiaries.

Twenty-fourth of March was the day that 30,000 infuriated steelworkers were expected to take to the streets in front of Deutsche Bank headquarters in Frankfurt. The night before, Krupp scrapped the takeover plan, pledging in writing that it would not make any further bid for Thyssen. At the same time, the two parties consented on holding talks on combining their steel interests (*Financial Times* 2002*a*); the talks led up to a merger agreement on 28 March.

In August, the public was taken by surprise when it learned that Krupp and Thyssen were holding talks about a full-fledged merger. The merger details were finalized in November and approved by the respective supervisory boards—that is, boards of non-executive directors—on 22 January 1998 (Thyssen), and 5 February 1998 (Krupp). Meanwhile, the public attention to the merger had all but died off.

The supervisory boards of Krupp and Thyssen approved the merger with thin majorities. Thyssen was subject to *Montan* codetermination, a regime of extensive labour representation on the supervisory board that dates back to the immediate post-war period. In *Montan* codetermination, which applies to an increasingly small, now single-digit number of companies in the coal and steel industries, labour and shareholder representatives each command the same number of votes; a so-called neutral member, who holds no interest in the corporation, casts a tie-breaking vote. All labour representatives on the

Thyssen supervisory board voted against the merger, making the neutral member pivotal in the decision. Similarly, on the Krupp supervisory board, all labour representatives, except for the representative of middle management ('leitende Angestellte'), opposed the transaction. Note that the Krupp supervisory board, which was subject to equal representation under the 1976 Codetermination Act, was able to outvote labour regardless of the ballot cast by middle management. Under the 1976 Codetermination Act, which generally applies to corporations with more than 2000 employees, there is no neutral member; rather, the chairman of the supervisory board can cast a second vote in a repeatedly tied ballot. Then again, there is generally strong reservation among shareholder representatives in using the tie-breaking vote— a manifestation of the German, consensus-oriented business model. It is worthy of note that the newly established, merged company, Thyssen-Krupp AG, is subject to the 1976 Codetermination Act, rather than *Montan* codetermination—a possible explanation of why the Thyssen workers resisted the merger so fiercely.

The roles played by Deutsche Bank and Dresdner Bank in this takeover battle remain controversial in Germany. When Krupp launched its takeover attempt on Thyssen, Wolfgang Röller, then ex-CEO of Dresdner Bank and chairman of its supervisory board, was a member of Thyssen's supervisory board. At the end of March 1997, when Röller's tenure at Thyssen ended, Bernhard Walter, a member of the Dresdner Bank management board—that is, the board of executive directors—succeeded him in this position. Even more delicate was the case of Ulrich Cartellieri, a member of the management board of Deutsche Bank and simultaneously a member of the Thyssen supervisory board. As a member of the Thyssen supervisory board, he had access to inside information that was potentially valuable to Krupp, a client of Deutsche Bank. As a member of the Deutsche Bank management board, he approved the takeover attempt. Cartellieri tried unsuccessfully to dispel accusations of a conflict of interest brought against him in the financial press; he retired from both board positions on 20 May 1997. The case highlights a general problem of financial conglomerates, universal banks in particular. What may be synergies to the universal bank may look like conflicts of interest in the eyes of the public or the financial regulator.

The Krupp–Thyssen takeover confirms and, at the same time, refutes the stereotypes the international financial press tends to associate with the German economic model of Rhineland capitalism. On one hand, public outrage and resistance from nearly all quarters of the political spectrum—save for a small libertarian faction—initially frustrated Krupp's unsolicited bid. On the other hand, the takeover eventually materialized. The takeover also highlights the intensely debated role of German universal banks in control changes. German universal banks maintain extensive networks of equity interests and board representation—a corporate structure dubbed 'Deutschland AG' in the financial press (*Financial Times* 2003c). The banks have long been accused of insulating incumbent management from the disciplining forces of the market for corporate control (Wenger and Kaserer 1998). In sharp contrast to this commonly held view, Jenkinson and Ljungqvist (2001) find that the German merger and acquisition environment, not least because of the active role of German universal banks, is in fact more hostile than frequently portrayed. The authors find that hostile stakes in Germany play a role similar to hostile tender offers in the United Kingdom. Then again, Boehmer (2000) finds that concentrated ownership—a corollary to block trades—increases the chances of value-reducing takeovers in Germany.

The 1999/2000 takeover of Mannesmann AG by Vodafone AirTouch plc of the United Kingdom is the second episode that highlights important particularities of the German takeover market. At the time, Mannesmann AG was an engineering group that had diversified into wireless communication and fixed-line phone service, making communications its core business. Like Vodafone, which was a communications purebred, Mannesmann pursued a strategy of aggressive geographic expansion in its wireless business in an attempt to realize economies of scope. On October 1999, Mannesmann made a friendly bid for Orange plc, the third-largest wireless communications company in the United Kingdom. Vodafone, on the other hand, had just become the largest wireless communications company in the world after merging with AirTouch of the United States.

From the perspective of Vodafone, a takeover of Mannesmann appeared worthwhile for two reasons. First, Mannesmann would allow Vodafone to expand into Germany and, second, Mannesmann was a conglomerate, which presumably traded at a discount in the stock market. Indeed, after the takeover materialized, Vodafone quickly auctioned off the Mannesmann automotive and engineering subsidiaries. Although Mannesmann in September 1999 announced plans of splitting itself into telecommunications and engineering units with separate stock market listings, the restructuring was overdue. It is open to debate whether Mannesmann in a more competitive corporate control environment than Deutschland AG would have been long pressured to dispose of its non-core businesses, making the company a less attractive takeover target.

In October 1999, rumours that Vodafone was preparing a takeover of Mannesmann started circulating in the stock market. On 14 November 1999, Chris Gent, CEO of Vodafone, travelled to Düsseldorf to present a takeover bid to the Mannesmann management board, offering 43.7 own shares per Mannesmann share. After the Mannesmann management rejected the offer, Vodafone on 19 November turned to the Mannesmann shareholders, offering 53.7 Vodafone shares per Mannesmann share. This bid granted the Mannesmann shareholders a 47.2 per cent participation in Vodafone. Also, the offer implied a 68.8 per cent takeover premium based on the share price implied in Mannesmann's bid for Orange and a whopping 84.4 per cent takeover premium over the €144.8 Mannesmann share price at close on the day the news about the takeover talks with Orange hit the market. On 28 November, the Mannesmann management board denounced the bid.

Meanwhile, German chancellor Gerhard Schröder, who was heading an SPD-led coalition government with the environmentalist party *Die Grünen* and who had campaigned on a pro-business platform akin to the one of UK prime minister Tony Blair, condemned the bid. On the day Vodafone announced the bettered offer to the Mannesmann shareholders, Schröder declared that hostile takeovers destroy the 'culture' of the target company. He went on saying that hostile bidders underestimate 'the virtue of co-determination' in German companies (*Financial Times* 1999a).

The matter came to a head in a meeting in Florence on 21 November between Tony Blair and Gerhard Schröder. There, the UK prime minister made it clear that shareholders, not the governments, ought to decide on takeover bids. Tony Blair was quoted saying that we 'live in a European market today where European companies are taking over other European companies, are taking over British companies, and vice-versa...That's the European Market'. On one hand, the German chancellor admitted that it 'is, for the time being, only an affair between companies'. Then again, Gerhard Schröder qualified: 'I would put emphasis on there being no hostile takeovers.' It is worthy of note that Mannesmann CEO Klaus Esser spoke out publicly against government interference (*Financial Times* 1999b).

On 23 December 1999, Vodafone formally submitted the announced (unconditional and unrestricted) tender offer; the deadline for tendering shares was set at 7 February 2000. At the time, the shares of Mannesmann were widely dispersed among small shareholders and institutional investors seeking portfolio investment; no single investor held a significant equity interest (*Hoppenstedt Aktienführer 2000*). A possible reason for the dispersed shareholder structure was a clause in Mannesmann's charter that limited to 5 per cent the fraction of votes a block holder could cast at shareholder meetings.

What followed was a highly controversial takeover battle. According to Beinert (2000: § 350), German corporate law, at the time, mandated that management take a neutral stance in a takeover attempt. What's more, Mannesmann had signed the Takeover Code, which stipulates that management shall abstain from actions that are not in the shareholders' best interest. Specifically, the Takeover Code demanded that, after a takeover attempt has been launched, the target's management abstain from actions that might cause exceptional price movements in the target's securities or the securities offered in exchange thereof. Then again, the German Takeover Code had no force of law—compliance was voluntary even for those companies that had signed on (Beinert 2000: §§ 158, 163). At least twice, the Mannesmann management hovered on the brink of violating the neutrality principle of German corporate law and the Takeover Code in particular. On 28 January 2000, Mannesmann disclosed to the public plans of taking a stake in AOL Europe; 2 days later

Mannesmann announced intentions of entering an Internet alliance with Vivendi of France. Neither business plan materialized.

Even more delicate than the defensive attempts of the Mannesmann management was the €15 million 'appreciation award' for Mannesmann CEO Klaus Esser, made to him by the compensation committee of Mannesmann's supervisory board on 4 February, one day after Esser dropped his objections to the bid. Germany, in its corporate law, imposes strict fiduciary duties on management, rendering severance payments to the target's management ('golden parachutes') prone to prosecution and litigation (Beinert 2000: § 345). In March 2000, the state prosecutor of North Rhine-Westfalia launched a criminal probe in this matter (*Financial Times* 2002e). In February 2003, the state prosecutor filed charges of breach of shareholders' trust against Esser and other former Mannesmann executive and non-executive directors. Among the charged are Josef Ackermann, present CEO of Deutsche Bank, and Klaus Zwickel, former chairman of IG Metall, Germany's largest trade union; both were members of the supervisory board compensation committee at the time (*Financial Times* 2003a). As this chapter was being written, the case was pending.

In the end, the Mannesmann management board was defeated by the company's shareholders, who overwhelmingly chose to tender. To many, the Vodafone–Mannesmann takeover dealt a debilitating blow to Deutschland AG—a presumably doomed economic concept that offers German corporations shelter from the chills of an unfettered market for corporate control. The *Financial Times*, on 4 February 2000, gave a telling description of the German post-Mannesmann takeover market, quoting an anonymous investment banker: 'Germany's hitherto unbreakable corporate world has finally been broken and many are going to be licking their lips.'

9.3. THE REGULATORY FRAMEWORK

The regulatory framework for business combinations in Germany has seen significant revisions during the period 1990–2002. Four laws for the promotion of financial markets ('Finanzmarktförderungsgesetze') have been passed under administrations of different political orientation in an attempt to increase the transparency and level the playing field in the market for corporate control. Also, a revised Reorganization Act ('Umwandlungsgesetz') entered into force in 1995, significantly lowering the transaction costs of business combinations and restructuring. Then, there is the mentioned Takeover Act ('Unternehmensübernahmegesetz'), which became effective in 2002. The takeover law provides, for the first time, a legal framework for tender offers; the law applies to domestic as well as foreign bidders for publicly traded German corporations. Other legislation of import includes antitrust law ('Gesetz gegen Wettbewerbsbeschränkungen') and corporate law ('Aktiengesetz, GmbH Gesetz'). What follows is an overview of legal provisions that are most germane to the merger and acquisition activity in Germany. A more detailed analysis is Beinert (2000).

Antitrust supervision in Germany resides with the Federal Cartel Office ('Bundeskartellamt'). Generally, all business combinations that have a measurable effect on the markets for goods and services are subject to German antitrust supervision, regardless of the respective companies' countries of origin. According to the Antitrust Act, there are four types of transactions by which an enterprise may establish a business combination—a term the Antitrust Act stretches considerably beyond its acceptation (Beinert 2000: § 185). The first type of transaction that may establish a business combination is an enterprise acquiring the assets of another enterprise in whole or in substantial part. The second transaction type relates to an enterprise seizing direct or indirect control over an enterprise or parts thereof. Cases of decisive influence— the legal definition of control—include contracts in which a company surrenders control ('Beherrschungsvertrag') or its profit ('Gewinnabführungsvertrag') to another company. The Stock Corporation Act legalizes such contracts if they are approved by a minimum of 75 per cent of the voting capital represented at the shareholder meeting. The third type of transaction relates to an enterprise raising its equity interest in another enterprise above the threshold of 25 or 50 per cent. Finally, the fourth type of business combination concerns transactions that enable an enterprise to exercise significant competitive influence over another enterprise.

The Federal Cartel Office must be notified of intended business combinations with German participation if the concerned enterprises in the latest completed fiscal year had sales (worldwide and consolidated) of more than €500 million or if at least one party had sales in Germany of more than €25 million. There are two exceptions to the notification requirement. The first exception pertains to a business combination where an acquirer is not legally part of a group of enterprises and, at the same time, billed worldwide sales of less than €10 million during the latest completed fiscal year. The second exception applies to a business combination in a market that has existed for at least 5 years and had sales volumes of less than €15 million during the latest completed calendar year.

Upon notification of an intended business combination, the Federal Cartel Office must examine the case within one month's time. The Federal Cartel Office either moves on to an investigation ('Hauptprüfverfahren') or the business combination may be consummated. If, during the investigation, the Federal Cartel Office does not disapprove of the intended business deal within 4 months of the original notification, the transaction may be executed.

The Federal Cartel Office must disapprove of a business combination if the transaction results in or strengthens a market-dominating position, unless the enterprises in question can demonstrate that the gain in market dominance is more than offset by an improvement of the competitive environment (Beinert 2000: § 195). Then again, should the Federal Cartel Office indeed enjoin a business combination, the parties concerned may file a petition with the federal minister of economics. The minister of economics may overturn the decision of the Federal Cartel Office if the intended business combination is in the country's economic or public interest (Beinert 2000: § 197). As of June 2001, there were sixteen petitions on record for the post-war period, six of them having been granted (Bundeskartellamt 2001: 14). Finally, the German Federal Cartel Office is incompetent in cases where European antitrust supervision applies.[2]

As mentioned, during the period 1990–2002, Germany passed four Acts on the Promotion of Financial Markets. The most significant of these four laws is the Second Act on the Promotion of Financial Markets from 26 July 1994. This law—by implementing the EC Insider Dealing Directive of 13 November 1989—created the Securities Trading Act ('Wertpapierhandelsgesetz') and established the Federal Securities Supervisory Office ('Bundesaufsichtsamt für den Wertpapierhandel'); the agency was folded into the newly established German Financial Supervisory Authority ('Bundesanstalt für Finanzdienstleistungsaufsicht') in May 2002.

The Securities Trading Act applies to all companies that are headquartered in Germany and, at the same time, trade at a stock exchange—that is, not exclusively over the counter—in the European Union or the European Economic Area. The most significant provisions of the Securities Trading Act pertain to the disclosure of information on the corporation's shareholder structure—superseding similar provisions in the Stock Corporation Act—as well as to insider trading and *ad hoc* disclosure.

The German Stock Corporation Act stipulates that an investor, upon crossing the thresholds of 25 per cent of the equity or 50 per cent of the votes, shall notify the company, which in turn must disclose to the public the shareholder's identity and the threshold crossed. The investors do not have to disclose the actual sizes of the equity stakes, except in cases of cross-shareholdings in excess of 25 per cent (Beinert 2000: § 133). The disclosure standards specified in the Securities Trading Act of July 1994, on the other hand, stipulate that an investor shall notify the Financial Supervisory Authority upon arriving at the 5, 10, 25, 50, or 75 per cent threshold levels of voting rights, be it from above or below. The information is then made available to the public on the Internet. There is an ongoing discussion about methodological issues in calculating these voting rights in complex shareholder structures, such as networks of cross-shareholdings and pyramids. There is also concern about the fact that investors do not have to notify the Financial Supervisory Authority of subsequent changes to their equity stakes so long as they do not cross a neighbouring threshold.

---

[2] European antitrust supervision rests on Council Regulation (EEC) No. 4064/89 from 21 December 1989, as amended by Council Regulation (EC) No. 1310/97 of 30 June 1997.

The Securities Trading Act of July 1994 has made insider trading a criminal offence in Germany. Pursuant to the Securities Trading Act, the former Securities Supervisory Office issued a code of conduct for institutions dealing in financial securities (Bundesaufsichtsamt für den Wertpapierhandel 1999). Most importantly, the former Securities Supervisory Office and Deutsche Börse AG—the corporation that operates the bourse in Frankfurt—released non-authoritative guidelines for insider trading and *ad hoc* disclosure (Bundesaufsichtsamt für den Wertpapierhandel and Deutsche Börse AG 1998). The *ad hoc* disclosure rules stipulate that the corporation shall publish immediately all newly arriving, private information that has the potential of significantly affecting the prices of its securities—the intent being to create a level playing field in the marketplace and prevent insider trading. The guidelines specify that 'complex decision-making processes, in particular those requiring approval of the supervisory board,' are exempt from *ad hoc* disclosure—a clause that provides for clandestine preparations of merger and acquisition transactions. 'Ad hoc disclosure does not apply until the final decision has been made, that is, upon approval of the supervisory board.'

Disclosure requirements for traded corporations beyond and above what is specified in the Securities Trading Act of July 1994 are detailed in the *FWB Rules and Regulations* of Deutsche Börse AG. The disclosure rules vary by market segment, of which there is *Amtlicher Handel, Geregelter Markt*, and *Neuer Markt*; there is also an over-the-counter segment called *Freiverkehr*. The most liquid stocks are traded in *Amtlicher Handel—Geregelter Markt* being the second-tier market. *Neuer Markt* is a market segment for small to medium-sized companies that agree to adhere to international accounting and disclosure standards as specified in *Rules and Regulations Neuer Markt (FWB 9)*. Effective 1 January 2003, Deutsche Börse reorganized *Amtlicher Handel, Geregelter Markt*, and *Neuer Markt* into two new market segments: General Standard and Prime Standard. The General Standard is designed for small and mid-sized companies that seek an inexpensive stock market listing and do not target international investors; these companies must meet the minimum legal requirements set forth for *Amtlicher Handel* or *Geregelter Markt*. The Prime Standard, on the other hand, has been established for companies willing to commit to international accounting standards and disclosure rules. Prime Standard companies may choose between IFRS (International Financial Reporting Standards) or US-GAAP accounting rules. Trading in the Prime Standard is a precondition for inclusion in Frankfurt's stock market indexes. Meanwhile, *Neuer Markt* was merged onto the Prime Standard and set to close at the end of 2003.

Frequently, merger and acquisition transactions lead up to restructuring. The transaction costs of business restructuring in Germany were lowered significantly when on 1 January 1995, the revised Restructuring Act went into force. The law provides a general framework for restructuring, independent of the legal status of the businesses under consideration. Accompanying changes to the tax law, some of which have subsequently been reversed in response to abusive practices, allow companies to restructure at book value, avoiding asset write-ups and the ensuing capital gains taxation (Beinert 2000: § 324). The Restructuring Act provides for four types of restructuring, which are mergers, break-ups, and various forms of spin-offs, transfers of assets, and changes of legal status. Most significant is the possibility to change the legal status at book value, a provision that allows for reorganizing public corporations into partnerships without invoking capital gains taxation (Beinert 2000: § 325).

The revised Restructuring Act considerably constrains the power of dissenting shareholders in corporate restructuring when compared with the Stock Corporation Act. Corporate restructuring requires a qualified majority of at least 75 per cent of the voting capital represented at the shareholder meeting—depending on the articles of association. The Stock Corporation Act generally allows shareholders to challenge in court any resolutions passed at shareholder meetings—possibly blocking the execution of restructuring decisions for years. The Restructuring Act, which supersedes the Stock Corporation Act if invoked, allows shareholders that feel disadvantaged in the conversion of their interests to sue for cash compensation only—the restructuring decision being impervious (Beinert 2000: § 322). Note that the Restructuring Act does not provide for squeeze-outs. In other words, the interests of dissenting shareholders can only be converted against their will, but not acquired (Beinert 2000: § 342).

Effective 14 July 1995, Germany implemented a Takeover Code ('Übernahmekodex')—a code of conduct for bidders and targets in public tender offers. The Takeover Code was drafted and watched over by the *Börsensachverständigenkommission* at the Ministry of Finance—a case of self-regulation akin to the UK Takeover Panel.[3] Like the UK City Code, the German Takeover Code called for mandatory tender offers—bids that investors are obligated to present to the residual shareholders upon obtaining control over the corporation.[4] Control was defined as manifest when an investor's equity interest conveys the majority of votes or, due to imperfect shareholder attendance, has represented 75 per cent of the voting capital at all of the past three annual shareholder meetings. The code was last revised effective 1 January 1998.

It was in particular the mandatory tender offer stipulation that made corporations hesitant to sign the Takeover Code. This is because mandatory takeovers do not allow companies to hold significant equity interests in subcontractors as a means of protecting relation-specific investments (Kojima

---

[3] *FWB Rules and Regulations* of Deutsche Börse AG made adherence to the Takeover Code a precondition for the listing at *Neuer Markt* or the inclusion in the stock market indexes DAX—the most popular German stock market index—and its mid-cap and small-cap siblings (MDAX, SDAX). Incumbents were 'grandfathered'.

[4] Rule 9 of the UK City Code stipulates that an investor shall make a tender offer to the residual shareholders once his equity interest reaches 30 per cent of the corporation's voting rights.

2000). Not surprisingly, four of the former thirty members of the German stock market index DAX (BMW, Hoechst, Viag, and Volkswagen) never signed on; as of February 1999, only sixty-eight of the DAX 100 companies had submitted to the code. What's more, referring to the poor acceptance and to numerous counts of violation of the Takeover Code by the signatories, the *Börsensachverständigenkommission* concluded that the code failed to establish a 'level playing field among the market participants'. The commission recommended writing the code (in modified form) into law (Börsensachverständigenkommission beim Bundesministerium der Finanzen 1999).

The German Takeover Act entered into force on 1 January 2002, rendering the Takeover Code ineffective. The law departs in two important ways from the Takeover Code. First, the Takeover Act (§ 29) associates control over the corporation with ownership of an equity interest that conveys 30 per cent of the votes—a threshold significantly below what had been specified in the Takeover Code. It remains to be seen how this rule plays out in the German market for corporate control—a market that has so far been characterized by high shareholder concentration and control changes facilitated through block trades (Köke 2000; Jenkinson and Ljungqvist 2001). Second, whereas the Takeover Code reinforced the principle that the management of the target shall take a neutral stance in a takeover attempt—a stipulation anchored in corporate law (Beinert 2000: § 350)—the Takeover Act (§ 33) explicitly allows for defensive measures.

Defensive measures permissible under the German Takeover Act include issuing shares to a 'friendly' third party with exclusion of pre-emptive rights ('Bezugsrechte'), share repurchases, selling businesses of import to the bidder to third parties, launching a counter-offer for the bidder's shares, and soliciting competing bids from 'white knights'. The latter measure is permissible without the approval of the supervisory board once an offer has been announced. Moreover, the shareholders may, with a qualified majority of 75 per cent of the voting capital, authorize management to take defensive measures at is own discretion within 18 months of the respective shareholder resolution. Note that the scope of defensive measures available to management is constrained by existing law—the fiduciary duties of the Stock Corporation Act in particular—and the explicit provision of the Takeover Act (§ 3) that management's actions be in the interest of the corporation.

Note that the Takeover Act (§ 33) rules illegal the bidder offering seductive severance payments (golden parachutes) to the management of the target company. The Takeover Act (§ 21) accommodates offers that are conditioned on the shareholder tendering a predetermined, minimum fraction of shares (conditional tender offers). The Takeover Act (§ 32) prohibits offers that are restricted to a certain fraction of shares (restricted tender offers) but aspire to crossing the control threshold of 30 per cent of the voting stock.

The introduction of the Takeover Act entailed only one change, albeit a significant one, to the Stock Corporation Act (§ 327). Shareholders can now pass a resolution that transfers the shares of the residual shareholders to an investor that holds at least 95 per cent of the corporation's equity capital; the residual shareholders are compensated in cash. This squeeze-out clause is a significant improvement over existing corporate law—a topic to be discussed in the following section.

9.4. TAKEOVER BARRIERS

Barriers to takeovers or, more generally, to transfers of residual cash flow rights on complex assets can be broken down into two categories. First, there are impediments that are systematic in that they are common to all corporations in Germany of a given type. Second, there are hurdles that companies may install at their discretion. Again, note that management may take measures to try to ward off a takeover attempt, be it imminent or not, but management has the duty to act in the corporation's best interest (Beinert 2000: § 379). The permissive stance of the German Takeover Act toward defensive actions notwithstanding, because shareholders, creditors, and labour may be regarded as sufficiently protected by existing law, management may find itself at risk of being sued for serving its own interests when employing anti-takeover measures (Beinert 2000: §§ 350, 379).

Barriers to transfers of residual cash flow rights that are systematic to public corporations in Germany originate predominantly from capital gains taxation, minority shareholder protection, qualified-majority rules, board entrenchment, and proxy voting. Defensive measures that companies might take to deter potential acquirers from launching a takeover attempt are shares whose registration is subject to the issuer's approval, voting restrictions, dual-class stock, stocks with multiple voting rights, cross-shareholdings, and pyramidal shareholder structures. In what follows we provide an overview on these two categories of barriers to control changes at German stock corporations.

The taxation of capital gains at the full corporate tax rate in the past was a major reason for German financial institutions, most importantly large insurers (Allianz AG and Munich Re) and large universal banks (Deutsche, Dresdner, and Commerzbank), to hold on to their equity stakes rather than selling them. The present value from deferring the realization of capital gains in order to avoid their taxation often outweighed the potential gain from reallocating the financial resources to projects with higher net present value before taxes. Effective 1 January 2002, divestitures of stakes held in other corporations are tax-exempt. It is noteworthy that, shortly after the legislation was passed and before it had entered into force, there were isolated cases in which corporations sold off equity stakes, deferring through complex legal and financial arrangements the recording of the sale on their books past 31 December 2001.

German corporate law grants dissenting shareholders the right to fight in court decisions made at shareholder meetings. The initiation of legal proceedings by minority shareholders against amendments of the articles of association, equity issues or repurchases, and control or profit transfer agreements may block the inscription of these decisions on the commercial register for years. Before the introduction of a squeeze-out provision in the Stock Corporation Act (§ 327) effective 1 January 2002, the only way a block holder could get rid of small shareholders was to liquidate the corporation with a 75 per cent majority and subsequently purchase the business (Beinert 2000: § 342). The purchase of the business has to be made at arm's length and the assets have to be written up to the purchase price, invoking capital gains taxation. As discussed above, the revised Reorganization Act, although it does not allow for squeeze-outs, limits the power of dissenting shareholders in business reorganizations considerably.

Generally, decisions at shareholder meetings are made with the simple majority of votes. For important decisions, in addition to the simple majority of votes, German corporate law requires a qualified majority of 75 per cent of the voting capital represented at the meeting. Among the decisions that, by default, require a qualified majority of the voting capital are, according to Beinert (2000: § 367), amendments to the articles of association, removal of shareholder representatives from the supervisory board, control agreements and profit transfer agreements, and mergers. Furthermore, a qualified majority of the voting capital is required for the aforementioned 18-month authorization for anti-takeover measures. Besides, there are decisions for which the company may specify qualified-majority rules in the corporate charter—an option rarely exercised (Beinert 2000: § 368). On the other hand, for some decisions, German corporate law allows companies to abandon in their charter the qualified majority in favour of the simple majority of the voting capital represented at the shareholder meeting. Simple majorities of the voting capital may be adopted for decisions on the removal of shareholder representatives from the supervisory board, certain amendments to the corporate charter, and equity offerings with pre-emptive rights.

In Germany, members of corporate boards are legally entrenched. This holds for both the board of executive directors (management board) and the board of non-executive directors (supervisory board). The supervisory board oversees the management board, appoints the members, and, should the situation arise, removes them. The supervisory board consists of labour and shareholder representatives. The workforce elects the labour representatives. The shareholders elect at least two-thirds of the shareholder representatives, whereas the remainder, if the company's articles of association so determine, become members by means of owning an equity interest. The management board runs the day-to-day operations. The chairman or, synonymously, speaker of the management board is the company's chief executive officer.

Neither the supervisory board nor the shareholders have authority to instruct the management board.

The composition of the supervisory board, and the balance of power between labour and shareholder representatives in particular, depends on the relevant codetermination regime. Among publicly traded corporations, only companies for whom the constitutional freedoms of faith and the free press are a business purpose are exempt from codetermination. For instance, the media company Springer AG has no labour participation in corporate decisions at the board level. Then, there is a handful of companies in the coal and steel industries that are subject to the 1951 *Montan* Codetermination Act. As mentioned, *Montan* codetermination determines equal representation of shareholder and labour representatives on the supervisory board; a so-called neutral member has a tie-breaking vote. For the remaining stock corporations, the 1976 Codetermination Act applies if they have more than 2000 employees; otherwise, the Stock Corporation Act is relevant. The 1976 Codetermination Act calls for equal representation on the supervisory board. The chairman, who is generally a shareholder representative, can cast a tie-breaking vote in a repeatedly tied ballot. The Stock Corporation Act, on the other hand, calls for a labour representative in only a third of the supervisory board seats. When equal representation applies, be it in the 1951 or the 1976 version, there is also a labour representative ('Arbeitsdirektor') on the management board.[5]

For traded corporations, the supervisory board has to meet twice per half calendar year. The supervisory board has far-reaching information rights. The corporate charter defines the areas in which management board decisions are subject to supervisory board approval. Supervisory board vetoes to management decisions can be overturned by a majority of 75 per cent of the votes at the shareholder meeting. At any time, the supervisory board can call for an extraordinary shareholder meeting if deemed in the company's interest.

The members of the management board are usually appointed for the legal maximum of 5 years, reappointment being permissible. During their tenure, members of the management board cannot be removed from the post, except for cause. Cause exists, according to the Stock Corporation Act, in cases of incompetence or acute negligence, or when shareholders cast a vote of no confidence 'for reasons that are not manifestly arbitrary' (Beinert 2000: § 55). In consequence, German management boards enjoy a fair amount of independence—a significant hurdle for an unwelcome bidder who tries to seize control over the corporation.

The members of the supervisory board usually serve for 5 years—the maximum tenure allowed by law. All labour representatives are elected at the

---

[5] Gorton and Schmid (2002) offer a detailed description of the German board system and an analysis of the influence of various degrees of codetermination on the performance of the corporation.

same time. Staggered terms, which spread attrition evenly over time, are possible for the shareholder representatives if provided for in the articles of association. Then again, corporations in Germany rarely opt for staggered terms to avoid the ordeal of electing (some) shareholder representatives at every annual meeting (Beinert 2000: § 373).

To an unwelcome bidder, attaining control over the supervisory board might prove a challenging task. For one thing, shareholders have no power of removing labour representatives. Also, a shareholder representative who is a member by way of owning an equity interest cannot be removed from the post, except by the actual owner of the equity interest, should the supervisory board member in question be a stand-in. Only supervisory board members that have been elected at the annual meeting can be voted out of office; this requires a qualified majority of 75 per cent, should the corporate charter not specify a different majority rule.

Proxy voting has long been one of the most hotly debated corporate control issues in Germany. Proxy voting originates from the fact that in Germany shares are predominantly bearer shares. Usually, small shareholders leave their shares in the bank that keeps their brokerage accounts. The bank, which knows the identity of its brokerage clients, typically solicits permission for voting on their behalf. Many shareholders grant this permission and go along with the pre-announced voting behaviour of the bank, rather than attending the shareholder meetings in person or giving the bank legally binding voting instructions. Not surprisingly, the large universal banks, which have the most extensive branch networks, garner most of the small shareholder's votes. It is thus not unusual that, at the annual meeting of a public corporation with a dispersed shareholder structure, the large universal banks taken together control the majority of votes. In fact, there have been instances when, as a group, the three largest universal banks at the time (Deutsche, Dresdner, and Commerzbank) cast the majority of votes at their own annual meetings—all due to proxy voting.[6]

The degree to which proxy voting constitutes a takeover barrier is debatable. Although banks exercise substantial amounts of proxy votes at annual meetings, little is known about how much power these votes confer and, if they do confer power, how banks use this lever. On one hand, it can be argued that proxy voting is derived, rather than genuine, voting power. That is to say, small shareholders rarely give banks voting instructions because the shareholders recognize that it is in their best interest to go along with the banks' announced voting behaviour. The banks anticipate that, if they announced a voting behaviour that suggested otherwise, the shareholders would issue

---

[6] The German Antitrust Commission ('Monopolkommission') investigated the influence of banks on the German corporate sector in its 1976/77 report *Fortschreitende Konzentration bei Großunternehmen* (Monopolkommission 1978) compiling the first extensive set of proxy voting data.

voting instructions. In this case, then, proxy voting does not contain information that is not subsumed in the shareholder structure and, consequently, has no measurable impact of its own. On the other hand, it could be argued that proxy voting gives banks genuine voting power, simply because, to the small shareholder, the marginal cost of issuing voting instructions exceeds the marginal benefit, which gives rise to free riding. Again, proxy voting would then simply be the flip side of a dispersed shareholder structure, having no bearing of its own on the corporation. As the case may be, empirically, proxy voting seems immaterial for the conduct of the corporation and, as a result, may not constitute much of a takeover barrier. Gorton and Schmid (2000), in an inquiry into the influence of proxy voting on the stock market valuation of the corporation, find no discernable impact. Jenkinson and Ljungqvist (2001), in a clinical study, find that banks in takeover battles do not always cast proxy votes in favour of the status quo. On one hand, Deutsche Bank drew on proxy votes in fending off an unsolicited bid of the Italian tire maker Pirelli SpA for its German competitor Continental AG in a bitter takeover battle that lasted from the initial Pirelli bid in September 1990 until March 1993. On the other hand, in the mentioned takeover of Hoesch by Krupp, Deutsche Bank, in spite of being Hoesch's *Hausbank*, cast the proxy votes in favour of the merger.

One of the most effective tools that a company can employ to discourage takeover attempts is to issue registered shares that can be transferred only upon approval of the corporation. By default, it is the management board that approves the inscription of this type of shares on the commercial register, called *vinkulierte Namensaktien*; the articles of association might bestow this right on the supervisory board or the annual shareholder meeting (Beinert 2000: § 65). Only *vinkulierte Namensaktien* may convey the aforementioned statutory right on a supervisory board seat. *Vinkulierte Namensaktien* are common in (and largely confined to) the insurance industry. Most recently, in the summer of 2002, this type of share turned out to be pivotal in a wrestle over the control of a 40 per cent equity stake in the aforementioned German media company Axel Springer AG. As reported by the *Financial Times* (2002*f*), WAZ Gruppe—a secretive German media group—in the summer of 2002 deliberated the acquisition of a 40 per cent stake in Springer AG from the insolvent media mogul Leo Kirch. Friede Springer, the widow of the company's founder, who—jointly with other members of the Springer family—controlled just over 50 per cent of Springer AG at the time, vowed to veto the inscription of the shares on the register should the transaction come about. As reported by the *Financial Times* (2002*g*), Munich's civil court ruled on 3 September 2002, that Leo Kirch could not transfer his 40 per cent stake without the consent of Axel Springer AG. In response to the court decision, WAZ Gruppe withdrew its interest. Meanwhile, Leo Kirch defaulted on a €720 loan from Deutsche Bank, for which he had pledged the Springer interest as collateral. On 8 October 2002, Deutsche Bank held an auction in which it acquired Kirch's equity stake. On the following day, Deutsche Bank traded a

10.4 per cent block to Friede Springer, who now is the sole majority shareholder of Springer AG. Deutsche Bank retained the remaining 29.9 per cent equity interest in Springer—a position just short of the mandatory takeover threshold laid down in the German Takeover Act.

In the past, German corporations could resort to voting restrictions as a means of discouraging takeover attempts. Voting restrictions limit the voting power of block holders to a certain percentage of the corporation's total voting stock. The Third Act on the Promotion of Financial Markets ('Drittes Finanzmarktförderungsgesetz'), introduced in 1998, prohibits the introduction of voting restrictions for public corporations and rules that voting restrictions, where they existed, would be ineffective as of 1 June 2000. Note that voting restrictions do not apply where corporate law or the articles of association call for a (simple or qualified) majority of the voting capital represented at the shareholder meeting, rather than a majority of the votes (Beinert 2000: § 70).

The legislation that outlaws voting restrictions for traded stock corporations exempts Volkswagen AG, which has a 20 per cent limit on the fraction of votes a shareholder can cast. The control structure of Volkswagen is governed by the Volkswagen Act, a law that legalized the privatization of Volkswagen in 1960 and was last revised in 1970.[7] The Volkswagen voting restriction preserves the voting power of the State of Lower Saxony—the state that harbours the Volkswagen headquarters. As of year-end 2001, the State of Lower Saxony owned 13.7 per cent of the Volkswagen voting stock. (Another 9.8 per cent of the voting stock was in the hands of Volkswagen-Beteiligungsgesellschaft mbH, a 100 per cent subsidiary of Volkswagen AG.) The degree to which the equity interest of the State of Lower Saxony, along with the voting restriction, serves as a barrier to a control change at Volkswagen can be read from the remarkable spread between the share prices of Volkswagen's voting and nonvoting stocks. Over the period 1997–2001, based on the share price of the last trading day of the year, the premium of voting over non-voting stock hovered between 30 per cent (1999) and 76 per cent (2000). Note that over the same period, the cash dividend on non-voting shares exceeded the cash dividend on voting shares by between 4.6 and 8.2 per cent (Volkswagen AG 2001). In the wake of the mentioned ruling of the European Court of Justice on golden shares on 4 June 2002, the Volkswagen governance structure has come under scrutiny (*Financial Times* 2002c).

German corporate law allows corporations to issue half of the stock as nonvoting stock. This provision allows founding families to remain in control even as the companies grow beyond the point where wealth constraints force the families' interests below the 75 per cent level—the level of voting stock ownership that delivers exclusive control. Well-known examples of corporations with a 50 per cent fraction of nonvoting stock are BMW AG—controlled

---

[7] Prior to the 1970 revision of the Volkswagen Act, the voting restriction at Volkswagen was 2 per cent.

by the Quandt family—and Porsche AG—controlled by the Porsche and Piëch families.

Schmid (2002) argues that, due to the qualified-majority rules written into German corporate law, dual-class stock might enhance social welfare if founding families enjoy large private control benefits. Nenova (2000) and Dyck and Zingales (2001) find that private control benefits are indeed significant in Germany. To illustrate the point, assume there is a wealthy individual, possibly an entrepreneurial competitor, who enjoys benefits from controlling an interest of 25 per cent plus one vote in a corporation where the founding family's stake has dropped below the 75 per cent level due to a binding wealth constraint. At a minimum, the intruder can thwart all motions at shareholder meetings that require—by law or corporate charter—a qualified majority of the represented voting capital; ironically, these decisions are the most critical ones for the performance of the corporation. If the loss of exclusive control weighs more heavily on the family than the gain in control weighs on the intruder, society finds itself worse off. As Schmid shows, the founding family has no capacity to ward off an intruder. If the family were sufficiently wealthy to control at least 75 per cent of the votes, the situation would not arise in the first place. Also, paying off potential intruders for dispensing of the equity interest or not acquiring it in the first place is not an option. 'Greenmailing' would only increase the incentive for copycat investors. Also, if financed with company funds, greenmailing is in violation of German corporate law (Beinert 2000: § 341). Taken together, nonvoting stock might be a welfare-enhancing countermeasure where qualified-majority rules are mandatory. Not surprisingly, non-voting stock figures prominently with corporations controlled by the founding families.

Another possible departure from single-class stock is shares with multiple votes. Then again, German corporate law no longer allows the issuance of multiple-vote stock. Multiple votes, where they exist, phased out by law on 1 June 2003 unless the shareholders voted otherwise (Beinert 2001: § 70).[8]

A further barrier to control changes in Germany is cross-shareholdings. Plain vanilla cross-shareholding pertains to cases where two companies own stock in each other. If the mutual equity stakes exceed 25 per cent, certain restrictions apply when it comes to exercising the votes at the annual shareholder meeting (Beinert 2000: § 382). More sophisticated cross-shareholding might involve complex networks of inter-corporate stock ownership. The most extensive network of cross-ownership in Germany is centred on two financial institutions: Allianz AG and Munich Re. It should be noted that Allianz AG is the most powerful financial institution in Germany as measured by market capitalization and the size and reach of its equity stakes, eclipsing Deutsche Bank. The Allianz network comprises mainly domestic financial institutions,

---

[8] Volkswagen AG is exempt from this legal provision (Beinert 2000: § 70). Currently, Volkswagen has no stock with multiple votes outstanding (Hoppenstedt Verlag 2001).

but also stretches into the domestic non-financial sector and the financial sectors of neighbouring European countries (Hoppenstedt Verlag 2001). Clearly, networks of cross-shareholdings are difficult to crack for outsiders and, hence, are highly effective takeover barriers. Then again, it is difficult to gauge the degree to which cross-shareholding is indeed motivated by anti-takeover considerations. First, cross-shareholdings might simply serve as a call option on a possible future merger. For instance, Allianz in the past has used some of its stakes to forge mergers in the banking and insurance industries— the 1998 merger of Bayerische Hypotheken- und Wechsel-Bank AG and Bayerische Vereinsbank AG into Bayerische Hypo- und Vereinsbank AG being a case in point. Second, cross-shareholding might serve as a means of bonding where contracts are incomplete, keeping the parties in question sufficiently vulnerable to uncooperative behaviour.

Attempts of management to engineer the corporation's shareholder structure are limited by the legal provision that seasoned offerings generally be endowed with pre-emptive rights. This stipulation holds both for shareholder pre-approved offerings (shelf registrations), which management may execute at its own discretion, and instant seasoned offerings. In consequence, existing shareholders generally cannot be excluded from seasoned equity issues. Then again, exclusion of pre-emptive rights, both for instant and pre-approved seasoned offerings, are possible if three legal requirements are met (Beinert 2000: § 363). First, shareholders authorize the share issue and the added-on exclusion of pre-emptive rights with a qualified majority of 75 per cent of the represented voting capital. Second, management submits to the shareholders in writing the reasons for the exclusion of pre-emptive rights. Third, the exclusion of the pre-emptive rights is in the corporation's best interest. Then again, Beinert (2000: § 365) argues that, from a legal perspective, only in special circumstances would an exclusion of pre-emptive rights be justifiably in the company's best interest. In particular, so the argument goes, engineering of the corporation's shareholder structure is likely to violate management's fiduciary duties toward the company.

One of the boldest moves in crafting an indulgent shareholder structure was undertaken in September 2000 by the management of Commerzbank, the fourth largest German universal bank. The barely disguised objective of this endeavour was to ward off a looming takeover attempt. At the time, Commerzbank's largest shareholder was CoBRa Beteiligungsgesellschaft, which was led by Hansgeorg Hofmann, a corporate raider. CoBRa had accumulated an equity interest of 17 per cent with the intent of auctioning off the stake to the highest bidder in a future takeover battle for Commerzbank— a case of merger arbitrage. Commerzbank's strategy was to issue shares— exclusive of pre-emptive rights—to two companies with which it had existing cross-shareholding relations: Assicurazioni Generali of Italy and Banco Santander Central Hispano (BSCH) of Spain. The intent of the transactions was to dilute CoBRa's stake and the free float.

On 1 September 2000, Commerzbank announced that Generali agreed to raise its stake from 5.1 to 9.9 per cent. At the same time, Mediobanca, the secretive Italian investment bank, agreed to notch up its holdings in Commerzbank to 2 per cent (*Financial Times* 2000b). The Generali transaction had a cash component of €600 million; another €360 million involved a transfer to Commerzbank of part of Generali's 1.8 per cent stake in BSCH (*Financial Times* 2000a). The Generali transaction strengthened existing cross-shareholdings with both Generali and BSCH. For one thing, in 1998, Commerzbank had acquired about 1.5 per cent of Generali, according to an officious AMB Generali Holding AG document (Schöllkopf 2002). What's more, Commerzbank's stake in BSCH rose to 2.3 per cent while, at the same time, BSCH owned about 5 per cent in Commerzbank (*Financial Times* 2000b).

The intended share issue to BSCH did not materialize. The talks ran into obstacles and failed in October 2000. The two banks could not agree on the value of CC Bank, a German subsidiary of BSCH that Commerzbank was supposed to acquire as part of the transaction (*Financial Times* 2000c).

According to an official Commerzbank (2001) investor relations document, as of 31 March 2001, Commerzbank had cross-shareholdings with four financial institutions. These financial companies were Assicurazioni Generali (1.4 per cent owned by Commerzbank and 9.9 per cent owned in Commerzbank), BSCH (2.4 and 4.8 per cent), Banca Commerciale Italiana (2.5 and 0.8 per cent), and Mediobanca (1.8 and 1.1 per cent). As the odds of cracking the network for possible Commerzbank acquirers grew longer, the interest for CoBRa's stake waned. In early April of 2002, CoBRa threw in the towel.

Related to cross-shareholdings are pyramidal shareholder structures. Pyramids are multiple layers of financial holding shells that are sandwiched between an investor and a company the investor wishes to control. The financial holding shells, which are often times obscure and privately held, frequently have two or three owners—typically banks or insurance companies. For matters of illustration, suppose an investor owns 25 per cent plus one vote in a financial holding shell, which in turn holds a similar stake in another holding shell, while this shell holds a similar stake in a target company. The investor at the bottom of the pyramid effectively holds a blocking minority interest in the company at the top of the pyramid, although the investor (indirectly) owns only 1.5625 per cent of the top layer's voting stock. The apotheosis of a shareholder pyramid is the former Mercedes-Automobil-Holding AG, which held a blocking minority in Daimler-Benz AG and was controlled by two layers of financial holding shells. At the bottom of the pyramid was a myriad of banks and insurance companies, as well as non-financial companies with close ties to the automobile industry. The pyramid, which is described in Franks and Mayer (2001), was established as an anti-takeover device in the aftermath of the first oil-price shock when OPEC countries started taking stakes in large public German corporations. In 1993, Mercedes-Automobil-Holding AG was dissolved. Franks and

Mayer find little evidence that pyramid structures can be used for control purposes.

To summarize, German corporations hide behind a host of takeover barriers, some of which are in place by virtue of law, whereas others are optional to the corporation. Some of these impediments have been removed during Germany's ongoing effort to modernize financial markets and corporate governance, among them shares with multiple votes and voting restrictions. Most of the mentioned barriers to transfers of cash flow rights on corporations have not been established or made available with the intent of fending off unsolicited takeover bids. Rather, these impediments to takeovers are artefacts of a financial system rooted in history that is inevitably highly path-dependent. Judging takeover barriers in isolation might lead to erroneous conclusions, as the case of dual-class stock in the presence of qualified majorities and private control benefits illustrates.

9.5. CONCLUSION

In the late twentieth century, Germany made great strides toward establishing sophisticated financial markets. Between 1990 and 2002, the federal legislature passed four laws for the promotion of financial markets. These laws increased the incentive of corporations to disclose critical information to investors, improved the transparency in financial markets, and extended the range of financial transactions available to corporations and investors. As a result, the import of financial markets in the savings and investment process of the German economy increased.

The financial modernization process in Germany occurred during a time period characterized by soaring stock markets and torrid merger and acquisition activity, both in North America and Europe (Gaughan 2002). When the stock markets of the United States and Europe started to crumble in the spring of 2000, the mergers and acquisitions wave ebbed. Ironically, Germany, which had gone a long way in creating competitive financial markets modelled after the United States, was caught in the eye of the hurricane. The percentage declines from the peaks in March 2000 to the latest troughs of the German *Neuer Markt* Nemax 50 and Nemax All Share indexes were considerably steeper than the per centage drops of their US counterparts, the Nasdaq 100 and the Nasdaq Composite indexes. While the US indexes declined by 82 and 78 per cent, respectively, the German indexes fell by a respective 97 and 96 per cent. Unable to stem the loss in investor confidence, Deutsche Börse AG on 26 September 2002 announced its intention of closing *Neuer Markt*.[9] Then

---

[9] The Nemax 50, Nemax All Share, Nasdaq 100, and Nasdaq Composite indexes had their all-time highs on 10 March 2000; they had their respective latest troughs on 7 October 2002 (Nasdaq 100), 9 October 2002 (Nasdaq Composite), and 12 March 2003. The percentage declines were calculated from daily values at close.

again, because the allocation of financial and real resources—and, consequently, the merger and acquisition activity—in Germany does not rely as much on financial markets as in the United States, the collapse of the stock market may prove less disruptive for the real economy in Germany. On one hand, in 2001, the merger and acquisition volume dropped to €163 billion, from €478 billion in 2000. On the other hand, while transactions dropped by volume, by number they increased by 10 per cent to a new all-time high of 2173.[10] Possibly, because the allocation of financial and real resources in Germany does not rely as heavily on financial markets as in the United States, there might be less spillover from boom and bust in financial markets into the real economy. For instance, in 2000, the ratio of stock market capitalization to GDP in Germany ran at only 67 per cent (World Federation of Exchanges 2001), while it equalled 150 per cent in the United States and averaged 89 per cent across the European Union (European Central Bank 2001).

References

Bebchuk, L., and Hart, O. (2002). 'A Threat to Dual-Class Shares', *Financial Times*, 31 May 2002: 11.

Beinert, D. (2000). *Corporate Acquisitions and Mergers in Germany*. 3rd ed. The Hague: Kluwer Law International.

Berklof, E., and Burkhart, M. (2002). 'Fighting the Wrong Problem', *Financial Times*, 31 May 2002: 11.

Boehmer, E. (2000). 'Business Groups, Bank Control, and Large Shareholders: An Analysis of German Takeovers', *Journal of Financial Intermediation*, 9(2): 117–48.

Börsensachverständigenkommission beim Bundesministerium der Finanzen (1999). *Standpunkte der Börsensachverständigenkommission zur künftigen Regelung von Unternehmensübernahmen*, 14 February 1999. http://www.kodex.de.

Bundesaufsichtsamt für den Wertpapierhandel (1999). *Guideline of the Federal Securities Supervisory Office on the details concerning the organizational duties of investment services enterprises pursuant to section 33 paragraph (1) of the Securities Trading Act of 25 October 1999*, 6 November 1999. http://www.bafin.de.

——, and Deutsche Börse AG (1998). *Insider Trading Prohibitions and Ad hoc Disclosure Pursuant to the German Securities Trading Act*, 2nd edn. Frankfurt.

Bundeskartellamt (2001). *Tätigkeitsbericht 1999/2000*. Deutscher Bundestag. Drucksache Nr. 14/6300. Berlin.

Commerzbank AG (2001). 5 October (2001). http://www.commerzbank.com/aktionaere/vortrag/charts_010510.pdf.

Die Welt (1997). 'Kohl mahnt zur Vernunft', 20 March 1997.

Dyck, A., and Zingales, L. (2001). 'Private Benefits of Control: An International Comparison', CRSP Working Paper No. 535.

[10] The previous all-time high was 2172 transactions, established in 1991—a year in which the merger and acquisitions activity in Germany was fuelled by the German reunification.

Emmons, W. R., and Schmid, F. A. (1998). 'Universal Banking, Control Rights, and Corporate Finance in Germany', *Federal Reserve Bank of St. Louis Review*, 80 (4): 19–42.

European Central Bank (2001). *The Equity Markets*, 20 August 2001. http://www.ecb.int.

Financial Times (1997). 'Mediators Chosen for German Steel Talks', 20 March 1997. Online Edition.

——(1998). *FT 500 1998*. 22 January 1998.

——(1999*a*). 'Schröder Weighs into Bid Battle', 20 November 1999. Online Edition.

——(1999*b*). 'Blair Enters Telecoms Battle', 22 November 1999.

——(2000*a*). 'Generali Lifts German Stake', 4 September 2000.

——(2000*b*). 'Commerzbank Builds Cross-Shareholdings', 17 October 2000.

——(2000*c*). 'Commerzbank and BSCH End Stake Talks', 24 October 2000.

——(2001*a*). 'Berlin Glee Greets Demise of EU Takeover Directive', 6 July 2001.

——(2001*b*). 'EU Establishes European Company Statute', 9 October 2001.

——(2002*a*). 'Krupp Drops Bid for Thyssen', 24 March 2002.

——(2002*b*). 'Europe Strikes a Balance Over Golden Shares', 5 June 2002.

——(2002*c*). 'EU Says Examining 10 Golden Share Cases Including VW', 20 June 2002.

——(2002*d*). 'Collapse of Babcock Unravels Germany's Way of Doing Deals', 10 July 2002.

——(2002*e*). 'Esser Sues Over 18-Month Investigation', 22 August 2002.

——(2002*f*). 'WAZ War of Words with Springer Escalates', 27 August 2002.

——(2002*g*). 'Kirch Attempt to Sell Springer Stake Halted', 4 September 2002.

——(2003*a*). 'Top Executives Charged in Mannesmann Case', 17 February 2003.

——(2003*b*). 'Court Rules Against "Golden" Shares', 14 May 2003.

——(2003*c*). 'Deutschland AG shrugs off Investor Protests', 15 May 2003.

Franks, J., and Mayer, C. (2001). 'Ownership and Control of German Corporations', *Review of Financial Studies*, 14: 943–77.

Gaughan, P. A. (2002). *Mergers, Acquisitions, and Corporate Restructurings*, 3rd edn. New York: John Wiley.

Gorton, G., and Schmid, F. A. (2000). 'Universal Banking and the Performance of German Firms', *Journal of Financial Economics*, 58: 29–80.

——, and ——(2002). 'Class Struggle Inside the Firm: A Study of German Co-determination', Working Paper. Wharton School, University of Pennsylvania.

Hoppenstedt Verlag (2001). *Hoppenstedt Aktienführer 2002*. Darmstadt: Verlag Hoppenstedt.

Jenkinson, T., and Ljungqvist, A. P. (2001). 'The Role of Hostile Stakes in German Corporate Control', *Journal of Corporate Finance*, 7(4): 397–446.

Kojima, K. (2000). 'Commitments and Contests: A Game-Theoretic Perspective on Japanese Vertical Integration', Kobe Economics and Business Research Series No. 15. Kobe University.

Köke, J. (2000). 'Control Transfers in Corporate Germany: Their Frequency, Causes and Consequences', Center for European Economic Research. Working Paper No. 00–67.

Monopolkommission (1978). *Fortschreitende Konzentration bei Großunternehmen*. Baden Baden: Nomos.

Nenova, T. (2000). 'The Value of Corporate Votes and Control Benefits: A Cross-country Analysis', Working Paper. Harvard University.

Schmid, F. A. (2002). 'Voting Rights, Private Benefits, and Takeovers', *Federal Reserve Bank of St. Louis Review*, 84(1): 35–46.

Schöllkopf, T. (2002). 'Strategische Überlegungen bei der Zusammenarbeit zwischen Banken und Versicherungen', *Vortragsreihe Institutionelles Asset Management*. RWTH Aachen. 22 January 2002. Aachen.

Volkswagen AG. (2001). *Annual Report 2001*.

Wenger, E., and Kaserer, C. (1998). 'The German System of Corporate Governance—A Model Which Should Not Be Imitated', in S. W. Black and M. Moersch (eds.), *Competition and Convergence in Financial Markets: The German and Anglo-American Models*. Amsterdam: North-Holland, 413–59.

World Federation of Exchanges (2001). 15, March 2001. http://www.world-exchanges.org.

PART III

REGULATION AND CORPORATE GOVERNANCE

10

Regulation and Competition in German Banking: An Assessment

KARL-HERMANN FISCHER* AND CHRISTIAN PFEIL

10.1. GERMAN BANKING—STABILITY AND MARKET POWER

10.1.1. Introduction

According to a widely held view, German banking in the past has been stable but not very competitive.[1] Although there have been difficulties with single banking institutions—Bankhaus Herstadt and Schröder, Münchmeyer & Hengst are well-known examples—no widespread systemic crisis has occurred for decades. It is only very recently that word of a 'banking crisis' has spread over Germany, a phenomenon which we will be discussing in more detail below.[2] Between the end of the Second World War and early 2002, however, the banking industry seemed to operate smoothly. Many observers believe that the second characteristic, that is, the lack of competitive pressure in Germany's financial system, was nothing less than the flip side of this medal. Bank regulation in Germany—so the argument goes—had achieved its stability goal mainly by restricting competition in the financial services sector and by sheltering Germany's universal banks from competition with foreign banks and non-bank suppliers of financial services. Furthermore, regulators and politicians

* Corresponding author; the authors would like to thank Martin Hellwig for very helpful comments and suggestions. We further would like to thank Horst Bertram, Hannah S. Hempell and Reinhard H. Schmidt for valuable comments and discussions. The provision of data from Deutsche Bundesbank, Verband der Vereine Creditreform e.V., Börsenzeitung, Worldbank, and our colleague Stefanie Franzke is greatfully acknowledged. All errors and inaccuracies remain—of course—our own responsibility.

[1] See Gual and Neven (1993), Saunders and Walter (1994), Rajan (1996), Beck (2000), or Allen and Gale (2000) for such evaluations!

[2] We will refer to this point in Section 10.3. At the time of writing in spring 2003, the 'German banking crisis' still remains in a somewhat unresolved state. While no serious banking failures have occurred to date, accelerating default rates among non-bank enterprises and a weak outlook for the German economy still raise fears that the danger of a systemic disruption of the banking system is not yet fully averted.

were believed to have fostered cartelization of the industry and to have favoured national champions. Like in other European countries, regulatory capture seemed to be a widespread phenomenon in the past.

In Germany a public discussion on the 'power of banks' has been going on for decades now with the term 'power' having at least two meanings. On the one hand, it denotes the power of banks to control public corporations through direct shareholdings or the exercise of proxy votes—this is the power of banks in corporate control. On the other hand, the market power derived from imperfect competition in markets for financial services is implied, which banks exercise *vis-à-vis* their loan and deposit customers.[3]

Given such a strong public perception inside and outside Germany, it is not surprising that the regulatory regime in Germany is most often interpreted as an attempt to trade off the stabilizing effects of bank market power against the efficiency benefits of more intense competition in financial services (Franke 2000). According to this view, bank regulators have used means of anti-competitive regulation to make banking a 'safe haven', that is, not vulnerable to excessive risk taking. More recently however, important measures towards deregulation of the banking industry were taken at the European level. Anti-competition regulations have been abolished and the remaining regulatory structure does more to directly address the primary goal of bank regulation, that is a reduction of risk of bank failures. As a consequence of deregulation, there is little doubt among industry observers that banking all over Europe, and in Germany as well, has become significantly more competitive.[4]

Although we find this overall assessment of the past and present of bank regulation in Germany convincing, we believe that there is more to the story. While deregulation in financial services has been greatly applauded by many economists and the public since its beginning in the mid-1980s, for some sceptics the joint occurrence of unfettered competition in banking on the one hand, and crisis-type phenomena observed around the world on the other, is more than just a coincidence. Furthermore, from our perspective, several of the more important questions have remained largely unanswered. Why have regulators' attitudes towards competition in financial services changed so dramatically? Will deregulation keep its promises? What will the long-term competitive effects of internationally harmonized prudential regulations (capital requirements, market discipline, supervision) be in national markets that have taken such different roads in the past? While cross-country empirical work has made significant contributions to recent research in this area, we believe that evaluations of the historical performance of single country banking systems are at least as important.

---

[3] Interestingly, in the political arena, most attempts to restrict bank powers in Germany in the past were aimed at restricting their dominance in corporate control.

[4] In addition, advances in information technology and applied finance have had a strong impact on competitive conduct in financial services.

This chapter, therefore, tries to shed some light on the development and current state of bank regulation in Germany.[5] In so doing, it tries to embed the analysis of bank regulation in a more general industrial organization framework. For every regulated industry, competition and regulation are deeply interrelated since most regulatory institutions, even if they do not explicitly address the competitiveness of the market, either affect market structure or conduct (see Vives 1991; Cerasi *et al.* 1998). Moreover, discussions on bank regulation, instead of referring to single regulatory institutions, might more usefully be directed towards what has recently been termed the regulatory regime. In addition to analysing the traditional instruments of bank regulation (capital requirements or deposit insurance), according to Llewellyn (2000) a regulatory regime perspective also takes the role of market discipline and banks' internal corporate governance arrangements into account. Therefore, throughout this chapter, a recurring theme will be specific types of governance structures that dominate in German banks and the role of the public banking sector in Germany in particular. We believe that the importance of these structural features of the banking system can hardly be overestimated. For instance, we will argue that 'government ownership of banks' might mean different things in different countries and we will point to several peculiarities of the German case.[6] While our approach is mainly descriptive we also try to uncover some of the specific relationships between monetary policy, government interference, and bank regulation on the one hand and bank market structure and economic performance on the other. We hope thereby to be able to point to several areas for fruitful research in the future. While our focus is on Germany, some of the questions that we raise and some of our answers might also be applicable to banking systems elsewhere.

To emphasize the relevance of our perspective, in Section 10.1.2 we first briefly review different approaches to interpreting anti-competitive regulation in financial markets. Whether standard theory provides useful guidelines for explaining the causes and consequences of bank regulation in Germany will then be discussed. In order to allow a first assessment, in Section 10.1.3 we take a bird's eye view of the history of bank regulation in Germany, outlining how it has evolved since its beginnings in the 1930s. This discussion of the sequence of regulatory activities allows us to identify both the fundamental structure of the regulatory regime, and the driving forces behind its adjustment over time. Section 10.1.4 reviews empirical evidence on market structure and market power in German banking. We then turn to a more detailed evaluation of the interrelationship between regulation on the one hand and competitiveness and bank market power on the other. In Section 10.2 our discussion

---

[5] Our focus, however, is on regulations pertaining to commercial banking activities and as such only provides a discussion on selected aspects of the regulation of universal banks.

[6] Given the importance of government ownership of banks around the world, every discussion about public regulation of banking should take public banking into account as well. See La Porta *et al.* (2002) for empirical evidence on the pervasiveness of government ownership of banks.

thus focuses on selected aspects of bank regulation and bank market structure in Germany and tries to provide data and empirical evidence whenever available. Based on our results, Section 10.3 concludes and discusses what might be expected for the future.

10.1.2. Public Interventions in Financial Services—the Public and the Private Interest

It is now well recognized that the regulation of banks has important implications for the shape and functioning of a financial system and the economy as a whole. While this claim seems to be widely accepted among economists, politicians, and bank regulators and supervisors, international differences in bank regulation indicate that there is much less consensus on how it best serves its goals and probably even what these goals are. Yet, what most discussions on bank regulation—academic or more policy oriented—have in common, is that they look at bank regulation from a 'public interest' perspective. Government intervention serves to cure market failures that would otherwise threaten the functioning of the financial system. The historical experience with banking crises in many countries strongly underlines the need to impose limitations on the discretion of bank owners and managers. Theoretical work has pointed to inherent instabilities of the banking business and highlighted the potential for severe problems based on asymmetries of information and asset substitution type risk-shifting (see Bhattacharya *et al.* 1998 for an overview). Banks throughout the world are highly leveraged and normally the base of investors in their debt instruments, that is, bank deposits, is widely dispersed. The large share of debt in banks' capital structures increases the risk of default and as a consequence might trigger excessive risk taking in certain economic environments. The wide dispersion of relatively small depositors limits the willingness of these debt-holders to act as an effective monitor. Furthermore, the social cost of the failure of banking institutions is perceived to be high.[7] All these fundamental reasons for regulating banks are well known and we need not reiterate them here in any more detail.[8] Historically, the rationale for bank regulation in Germany is also in keeping with these arguments and is primarily aimed at protecting depositors as well as safeguarding the viability of banks and the functioning of the financial sector as a whole.[9] However, from this prudential perspective, it is not immediately clear where a trade-off between competition and stability could arise. Why should bank regulators, pursuing the

---

[7] The 'shock waves' generated by banking crises often affect the whole economy. See Stiglitz (2001) for a discussion.

[8] See Dewatripont and Tirole (1994), Freixas and Rochet (1997), or Bhattacharya *et al.* (1998) for in-depth discussions.

[9] It is assumed that the banking business is especially sensitive to depositor confidence. Moreover, bank regulation has a strong social impetus as the small depositor is seen as being in need of protection against losses caused by bank failures.

public interest (stability of the financial system and protection of depositors), choose to restrict competition in banking, thereby laying a well-known burden on society as a whole? One explanation that has gained prominence recently may be summarized as follows: Bank regulation is best described as taking place in an environment of asymmetric information between depositors and banks, and is therefore characterized by moral hazard and asset-substitution type risk-shifting incentives on the part of banks. There is, of course, a long history of widespread banking crisis, sustained periods of lack of depositor confidence and many examples of outright fraud. One possible and forceful regulatory remedy to these problems is to restrict competition in financial services and to create positive bank charter values. A franchise value of banks, caused by imperfect competition in banking markets, gives bankers something to lose in case of default.[10] The threat of losing a valuable charter whenever a bank is closed by regulators makes bankers more conservative and deters excessive risk taking. Recent regulatory reforms, by putting more emphasis on safety and soundness of banks and abolishing anti-competition regulations, might, therefore, be based on the implicit assumption that the informational gap between financial markets, bank depositors, and bank regulators on the one hand and bank managers and owners on the other has become narrower over the last two decades.

A less naive alternative to the public interest view is the capture theory or 'private interest view' that interprets regulation as the attempt by a well-organized regulated industry to use the sovereign power of the state to capture rents at the expense of customers and society as a whole.[11] This perspective seemed to have played an important role among industry observers and academics in explaining the perceived low degree of competitiveness in European banking in the past. In 1991 Xavier Vives predicted '[...] the main effect of integration will be to change the focal point of the strategies of banks from collusion and regulatory capture to competition' (Vives 1991). Given that the banking industry seems to have well-organized lobbying instruments at its disposal, to what extent was regulation in the past triggered by the industry's desire to deter competition in financial services?

There might also be a different type of regulatory capture in banking, combining two of the aspects of public and private interest mentioned above. In the United Kingdom, for instance, the Cruickshank report suspected that there has been 'an informal contract between successive governments and banks, designed to deliver public confidence in the banking system. In return for cooperating in the delivery of Government objectives, the banking industry escaped the rigors of effective competition' (Cruickshank 2000).

Finally, a closely related view on regulation might be termed the 'grabbing hands view'.[12] From this perspective neither the public interest nor the

---

[10] See the paper by Demsetz *et al.* (1996) for instance.

[11] See Stigler (1971) and for a brief sketch Kroszner and Strahan (1999).

[12] This term is adopted from Shleifer and Vishny (1999).

regulated industry, but rather politicians and state officials drive regulatory actions and interfere with the regulated industry in order to extract benefits and pursue their own interests. As Hellwig (2000) points out, the banking industry is especially vulnerable to encouraging greediness on the part of politicians. Politicians like to exercise control over banks because the banking business provides a unique and most direct opportunity to spend money and fund projects that serve the politicians' own purposes. It is worth noting here and for the remainder of this chapter that while we primarily address bank regulation our regulatory regime perspective necessarily leads us to consider government ownership of banks as well. The interrelationships between regulation and government ownership of banks are at least threefold. First, governance and incentive structures in government-owned banks are likely to be different from those in privately owned, value-maximizing banks that have traditionally been the focal point of almost all discussions on bank regulation. Second, in a country where a large share of bank assets is already under the control of the state, politicians' attitudes towards regulating banks might be different by comparison to a private banking system. For instance, the nationalization of single banks or the banking system as a whole has historically been one forceful governmental remedy for banking crises, and can thus be interpreted as a means of bank regulation itself. Third, one has to ask how competition in financial services is affected when some banks are state-owned while others are not.

Recent cross-country empirical work by La Porta *et al.* (2002) analyses the consequences of government ownership of banks and indicates that a higher share of bank assets controlled by government negatively correlates with subsequent financial development and subsequent rates of growth in GDP. These findings can be interpreted as evidence supporting the capture theory of regulation or the 'grabbing-hands view' of government intervention in financial markets, and thus reinforce a commonly held notion: Government involvement in the capital allocation process yields inefficient outcomes because it distorts the price system, favours corruption, and undermines the functioning of the market.

At first glance, the structure of the German banking system seems to be especially exposed to inefficiencies arising from regulatory capture and politicians' grabbing hands. A significant share of bank assets in Germany is under the control of the state. La Porta *et al.* (2002) measure the share of government ownership in Germany as 51.90 per cent in 1970 and 36.36 per cent in 1995. Although only based on observing the ten largest banks in the country, these figures capture the overall share of public ownership fairly well. At the end of 2001 the share of *Landesbanks* (central giro institutions of the Federal States) in total bank assets in Germany was 19.9 per cent and that of municipal savings banks was 15.4 per cent. Adding public mortgage banks, public building societies and public special purpose banks, the share of public banks in total banking assets is estimated to be somewhat above

40 per cent.[13] While La Porta *et al.* (2002) use the term 'government ownership', we will refer to these institutions as 'public banks' in the remainder of this chapter.[14] From our perspective, this is more than just a terminological note because in Germany all levels of regional authorities own and control banks. While municipalities own more than 500 savings banks, almost all German states[15] hold ownership stakes in one of the twelve *Landesbanks* and besides often own state-level development banks. In addition, the Federal Government owns Kreditanstalt für Wiederaufbau (KfW) and Deutsche Ausgleichsbank (DtA), two large development banks.

Politicians, especially at the municipal and state level, thus, often seemed in the past to exert direct control over bank assets because states and municipalities acted as guarantors for the liabilities of the savings banks and *Landesbanks* (guarantee obligation or *Gewährträgerhaftung*) and by law were required to ensure the viability of these public enterprises (maintenance obligation or *Anstaltslast*). For example, they had to provide capital in the event of a reorganization.[16] State governments use the *Landesbanks* as their own development banks and directly pursue what is officially stated to be the interest of the state in terms of regional economic development. The same can be said about public savings banks and the influence exerted by politicians at the municipal level. As is well known, in 2002 an agreement was reached between the European Commission, the German authorities and the public banking sector to abolish state and municipal guarantees and significantly modify obligations to ensure the banking institution's viability. We will address these more recent developments and their likely consequences in Section 10.3 below.

It is important to note, however, that ownership in most public banks is far from monolithic. While municipal savings banks are usually owned by groups of municipalities, *Landesbanks* in aggregate are owned by states and the regional associations of municipal savings banks. Furthermore, cross-ownership is important among *Landesbanks*. The process of decision-making within *Landesbanks* might as a consequence be characterized by conflicts of interest. It is, therefore, not immediately clear how different interest groups—politicians, public banks' managers, as well as the public banks' associations at the state or federal level—contribute to what could be termed the corporate governance of German public banks. Also, in addition to the 'grabbing hands' hypothesis on public interference in banking, there is a competing view, termed the

---

[13] As of year end 2000, five of the ten largest banks and nine out of the fifteen largest banks belong to the public sector. In terms of total assets and measured for the ten largest banks the figure comparable to La Porta *et al.* (2002) for 2000 is 33 per cent.

[14] Obviously, with 'public banks' we are not referring to banks who have issued shares of common stock and whose shares are traded on exchanges.

[15] Only the state of Rhineland-Palatine does not hold ownership stakes in a Landesbank.

[16] This is often termed 'maintenance obligation'. As public sector banks in trouble are always rescued because of the maintenance obligation, the guarantor obligation has never been called for. For further discussion see Hackethal's (2003) contribution in this volume.

'development view' by La Porta *et al.* (2002). Based on the notion that financial markets are characterized by important market imperfections and given that financial development is beneficial in that it fosters economic growth, governments might also have a positive role to play. From a theoretical point of view, it cannot be entirely ruled out that public banks would be better able to provide financial services to certain groups of customers when market imperfections are significant. Moreover, private shareholder value-maximizing banks in such a market environment might be forced to focus their supply of financial services on the least risky and most profitable customers, leaving others 'unbanked'. Thus, it is the case that savings banks and state owned *Landesbanks* have a disproportionately larger market share in financing small, young, and risky corporate customers.[17]

Whether the 'grabbing hands' view or the 'development view' does a better job in explaining the history of public banks in Germany and whether the results of La Porta *et al.* (2002) also apply in the German case remains an open question and more research is definitely required. Did the existence of such a large public banking sector cause capital to be allocated inefficiently and as a consequence lead to lower economic growth?[18] As we are primarily interested in regulation we also have to ask whether inefficient public banks lead regulators and policy-makers to restrict competitive pressure in order to allow these institutions a 'quiet life'.

Answers to all the questions raised in this section are far from being straightforward, but we will try to discuss them in more detail in Section 10.2 when we assess single regulatory instruments. It is important to note, however, that from the researcher's perspective it is inherently difficult to analyse how a given regulation affects industry profits[19] and even more so, to find out how different interest groups contribute to the regulatory process. Unfortunately once again, empirical work on this issue is virtually non-existent in Germany.[20] In what follows, we therefore first briefly review the history of bank regulation in Germany. Our aim is to sketch the fundamental structure of the regulatory regime as well as the driving forces behind its adjustment over time.

---

[17] Municipal savings banks, for instance, do grant 64 per cent of all loans to small craftsmen and provide around 50 per cent of financing to newly created enterprises.

[18] Two questions are of importance here. (1) Does corporate control exercised by politicians lead to the inefficient allocation of capital? And more fundamentally, (2) does the governance structure of public banking institutions by its very nature lead to inefficient outcomes?

[19] This task is further complicated by the possibility that certain stakeholders might extract part of these rents.

[20] Analyses of the effect of regulation on industry profits often use the event study method, measuring the stock price reaction of regulated firms to regulatory announcements. One such study conducted by one of the authors will be presented in Section 10.2.2. Further, in the US several studies analyse congressional voting behaviour to indirectly infer interest group influence. See Kroszner and Strahan (1999) as an example for the latter group of studies. Unfortunately there is no comparable empirical work for Germany.

10.1.3. Regulation in German Banking—a Short Historical Overview

The beginning of banking regulation in Germany dates back to 1931, when licensing requirements and bank supervision were first introduced on a general scale and a supervisory authority was set up. Before that, only public sector savings banks and mortgage banks had been subject to regulation and supervision. Like in many other countries, bank regulation in Germany can be interpreted primarily as a response to banking crises. The 1931 initiatives, for example, followed the general banking crisis culminating in the default of the Danatbank. As a further response and in an attempt to consolidate the provisions passed so far, the first German banking law was enacted in 1934.

It is important to note that when bank regulation began in the 1930s the fundamental structure of the German banking system, a mix of private, public, and cooperative institutions, was already in place. Moreover, all three groups of banks had already established banking associations at the national as well as the regional level.

While in the United States or United Kingdom, mandatory capital requirements were first implemented in the 1980s, regulation of bank capital has a long tradition in Germany.[21] For example, mortgage banks were subject to structural norms tied to an institution's equity capital as early as 1899. The German Banking Act of 1934 defined a credit institution's capital, termed 'liable capital', by enumerating respective balance sheet items. Further it made 'liable capital' a point of reference for specific horizontal as well as vertical structural balance sheet rules. Interestingly, the early capital requirements primarily served the purpose of limiting maturity mismatch between banks' assets and liabilities by requiring banks to hold capital in relation to the difference between customer liabilities and liquid assets. Regulators as well as academics at that time were well aware of the potential losses that banks could suffer whenever they were forced to sell off their illiquid loans. Therefore, instead of requiring banks to hold capital in relation to an overall measure of asset risk, two further structural norms of the 1934 Banking Act limited the amount of lending to single borrowers and an institution's investment in real estate and long-term participating interest to a certain proportion of capital.

Supported by the Nazi government, in 1937 German banks entered into a cartel-like agreement on interest rates, fees, and advertising. The Central Credit Committee (*Zentraler Kreditausschuss*) was established as a platform for private, cooperative, and public banks in 1936 in order to coordinate banks' business decisions and ceilings on loan and deposit interest rates. Although no such cartels have remained in place, today the Central Credit Committee still exists and serves as an integrated lobbying platform for all German banking associations—cooperative, public, and private—as well as a contact to the banking industry for regulators and administrative institutions.

---

[21] See Krümmel (1983) for a short survey of the history of capital regulation.

After the Second World War the 1934 Banking Act also formed the basis for bank regulation, which was first exercised by the western allies' military administration and then passed over to the states and their authorities. In a remarkable step in 1958 branching restrictions were abolished and banking institutions were free to open branches everywhere in the country without passing a public needs test. However, because public savings banks are closely tied to their municipalities' market areas and in general do not invade each others' local markets, the economic effect of this deregulation might not have been as significant as comparable measures taken by US states during the 1978–92 period.[22]

With the passage of the new German Banking Act ('Kreditwesengesetz') in 1961 bank supervisory activities were centralized at the federal level and passed over to the newly established Federal Banking Supervisory Office ('Bundesaufsichtsamt für das Kreditwesen' or FBSO in what follows). From its beginning the law required the *Bundesbank* to be involved in the supervisory process.[23] In addition, in every single state there has to be a supervisory authority for public savings banks. The FBSO is responsible for supervising banks; it grants and revokes banking licences and supervises the ongoing business activities of banks. The FBSO has far-reaching rights to obtain information, intervene into management decisions, recall bank managers, impose moratoria, and close a bank. It is worth emphasizing that in Germany there is a supervisory agency which is separate from the central bank but the *Bundesbank* is actively involved in banking supervision and significantly supports the FBSO.[24] The *Bundesbank* plays an important role in virtually all areas of banking supervision with a special emphasis on activities related to collecting and processing relevant information. In particular, it is involved in 'the issuing of general rules (such as principles and regulations), the process of ongoing supervision, with the exception of (sovereign) individual regulatory measures *vis-à-vis* institutions, prudential audits and international cooperation/ coordination in the prudential field'.[25] The *Bundesbank* also plays an important role in crisis management.[26]

One of the main arguments in favour of involving the *Bundesbank* in the supervisory process lies in the informational economies of scope between

---

[22] See Berger *et al.* (1995) and Jayaratne and Strahan (1996) for an evaluation of branching deregulation in the United States. We will highlight the role and structure of the bank branching network in Germany further below.

[23] An interesting remark concerns the fact that the law was enacted against the will of the states, who instituted proceedings against it at the Federal Constitutional Court (Bundesverfassungsgericht). In its opinion the Court emphasized that bank supervision is an integral part of a central bank's area of responsibilities.

[24] In several European countries—for instance, in Greece, Ireland, Italy, the Netherlands, Portugal or Spain—the central bank is the only supervisory agency.

[25] See *Bundesbank* (2000) and the *Bundesbank*'s (www.bundesbank.de) website for further details.

[26] For readers interested in the subject, we have listed several websites on German banking in the Appendix. The *Bundesbank*'s website address is also listed there.

monetary policy, bank supervision, and crisis management in particular.[27] While the allocation of supervisory duties is relatively clear, the question of who actually 'makes regulation' in Germany is much harder to answer, with the German Parliament, the Ministry of Finance and the supervisory authorities (FBSO and the *Bundesbank*) all being involved. Furthermore and as already mentioned above, the role played by the banking industry itself should be critically assessed.

According to the Banking Act, the FBSO is required to draw up principles allowing it to assess whether a bank's liquidity and capital is adequate. From 1961 onwards, therefore, German credit institutions were subject to the so-called Principle I that limited a bank's credit risk by requiring them to hold an appropriate amount of capital relative to the sum of risk-weighted assets. Principles II and III, like their predecessors in the Banking Act of 1934, were primarily concerned with maturity mismatch and required assets of certain maturity to be related to liabilities of similar maturity. With respect to interest rates, cartel-like agreements among banks remained in place until 1965. Although the 1961 Banking Act already formed the legal basis for federal interest rate regulations, the FBSO made use of it only during the 1965–67 period. In 1967 all regulations on interest rates were abolished and since then loan and deposit rates have been free to adjust to market conditions.[28] In addition to its involvement in the supervisory process, the *Bundesbank* has always been an important player in every decision on financial market regulation and in some instances has protected German banks from foreign or non-bank competition. For example, at the end of the 1960s the increased desire of foreign entities to issue bonds denominated in DM posed a threat to the *Bundesbank*'s strategy to prevent the DM from becoming an international reserve currency. In 1968, therefore, the *Bundesbank* settled an agreement with the German banks—the so called 'Gentlemen's Agreement'—that only a German bank could act as lead underwriter of DM-denominated issues of foreign entities. This effectively restricted competition from foreign banks.[29] The scope of the 'Gentlemen's Agreement' was expanded further in 1980 before it was abolished in 1985.

The 1961 Banking Act remained largely unchanged until the next significant crisis occurred in 1974, when Bankhaus Herstatt collapsed as a consequence of large speculative positions in foreign exchange. The Herstatt crisis, which according to Herring and Litan (1995) had a significant effect, despite the small size of the bank, on banks worldwide, led to several new regulatory initiatives: Firstly, a system of group-specific deposit insurance schemes was

---

[27] See also Vives (2000).

[28] Reserve requirements on bank deposits, however, still drive a wedge between money market rates and bank deposit rates.

[29] Proceeds from the issues were immediately converted into the issuer's home currency and transferred to him. Bilateral agreements with other central banks further ensured that no DM-bonds were issued outside Germany. See Franke (2000) for further details.

established. It replaced the rudimentary systems that had existed since 1969. The newly created system of deposit insurance schemes was unique in that deposit insurance was and still is entirely in the hands of the banking groups (cooperatives, public, and private banks) themselves. We will provide a more detailed analysis of deposit insurance in Germany further below. As a further response to the Herstatt crisis, the so-called liquidity bank ('Liquidi- tätskonsortialbank') was founded in order to assist solvent but illiquid private banks. New structural norms, termed Principle Ia, were introduced by the FBSO to tie open positions in foreign exchange and precious metals to a bank's capital. The 1976 amendment to the Banking Act further authorized the FBSO to audit single institutions without special reason and defined limits on losses experienced by credit institutions that lead to mandatory closure by the FBSO. Finally, in 1974 an expert group was implemented to consult the government with respect to fundamental questions of the banking industry.[30]

It may, however, be seriously doubted whether any of these reforms directly addressed the weaknesses in the supervisory system that the Herstatt crisis had uncovered, namely that of timely and accurate information in the hands of the supervisors. This information necessarily forms the basis of a functioning early warning system. Whether the supervisory agency's ability to detect problems in single banks has since improved, remains somewhat unclear. According to Beck (2001), when Bankhaus Schröder, Münchmeyer & Hengst nearly failed in 1983 due to large loan losses, these problems were first discovered by the Association of Private Banks ('Bundesverband deutscher Banken'), not by the FBSO![31]

The third amendment to the Banking Act came into force in 1985 and required capital adequacy regulations to be met both by individual institutions as well as on a consolidated basis. Prior to 1985 banks were permitted to build up credit pyramids through their subsidiaries without adequately adjusting the parent bank's capital base. Furthermore, and as a direct response to the Schröder, Münchmeyer & Hengst case, the limit for lending to a single borrowing entity was reduced from 75 to 50 per cent of capital. Principle Ia that tied a bank's exposure in foreign currencies and precious metals to its capital was revised in 1990 to also cover price risk from derivatives and interest rate exposures.

Further amendments to the Banking Act primarily served to transpose European Directives into German law. The fourth amendment in 1993 imple- mented the Solvency Ratio and first Capital Adequacy Directive and raised the threshold of the reporting requirement for large loans from around €500,000 to €1,500,000. Since the mid-1930s German banks have been required to report all large loans to a central credit register maintained by the central bank. After consolidating these reports, the *Bundesbank* notifies the lending banks of the overall indebtedness of their borrowers. It is interesting to note that the first Basle Accord, underlying the Capital Adequacy Directive, was accompanied by

---

[30] See Krümmel (1980) for a report.
[31] Schröder, Münchmeyer & Hengst had lent heavily to building machinery group IBH. See Goodhart and Schoenmaker (1993) for a short description.

heavy discussions with respect to its effect on the international competitiveness of German banks.[32] While the competitiveness of domestic banks in the international marketplace was still an issue when the so called Basle II programme was made public in 1999, in Germany discussions on Basle II now focus much more attention on questions related to capital requirements, internal rating systems, and bank loan supply to SMEs (small and medium-sized enterprises).

In 1994 and after 6 years of intense debate, money market mutual funds were allowed to operate in Germany posing a serious competitive threat to German banks' deposit business. In the preceding years the *Bundesbank* especially had strongly opposed the necessary changes to the Investment Company Act because of monetary policy considerations.[33] In Section 10.2 below, we will use this episode of financial market regulation to clarify further the role of the monetary authority in protecting banks' deposit franchise.

Another revision of the Banking Act occurred in 1995 and led to changes in the rules on consolidation and large-credits. A major innovation was brought about by the sixth amendment to the Banking Act in 1998 that implemented three European Directives: the Investment Services Directive, the Capital Adequacy Directive, and the so called Post-BCCI Directive. As a consequence of the 1998 reform, like in other European Countries, investment firms are now supervised according to the same rules as credit institutions. Also the concept of the trading book was introduced and Principle I was changed accordingly.[34] Banks are now allowed to use their own internal models to assess their risk position with respect to the trading book. In 1998 the Directive on Depositor Guarantee and Investor Protection was implemented. A statutory system compensating depositors in the event of bank default was established that complements the already existing group specific schemes.[35] In 1999 the FBSO changed its internal structure and, among other things, established a new division concerned with 'complex groups', that is with large international financial conglomerates. In 2002 a major reform in financial market supervision occurred, when a new integrated financial services supervising authority was established that comprises the formerly separated supervisory offices for banking, insurance and securities trading.[36] Obviously the Ministry of Finance has thus made a serious attempt to track the organizational complexity of today's financial services industry.

Table 10.1 summarizes the most important events in German bank regulation since the Second World War.

---

[32] While the implementation of this directive in 1993 did not materially change Principle I, the question of what types of equity capital German authorities would allow to consider as 'liable capital' was hotly debated.

[33] This point is also emphasized by Saunders and Walter (1994).

[34] Tier 3 capital was defined and an institution's own funds were introduced as an adjustment to its liable capital.

[35] A discussion of the private deposit insurance scheme in Germany is provided further below.

[36] The role of the *Bundesbank* in banking supervision has formally remained unaltered by this restructuring.

Table 10.1. *Bank Regulation in Germany—a selective overview*

Year	Event
1957	Bundesbank Act
1958	Branching restrictions abolished
1961	German Banking Act
1965	Interest rate regulation by FBSO replaces cartel agreements among banks
1967	Interest rate regulation completely abolished
1968	German banks and Bundesbank enter into so called 'Gentlemen's Agreement' effectively prohibiting foreign banks from underwriting issues of DM-denominated bonds by foreign issuers
1969	Introduction of first group specific deposit insurance schemes
1974	Default of Bankhaus Herstatt
	Introduction of Principle Ia that limits open positions in forex and commodities to 30% of bank capital
	Establishment of the Liquiditäts-Konsortialbank GmbH
	Expert group on 'Grundsatzfragen der Kreditwirtschaft' (fundamental issues of the banking industry)
1976	Second Amendment to the German Banking Act
	• new rules for large loans to single borrowers
	• new rules on credit files
	• FBSO authorised to audit single institutions without specific reason
	• explicit limits on bank losses that oblige FBSO to close the bank
1974–77	Enlargement/adjustment of group-specific deposit insurance schemes for private banks, public banks, and cooperative banks, respectively
	• 1975 public savings banks
	• 1976 private banks
	• 1977 cooperative banks
1980	Expansion of the 'Gentlemen's Agreement'
1983	Near collapse of Bankhaus Schröder, Münchmeyer & Hengst
1985	Third amendment to the German Banking Act
	• Capital requirements to be met on consolidated basis
	• New limit for lending to a single borrowing entity
	Abolition of the 'Gentlemen's Agreement'
	Permission to issue DM-denominated zerobonds
1986	Permission to issue DM-denominated Certificates of Deposit
1990	First Financial Market Promotion Act
1993	Fourth amendment to the Banking Act implementing the EU
	• Solvency Directive and
	• Capital Adequacy Directive
	• Threshold for large loans to be reported to the *Bundesbank's* credit register raised from €500,000 to €1,500,000
1994	Second Financial Market Promotion Act
	• Introduction of Money Market Mutual Funds (Amendment to the Investment Company Act)

Table 10.1. *Continued*

Year	Event
	• Prohibition of insider trading
	• Establishment of Federal Supervisory Office for Securities Trading
1995	Fifth amendment to the Banking Act implementing new rules on consolidation and large credits
1998	Sixth amendment to the Banking Act implementing EUs
	• Investment Services Directive
	• Capital Adequacy Directive and
	• Post-BCCI Directive
1999	FBSO creates division supervising 'complex groups'
2002	Establishment of an integrated financial services supervisor—the Federal Financial Supervisory Authority—integrating the formerly separated supervisory offices for banking, insurance, and securities trading

With respect to the fundamental structure of the regulatory regime and the driving forces for its adjustments over time, the following is worth emphasizing and will be discussed in more depth in Section 10.2.

Banking regulation in Germany, at least since the Second World War, has rested on two strong pillars: licensing and supervision on the one hand and capital requirements on the other. Limits on banking activities, portfolio composition or lending activities, ceilings on deposit interest rates, or restrictions on bank branching in contrast have either not played a significant role from the outset, or were abolished much earlier than in other countries. In some sense these observations seem to contradict the notion of particularly anti-competitive bank regulation in Germany. Although the regulatory frame was relatively stable until the early 1990s, amendments to the Banking Act before 1990 were triggered primarily by problems of single institutions. Reforms that were enacted after 1990 in contrast were motivated in the first instance by the necessity to transpose EU directives into German law. With respect to identifying key players in the regulatory arena, it is worth noticing that on several occasions the *Bundesbank* prevented the introduction of securitized money market instruments (money market funds, DM-denominated CDs) for monetary policy reasons. Furthermore, it effectively deterred entry by foreign banks in DM-denominated bond underwriting activity.

10.1.4. Market Structure and Conduct: Empirical Evidence on the Competitiveness of German Banking

In the introduction it was stated that German banking in the past was often considered as stable but not very competitive. If assessments of the stability of banking are based on the number of failures and the occurrence of systemic banking crises, the notion of the relative stability of German banking since the Second World War cannot easily be rejected. By comparison, the empirical evidence on the degree of competition among German banks is somewhat more ambiguous.

10.1.4.1. *Market structure and industry concentration in a universal banking system*

An important aspect of the German tradition of bank structure and regulation is that regulators impose only few restrictions on the range of services banks are allowed to offer to their customers. It seems fair to say that Germany is perceived to be the prototype of a universal banking system. The most direct tool for regulating the structure of banking and financial services, namely the centrepiece of all banking legislation, therefore lies in the definition of what constitutes a bank. This definition is crucial as it defines the scope of activities and products subject to regulation. And on the other hand, it also implicitly defines a group of non-bank suppliers of financial services that remain unregulated or are subject to some other form of public intervention.[37] The German Banking Act defines a credit institution as an enterprise commercially active in at least one of twelve fields of business, which include deposit taking, loan granting, discounting of bills of exchange, investment fund business, securities underwriting and the like.[38] Edwards and Fischer (1994) note that '[...] the legal definition of banking business is so broad that most financial institutions are, by definition, banks'. Only banks' insurance activities, mortgage banking and activities of building societies require legally separate subsidiaries.

However, data compiled by Barth *et al.* (2001) shows that from 1999 onwards universal banking was common in EU countries. One of their indices summarizes information about the restrictiveness of bank participation in specific financial services activities (securities, insurance, and real estate) and about whether banks are allowed to own non-financial firms. An index value of 1 indicates that no restrictions are imposed on banks, whereas a value of 4 would indicate that all activities in these areas are prohibited.[39] While Germany is among the countries with a low index (1.25), the average index value for EU countries is 1.82, which is significantly lower than in the rest of

---

[37] See also Barth *et al.* (2001).

[38] Besides, the Banking Act also defines a group of financial services institutions (portfolio management, investment trading, own-account trading) and financial enterprises (leasing, consulting (M&A etc.)).

[39] In computing this index Barth *et al.* (2001) use detailed information on bank regulation in a large cross-section of countries. Barth *et al.* (2001) proceed as follows. For every country in their dataset they rank the degree of restrictiveness imposed on banks when entering a certain line of activity. They consider securities activities, insurance, and real estate activities. Further they look for restrictions on the ability of banks to own and control firms. For all these activities they assign values ranging from 1 (unrestricted) to 4 (prohibited). The indices mentioned in the text above are just the average of these ranks.

the world (1 per cent level of significance).[40] The worldwide average of the restrictiveness index is 2.5. It is 2.3 for European non-EU countries, 2.9 for African countries, 2.5 for American countries, and 2.7 for Asian countries in the Barth *et al.* (2001) data set. Continental European banking markets in general now seem to be characterized by a universal banking approach. However Berger *et al.* (2001) suspect that the Single Market Programme (SMP), and the rule of mutual recognition in particular, has made universal banking the norm in the EU because remaining restrictions at the national level might put domestic banks at a disadvantage.[41] If this notion were true, for some observers universal banking might appear as the best practice benchmark and competition would lead to strong convergence towards unrestricted bank activities.

Theoretically, there seem to be several reasons why universal banks could be more efficient than specialized banking institutions that are restricted in the scope of their activities.[42] Rajan's (1996) discussion, however, should make us somewhat cautious here: His argument points to the relevance of the legal and financial framework within which universal banks are allowed to operate. Following his argument, in a financial system that is fairly competitive, where a full range of financial services providers are allowed to operate and where there are meaningful disclosure requirements as well as political checks and balances and a working regulatory framework, universal banking could hardly be harmful to the economy. In such a framework competition decides whether universal banking or more specialized financial institutions will be the most efficient vehicles for providing firms and households with financial services. But in a country where these requirements are not met, the historical predominance of a few large universal banks might have seriously hindered the emergence of securities markets, financial innovations, and more specialized suppliers of financial services.[43] As yet these idiosyncrasies of universal

---

[40] These figures are based on our own computations using the Barth *et al.* (2001) data base. Access to their data is gratefully acknowledged.

[41] Unfortunately we were not able to exactly follow the development of regulations on banks' activities in EMU countries. A partial sketch of these developments is provided by OECD (1992: table 10.4, 51–4).

[42] These range from economies of scope to the more efficient use of customer specific information and finally to arguments involving the diversification of business risk. See Rajan (1996) for an overview and Vander Vennet (2002) for empirical evidence in favour of this hypothesis.

[43] Market power as well as political power and regulatory capture might be responsible for such a negative effect on financial development. See Rajan (1996) and also Barth *et al.* (2002). Similarly Boot and Thakor (1997) offer several reasons why stand-alone banks might be at a disadvantage in universal banking systems. Obviously questions of this type are of central importance for any assessment of the financial system in Germany and its historical performance. See for instance the contribution by Franzke *et al.* (2004) in this volume for an in-depth analysis. Although such a discussion goes far beyond the scope of this chapter, it might nevertheless provide some guidance for a discussion of bank regulation and competition. First, an assessment of the regulatory framework within which universal banks are forced to operate, might turn out to be a useful intermediate step towards a better understanding of universal banking. Second, it is important to

banking systems are not well understood.[44] This is especially true for an analysis of the competitive effects of universal banking and its likely repercussions in the regulatory framework. Although our ability to analyse questions of this type is limited, we will proceed by describing the competitive structure of the German universal banking system in order to provide a first step towards a better understanding.

Hackethal (2004) gives a detailed description of the structure of the banking market in Germany highlighting the role of private, public, and cooperative banks. For a basic understanding of this so-called three-pillar system we refer the reader to his contribution to this volume, which we take as a starting point for our discussion in the remainder of this section.

In light of standard oligopoly theory, measures of market structure and especially indices of bank concentration might serve as first indicators for the degree of competitiveness. This is exactly why indices of market concentration, for example, concentration ratios and the Herfindahl index, play such an important role in almost all recent assessments of US and European banking markets. They are also widely used in empirical work. Data presented in the literature, however, does not draw a clear and reliable picture. For example, figures for the three-firm concentration ratio CR3, the combined market share of the three largest institutions, for the German banking market range from 89.5 per cent in Allen and Gale (2000) to 27 per cent in Cetorelli and Gambera (2001) and even to a low value of less than 17 per cent in Danthine *et al.* (1999). While a three-firm concentration ratio of around 90 per cent would lead us to conclude that Germany is among the most highly concentrated banking markets in the world, a figure of less than 17 per cent would indicate exactly the opposite and make Germany one of the least concentrated banking industries worldwide. What is the underlying problem in interpreting these measures of market concentration? Although this question is almost impossible to answer precisely, as we see it, more attention should be devoted to traditional questions related to the delineation of the relevant market in terms of geographic reach as well as in terms of the set of relevant competitors. For example, it seems to be widely accepted that retail banking markets are local in nature.[45] Markets for investment banking services in contrast seem to have grown beyond national boundaries and today are perceived to be of almost global dimension. Furthermore, while the majority of German banks is active in the retail segment, only a few of them offer investment banking services.[46] Most of these retail banks conduct their business in narrowly defined regional

---

keep in mind that 'allowing' universal banking need not necessarily lead to actually 'observing' universal banking.

[44] See also Rajan (1996) for such an assessment.

[45] See Amel and Starr-McCluer (2001) or Cruickshank (2000), chapter 5.

[46] If the retail market were indeed national in scope and all banks would compete in retail services, then a CR3 around 12–13 per cent would be a reliable estimate for the year 2000. The Herfindahl based on balance sheet total would then be around 0.015. See *Bundesbank* (2001).

markets as they belong to either the cooperative or the public banking sector. Since these banking institutions do not invade each others' regional markets, within-group competition is of only minor importance. Finally, as pointed out by Hackethal (2003) competition in German financial services might be described as competition among groups of financial conglomerates. Besides the few big banks the cooperative as well as the public banking sector could also be viewed as one large competitor that offers almost all types of financial services. Whether the group character of competition softens competitive pressure or even intensifies it, is an open but extremely important question.

10.1.4.2. *Retail banking*

Let us turn to retail markets first. Table 10.2 contains Herfindahl indices for German administrative regions called *Landkreise* for the years 1996, 1998, and 2000. These regions might be a useful approximation for local banking markets relevant to retail banking in Germany. Because market share data for banks is generally not available at this level of disaggregation, branching data was used instead.[47] $MS_{i,j}$ denotes bank i's market share in local market j. We approximated $MS_{i,j}$ by the number of branches that bank i operates in j divided by the total number of bank branches operated in market j. Individual bank market shares in a given administrative region were squared and summed.

Although the figures in Table 10.2 are not directly comparable with data from other countries, three conclusions can be drawn.[48] First, local banking markets in eastern Germany are much more concentrated than their western counterparts. There are structural differences between eastern and western markets which might account for the differences in concentration. For example during the 1990s per capita income was lower and default rates were higher in the eastern part of the country.[49] It might, nevertheless, be interesting to note that with German reunification in 1990 public savings banks and credit cooperatives were inherited from the former German Democratic Republic. Although these institutions had to be reshaped in several dimensions, market entry in the sense of opening branches was primarily observed with private banks. Second, and unlike the United States, there seems to be no clear-cut rural–urban pattern.[50] One reason is the large number of relatively small

[47] As Fischer (2001) shows for US Metropolitian Statistical Areas, Herfindahl indices based on branching data provide a reasonable approximation of the more common Herfindahl indices based on deposit market shares.

[48] Fischer (2001) computes Herfindahl indices based on branching data for 212 Metropolitan Statistical Areas in the United States. The average Herfindahl for these local US markets is 0.1135, and is thus considerably lower than the 0.2 for densely populated areas in western Germany.

[49] A two-stage game of banking competition comprising an entry stage where banks decide whether to conduct deposit and loan business in a certain local market and in the second stage compete in prices or quantities, would normally predict that less banks enter whenever borrower default risk is higher or households are less wealthy.

[50] In the United States, for example, the rural county markets show significantly higher bank concentration than the more urban MSA markets.

Table 10.2. *Measures of local banking market concentration—Herfindahl indices based on branching data*

Markets	No. of local markets	Average Herfindahl		
		1996	1998	2000
Western Germany	328	0.198	0.200	0.206
Eastern Germany	112	0.280	0.302	0.325
Among them:				
Cities (Eastern and Western Germany)	111	0.210	0.214	0.212
Western Germany				
Densely populated areas	120	0.200	0.202	0.205
Urbanized areas	140	0.196	0.197	0.205
Rural areas	68	0.199	0.202	0.211
Eastern Germany				
Densely populated areas	30	0.284	0.298	0.329
Urbanized areas	47	0.296	0.321	0.338
Rural areas	35	0.255	0.280	0.306

Source: Fischer (2001).

cooperative banks in rural areas which lead to more fragmented market structures. Third, during the 1996–2000 period, the process of industry consolidation was much more pronounced in rural areas (especially in the eastern part of the country), and this might also be seen as a consequence of the fragmented structure of cooperative banks in rural areas. As already mentioned above, the retail market is quite fragmented as the public and cooperative banks among themselves do not in principle invade each others' regional markets. Table 10.3 provides an initial basic impression which further illustrates the typical structure of a local banking market in Germany. In order to enable a better comparison we took into account all eighty-three German cities with more than 100,000 inhabitants. As a subsample of all markets considered in Table 10.9, these densely populated city areas are relatively homogeneous and might well serve as useful approximations for local banking markets.

On average there are twenty-five banks present in these local markets. In sixty-three of the eighty-three cities considered there is only one savings bank present, whereas there are on average six cooperative banks and seventeen private banks. This reinforces the widely held notion that the principle of market demarcation is almost perfect among the local savings banks. Savings banks are strictly tied to the local market, which is identical to the jurisdiction of the municipalities that act as their guarantors. Market areas of cooperative banks in contrast show much more regional overlap. On average 40 per cent of all branches in these local markets are operated by savings banks and 22 per cent are operated by cooperative banks. Measured this way, the market

Table 10.3. *Bank market structure in largest German cities (# 83)*

	Mean/median	Minimum/maximum
# of banks that operate branches in a local market	25/20	6/87
# of savings banks that operate branches in a local market	1.3/1	1/7
# of Landesbanks that operate branches in a local market	0.6/0	0/4
# of cooperative banks that operate branches in a local market	6/5	1/19
# of private banks that operate branches in a local market	17/12	4/68
# of bank branches	112/69	26/867
Branches per 1000 capita	0.39/0.39	0.21/0.67
Branches per square kilometre	0.64/0.59	0.20/1.86
Herfindahl (based on branch data)	0.21/0.20	0.09/0.41

Source: Authors' own calculations based on data from Fischer (2001).

share of the four large private banks is approximately 21 per cent in these eighty-three markets.

Looking at local banking markets as the relevant market in retail banking business thus reveals that the large private banking institutions, that is, Deutsche Bank, Dresdner Bank, Hypovereinsbank, and Commerzbank, which are often perceived as being the most powerful and dominant players in German financial services, are better described as fringe players in many local markets (the average share of the branch network in the eighty-three markets considered amounted to 7 per cent for Deutsche Bank, 5 per cent for Dresdner Bank, 5 per cent for Commerzbank and 3 per cent for Hypovereinsbank), whereas savings banks and cooperative banks seem to dominate the retail market. In all eighty-three city markets considered, the largest supplier in terms of branch networks is the local savings bank. Figure 10.1 displays average concentration ratios from CR1 to CR10 for cities with populations above 100,000. On average the local savings bank operates 40 per cent of all branches (ranging from 20 to 60 per cent within our sample of densely populated cities); the next largest banks all operate considerably smaller branch networks.

The important issue here is how these structural aspects affect competition in retail banking. In addition to the question of how German banking compares to its European peers, there might also be a specific interest in intra-industry studies of concentration and price.[51] Retail banking markets are

---

[51] In his survey on structure–performance studies Schmalensee (1989) concludes 'In cross-section comparisons involving markets in the same industry, seller concentration is positively related to the level of price and since studies of price have fewer obvious weaknesses than studies

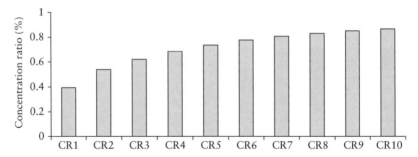

Figure 10.1. *Concentration ratios in large German cities (# 83). Concentration ratios in local banking markets (German cities with population greater than 100,000).*
Source: Fischer (2001).

particularly well suited to this type of analysis because there is strong evidence—anecdotal as well as analytical—that markets can be separated by location. Moreover, studies using data from only one national market might lead to more accurate conclusions concerning the influence of market structure on price because omitted variables with respect to the legal and regulatory environment are less likely to play a role. As already mentioned above, surveys among households and small enterprises in the United States conducted by the Federal Reserve Board offer convincing evidence that loan and deposit customers shop for banking services in rather narrowly defined markets. In most empirical work in the United States so-called metropolitan statistical areas or counties serve to approximate these local markets. Studies such as Berger and Hannan (1989), Neuberger and Zimmermann (1990) or Neumark and Sharpe (1992) have all found strong evidence in favour of the concentration price relationship at the intra-industry level. For Europe to date only a few such studies exist. Fischer (2001) analyses this relationship for local retail banking markets in Germany from 1992 to 1995. Since market share data in deposit and loan markets is not available, he computes measures of supplier concentration based on branching information. For most bank products considered, the study finds a significant concentration price correlation that points to the exercise of market power in more concentrated markets. Deposit rates, especially those on time deposits and savings deposits, are lower in more concentrated markets (i.e. the margins earned by banks are higher). Rates on loans to small firms are significantly higher in these markets. As a further illustration, Table 10.4 displays results of concentration-price regressions using data from Fischer (2001).[52] Table 10.4 contains results of pooled regressions for three specific bank products for the 1992 to 1995 period using

of profitability [this] seems to provide the best evidence in support of the concentration-collusion hypothesis', see Schmalensee (1989: 988).

[52] The specification 'and estimation' used here, however, is different from Fischer's (2001).

Table 10.4. *Bank market concentration as a determinant of bank interest margins—regression results*

	Margin savings deposits	Margin time deposits	Margin discount loans
1YEARGRO	0.08	−0.09	0.53[*]
PCINC	−0.10[*]	0.03	−0.36[*]
POPGRO	0.47	−0.89	6.06[*]
UNEMPLOY	−0.95[*]	0.04	−2.21[*]
RURAL	0.08	0.03[***]	0.12[**]
HERF	0.15[**]	0.09	2.03[*]
# Obs./R^2	5873/0.94	5943/0.52	5500/0.20

Notes:

1YEARGRO: Percentage growth in respective product category of all cooperative and savings banks' headquarters located in the local market.

PCINC: Average annual per capita income in local market.

POPGRO: Annual growth in population in local market.

UNEMPLOY: Average annual rate of unemployment in local market.

RURAL: Dummy variable indicating rural market.

HERF: Herfindahl index of local bank concentration based on branching data.

Pooled-OLS-regressions include a constant, fifteen quarterly dummies, and ten dummies for states (coefficients not reported).

[*] Significantly different from zero at 1% level.

[**] Significantly different from zero at 5% level.

[***] Significantly different from zero at 10% level.

Source: Authors' own calculations based on data from Fischer (2001).

end-of-quarter observations on discount loans to small borrowers (with loan volumes below €50,000), savings deposits and time deposits with maturities between one and three months.[53] The dependent variable is the difference between the product interest rate and the 3-month money market rate (FIBOR).[54] Control variables are all observed at the local market level; as in other studies that estimate reduced form price equations, the coefficients of most of the control variables are difficult to interpret.[55] However, confirming empirical results from other countries and in line with standard oligopoly theory, the Herfindahl index of local market concentration seems to be positively related to gross margins earned by German banks and is significant in two regressions (savings deposits and discount loans).[56]

[53] For further results and some other specifications and estimation techniques see Fischer (2001).

[54] For the two deposit products the margin is computed as 'money market rate minus deposit rate'; the loan margin is 'loan rate minus money market rate'.

[55] See Berger and Hannan (1989), Borenstein (1989), or Neuberger and Zimmerman (1990) for similar problems.

[56] Further evidence on the concentration–price relationship in Germany comes from an empirical analysis of the price effects of local bank mergers. Mergers that lead to stronger increases in local bank concentration also show stronger subsequent price effects to the disadvantage of loan and deposit customers; see Fischer (2001).

Table 10.5. *Market structure in German IPO underwriting*
(1990–2000)—bookrunners

Year	IPO volume (Euro mio) [# of IPOs]	Herfindahl— bookrunners	# of Banks acting as lead underwriter	CR3— Bookrunners	% Share of foreign banks in total volume
1990	1545.13 [34]	0.32	5	90.05	0
1991	1494.84 [19]	0.30	7	84.81	0
1992	373.98 [9]	0.34	4	89.34	0
1993	475.78 [11]	0.37	4	94.41	0
1994	596.73 [15]	0.28	7	77.44	1.01
1995	3583.03 [20]	0.29	10	89.12	35.64
1996	9054.48 [14]	0.32	9	98.65	33.24
1997	2529.75 [36]	0.13	16	47.07	26.42
1998	4098.87 [79]	0.08	29	38.52	27.09
1999	12731.013 [175]	0.11	46	47.47	50.12
2000	25556.29 [153]	0.17	43	65.12	44.03

Source: Authors' own calculations based on data kindly provided by Stefanie Franzke (Center for Financial Studies). In measuring market shares, whenever two or more banks act as bookrunner for one single issue, we double counted the volume of that issue.

10.1.4.3. *Investment banking*

To derive comparable structural measures of the market for investment banking services is somewhat more difficult. What is the geographic scope of this market? Should, for example, in underwriting corporate bonds and equity a global approach be taken and should these issues be considered with respect to European or only to German entities? For the following analysis we considered issues involving German entities only, thus allowing a more focused interpretation of the results. Table 10.5 shows Herfindahl indices for banks acting as lead underwriters in IPOs in Germany during the 1990–2000 period.[57]

As can be seen from Table 10.5, the market for lead underwriting services was highly concentrated at the beginning of the 1990s. Only few IPOs were brought to the market and the large German banks (Deutsche Bank, Dresdner Bank, and Commerzbank) dominated in equity underwriting. Of the Landesbanks, only WestLB had a noticeable market share. During the 1990s, however, the development towards strong market fragmentation began.[58] As the IPO market grew considerably, more and more banks entered, and the market share of foreign banks especially increased dramatically. Comparable

---

[57] For more evidence and an in-depth discussion on IPOs in Germany see Franzke *et al.* (2004: this volume).

[58] Market fragmentation as a response to market growth is a standard result in IO; see Sutton (1991) for further details.

Table 10.6. *Market structure of Euro-denominated bond underwriting (2001)—bookrunners*

Position	Bank	Volume in EURO mio	# of issues	% Share in volume
1	Dresdner Kleinwort Wasserstein	26.552	168	10.45
2	Deutsche Bank	24.209	113	9.53
3	JP Morgan	21.617	40	8.51
4	Merrill Lynch & Co.	21.446	68	8.44
5	Salomon Smith Barney Int.	16.113	59	6.34
6	Morgan Stanley Dean Witter	16.047	68	6.32
7	Goldman Sachs & Co.	13.660	53	5.38
8	Commerzbank Sec.	10.180	92	4.01
9	Barclays Capital	9.866	74	3.88
10	UBS Warburg	8.077	27	3.18

Source: Börsenzeitung based on Capital Data. Calculations of market share excluding own issues and based on total volume of top thirty bookrunners.

market structure data for bond markets is harder to find. As an example, therefore, Table 10.6 lists the top ten bookrunners of Euro-denominated bonds issued or guaranteed by German entities in 2001.

A similar picture emerges here. While Deutsche Bank and Dresdner Bank's investment banking subsidiaries take the lead positions and Commerzbank ranks No. 8 in bond underwriting with German issuers, no other German bank is among the top ten underwriters. Again US investment banks have gained significant market shares in recent years. In M&A advisory mandates related to Germany a similar picture emerges as only Deutsche Bank and Dresdner Bank play a role of any importance in these transactions (for the sake of brevity, we do not report market share data here). Overall, in investment banking services the following picture emerges. Investment banking business— even with German corporate customers—was heavily invaded by US investment banks during the 1990s. Building on their skill and reputation, these banks have recently increased their capacities to a considerable extent all over Europe. Apart from large players like Deutsche and Dresdner, whose strategy is explicitly orientated towards investment banking, most German banks by comparison have difficulty in establishing a significant role for themselves in this market segment. To date even the *Landesbanks* are of minor importance. Although often deemed to be the prototype of a universal banking system, a closer look at banks in Germany reveals that there is much more separation of business activity among banking institutions. Historically investment banking has not been a significant area of business for most German banks. Moreover, many of them are doing business in rather narrowly defined local markets. Only a few large banks are supra-regional in scope or offer true investment banking services. Another peculiarity of the German case is that competition is among integrated groups of financial services providers rather than among single banking institutions. While these structural peculiarities are quite obvious, their influence on market outcomes and economic performance is by no means clear.

10.1.4.4. *Competitiveness in German banking*

To assess the competitiveness of a market, the empirical industrial organization (IO) approach can be applied as it offers a range of techniques from traditional structure–performance studies to the more recently developed new empirical IO methods.[59] In the US questions related to the industrial organization of banking have always been of great interest to both academics as well as bank regulators. By comparison in Europe there is not yet much empirical evidence on the issue, despite the widespread belief that considerable market power is exercised by banks. Given the purpose of this section two questions seem to be of importance. First, what can be said about the competitiveness of German banking when compared to other countries, most importantly its European peers? Second, are there any differences in terms of conduct between banking groups (cooperative, public, and private) within the German financial system?

Courvoisier and Gropp (2002) use the more traditional structure–performance approach to analyse the relationship between bank retail margins and measures of national industry concentration for the 1993–99 period. Their study comprising observations from ten European countries finds a statistically and economically significant correlation between margins and product specific measures of industry concentration. Given that their estimate of a national German Herfindahl index is low and Germany is the least concentrated market in the Courvoisier and Gropp (2002) data set, a possible interpretation of their results is that Germany is one of the most competitive banking markets in Europe and margins in deposit and loan markets are low in international comparison.[60]

Several empirical studies apply the methodology proposed by Panzar and Rosse (1987) estimating reduced form revenue functions and using the sum of estimated factor price elasticities—the *H*-statistic—as an indicator of competitiveness. According to Panzar and Rosse (1987) the *H*-statistic is 1 in the case of perfect competition and negative in the case of monopoly behaviour, intermediate values refer to monopolistic competition. Hempell (2002) uses a large panel data set covering almost all banks reporting to the *Bundesbank* for its monthly banking statistics. Like Lang (1997), who uses a subset of German private, cooperative and public savings banks, her analysis focuses on the differences between German banking groups and the differences over time.

---

[59] See Bresnahan (1989) for an overview.

[60] We have already noted the large differences in measures of German bank market concentration to be found in the literature.

Bikker and Groeneveld (2000), De Bandt and Davies (2000), and Molyneux *et al.* (1994) in contrast analyse competition in a cross section of European countries using Fitch IBCA's data bank. All these studies find intermediate values for the *H*-statistic for German banks, which do not allow for a very precise interpretation of the mode of industry conduct. In Hempell (2002), Lang (1997) and De Bandt and Davies (2000) *H*-statistics are larger (indicating more competitive behaviour) for larger banks than for smaller ones and for private banks compared to savings banks and credit cooperatives. A possible interpretation is that smaller banks, savings banks as well credit cooperatives, exercise market power due to their strong competitive position in local retail markets and the type of spatial differentiation that comes with it.[61] From those three studies that use cross-country data it is hard to judge how Germany compares to other European countries. With only a few exceptions, across Europe all estimated *H*-statistics are between 0 and 1, indicating monopolistic competition; no further comment can be made. However, lack of robustness across specifications or time, large standard errors and most notably problems in interpreting intermediate values of *H* render pairwise comparisons inconclusive. For example, in Bikker and Groeneveld's study almost all country-specific estimates are well above 0.75 with only a few that are indistinguishable from 1 (perfect competition).

In empirical IO a widely accepted measure of the degree of market power, or alternatively an inverse measure of competition, is the Lerner Index *L*. With *P* for price, MC for marginal cost and $\eta(p)$ denoting the price elasticity of demand, the Lerner Index computes as

$$L = \frac{P - \text{MC}}{P} \eta(p).$$

As an alternative to the Rosse and Panzar methodology, one could as well attempt to measure this index more directly. A quick and simplistic method uses accounting data on revenues or price data and imposes restrictive assumptions with respect to marginal cost.[62] A more sophisticated alternative, however, tries to estimate the Lerner index econometrically from structural models of oligopoly behaviour based on conjectural variations.[63] There are several applications of this methodology in banking markets.[64] Neven and Röller (1999) for example, investigate industry conduct in European loan markets and find significant exercise of market power in corporate loan and household

---

[61] However, it must be noted that systematic differences in the maturity structure of loans and deposits between banking groups might also contribute to this result as they obviously influence measured factor price elasticities.

[62] For example, see Domowitz *et al.* (1986) for manufacturing industries, or Gual and Neven (1993) using price data for European banking.

[63] See Bresnahan (1989) for an overview and Genesove and Mullin (1998) for an application that provides evidence in favour of the accuracy of the methodology.

[64] See, for example, Neven and Röller (1999), Shaffer (1993) for Canada, Spiller and Favero (1984) for Uruguay, Ribon and Yosha (1999) for Israel or Angelini and Cetorelli (2003) for Italy.

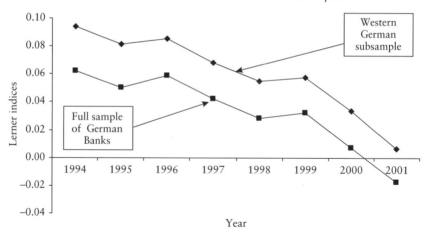

Figure 10.2. *Market power in German banking—Lerner indices.*
Source: Fischer/Hempell (2003).

mortgage markets. Given their estimate of the elasticity-adjusted Lerner index close to 1, they cannot reject the hypothesis of collusive conduct in Europe. However, their data and technique do not allow for the separate estimation of conduct parameters for the countries that comprise their sample and it is thus not possible to compare Germany to its European peers.

Angelini and Cetorelli (2003) and Ribon and Yosha (1999) analyse the effect of banking deregulation on industry conduct in Italy and Israel respectively. Both studies find significant shifts towards more competitive industry conduct throughout the 1990s. Fischer and Hempell (2003) employ a methodology quite similar to Angelini and Cetorelli's (1998) cross-sectional study and investigate industry conduct in Germany for the 1994–2001 period for a sample which includes almost all German banks that report their P&L accounts to the *Bundesbank*. Estimated Lerner indices for implied prices of compound banking services, including both interest and non-interest income, are displayed in Figure 10.2 for all banks in the sample and for banks from western Germany separately.[65]

The Lerner indices in Figure 10.2 are not adjusted for the elasticity of demand for the compound banking service, and thus should be interpreted with some caution.[66] Also, the use of accounting data in Fischer and Hempell

---

[65] The estimated model consists of a price equation derived from the first-order condition of a profit maximizing oligopolist in a static conjectural variation equilibrium and a cost function of the translog functional form. The cost function includes three factor prices as explanatory variables. The system was estimated with 3SLS instrumental variables procedures. See Fischer and Hempell (2004).

[66] However, most econometric estimates of, for example, the interest rate elasticity of loan demand yield values well below 1. See Ribon and Yosha (1999) for one such example.

(2003) raises some specific problems. For example, as their measure of price is derived from banks' fee income and interest income figures, unexpected losses due to borrower distress bias the measure of bank market power downward.[67] Furthermore, the maturity structure of a loan portfolio might seriously affect this measure of price.[68]

Taking all these difficulties into account, the Lerner indices reported by Fischer and Hempell (2004) seem to be moderate and are well below 0.10 during the sample period. There is a marked decline in the Lerner indices both for the full sample of German banks and the western German subsample, indicating an intensification of competitive rivalry throughout the 1990s. Moreover, higher Lerner indices for the subsample of banks from the western part of the country may be interpreted as preliminary evidence of less market power exercised by eastern German banks.

These figures, thus, do indeed support the notion that German banking has been quite competitive during the second half of the 1990s. Whether a similar conclusion could also be drawn for the 1970s and 1980s, remains an open question. Obviously, caution should be exercised in drawing strong conclusions from the few studies that are currently available and it is wise to be well aware of the fact that the empirical estimation of market power and competitiveness entails many methodological problems. Summing up, however, it can be concluded that the existing empirical evidence does not lend much support to the widely held notion of significant market power exercised by German banks.

10.2. A CLOSER LOOK—SELECTED ISSUES IN GERMAN BANK REGULATION

10.2.1. Introduction

We first of all review an episode of German financial market regulation—the introduction of money market mutual funds in 1994—in order to throw more light on the role of the *Bundesbank* and of monetary policy considerations. Next we focus on the building blocks of modern prudential regulation, that is, capital requirements, the supervisory process and deposit insurance. While the first of these issues is now fully harmonized internationally, the other two still display important peculiarities in Germany. In particular in supervision and deposit insurance, aspects of industry self-regulation still seem to play a noticeable role.

---

[67] There is little dispute that the frequency of such events has steadily increased during their sample period. Furthermore, it must be noted, that as an *ex post* measure of market power, these Lerner indices could also be negative for some sub-periods.

[68] See Hempell (2002) for further discussions.

10.2.2. Money Market Funds, Bank Deposits, and the Role of the *Bundesbank*

One of the relationships that seemed to have played an important role in the design of financial market regulation in Germany stems from the natural conflict of interest between bank regulation and monetary policy. Since the Second World War and owing to the trauma of two hyperinflations, there has been a strong desire on the part of German central bankers to pursue their anti-inflationary policy independently not only of political interference, but also of the short-term effects that it might have on financial markets and on real economic activity.

From a very general perspective, every central bank would prefer higher banking industry profits to lower ones, simply because higher profits lower the probability of bank failures, and thus of financial instability.[69] Given that financial stability is an important prerequisite for the independent conduct of monetary policy, a central bank might, in one way or another, influence matters in favour of incumbent banks' profitability. The argument that applies to the *Bundesbank*, however, is somewhat more specific and based on the viability of monetary targeting on the one hand and a natural conflict of interest between monetary and regulatory objectives on the other. This latter point—often overlooked—is made precisely in Goodhard and Schoenmaker (1993) who note: 'It is the German tradition which exhibits the greatest concern about conflicts of interest, and the greatest desire for separation of responsibilities; yet it is the German system, dominated by an oligopoly of enormously powerful universal banks, with relatively underdeveloped, competitive wholesale financial markets, in which such "conflicts" of interest will be least bothersome.'[70] The *Bundesbank* has always played a significant role in the regulatory process.[71] Besides its involvement in bank supervision, the central bank has had a powerful say in almost every discussion about financial market reform.[72] As an example, the *Bundesbank* always strongly opposed the introduction of securitized money market instruments issued either by the government or by private entities. The *Bundesbank* argued that these instruments would affect the accuracy and empirical basis of monetary targeting as well as the effectiveness of reserve requirements as an instrument of its monetary policy. Furthermore, the *Bundesbank* repeatedly maintained that such instruments would introduce

---

[69] See Cukierman (1992) for a discussion.

[70] Goodhart and Schoenmaker (1993) provide a nice description of the manifestation of this conflict of interest.   [71] See also Franke (2000).

[72] According to the German Banking Act, participation of the *Bundesbank* in the regulatory process is limited and, depending on the specific case considered, ranges from its participation in official hearings to the requirement that it explicitly agrees to regulatory actions undertaken by the Federal Banking Supervisory Office (FBSO). Especially in the legislative process the *Bundesbank* only acts as an advisor to the Federal Government and occasionally expresses its opinion. In reality, however, its influence has always been much stronger and was well beyond what could be derived simply from its legal status.

'short-termism' into the financial sector. In a Monthly Report in 1997 this was stated as follows: 'If a major part of credit terms is geared to short-term interest rates, however, the impact of the central bank's interest rate policy measures on the real economy increases, as does the risk of conflicts of interest'.[73] By preventing these short-term instruments from being marketed, however, the *Bundesbank* effectively protected the deposit franchise of German banks.

A nice example that further illustrates this point is the struggle for the introduction of money market mutual funds at the beginning of the 1990s. In 1988 the state of Lower Saxony proposed changing the law on investment companies and allowing money market mutual funds to operate. Until then, the Investment Company Act stipulated that funds were not allowed to invest in short term instruments with maturity below one year. From the beginning of the discussion on money market funds, the political side, that is, all political parties at the federal as well as at the state level, had a strong preference in favour of the proposed reform. The *Bundesbank* strongly opposed. It is striking that this veto was enough to stop any further legislative initiative for a couple of years. As in many previous instances, the federal government, in particular, regarded the *Bundesbank*'s veto as imperative. But in January 1992 the Ministry of Finance surprisingly launched another attempt to allow market funds to operate in Germany. In its outline for financial market reform, the Ministry explicitly proposed changing the law on investment companies accordingly. The *Bundesbank* responded almost immediately and a couple of weeks later it declared money market mutual funds as 'unwelcome' and refused all further attempts to introduce these instruments. The Ministry of Finance, in reaction, then withdrew its proposal and stated that it did not intend to allow money market mutual funds in the near future. In 1994, however, harmonization activities at the European level forced the *Bundesbank* to change its position. European negotiations on the so called OGAW Directive made it clear that national resistance against money market funds could no longer be sustained. However, when the *Bundesbank*'s decision to put aside its reservations against money market funds became public, this came as a real surprise to the market. Upon announcement of the *Bundesbank*'s retreat, German banks experienced significantly negative stock price reactions. Table 10.7 displays the authors' own estimates of cumulative abnormal returns for three bank portfolios around the announcement date.[74]

---

[73] See *Bundesbank* (1997).

[74] Unfortunately the announcement of the *Bundesbank*'s retreat is contaminated by a downward change in the discount rate and Lombard rate, which occurred the same day. This contamination however is most likely to lead to an upward bias of our estimate of a negative stock price reaction. Kaen *et al.* (1997), for example, show that during the 1987–93 period, a downward change in either the discount rate or the Lombard rate in every single case led to positive price reactions of banks' stock. Taking this into account, the actual stock price reaction upon announcement of the *Bundesbank* decision with respect to money market funds might have been even more negative than those documented in Table 10.7.

Table 10.7. *Capital market reactions to introduction of money market mutual funds in Germany—market value of banks*

Portfolio	Equally weighted bank portfolio	Portfolio of small banks	Portfolio of large banks
CAR [day$_0$,day$_{+2}$]^a (%)	−2.4*	−1.2*	−3.6*

* Significantly different from zero at 1% level.

^{a} Based on authors' own analysis; cumulative abnormal return for the three-day period [0, + 2] upon announcement that the Bundesbank puts aside its reservations against allowing money market funds in Germany in April 1994. The estimated market model includes the daily return on an equally weighted market index (DAFOX), the daily change in the long-term government bond yield and the daily change in the 3-month money market rate as explanatory variables; stock price data from Deutsche Kapitalmarktdatenbank, Karlsruhe; data on interest rates from Deutsche Bundesbank.

CARs in Table 10.7 indicate that the three large banks (Deutsche Bank, Dresdner Bank, and Commerzbank), which comprise the large bank portfolio (right column of Table 10.7) experienced more negative abnormal returns compared to smaller banks. This might be due to 'cannibalization' effects, since these banks have large investment companies as their subsidiaries, who were among the first to offer money market funds to their customers and thus created in-house competition for depositors' funds. An examination of the abnormal returns of single banks indicates that negative stock price reactions seem to be related to the share of savings deposits in a bank's financial structure (not shown here).[75] Although only based on a sample of thirteen banks whose stock traded on an exchange at that time, these results could be seen as an indication of more competitive pricing behaviour in bank deposit markets following the introduction of money market mutual funds. Some supporting evidence for this hypothesis can further be found in banks' pricing behaviour following the licensing of the first of those funds in August 1994. Bank deposit margins, defined as the difference between money market rates and rates on time and savings deposits of equal maturity, dropped significantly as shown in Figure 10.3. This figure displays an equally weighted index of gross deposit margins comprising different types of savings and time deposit products (the line in Figure 10.3). It also shows the number of money market mutual funds that were licensed by the FBSO and subsequently offered to the public (the bars in Figure 10.3). It might have been the introduction of money market funds that led to a significant decline in bank deposit profitability.

This story about the introduction of money market mutual funds covers just one episode of financial market regulation in Germany. It might, nevertheless, be seen as comprising two important aspects that have been of more general

[75] This is interesting because after the introduction of money market funds especially savings banks and cooperative banks offered new products in the field of savings deposits, which significantly increased the interest paid on these accounts. See also *Bundesbank* (1997).

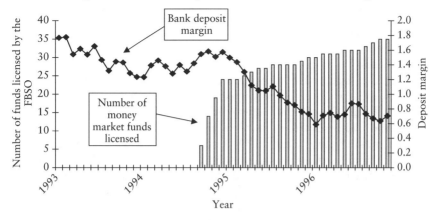

Figure 10.3. *Bank deposit margins and money market mutual funds.*
Source: Authors' own calculations; data from Deutsche Bundesbank, Monthly Reports.

meaning in the past. On the one hand, there is the strong role of the *Bundesbank* and monetary policy considerations which, intentionally or otherwise, might have had the effect of protecting banks' oligopolistic rents. On the other hand, there is the indisputable influence of harmonization initiatives at the European level that exerted considerable pressure on policy-makers in Germany.

10.2.3. Capital Requirements and the Supervisory Process

10.2.3.1. *Capital requirements*
As laid out in Section 10.1.3 above, most amendments to bank capital regulation (Principle I and the respective sections of the Banking Act) during the 1990s served to transpose European Directives into the domestic legal framework. As these developments are well documented in the international literature, and capital requirements can now be seen as the predominant and most harmonized of all bank regulations, we will forego further descriptions here. Nevertheless several remarks are in order. From a very basic and rather mechanical perspective, when a bank's asset risk is assumed to be exogenous, capital serves as a buffer stock against losses resulting from risky assets and thus reduces the risk of bank failure.[76] Tightening capital standards, therefore, forces banks to either raise new equity, boost retained earnings or alternatively to cut back on investing in those risky assets (e.g. corporate loans).

However, as Rochet (1992) points out, this perspective is too simplistic, as it does not take into account that bankers, as a response to mandatory capital requirements, might be induced to systematically reallocate their

---

[76] Capital requirements might as well effectively limit the amount of risk a bank can assume.

portfolios.[77] In the introduction to this section it was mentioned that asset-substitution type risk-shifting incentives are perceived to be an especially virulent problem in banking. The high leverage of limited liability banks creates incentives to take excessively risky positions. Flat premium deposit insurance that undermines deposit market discipline might even accentuate this problem. It is generally perceived that a primary objective of bank regulation is to deal with these unwanted incentives of bankers. Bank capital regulation not only serves to reduce the risk of bank failure directly, but is also aimed at making these incentives less severe. This is why the more indirect effects of capital regulation have to be carefully assessed. Whether capital requirements trigger perverse incentives in the sense that such reallocations lead banks to invest in even riskier assets, is still an open question and theoretical work yields ambiguous results. While some work supports the traditional notion that more onerous capital requirements lead banks to reduce their risk-taking,[78] others argue that capital requirements will do exactly the opposite and make banks pursue more risky strategies instead.[79] Unfortunately as is often the case in contemporary economics, theoretical analysis in this area delicately depends on the details of the modelling framework.

Moreover, one further assumption implicit in almost all theoretical models needs to be critically assessed: For all the arguments offered in the literature to be applicable, control over banks needs to be exercised by residual claimants with limited liability. Moreover, these owners have to be actively involved in bank management and have control over bank assets. However as Boot (2001) and Schmidt (2001) note, this is not a good description of the corporate governance of real world banks in most countries. In Germany, for example, a significant share of all banking institutions could be characterized as being manager controlled. The exercise of control rights by residual claimants in these institutions is weak at best. In some cases, notably in public banks like local savings banks and *Landesbanks*, a residual claimant in the usual sense does not even exist.

As well as cooperative and public banks, even the large private banks operated in the legal form of a stock corporation might fall into this category of manager controlled institutions. For example, the large private banks display ownership structures that are rather untypical for Germany in that they have widely dispersed ownership bases. Restrictions on voting rights have been commonplace in the past[80] and a majority of voting rights in the annual meeting is exercised by the bank's own management (via proxy votes) and the management of other banks. In cases where some form of concentrated long-term participating interest was evident in the past, this was mostly held by other

---

[77] See Santos (2000) for a survey of the literature.
[78] See Furlong and Keeley (1989, 1990) for example.
[79] See, for instance, Kim and Santomero (1988).
[80] See Drukarczyk (1986) for a short description of the case of Deutsche Bank AG in 1975.

banks or by one of the large insurance companies. As a result, bank managers were in a particularly strong position and in the event that outside control was exercised, this was by their colleagues rather than by their shareholders. Bank managers, however, might have incentives quite different from those of limited liability residual claimants.[81] Furthermore, for the risk-shifting problem to be virulent, it is important to have residual claimants whose ability to appropriate the gains from risky and successful strategies is not restricted in any way. Moreover, their liability needs to be limited in cases when the risky strategy turns out to be a disaster. In public banks as well as credit cooperatives there are no such owners, at least in the usual sense.[82] For public banks, the absence of residual claimants is even more obvious. Here, for example, the fundamental ownership right of selling off the asset is legally not defined. Given the current state of the law of savings banks in most states, a municipality would neither be able to decide to sell the local savings bank to some outside investor,[83] nor could it force the managers of the savings bank to pay out dividends in excess of the limits defined by the respective state's Savings Banks Act. In the fiscal year 2000 only 2–3 per cent of the profits of all savings banks were distributed to their guarantors.[84] Furthermore, because of the guarantee and maintenance obligation, in the past municipalities and states were fully liable with respect to any losses borne by the bank's creditors. There is considerable anecdotal evidence that because of the negative effects on public budgets and the burden for the tax payer, distress of savings banks or *Landesbanks* has a non-negligible impact on the re-election of mayors and state governments.[85] Furthermore, as already mentioned above from our perspective it is an oversimplification to classify *Landesbanks* as 'government owned' institutions as in La Porta *et al.* (2002). Closer examination of ownership structures of *Landesbanks* shows that on average the German states, the regional association of savings banks and other *Landesbanks* all hold around 30 per cent of all ownership rights assigned.[86]

---

[81] Except for the case where their labour contracts display high powered incentive schemes. But there is no evidence that high powered contracts were in place in the past.

[82] For example, in a cooperative bank, except in the case where the bank is liquidated, no member is able to participate in increases in the banking firm's market value. When leaving the cooperative a member can only redeem her participation at par. Although many cooperatives pay out dividends, this does not seriously contradict our argument.

[83] The same holds true for the states and their *Landesbanks*. However, we have to note here, that as a consequence of interventions by the European Commission, most states are currently reforming their savings bank law with likely consequences for restrictions on dividend distributions and basic ownership rights.

[84] We thank 'Deutscher Sparkassen- und Giroverband' for providing this non-public information.

[85] A recent example is the state of Berlin, where the state-owned Bankgesellschaft Berlin nearly defaulted, which led to considerable cuts in public spending. As one consequence, the former state government was not re-elected.

[86] While these institutions themselves are state owned, conflicts of interest are likely to play a role here. For example, business relationships between savings banks and Landbanks are very close.

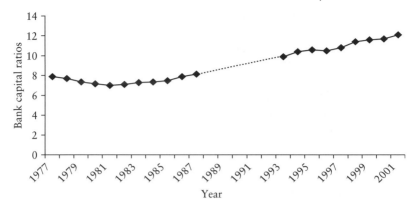

Figure 10.4. *Regulatory capital positions of German banks (1977–2001).*

Source: Regulatory bank capital ratio of all German banks. Figures for 1977–88 adapted from Rudolph (1992); figures for 1989–92 not available. Figures for 1993–2001 period kindly provided by Deutsche Bundesbank.

During the 1990s, there was a remarkable capital build-up of banks in industrialized countries. Jackson *et al.* (1999) show that in G-10 countries average bank capital ratios increased from 9.3 to 11.2 per cent during the 1988–96 period. Interestingly, this rise in capital ratios coincided with the agreement and implementation of the first Basle Accord. In Germany a similar pattern could be observed. Figure 10.4 above displays capital ratios (ratio of banks' capital to risk assets) for all German banks over the 1977–2001 period. Unfortunately data for the 1988–93 period is missing but a likely path of the development of capital ratios is indicated by the dotted line. Besides regulatory requirements following the first Basle Accord, several other explanations for this capital build-up are offered in the literature, market discipline being one of them.[87] Closer scrutiny of German data reveals interesting patterns, whose interpretations should take into account the specific features of the German banking system. Table 10.8, therefore, contains information about bank capital ratios, growth in total assets, loans to non-banks and book equity, broken down according to bank group.

As becomes apparent from Table 10.8, during the 1990s all groups of banks seem to have improved their regulatory capital position. However, capital ratios in 1993 as well as in 2001 were higher for private banks than for public banks.

This might be interpreted as support for the widely accepted notion that state and municipal guarantees undermine market discipline and provide public banks with a competitive advantage. Despite these lower capital ratios,

[87] Flannery and Rangan (2002) provide evidence in favour of the market discipline hypothesis for US banks.

Table 10.8. *Regulatory capital positions of German banks—results for different banking groups*

Bank group	Regulatory capital ratio[a]		% rate of growth		
	1993	2001	Total assets	Loans to non-banks	Book equity
Large private banks	10.2	13.9 }	2.78}	7.49}	9.86
Other private banks	10.3	12.9 }			
Savings banks (public)	8.9	10.8	4.62	5.18	6.76
Cooperative banks	8.9	11.1	4.33	4.28	6.84
Landesbanks (public)	9.7	11.3	10.1	7.55	14.31
Cooperative central banks	10.4	14.5	7.84	6.78	9.98

[a] According to the FBSO's Principle I. The definition of 'liable capital' and a bank's risk assets is largely in line with the first Basle Accord of 1988 and the respective European Directive.

Note: Per cent rate of growth is the nominal average annual growth rate over the 1993–2001 period.

Source: Deutsche Bundesbank.

German *Landesbanks*' long-term credit rating, for example, has been one or two notches above that of their private banking competitors.[88] According to Sironi (2003), investors' required return on subordinate debentures issued by European public banks is around 40 basis points lower than for otherwise comparable issues by private banks.[89] Especially for the larger banks active in the large-volume–low-margin wholesale market this turns out to be a remarkable competitive advantage. Interestingly, the capital build-up indicated in Figure 10.4 and Table 10.8 is stronger for large banking institutions that refinance a larger part of their assets in the capital market. This is also true for the *Landesbanks* and cooperative central banks. By comparison the smaller retail banks refinanced more heavily by customer deposits have lower regulatory capital ratios.

10.2.3.2. *Licensing, supervision, and interventions*

Besides capital requirements, the second building block of bank regulation as laid down by the Banking Act is a supervisory process that accompanies a financial institution's life from the 'cradle to the grave', that is, from licensing to (voluntary or forced) bank closure. Conducting banking business or providing financial services without being licensed by the FBSO is a punishable offence. Central aspects of the licensing procedure are concerned with the

---

[88] Moody's financial strength rating that disregards third party guarantees is C for most *Landbanks*, while it is B for four of the five private banks rated by this rating agency.

[89] It is important to note here that even private banks might benefit from an implicit guarantee by the government.

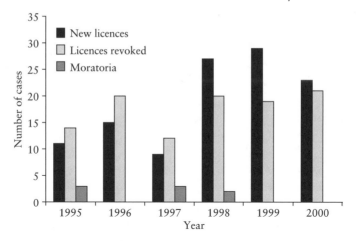

Figure 10.5. *Entry and exit in German banking—licensing by the FBSO.*
Source: Federal Banking Supervisory Office—Annual Reports.

applicant's minimum initial capital, number, qualification, and trustworthiness of managers and owners. Since 1976 licences are no longer granted to sole proprietorships, but in general restrictions with respect to legal form do not exist. Interestingly, the group-specific deposit insurance schemes also have a role to play in the licensing process. The FBSO is required by law to consult them whenever a new licence is granted. We will discuss the structure and role of deposit insurance in Germany further below. Whether the process of licensing by the FBSO, that is, the indisputable degree of discretion left to the authority, has the effect of reducing the rate of entry into banking below the level already implied by the explicit regulations of the Banking Act themselves, is difficult to analyse. Similarly it is hard to analyse whether the licensing procedure is especially tough in Germany compared to other countries.[90] As indicated by Figure 10.5, and given that during the 1995–2000 period there were roughly 3,000 credit institutions in Germany, entry into and exit out of the banking business was moderate at best. The number of new licences granted by the FBSO was in the range of 20–30 per year. The category of returned licences as displayed in the figure includes cases of failed banks as well as those that were closed for other reasons. It is a well-known fact in most countries that failure of banking institutions does not necessarily lead to market exit. In most cases failed institutions will instead be merged or taken over. This type of crisis resolution is also predominant in Germany's public

[90] The Barth *et al.* (2001) data set on bank regulation has something to say about entry and licensing. However despite the impressive amount of information collected there, we would find it hard to make any judgement about effective entry restrictions on that basis.

banking as well as cooperative banking sector, where such transactions are orchestrated by the regional association of public or cooperative banks respectively. Especially among cooperative banks a significant share of all mergers that take place can be interpreted as rescue transactions.[91] While this strategy of failure resolution leads to a reduction in the number of banks, it does not necessarily lead to market exit in terms of banking industry capacity (branches, employees, ATMs, etc.).

Also displayed in Figure 10.5 are the number of moratoria imposed by the FBSO. Such strong interventions by supervisors, however, require that the supervisory agency be equipped with all the relevant information. No matter how tight the regulatory rules in restricting banks and no matter how serious the regulatory authority is in enforcing them, information continues to be asymmetrically distributed between supervisors and banks. Narrowing this informational gap, therefore, is of considerable importance for the effectiveness of bank supervision. The timeliness and accuracy of information largely determines whether supervisors are able to detect problems and take appropriate measures. For example, the overall costs of a banking crisis to be borne by society are significantly determined by the existence of a functioning early warning system. Furthermore, 'gambling for resurrection' becomes a more serious problem the closer a bank is to default. If regulatory information is inaccurate and outdated, 'zombie banks' are likely to stay in business and pursue excessively risky strategies thereby significantly increasing the cost of a banking crisis.[92] On the other hand, maintaining a system of reports, audits, and examinations is also a costly endeavour. In Germany the system of transferring information between banks and supervisory authorities (FBSO and the *Bundesbank*) is especially close and presumably relatively costly. Unfortunately no estimates of those costs are available. Supervisory authorities have far-reaching rights to obtain information and significant obligations to give information are imposed on credit institutions. It is remarkable, however, that neither the FBSO nor the *Bundesbank* have built up their own staff for audits and examinations and that they rely heavily on external auditors to perform these tasks. It is only recently, since on-site examinations of trading activity and internal market risk models have increased in importance, that these authorities have built up their own capacities. In the near future, the Basle II framework will necessitate further expansion of capacity for on-site examinations.

Credit institutions' obligations to provide information, either in the form of regular reports or upon the occurrence of specific events, are considerable. According to the *Bundesbank* (2000), in 1999, for example, there were 2,254,194 reports on large loans (pursuant to section 13 and 14 of the German Banking Act), 43,091 announcements of banks because of special events

---

[91] See also 'Federal Banking Supervisory Office' (2000).

[92] A 'zombie bank' is a bank that is already dead from an economic point of view, but still around in the marketplace.

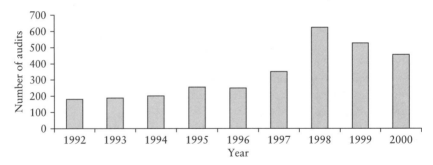

Figure 10.6. *Frequency of special audits by the FBSO (1992–2000).*
Note: Audits by the FSBO according to Section 44 of the German Banking Act.
Source: Federal Banking Supervisory Office—Annual Reports.

(section 24 of the German Banking Act), 213,172 reports in compliance with solvency and liquidity regulations (Principles I and II), 46,301 monthly reports on balance sheet items, 3401 annual accounts and 2690 auditors' reports on these annual accounts. Despite the large number of information items submitted to the supervisory agencies, external auditors' reports on the annual accounts remain the centrepiece of the information flow. External auditors have to comply with detailed auditing guidelines laid down by the FBSO and are subject to special duties according to the Banking Act (Section 29). While private banks are audited by independent third party auditors, the regional associations of savings banks as well as those of the cooperative banks have their own auditing staff. It is important to point out that for public banks as well as cooperative banks auditors commissioned by the FBSO are in most cases those of the regional associations of public and cooperative banks respectively.[93]

Among all information items available to the supervisory agencies, a distinguishing feature of auditor reports on annual accounts of banks is that they provide an assessment of risk, whereas most other reports do not. For example, the monthly reports submitted to the *Bundesbank* provide information on the volume of specific balance sheet items, but do not allow an assessment of price or credit risk to be made. By their very design instead, these reports seem to be much more useful as an empirical basis for monetary analysis. One weakness of auditors' reports, however, is the low frequency at which they are made available by audits of the annual accounts.

Pursuant to section 44 of the Banking Act the FBSO has the right to order special audits without specific reason at every credit institution. There is some indication that the relevance of these special audits has been increasing throughout the 1990s. Supervisors thus try to intensify the flow of information from problem institutions. As Figure 10.6 indicates the number of special

---

[93] This is indeed a very special feature of audits of German banks and might raise doubts on auditors' independence.

audits according to section 44 has steadily increased from 1992 to 2000 with a peak in 1998. Whereas in 1992 around 6 per cent of all licenced credit institutions were subject to special audits, the share of audited institutions grew to around 15 per cent in 2000 (20 per cent in 1998). The largest part of these auditing activities can be attributed to cooperative banks that have faced serious difficulties in recent years.

10.2.4. Deposit Insurance—the Private Club Model

As mentioned in Section 10.2 of this chapter, there might be a certain tendency to allow self-regulation of the banking industry in Germany. This can be illustrated by looking at the private club model of deposit insurance. In order to prevent the German government from implementing a publicly managed deposit insurance scheme, after the Herstatt crisis in 1974 the banking industry agreed to build up group-specific insurance systems.[94] The scheme of the private banks was established and is operated by the representative body of private banks, the German Bank Association ('Bundesverband deutscher Banken e.V.'). Public savings banks and cooperative banks have their own group-specific schemes operated by their regional associations.[95] Recent initiatives to be further discussed in Section 10.3.2 will lead to a replacement of main-tanance obligation and an abolition of guarantee obligations. This will probably increase the importance of the deposit insurance support fund of savings banks in the future. Rather than only protecting non-bank deposits, these schemes are safeguarding the viability of the institution as a whole, and are thus better described as support funds. Given that public banks are completely protected by guarantees and maintenance obligations by municipalities and states, a group-specific deposit insurance system can at best have subsidiary character and at first glance should not be expected ever to be required to pay out depositors. Although there is a clear priority of maintenance obligation and guarantee obligation (that is obligations of the municipality) over the deposit insurance scheme/support fund, these funds do indeed have a role to play. Most municipalities in Germany have large budget deficits and in the event of the failure of a savings bank, when the maintenance (and guarantee) obliga-tion is called for, they must refinance the necessary capital infusion in the capital market. This is where the deposit insurance/support fund of the regional association of savings banks steps in and often lends to the munici-pality at below market rates.

In what follows, our discussion will deal primarily with the insurance scheme for private banks, although some of the arguments apply as well to the cooperative and public banks' schemes. At first glance the most important peculiarity of the German deposit insurance system is its private organization. With respect to membership, several points deserve to be mentioned. First, the

---

[94] See Beck (2000) for a more detailed evaluation of the system of deposit insurance in Germany.
[95] These regional funds, however, are tied together by so called 'overflow agreements'.

FBSO is by law required to consult the deposit insurance schemes before granting a banking licence. This gives the deposit insurance scheme a quasi-official status in the licensing process. Interestingly, in the past there have been a few cases where the FBSO granted a licence but the private banking association denied membership and insurance protection. Second, membership in the private banks' insurance scheme is voluntary but mandatory for members of the German Bank Association. Subsidiaries of foreign banks that are association members can, however, opt not to participate in the insurance scheme but only a few have chosen to do so.[96] In principle the private banks' deposit insurance scheme could, thus, be used as an entry deterring mechanism, that is *de novo* banks could simply be denied membership, and thus be put at a serious disadvantage in competition for depositor's funds. In fact, from the perspective of competition policy the deposit insurance scheme is seen as a cartel, and thus is under the permanent scrutiny of the German Cartel Authority ('Bundeskartellamt').[97] Whether admission to the German Banking Association and its deposit insurance scheme was used by the incumbents as a means to keep competitors out of the market, is not easy to answer. Refusals of membership applications have not occurred very frequently in the past and among the 245 member institutions there are eighty subsidiaries of foreign banks. One such example, however, has been the case of Mody Bank AG in Hamburg. Although licensed by the FBSO, the German Bank Association repeatedly refused this small bank membership in its insurance scheme. After a newspaper report in 1995 about unsound business practices and mention of the fact that Mody's deposits were not insured, the bank experienced a 'run by its depositors' and was subsequently closed by the FBSO. Denials of membership applications also occurred in the cooperative banking scheme.

Protection of non-bank deposits is almost complete and amounts up to a limit of 30 per cent of the capital of the credit institution in question.[98] Given that there is no retention or coinsurance, coverage of the German system is by far the highest in the world.[99] The system is financed solely by contributions of member institutions who pay a minimum premium of 0.03 per cent of all customer liabilities (sight, savings, and time deposits as well as savings certificates). In 1997 risk sensitive insurance premiums were introduced; Member banks are now rated annually according to a five notch rating system (A, B, and C1–C3) and institutions with ratings other than A have to pay

[96] Voluntary scheme membership of foreign bank subsidiaries might thus be seen as an indication that being a club member provides banks with certain benefits.

[97] For example, every amendment of the deposit insurance scheme's charter will be examined and needs to be approved by the cartel authority.

[98] According to the German Banking Act, the minimum capital of a credit institution is €5 million, so that every single non-bank deposit account is protected up to a limit of €1.5 million.

[99] However, it must be noted that reimbursement of depositors is non-statutory. There is no legally enforceable claim of depositors and troubled banks against the deposit insurance fund. The reason for this peculiarity is not to introduce uncertainty in order to foster market discipline by depositors, but rather to keep the fund from being subject to the regulations of insurance companies.

premiums higher than 0.03 per cent.[100] The annual report of the deposit insurance fund has to be submitted to the supervisory authorities but unfortunately it is not made public.

Apart from the involvement of the German Bank Association in the process of licensing, it is also significantly involved in the process of market exit. Again this involvement is accomplished through the deposit insurance scheme. In the event that a private bank and member of the insurance scheme fails, the insurance scheme pays out depositors of that institution and in turn becomes the largest and most important creditor of the failed bank. It, thus, gains control over the failed institution and has to make the decision either to liquidate or reorganize. In the case of Schröder, Münchmeyer & Hengst, for example, the deposit insurance scheme had to put up roughly €176 million to pay out depositors and decided to split the bank into two parts, one of which was liquidated while the other was sold to a foreign bank.[101]

According to the EU's Deposit Guarantee Directive of 1994, every EU member country is required to implement a statutory deposit insurance scheme on the basis of public law. It was implemented in Germany in 1998 and again used the established organizational structure of the relevant banking associations. Thus, even the statutory system is operated under the roof of the respective banking association. Because of their far-reaching characteristic of safeguarding the viability of every single institution, public savings banks and cooperative banks are exempt from the requirement of establishing a statutory scheme.[102] The new statutory scheme covering 90 per cent of deposits up to a maximum amount of €20,000 takes the first hit, while the already existing schemes remain in place and supplement the statutory scheme. As a consequence of this implementation, the system of deposit insurance in Germany has not changed in any material way.

10.2.5. Bank Competition and SME Financing

Given our discussion above, the central issue of whether bank competition might be socially beneficial after all, and thus whether 'more competition' can be regarded as a valid goal of bank (de)regulation, remains to be discussed. Standard economic thought predicts that more intense competition will lead to more efficient market outcomes in terms of price and quantities. This notion has implicitly underpinned our discussion so far and no specific attention was given to the many different market segments and customer groups served by

---

[100] As Beck (2000) reports, this premium can be 'doubled or set at zero' depending on the financial condition of the insurance fund. Furthermore, there is a one-time payment of 0.09 per cent for new members. See Beck (2000) for the details.

[101] See Beck (2000) for the details.

[102] Two new systems have been established: one for private banks and one for special purpose public banks that are not members of the support fund of the savings banks.

(universal) banks. However, in the real world, all these markets are far from being perfect in terms of the absence of barriers to entry, the homogeneity of products and services and the distribution of information among market participants.[103] Note here that the mere existence of banks and other financial intermediaries is generally explained by significant imperfections in financial markets. Asymmetries of information, the incompleteness of contracts and non-contractable liquidity risk, for example, are at the heart of the modern theory of the banking firm. As a consequence, this theory itself paves the way for arguments that cast doubt on conventional wisdom. In a static sense, therefore, perfectly competitive banking markets could yield capital allocations that are dominated by those that result from oligopoly market structures in terms of credit availability, growth and stability.[104] Furthermore, in a dynamic sense, and even if competition were unambiguously socially beneficial, deregulating financial services by simply lifting formerly imposed restrictions need not necessarily lead these markets to converge towards the competitive benchmark. A more recent strand of the economic literature at the interface between finance and IO, therefore, analyses bank competition in imperfect markets for financial services. In the remainder of this section we will focus on SMEs and their external financing needs, and will thus consider only one of the many markets and customer groups to be served by banks. From our perspective, there are several reasons why providing loans to SMEs is especially well suited to analysing the effects of bank competition. Informational problems that are of great theoretical interest play a significant role in SME financing and might in turn have a considerable influence on equilibrium market structures.[105] Furthermore, borrower size might be somehow related to bargaining power in loan negotiations.[106] Even small differences in bank competitiveness across markets might therefore have a pronounced effect on SME financing. Besides, SMEs represent an important part of the German economy in terms of investment, value added, employment, and innovative activity.[107]

---

[103] To put it differently, what market outcomes should be expected in financial markets when the assumptions underlying the fundamental welfare theorems are not met? See also Laffont (1998) for this problem.

[104] See Perrotto and Cetorelli (2000) and Caminal and Matutes (2000a, b) for examples.

[105] Guided by the modern theory of the banking firm one might argue that this is exactly why bank loans play such an important role empirically in SME financing. On the other hand, informational problems might well feed back into bank market structures because inter-temporal aspects of business relationships to SMEs might constitute serious barriers to entry.

[106] Most empirical studies that regress corporate loan rates on a set of explanatory variables reveal that borrower size (sales, total assets or loan size) is a statistically and economically significant determinant of loan rate margins even if borrower default risk is accounted for. See the evidence in Elsas and Krahnen (1998) or Hanser (2001) for Germany and Berger and Udell (1995) or Berlin and Mester (1999) for the United States. The fixed cost of granting loans could be seen as an alternative explanation for this phenomenon.

[107] According to Deutscher Sparkassen- und Groverband the 3.3 million SMEs in Germany (sales below €5 million) account for 50 per cent of gross investment, 60 per cent of total assets and even 70 per cent of employment.

In a widely cited paper Petersen and Rajan (1995) argue that bank market power positively affects bank credit availability especially for young and risky borrowers. Given that informational and related incentive problems are a major obstacle to lending to these firms, banks with market power could weaken such problems by lending at concessionary rates when problems threaten to be severe. It is well known that in a perfectly competitive market problems of this type could lead to credit rationing. In a less than perfectly competitive credit market, however, firms with lower credit quality might be able to obtain funding. The argument is based on an inter-temporal smoothing effect. In later periods and by virtue of their market power, banks are able to extract a larger part of the project surplus from the good customers who survive. In the first period, therefore, banks grant loans even to the more risky loan applicants, because lender market power is like an implicit equity stake in the firm.

The empirical evidence in Petersen and Rajan (1995) indicates that small US firms located in more concentrated banking markets (*i*) show a stronger reliance on debt financing by financial institutions, (*ii*) take early payment discounts more frequently, and (*iii*) pay lower loan rates when young, and higher loan rates when old compared to similar firms based in more competitive markets. More recently Zarutskie (2003) finds that small US firms use more bank debt and less debt provided by firm insiders in more concentrated markets, confirming evidence in Petersen and Rajan (1995). A similar but more differentiated picture is drawn by Cetorelli and Gambera's (2001) study. These authors use cross-country, cross-industry data to assess the effects of banking market concentration on growth of non-financial industries. The cross-country dimension of their data allows them to measure the impact of more or less concentrated banking market structures on the growth of the average industry. The within-country cross-industry dimension raises the more intriguing question of whether this effect is equal across all industries considered.[108] From Cetorelli and Gambera (2001) two results emerge. First, the standard argument that market power by banks depresses the growth of loan customers cannot be rejected. This is in line with conventional wisdom. Second, there are some industries that might benefit from a less competitive banking environment as this improves the availability of bank loans as a source of external finance. It must, however, be noted that the empirical work in Cetorelli and Gambera (2001) or Petersen and Rajan (1995) is not fully able to discriminate among different possible hypotheses that link bank market power and credit availability.

Are there indications that similar results also apply in Germany? Do small and medium-sized enterprises more readily find access to bank credit in more

---

[108] Cetorelli and Gambera (2001) are especially interested in the cross-industry differences in external financing needs of young enterprises. The dependent variable in their regressions is the average (compounded) rate of growth of real value added for each industrial sector in each country between 1980 and 1990.

Table 10.9. *SME financing and banking market concentration*

	Firms in local markets with low concentration of banks	Firms in local markets with high concentration of banks	*t*-statistic (*P*-value)
Western German subsample			
Ratio of bank loans to total assets (# of observations)	0.17 (776)	0.22 (776)	3.17 (0.00)
Share of firms with bank loans in capital structure (# of observations)	0.55 (776)	0.59 (776)	1.49 (0.14)
Eastern German subsample			
Ratio of bank loans to total assets (# of observations)	0.21 (626)	0.28 (626)	4.70 (0.00)
Share of firms with bank loans in capital structure (# of observations)	0.70 (626)	0.78 (626)	3.40 (0.00)

Source: Authors' own calculations; data: Verband der Vereine Creditreform e.V.

concentrated banking markets? Given the importance of SMEs, banks, and bank loan financing in Germany, this seems to be a question of considerable interest.

To give a first basic impression, Table 10.9 displays summary statistics from a widely used commercial database provided by *Verband Creditreform*, the largest credit bureau for corporate customers in Germany.[109] From this data bank we select all firms that belong to manufacturing, construction, and mining with balance sheets that are available at least once during the 1994–97 period and annual sales below €25 million.[110] We split the group of firms into two subsamples according to whether the firms' headquarters are located in the eastern or western part of Germany. As shown in Table 10.2 above, local banking markets in eastern Germany are much more concentrated than their west German counterparts. Thus in order not to bias results, a sample split is warranted. In a second step these subsamples are split according to our measure of local banking market concentration. For the west German subsample a threshold level of 0.17 for the local Herfindahl was used, while for the east German subsample the respective value was 0.28. For every pair of observations, the average ratio of bank loans to total assets is higher for firms located in those areas where banking is more concentrated. Similarly, the share of firms that use bank loans as a source of funding is significantly higher in these markets. Although this evidence is more anecdotal,[111] it is, nevertheless, remarkable that it is in such stark contrast to conventional wisdom which

---

[109] We thank Verband der Vereine Creditreform e.V. for providing the data.

[110] For computing the following variables, we average over years to construct a cross-sectional data set.   [111] In particular, we have not controlled for any form of sample selectivity!

suggests that bank concentration will lead to higher loan rates and lower loan volume.

As already mentioned above,[112] the relationship between concentration and bank loans as a source of SME financing displayed in Table 10.9 could as well be driven by reverse causality. According to this, banking markets are more concentrated simply because firms located in these markets are more risky and less transparent. Given that the cost of granting loans to these firms is higher, only few banks have entered because only few of them could operate profitably. Furthermore, these more risky and opaque firms have few alternatives to bank loans when looking for sources of outside finance because banks specialize in lending to risky and opaque borrowers. The relationship between concentration and bank loans displayed in Table 10.9 might therefore arise as a natural consequence of the uniqueness of bank loan financing. This latter point is a centrepiece of the modern theory of the banking firm.[113] However, while the average quality of borrowers in a market is a determinant of bank market structure, banks should be expected to devote considerable resources to distinguishing good borrowers from bad ones. If this holds true, differences in average borrower quality between high and low-concentration markets should not be sufficient to explain the pattern in Table 10.9. Instead, for the reverse causality story to have any meaning, the quality of firm used to build the subsamples in Table 10.9 should be different, with the frequency of 'lemons' being higher in more concentrated markets. Matching subsamples of firms of comparable quality could, therefore, be one way to check whether the theory in Petersen and Rajan (1995) explains at least part of the patterns in Table 10.9. Unfortunately, with only balance sheet data at hand, the risk and opaqueness of firms is not easy to assess. As a crude proxy, we use industry classification and firm size (measured by total assets) to control for firm opaqueness. Overall the results displayed in Table 10.9 seem to hold even after controlling for firm size and industry. As an example Table 10.10 shows averages of the ratio of bank loans to total assets for all sample firms belonging to the construction sector[114] where the subsample is split according to firm size (measured by total assets).

The relationship between bank loan financing by SMEs in the construction sector and local banking market concentration seems to hold across all size classes. Similar results are obtained for manufacturing firms.[115]

Although providing only anecdotal evidence, the pattern that shows up in Tables 10.9 and 10.10 is very much in line with the predictions derived from Petersen and Rajan's theory. Furthermore it confirms empirical evidence from

---

[112] See footnote 51 further above!   [113] See Diamond (1984, 1991).

[114] According to German industry classification WZ93.

[115] Since manufacturing firms are more heterogeneous, we also switched to finer industry classification. Unfortunately the number of firms in each size industry cell rapidly becomes insufficient to obtain meaningful statistical inferences.

Table 10.10. *SME financing and banking market concentration—firms from construction sector*

Group of firms according to total assets	Firms in local markets with low concentration of banks	Firms in local markets with high concentration of banks
Western German subsample		
Ratio of bank loans to total assets (# of observations) — Largest firms	0.20 (64)	0.25 (62)
Ratio of bank loans to total assets (# of observations) — Firms of medium size	0.19 (70)	0.21 (77)
Ratio of bank loans to total assets(# of observations) — Smallest firms	0.11 (134)	0.16*** (117)
Eastern German subsample		
Ratio of bank loans to total assets (# of observations) — Largest firms	0.18 (69)	0.24*** (68)
Ratio of bank loans to total assets (# of observations) — Firms of medium size	0.19 (158)	0.23 (127)
Ratio of bank loans to total assets (# of observations) — Smallest firms	0.15 (174)	0.22* (160)

* Difference between markets with high and low bank concentration significantly different from zero at 1% level

*** Difference between markets with high and low bank concentration significantly different from zero at 10% level

Source: Authors' own calculations; Data: Verband der Vereine Creditreform e.V.

the United States.[116] Interestingly, the results seem in general to be stronger in eastern Germany where firms are significantly younger and riskier than in the western part. In Petersen and Rajan (1994) and (1995) the share of early payment discounts taken by the firm is also used as a measure of credit availability and it is found that this share is higher for firms located in more concentrated banking markets. Using a similar variable and survey data for small and medium-sized firms in Germany, Fischer (2000) finds a positive relationship between local banking concentration and the frequency of early payment by these German firms. According to Petersen and Rajan (1995), for example, banks with market power are better able to provide liquidity because of their ability to lend at concessionary rates in troubled times and extract larger parts of the project surplus during successful periods.

There is, however, a closely connected notion and complementary mechanism that might drive these results. It points to the relationship between bank

[116] See Petersen and Rajan (1995) and Zarutskie (2003).

market power and the incentives to invest in borrower specific information.[117] If close informational ties between banks and borrowers are value enhancing, then market power enables banks to appropriate a larger share of that incremental value via higher loan rates, which in turn makes information acquisition and relationship lending more profitable from the bank's perspective. Fischer (2000) puts this hypothesis to the test and finds that in Germany information acquisition by banks is more intense in more concentrated markets. In a loan application situation firms located in these areas have to disclose more private information to their banks. The study uses data on information items transmitted to the lending bank in a loan application situation. Besides merely measuring the number of information items, it also distinguishes between what could be termed hard and soft information. All regressions control for firm variables, loan variables, relationship variables and other variables related to the local market. Bank market concentration has a positive effect on the amount of information disclosed to the bank and further makes transmission of soft information significantly more likely.[118]

The reusability feature of information, in turn, allows these better informed banks to provide liquidity at short notice without incurring any additional costly transfer of information. Firms that have experienced a liquidity shock, therefore, provide an opportunity to conduct a natural experiment on the concentration–information relationship. If it were true that banks in more concentrated markets systematically acquire more information about their customers and if this information is somehow reusable in later periods, these firms should be expected to submit less additional information to their lenders whenever they are in need of liquidity at short notice. The empirical evidence in Fischer (2000) strongly supports this notion. Overall there seem to be benefits and costs of more intense competition among banks. While the benefits are well understood, the costs have only recently become the subject of economic discussion and have begun to be analysed. The incentives to acquire information about borrowers, thus incurring higher costs within the credit process as a result, might be one such source for the likely social benefits of market power of banks. The implications of these findings on information acquisition and monitoring intensity, however, go well beyond the analysis of the effects of bank competition for small firm finance. Of equal importance are the consequences related to bank soundness and loan portfolio risk.[119] Moreover, to date we do not have a very good understanding of how monitoring, diversification, and other aspects of bank credit policy contribute to a loan portfolio's risk–return profile.[120]

---

[117] See for example Caminal and Matutes (2000*b*).   [118] For details see Fischer (2000).

[119] Thus, for example, in an environment with aggregate risk Caminal and Matutes (2002) analyse the effect of bank competition on monitoring incentives and the probability of bank failure.

[120] See Winton (1999) for a discussion and a model of the interaction between loan monitoring and diversification.

10.3. CONCLUSION

10.3.1. How Should we Interpret the Past and Present?

When German bank regulation was first established in the 1930s and re-established after the Second World War, it faced a banking industry characterized by inherited structural peculiarities in both instances. The German banking system was and still is characterized by the existence of three strong groups or networks of suppliers of financial services: A host of small retail banks was historically tied together within the multilayer organizations of the cooperative and public banking sector. The group of private banks was dominated by a few large universal banks. The group character is least strong and least obvious for private banks, but as our discussion of the deposit insurance scheme has suggested, it also shows important features of peer control and self-regulation. In general, there has been a tendency to allow these groups to build their own systems, to monitor each other, and even to organize the bail-out of a failed institution within the group, rather than with the assistance of regulatory authorities. In some sense, regulators have made use of these banking sub-systems and even delegated quasi-regulatory responsibilities (e.g. auditing, deposit insurance, bail-out policies) to them.

It is not only that the actual implementation of regulatory activity has somehow adjusted to this inherited structure of the banking market. It is also that competition in German banking might still be best described as competition primarily among groups of banks. As a further consequence of this peculiarity, the larger part of all structural adjustments in the past has taken place within these groups rather than by shifting the boundaries dynamically between them. This is not only true for structural adjustments related to the banking business itself (with respect to products, markets, technology, etc.), but it also holds for challenges posed by regulation. Despite the fact that the banking industry has faced serious challenges during the decades since the Second World War, market shares and the relative importance of the cooperative, public and private banking sectors have, thus, been remarkably stable over time. Germany's banking associations have become enormously important in coordinating the industry and industry's interactions with regulators. Furthermore, they provide vehicles that perform certain tasks characterized by considerable economies of scale. For example, they currently play an enormously important role in building internal rating systems that fit into the Basle II framework to assess a borrower's probability of default.[121]

Since the Second World War monetary policy by the *Bundesbank*, that is, its overall strategy and specific form of conduct have also had a role to play. On several occasions, the monetary authority undermined financial innovation, involving the introduction of short-term securitized money market instruments

---

[121] See Schenk (2002) for further details.

and derivative instruments in particular, thereby preventing bank charter values and preserving the inherited structure.[122] What is even more important is that this structural stability has also conserved manager-oriented as well as interbank-oriented governance structures. High powered, owner-oriented incentive schemes, in turn, did not have much of a role to play in the past. The group character and the specific governance structures might have contributed more to the stability and soundness of German banking than any market power German banks were suspected to exercise.

In the introduction to this chapter it was noted that many observers considered German banking to be stable but not very competitive and further suspected that both these characteristics might be somehow interrelated. With respect to the competitive issue, caution should be exercised before deriving strong conclusions from anecdotal[123] as well as econometric evidence. While there is a strong public perception about the 'power of banks' in Germany, empirical IO could hardly be interpreted as offering strong supportive evidence. Even if the methodological problems of this research are taken into account, German banking, at least in recent years, seems to have been fairly competitive. International comparisons also indicate that German banking is competitive relative to most other European markets. Whether this was also the case in earlier times, remains somewhat unclear. Further research applying more sophisticated empirical methods is urgently required. However, a prerequisite for constructing good models might be a better understanding of the implications of the specific structural features of the German banking system. What does it mean to have a strong public banking sector acting like a large financial conglomerate, displaying features of political interference as well as self-regulation? The same question can be raised with respect to the stability issue. What are the implications of this banking business structure for future developments?

10.3.2. What the Future Might Bring

What does all this imply for the future of German and European banking? What are the implications of this banking business structure for future developments? One implication might be that the most dramatic changes in German banking are to be expected, whenever the boundaries between the banking groups shift. One such occasion could be the implosion of a banking group, when widespread defaults could not be handled within the group system any more and some outside help would be required. Although it is classified as an extreme scenario, taking a look at recent banking crises elsewhere

---

[122] This point is highlighted by Franke (2000).

[123] Besides a widely recognized but fairly general public discussion about the 'power of banks', this issue has also kept occupied parliamentary committees as well as political parties in Germany for decades.

suggests that events of this type should not be ruled out entirely in the future. In the introduction to this chapter we already made brief reference to the current notion of a general banking crisis in Germany.[124]

While some would argue that this crisis is 'systemic', and thus a serious threat to the overall economy, others do not expect German banks to be severely hit by a solvency or liquidity crisis in the near future.[125] Overall, however, there is little doubt that the German banking system is in dire straits, a fact that may be attributed to two main reasons, economic and structural.[126] On the economic side, the German economy is performing poorly, even by comparison to other continental European countries. Stock markets have plummeted and bank profits from trading, underwriting and M&A advisory services, for example, have deteriorated. Furthermore, profitability of traditional loan-related business has been seriously affected by non-performing loans as well. As a consequence of the poor economic conditions in Germany, borrower default rates are at record levels. According to Creditreform, 37,700 firms defaulted in 2002 (26,600 in western Germany and 11,100 in the east), with a rate of growth of 16.4 per cent compared to the previous year and 41.6 per cent as compared to 1999.[127] Bad-loan provisions by German banks have recently increased dramatically.

On the structural side, the low earning power of German banks seems to be systematically affected by the high level of market fragmentation.[128] As already mentioned, even the largest German banks have domestic market shares that are considerably smaller than their counterparts in other European countries. However, the fragmented structure of the German market is most directly related to the role of the public banking sector. Municipalities and states own banks that are allowed to offer a full range of relevant banking services and furthermore provide them with guarantees that lower their cost of capital. For many observers, this is a major obstacle to private banks' profitability. It is indeed questionable whether public and cooperative banks, classified as non-profit making entities have, in the past, put enough emphasis on pricing their products in order to achieve returns that are appropriate for the risks that they take.[129] On the other hand, in a world of capital requirements,

---

[124] Even the IMF has recently scrutinized the German banking system within its Financial Stability Assessment Program (FSAP).

[125] As an example of this perspective, see Sam Theodore (2003) of Moody's, who in March 2003 did not expect the rating of major German banks to slide below the 'mid to low A/Prime-1 range'.

[126] We again refer to Hackethal's (2003) contribution to this volume for empirical evidence on the low profitability of German banks in recent years.

[127] Banks in turn have become much more cautious in their loan granting policies. Survey data from different sources seem to indicate that especially small firms had difficulty obtaining credit in 2002. For the first time in Germany therefore, there is strong indication that a 'credit crunch' might accentuate the economic downturn and exert an important pro-cyclical effect.

[128] See Section 10.1.4 of this chapter further above.

[129] This might have had the effect of keeping margins down.

these institutions have always been forced to fully retain earnings in order to strengthen their capital base and be able to grow.[130]

When this chapter was written in spring of 2003, the German banking crisis was still in a somewhat unresolved state. While no serious bank default had occurred to date, the weak economic outlook for Germany and the rest of Europe has made us cautious with respect to making any premature assessment of the German experience.

With respect to changing industry structures, a less extreme but much more likely scenario than a severe crisis can be seen in the widespread willingness to privatize public banks or de-mutualize cooperative banks in Germany. Privatization of public banks has not yet taken place but has been the subject of intense discussions for quite some time now. What is, therefore, required is a serious evaluation of the advantages and disadvantages of having and maintaining a public banking sector in a developed country like Germany. An evaluation of this kind would also require public banks' performance in stimulating and stabilizing regional development to be evaluated. This issue is particularly important with respect to SMEs and low income households. Given that German SMEs are often seen as the backbone of economic activity, this discussion will be of vital importance for the future.

In the United States as well as in the United Kingdom there have been serious discussions in the recent past about whether banks need be required to target at least part of their retail business policies towards their own community and the SMEs and households located there. The Community Reinvestment Act of 1977, which was revised in 1995, was intended to encourage US banks to meet the credit needs of the low and moderate income neighbourhoods in their communities. In the United Kingdom, the Cruickshank report proposed to take measures that improve the access to basic banking services by low income individuals and households.[131]

Public savings banks in Germany have convincingly argued that such policy measures were unnecessary in the past because savings banks, pursuing a public mission and acting in their home community's best interest, provide a stable source of financial services to all groups of customers. Their business strategies are especially tailored to cater for private customers and SMEs. Basic descriptive statistics are sufficient to show that public banks are especially active in financing young and small enterprises as well as households of all income levels. From an economic point of view, however, the relevant question is whether this is merely a crowding out effect due to the competitive advantages provided by government guarantees.

As is well known, in 1998 German private banks initiated proceedings against the system of state and municipal guarantees for public banks at the

---

[130] In Section 10.1.3 of this chapter we noted that general mandatory capital requirements for banks were introduced as early as 1934 in Germany.

[131] See Cruickshank (2000: Executive Summary, pp. xxiv).

European Commission. Although much more fundamental in its significance, the actual complaint was triggered by a transfer of a state-owned building and real estate company from the state of North-Rhine-Westphalia to WestLB ('Westdeutsche Landesbank'), thereby strengthening WestLB's capital base. In 2001 the Commission required the German government to adopt 'appropriate measures' to make the whole system of guarantees compatible with state aid rules in the EU treaty. In February 2002 the European Commission, the German Federal Government and State Governments as well as the Association of Savings Banks and *Landesbanks* reached an agreement to restructure the guarantee mechanisms for public banks in Germany. According to this agreement the maintenance obligation will be replaced and the guarantee obligation will be abolished.[132] This will make financing in international capital markets significantly more costly for *Landesbanks*.[133] As a consequence of this agreement, there is little doubt that *Landesbanks* have come under heavy pressure to cut operating costs and restructure their business portfolio. While many *Landesbanks* were active in wholesale banking in the past, without state guarantees this does not seem to be profitable anymore. Many observers thus recommend that they tie in with the savings banks in their region to integrate retail business activities.[134] However, it seems highly doubtful whether savings banks will be willing to share even a small portion of retail business activities with them.

It is not at all clear what all this means for the future of public banking in Germany. Rather than an immediate shift in the ownership structures of public-sector banks, privatization of public banks will occur gradually over longer periods of time. In general, such conversion of legal forms may be seen as a prerequisite for further and intensified M&A activity, which might be an important option for the future restructuring of the industry. Especially in the retail segment, we expect considerable pressures towards industry consolidation and re-organization to arise in the future.

References

Allen, F., and Gale, D. (2000). *Comparing financial systems*. Cambridge: MIT Press.

Amel, D. F., and Starr-McCluer, M. (2001). 'Market definition in banking: Recent evidence', Board of Governors of the Federal Reserve System. Working Paper.

[132] Existing liabilities (as of 18 July 2001) will be fully covered by the guarantee obligation (Gewährträgerhaftung) until their final date of maturity (grandfathering). The maintenance obligation has to be replaced by a 'normal commercial owner relationship governed by market economy principles'. The latter makes necessary a reform of the Law of Savings Banks in all German states.

[133] WestLB was the first Landbank to restructure in response to these new challenges. In September 2002 WestLB split up into two independent banks that will be associated in a parent–subsidiary relationship. WestLB will continue to be an internationally active universal bank, while NRW will be a development bank with a 'public mission'

[134] Especially the rating agencies recommend such refocus. See Skelly (2002).

Angelini, P., and Cetorelli, N. (2003). 'The effects of regulatory reform on competition in the banking industry', *Journal of Money, Credit, and Banking*, 35: 663–84.

Barth, J., Caprio, G., and Levine, R. (2001). 'The Regulation and Supervision of Banks Around the World—A New Database', World Bank. Working Paper.

——, ——, and —— (2002). 'Bank regulation and supervision—What works best?', World Bank. Working Paper.

Beck, T. (2000). 'Deposit insurance as private club. Is Germany a model?', World Bank. Working Paper.

Berger, A. N., De Young, R., and Udell, G. F. (2001). 'Efficiency barriers to the consolidation of the European financial services industry', *European Financial Management*, 7: 117–30.

Berger, A. N., and Hannan, T. H. (1989). 'The Price Concentration Relationship in Banking', *Review of Economics and Statistics*, 71: 291–9.

——, and Udell, G. F. (1995). 'Relationship lending and lines of credit in small firm finance', *Journal of Business*, 68 (3): 351–81.

——, Kashyap, A. K., and Scalise, J. M. (1995). 'The Transformation of the US Banking Industry: What a Long Strange Trip It's Been', *Brookings Papers on Economic Activity*: 55–218.

Berlin, M., and Mester, L. J. (1999). 'Deposits and Relationship Lending', *Review of Financial Studies*, 12: 579–607.

Bhattacharya, S., Boot, A. W. A., and Thakor, A. V. (1998). 'The Economics of Bank Regulation', *Journal of Money, Credit and Banking*, 30: 745–70.

Bikker, J. A., and Groeneveld, J. M. (2000). 'Competition and concentration in the EU banking industry', *Kredit und Kapital*, 33 (1): 62–98.

Boot, A. W. A. (2001). 'Regulation and banks' incentives to control risk', *Sveriges Riksbank Economic Review*, 2: 14–24.

——, and Thakor, A. V. (1997). 'Banking scope and financial innovation', *Review of Financial Studies*, 10: 1099–131.

Borenstein, S. (1989). 'Hubs and high fares: dominance and market power in the US airline industry', *RAND Journal of Economics*, 20(3): 344–65.

Bresnahan, T. F. (1989). 'Empirical studies of industries with market power', in R. Schmalensee and R. D. Willig (eds.), *Handbook of Industrial Organization*. North-Holland, Amsterdam, 1011–55.

Bundesbank (1997). 'The longer-term trend in savings deposits and its implications for monetary targeting', *Monthly Report* (May).

—— (2000). 'The *Bundesbank*'s involvement in banking supervision', *Monthly Report* (September).

—— (2001). 'Bank balance sheets, bank competition, and monetary transmission', *Monthly Report* (September).

Caminal, R., and Matutes, C. (2000). 'Can competition in the credit market be excessive?', Center for Economic Policy Research. Working Paper No.1725.

——, and —— (2002). 'Bank solvency, market structure, and monitoring incentives', *International Journal of Industrial Organization*, 20: 1341–61.

——, and —— (2002). 'Market power and banking failures', *International Journal of Industrial Organization*, 20(9): 1341–61.

Cerasi, V., Chizzolini, B., and Ivaldi, M. (1998). 'Sunk costs and competitiveness of European banks after deregulation', London School of Economics, Financial Markets Group. Working Paper.

Cetorelli, N., and Gambera, M. (2001). 'Bank market structure, financial dependence and growth: International evidence from industry data', *Journal of Finance*, LVI (2): 617–48.

Courvoisier, S., and Gropp, R. (2002). 'Bank concentration and retail interest rates', *Journal of Banking and Finance*, 26: 2155–89.

Cruickshank, D. (2000). 'Competition in UK banking—A report to the Chancellor of the Exchequer', Norwich.

Cukierman, A. (1992). *Central Bank Strategy, Credibility, and Independence*. Cambridge: MIT Press.

Danthine, J.-P., Giavazzi, F., Vives, X., and von Thadden, E.-L. (1999). *The future of European banking*. London: CEPR.

De Bandt, O., and Davies, A. E. P. (1999). 'European banking sectors on the Eve of EMU', *Journal of Banking and Finance*, 24: 1045–66.

Degryse, H., and Ongena, S. (2001). 'Distance, lending relationships, and competition', Tilburg. Working Paper.

Demsetz, R. S., Saidenberg, M. R., and Strahan, P. E. (1996). 'Banks with something to lose: The disciplinary role of franchise value', *Economic Policy Review Federal Reserve Bank of New York* (October): 1–14.

Dewatripont, M., and Tirole, J. (1994). *The Prudential Regulation of banks*. Cambridge: MIT Press.

Diamond, D. W. (1984). 'Financial intermediation and delegated monitoring', *Review of Economic Studies*, 51: 393–414.

—— (1991). 'Monitoring and reputation: The choice between bank loans and directly placed debt', *Journal of Political Economy*, 99: 689–721.

Domowitz, I., Hubbard, R. G., and Petersen, B. C. (1986). 'Business cycles and the relationship between concentration and price-cost margins', *RAND Journal of Economics*, 17(1): 1–17.

Drukarczyk, J. (1986). Finanzierung, 3rd edition, Stuttgart: Fischer Verlag.

Edwards, J., Fischer, K. (1994). Banks, Finance and Investment in Germany. Cambridge/UK: Cambridge University Press.

Elsas, R., and Krahnen, J. P. (1998). Is relationship lending special? Evidence from credit file data in Germany', *Journal of Banking and Finance*, 22: 1283–316.

Federal Banking Supervisory Office (2000). *Annual Report 1999*. Bonn.

Federal Banking Supervisory Office (2001). *Annual Report 2000*. Bonn.

Fischer, K.-H. (2000). 'Acquisition of information in loan markets and bank market power—An empirical investigation', Goethe University Frankfurt. Working Paper.

—— (2001). *Banken und unvollkommener Wettbewerb – Empirische Beiträge zu einer Industrieökonomik der Finanzmärkte*. Dissertation. Goethe University Frankfurt.

——, and Hempell, H. S. (2004). 'Oligopoly and conduct in German banking', Goethe University Frankfurt. Working Paper, forthcoming.

Flannery, M. J., and Rangan, K. (2002). 'Market forces at work: Evidence from the capital build up in the 1990s', University of Florida. Working Paper.

Franke, G. (2000). 'Deutsche Finanzmarktregulierung nach dem Zweiten Weltkrieg zwischen Risikoschutz und Wettbewerbssicherung.' Center for Econometrics and Finance, University of Konstanz. Working Paper.

Franzke, S., Grohs, S., Laux, C. (2004). 'Initial public offering and venture capital in Germany', in Jan Pieter Krahnen and Reinhard H. Schmidt (eds.), *The German Financial System*. Oxford: Oxford University Press.

Freixas, X., and Rochet, J.-C. (1997). *Microeconomics of Banking*. Camridge: MIT Press.

Furlong, F. T., and Keeley, M. C. (1989). 'Capital regulation and bank risk taking: A note', *Journal of Banking and Finance*, 13: 883–91.

——, and —— (1990). 'A reexamination of mean-variance analysis of bank capital regulation', *Journal of Banking and Finance*, 14: 69–84.

Genesove, D., and Mullin, W. P. (1998). 'Testing static oligopoly models: Conduct and cost in the sugar industry, 1890–1914', *RAND Journal of Economics*, 29(2): 355–77.

Goodhart, C. A. E., and Schoenmaker, D. (1993). 'Institutional separation between supervisory and monetary agencies', in *Prudential Regulation, Supervision and Monetary Policy* (eds.), F. Bruni. Milano: 353–439, reprinted in Goodhart, C. A. E. (1995). *The Central Bank and the Financial System*. Basingstoke: MacMillan Press.

Gual, J., and Neven, D. (1993). 'Deregulation in the European banking industry, 1980–1990', *European Economy*, 3: 151–82.

Hackethal, A. (2004). 'Banks and banking structure', in Jan Pieter Krahnen and Reinhard H. Schmidt (eds.), *The German Financial System*. Oxford: Oxford University Press.

Hanser, F. (2001). *Die Struktur von Kreditbeziehungen*. Wiesbaden: Gabler.

Hellwig, M. (2000). 'Banken zwischen Politik und Markt: Worin besteht die Volks-wirtschaftliche Verantwortung der Banken?' *Perspektiven der Wirtschaftspolitik*, 1(3): 337–56.

Hempell, H. S. (2002). 'Testing for competition among German banks', Deutsche Bundesbank, Frankfurt. Discussion Paper No. 04.

Herring, R. J., and Litan, R. E. (1995). Financial regulation in the global economy, The Brookings Institution, Washington DC.

Jackson, P. *et al.* (1999). 'Capital requirements and bank behaviour—The impact of the Basle accord', Basle Committee. Working Paper.

Jayaratne, J., and Strahan, P. E. (1996). 'The finance-growth nexus: Evidence from bank branch deregulation', *Quarterly Journal of Economics*, 111: 639–70.

Kaen, F. R., Sherman, H. C., and Teheranian, H. (1997). 'The effects of Bundesbank discount and lombard rate changes on German bank stocks', *Journal of Multi-national Financial Management*, 7: 1–25.

Keeley, M. C., and Furlong, F. T. (1990). 'A re-examination of the mean-variance analysis of bank capital regulation', *Journal of Banking and Finance*, 14: 69–84.

Kim, D., and Santomero A. M. (1988). 'Risk in banking and capital regulation', *Journal of Finance*, 43: 1219–33.

Kroszner, R. (2001). 'The motivations behind banking reform: Why do lawmakers pursue deregulation?', *Regulation*, 24(2) (Summer): 36–41.

——, and Strahan, P. E. (1999). 'What drives deregulation? Economics and politics of the relaxation of bank branching restrictions', *Quarterly Journal of Economics*, 114: 1437–67.

Krümmel, H. J. (1980). 'German universal banking scrutinized', *Journal of Banking and Finance*, 4: 33–45.

—— (1983). *Bankenaufsichtsziele und Eigenkapitalbegriff*. Frankfurt: Fritz Knapp.

Laffont, J.-J. (1998). 'Competition, information and development', Annual World Bank Conference on Development Economics, in B. Pleskovic and J. E. Stiglitz (eds.), Washington DC: The World Bank, 237–57.

Lang, G. (1997). 'Wettbewerbsverhalten deutscher Banken- Eine Panelanalyse auf Basis der Ross-Panzar Statistik', *Jahrbuch für Wirtschaftswissenschaften—Review of Economics*, 48: 21–38.

La Porta, R., Lopez-de-Silanes, F., and Shleifer, A. (2002). 'Government ownership of banks', *Journal of Finance*, 57: 265–301.

Levine, R. (1997). 'Financial development and economic growth: Views and agenda', *Journal of Economic Literature*, 35: 688–726.

Llewellyn, D. T. (2000). 'Alternative approaches to regulation and corporate governance in financial firms', in R. A. Brealey, A. Clark, C. Goodhart, J. Healey, G. Hoggarth, D. T. Llewellyn, C. Shu, P. Sinclair, and F. Soussa (eds.), *Financial Stability and Central Banks: A global perspective*. London and New York: Routledge.

Molyneux, P., Lloyd-Williams, D. M., and Thornton, J. (1994). 'Competitive conditions in European banking', *Journal of Banking and Finance*, 18: 445–59.

Neuberger, J. A., and Zimmerman, G. C. (1990). 'Bank pricing of retail deposit accounts and the California rate mystery', *Economic Review*. Federal Reserve Bank of San Francisco. (Spring): 3–17.

Neumark, D., Sharpe, S. A. (1992). Market structure and the nature of price rigidity: Evidence from the market for consumer deposits, Quarterly Journal of Economics, 107: 657–680.

Neven, D., and Von Ungern-Sternberg, T. (1998). 'The competitive impact of the UBS-SBC merger', University of Lausanne. Working Paper.

——, and Röller, L.-H. (1999). 'An aggregate structural model of competition in the European banking industry', *International Journal of Industrial Organization*, 17: 1059–74.

OECD (1992). *Banks Under Stress*. Paris: OECD.

Panzar, J. C., Rosse, J. N. (1987). 'Testing for monopoly equilibrium', *Journal of Industrial Economics*, 35: 443–56.

Perotto, M., and Cetorelli, N. (2000). 'Oligopoly Banking and Capital Accumulation', Federal Reserve Bank of Chicago. Working Paper.

Petersen, M. A., and Rajan, R. G. (1994). 'The benefits of firm-creditor relationships: Evidence from small business data', *Journal of Finance*, 49: 3–37.

——, and —— (1995). 'The effect of credit market competition on lending relationships', *Quarterly Journal of Economics*, 110: 407–43.

Rajan, R. G. (1996). 'The entry of commercial banks into the securities business: A selective survey of theories and evidence', in A. Saunders and I. Walter (eds.), *Universal Banking*. Chicago: Irwin.

Ribon, S., and Yosha, O. (1999). 'Financial liberalization and competition in banking: An empirical investigation', Tel Aviv University. Working Paper.

Rochet, J. C. (1992). 'Capital requirements and the behaviour of commercial banks', *European Economic Review*, 36: 1137–78.

Rudolph, B. (1992). 'Capital requirements of German Banks and the European Economic Community proposals on banking supervision', in J, Dermine (ed.), *European Banking in the 1990s*, 2 ed., Oxford: Oxford University Press, 1993: 373–85.

Santos, J. (2000). 'Bank capital regulation in contemporary banking theory: a review of the literature', Bank for International Settlement. Working Paper.

Saunders, A., and Walter, I. (1994). *Universal banking in the United States*. Oxford: Oxford University Press.

Schenk, C. (2002). 'Banding together for SME credit risk analytics', *Risk* (November): 24–6.

Schmalensee, R. (1989). 'Inter-industry studies of structure and performance', in R. Schmalensee and R. Willig (eds.), *Handbook of Industrial Organization*. Amsterdam: North Holland, 951–1001.

Schmidt, R. H. (2001). 'The future of banking in Europe', *Financial Markets and Portfolio Management*, 15: 429–49.

Shaffer, S. (1993). 'A test of competition in Canadian banking', *Journal of Money, Credit, and Banking*, 25: 49–61.

Shleifer, A., and Vishny, R. (1999). *The Grabbing Hand*. Cambridge: Harvard University Press.

Sironi, A. (2003). 'Testing for market discipline in the European banking industry: Evidence from subordinated debt issues', *Journal of Money, Credit, and Banking*, 35: 443–72.

Skelly, J. (2002). 'Change now or lose business later', *European Banker* (October): 2.

Spiller, P., and Favero, E. (1984). 'The effects of entry regulation on oligopolistic interaction: The Uruguayan banking sector', *RAND Journal of Economics*, 9: 305–27.

Stigler, G. J. (1971). 'The theory of economic regulation', *Bell Journal of Economics and Management Science*, 2: 1–21.

Stiglitz, J. E. (2001). 'Principles of financial regulation: A dynamic portfolio approach', *The World Bank Research Observer*, 16: 1–18.

Sutton, J. (1991). *Sunk Cost and Market Structure*. Cambridge: MIT Press.

Theodore, S. (2003). 'Caution reigns over Germany for 2003', *The Banker* (March): 12.

Vander Vennet, R. (2002). 'Cost and profit efficiency of financial conglomerates and universal banks in Europe', *Journal of Money, Credit, and Banking*, 34: 254–82.

Vives, X. (1991). In A. Giovannini and C. Mayer (eds.), *Banking Competition and European Integration, European Financial Integration*. Cambridge: Cambridge University Press, 9–31.

—— (1999). 'Lessons from European banking liberalization and integration', Institut d'Analisi Economica, Barcelona. Working Paper.

—— (2000). 'Central banks and supervision (with an application to financial architecture in EMU)', Institut d'Analisi Economica, Barcelona.

Winton, A. (1999). 'Don't put all eggs in one basket: Diversification and specialization in lending', University of Minnesota, Working Paper.

Zarutskie, R. (2003). 'Does bank competition affect how much firms can borrow? New evidence from the U.S.', Working Paper. MIT.

11

Corporate Governance: Legal Aspects

OLIVER RIECKERS AND GERALD SPINDLER

11.1. INTRODUCTION

German corporate governance has always fascinated the Anglo-American world, both positively and negatively. On the one hand, in the 1980s some observers considered the German corporate governance system as a model for the struggling American economy to follow. By doing so, these observers argued, American companies might be able to overcome problems resulting from their excessively short-term oriented policies.[1] German codetermination and the insulation of top management from shareholders' demands for higher dividends as well as the opportunities for pursuing long-term strategies seemed to give German corporations the upper hand over their American competitors at a time when long-term investments and developments in high-technology markets were considered crucial for corporate performance and economic growth.

However, things started to change in the mid- to late 1990s when the performance of the American economy surpassed those of all other nations, including Germany and Japan. American spectators began to wonder about the seemingly outdated corporate structures, especially the strange German model of corporate governance, that did not seem to be able to adapt to the requirements of modern capital markets. In particular, the German model of codetermination at the supervisory board level is nowadays typically perceived by foreign observers in exactly the opposite way to how it was viewed in the early 1980s, and is often looked upon as a hindrance to necessary changes in corporations. Furthermore, the German focus on the corporation itself, and not on capital market requirements, is regarded as an obstacle to unfriendly takeovers, which in turn have for some time been considered a necessary element of any efficient corporate governance system. Furthermore, due to the globalization of capital markets, institutional investors have made their way to

---

[1] See Roe, 109 Harv. L. Rev. 641 (1996) with a summary and more references; Roe, Some Differences in Corporate Governance in Germany, Japan, and America, *in* Institutional Investors and Corporate Governance 23 et seq. (Theodor Baums *et al.* eds., 1994).

German corporations and their boards, demanding an internationally compatible corporate governance that can be understood by foreign investors. All of these factors have led to developments which range from the introduction of American accounting principles to the creation of a corporate governance code with legal backing. It seems that Germany is currently confronted with a corporate governance system in transition.[2] The traditional German model of governing corporations and monitoring top managers by closely knit webs of banks and other stakeholders seems to be in the process of being replaced by a more capital market-oriented governance model.[3]

The very notion of 'corporate governance' is far from being clear in Germany. In the legal discussion it is typically used to denote the internal legal structure of the corporation, that is, the system of checks and balances between shareholders, directors, and other agents or stakeholders, such as worker representatives. Sometimes, however, the concept of corporate governance is understood to encompass even more than that, namely the whole structure of the corporation and its relationships to its environment, including the capital markets and the labour market. In this brief survey, we concentrate on the internal structure of the corporation and the impact of the legal framework on the control of directors.

In legal terms, the potential shift of paradigm towards a more capital market-oriented corporate governance is reflected in the actual debate that considers problems of internal organization to be the result of capital market processes—in sharp contrast to the discussions of the 1970s and 1980s when a more 'internal' view of the corporation prevailed.[4] However, it is too early to declare that the German corporate governance system is actually dominated by capital markets; the remnants of a highly institutionalized system of insider-controlled governance still remain, such as the dual board system and codetermination at the level of the supervisory board.

To facilitate a better understanding and an assessment of the impact the recent legal developments might have on the German model of—legal— corporate governance, the chapter starts by providing a brief overview of the basic legal principles of the German corporate governance system in Section 11.2. In Section 11.3, the legal aspects of the organization of the German stock corporation are described in detail, focusing on the dual-board system and codetermination. Section 11.4 outlines the German law of corporate groups,

---

[2] Heeren/Rieckers, 14 European Business Law Review [EBLR] 595, 625 et seq. (2003); Merkt, 48 Die Aktiengesellschaft [AG] 126 et seq. (2003).

[3] Cf. R. H. Schmidt, Kontinuität und Wandel bei der Corporate Governance in Deutschland, in: Lassmann, Gert (ed.), Neuere Ansätze der Betriebswirtschaftslehre, Zeitschrift für betriebswirtschaftliche Forschung, Special Issue No. 47, 61 et seq. (2001) with more references; Merkt, 48 Die Aktiengesellschaft [AG] 126, 128 et seq. (2003).

[4] On the reasons for this change of perspective see Merkt, 48 Die Aktiengesellschaft [AG] 126, 127 (2003).

which is a unique feature of German corporate law and has important implications for German corporate governance. Section 11.5 addresses some current issues that may be considered as highly relevant for the ongoing transition to a more capital market-oriented governance regime. Among other topics, this section will discuss the impact of modern communication technology on corporate governance and questions related to the new German takeover law. The chapter concludes with an outlook on the future development of the German corporate governance system, especially in the context of its legal aspects. These legal aspects are indeed important. In this respect, we clearly share the views expressed by LaPorta et al. in a series of influential papers.[5] However, we are less convinced than these authors seem to be that the legal side is the exogenous element of any corporate governance system. Instead, this chapter is shaped by the assumptions that the legal and economic aspects of corporate governance are interrelated and that both are a reflection of more general developments such as technological progress and the increasing internationalization of markets for capital, goods, and services.

As the greater part of the German corporate governance system is still based on corporate law, we will only address selected aspects of securities law and their impact on the legal structure of the stock corporation. Moreover, as German stock exchanges still have little power to require listed stock corporations to establish internal corporate structures, such as audit committees or supervisory boards, there is (still) no need to inquire deeply into the nature of stock exchange regulations regarding the governance structure of listed corporations.[6] However, in this respect an innovation can be seen in the revision of the Stock Exchange Act completed in 2002.[7] This amendment provides stock exchanges with the opportunity to integrate regulations into their by-laws in order to enable them to react in a rapid and flexible way to changing requirements and standards. Backed by the force of law, German stock exchanges may now impose additional regulations on supervision and transparency for certain high quality sections of the market concerning lock-up-periods, accounting standards, and free-float requirements.

---

[5] See the references in the chapter by Eric Nowak in this book.

[6] Capital market regulation and investor protection are covered in the chapter by Eric Nowak in this book.

[7] In force since July 1, 2002; see Fürhoff/Schuster, 3 Bank- und Kapitalmarktrecht [BKR] 134 et seq. (2003); Fenchel, 32 Deutsches Steuerrecht [DStR] 1355 et seq. (2002); Fleischer, 55 Neue Juristische Wochenschrift [NJW] 2977 et seq. (2002); Zietsch/Holzborn, 56 Wertpapier-Mitteilungen [WM] 2356 et seq. (2002); Beck, 2 Bank- und Kapitalmarktrecht [BKR] 699 et seq. (2002); on the draft see Möller, 55 Wertpapier-Mitteilungen [WM] 2405 et seq. (2001); on the implementation by the Frankfurt Stock Exchange see Schlitt, 48 Die Aktiengesellschaft [AG] 57 et seq. (2003).

11.2. PRINCIPLES AND PECULIARITIES OF GERMAN CORPORATE GOVERNANCE

In this section we present and briefly characterize five characteristic and fundamental features of German corporate law, which are highly relevant for German corporate governance. We have selected these five features, not so much because they are legal principles, but rather because, according to our experience with lawyers, economists, and business people with an Anglo-American background, they are the least understood elements of the German system.

11.2.1. A Limited Set of Legal Forms for German Corporations

As in most EU legislations, German corporate law is based on a formal division between stock corporations ('Aktiengesellschaft' or 'AG') and private limited companies ('Gesellschaft mit beschränkter Haftung' or 'GmbH'). The two types of corporation are governed by different acts. The AG is governed by the Stock Corporation Act of 1965 ('Aktiengesetz' or 'AktG'), the GmbH by the Limited Liability Companies Act of 1892 ('GmbH-Gesetz' or 'GmbHG'). Although the distinction between stock corporations and limited liability companies does not refer to the size of the company, the latter type is typically chosen for purposes of small or medium-sized enterprises since the GmbH-Law provides a more flexible internal regime. However, unlike the stock corporation, a limited liability company cannot issue stock on the capital markets. Thus the legal form by itself limits its ability to raise equity capital from the general public. This is the primary reason why the stock corporation is the legal form for large publicly held firms with widely distributed ownership.[8]

In contrast to the limited liability company, the German stock corporation is characterized by a mandatory internal regime that permits only slight modifications by its shareholders (see Sect. 23 (5)). Thus, shareholders are scarcely able to opt for a different internal corporate governance regime other than the one provided by the Stock Corporation Act. Neither specific minority nor majority rights are allowed; the bulk of the internal corporate governance system continues to be mandatory, even though the strengthened capital market influence on corporation law might suggest otherwise.[9]

---

[8] In this chapter, references to the law are always references to the Aktiengesetz (AktG), unless otherwise indicated.
[9] Cf. Spindler, 43 Die Aktiengesellschaft, [AG] 1998, 63 et seq. 1998 with further references.

11.2.2. Lack of Clear Distinction Between Listed Open and Non-Listed Close Companies

It is a peculiar feature of the German legal and financial system that the impact of the capital markets on the legal framework for stock corporations is still modest at best. This feature is reflected in the lack of legal distinction between listed companies and companies not quoted on a stock exchange. However, although this feature is still not questioned as a principle, the situation is about to change slightly as an increasing number of scholars and judges are beginning to recognize the close relationship between corporate governance, internal corporate structures, and capital markets. Thus, slowly but surely, the unified legal concept of the stock corporation is being subdivided into two categories, namely that of the public exchange-listed stock corporation on the one hand and the close stock corporation, typically dominated by family groups, on the other. Even the Stock Corporation Act has already begun to introduce this distinction by referring to the so-called 'small stock corporation' ('Kleine AG') on the one hand and to certain obligations of the board which only apply in the case of being listed on a stock exchange on the other, such as the so-called 'comply-or-explain' approach in the recently introduced Sect. 161 (see 11.5.3).

Moreover, securities law is beginning to 'invade' and supersede corporate law. The most important example for this trend is the Securities and Takeover Act ('Wertpapierübernahmegesetz' or 'WpÜG'), which obliges the board of directors to follow certain rules of neutrality during a takeover fight (see Section 11.5.5). Other acts provide for disclosure to the capital market—thus, coming into conflict with certain corporate law rules, which tend to ensure that certain corporate information is only provided to a restricted audience.

11.2.3. Dual-board System and Mandatory Codetermination

Besides the rigid statutory regulation and the limited role of capital market law, another structural principle regarding the governance of German stock corporations is the dual-board system. It distinguishes strictly between a management board of inside directors ('Vorstand') and a supervisory board of outside directors ('Aufsichtsrat'). The dual-board system is mandatory for stock corporations and certain large limited liability companies. Embedded in this system of decision-making bodies inside the corporation is the further specialty of German corporate governance, namely the regime of codetermination that affects the composition of the supervisory board. Workers' interests are, thus, represented directly in the supervisory board, influencing in part corporate policy and strategy.

Closely related to the mandatory dual-board system, and at the same time a pivotal element of the German stock corporation, is the almost complete independence of the management. Sect. 76(1), a central rule of the Stock Corporation Act, states that the management directs the company under its sole responsibility. Shareholders have no (legal) right to instruct the directors to act in their interest. The inside directors have to report in a direct manner only to the supervisory board. Moreover, according to Sect. 131(1), shareholders cannot demand that inside directors provide information about the corporation outside the shareholders' general meeting ('Hauptversammlung'). As a consequence of this strong and independent position of the management board, the German corporate governance system can be characterized as managerialism subject to limits and control—limits imposed by law to protect certain stakeholder groups, and control exercised by key groups, such as shareholders, important lenders, and employees.[10]

11.2.4. Minority Protection—Largely but not Fully Neglected

The Stock Corporation Act does not offer a complete concept of minority protection. On the one hand, it provides detailed rules for the protection of minority shareholders of a subsidiary against various kinds of disadvantageous influences exercised by the holding company in a group of companies. But on the other hand, in many areas the protection is still insufficient. For instance, the admissibility of shareholders' derivative actions is strictly limited (see Sect. 147 for details). Although important decisions of the shareholders' general meeting regularly demand a qualified majority, the requirement of a blocking minority exceeding 25 per cent of the share capital present at a general meeting usually leaves shareholders with smaller holdings unprotected. To compensate for this deficiency, the rules of the Stock Corporation Act are supplemented with judge-made law, making use of general legal notions like the fair use of shareholders' rights (control of majority votes) and an extensive duty of loyalty between the individual shareholders.[11]

11.2.5. Creditor Protection through the Protection of the Share Capital

Due to the fact that the liability of a stock corporation is limited to its assets or, at the same time, that the liability of the shareholders is limited to the capital they have committed themselves to contribute by subscribing to shares and have in most cases paid in, one of the traditional purposes of the German Stock Corporation Act is the protection of creditors. The most important expression of this principle of creditor protection is a detailed regulation to

---

[10] See Charny, Colum. Bus. L. R. 145, 149 (1998).

[11] See BGHZ 103, 184 (189 et seq.)—Linotype; BGHZ 129, 137 (141 et seq.)—Girmes; see also Hennrichs, 195 Archiv für die civilistische Praxis [AcP] 221 et seq. (1995); Henze, *in* Festschrift für Alfred Kellermann 141 et seq. (Marcus Lutter *et al.* eds., 1991); Hüffer, *in* Festschrift für Ernst Steindorff 59 et seq. (Jürgen F. Baur *et al.* eds., 1990); Kübler, Gesellschaftsrecht § 15 II 3 c (5th ed. 1998); Timm, 45 Wertpapier-Mitteilungen [WM] 481 et seq. (1991).

ensure that the share capital[12] is paid up and maintained. Sect. 9(1) forbids the issue of shares below par. Furthermore, the rendering of non-cash contributions is strictly regulated to ensure that their value at least equals the share capital to which it relates (Sect. 27). Moreover, according to Sect. 66(1), the discharge of a shareholder from his obligation to make contributions is prohibited. In order to preserve the share capital, the Stock Corporation Act further forbids the refund of paid-in contributions. According to Sect. 57(3), only the net income of the year may be paid out as dividends. Closely related to the protection of creditors by preserving the capital of the corporation are the accounting principles laid down in the Commercial Code ('Handelsgesetzbuch' or 'HGB'). As Leutz and Wüstemann explain in their contribution to this volume, in contrast to the generally accepted accounting principles (GAAP) of the United States, the accounting rules of the HGB are much more oriented towards the protection of creditors than towards informing investors. However, these means to protect creditors via a far-reaching protection of the corporation's capital are no longer unquestioningly accepted in Germany. The discussion has been opened about whether other means to achieve creditor protection, such as extended liability of shareholders, might not be more appropriate.[13]

11.3. THE STRUCTURE OF THE GERMAN STOCK CORPORATION

The internal structure of the German Stock Corporation consists of three institutions: the shareholders' general meeting (covered in Sect. 118–147), the supervisory board (Sect. 76–94), and the management board (Sect. 95–116).

11.3.1. General Meeting and Shareholders' Rights

Shareholders' rights can be subdivided into administrative rights and pecuniary rights. The Stock Corporation Act strictly limits the latter, that is, Sect. 58(4) grants shareholders the right to participate in the net income as determined by the traditional German accounting standards which are, generally speaking, quite one-sidedly creditor-friendly. Sect. 271(1) states a comparable right regarding the assets remaining after liquidation. In addition, the dividend claim is limited by the obligation to set up a statutory reserve (Sect. 150). The distribution of the net income to the shareholders can be further restricted by the articles of association or by resolutions of the shareholders' general

---

[12] See Sect. 1(1) Sentence 2 AktG; according to Sect. 7 AktG the required share capital must be at least €50,000.

[13] See Kübler 39 Die Aktiengesellschaft [AG] 141, 145 et seq. (1994); Escher-Weingart, Reform durch Deregulierung im Kapitalgesellschaftsrecht, 107 et seq., 174 et seq. (2001).

meeting. According to Sect. 57(1), the refund of shares in the corporation is strictly prohibited.

The administrative rights include the right to demand information, which is quite restricted, as we said before. Shareholders also have the right of rescission (Sect. 243–248). The most important administrative right, though, is the right to vote. The number of votes attached to a share depends on the share's par value. For shares without par value the rule that each share carries one vote applies. Neither multiple voting rights nor the so-called 'golden shares' (preferential voting rights which cannot be overruled) exist. Moreover, in a listed stock corporation maximum voting rights are also prohibited.[14] There are only a few exceptions, partly of a temporary character, such as the provision of grandfathering voting rights granted to urban communities owning utility stock corporations, partly due to special acts, such as the Volkswagen Act, which limits the voting rights for each shareholder, and thereby serves to prevent an unwelcome takeover. However, these special acts are currently being scrutinized by the EU Commission as a potential violation of fundamental EU liberties.[15]

As a rule, shareholders can exercise their administrative rights only at the general meeting (Sect. 118(1)). At least once a year the shareholders' general meeting is to be convened by the management board, which also sets the agenda. A quorum of shareholders is entitled to demand the convocation of a general meeting and the extension of the agenda. Each shareholder is entitled to participate in the general meeting, to take the floor on matters on the agenda, and to submit materially relevant questions and proposals. However, as already mentioned, neither individual shareholders nor the assembly of shareholders as it is convened at the general meeting have the (formal) right to instruct the management board. Nevertheless, a strong de facto influence of a majority shareholder cannot be denied.

The shareholders' general meeting is restricted to taking basic decisions on issues listed in Sect. 119(1). According to Sect. 119(2), it may also decide on regular management issues, but only at the management board's request. In principle, shareholders' resolutions require a simple majority of more than 50 per cent of the share capital present at the general meeting, unless mandatory law requires a greater majority or the consent of certain shareholders. Additionally, the by-laws may also provide otherwise. Whereas the law seems to be clear—and highly restrictive—on the authority of the shareholders' general meeting, in the well known Holzmüller decision the Federal Supreme Court granted shareholders the competence to vote on fundamental issues of the corporation, such as the transfer of the corporation's most important

---

[14] Cf. Sect. 134(1) Sentence 2 AktG.
[15] See Frankfurter Allgemeine Zeitung [FAZ], 20 March 2003, p. 13; Frankfurter Allgemeine Zeitung [FAZ], 14 March 2003, p. 13; Frankfurter Allgemeine Zeitung [FAZ], 6 March 2003, p. 11, 13; Frankfurter Allgemeine Zeitung [FAZ], 20 June 2002, p. 13.

assets to a subsidiary (BGHZ 83,122). However, in practice, a great deal of uncertainty concerning the extent of this doctrine still remains.

On a shareholder's request, the management board is obliged to provide information on the corporation's affairs to the general meeting. However, there is a limit even to this basic information right. The management board may refuse to provide the requested information under certain circumstances, especially if giving the information would be likely to cause damage to the corporation.[16] Although shareholders may bring an action to declare void a resolution passed at the general meeting if a demand for information is wrongfully rejected, the general right of information seems to be difficult to enforce in practice.

The management board submits the annual financial statements and the consolidated financial statement to the general meeting, and the general meeting resolves on the appropriation of the net income, especially the dividends to be distributed. The general meeting also elects the shareholders' representatives to the supervisory board, which suggests that the elected members are representatives of the shareholders. But at least in a legal sense this understanding of their role is not appropriate as will be discussed at greater length in the next subsection. It was not before the late 1990s that the general meeting of shareholders was also given the right to elect the auditors.

The shareholders' general assembly also resolves on the articles of association and their changes, essential corporate measures such as the issue of new shares, the authorization to purchase the company's own shares, intercompany agreements, and transformations into other corporate forms.[17] This right to vote on changes of the articles of association is much more than a formality. The business purpose of a corporation as well as the equity capital are laid down in these articles. Therefore, the issue of new shares always requires a vote of the shareholders, which imposes certain limitations on the freedom of top management.

All in all, the factual and legal position of the shareholders' general meeting is quite weak, although at least according to the traditional legal doctrine in Germany this is not regarded as a weakness but rather as part of a carefully designed system. Shareholders' rights are accompanied by some duties of which the most important is the obligation to make contributions to the share capital. Moreover, shareholders have to observe the duty of loyalty mentioned above. However, this duty applies primarily to majority stockholders and only under exceptional circumstances to minority stockholders.[18]

---

[16] Sect. 131(3) AktG; see Hüffer, Aktiengesetz § 131 at n. 23 et seq. (5th ed. 2002) for details.

[17] Cf. Kübler, Gesellschaftsrecht § 15 V 1 a (5th ed. 1998) with further references.

[18] Cf. BGHZ 129, 136 (145 seq.)—'Girmes'; Lutter, 50 Juristenzeitung [JZ] 1053 et seq. (1995); Altmeppen, 48 Neue Juristische Wochenschrift [NJW] 1749 et seq. (1995); Marsch-Barner, 17 Zeitschrift für Wirtschaftsrecht [ZIP] 853 et seq. (1996); Bungert, 48 Der Betrieb [DB] 1749 et seq. (1998).

11.3.2. Functions and Composition of the Supervisory Board

11.3.2.1. *Main functions*

The main task of the supervisory board is to regularly advise and to supervise the management board within the limits determined by Sect. 111. While the supervisory board is not allowed to interfere with the company's day-to-day business, certain categories of transactions may be subjected to the supervisory board's prior approval by the articles of association or by a decision of the supervisory board.

Another major task of the supervisory board is the appointment and dismissal of the members of the management board. The preparations for the appointment of inside directors may be delegated to a committee, which also can determine the conditions of the employment contracts including compensation. The actual appointment, though, is a task of the entire supervisory board and cannot be delegated. The supervisory board represents the corporation in legal dealings with the management board (Sect. 112). Finally, it reviews and approves the annual financial statement. A chairperson coordinates the work within the supervisory board.[19] According to Sect. 107(1) the chairperson is elected by the members of the supervisory board and thus not by the shareholders' general meeting.

All corporate law reforms, which date back to the beginning of the last century,[20] had more or less the same goal, namely to make the board more effective in its supervisory role. The last efforts to improve the supervisory function—the KonTraG (the Act on Control and Transparency of Enterprises) and the TransPuG (the Transparency and Disclosure Act)—introduced additional rights of the supervisory board as well as additional obligations of the managing directors, such as substantial reporting to the supervisory board. Whether these recent developments will really help to improve the control of the directors, remains to be seen; fundamental changes, such as the introduction of a class action for gross negligence by the directors (breaches of the duty of care, mismanagement) are still being heavily debated (see Section 11.3.2.4 for details).

11.3.2.2. *Composition and compensation*

The members of the supervisory board who are not workers' representatives in a corporation under a codetermination regime are elected by the shareholders' general meeting. Their term of office is typically between 4 and 5 years. They are outside directors and as such not allowed to serve on the management

---

[19] Hüffer, Aktiengesetz § 107 at n. 5 (5th ed. 2002).

[20] For an overview see Spindler, Recht und Konzern, 56 et seq. (1993); see also Wiethölter, Interessen und Organisation der Aktiengesellschaft im amerikanischen und deutschen Recht, 278 et seq. (1961); Mestmäcker, Verwaltung, Konzerngewalt und Rechte der Aktionäre, 83 et seq. (1958); Hopt, *in* Recht und Entwicklung der Großunternehmen im 19. und frühen 20.Jahrhundert, 231 et seq. (Norbert Horn and Jürgen Kocka, eds., 1979).

board of the same company or a subsidiary at the same time. According to Sect. 103, they may be dismissed either by a 75 per cent majority of votes in the shareholders' general meeting, by the appointing shareholder in those cases in which a specific right to appoint is contained in the articles of association, or by a court for cause upon the initiative of the other board members. Note that a simple majority of shares is not sufficient to replace board members before their term has ended.

The compensation of the supervisory board's members is either specified by a resolution of the general meeting or by the articles of association. It should take into account the responsibility and the scope of tasks of the outside directors as well as the economic situation and performance of the corporation.[21] The average compensation for members of the supervisory board has traditionally been relatively modest in Germany.[22] But recently it has increased considerably.[23] It is still debated whether the compensation for members of the supervisory board may encompass stock options, as Sect. 192(2) seems to refer only to the board of (managing) directors, but not to the supervisory board.[24]

The number of supervisory board members depends on the codetermination regime of the corporation in question: If the corporation is not codetermined, the supervisory board must consist of three members or a multiple of three. If the corporation is codetermined according to the Codetermination Act of 1976 and has more than 10,000 employees, then there must be at least twelve members. As the vast majority of German corporations falls into this category, German supervisory boards tend to be large. Many people, especially industry spokespersons, are inclined to add that for this very reason German boards are also notoriously inefficient.[25] According to these critics, large supervisory

---

[21] See Hüffer, Aktiengesetz § 113 at n. 4 (5th ed. 2002).

[22] See Hoffmann-Becking, *in* Festschrift für Hans Havermann 229, 245 et seq. (Josef Lanfermann *et al.* eds., 1995); Hüffer, Aktiengesetz § 113 at n. 4 (5th ed. 2002); Peltzer, *in* Festschrift für Carl Zimmerer 377, 378 (Carsten P. Claussen *et al.* eds., 1997).

[23] The Frankfurter Sonntagszeitung, the Sunday edition of Frankfurter Allgemeine Zeitung, reports on 6 May, 2003 that the compensation of the chairmen of the supervisory boards of most Dax-30 corporations has almost doubled in the past year or two and can therefore hardly be called modest anymore.

[24] LG München 24 Zeitschrift für Wirtschaftsrecht [ZIP] 287, 289 (2003); Frey, *in* AktG, Großkommentar § 192 at n. 97 (Klaus J. Hopt and Herbert Wiedemann eds., 4th ed. 2001); Krieger, *in* Münchener Handbuch des Gesellschaftsrechts, Band 4, Aktiengesellschaft § 63 at n. 31 (Michael Hoffmann-Becking, ed., 2nd ed. 1999); Wiechers, 56 Der Betrieb [DB] 595, 595 et seq. (2003); see, however, OLG Schleswig 48 Die Aktiengesellschaft [AG], 102 (2003): the court held that stock options for supervisory board members do not contradict the restrictions in Sect. 192.

[25] Bernhardt, 159 Zeitschrift für das gesamte Handels- und Wirtschaftsrecht [ZHR] 310 et seq. (1995); Graf Lambsdorff, *in* Corporate Governance (Dieter Feddersen, Peter Hommelhoff and Uwe H. Schneider eds., 1996), 217, 226 et seq; see also Ulmer, 166 Zeitschrift für das gesamte Handels- und Wirtschaftsrecht [ZHR] 271, 275 (2002).

boards tend to transform their character into some sort of a political arena, while the essential work is shifted to committees.

11.3.2.3. *Codetermination*

A unique and much criticized feature of the German system is legally mandated codetermination.[26] There are three different forms or models of codetermination: the one-third model, the full-parity model, and the quasi-parity model.

The one-third model is based on the Works Council Constitution Act of 1952 ('Betriebsverfassungsgesetz 1952' or 'BetrVG 1952') and principally applies to all corporations—AGs as well as GmbHs—with more than 500 employees. As the name indicates, one-third of the supervisory board members is elected by the employees, and the rest by the shareholders.

The full-parity model applies only to corporations in the mining and steel-making industries. Under this model, labour side and capital side send an equal number of persons to the board, and the majority of these members jointly select a neutral so-called 'eleventh man'. Under this model, there is simply no majority for the capital side.

The most important case of legally mandated codetermination is that of quasi-parity. It is based on the Codetermination Act of 1976 ('Mitbestimmungsgesetz' or 'MitbestG') and is applicable to stock corporations and private limited companies outside the mining industry with more than 2,000 employees. The Codetermination Statute states that one half of the supervisory board members is elected by the employees, the other half by the shareholders. The members elected by the employees must include a certain number of representatives of the relevant unions.[27] A peculiarity of the quasi-parity model is that the chairman of the supervisory board has the deciding vote in the event of a tie.[28] The voting procedure set forth in the Codetermination Act is designed in such a way that the chairman may not be elected against the wishes of the share-holders' representatives on the supervisory board. In combination with the chairman's casting vote this procedure ensures a slight superiority of the shareholders, which explains the term 'quasi-parity'. In practice, in almost all corporations the chairman is a representative of the shareholders' side, whereas the vice-chairman is elected by the workers' representatives.

Although the impact of codetermination on corporate performance has been frequently discussed in the German legal and economic literature,[29] codetermination as a whole is currently not questioned, at least not publicly, in Germany. As it seems, German unions consider it as one of their main assets.

---

[26] Cf. Roe, 5 Colum. J. Eur. L. 199 et seq. (1998); see also the comment by Kübler, 5 Colum. J. Eur. L. 213 et seq. (1998). [27] Cf. Sect. 7(2) MitbestG.

[28] Sect. 29(2) MitbestG; cf. Kübler, Gesellschaftsrecht § 32 III 3 b (5th ed. 1998).

[29] See Wiedemann, Gesellschaftsrecht § 11 I 2 (1980) with further references to the legal literature and Schmidt, this volume, with further references to the economic literature.

Even the last commission which was mandated by the German government to look into the German corporate governance system from a mainly legal standpoint and to suggest specific improvements, the so-called Baums-Commission, excluded this topic from its deliberations as it was considered too controversial.[30]

11.3.2.4. *Conflicts of interest and liability*

Like the members of the management board (see below), those of the supervisory board are obliged to act in the enterprise's best interests.[31] However, as long as the interests of the workers' side and the general public are not inappropriately restrained, this restriction does not exclude the possibility to pursue specific interests within a pluralistic supervisory board (e.g. the employees' representatives in a codetermined supervisory board may support the interests of the employees).[32] Hence, a rule to act exclusively in the (long-term) interest of shareholders or even to strictly maximize shareholder value is not only not contained in the law, it would even be incompatible with German corporate law.[33]

Members of the supervisory board neglecting their duties are liable to the company.[34] However, in the case of a conflict of interest it has to be considered that, unlike the managing directors, the members of the supervisory board only work on a sideline basis.[35] Therefore, they may pursue personal interests to the extent that the exercise of their mandate is not compromised.[36]

11.3.3. Functions and Powers of the Management Board

11.3.3.1. *General rules*

The management board represents the company in its business dealings and legal affairs (Sect. 76–78). It bears the sole responsibility for managing the

[30] Regierungskommission Corporate Governance ('Baums-Commission') in Baums, Bericht der Regierungskommission Corporate Governance, at n. 3 (2001).

[31] Cf. BGHZ 64, 325 (329 et seq.)—Bayer; Kübler, Gesellschaftsrecht § 15 IV 3 b (5th ed. 1998).

[32] Cf. Kübler, Gesellschaftsrecht § 32 III 4 a (5th ed. 1998).

[33] Hefermehl/Spindler, *in* Münchener Kommentar zum AktG, § 76 at n. 46 et seq. (Kropff and Semler eds., 2nd ed. 2003); Mertens, *in* Kölner Kommentar § 76 at n. 16 (Wolfgang Zöllner ed., 2nd ed. 1996); Semler, Leitung und Überwachung der Aktiengesellschaft, at n. 51et seq. See also below note 47 seq. with further references. For one of the critics of this concept see Zöllner, 48 Die Aktiengesellschaft [AG] 2, 7 (2003).

[34] Sect. 116, 93(2) AktG.

[35] Cf. Hoffmann-Becking, *in* Münchener Handbuch des Gesellschaftsrechts, Band 4, Aktiengesellschaft § 22 at n. 49 (Michael Hoffmann-Becking, ed., 2nd ed. 1999); Hüffer, Aktiengesetz § 116 at n. 4 (5th ed. 2002); Kübler, Gesellschaftsrecht § 15 IV 3 b (5th ed. 1998); Ulmer, 43 Neue Juristische Wochenschrift [NJW] 1603, 1605 et seq. (1980).

[36] Kübler, Gesellschaftsrecht § 15 IV 3 b (5th ed. 1998); see also R. H. Schmidt, Chapter 12 in this volume.

enterprise. This is laid down in Sect. 76(1), and it is the legal foundation of the far-reaching independence of the management board. In fulfilling its task, the management board as well as its individual members are obliged to act in the company's best interests and to undertake to increase the sustainable value of the enterprise (Sect. 93(1)). This notion is, however, not equivalent to shareholder value, implying that by law the management does not have the sole task of acting in the shareholders' interests. The 'interest of the enterprise', to which management is committed, can be understood as a compromise between shareholders' interests, creditors' interests, and employees' interests—a notoriously vague legal concept.[37] The independence of the management board implies, from a legal perspective, that neither the shareholders nor the supervisory board may issue directives to the inside directors regarding the management of the corporation. However, in practice, this does not prevent majority stockholders from strongly influencing the board of directors. Moreover, the powers of the management board may be limited by the articles of association or by the supervisory board. However, such limitations do not affect third parties (Sect. 82).

11.3.3.2. *Composition*
The members of the management board are appointed by the supervisory board for a term of 5 years at the most (Sect. 84(1)). The appointment can be renewed for additional periods of up to 5 years. The inside directors can also be dismissed by the supervisory board, but only for due cause. The mere fact that the supervisory board has lost its trust in the capabilities of the directors or the management board as a whole would not be sufficient reason to dismiss the elected directors; this reflects again the strong position of the board and the directors' independence. Moreover, shareholders may not issue instructions to the members of the supervisory board as to which directors should be appointed.[38] Even agreements between shareholders on the composition of the management board cannot bind the members of the supervisory board. In practice, however, informal consultations between majority shareholders and the supervisory board usually occur, and therefore it is unlikely that the latter will appoint inside directors who are unacceptable to the majority shareholders.

The management board usually comprises several persons. Only individuals may serve on the board. Pursuant to Sect. 33 of the Codetermination Act of 1976, a stock corporation with more than 2,000 employees must have a director representing the employees ('labour director') as a member of the management board responsible for employment affairs. The management board may have a speaker or chairman. If so, the position and influence of the

---

[37] Cf. Schmidt/Spindler, *in* Wirtschafts- und Medienrecht in der offenen Demokratie, Freundesgabe für Friedrich Kübler 515 et seq. (Heinz-Dieter Assmann *et al.* eds., 1997) with further references. [38] Cf. Hüffer, Aktiengesetz § 84 at n. 5 (5th ed. 2002).

latter is not comparable to that of a US-style CEO since he can neither hold a seat in the supervisory board nor can he decide against the majority of inside directors.[39]

11.3.3.3. Compensation

Compensation of the management board's members is determined by the supervisory board at an appropriate amount based on a performance assessment. Most supervisory boards have delegated the task of determining the compensation and of drafting the contracts with the directors to a special committee, sometimes called the compensation committee. Criteria for determining the appropriateness of compensation are, in particular, the tasks of the director, his or her performance, the economic situation and the performance and outlook of the enterprise.[40]

One of the main topics concerning compensation refers to the means to overcome the principal–agent-conflict, since the characteristic feature of the publicly held corporation is the separation of ownership and control.[41] The management consists of persons who are experienced in business and involved in it on a full-time basis, whereas the typical shareholder is neither knowledgeable about the business of the firm, nor does he derive an important part of his livelihood from it. Like a bondholder, the typical shareholder is a passive investor with a mere financial rather than a managerial interest. Nevertheless, shareholders are more vulnerable than bondholders. Since the latter have a superior claim on their interest and repayments, their concern is primarily that the firm is not being so badly mismanaged that it defaults on its interest payments or is unable to repay a loan or a bond when it matures. In contrast, shareholders' returns are directly related both to how well the firm is managed and to how scrupulously the managers allot a portion of the firm's income to the shareholders. The danger of disloyalty is more serious for shareholders than that of mismanagement, since the latter is not in the directors' own interests. Although managers have a strong incentive to manage the firm well, their incentive to deal fairly with shareholders is weaker.[42]

A way to counteract this problem is to align directors' self-interest with that of the shareholders through performance-based compensation. Until quite

---

[39] Note, however, that actually the Deutsche Bank AG is trying to install a CEO who chairs not only the board, but also the so-called group executive committee. This committee performs many of those functions which in most other cases are board functions, and in this committee, the speaker of the management board of Deutsche Bank may overrule the other members. Whether courts will undermine this structure remains to be seen.

[40] Hefermehl/Spindler, *in* Münchener Kommentar zum AktG, § 87 at n. 42 (Bruno Kropff and Johannes Semler eds., 2nd ed. 2003); Mertens, *in* Kölner Kommentar § 87 at n. 12 (Wolfgang Zöllner ed., 2nd ed. 1996); Hüffer, Aktiengesetz § 87 at n. 7 (5th ed. 2002).

[41] Cf. Easterbrook/Fischel, The Economic Structure of Corporate Law 90 et seq. (1991); Posner, Economic Analysis of Law § 14.7 (6th ed. 2002).

[42] See Posner, Economic Analysis of Law § 14.7 (6th ed. 2002).

recently, the performance-dependent compensation usually consisted solely of a participation in profits or in bonus schemes. In recent years, though, market-oriented compensation mechanisms have become more popular as a variable salary component with long-term incentive effects. The alignment of managers' self-interest with that of shareholders is widely held to be a better-suited device for preventing the violation of contractual or statutory duties than liability instruments. Whereas stock option plans are well known in the United States and the United Kingdom, German corporations did not offer participation in such schemes until very recently.[43] The main reason for this reluctance has been the former restrictive rules of the Stock Corporation Act concerning remuneration schemes for board members. It was not until 1998 that the admissibility of stock option plans was acknowledged by the German legislature in an amendment to the Stock Corporation Act called Act on Control and Transparency of Enterprises (KonTraG).

The new regulation has been widely approved by commentators.[44] Besides the extended opportunities to create incentive schemes for members of the management board, it also helps to adjust German corporate law to international standards. With markets becoming increasingly international, executives are sought after on an international basis. This fact makes it necessary to be able to offer remuneration packages which are attractive by international standards.

This development can be deemed as another manifestation of the transition of German corporate law to a more capital market-oriented governance regime. However, even today the legal and practical limits to the use of stock options are not yet clear; several issues remain to be resolved by the Federal Supreme Court.

The shareholders' general meeting decides on the establishment of a stock option plan and, according to Sect. 193(2), on the distribution of the stock options among the members of the management board and the employees. Note that even if a stock option plan is set up by the general meeting, only the supervisory board decides whether stock options should be a variable component of the managing directors' compensation.

11.3.3.4. *Conflicts of interest*

During their employment for the enterprise, members of the management board are subject to a comprehensive non-competition obligation.[45] Furthermore, no inside director may pursue personal interests in his decisions or personally use business opportunities intended for the enterprise. The

---

[43] Cf. Fleischer, 30 Zeitschrift für Unternehmens- und Gesellschaftsrecht [ZGR] 1, 9 (2001); *see also* Adams, 23 Zeitschrift für Wirtschaftsrecht [ZIP] 1325 et seq. (2002).

[44] See Hüffer, Aktiengesetz § 192 at n. 17 (5th ed. 2002) with further references.

[45] Sect. 88 AktG. On the details see Hefermehl/Spindler, *in* Münchener Kommentar zum AktG, § 88 at n. 1 et seq. (Bruno Kropff and Johannes Semler eds., 2nd ed. 2003).

members of the management board are obliged to act in the enterprises' best interests. The broad scope given to the inside directors by Sect. 76(1) requires them to take into account not only the interests of shareholders, but also those of other stakeholders, such as employees, creditors and even the general public. The management board has to aim at a reconciliation of interests for each individual case.[46]

Recently, a broad discussion among German legal scholars emerged on the question whether the articles of association can authorize the management board to act on the basis of the so-called 'shareholder value' concept.[47] This concept would oblige the directors to undertake those and only those measures which would raise the value of a company's shares. The supporters of this concept point out that the realization of profits is the typical objective of a stock corporation,[48] whereas the opponents mainly refer to the history of today's Sect. 76.[49] They argue that the predecessor of Sect. 76 committed the directors explicitly to the well-being of the enterprise and its employees and also to the good of the public. The legislator of 1965 stated that the legislative intent for the new rule of Sect. 76 was only a terminological change, not a change in substance,[50] and that the broader mandate of the management board was so self-evident in the first place that it did not need to be restated in the law. In the final analysis even the supporters of a strong profit or share-holder value orientation concede that long-term effects have to be taken into consideration, thus rendering the concept of shareholder value very vague.

11.3.3.5. *Liability*

The members of the management board are liable to the company for the intentional or negligent breach of a contractual or statutory duty owed to the

---

[46] See Hopt, *in* AktG, Großkommentar § 93 at n. 151 (Klaus J. Hopt and Herbert Wiedemann eds., 4th ed. 1999); Hüffer, Aktiengesetz § 76 at n. 12 (5th ed. 2002); Mertens, *in* Kölner Kommentar § 76 at n. 19 (Wolfgang Zöllner ed., 2nd ed. 1996); Ulmer, 202 Archiv für die civilistische Praxis [AcP] 143, 155 et seq. (2002).

[47] See Groh, 53 Der Betrieb [DB] 2153 et seq. (2000); Hommelhoff, *in* Festschrift für Marcus Lutter 95, 102 et seq. (Uwe H. Schneider *et al.* eds., 2000); Kübler, *in* Festschrift für Wolfgang Zöllner I 321 et seq. (1998); Mülbert, 26 Zeitschrift für Unternehmens- und Gesellschaftsrecht [ZGR] 129 et seq. (1997); Ulmer, 202 Archiv für die civilistische Praxis [AcP] 143, 155 et seq. (2002).

[48] Groh, 53 Der Betrieb [DB] 2153, 2156 et seq. (2000); see also Busse von Colbe, 26 Zeitschrift für Unternehmens- und Gesellschaftsrecht [ZGR] 279, 289 et seq. (1997); Kübler, *in* Festschrift für Wolfgang Zöllner, Band I 321, 334 et seq. (Manfred Lieb *et al.* eds. 1998); Mülbert, 26 Zeitschrift für Unternehmens- und Gesellschaftsrecht [ZGR] 129, 140 et seq. (1997); Wymeersch, 30 Zeitschrift für Unternehmens- und Gesellschaftsrecht [ZGR] 294, 303 et seq. (2001).

[49] Hüffer, Aktiengesetz § 76 at n. 12 (5th ed. 2002); Mertens, *in* Kölner Kommentar § 76 at n. 19 (Wolfgang Zöllner ed., 2nd ed. 1996); Raiser, Recht der Kapitalgesellschaften § 14 at n. 11 (3rd ed. 2002); see also Hüffer, 161 Zeitschrift für das gesamte Handels- und Wirtschaftsrecht [ZHR] 214, 217 (1997).

[50] See Legislative Intent at *Kropff*, Aktiengesetz 97 (1965).

company. Liability presupposes that the breach has caused damage to the corporation. In theory, German law differentiates between the breach of a contractual or statutory duty and the question whether the member of the management board acted negligently. In practice, however, both aspects are combined in the question how a prudent and diligent manager would have acted. Directors need to take all possible care, which is more than the usual care to be expected of an ordinary person (Sect. 93(1)). German judges have adopted the distinction, known from common law systems, between a duty of care and a duty of loyalty. Recently, the Federal Supreme Court explicitly acknowledged a business judgement rule with a corresponding judicial self-restraint.[51]

The Stock Corporation Act strictly limits the enforcement of directors' duties by shareholders. As a rule, the individual shareholder cannot bring a derivative action against the members of the management board on behalf of the company. Only the general shareholders' meeting can decide that the management may be sued either by the supervisory board or by a special representative. Furthermore, Sect. 147(3) provides that a minority representing at least 5 per cent of the share capital or €500,000 of share capital can demand that the supervisory board or a special representative take action against members of the management board. A problem concerning this rule is that the shareholders who bring the action have to bear all the costs and expenses of the other party and the company if the action should be dismissed. However, the introduction of some sort of class action is heavily debated in Germany, even by the legislature.[52]

In legal proceedings against members of the management board, the stock corporation is represented by its supervisory board. However, in practice, members of the supervisory board will be hardly inclined to sue the members of the management board in case of negligence as the supervisory board could also be blamed for not having fulfilled its monitoring task correctly. Thus, they will often be reluctant to take action against the inside directors. However, the Federal Supreme Court held that under certain circumstances the supervisory board is obliged to claim damages from the members of the management board.[53]

Court decisions regarding the liability of inside directors are comparatively rare, although in recent years an upward tendency has developed. Nevertheless,

---

[51] BGHZ 135, 244 (253 et seq.)—ARAG/Garmenbeck.

[52] Baums, *in* Verhandlungen des Dreiundsechzigsten Deutschen Juristentages [63. DJT], Gutachten F, 240 et seq., 256 et seq. (2000); Lutter, 159 Zeitschrift für das gesamte Handels- und Wirtschaftsrecht [ZHR] 287, 304 et seq. (1995); Lutter, 27 Zeitschrift für Unternehmens- und Gesellschaftsrecht [ZGR] 191, 219 (1998); Hopt, *in* Festschrift für Ernst Joachim Mestmäcker, 909, 925 et seq. (Ulrich Immenga *et al.* eds. 1996). Ulmer, 163 Zeitschrift für das gesamte Handels- und Wirtschaftsrecht [ZHR], 290, 329 et seq. (1999); Bayer, 53 Neue Juristische Wochenschrift [NJW], 2609, 2618 et seq. (2000); Sünner, 163 Zeitschrift für das gesamte Handels- und Wirtschaftsrecht [ZHR], 364, 372 et seq. (1999).

[53] See BGHZ 135, 244 (251 et seq.)—ARAG/Garmenbeck.

this does not say anything about the practical importance of directors' liability under German law. Many disputes between directors and their companies are settled out of court. Thus, the liability rules of the Stock Corporation Act can have an important pre-emptive function, which is, however, hard to prove empirically.

11.3.4. Disclosure

The strengthened focus on capital market issues and the control of the corporation via the capital market is reflected by several disclosure duties to be obeyed by a stock corporation, which are stated in the German Securities Exchange Act ('Wertpapierhandelsgesetz' or 'WpHG'). According to Sect. 15(1) WpHG, a stock corporation is obliged to immediately disclose any new facts, which have arisen in the enterprise's field of activity and which are not known publicly, provided that such facts could substantially influence the price of the company's securities. Further disclosure duties arise in connection with the purchase and sale of stock. If an individual acquires, exceeds or falls short of 5, 10, 25, 50, or 75 per cent of the voting rights in the company by means of purchase, sale or any other manner, he has to disclose this fact without delay to the company and the Federal Supervisory Authority. If a stock corporation receives such a notification it is also obliged to disclose it without delay. The chapter by Leutz and Wüstemann in this volumes provides additional information on a corporation's obligation to provide information via the disclosure of accounting information to its shareholders and the general public. As these authors show in detail, the current shift in accounting rules from a strict creditor-based view to a more shareholder-oriented perspective reflects the aforementioned transitional stage of the German corporate governance system. Strong remnants of the creditor protection principle are still there since the basic German accounting principles still apply; they are, however, overlaid by the international accounting principles which are driven by a focus on the informational needs of capital markets.

11.4. THE LAW OF CORPORATE GROUPS

German corporate law is probably unique in the world with respect to the way in which it deals with conflicts and dangers that arise in connection with corporate groups, in particular concerning minority shareholders and creditors. As other legal systems use other concepts to cope with these problems the main features of the German system need to be analyzed in short—not least in order to show that also in this respect the German system focuses on the inner structures of the corporation.

   In Germany, the law of corporate groups has a long history. It was already discussed in the early twentieth century. The dominant questions of that time revolved around the forms of organization best suited to combining the interests of different enterprises.[54] In the 1950s, the policy of using group law as a means to provide the safeguards needed when companies combine their organizations became the main subject of discussion among corporate lawyers. With the introduction of specific rules regarding corporate groups into the Stock Corporation Act of 1965, Germany became the first country to have a codified law of corporate groups.

The rules of the Stock Corporation Act referring to groups of companies relate exclusively to combinations involving a stock corporation or a partnership limited by shares ('Kommanditgesellschaft auf Aktien' or 'KGaA').[55] Groups of companies which only include enterprises in other legal forms are not covered by the law. Groups of private limited companies have instead been subject to leading judgements of the Federal Supreme Court. These judgements have developed mechanisms for the protection of minority shareholders and creditors of companies that are part of such a group. Note, however, that German corporate law has always focused on the control of a corporate group *in being*; the act of *forming* a corporate group—be it by a takeover or by establishing a new subsidiary—did not receive special attention in the German corporate law statutes until recently. Hence, once again the focus had been on the inner structure of the corporation and the internal legal relationships as well as on the protection of creditors. Control over corporate groups by means of capital market mechanisms, e.g. in takeover fights, was not on the mind of German regulators and legislators when the law of corporate groups was enacted.

The Stock Corporation Act differentiates, in principle, between corporate groups built on a contractual basis (Sect. 291–307) and groups built merely on majority holding, so-called de facto groups (Sect. 308–318).

11.4.1. Control by 'Enterprise Contracts'

Although shareholdings are the prime basis of links between companies, it has always been a peculiarity of German Corporate Law that groups may also be created by means of a contract. The Stock Corporation Act recognizes two categories of such contractual agreements. Sect. 291(1) mentions a domination contract (i.e. an agreement whereby a stock corporation submits its own management to that of another enterprise) and a profit transfer agreement. In practice, these two contracts are usually combined. In Sect. 292 the law also mentions other contract types such as profit-pooling or company lease agreements. The most important contractual agreement between two

---

[54] Cf. Spindler, Recht und Konzern (1993); Emmerich/Sonnenschein/Habersack, Konzernrecht § 1 II 2 (7th ed. 2001).

[55] The KGaA is a hybrid form with at least one general partner whose liability is unlimited and limited shareholders who have an interest in the stated capital divided into shares, see Sect. 278(1) AktG.

companies, though, is the domination contract. The essential feature of such an agreement is the close attachment of the controlled enterprise to the interests of the parent company: In contrast to Sect. 76(1), a domination contract grants the parent company the right to issue directives to the management of the subsidiary even if they are detrimental to the subsidiary and its shareholders (Sect. 308(1)). This right involves a corresponding duty for the subsidiary's management board to follow the respective directives. The only condition is that the directive serves the interests of the group as a whole.[56] Hence, the Stock Corporation Act allows an explicit priority of the group interest if the group is based on a domination contract.

11.4.1.1. *Protection of minority shareholders*
Due to this influence, the business independence of the controlled company can be largely eliminated. Since the interests of the controlled company are no longer the standard by which the objectives of its management are determined and since, therefore, the adherence to this standard can no longer provide protection for the interests of minority shareholders and creditors, special rules to provide such protection are required. Hence, to compensate for the influence of the parent company, Sect. 304 and 305 state that one of the following two types of security must be offered to minority shareholders: either security in the form of a guaranteed dividend based on past and future profit prospects of the no longer independent corporation, or, where the controlling company is a stock corporation, a claim to the annual dividends of the parent company (Sect. 304). If the minority shareholders prefer to exit the controlled company, Sect. 305 gives them the right to do so and to demand compensation. If the parent company is not controlled by another company, compensation may take the form of shares of the said company. In the remaining cases shareholders are entitled to a cash compensation. To ensure the adequacy of the compensation offered pursuant to Sect. 304–306, the Stock Corporation Act provides the possibility of judicial review.

11.4.1.2. *Protection of creditors*
The authority to give instructions to the management board of a subsidiary gives the parent company the power to dispose of the subsidiary's assets. However, the Stock Corporation Act does not impose any direct liability on the parent company for claims against the subsidiary.[57] The main instrument to compensate the influence of the parent company is an obligation to balance the subsidiary's net loss for the year (Sect. 302(1)). The year's net loss may be made up out of the subsidiary's free reserves only to the extent that they

---

[56] Cf. Sect. 308(2) Sentence 2 AktG, see Hüffer, Aktiengesetz § 308 notes 15 et seq. (5th ed. 2002) for details on the limits of the authority to give instructions.

[57] Sect. 322(1) AktG imposes direct liability of the parent company only in the case of integration, see Sect. 319–327 for details on integration.

were created during the existence of the domination contract (Sect. 302(1)). The rightful claimant is solely the controlled company; its creditors have no right of action.[58] If a domination contract is terminated, the parent company is obliged to provide security for creditor claims that have been constituted before the termination was entered in the Commercial Register. The duty to balance the year's net loss of the subsidiary is supplemented by certain rules regarding the creation of reserves in the controlled company. Further, Sect. 301 states certain rules and limitations for profit transfer agreements.

Whereas the protection of creditors in the situation of a de facto group is primarily based on the compensation of damage resulting from single detrimental measures, the respective rules of the Stock Corporation Act are extremely controversial in their very concept and considerable doubt has been expressed about their effectiveness.[59] The first problem is the ascertainment of a detrimental measure. The rules of the Stock Corporation Act on ensuring compensation for detriment are also subject to criticism. Especially the significance of the dependence report is considered to be extremely low.[60]

To compensate the deficiencies of Sect. 311–318, the institute of a 'qualified' de facto group had been developed by German scholars and the Federal Supreme Court.[61] Qualified control was defined as a situation in which the interests of the dependent company are affected in a negative way by the influence exerted by the controlling company to the same extent as they would be under a domination contract.[62] This means that the controlled company is treated as if it were a mere branch of its parent company. According to the supporters of the theory of 'qualified' control, the controlling company was obliged to compensate the loss of the subsidiary based on an analogous application of Sect. 302.[63]

In recent years, the theory of 'qualified' control was only slightly modified by the Federal Supreme Court and not questioned in general, by either German jurisdiction or commentators. However, in a judgement from 2001, the

---

[58] Altmeppen, *in* Münchener Kommentar zum AktG, § 302 at n. 74 et seq. (Bruno Kropff and Johannes Semler eds., 2nd ed. 2000); Emmerich/Sonnenschein/Habersack, Konzernrecht § 20 V 6 a (7th ed. 2001); Hüffer, Aktiengesetz § 302 at n. 15 (5th ed. 2002); Koppensteiner, *in* Kölner Kommentar § 302 at n. 23 (Wolfgang Zöllner ed., 2nd ed. 1987).

[59] Cf. Immenga, The Law of Groups in the Federal Republic of Germany, *in* Groups of Companies in the EEC 85, 108 (Eddy Wymeersch ed., 1993) with further references.

[60] See Kübler, Gesellschaftsrecht, 5th ed. (1998), § 30 II 3 b, and Hommelhoff, 156 Zeitschrift für das gesamte Handels- und Wirtschaftsrecht [ZHR] 295, 296 (1992) with further references.

[61] See BGHZ 95, 330 (341 et seq.)—Autokran; Assmann, 41 Juristenzeitung [JZ] 881 et seq., 928 et seq. (1986); Kübler, Gesellschaftsrecht § 30 II 6 a (5th ed. 1998); K. Schmidt, Gesellschaftsrecht § 31 IV 4 (3rd ed. 1997).

[62] See Immenga, The Law of Groups in the Federal Republic of Germany, *in* Groups of Companies in the EEC 85, 110 (Eddy Wymeersch ed., 1993).

[63] BGHZ 95, 330 (341 et seq.)—Autokran; K. Schmidt, Gesellschaftsrecht § 31 IV 4 a (3rd ed. 1997).

Federal Supreme Court dropped the doctrine of 'qualified' de facto groups.[64] The court decided that the statutory regulations to protect the creditors of a private limited company are sufficient and need no supplementation by an analogous application of Sect. 302. Only if the majority shareholder undertakes measures endangering the existence of the controlled company, is the latter entitled to claim for damages.[65] The actual impact of this decision and of its successors seems to be a return to old categories of 'piercing the corporate veil'; it already seems to be apparent that issues of creditor protection will be some of the most controversially discussed questions regarding the law of corporate groups in the near future. This return to the 'roots' of the misuse of the corporate form renders the analysis of liability risks in a corporate group even more complex.

11.4.2. Control by Majority of Votes or Capital

Control of another corporation cannot only be exerted on a contractual basis, but also on the basis of mere majority holding (of votes and/or share capital). The law accepts the fact that mere majority holding results in a strong influence on the board of managing directors even if the direct instructions of shareholders to directors are not legally binding. The Stock Corporation Act allows a parent company to issue detrimental directives if the group is formed on a contractual basis, but only at the price of a duty to balance the subsidiary's net loss. If de facto control could be used to appropriate the resources of the controlled company without accepting the specific obligations implicit in a contract-based group, the option of concluding a domination contract would certainly not be chosen. A major difference between a corporate group formed upon a contractual basis and a de facto group is that in the case of mere majority holding Sect. 76(1) is fully applicable. Hence, in theory, the management board of the subsidiary is not obliged to follow directives of the parent company. However, if the directors of such a de facto controlled subsidiary do not act in the mere interest of the enterprise but instead follow the wishes of the majority stockholder, the latter has to reimburse the subsidiary as described above.

Whereas the factual control of the corporation triggers the obligation for the parent to reimburse disadvantages of the subsidiary, there are no means provided by the Stock Corporation Act to regulate the act of forming a de facto group, in particular in the takeover situation.[66] The rules of de facto

---

[64] BGHZ 149, 10 (16)—Bremer Vulkan.

[65] The decision refers to a de facto group consisting of private limited companies, but is also relevant for stock corporations.

[66] Takeovers are nowadays regulated by the Securities Acquisition and Take Over Act (Wertpapierübernahmegesetz—WpÜG), see below Section 11.5.5. and the chapter by Eric Nowak, this volume.

influence are based on the existence of control. A corporation is presumed to be controlled by another company if the latter owns a majority share in it (Sect. 17). According to Sect. 311(1), the controlling company is not allowed to use its influence to the detriment of the controlled corporation. However, Sect. 311(2) makes an exception from this prohibition if the detriment is compensated by the parent company. To secure these composition proceedings, according to Sect. 312 the management board of the controlled company is obliged to provide an annual dependence report giving details of transactions between the linked enterprises and all steps taken at the insistence of the controlling company. The management board must state whether, in its opinion, the subsidiary has suffered detriment or whether any detriment was suitably compensated. The dependence report is examined by the auditor and the supervisory board. Sect. 317 and 318 grant the controlled company and its shareholders a claim for damages if the parent company omits to compensate a measure that is not in the subsidiary's interest. The liability is excluded, however, if the management board of an independent corporation would have carried out the measure as well.

11.4.3. Corporate Groups and the Capital Market

To sum up, German corporate law still focuses on the protection of shareholders already owning stock of the corporation as well as on the protection of creditors. The principal means for achieving these goals is to secure the capital of the corporation by providing for claims against the parent in control of the subsidiary. In contrast, capital market-based law primarily focuses on the investment decision, that is, the time before the shareholder actually becomes involved. Hence, capital market-driven law accentuates the information, true and timely given, in order to avoid misled decisions. Alternatively—for example, in takeover regulation—the shareholder receives a substantial reimbursement if the corporation is taken over (Sect. 35 WpÜG), or if the remaining shareholders are squeezed out (Sect. 327a et seq.).[67] Hence, minority issues and creditor protection are in principle out of the range of capital market-based legal approaches; once the investor has decided to buy shares—provided that he had all substantial information—he acts on his own risk.

It seems that neither German law nor foreign legal regimes can stand their ground by focusing on only one approach. On the one hand, German law has recently adopted capital market-oriented approaches, such as the regulation of takeover fights as well as provisions for a timely and substantial disclosure for investment decisions, thus adding to the traditional concept of minority protection the *ex ante* view that focuses on the investment decision. On the other hand, foreign legal regimes like the US corporate law—traditionally more

---

[67] Mülbert, Aktiengesellschaft, Unternehmensgruppe und Kapitalmarkt (2nd ed. 1996), 105 et seq. with further references.

focused on capital market issues—seek to solve the minority and creditor protection problems by utilizing common law doctrines, such as 'piercing the corporate veil', fiduciary duties etc.[68] At the moment, a modernization of corporate law, as far as corporate groups are concerned, is not planned by the German legislature; the focus in this field is explicitly on securities law.

11.5. CURRENT ISSUES

The preceding survey of the German corporate governance system has already provided a glimpse of the elements of transition in German corporate law. This analysis will now be taken further by looking at some current issues in the field of corporate governance.

11.5.1. Conflict of Laws and the Emerging Competition in Corporate Law in Europe

One of the topics widely discussed, and with an importance not easy to assess, is the revolution regarding conflicting laws of Member States in the area of corporate law. The European Court of Justice (ECJ) is apparently accepting more and more a doctrine similar to its counterpart in the United States, the doctrine of incorporation. This may lead to the same effects that can be observed in the United States—the famous Delaware effect and a competition between Member States concerning corporate law.[69]

Questions concerning the applicability of German Corporate Law have arisen lately as a result of the so-called 'Centros' decision of the ECJ.[70] In the 'Centros' case, a Danish couple set up a private limited company in the United Kingdom and applied for the registration of a branch of the respective company in Denmark. The registration authority refused this request as the branch was in fact set up for no reason other than to circumvent the Danish capital requirements for setting up a private limited company.

The ECJ decided that it is contrary to Art. 52 [43] and 58 [48] of the EU Treaty for a Member State to refuse to register a branch of a company formed

---

[68] On the application of veil-piercing and related doctrines in connection with corporate groups see Blumberg, The Law of Corporate Groups: Substantive Law, *passim* (1987); on US directors' fiduciary duties with respect to takeover defences and corporate control transactions see *Unocal Corp. v. Mesa Petroleum Co.*, 493 A.2d 946 (Del. 1985); *Revlon, Inc. v. MacAndrews & Forbes Holding, Inc.*, 506 A.2d 173 (Del. 1986); *Paramount Communications, Inc. v. QVC Network Inc.*, 637 A.2d 34, 43 (Del. 1994); for the leading Delaware fiduciary duty decision regarding freeze-out mergers see *Weinberger* v. *UOP, Inc.*, 457 A.2d 701 (Del. 1983).

[69] Kieninger, Wettbewerb der Rechtsordnungen 106 et seq. (2002); Grundmann, 30 Zeitschrift für Unternehmens- und Gesellschaftsrecht [ZGR] 783, 785 et seq. (2001); Eidenmüller, 23 Zeitschrift für Wirtschaftsrecht [ZIP] 2233 et seq. (2002); Dreher, 54 Juristenzeitung [JZ] 105 et seq. (1999); Freitag, 9 Europäische Zeitschrift für Wirtschaftsrecht [EuZW] 267 et seq. (1998).

[70] Case C-212/97, *Centros Ltd.* v. *Erhvervs-og Selskabsstyrelsen*, (1999) E.C.R. I-1459.

in accordance with the law of another Member State, in which it has its registered office, but in which it conducts no business. This applies even if the branch is intended to enable the company in question to conduct its entire business in the Member State in which the branch is to be created avoiding the need to form a company there, thus evading the application of the respective rules governing the formation of companies. According to the ECJ, however, this interpretation does not prevent the authorities of the Member State concerned from adopting any appropriate measure to prevent or penalize fraud, provided that the measure is non-discriminatory, justified in the general interest, suitable for securing the objective and does not go beyond what is necessary.

To understand the relevance of the 'Centros' decision for the German corporate governance system, it is essential to take a look at German private international law. To determine the applicable law, German courts used to apply the so-called 'real seat' doctrine ('Sitztheorie').[71] Pursuant to this theory companies are governed by the law of the state where their administration office, the center of management, is situated. The counterpole of the 'real seat' theory is the 'incorporation' theory ('Gründungstheorie'). According to the latter, company matters are governed by the law under which the company has been duly incorporated.

The 'Centros' decision is commonly interpreted as a refusal of the 'real seat' theory. Such an interpretation would have far-reaching consequences for German corporate law, not least for its creditor protection devices, (e.g. the requirement of a certain capitalization), the system of codetermination and the dual-board structure.[72] To evade the Stock Corporation Act's strict regulations, a company could be founded in a Member State with less rigorous standards and afterwards apply for the registration of a branch in Germany. This could evoke a race to the bottom between the individual Member States. To shed some light on the situation, the German Federal Supreme Court asked the following preliminary questions to the ECJ:[73] (i) Does the application of the 'real seat' theory infringe upon the freedom of establishment which is granted by Art. 43 and 48 of the EU Treaty? (ii) If so, does freedom of establishment impose the duty upon authorities of the Member States to apply the 'incorporation' theory to companies duly incorporated in another Member State?

In its 'Überseering' decision,[74] the ECJ once and for all rejected the 'real seat' theory as far as the legal capacity and the capacity to be a party to legal

---

[71] BGHZ 25, 134 (144); BGHZ 51, 27 (28); BGHZ 53, 181 (183); BGHZ 53, 383 (385); BGHZ 97, 269 (271 et seq.); see also Assmann, *in* AktG, Großkommentar Einl. at n. 532 et seq. (Klaus J. Hopt and Herbert Wiedemann eds., 4th ed. 1992), and Kübler, Gesellschaftsrecht, § 34 II 1 (5th ed. 1998). [72] Cf. Sandrock, 57 Betriebs Berater [BB] 1601 et seq. (2002). [73] BGH 46 Recht der internationalen Wirtschaft [RIW] 555 (2000). [74] ECJ 55 Neue Juristische Wochenschrift [NJW] 3614 (2002); see also the final motions of the Advocate-General Dámaso Ruiz-Jarabo Colomer, Case C-208/00 *Überseering BV* v. *NCC Nordic*

proceedings are concerned. Although 'Überseering' gave rise to an active debate among commentators,[75] the practical implications of the decision are not yet fully foreseeable. The future will show, if the ECJ really laid the foundation for a race to the bottom between European corporate laws.

11.5.2. The European Stock Corporation

Surprisingly, a long enduring discussion referring to the introduction of the European Stock Corporation recently came to an end. After more than 30 years of deliberations the European Union finally adopted an ordinance—not a directive (!)—that provides a new legal entity, the European Stock Corporation. However, the notion of 'European' is somehow misleading as only some basic principles for the corporation and its structure are laid down in the ordinance whereas the bulk of rules for fully operating the European Stock Corporation still have to be adopted by the respective national legislators. Hence, there will be as many variants of the 'European Stock Corporation' laws as there are Member States.

Keeping this fact in mind, the European Stock Corporation might play a similar role for the competition of Member States concerning corporate law as the breakthrough of the European Court of Justice in the area of conflict of laws. Furthermore, the European Stock Corporation forces German corporate law to introduce for the first time the option of a monistic board system as the European Stock Corporation ordinance explicitly provides fo a choice in *each* (!) Member State to opt either for a dualistic system—such as the German one (supervisory board and board of managing directors)—or for a monistic system (one board of directors, exercising supervisory functions as well as managing tasks).[76] Once again, the former strict structures of German corporate law are somewhat broken up by offering more freedom and more institutional choices to potential investors than before.

11.5.3. The Diminishing Role of German Universal Banks

Another phenomenon—closely related to the transitional stage of the actual German corporate governance system—is the declining influence of German

---

Construction Company Baumanagement GmbH, 6 Neue Zeitschrift für Gesellschaftsrecht [NZG] 16 et seq. (2002).

[75] Cf. Lutter, 58 Betriebs Berater [BB] 7 et seq. (2003); Eidenmüller, 23 Zeitschrift für Wirtschaftsrecht [ZIP] 2233 et seq. (2002); Hirte, 13 Europäisches Wirtschafts- und Steuerrecht [EWS] 573 et seq. (2002); Schanze, 48 Die Aktiengesellschaft [AG] 30 et seq. (2003); Kersting, 7 Neue Zeitschrift für Gesellschaftsrecht [NZG] 30 et seq.(2002).

[76] Neye/ Teichmann, 48 Die Aktiengesellschaft [AG] 169, 176 et seq. (2003); Teichmann, 31 Zeitschrift für Unternehmens- und Gesellschaftsrecht [ZGR] 383, 441 et seq. (2002); Lutter, 57 Betriebs Berater [BB] 1, 5 (2002); Hirte, 6 Neue Zeitschrift für Gesellschaftsrecht [NZG] 1, 5 et seq. (2002).

banks, that is, their diminishing role in the former network of checks and balances in the German economic system. Essentially, three topics are involved here.

11.5.3.1. *Depositary voting right*

For a long time, the role of German universal banks was a widely criticized feature of the German corporate governance system.[77] Besides their role as creditors, German banks own a significant number of large equity stakes in public companies and are represented on the supervisory boards of most large German corporations.[78] Their influence is extended by the so-called depositary voting right ('Depotstimmrecht'). By tradition, banks have acquired the right to vote on behalf of their customers who have shares kept in their custody. A first attempt to regulate such voting rights was made by the Stock Corporation Act of 1937. The rules regulating the depositary voting rights were amended and extended in 1965, when the new Stock Corporation Act came into effect.[79] Recent amendments were made by the Act on Control and Transparency of Enterprises ('Gesetz zur Kontrolle und Transparenz im Unternehmensbereich' or 'KonTraG') and by the Act on Registered Shares and the Exercise of Voting Rights ('Namensaktiengesetz' or 'NaStraG'), which introduced a German type of proxy voting.

Pursuant to Sect. 135(10) a bank offering to vote with respect to its clients' shares is obliged to secure a client's request to cast the vote for him. The appointment of a proxy has to be in writing. It may not be included in the general standard form contract governing the bank–customer relation.[80] If a bank intends to cast the votes of its customers, it is further obliged to submit proposals on how to exercise the voting rights (Sect. 128). The bank must devise such proposals in accordance with the assumed interests of an average customer and take organizational measures to ensure that the bank's own interests do not influence the proposals. In particular, the bank must appoint a member of its management board who is responsible for compliance with the aforementioned duties and who must supervise the orderly exercise of the voting rights and the recording thereof. A bank may not exercise the voting rights of its customers in stock corporations in which it holds more than 5 per cent of the share capital unless it has specific instructions from the

[77] Cf. Baums, The German Banking System and its impact on Corporate Finance and Corporate Governance, *in* The Japanese Main Banking System 409 et seq. (Masahiko Aoki and Hugh Patrick eds., 1994); Köndgen, Duties of Banks in Voting their Clients' Stock, *in* Institutional Investors and Corporate Governance 531 et seq. (Theodor Baums *et al.* eds., 1994).

[78] Cf. Hopt, The German Two-Tier Board (Aufsichtsrat)—A German View on Corporate Governance, *in* Comparative Corporate Governance 3, 11 (Klaus J. Hopt and Eddy Wymeersch eds., 1997).

[79] See Köndgen, Duties of Banks in Voting their Clients' Stock, *in* Institutional Investors and Corporate Governance 531, 532 et seq. (Theodor Baums *et al.* eds., 1994) with further details on the history of the German depositary voting rights.

[80] See Köndgen, Duties of Banks in Voting their Clients' Stock, *in* Institutional Investors and Corporate Governance 531, 533 et seq. (Theodor Baums *et al.* eds., 1994).

customer or if it does not exercise its own rights (Sect. 135(1)). The institution of the depositary voting right had shifted the voting power of shareholders to the banks for a long time; today, however, German banks are more and more reluctant to accept their role as a proxy voter for shareholders as they face the above mentioned restrictions as well as high costs for preparing their votes. Closely related to this process is the introduction of proxy voting.

11.5.3.2. *Proxy voting*

Voting stock in person is normally not worthwhile for the average minority shareholder. Given the single shareholder's influence on the outcome of a vote, his expenses would greatly outweigh any expected benefit from casting his vote personally. The consequence of this circumstance is a rational apathy on the part of small minority shareholders. Modern corporation laws have developed various devices to cope with this problem and generally allow shareholders to have their vote cast by some sort of proxy. The most widely known is the Anglo-American proxy system with its often spectacular proxy fights.[81]

Until quite recently, the compatibility of American-style proxy voting with the rules of the Stock Corporation Act was the subject of controversial discussions in the German legal literature. It had been commonly believed that German law strictly forbids proxy voting in order to prevent manager-controlled corporations.[82] This discussion was put on a new basis after the modification of Sect. 134(3) by the Act on Registered Shares and the Exercise of Voting Rights ('Namensaktiengesetz' or 'NaStraG'). Although the new Sect. 134(3) does not explicitly legalize proxy voting, it implies its admissibility.[83] According to Sect. 134(3) Sentence 3, the company can name a proxy, who is to be authorized by the shareholders, to exercise their voting rights. However, proxy voting is only permissible if a shareholder gives explicit instructions regarding the subject of the resolution.[84] In practice, most large corporations have already made use of the new proxy voting by inaugurating proxy committees consisting of employees of the respective corporation, mostly combined with Internet voting. However, German Securities Law, unlike the SEC rules, still does not provide any regulations concerning the thorough information of shareholders in proxy contests. It remains to be

---

[81] However, proxy contests are of declining importance in the United States, see Bainbridge, Corporation Law and Economics § 12.7, at 652–54 (2002).

[82] See v. Radow, 19 Zeitschrift für Wirtschaftsrecht [ZIP] 1564, 1565 et seq. (1998); Singhoff, 2 Neue Zeitschrift für Gesellschaftsrecht [NZG] 670, 673 (1998); Zöllner, *in* Festschrift für Martin Peltzer 661, 664 et seq. (Marcus Lutter *et al.* eds., 2001).

[83] Hüffer, Aktiengesetz § 134 at n. 26a (5th ed. 2002).

[84] Habersack, 165 Zeitschrift für das gesamte Handels- und Wirtschaftsrecht [ZHR] 172, 187 et seq. (2001); Hüffer, Aktiengesetz § 134 at n. 26b (5th ed. 2002); Noack, 22 Zeitschrift für Wirtschaftsrecht [ZIP] 57, 62 (2001).

seen whether the German legislature will enact informational and voting rules, as proxy voting may become more widespread in the near future.

11.5.3.3. *Methods of financing*

The instrument of depositary voting rights goes along with the (long-time) typical financial structure of German stock corporations, thus according banks the combined power of their position as creditor and as quasi-shareholder (via the exercise of voting rights). Therefore, it is useful to take a glance at the legal framework governing the financing of corporations.

Like any other enterprise, the stock corporation can raise its required capital either by equity or by debt financing. In general, it is completely up to the discretion of the shareholders whether they wish to finance their company with equity or debt.

Sect. 7 lays down the requirement of a minimum share capital of €50,000. Shares may be issued either with a par value of at least €1 per share or multiples thereof ('Nennbetragsaktien') or without a par value ('Stückaktien', Sect. 8(2, 3)). Since 1998, multiple voting rights are no longer permitted—an essential barrier for takeovers has thus been removed. Existing multiple voting rights expire on 1 June, 2003. Pursuant to Sect. 10(1) either bearer shares ('Inhaberaktien') or registered shares, where the name of the shareholder has been registered ('Namensaktien'), can be issued, so that the listing on foreign stock exchanges, such as the NYSE, will be easier. The transfer of bearer shares cannot be restricted, whereas, according to Sect. 68(2), the by-laws can provide that registered shares may not be transferred without the corporation's consent. Hence, takeovers may be hampered to a certain extent.

The traditional method of financing involved taking out bank loans or issuing bonds, thus granting the bank power in its role as a *Hausbank*. This role was often combined with holding a seat in the supervisory board. However, the so-called 'covenants' (i.e. an arrangement in a credit agreement, which grants the creditor insight into and influence on the decisions of the borrowing company's management[85]) are incompatible with the management board's sole responsibility for managing the enterprise if they interfere with the management's discretion to manage the enterprise according to Sect. 76(1). Like all kinds of debt, bonds issued by the corporation entitle the holder to claim payments of a certain amount including interest and repayment after a previously defined period of time. According to Sect. 793 Civil Code ('Bürgerliches Gesetzbuch' or 'BGB') the corporation can issue bearer bonds. Furthermore, according to Sect. 221(1) bonds may be issued as convertible bonds (which may be converted into shares), option bonds (which entitle the holder to subscribe to shares), or profit-sharing bonds (where the bondholder also participates in the profit of the corporation). Treated as

---

[85] Cf. Fleischer, 19 Zeitschrift für Wirtschaftsrecht [ZIP] 313 (1998); Smith/Warner, 7 J. Fin. Econ. 117 (1979).

equivalent to convertible bonds, option bonds and profit-sharing bonds are corporate profit participation rights. The Stock Corporation Act does not provide a legal definition of corporate profit participation rights.[86] Therefore, the terms and conditions of such rights may be freely agreed on. If corporate profit participation rights are redeemable or if the holder of such rights is entitled to claim repayment of a fixed nominal amount after a certain period of time, they qualify as loan capital rather than as equity.[87] In sum, the discretion of the board of directors to opt for bank financing and the strong role of banks inside the supervisory board have both strengthened the role of banks and the independence of directors from the influence of capital markets, and thus of shareholders.

However, in the last 20 years the practice of financing a corporation via a banking loan has become more risky for a bank that acts at the same time as a major stockholder. If a loan granted to a corporation by one of its share-holders serves the same purpose in economic terms as equity, it is to be considered as such. A shareholder's loan is considered to be 'equity replacing' if it is provided while the corporation is in financial difficulties, that is, the corporation would not have obtained such a loan from an unrelated third party under the market conditions prevailing at the time. If it was granted prior to such difficulties, it nevertheless becomes equity replacing if the shareholder allows it to remain with the corporation after the financial difficulties have occurred.[88] Repayment of equity replacing loans is subject to several restrictions, which essentially result in a subordination of the shareholder's loan. Prior to the commencement of insolvency proceedings, the shareholder may not claim repayment of that part of the loan by which the net assets of the corporation would fall below its share capital. During insolvency proceedings the lending shareholder may demand repayment only after repayment of all third party debts.[89] Security provided by the corporation for the loan in question may not be realized.

Moreover, the rules for equity-replacing loans may also apply if a third party's loan serves as an economic equivalent to a shareholder's loan. This requires that the third party involved indirectly holds a stake in the corpora-tion and participates in fundamental decisions: The third party has to act on a shareholder's account or form an economic unit with one of the corporation's shareholders.[90] Therefore, the rules can apply to affiliates of the shareholder, shareholders or dormant partners of the shareholder and to trustees.

The rules for equity replacing shareholders' loans were originally developed for limited liability companies, but are now deemed to also apply to stock

---

[86] Cf. Hüffer, Aktiengesetz § 221 at n. 23 (5th ed. 2002).

[87] See Hüffer, Aktiengesetz § 221 at n. 31 et seq. (5th ed. 2002).

[88] Hüffer, Aktiengesetz § 57 at n. 16a (5th ed. 2002).

[89] K. Schmidt, Gesellschaftsrecht § 29 I 2 (3rd ed. 1997).

[90] K. Schmidt, Gesellschaftsrecht § 29 I 2, § 37 IV 3 b (3rd ed. 1997).

corporations.[91] However, in case of a stock corporation the application differs in one significant point. Owing to the fact that minority shareholders have no substantial influence on the management and capitalization of the corporation, only loans from shareholders with a shareholding interest exceeding 25 per cent of the share capital, or loans from shareholders who, by other means, exert a substantial influence on the management of the corporation, may qualify as equity replacing loans.[92]

Summing up, we can again observe the tendency towards capital market-based approaches as far as the role of banks is concerned. The augmented risk of lending money to the corporation, the introduction of proxy voting rights, and the restrictions placed on depositary voting rights are some of the factors that weaken the former strong position of banks.

11.5.4. German Corporate Governance Code

In order to align Germany as a financial centre more closely to the requirements of the international capital markets and to make it more attractive for investors, especially foreign institutional investors, the German Minister of Justice mandated a commission, the so-called Baums Commission,[93] with the development of new proposals for stock corporation and securities law. The commission adhered to the basic approach of German stock corporation law, but recommended multiple enhancements in detail to take account of the growing capital market impact on corporations. One of the major proposals of the commission was to introduce a German Corporate Governance Code (in analogy to the Financial Services Act in the United Kingdom), which is not mandatory, but can be adopted by any corporation. In the event that a management board is reluctant to accept the Corporate Governance Code, it is obliged to 'explain' to the capital market why it wants to deviate from the given code, thus creating pressure on corporations to restructure themselves, in particular the board of directors, according to internationally recognized standards.

On this basis, a second commission (the Cromme Commission) consisting of high-level national experts, mainly from various industries, was established in order to develop a code of practice. On 26 February 2002, the commission (which is not a governmental one, but privately constituted and supported by the government) presented the final version of a German Corporate

---

[91] BGHZ 90, 381 (385 et seq.)—BuM; Hüffer, Aktiengesetz § 57 at n. 17 (5th ed. 2002); K. Schmidt, Gesellschaftsrecht § 29 I 2 (3rd ed. 1997).

[92] BGHZ 90, 381 (390 et seq.)—BuM; Hüffer, Aktiengesetz § 57 at n. 18 (5th ed. 2002); Lutter, *in* Kölner Kommentar § 57 at n. 93 (Wolfgang Zöllner ed., 2nd ed. 1988); Rümker, *in* Festschrift für Walter Stimpel 673, 677 et seq. (Marcus Lutter *et al.* eds., 1985); K. Schmidt, Gesellschaftsrecht § 29 I 2 (3rd ed. 1997).

[93] See Bericht der Regierungskommission Corporate Governance (Theodor Baums ed., 2001).

Governance Code.[94] The Minister of Justice restricted herself to setting the legal framework, and thus gave the German business world the opportunity to propose a code containing nationally and internationally recognized standards of good and responsible corporate governance.

An explicit aim of the German Corporate Governance Code is to create transparency for foreign investors and to make the German corporate governance system understandable to them. The Code presents essential statutory regulations for the management and supervision of listed companies to clarify the duties of the management and the supervisory board as well as the rights of shareholders. Besides the reproduction of rules to be observed under applicable law, the Code also contains recommendations on standards and disclosure duties for listed companies that are marked in the text by use of the word 'shall'. Companies can deviate from them, but are then obliged to disclose this annually.[95] The Code also contains suggestions that can be deviated from without explanation. These suggestions are marked by use of terms such as 'should' or 'can'. The Code will be reviewed annually against the background of national and international developments and will, if necessary, be adjusted.

The legal impact of the German Corporate Governance Code, however, remains to be assessed more clearly. The management and the supervisory board must declare publicly whether the corporation intends to comply with the rules of the Code or to deviate. Thus, in theory, capital markets should decide which corporation has the 'best' principles of corporate governance. However, the Code may have a legal impact not only on the board members' duty of loyalty and duty of care, but also on their liability towards investors, particularly if the corporation has violated the Code in contrast to a former compliance declaration.[96] Furthermore, the indirect legal impact of the Code has given rise to constitutional doubts because the commission issuing the rules is not an institution with democratic authorization.

11.5.5. Shareholders' General Meeting via the Internet

Another new way of coping with minority shareholders' rational apathy, closely related to proxy voting, is the holding of general meetings via the Internet. Traditionally, the shareholders' general meeting is an event characterized by the shareholders' presence, either in person or represented by a proxy. In recent years, however, more and more corporations have started to

---

[94] The final version of the German Corporate Governance Code can be downloaded at www.corporate-governance-code.de.

[95] With the commencement of the Transparency and Disclosure law, the so-called 'comply or explain' rule was integrated within the new Sect. 161 AktG.

[96] Cf. Lutter, *in* Festschrift für Jean Nicolas Druey 463, 469 et seq. (Rainer J. Schweizer *et al.* eds., 2002).

transmit the general meeting via the Internet. Moreover, the new German Corporate Governance Code suggests that the company should make it possible for shareholders to follow the general meeting using modern communication media. This suggestion is accompanied by recent legislation. The Transparency and Disclosure Act ('Transparenz- und Publizitätsgesetz' or 'TransPuG'), that came into effect on 26 July 2002, amends Sect. 118. The new Sect. 118(3) states that the articles of association or the rules of procedure can require the shareholders' general meeting be transmitted audio-visually. Although this amendment of the Stock Corporation Act permits general meetings to be held online, it is, however, still not possible for shareholders to cast their votes directly via the Internet.[97] In practice, proxies are used for voting via the Internet as shareholders can instruct their representatives throughout the meeting, thus achieving the same result as by direct votes. For the future, it would be recommendable to further amend the Stock Corporation Act in order to enable shareholders to participate directly in the general meeting without either being present or using a proxy and to exercise all or certain rights by means of electronic communication.[98]

11.5.6. The Securities Acquisition and Takeover Act

As stated above, the Stock Corporation Act provides no rules to control the formation of de facto groups. However, a certain mechanism for doing so was recently established by the new German Securities Acquisition and Takeover Act ('Wertpapiererwerbs- und Übernahmegesetz' or 'WpÜG').[99] The Takeover Act deals with public offers to acquire securities of a German stock corporation or a partnership limited by shares listed on an organized market in the European Economic Area.[100] Germany enacted the Takeover Act after the initial failure of the European Union to agree on a Takeover Directive.

The Takeover Act distinguishes between basic purchase offers, offers to acquire a controlling interest (takeover bids) and mandatory offers. Offers to acquire a controlling interest are defined as offers to acquire directly or indirectly more than 30 per cent of the voting rights of the target company.[101] Shareholders holding more than 30 per cent of a target company must make a mandatory offer to acquire all other issued and outstanding stock, if the controlling interest was not acquired by means of a takeover offer.[102] In order to secure the interests of the shareholders addressed by an offer, the Takeover

---

[97] See Noack, 55 Der Betrieb [DB] 620, 624 et seq. (2002).

[98] See Bericht der Regierungskommission Corporate Governance at n. 115 (Theodor Baums, ed., 2001); Noack, 55 Der Betrieb [DB] 620, 624 et seq. (2002).

[99] For details, see the chapters by Schmid and Wahrenburg and by Nowak, this volume.

[100] Cf. Sect. 1 WpÜG *and* Sect. 2(3, 7) WpÜG.   [101] Sect. 29 WpÜG.

[102] Sect. 35(1) WpÜG.

Act lays down certain procedural rules. Special rules regarding the target company's shares apply to takeover bids and mandatory offers.

These must be offered in cash if the offeror has directly or indirectly purchased at least 5 per cent of the target company's shares in exchange for monetary payment within 3 months prior to the publication of the decision to acquire shares or has purchased at least 1 per cent of the stock or the voting rights in exchange for monetary payment between publication of the decision to acquire stock and expiry of the acceptance period. The consideration for all stockholders will be adjusted accordingly should the offeror have acquired or agreed to acquire shares for a higher price between publication of the offering document and publication of the offer's final result. If the offeror has acquired shares of the target company at a higher price within one year after publication of the offer's final result, he is, in principle, required to pay the difference to all shareholders having accepted the original cash offer.

The most controversial issue regarding German takeover law is the management board's obligation to neutrality. Unlike the previously submitted drafts of the Takeover Directive that opted for strict neutrality with only narrow exceptions, Sect. 33 WpÜG grants the target company's management board substantial powers to oppose a takeover bid. Prior to the publication of the decision to make a public offer, the shareholders of the potential target company may resolve to authorize the management board to take certain actions if an offer is made that would otherwise fall within the authority of the general meeting. The authorization can be issued for up to 18 months by a shareholders' resolution requiring three fourths of the present share capital.[103] After the announcement of the decision to make a public offer, the management board is, in principle, prohibited from taking any actions that might prevent the success of the transaction. However, according to Sect. 33(1) Sentence 3 WpÜG, the management board is not restricted from carrying on with the day-to-day business and may also seek a competing offer ('white knight'). Moreover, preventive actions are allowed if they are approved by the supervisory board.[104] This German specialty causes a lot of problems. Since this rule does not apply if the defence action comes within the authority of the general meeting, in most cases a demarcation of the authorities of the

---

[103] Sect. 33(2) Sentence 3 WpÜG; cf. Krause, 57 Betriebs Berater [BB] 1053 et seq. (2002); Röh, *in* Öffentliche Übernahmeangebote § 33 at n. 98 et seq. (Wilhelm Haarmann *et al.* eds., 2002); Schwennicke, in Wertpapiererwerbs- und Übernahmegesetz (WpÜG) § 33 at n. 57 (Stephan Geibel and Rainer Süßmann eds., 2002).

[104] The requirements for such an approval are disputed, cf. Röh, *in* Öffentliche Übernahmeangebote § 33 at n. 120 et seq. (Wilhelm Haarmann *et al.* eds., 2002); Schneider, 47 Die Aktiengesellschaft [AG] 125, 129 (2002); Schwennicke, in Wertpapiererwerbs- und Übernahmegesetz (WpÜG) § 33 at n. 49 et seq. (Stephan Geibel and Rainer Süßmann eds., 2002); Winter / Harbarth, 23 Zeitschrift für Wirtschaftsrecht [ZIP], 1, 8 et seq. (2002).

general meeting and the board is required.[105] However, it remains to be seen whether the current German takeover law is only of a transitive character as the EU-Commission still plans to draft a directive concerning takeover issues (after several failures), and has therefore called for the help of a high-level expert commission, which is also in charge of an inquiry into corporate governance in Europe.[106]

11.6. CONCLUSION

German corporate governance is indeed in a transitional stage. Whereas German corporate law has long been dominated by a perspective focused on the internal relationship between shareholders, directors, and creditors, the link to capital markets is now being recognized and integrated step by step into German stock corporation law. The former mandatory internal structures are softened little by little; capital markets are regarded as a means to control directors; liability instruments concerning false disclosures towards investors have been introduced, etc.[107] What we observe today in Germany is the slow, but steady transformation towards a more capital market-oriented corporate law that will be fit to offer options for large, publicly held corporations as well as options for smaller enterprises not wishing to go public. Thus, German stock corporation law, nowadays, encompasses different types of stock corporations that are not governed by the same set of rules anymore; only the common basis has remained in place. The introduction of the new German takeover law and the German Corporate Governance Code may accelerate these developments. However, the final outcome of this process still cannot be assessed clearly, although the tendency is already shaped.

---

[105] Hirte, *in* Kölner Kommentar zum WpÜG (Heribert Hirte and Christoph von Bülow eds., 2002) § 33 at n. 80.

[106] The first report of the High Level Group of Company Law Experts on Issues Related to Takeover Law can be viewed at http://europa.eu.int/comm/internal_market/en/company/company/news/hlg01–2002.pdf.; on this report Heeren/Rieckers, 14 European Business Law Review [EBLR] 595, 625 et seq. (2003); Wiesner, 23 Zeitschrift für Wirtschaftsrecht [ZIP], 208 et seq. (2002); see also the Proposal of a Directive of the European Parliament and of the Council on takeover bids from 2 October 2002, COM 2002, 534 at http://europa.eu.int/eur-lex/ en/com/pdf/2002/com2002_0534en01.pdf; on this directive Lehne/Haak, 1 Der Konzern, 163 et seq. (2003); Dauner-Lieb/Lamandini, 1 Der Konzern, 168 et seq. (2003); Zinser, 14 Europäische Zeitschrift für Wirtschaftsrecht [EuZW] 10 et seq. (2003).

[107] See also Merkt, 48 Die Aktiengesellschaft [AG] 126, 130 et seq. (2003).

12

Corporate Governance in Germany: An Economic Perspective

REINHARD H. SCHMIDT

12.1. THE PROBLEM

A financial system can perform its main function of channelling funds from savers to investors only if it offers sufficient assurance to the providers of the funds that they will reap the rewards which have been promised to them.[1] To the extent that this assurance is not provided by contracts alone, potential financiers will want to monitor and influence managerial decisions. At least they will want to be sure that some persons, institutions, or mechanisms have assumed the role of monitoring and influencing the activities of the firm and its management, and are performing that role in their, the financiers', best interests. If they do not have this assurance they will abstain from providing capital in the first place. Therefore, corporate governance is an essential part of any financial system.

It is obvious that providers of equity have a genuine interest in the functioning of corporate governance. However, corporate governance encompasses more than investor protection. Considerations similar to those which underlie the logical link between equity capital and governance also apply to other stakeholders who invest their resources in a firm and whose expectations of later receiving an appropriate return on their investment also depend on decisions at the level of the individual firm which would be extremely difficult to anticipate and prescribe in a set of complete contingent contracts. Lenders, especially long-term lenders, are one such group of stakeholders who may also want to play a role in corporate governance; employees, especially those with high skill levels and firm-specific knowledge, are another. The German corporate governance system is different from that of the Anglo-Saxon countries insofar as it is based on the notion that it is possible, or indeed necessary, to integrate lenders and employees into the

---

[1] This is the starting point for the influential series of papers by La Porta *et al.* See especially their 1997 article on 'legal determinants of external finance', and also Shleifer and Vishney (1997).

governance of large corporations; and this is one of the reasons why the German corporate governance system has for a long time appeared to be somewhat anomalous. As Rieckers and Spindler also point out in their companion chapter in this book, because of its peculiarities the German corporate governance system was considered to be one of the strengths of the German economy some years ago, whereas nowadays it tends to be perceived as more of a burden.

German corporate governance is shaped by a legal tradition that dates back to the 1920s and regards corporations as entities which act not only in the interests of their shareholders, but also have to serve a multitude of other interests. These views may sound somewhat outdated today, but they have left their mark. A narrow orientation toward shareholder value in the sense of an exclusive commitment of management to shareholders' interests is still not part of German business culture, nor is it in line with actual practice or with the law (Charkham 1994).

The German corporate governance system is generally regarded as the standard example of what Franks and Mayer (1994) have called an insider-controlled and stakeholder-oriented system. Moreover, only a few years ago the German corporate governance system was a consistent system in the sense of being composed of complementary elements which fit together well. The first objective of this chapter is to show why and in which respect these characterizations were once appropriate. Today, however, they may no longer be appropriate. It is worthwhile, and indeed necessary, to investigate whether German corporate governance has recently changed in a fundamental way. More specifically one can ask which elements and features of German corporate governance have in fact changed, why they have changed and whether those changes which did occur constitute a structural change which has transformed the old insider-controlled system into an outsider-controlled and shareholder-oriented system, or has at least deprived the system of its former consistency.

Two of the factors which drive the evolution of financial systems in general, and specifically of national corporate governance systems, are European integration and globalization. It is often argued that these factors expose countries to the pressure of adopting a 'good' corporate governance system, and very often a good system is assumed to be one that comes as close as possible to the capital market-based Anglo-Saxon model of a financial system and the outsider-controlled model of a corporate governance system.[2]

The past decade has seen a wave of developments in the German corporate governance system. At least from a common-sense standpoint, it can be assumed that these innovations, for which not only this chapter, but also those by Rieckers and Spindler and by Nowak in this volume provide

---

[2] See Walter (1993) and recently chapter 7 of Walter and Smith (2000), Bebchuk and Roe (1999), and Roe (1996).

evidence, are shifting the general structure of German corporate governance towards the Anglo-Saxon model. But common sense may not be enough to substantiate such an assessment. Therefore, the second purpose of this chapter is to investigate in detail what the main recent developments in German corporate governance have been and whether they indicate that such a paradigm shift is already happening, or indeed has already taken place.

This chapter summarizes and extends my earlier work with various co-authors[3] on German corporate governance. Section 12.3 summarizes the earlier work which attempted to demonstrate the inner logic of the German system, and Section 12.4 extends it and discusses whether recent changes can be qualified as constituting a fundamental transformation.

12.2. BASIC CONCEPTS

In this section, we define and briefly explain the core concepts of this chapter. They are the concepts of corporate governance and of complementarity and consistency. A corresponding definition of the financial system, of which corporate governance is a part, has already been presented in Chapter 2 of this book.

We use a broad concept of *corporate governance*. In our definition, corporate governance denotes the entire range of mechanisms and arrangements that shape the way in which key decisions are made in (large) corporations. Corporate governance takes in legal regulations and arrangements regarding the way in which the highest-level decision-making rights are distributed in a company; it also encompasses other aspects of company law, the product markets, the markets for capital and labour, and finally, both the formal organizational structure of a company and any informal organizational arrangements which may exist and function alongside the formal structures.[4]

---

[3] See especially Schmidt and Grohs (2000), Schmidt (2001) and the references given there, as well as Schmidt and Spindler (2002) and Hackethal *et al.* (2003) with respect to corporate governance systems, and Hackethal and Schmidt (2000), Tyrell and Schmidt (2001) and Schmidt *et al.* (2002) with a broader focus on financial systems. Mann (2002) is also part of this research programme, which received financial support from the German Science Foundation. The strong role of my various co-authors in this area is the reason why I write 'we' instead of 'I', which is of course not meant to imply that others bear responsibility for any errors I may have made.

[4] See Prigge (1998) on different definitions of corporate governance and their implications. Most of the American literature on corporate governance uses a narrower concept than the one introduced here. For authors like Shleifer and Vishny (1997) corporate governance is mainly concerned with the Berle-Means question of how management can be made to act strictly in the interests of shareholders. This narrower concept reflects a normative assumption, namely that management should act strictly in the interests of shareholders. From a non-US perspective, a statement like this might be the outcome of a discussion or an investigation, but it certainly cannot be taken as a premise, let alone as a premise which is not even made explicit. However, some American authors do apply broader concepts of corporate governance similar to those used in the present text; see example Blair (1995) and Zingales (1998).

In discussing corporate governance systems—and financial systems (see Chapter 2)—we use the term 'system' in a specific way. A system is not just any collection of elements and their relationships, but one in which there is complementarity between the various elements or at least between the main elements, and possibly also consistency. *Complementarity* denotes an attribute of the relationships between the elements of a system, while *consistency* represents an attribute of an entire system in which complementary elements take on specific values maximizing a given objective or evaluation function.[5]

Two or more elements of a system are complementary to each other if, and only if

(1) the positive effects of the values taken on by the elements mutually reinforce each other and the negative effects mutually mitigate each other; that is

(2) a higher value for one element increases the benefit yielded by an increase in the value for the other element (and vice versa); and

(3) as a result, the 'quality' or the 'workability' or the 'value' of a system depends on the extent to which the values taken on by its (complementary) features are compatible with each other or, put simply, the extent to which the values 'fit together'.

The definition of complementarity implies that there is a potential for securing a benefit if the values taken on by the features or elements of the system are well adjusted to each other. It does not, however, presuppose that this potential is also exploited. This is precisely the aspect covered by the concept of *consistency*: A system composed of complementary elements is called consistent if the various elements—or at least the most important ones—take on values which exploit the potential which complementarity offers, that is, if these values fit together. Taken together the concepts of complementarity and consistency suggest a number of implications which are particularly relevant to the topic of this chapter. First of all, if complementarity prevails, there is a distinct possibility that multiple 'good' systems will coexist. In the case of corporate governance, two consistent systems or two types of systems are known. They come close to the typology of insider-controlled and outsider-controlled systems (Franks and Mayer 1994). Second, if there are two or more consistent or (locally) efficient configurations of system elements, 'middle-of-the-road systems' can be quite 'bad'.[6] Third, systems characterized by complementarity have specific ways of changing over time; there may be path dependence, and changes, when they occur, may be abrupt and far-reaching

---

[5] Formal definitions of these terms and relevant sources are extensively discussed in Hackethal (2000) and Hackethal and Schmidt (2000). The concepts of complementarity and consistency have already been introduced in Chapter 2 of this book.

[6] Note however that this need not be the case; it is not an implication of complementarity and consistency that middle-of-the-road systems *are* 'bad', but only that they *can be* 'bad'.

(Schmidt and Spindler 2002). It is precisely because of these implications that the concepts of complementarity and consistency help us to assess the efficiency of systems and to understand how they develop over time. Finally, the concepts provide an understanding of the 'fundamental' structure of a system, and therefore also a notion of what might be a 'fundamental' or 'structural' change in that system (Hackethal and Schmidt 2000).

12.3. GERMAN CORPORATE GOVERNANCE FROM A SYSTEMIC PERSPECTIVE

12.3.1. Corporate Governance from a Systemic Perspective

Firms are pools of resources. Pooling and employing resources in a firm can generate rents and quasi-rents. How large these rents will be depends on decisions which have to be made in the future. However, in part these residual decisions influence not only the size of the total rent, or the size of the proverbial pie which can be shared by the providers of the resources, but they also influence the distribution of the rent among them, that is, how big a slice of the pie each one gets. Thus, the providers of the resources have something 'at stake', which makes them stakeholders, and as such they have a 'natural' interest in monitoring as well as influencing management and its decisions.

Shareholders are an important group of stakeholders. Few would question that they are also the most important stakeholder group. But also employees, especially those who have undertaken firm-specific investments in their human capital or have built a house at the firm's location and cannot relocate easily, are stakeholders in this sense; so are creditors who have extended not fully secured loans. If too much is at stake, potential providers of critical resources might be worried that future decisions could violate their interests, and they might therefore abstain from contributing their resources to the pool. This is a precautionary reaction which others may want to avoid, and they may therefore agree that those stakeholders who might be exposed to moral hazard are given a governance role (Hart 1993, 1995; Schmidt 1997; Tirole 2001). Formally speaking, governance problems arise from the incompleteness of the contracts which tie together a corporation and its various providers of resources or its stakeholders and which, at the same time, create a network of relationships and interdependencies between the stakeholders.

Essentially, corporate governance is about the distribution of decision and control rights; it is about governing and monitoring management, which typically has important residual decision rights; it is about influencing business policy; and it is about protecting stakes which are exposed to the risks arising from the incompleteness of contracts and markets and the asymmetric distribution of information and decision rights.

If one wants to characterize a corporate governance system like that of large corporations in Germany in economic terms, one has to find answers to the following three sets of questions:

1. Which *stakeholder groups* are able to influence—and do actually influence—the important decisions which need to be taken in a corporation and on its behalf?
2. Which *instruments* do the various stakeholder groups, including those who are not active in influencing and controlling management, have at their disposal? How do they use their instruments, and in what way are these instruments effective? In other words, what are the *mechanisms* through which the individual stakeholder groups can and do participate in corporate governance?
3. How and to what extent do these two building blocks, that is, the roles on the one hand, and the arrays of instruments and the mechanisms for using them on the other, fit together? Are they *complementary and consistent*? Are they really 'a system' in the sense defined above?[7]

Real corporate governance systems differ with respect to the answers to these three questions. They can distribute influence among several stakeholder groups, or concentrate it in the hands of just a few; they can give active and non-active stakeholders few instruments of influence, or many; and they can distribute those instruments in a way which is largely consistent or rather inconsistent.

Monitoring management is a key issue in corporate governance. For various reasons, many decisions, including very important ones, need to be delegated to professional managers. Blind faith in managers is not a sound basis for securing business success. Rather, it makes sense for management,[8] as the main decision-making body, to be exposed to strong market pressures, or to be given general directions by the stakeholders and also to be monitored by them to a certain extent. However, whether this is really better in terms of its effect on the success of the company and on the benefits for all resource providers, depends in no small measure on which groups of stakeholders have the right to actively exercise influence and control, and also on which instruments or weapons the various groups of stakeholders have at their disposal to monitor, control, and influence management and to protect their claims.

Note that stakeholders' actively exercising influence over management, and especially the presence of different stakeholder groups with this capability, is not a feature of all corporate governance systems. In an ideal market-based or outsider control system no group has—or needs—the power to actively exercise influence, because market signals provide direction to management,

---

[7] If they are consistent, Mann (2002) calls such a system a corporate governance regime.

[8] In this chapter we mostly use the term 'management' to refer to top management.

because management is monitored by anonymous market forces, and because stakes are protected by complete and easily enforceable contracts and markets which provide exit opportunities for all stakeholders. In an insider control system, in contrast, markets play a less important role, as contracts are incomplete or unenforceable and some markets are imperfect, which makes it important to have the power to exercise active influence and control.

The economic effectiveness of control depends in a crucial way on the consistency of the governance system, because its elements are complementary. There are at least two systemic aspects or types of complementarity which need to be kept in mind in the present context.

The first systemic aspect, or the first respect in which complementarity and consistency are important, is related to the set of instruments or the arsenal of weapons which a given group of stakeholders has at its disposal and which it can use to protect its claims. How effective each individual instrument can be depends on which other instruments this group has, how they can be used and how they are, in fact, used. Each individual stakeholder group has an interest in ensuring that its arsenal is composed of weapons which reinforce each other in their effectiveness both in influencing management and in the distributive fight with other stakeholder groups.

The second systemic aspect refers to the interaction of the various stakeholder groups and their arsenals. There are different stakeholder groups with different arsenals of weapons to influence management and to protect their interests. Like the instruments or weapons in each arsenal, the various arsenals are complementary to each other. They may support each other, or they may be mutually destructive. Thus, the various groups may tend to cooperate or they may tend to act antagonistically towards each other, not only in their joint efforts to monitor management, but also in pursuit of their own respective interests. One group may strive to gain benefits for itself largely at the expense of other groups, or it may do so in a way which impinges less on the interests of others.

This characterization of the two systemic aspects has made reference to a standard of evaluation for the weapons and the arsenals without making this standard explicit. It is important to distinguish between two standards. One standard is the overall effectiveness of corporate governance as a determinant of the rents that can be distributed to all parties involved, which is measured by asking 'What is the contribution to the overall quality of corporate governance, and indirectly to corporate success, of assigning certain rights and opportunities to certain stakeholder groups?' We call this standard 'productive relevance'. A good corporate governance system provides instruments and assigns an *active* role to those stakeholders—and only to those—that have incentives and strategies for using their instruments in such a way that management is made to follow a business policy which benefits all groups of stakeholders or at least affords them so much protection that they all find it attractive to contribute their respective resources to the pool that is called the firm. The second standard is the size of the *share* of the rent, or the slice of the pie, which a given stakeholder group can secure for itself by using its instruments. We call this the 'distributive relevance'. The importance of distributive relevance should be self-evident. The focus of the discussion in this chapter is, therefore, on productive relevance.

12.3.2. Characteristic Features of German Corporate Governance

The starting point for our analysis of German corporate governance is the legal structure and the division of roles in a German joint stock corporation ('Aktiengesellschaft').[9] The Stock Corporation Act ('Aktiengesetz') gives the management board ('Vorstand') considerable power. According to Sect. 76(1), it has to manage the company in its own responsibility ('in eigener Verantwortung'). Most scholars of corporate law interpret this as saying that not only shareholder interests, but a wider array of interests should determine how a large company is to be managed. This is sometimes expressed as management having to act in the interests of the enterprise ('im Unternehmensinteresse').[10] Thus, stakeholder orientation is consistent with German company law. As Rieckers and Spindler discuss in their chapter in this book, it would even be against the law if the management board considered strict and exclusive shareholder value maximization as its goal. However, this does not call into question the fact that shareholder interests are very important in a legal sense and that they may also be the most important element in a complex set of related objectives.

Stakeholder orientation is also consistent with the distribution of power in large German corporations. As a complement to the strong role of the management board, corporate governance power in Germany is vested in the supervisory board. The supervisory board does not have the formal right to give specific instructions to the management, but management is required to report to the supervisory board at regular intervals and must seek its approval for certain classes of important decisions.[11] Moreover, one of the main functions of the supervisory board is to appoint and to dismiss the members of the management board, whose regular term is 5 years, and to determine management remuneration. For this reason alone it can be safely assumed that in its decisions the management board will tend to give due consideration to what the supervisory board and its members think.

---

[9] The following exposition is intentionally brief and necessarily incomplete; an extensive discussion of the legal aspects of German corporate governance law is not intended. Interested readers are referred to the chapter by Rieckers and Spindler in this volume and to Kübler (1998).

[10] For a critical discussion of this extremely vague concept in economic terms see Schmidt and Spindler (1997) and the references provided there.

[11] An older empirical study by Gerum *et al.* (1988) demonstrated that in the past the approval of the supervisory board was not important in practice. However, a recent amendment to the law may change this situation in the near future.

Evidently, the composition of the supervisory board is of crucial importance. It determines which stakeholder groups—alongside, or as a counterweight to, top management—can be active and have power. Three groups of stakeholders deserve special attention.

The first group consists of the shareholders. Within this group it is important to distinguish between blockholders and other, 'dispersed' shareholders. In 1990, the fraction of shares held directly by individual households stood at 18 per cent. By 2000, it had fallen to 12 per cent. The decline in direct ownership largely corresponds to the growth of indirect holdings via investment funds.[12]

Almost all large German corporations have one or a few major shareholders, which may be other companies, wealthy families or banks and insurance companies. According to a study by Böhmer and Becht (2001), which is based on the most detailed investigation of share ownership concentration to date, in the mid-1990s two-thirds of all listed companies in Germany had one blockholder with a stake exceeding 25 per cent. A share of 25 per cent gives a blockholder the power to veto important decisions, since in Germany many key decisions require a change in the corporate by-laws which in turn require the consent of more than 75 per cent of the votes at the general meeting. Voting power was even more concentrated than share ownership in the mid-1990s. In more than four-fifths of German listed corporations one blockholder had more than a quarter of the voting rights.

It is not easy to determine exactly which individuals or entities are 'really' the ultimate owners of share blocks, since in many cases wealthy families use corporations as legal vehicles to bundle their shares, and corporations can hold shares in other corporations via various subsidiaries within their group of companies. Nevertheless, it seems clear from the data (Böhmer and Becht 2001) that—in contrast to what is generally assumed about German ownership structures—the most important blockholders are other business enterprises. These blocks of shares held by other corporations are not part of the complex structures of groups of companies which Rieckers and Spindler explain in their chapter; instead they are blocks of shares in 'unrelated' firms.

The second largest group of blockholders are wealthy families, often those of the company's founder or founders. Financial institutions follow as a distant third. Especially the big commercial banks (Deutsche Bank, Dresdner Bank, Commerzbank, and HypoVereinsbank) and a few large insurance conglomerates (Allianz and Munich Re) used to have large portfolios of sizeable equity participations in corporations from various industries. What makes it very difficult to properly assess the extent to which financial firms, as blockholders, have the potential to influence corporate management is not

---

[12] It is important to note that investment funds in Germany are managed by investment management companies almost all of which are closely related to banks or groups of banks, or to insurance companies.

only the fact that until quite recently they held shares in non-financial corporations, but also the fact that there were many instances of complex cross-shareholdings among the big financial firms.[13] As will be discussed later, the complex web of cross-shareholdings within the financial sector is currently being dismantled.[14]

All large German corporations are subject to mandatory codetermination, and almost all of them are heavily dependent on banks as lenders and as active players in corporate governance. In the standard case of a large publicly held corporation, employee representatives make up half of the membership of the supervisory board. On paper, only a certain fraction of the employee representatives on the board are selected by the respective labour union or unions, whereas in practice most board members representing the labour side are union-affiliated. Typically, the chairperson of the supervisory board, who has a second vote in the case of a tie, will be a representative of the capital side, while his or her deputy will come from the labour side.

The governance role of banks and their potential to exercise influence emanate from four sources. One is lending: measured in terms of flows, bank loans constituted close to 80 per cent of long-term external funding to business in Germany in the 1990s.[15] The second source of the German banks' power to exercise influence is the fact that they traditionally exercise depositary voting rights on behalf of their clients. Third, banks (and insurance companies) themselves own shares in the companies concerned. And fourth, they hold seats on the companies' boards. Due to the depositary voting rights of the various big banks and probably also to their tradition of mutually supporting each other in their governance roles, the number of board seats and especially of chairs held by bankers far exceeds the number which one might expect merely on the basis of their shareholdings.[16]

Thus, there are three groups of powerful and 'influential' stakeholders— blockholders, employee and/or union representatives, and banks. They are represented on the typical German supervisory board, and they play an active role there. Moreover, former top managers of the respective companies are

---

[13] There exist various versions of a graphical representation of the almost unbelievably complex network of cross-shareholdings among the 'big players' in the so-called *Deutschland AG* (Germany Inc.). Dr Jens Massmann, now with Price Waterhouse Coopers, claims that he produced this graph while he was a research assistant. For one version see Adams (1999).

[14] Besides Böhmer, the distribution of shareholdings and especially blockholdings is discussed in Deutsches Aktieninstitut (2001), Davis (2002), Faccio and Lang (2002), and Adams (1999).

[15] This fraction is about the same in Japan, and stands in a sharp contrast to that in the United States (12 per cent). See Hackethal and Schmidt (2002) for the methodology employed to determine these fractions and for further results. The chapter by Elsas and Krahnen in this book contains more information on the influence of banks on corporations resulting from their close relationships.

[16] On the role of banks, especially the traditional large banks ('Grossbanken'), in the governance of many large corporations, see for example Emmons and Schmid (1998), Seger (1997), and Prigge (1998).

occupying an increasing number of seats on supervisory boards. One can consider this group as representing, at least indirectly, the current management. These three to four groups constitute what one might call the 'governing coalition' in most large German corporations. Still today, small shareholders and institutional shareholders who are not affiliated with banks do not play an important role on German supervisory boards; they are not part of the coalition. This answers the question of who the active and influential stakeholders in German corporate governance are. We now turn to the second question: How can and do they bring their interests to bear?

As Rieckers and Spindler (this volume) also acknowledge, the members of the supervisory board have a dual obligation. On the one hand, they are obliged to act in the best interests of the firm—whatever this may mean precisely—while on the other hand they have a certain amount of leeway to further the interests of their specific constituencies. Thus, there is a mixture of shared and divergent or even conflicting interests at work. This situation raises the important question of how the supervisory board can influence and monitor the management board at all.

Monitoring and control are made difficult by the fact that the task of management—namely to act in the best interests of the enterprise—is not at all well defined. But at the same time, monitoring and control are made relatively easy by the fact that the groups which form what we have called the governing coalition have a largely similar long-term objective. It does not consist in the maximization of shareholder value, but rather in ensuring stability and growth, or stable growth: Banks want their loans to be secure; employee and union representatives want job security and advancement opportunities for the staff and the protection of the human capital; families as blockholders want the family name and family involvement to last; top managers of other firms want stable structures in the entire German economy, and ex-top managers will probably wish to protect their successors and the firms to which they have dedicated an important part of their life. The common interests of the powerful groups may amount to what some legal scholars call 'the interests of the enterprise'.

The members of the active groups of stakeholders can act on the basis of much better information than the general investing public can ever have at their disposal, as Leuz and Wüstemann explain in their chapter in this book. Membership of a supervisory board is an important source of privileged and valuable information.

One last element of what the German corporate governance system used to be needs to be added even to the briefest of accounts: In the past there has *not* been an active *public* takeover market that could function as a market for corporate control. However, this does not imply that there has been no market for control at all. In Germany, this market took the form of a market for blocks of shares. As Franks and Mayer (2001) report, this market is active and at times quite hostile to incumbent management. Again, the participants in this market belong to the governing coalition, and therefore one might expect that adherence to the goal of making their firms successful from the perspective of several stakeholder groups would be advisable for incumbent managers, and it might be more advisable than 'mere' shareholder value orientation.

12.3.3. German Corporate Governance as a 'System'

Our brief description of the characteristics of German corporate governance, as it was in the mid-to-late 1990s and as it may still be today, provides a first glimpse of its fundamental features and its 'inner logic'.

1. It is a system based on stakeholder orientation as opposed to one-sided shareholder orientation. It is an insider control system as opposed to an outsider control system. Its functioning rests on internal, non-public information as opposed to public information. Evidently, these features of the system are complementary and consistent.
2. The set of active participants in the corporate governance of large publicly traded German corporations is compatible with the distribution of power and influence. There are several influential groups, and they are forced by the institutional design of the German *Aktiengesellschaft* (stock corporation) to use the supervisory board as the forum for their cooperation.
3. Moreover, these two features make the system stakeholder-oriented, and this conforms to the legal norm that the management shall be committed to serving 'the interests of the enterprise'.
4. The influential stakeholder groups can exercise their influence through the supervisory board, and they can do this on the basis of information which would be much too detailed to be presented to the general investing public.
5. Under this general rule, it is consistent that banks as long-term lenders and employees are part of the 'governing coalition'. At least some of their investments are relationship-specific or firm-specific. This shows that at least in principle the strange feature of mandatory codetermination and the traditional 'power of banks' are not inconsistent with the logic of this system.
6. As has been explained in Chapter 2 of this book, the German corporate governance system is also consistent with the general features of the German financial system.

One can take this analysis further and compare the ways in which the members of the governing coalition and their respective constituencies participate in the firm and its governance.[17] Not market forces and outside

---

[17] The following is based on Hackethal and Schmidt (2000).

opportunities—or 'exit' according to Hirschman's (1970) well known dichotomy—but internal mechanisms or 'voice' provide influence and protection for each of the three groups of active stakeholders, and this is why they find it in their interest to be active in governance. Blockholders as the most important group of shareholders seem to prefer control over liquidity.[18] German banks as lenders seem to prefer long-term lending and complex relationships to arm's length lending. For core employees and especially for staff with considerable firm-specific human capital there are advantages in a system in which internal labour markets are more important than external ones, and cooperative labour relations and codetermination predominate over adversarial relations and relations in which loyalty does not play much of a role.

The concept of complementarity suggests why each of the three stakeholder groups has an observable preference for its specific mode of participation in a firm:[19] The choice of the other groups suggests what is best for each group. For instance, the fact that important shareholders opt for control instead of liquidity and that banks engage in long-term lending relationships instead of arm's length lending makes it easier and more attractive for employees to rely on internal promotion and low-powered financial incentives, to act as partners in a codetermination regime and to invest in firm-specific human capital. The willingness of banks and core employees to support long-term relationships with the corporations makes it easier and more attractive for shareholders to take a long-term view and creates incentives to become blockholders in the first place; and long-term lending is less risky, and therefore more attractive for banks in a situation in which the shareholder structure is stable and in which employees have reasons to be loyal.

If, in contrast, the most important shareholders preferred liquidity and banks opted for arm's length lending, it would be better for employees to rely on external instead of internal labour markets, to act in an adversarial way in wage bargaining and to avoid even the appearance of being involved in anything which might resemble a codetermination regime, as the examples of the United Kingdom and the United States clearly show. Lending at arm's length would be more appropriate for banks if employees and shareholders were less committed; and one could expect shareholder structures to be less stable and shareholders to be more short-term oriented if employees and banks as lenders were less relationship-oriented.

In the case of Germany, control by blockholders, relationship lending by banks and internal labour markets supported by codetermination form a consistent set, which conforms to the stakeholder system of governance and to internal mechanisms of control based on privileged information for those who

---

[18] See Bolton and von Thadden (1998).

[19] See Hackethal (2000), who explains why the respective modes of participation are advantageous, and provides evidence to the effect that these modes are indeed preferred and chosen.

actively participate in governance. On a general level, the traditional German system of corporate governance appears to be a well designed institutional arrangement, or a consistent system of complementary elements.

However, there are also conflicting interests, and it is necessary to leave room for them. What mechanisms are in place to minimize the pursuit of particular interests and the level of conflict, and thus to ensure that the common interest prevails? The answer lies in at least five features of the traditional German corporate governance system.

(1) As has already been mentioned, the governing coalition is composed of groups with largely similar long-term objectives. Note that until today the typical small shareholders as well as independent institutional investors, who are only interested in dividends and share price appreciation, are either not represented on the supervisory boards of large corporations or, if they are represented, hardly have any influence. Their interests would be more difficult to reconcile with those of lenders and qualified staff, or with those of managers, unless the latter group were compensated with sizable stock option programmes.

(2) The participants of the 'governing coalition' seem to benefit from a situation which allows them to work together when they perform their job of monitoring management and of providing directions to management. But it seems that they can also reap private benefits of various kinds, and the expectations of these benefits may motivate them to be active players in corporate governance. For this reason, and because of the small number of active participants in the coalition, free riding among the coalition members is not to be expected.

(3) The instruments through which the individual groups can pursue their specific interests are consistent in the sense that their use tends to hurt other groups only to a limited extent. Examples of this kind of consistency include the following facts: In Germany wage bargaining is strictly separated from all issues of codetermination; dividends are limited to accounting profits determined under the conventional 'cautious' German accounting standards; and at least in the past, certain big banks were expected to play a supporting role in the event of a financial crisis in those companies for which they had traditionally been the main banker.

(4) Seen as social groups and even as individuals, the members of the 'governing coalition' not only interact on the supervisory board of a single corporation; rather, they are likely to meet again next month at the board meeting of another big corporation. This repeated and multifaceted interaction creates a sense of cohesion and joint responsibility for the common task of monitoring management and giving general directions of the kind described above; and it offers many opportunities to conclude and honour implicit deals, and thus balance interests over the longer term.

(5) Since there is room for conflict on the supervisory board, there is a possibility that, on a short-term basis, the balance of power might shift from one coalition of groups to another. Consequently, even the preferences within the board with respect to medium-to-long term strategies might occasionally change without such changes being justified by changing business conditions and prospects. Under these circumstances it could be difficult to design and implement a long-term strategy if the supervisory board had the right and the duty to directly influence the policy and strategy of corporations. The German system takes account of this potential problem by denying the supervisory board the formal right to intervene in the business decisions of the management.

At first glance, it might appear as if the traditional German corporate governance system were inimical to 'small' shareholders and therefore simply not good by international standards. This assessment is clearly right in the sense that these shareholders have no active corporate governance role. In the past investor protection was indeed rather weak in Germany. Moreover, analysis of the entire German corporate governance system suggests that there is no mechanism which would ensure that shareholders' interests were the sole or at least the dominant concern of those who run big corporations. This too is indeed the case. However, giving shareholders a *much* stronger role might be incompatible with the inner logic of the system of stakeholder orientation and restricted profit orientation. This is why even the absence of a public takeover market, which is generally perceived as a characteristic weakness of the German corporate governance system, is consistent with the fundamental structure of this system. If it existed and functioned very well, a market for corporate control based on public tender offers would put management under too much pressure to act in a shareholder value-maximizing way, and might thereby prevent it from honouring the implicit agreements with the other stakeholder groups, which, as we have seen, are an essential element of the system as a whole. Moreover, it would imply that banks and employees, in their capacity as stakeholders, would face the danger of a new owner possibly breaking the largely implicit contracts after a successful hostile takeover (Shleifer and Summers 1988). Both effects of an active takeover market could be anticipated by the other stakeholders. If banks and employees anticipated these possible effects of a takeover threat, they would probably not enter into relationships which would be dangerous for them.

However, one should not throw the baby out with the bathwater. The 'purely investing' public has not fared badly in the normal course of affairs in Germany. The financial rewards for investing in shares in publicly traded corporations have been in line with those available in other countries. In a comparative analysis of global stock markets, Jorion and Goetzmann (1999: 961) make the point that 'Germany experienced a steep run-up in stock market prices, 6 per cent in real terms, over the period 1950 to 1996'.

Table 12.1. *Real annual returns on domestic security portfolios in four countries (1960–2000)*

	Stocks (%)	Bonds (%)	50:50 (%)
Germany	5.1	4.1	4.6
France	5.2	3.0	4.1
UK	5.5	2.9	4.2
USA	5.9	2.4	4.2

Source: Jorion und Goetzmann (1999) and own calculations.

Table 12.1, which is based on data provided by Jorion und Goetzmann (1999), shows that the performance of domestic portfolios in different countries over the past 40 years did not support the view that German shareholders who were not blockholders were in a relatively weaker position.

12.3.4. An Assessment

In the preceding subsection, we presented a rather one-sided and positive view of the traditional German corporate governance system. It used to be a largely consistent insider control system with all of the typical strengths of such a system, allowing management to take a longer-term perspective in its planning and strategies. Because of the need to conclude incomplete and implicit contracts, it offered the advantage of flexibility, and it created stronger incentives to undertake relationship-specific investments, including those in firm-specific human capital, than a market-based and purely shareholder-oriented outsider control system. However, there can be no doubt that this system also had its weaknesses. Critics maintain that its centrepiece, the supervisory board, does not function in the way in which it was supposed to function. As we will see later, this concern was the main motive for the efforts in the late 1990s to strengthen the German corporate governance system. Among the chief weaknesses of an insider control system, which relies heavily on informal contracting, are its lack of transparency and its anti-competitive effects. It also leads to a systematic neglect of the stock market, and it offers opportunities to abuse power. Even more importantly, there is a real danger that such a system is inimical to all reforms, even those which might improve its functioning without altering its fundamental structure.

Unfortunately, there is no way of determining in general terms whether an insider control system is better than an outsider control system, either universally or in the specific case of Germany.

There have been several attempts to identify by econometric methods the effects of certain features of the German corporate governance system on various measures of corporate performance. For instance, the effect of

Table 12.2. *Market for corporate control and executive turnover (various years)*

	# of hostile bids	Block transfers (%)	Executive turnover (%)
Germany	4	10	12
France	n.a.	10	11
UK	148	9	9
USA	150	7	n.a.

ownership concentration has been studied and found to be positive (Edwards and Nibler 2000; Gorton and Schmid 2000*a*; Edwards and Weichenrieder 2003); the effect of codetermination has been analysed and found in some studies to be slightly negative (Seger and Schmid 1998; Gorton and Schmid 2000*b*; cf. Sadowski *et al.* 2001); and the effect of bank ownership—or more generally the effect of banks' playing a strong role in the governance of non-financial firms—has been analysed and found to be slightly positive (Gorton and Schmid 2000*a*). However, for almost every study showing one effect, there is a competing study which points in the opposite direction. This is not all that surprising when one considers that none of these studies takes into account how the various elements of the German corporate governance system are related to each other. As Börsch-Supan and Köke (2002) argue, the econometric studies on the effects of certain features of corporate governance have so far not been able to come to grips with the econometric problems which they aspire to overcome. Most importantly, in the view of the present author, they have so far largely failed to take into account how the different elements and features of such a system interact.

Instead of drawing econometric inferences, one can use simple descriptive statistics. For instance, Table 12.2 shows that although Germany does not have a really active public market for corporate control, management turnover is not lower in Germany than in other comparable countries with different governance systems.[20] One can interpret this as indicating that management is not under less control and pressure in Germany than in countries with much more hostile takeover activity.

In summing up, one can say that the traditional German corporate governance system was, and perhaps still is, a consistent insider control system. For insiders, exit options are typically not good. The insider control system

---

[20] Number of takeover bids are taken from Lipton (2001) who reports number of deals with US targets over $100m. Block transfers (exceeding 10 per cent of total equity) Germany (89–94): Köke (2001), France (89–91): Dherment-Ferere *et al.* (2001), UK (89–94): Franks *et al.* (2001), US (80–89, threshold 5 per cent): Bethel *et al.* (1998), Executive turnover: Dherment-Ferere *et al.* (2001).

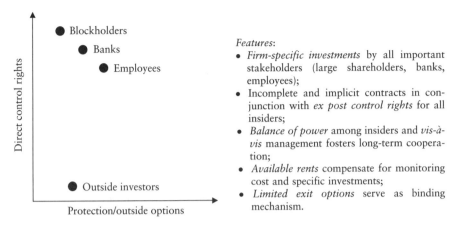

Figure 12.1. *Insider control system with the supervisory board as the centre of power.*

encourages firm-specific investments by lenders, employees and large share-holders and—as a necessary counterweight—gives control rights to the pro-viders of important and often firm-specific resources. It allows for a certain balance of power among the different groups of insiders and *vis-à-vis* man-agement, and thereby fosters long-term cooperation. It helps to create vents which can serve to compensate those who undertake firm-specific or rela-tionship-specific investments and who are—and need to be—active monitors of management for the risks of their investment and for their monitoring costs. Where does this compensation come from? In part it comes from the economic benefits of having a smoothly running and relatively efficient system. But in part it may also come from the 'exploitation' of those share-holders who are not insiders, that is, the small shareholders and possibly also some institutional investors. There is no doubt that shareholder protection has been weak in Germany for a long time. At first glance this may appear simply to be a weakness of the system. However, in functional terms, it may have been necessary since with a very high level of investor protection in place it might not have been possible to compensate the active stakeholders for their monitoring effort, and thereby to provide them with incentives to monitor management. Figure 12.1 is an intuitive representation of how we see the structure of German corporate governance in the recent past and why we tend to think that it used to be consistent and have positive economic effects. Later on we will present a similar graph in order to show how we assess the changes which have been taken place recently.

12.4. DEVELOPMENTS IN GERMAN CORPORATE GOVERNANCE

In this section we attempt to discuss the developments that appear to have taken place in corporate governance in Germany during the last decade as a consequence of a series of political measures. We start by looking back over the past 30 years, then address recent developments and conclude with a conjecture concerning the possible future course of events.

12.4.1. The longer-term development of German corporate governance in the past

Looking back over the last 30 years, but ignoring for the moment the last half-decade, we find a surprising degree of stability in the German corporate governance system. In the European context, or indeed anywhere in the world, hardly any other country exhibits so much stability in this area (Schmidt and Grohs 2000). The legal structure of the joint-stock corporation has remained almost untouched, the role of banks has hardly changed, and codetermination has not been seriously questioned. On a more general level, the specific mixture of conflict and cooperation between the various groups which play an active role in corporate governance in Germany has remained the same over decades. Finally, there has also been no change in the fact that small shareholders' interests tend to receive relatively little attention.

This unusual degree of stability calls for an explanation. One might be inclined to assume that change did not occur because the traditional system was not at all bad for all parties and that the players have understood its merits. This may indeed be the case, and the consistency of the system, which we have tried to demonstrate here, may have contributed to the success on which the stability may be partly based. But this cannot be the whole story. There is also a specific effect of complementarity and consistency on the propensity of a system to develop and to adapt to new circumstances. Complementarity and consistency prevent changes, especially gradual changes; they are a cause of path-dependence, as Schmidt and Spindler (2002) have argued in a response to Roe (1996) and Bebchuk and Roe (1999). In reality, reforms typically start as partial reforms; as long as there is not an extreme problem, reforms are not 'revolutions'. If complementarity is strong and if a given system is largely consistent, and therefore does not function too badly, partial reforms will rarely succeed even though they may seem to hold the potential for improvement. The reason for this resilience is that partial reforms would tend to reduce consistency, which comes with a cost in terms of economic efficiency, and this inconsistency may weigh more heavily than the benefits which the reform in question could bring if it were not part of a complex system.

However, instead of the seemingly positive features of stability and relative efficiency one could also diagnose stagnation, even ossification and an inability to reform in the German corporate governance system. If this negative assessment were appropriate—an issue which we are not in a position to decide—the German system might be one which faces extinction under the pressure of European integration and the globalization of financial markets.

12.4.2. Recent Developments and their Isolated Assessment

Recent developments, to which we now turn, indicate that something is being done to counter the danger of an ossification of the German corporate governance system. We will now look at individual aspects and areas of change which relate to corporate governance in Germany, and we start by discussing those developments which hold the greatest potential to contribute to a structural change of the German system, that is, to its transformation into a 'modern' capital market-based and outsider controlled system.[21] It is not our intention here to offer a broad and balanced description of the developments to be discussed. Rather, this section is highly selective in that it focuses exclusively on the possibility that the German system has already changed in a fundamental way or that a transformation of the traditional relationship-based insider control system into a market-based outsider control system is imminent.

The presentation of the individual developments is immediately followed by an assessment of the relevance of each development to the topic of this paper. But note that such an assessment is necessarily *ad hoc*, as it ignores the wider systemic perspective. Accordingly, in the next section we will assess these developments in a systemic context.

12.4.2.1. *The political debate*

The potentially most important—and certainly most topical—recent developments have taken place in the political arena. Four influential groups of high-level experts have recently deliberated on the basic issues of corporate governance in Germany and have produced four documents: the 'Frankfurt principles' and the 'Berlin principles', two sets of corporate governance principles named after the places where they were elaborated; the report of a high level 'Government Commission on Corporate Governance' published in 2001; and the Corporate Governance Code issued by the so-called Cromme Commission early in 2002.[22]

---

[21] This section draws on Hackethal *et al.* (2003).

[22] See Grundsatzkommission Corporate Governance (2003), Berliner Initiativkreis (2003), Government Commission on Corporate Governance (2001), and German Corporate Governance Code (2002).

The two sets of principles reflect different philosophies. The 'Frankfurt principles' seem to have been prepared under the premise that much more—or perhaps even exclusive—shareholder orientation and capital market orientation are desirable and that more elements of the Anglo-Saxon governance model should be introduced in Germany. But surprisingly this premise and its implications are not even mentioned in the published 'principles'. The 'Berlin principles', in contrast, retain the traditional stakeholder perspective as their normative basis. Top management, that is, the managing board ('Vorstand') is seen as the main actor here, and it is regarded as having a commitment to a broader set of 'legitimate' interest groups than merely the shareholders. Moreover, it is acknowledged that in order to fulfil its mandate, the managing board needs to have, and should have, considerable freedom to determine what it sees as being in the overall interests of the respective corporation or rather the respective enterprise.[23]

According to several statements by its chairman, Professor Theodor Baums, the 'Government Commission' had the political mandate to come up with recommendations supported by all committee members. This seems to have led it to leave aside the crucial but controversial question of what might be the best model of corporate governance for Germany. In its introduction the published report even states explicitly that the fundamental structure of corporate governance in Germany, that is, the law-based approach, the dual board system, mandatory codetermination, considerable autonomy of the management board, and the reliance on internal mechanisms of corporate governance, need not be altered.

In its refusal to take an explicit stand on the 'fundamental issues', the 'Corporate Governance Code' of the Cromme Commission goes even further. Indeed, the very composition of the Commission made this outcome seem virtually inevitable. It included fervent advocates of the old German model as well as outspoken 'modernists'.

All in all, in their widely publicized attempts to address 'the corporate governance problem' in Germany, the four groups of experts appear to have come to a rather simple conclusion: There does not seem to be a need to modify the basic structure of corporate governance in Germany. Of course, all shareholders should be treated fairly and small shareholders in particular should certainly be treated better than in the past, but none of the expert groups has made an attempt to reinstate shareholders as the supreme, let alone the only, authority in corporate governance matters.[24]

---

[23] See Schmidt and Spindler (1997) on the distinction in the German legal tradition between 'the interests of the corporation', that is, of the association of the shareholders, and 'the interests of the enterprise'.

[24] This assessment refers only to the documents' conclusions regarding 'the fundamental problem'; it should not be misinterpreted as implying that these documents did not have useful roles of their own or that they did not succeed in fulfilling these roles. The 'Government Commission'

12.4.2.2. *Investor protection and capital market law*

One of the main functions of capital market law is to protect investors, especially 'small' and 'unsophisticated' investors, from the hazards which might be entailed in buying, holding, and selling shares and other financial instruments; another is to attract institutional investors to the national capital market. Before 1990, there was no capital market law in Germany in the strict technical sense of the word. In 1994, insider trading was legally prohibited and a Federal Authority supervising certain elements of stock market activity was created; and in 2001 a mandatory bid was incorporated into the new German takeover law. These are just the most important regulatory changes of the past decade, and without doubt they are important innovations. In combination with the institutional improvements at the level of the German stock exchange system, these developments have greatly improved the quality of investor protection. The traditional assessment that the German capital markets are 'underdeveloped' no longer appears justified today.[25] Also the devastating rating of German investor protection by La Porta *et al.* does not seem to apply any more.[26]

However, the new supervisory authority which came into existence in 1995 did not have the broad mandate of the SEC—to oversee all relevant aspects of stock market activity—and it largely lacks enforcement powers.[27] This limits the effectiveness of legally mandated investor protection,[28] and this fact alone makes it difficult to argue that the new elements of capital market law already constitute, or at least pave the way for, a capital market-based system of corporate governance.

12.4.2.3. *Developments in corporate law*

In a process which is still going on, the law governing joint-stock corporations has been modified to a considerable extent. The most important part of this

contains a wealth of specific proposals on how the German Stock Corporation Act can and should be modernized; the Cromme Commission seems to have had the function of helping foreign investors to understand the nature of the German corporate governance system from a legal point of view and even encouraging them to appreciate that it is not so bad after all; and all four documents have the common function of making managers, supervisory board members and others aware of their respective obligations.

[25] See Chapters 13, 11, and 5 by Nowak, Rieckers and Spindler, and Theissen in this book for details underpinning this assessment.

[26] See e.g. La Porta *et al.* (1998) and our reassessment of the current situation along their lines in the Appendix (Table 12A.1). It is important to note here that many German experts find the assessment of La Porta *et al.* inappropriate on a purely factual basis even for the time to which these authors refer explicitly.

[27] The Bundesaufsichtsamt für den Wertpapierhandel, BAWe (since 2002 incorporated into the new Bundesanstalt für Finanzmarktaufsicht, BAFin) is not allowed to pursue violations of the insider trading prohibition and has to transfer cases of presumed violations to the public prosecutor. Since 1995 there have been only two convictions (Bundesaufsichtsamt für den Wertpapierhandel 2001: 57).

[28] A more general criticism of the lack of enforcement is presented in Ehrhardt and Nowak (2002).

modernization process is the 'Law for the Strengthening of Control and Transparency' (KonTraG) of 1998. The main intention of the law was to improve the effectiveness of supervisory boards and to strengthen them in their role as monitors of top management. The KonTraG has led to a certain shift of power in favour of the supervisory board, thus limiting the powers of the management board. Moreover, it curtails the influence of banks. However, it did not address the questions of how the board is to be composed and what the respective legal obligations of the management and the supervisory boards should be. As this law has a clear and exclusive focus on improving internal governance mechanisms, it would also be inadmissible to claim that the KonTraG has contributed to a paradigm shift from insider to outsider control. On the contrary, it is an important step towards streamlining and strengthening the corporate governance system in its old format.

Accounting rules are a part of corporate law in Germany. Since 1998, corporations are permitted to use international accounting standards for their group accounts, and in a few years' time, listed companies will even be obliged to adhere to these standards. It may be true that American or International Accounting Standards ensure greater transparency. But even this claim seems hard to really substantiate. Furthermore, Wüstemann (2001) argues convincingly that the adoption of international accounting principles needs to be distinguished from the adoption of American-style disclosure. SEC disclosure rules go much further than those implied by US-GAAP. While many German top managers seem to be strongly in favour of American accounting standards, which tend to increase profits and possibly bonuses and the value of stock options, they seem less enthusiastic about the idea of having to conform to the far-reaching SEC disclosure rules. The adoption of these rules and requirements has not even been considered in Germany so far.

Mandatory codetermination constitutes one of the most remarkable peculiarities of German corporate governance and is a backbone of the stakeholder-oriented insider control system. Codetermination has not been challenged greatly during the past decade. This may be a matter of political correctness, but it seems more likely that codetermination owes its durability to the fact that it has worked reasonably well within the traditional system.[29] Another commission (Kommission Mitbestimmung 1998) composed of experts from the business community, unions, and other sections of society has recently given a clear endorsement to the fundamental structure of German codetermination. Indeed, in 2002 the law on works councils was actually tightened and at the same time streamlined. A recent newspaper article reports that, contrary to widespread expectations and fears, this seems to have had beneficial effects.[30]

---

[29] This applies particularly to shop floor level codetermination; see Frick and Lehmann (2001) and Sadowski *et al.* (2001).

[30] *Frankfurter Allgemeine Zeitung*, 19 September 2002.

12.4.2.4. *Takeovers and hostile bids*

The Mannesmann-Vodafone takeover battle of 1999 and 2000 was indeed a hostile one, and it was consummated in the form of a public tender offer, not in the form of block sales.[31] Its ultimate success seems to have marked a watershed and given a clear and simple signal of 'modernization': Hostile takeovers in the form of an offer to the broad shareholding public are possible in Germany.

For a number of reasons, the success of Vodafone in its attempt to take over Mannesmann does not imply that the curtain has risen on an active public market for corporate control in Germany.[32] First of all, the battle over Mannesmann does not seem to have had anything to do with sanctioning and ultimately removing bad management. Especially from a shareholder perspective, the former Mannesmann management had been remarkably successful long before the takeover bid by Vodafone and was even more successful after the bid. Second, many observers expected the outcome of the Mannesmann-Vodafone case to unleash a wave of tender offers, possibly governance-related and hostile. So far, there has been hardly a ripple since February 2000, and certainly no wave. Third, several of the reasons which had always made hostile tender offers difficult in Germany, especially the legal structure of German joint stock corporations and codetermination as a part of it, still apply.

An important recent legal development is the adoption of a German takeover law in 2002. It was enacted immediately *after* the narrow defeat of the EU takeover directive in the European Parliament (EP) in 2001. The main point of controversy which had led to the decision of the EP was that the defeated EU directive strictly prohibited incumbent management from taking measures against a takeover bid which it considered not to be in the interests of 'the company' or of those constituencies to which management has a legal commitment.[33] The German law contains most of the elements of the EU directive, including a mandatory bid rule, but stops short of disallowing all counter moves. Thus, it is evidence of an attempt to balance improved investor protection with the old conviction that not only shareholder interests matter.

This concludes our overview of recent political and regulatory developments. For reasons which we have not explained here and which are covered in other chapters of this book, these developments can be assessed as having many positive effects. They are bold steps towards improving investor protection and the functioning of the capital markets, but they do not constitute

---

[31] Block sales have always been customary in Germany, and they can indeed be quite 'hostile' towards the incumbent management. See Franks and Mayer (2001) and Jenkinson and Ljungqvist (2001).

[32] See Höpner and Jackson (2001) for details and empirical material, as well as Chapter 9 by Schmid and Wahrenburg in this book.

[33] Germany is expected to fight once again the new takeover directive draft (see The Wall Street Journal Europe, 25 September 2002: A3).

a decisive move towards introducing a capital market-based system of corporate governance in Germany.

12.4.2.5. *Ownership and direct influence*
The degree of ownership concentration and the extent of cross-ownership in the German business world are still very high by international standards (Ulrich 2002). It seems that they have decreased in the recent past, but these changes have not affected the extent of non-financial corporations' participations in other non-financial firms nearly as much as the shareholdings of financial institutions. In particular, there is a clear trend towards unravelling the overly complex web of participations within the financial sector itself.[34]

The corporate tax reform law of 2000 abolished the tax on profits from the sale of equity participations. This tax reform took effect at the beginning of 2002. Before that date it had generally been expected that the new legislation would encourage firms to sell off their big share blocks on a large scale. But so far, this has not happened. This reluctance may well be a consequence of the stock market situation in 2002 and early 2003, but it may also be due to a reluctance on the part of big corporations to fully relinquish their old roles.

Supervisory board composition has changed slightly in recent years. The number of positions and especially chairmanships held by top bankers has decreased during the last decade, while—interesting enough—the role of managers of other companies and especially that of former managers of the same company has increased. Höpner (2001) provides data which show that the retreat of bankers from corporate boards is matched almost one to one by the arrival of former members of the management board, a trend that is particularly pronounced in the financial sector. Thus, the role of management seems to have been strengthened—hardly a move towards greater capital market control. The fraction of seats on supervisory boards held by genuine shareholder representatives has not increased, while the fraction of shares held directly by households has reached an all-time low.[35] Institutional investors are not (yet) active in German corporate governance as far as board representation is concerned. Thus, once again, the facts do not support the proposition that the insider control system is giving way to a market-based system.

12.4.2.6. *Shareholder orientation*
There are strong indications that in the course of time, at least the professed degree of shareholder orientation has increased in most German companies. While the stock market was booming, firms and experts were almost euphoric

---

[34] See Appendix (Table 12A.2) based on Faccio and Lang (2002) for details. Our view seems to be shared by Deutsch *et al.* (2001), a group of researchers at Deutsche Bank. Developments in the past few weeks before this book went to press support the observation that financial institutions are tending to reduce their crossholdings.

[35] Deutsches Aktieninstitut (2001: chart 08-1-1°).

about shareholder value. In part, this may be due to increased informal pressure from institutional investors. As social and political analysts who study the German system argue, it may also be a consequence of the introduction of stock option programmes in most large corporations, or a complement to the introduction of new concepts of value-based internal management, or simply a fashion among managers.

It is, however, extremely difficult to distinguish rhetoric from fact in this area. For instance, Deutsche Bank, whose former CEO Rolf E. Breuer has, for a long time, been one of the most outspoken advocates of a reorientation of German corporate governance towards more emphasis on shareholder interests and capital markets, nevertheless, seems to support a moderate form of stakeholder orientation as the relevant principle of corporate governance. In its own corporate governance principles, Deutsche Bank (2002) proclaims that its board and management consider themselves responsible to four stakeholder groups, among which the shareholders are only the *primus inter pares*.

12.4.2.7. *Pension reform*

The recent German pension reform (see Chapter 4 by Maurer) seems to have followed the general tendency in the late 1990s to assign increasing importance to the stock market and to the interests of shareholders, and may have thus contributed, at least indirectly, to a change of the governance regime. To a certain extent this may have indeed happened, and it might gain momentum in the years to come, as we will argue in the concluding chapter of this book. But based on the plans presented so far, the extent to which the German pension system will in the future rely on capital-funded private pensions stops far short of the British or American levels. We therefore doubt that the pension reform will have a 'structural' impact on German corporate governance in the medium term.[36]

12.4.2.8. *The financing of business*

For a long time, the pattern of firm financing in Germany has been remarkably stable. Bank financing was the dominant source of long-term external financing for German companies, and large corporations were the favourite clients of the big banks. At a general level, the role of bank financing does not seem to have changed so far.[37] But there is a need to differentiate. Two aspects merit particular emphasis. First, large corporations, on which most discussions of corporate governance focus, have become increasingly independent of permanent long-term bank financing. Second, especially the big banks, which have traditionally played an important role in the governance of the very large corporations, seem to be reducing their corporate lending activities. These two developments together might motivate the big

[36] See Tyrell and Schmidt (2001) for details.
[37] See Hackethal and Schmidt (2000, 2003) for details.

banks to reduce their active involvement in corporate governance. Moreover, competition in the banking sector seems to be becoming stiffer, and this might undermine the willingness of the big banks to act in a co-ordinated way in their governance roles. Taken together, these developments might ultimately be the most important ones when it comes to identifying a possible fundamental change in the German corporate governance system. We will return to this point below.

In summing up, one can say that indeed much has changed which appears to be more or less closely connected to corporate governance in Germany. Especially investor protection and the institutional basis for the monitoring of management seem to have improved considerably. However, some of the developments which appear to be relevant may not in fact stand up to empirical scrutiny, or they may not last; other developments which clearly do have empirical reality are unlikely to have an impact on the German corporate governance system; and still others are not sufficiently significant to support the claim that a fundamental shift is taking place.

We could leave it at that and conclude by saying that in our view the proverbial glass, which others may regard as being still half full or already half empty (depending on their point of view), is in fact still three quarters full. However, as we said before, looking at the individual developments may provide a distorted picture. In the final analysis, the effects that a given change in the relevant factors, elements and features may have depends very much on other—stable as well as changing—elements of the entire governance system. This is the level at which our main question needs to be answered, and to this we now turn our attention.

12.4.3. Assessing Recent Developments from a Systems Perspective

12.4.3.1. *The general proposition*

In Section 12.3 we intentionally painted an idealized and almost 'idyllic' picture of German corporate governance as it existed until the mid-to-late 1990s. In Section 12.4.2, we discussed individual recent developments. We tried to show that when they are looked at in isolation, most of them do not seem to have a direct effect on the *fundamental structure* of German corporate governance. Can this assessment be sustained when we look at the entire system 'as a system'? To answer this question, we invoke the concept of 'productive relevance' from Section 12.3.1. This concept refers to the role that certain facts and instruments which are in place or have been given to certain stakeholder groups play in making the *entire* corporate governance system function for the benefit of all stakeholders or, as German lawyers might say, 'in the interests of the enterprise'. Productive relevance is evidently a feature which can only be assessed with reference to the entire corporate governance system of a country and to the way in which it functions.

The overarching question of this section is this: Is the fundamental way in which corporate governance seems to have functioned in the past, its 'inner logic', changing, or has it already changed, or is it likely to change, as a consequence of the developments described above? Structural or fundamental change can only be brought about by introducing new elements of a new system one at a time so that the new system can finally 'take over' (Witt 2001) or, alternatively, by undermining the functionality of the old system.

We first look at a possible transition based on the introduction of new elements or features of the governance system. Have they already led to a fundamental change, or are they likely to lead to such a change? At this general level the answer seems to be a straightforward No. The 'governing coalition' of blockholders, labour representatives and banks which supported the insider control system and benefited from the way it functioned does not seem to be affected in an essential way by the recent developments. Stakeholder orientation has not been replaced by radical shareholder orientation. Those who are active in governance still seem to act on the basis of privileged private information. In spite of the enormous improvements in its capacity as a secondary market, the stock market has not taken over an important role as a primary market and as a market for corporate control. The official proclamation of the end of the *Neuer Markt* epitomizes clearly that Germany has not yet become a shareholder society, and the downturn of the stock market since early 2000 may have interrupted any development in that direction for quite some time. Among the most important developments, we have singled out the strengthening of the supervisory board in its capacity as a monitor of management. This development even points in the opposite direction, indicating as it does that the insider control regime has been made more effective. Moreover, many of those elements in the larger economic system which support the traditional governance system, such as labour law, labour relations, and the overall financial system, have largely remained unchanged in Germany so far.

However, one important reservation needs to be made at this point. The more far-reaching recent developments include not only the strengthening of the role of the supervisory boards, but also considerable improvements in transparency and investor protection. Clearly, transparency and investor protection are crucial elements of an outsider control system. Do changes in these fields play a *constructive* role in inducing a transformation of the German system? We think that they do not, because our reconstruction of the mechanism according to which insider control systems function shows that those shareholders who only invest and only expect dividends and share price appreciation in return do not play a governance role at all in Germany. Improvements in investor protection will probably contribute to a change in 'distributive relevance' as defined above, but not in productive relevance. Creating more transparency and more protection for these investors does not exert pressure on management to adjust its strategies.

12.4.3.2. *The uneasy case of investor protection*

As stated above, structural or fundamental changes in a system composed of complementary elements can also be caused by undermining the functionality of the old system, thereby greatly increasing the pressure to adapt to new circumstances. We now turn to this possibility. Have the recent changes weakened Germany's insider control system to such an extent that it might cease to function, and therefore create space for the introduction of a new system?

One topic which is clearly relevant in this context is investor protection. In the public and political debate the presumed fact that small investors have, for a long time, been insufficiently protected in Germany[38] is considered a problem. But even if this is the case, what exactly is the nature of the problem here? First of all, it is certainly a problem for those individuals who are adversely affected by the relative lack of protection. Exploiting them is simply unfair and politically unacceptable. Second, it may be a public policy problem which stands in the way of all efforts to achieve a broad-based distribution of share ownership in the German population. Third, it may also create a financing problem for firms, insofar as it makes it difficult for them to raise equity capital from the general public. However, it is not necessarily a problem of corporate governance, since investors who do not have any other role and seek only dividends and share price appreciation simply do not have productive relevance in an insider control system. As the history of the so-called economic miracle in Germany shows, a lack of investor protection may also not be a problem as far as the competitiveness of the German economy and the individual firms is concerned. The economic advantages of a governance system based on consensus and cooperation among those who do wield power, 'undisturbed' by small shareholders in pursuit of their specific objectives, might well outweigh the difficulties of raising outside equity from relatively unprotected investors.

But how large are the possible benefits of having an insider control system for all stakeholders, including small investors, and how would these benefits need to be shared between on the one hand the active players, who in the German case are the traditional governing coalition, and on the other hand the—possibly 'free riding'—non-influential small shareholders, in order to keep the system operating? Or, to rephrase the same question: How much shareholder value orientation, as opposed to profit-based growth and stability orientation, how much investor protection and how much transparency is compatible with the functioning of a stakeholder-oriented insider control system? How important is it for the continuous involvement and the active monitoring efforts of those who are active players in the internal corporate governance that management pursues stability and growth enhancing strategies rather than value-maximizing strategies? How much do their

---

[38] Empirical support can be found in the work of Wenger, for example, Wenger and Hecker (1995).

cooperation and involvement rely on their ability to earn 'private benefits' or, as one could also put it, their ability to exploit small shareholders?

We simply have no answers to these questions. Optimists might think that the economic benefits of a functioning insider control system of corporate governance that accrue to all stakeholder groups are enough to ensure their continuing involvement in either an active or a passive role, so that the 'rewards' reaped by the active players for their activism are financed with the value created by their activity and therefore, in the final analysis, do not hurt shareholders. However, sceptics will question this view: They will merely see excessive private benefits on the one side and expropriated current share-holders and reluctant potential shareholders on the other. Nostalgia may lead one to think that in the past the net benefit was large enough to ensure the cooperation of all parties in their respective roles, whereas nowadays, as a consequence of the highly publicized changes that have taken place in the overall economy, including globalization, liberalization and increasing share-holder demands, the surplus left over for distribution may simply no longer be large enough to compensate active stakeholder–monitors and keep the old system viable.

12.4.3.3. *The diminishing role of banks in German corporate governance*

In the past, private benefits have existed in Germany, and as it seems, they have decreased in recent years. Figure 12.2 shows the development of the value

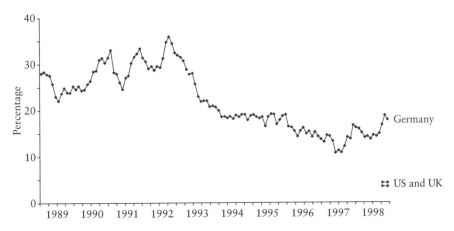

Figure 12.2. *The value of control rights in Germany. Difference between voting and preferred stock prices in Germany (1989–98).*

Sources: For US and UK, Nenova (2000) and Dyck/Zingales (2002) both report that average premiums for US and UK corporations are below 5 per cent. The data for Germany was kindly provided by Humboldt University, Institut für Bank- und Börsenwesen. Note that the measurement methods employed in the various sources are not the same.

Humboldt University, Institut für Bank- und Börsenwesen.

of control rights during the course of the 1990s. There is a marked decline, but control premiums, which are generally regarded as an indicator of the size of private benefits, remain substantial.

The decline in the value of control rights can be interpreted as empirical evidence showing that investor protection has improved. However, the considerations in the preceding subsection imply that those who play an active—and perhaps beneficial—role in corporate governance might require a certain compensation, and this compensation might come in the form of private benefits. More transparency and better investor protection might lead to a reduction of this compensation and ultimately even to less willingness on the part of those with an active role to continue playing this role.

Are there already signs of core players reducing their involvement or their willingness to cooperate in the governing coalition? There are indeed such signs. Deutsche Bank is actively reducing its corporate governance role. It has given up several board seats and has introduced the rule that its own top managers should avoid chairmanships of the boards of other corporations. Deutsche Bank has also undertaken several steps to reduce its own shareholdings and cross-ownerships. There are various reasons for these moves. One is that, like other big banks, Deutsche Bank is also substantially cutting back on its lending to large corporations, and at the same time is trying to become what might almost be described as an investment bank. The new Deutsche Bank simply no longer benefits much from its traditional governance role. This old role, which consisted in being the main bank or house bank of the leading German corporation in each industry, even seems to stand in the way of the current strategy. Another reason for the partial withdrawal of the big private German banks from their governance role in other corporations may be that recent reforms have restricted the scope for banks' active involvement in the governance of non-financial corporations.

Competition and rivalry in the banking sector have increased. This trend also tends to undermine the banks' old established practice of acting cooperatively in governance matters and in cases where big non-financial enterprises run into financial difficulties. The conflicts between the various big banks in the recent Holzmann and Kirch insolvency cases suggest that this traditional model of behaviour is no longer valid, and with it a key element of the old governance system may be about to vanish.

There are also indications that some of the core players of the traditional system are already looking for different ways of protecting themselves as an alternative to playing an active governance role. For example, changing practices of financing indicate that especially the big banks are tending to opt out of the system. It is an open, but extremely important question whether the aggregate effects of these attempts, which are certainly inspired by the changing economic environment, will, under changed circumstances, be as consistent with each other as their efforts to secure their interests have been in the past. And more directly, it is an open question whether this partial withdrawal of the banks from their former role reduces the 'productive relevance' of their involvement.

Traditionally, the big banks have been the incarnation of the proverbial *Deutschland AG* (Germany Inc.), which many observers now consider to be an outdated model and which they are happy to see disappear. The banks have indeed been the spider in the web of power and influence in Germany for several decades. However, even if this may not be politically correct, in functional terms one can also see their traditional role more positively: It seems to have been their role to keep the governing coalition stable and working, and thus to assure at least a certain level of control over management. It remains to be seen what will happen if the big banks should really give this role up, as they seem to be doing already. One possible consequence would be a—hopefully rapid—transition to a—hopefully well functioning—full blown market-oriented corporate governance system along Anglo-Saxon lines. But the necessary conditions for this to happen are not in place and not even in sight.

A more probable consequence in the medium term is that the effectiveness of the existing governance system will decrease and *no* new system will replace it any time soon. In spite of all political declarations and ambitions, monitoring of management might effectively be reduced, and instead of 'better governance' and more investor protection we might see an emerging control vacuum. The fact that today more chairpersons of large German corporations are former CEOs of the same corporation than ever before and that former top managers are systematically replacing bankers as board members suggests that the power of management is steadily increasing, a development which is not exactly what one would regard as a move toward good governance. The emphasis on shareholder value orientation, which some management teams seem to endorse to a large extent, could intensify and reshape the conflict between management and the remnants of the old control system, and a less co-ordinated and less powerful group of stakeholders would have little means of opposing the increasing autonomy of management and protecting their stakes. If the providers of critical resources see things this way, they might be inclined to reduce their exposure to the risk of being exploited by management, which they can do by reducing relationship-specific investments.

The growing instability of the German business environment and especially the enormous increase in the level of average top management compensation packages in recent years suggest that we may have already reached this point and that the old Berle–Means problem is reappearing in a more modern guise. However, this is not the only scenario of how corporate governance in Germany might develop. A further scenario will be briefly sketched in the concluding section.

12.5. CONCLUDING REMARKS

In this paper we have tried to demonstrate that German corporate governance was—and possibly still is—a system, in the sense of a consistent configuration of complementary elements. It was and is an insider control system with a clear stakeholder orientation. Governance was, and possibly still is, exercised by a coalition of active stakeholder groups. To a certain extent, this system seems to have functioned well because of features such as cross-ownership and shareholder concentration, and multiple relationships between the stakeholders and the companies in question. However, there are many reasons to regard these very features as highly ambivalent. The German corporate governance system of the past can also be seen as a system which functioned mainly in the interests of the active stakeholders and also at the expense of others, notably the general investing public.

The past decade has witnessed several important reforms of German corporate governance as such or elements of it. Seen in isolation, these reforms have gone a long way, without challenging the fundamental structure of German corporate governance. Some reforms have even helped to improve the traditional system. This assessment is confirmed when one looks at the recent developments in a systemic context: The fundamental structure—that is, the set of incentives, restrictions, and opportunities for the various stakeholders to secure their interests, among other things by controlling and monitoring management, and the way in which they complement each other—seems to be intact. A transition to a more modern capital market-based outsider control system is not yet in sight. While most other observers tend to think that the proverbial glass formerly filled with the strange brew of typically German corporate governance is already half empty because of capital market-friendly reforms and that it is in the process of becoming ever more empty, we think that it is still almost full. That is, the old system may still be largely intact.

However, the cautioning word 'largely' needs to be taken seriously. In economic terms, the old system was and possibly still is, a fragile equilibrium. This consideration suggests a different scenario. The reforms of the past decade and other pertinent developments may already have undermined the stability of the traditional German system of corporate governance. For instance, the willingness of big banks to finance hostile takeovers is simply inconsistent with the traditional role of bankers on the supervisory boards of corporations which may be targets in bank-financed takeover contests. If this is really the case, the traditional German system might soon simply cease to function as well or as badly as it did in the past. Figure 12.3, which is drawn in analogy to Figure 12.1, shows how one can see the current situation: The governing coalition seems to have become weaker, and the opportunities available to the passive investors seem to have increased. This leaves less

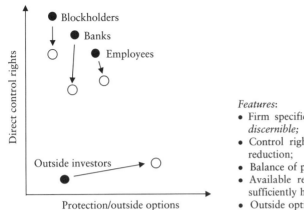

Features:
- Firm specific investments: *no clear trend discernible;*
- Control rights for insiders: simultaneous reduction;
- Balance of power: intact;
- Available rents: lower but arguably still sufficiently high;
- Outside options: slowly increasing.

Figure 12.3. *Impact of changes on core elements of German corporate governance system.*

'private benefits' for those with an active role in governance and might make them unwilling to continue playing their traditional role.

A possible breakdown of the traditional system would not imply that a market-based governance system is already in place and functioning, thus superseding the old system. It might therefore create a lack of any form of functioning governance. One can call this situation a systemic 'crisis' (as do Schmidt and Spindler 2002). As a functioning corporate governance system is probably indispensable in any modern economy, such a crisis would create the urgent need to restore some form of order or to regain some kind of consistency. In principle, both the return to the traditional system and a rapid or even immediate transition to the alternative of a market-based outsider control system would be ways to regain consistency. We simply do not know which of the two alternatives would be better. Therefore, we leave this question open. However, the two alternatives would not be equally attainable if one started from a governance crisis. The traditional German corporate governance system relied to a large extent on compatible mutual expectations, on long-term cooperation and on implicit deals with a give and take between parties that know each other and to a certain extent trust each other. Recent developments in the real world of German business suggest the basis for this kind of cooperation has disappeared. Since mutual trust cannot easily be restored, as Schmidt and Spindler (2002) explain, the only real option would be the transition to the Anglo-Saxon model of market-based corporate governance—not because it is better than the alternative, but rather because the old system cannot be restored.

Appendix

Table 12A.1. *Rating of German investor protection—shareholder rights as measured by La Porta* et al. *approach (1 = protection is in the law)*

	1998			2002
	USA	UK	Germany	Germany
1. One-share-one-vote	1	1		1[a]
2. Proxy by mail allowed	1	1		1
3. Shares not blocked before meeting	1	1		1[b]
4. Cumulative voting/proportional representation	1			
5. Oppressed minorities mechanism	1	1		
6. Preemptive rights		1		
7. Possibility to call an extraordinary SGM with less than 10% of the share capital	1	1	1	1
Total	6	6	1————→4	

[a] Excluding German-style preferred stock.
[b] Registered shares.

Source: La Porta *et al.* (1998), own investigations.

Table 12A.2. *Ownership concentration in Germany—ultimate ownership by sectors (%)*

	Sector holdings in total equity of nonfinancial corporations (various years)				
	< 20%	> 20%			Average voting rights[a]
		Family	Bank/Inst.	Other	
Germany	10	65	9	16	55
France	14	65	11	10	48
UK	63	24	9	4	25

[a] Share of total voting rights controlled by largest shareholder (5% threshold).

Source: Faccio and Lang (2002).

References

Adams, M. (1999). 'Cross Holdings in Germany', *Journal of Institutional and Theoretical Economics*, 155: 80–109.

Bebchuk, L. A., and Roe, M. J. (1999). 'A Theory of Path Dependence in Corporate Ownership and Control', *Stanford Law Review*, 52: 775–808.

Berliner Initiativkreis (2003). 'German Code of Corporate Governance (GCCG).' 2 August 2003. http://www.gccg.de/eng_German-Code-of-Corporate-Governance.pdf.

Bethel, J. E., Liebeskind, J. P., and Opler, T. (1998). 'Block Share Purchases and Corporate Performance', *Journal of Finance*, 53(2): 605–34.

Blair, M. M. (1995). *Ownership and Control: Rethinking Corporate Governance for the 21st Century*. Washington, D.C. Brookings Institution Press.

Böhmer, E., and Becht, M. (2001). 'Ownership and Voting Power in Germany', in F. Barca and M. Becht (eds.), *The Control of Corporate Europe*. London: Oxford University Press.

Bolton, P., and von Thadden, E. L. (1998). 'Blocks, Liquidity and Corporate Control', *Journal of Finance*, 53: 1–25.

Börsch-Supan, A., and Köke, J. (2002). 'An Applied Econometrician's View of Empirical Corporate Governance Studies', *German Economic Review*, 3: 295–326.

Bundesaufsichtsamt für den Wertpapierhandel (2001). Annual Report.

Charkham, J. (1994). *Keeping Good Company: A Study of Corporate Governance in Five Countries*. Oxford: Clarendon Press.

Davis, E. P. (2002). 'Institutional Investors, Corporate Governance and the Performance of the Corporate Sector', Working Paper. The Pensions Institute, Birkbeck College, London.

Deutsch, K. G., Nassauer, F., and Quitzau, J. (2001). 'Farewell to "Germany Inc."?', *Frankfurt Voice*, Deutsche Bank Research 5.

Deutsche Bank. (2002). 'Corporate Governance Grundsätze 2002', 2 August 2003. http://ircontent.db.com/ir/data/corpgovernance_de.pdf.

Deutsches Aktieninstitut (2001). *DAI Factbook*.

Dherment-Ferere, I., Köke, J., and Renneboog, L. (2001). 'Corporate Monitoring By Blockholders In Europe: Empirical Evidence of Managerial Disciplining in Belgium, France, Germany, and the UK', ZEW Discussion Paper No. 01-24. Mannheim.

Dyck, A. I. J., and Zingales, L. (2002). 'Private Benefits of Control: An International Comparison', NBER Working Paper 8711.

Edwards, J. S. S., and Nibler, M. F. (2000). 'Corporate Governance in Germany: The Role of Banks and Ownership Concentration', *Economic Policy*, 31: 237–60.

——, and Weichenrieder, A. J. (2003). 'Ownership Concentration and Share Valuation', mimeo.

Ehrhardt, O., and Nowak, E. (2002). 'Die Durchsetzung von Corporate-Governance-Regeln', *Die Aktiengesellschaft*, 47 (6): 336–45.

Emmons, W. R., and Schmid, F. A. (1998). 'Universal Banking, Control Rights, and Corporate Finance in Germany', *Federal Reserve Bank of St. Louis Review*, 80(4): 19–42.

Faccio, M., and Lang, L. H. P. (2002). 'The Ultimate Ownership of Western European Corporations', *Journal of Financial Economics*, 65: 365–95.

Frankfurter Allgemeine Zeitung (2002). 'Deutlich mehr Betriebsräte: Neuer Streit um die Mitbestimmungsreform /Exportschlager oder Last?', 19 September 2002: 12.

Franks, J., and Mayer, C. (1994). 'Corporate Control: A Comparison of Insider and Outsider Systems', Working Paper. London Business School.

——, and —— (2001). 'Ownership and Control of German Corporations', *Review of Financial Studies*, 14: 943–77.

Franks, J., Mayer, C., and Renneboog, L. (2001). 'Who disciplines management in poorly performing companies?', *Journal of Financial Intermediation*, 10: 209–48.

Frick, B., and Lehmann, E. (2001). 'Corporate Governance in Germany: Problems and Prospects', Paper presented at the 2nd ESF-SCSS Workshop on 'European Corporate Governance and Human Resource Management', Manchester. June 2001.

German Corporate Governance Code (2002). Düsseldorf. 26 February 2002.

Gerum, E., Steinmann, H., and Fees, W. (1988). *Der mitbestimmte Aufsichtsrat: eine empirische Untersuchung.* Stuttgart: Schäffer Verlag.

Gorton, G., and Schmid, F. A. (2000a). 'Universal Banking and the Performance of German Firms', *Journal of Financial Economics*, 58: 29–80.

——, and —— (2000b). 'Class Struggle Inside the Firm: A Study of German Codetermination', NBER Discussion Paper 7945.

Government Commission on Corporate Governance (2001). *Bericht der Regierungs-Kommission Corporate Governance.* Köln: Verlag Otto Schmidt.

Grundsatzkommission Corporate Governance (2003). 'Corporate Governance-Grundsätze ('Code of Best Practice') für börsennotierte Gesellschaften', 2 August 2003. http://www.dai.de/internet/dai/dai-2-0.nsf/dai_suche.htm.

Hackethal, A. (2000). *Banken, Unternehmensfinanzierung und Finanzsystem.* Frankfurt: Peter Lang.

——, and Schmidt, R. H. (2000). 'Komplementarität und Finanzsystem', *Kredit und Kapital', Supplement 15: Neue finanzielle Arrangements: Märkte im Umbruch.'*

——, and —— (2003). 'Financing Patterns: Measurement Concepts and Empirical Results', Working Paper Series: Finance and Accounting No. 33 (revised). University of Frankfurt.

——, ——, and Tyrell, M. (2003). 'Corporate Governance in Germany: Transition to Modern Capital Market-Based System?' Forthcoming in the *Journal of Institutional and Theoretical Economics*, 159(4). December 2003.

Hart, O. (1993). 'An Economist's View of Fiduciary Duties', LSE Discussion Paper.

—— (1995). *Firms, Contracts, and Financial Structure.* Oxford: Clarendon Press.

Hirschman, A. O. (1970). *Exit, Voice and Loyalty.* Cambridge: Harvard University Press.

Höpner, M. (2001). 'Corporate Governance in Transition: Ten Empirical Findings on Shareholder Value and Industrial Relations in Germany', Discussion Paper 01/5. Max-Planck-Institut für Gesellschaftsforschung.

——, and Jackson, G. (2001). 'An Emerging Market for Corporate Control? The Mannesmann Takeover and German Corporate Governance', Discussion Paper 01/4. Max-Planck-Institut für Gesellschaftsforschung.

Jenkinson, T., and Ljungqvist, A. P. (2001). 'The Role of Hostile Stakes in German Corporate Control', *Journal of Corporate Finance*, 7: 397–446.

Jorion, P., and Goetzmann, W. N. (1999). 'Global Stock Markets in the Twentieth Century', *Journal of Finance*, 54: 953–80.

Köke, J. (2001). 'Control Transfers in Corporate Germany: Their Frequency, Causes and Consequences', ZEW Discussion Paper No. 00-67. Mannheim.

Kommission Mitbestimmung (1998). *Mitbestimmung und neue Unternehmenskulturen—Bilanz und Perspektiven.* Gütersloh: Verlag Bertelsmann Stiftung/Hans-Böckler-Stiftung.

Kübler, Friedrich (1998). *Gesellschaftsrecht*, 5th edn. Heidelberg: Müller.

La Porta, R., Lopez-de-Silanes, F., Shleifer, A., and Vishny, R. W. (1997). 'Legal Determinants of External Finance', *Journal of Finance*, 52(3): 1131–50.

——, ——, ——, and ——(1998). 'Law and Finance', *Journal of Political Economy*, 106: 1113–55.

Lipton, M. (2001). *Mergers: Past, Present and Future*. Wachtell, Lipton, Rosen & Katz Archives.

Mann, A. (2002). *Corporate Governance-Systeme: Funktion und Entwicklung am Beispiel von Deutschland und Großbritannien*. Berlin: Duncker & Humblot.

Nenova, T. (2000). 'The Value of Corporate Votes and Control Benefits: A Cross-country Analysis', Working Paper. Harvard University.

Nowak, E. (2001). 'Recent Developments in German Capital Markets and Corporate Governance', *Journal of Applied Corporate Finance*, 14: 8–21.

Prigge, Stefan (1998). 'A Survey of German Corporate Governance', in K.J. Hopt et al. (eds.), *Comparative Corporate Governance—The State of the Art and Emerging Research*. Oxford: Clarendon Press, 943–1044.

Roe, Mark J. (1996). 'Chaos and Evolution in Law and Economics', *Harvard Law Review*, 109: 641.

Sadowski, D., Junkes, J., and Lindenthal, S. (2001). 'Gesetzliche Mitbestimmung in Deutschland: Idee, Erfahrung und Perspektiven aus ökonomischer Sicht', *Zeitschrift für Unternehmens- und Gesellschaftsrecht*, 30: 110–45.

Schmidt, R. H. (1997). 'Corporate Governance: The Role of Other Constituencies', in A. Pezard and J.M. Thiveaud (eds.), *Corporate Governance: Cross Border Experience*. Paris, Montchrestien, 61–74.

——(2001). 'Kontinuität und Wandel bei der Corporate Governance in Deutschland', *Zeitschrift für betriebswirtschaftliche Forschung*, Special issue 47: 61–87.

——, and Grohs, S. (2000). 'Angleichung der Unternehmensverfassung in Europa—ein Forschungsprogramm', in S. Grundmann (ed.), *Systembildung und Systemlücken in Kerngebieten des Europäischen Privatrechts*. Tuebingen: Mohr Siebeck, 145–88.

——, Hackethal, A., and Tyrell, M. (2002). 'The Convergence of Financial Sytems in Europe', *Schmalenbach Business Review*, Special Issue 1-02: German Financial Markets and Institutions: Selected Studies: 7–53.

——, and Spindler, G. (1997). 'Shareholder-Value zwischen Ökonomie und Recht', in H.D. Assmann et al. (eds.), *Wirtschafts- und Medienrecht in der offenen Demokratie—Freundesgabe für Friedrich Kübler*. Heidelberg: C.F. Müller, 515–55.

——, and ——(2002). 'Path Dependence, Corporate Governance and Complementarity', in J. Bebchuk and M.J. Roe (eds.), *Convergence and Persistence in Corporate Governance Systems*. Chicago: University of Chicago Press.

Seger, F. (1997). *Banken, Erfolg und Finanzierung—Eine Analyse für deutsche Industrieunternehmen*. Wiesbaden: Deutscher Universitätsverlag.

——, and Schmid, F. A. (1998). 'Arbeitnehmermitbestimmung, Allokation von Entscheidungsrechten und Shareholder Value', *Zeitschrift für Betriebswirtschaft*, 68: 453–73.

Shleifer, A., and Summers, L. (1988). 'Breach of Trust in Hostile Takeovers', in A.J. Auerbach (ed.), *Corporate Takeovers: Causes and Consequences*. Chicago: Chicago University Press.

Shleifer, A., and Vishny, R. W. (1997). 'A Survey of Corporate Governance', *Journal of Finance*, 52(2): 737–83.

The Wall Street Journal Europe (2002). 'Germany is expected to fight once again the new takeover directive draft', 25 September 2002, A3.

Tirole, J. (2001). 'Corporate Governance', *Econometrica*, 69: 1–35.

Tyrell, M., and Schmidt, R. H. (2001). 'Pension systems and financial systems – a comparison under the aspect of complementarity', *ifo – Studien*, 47: 469–503.

Ulrich, J. (2002). 'The German System of Corporate Governance—Characteristics and Changes', Working Paper FS II 02-203. Wissenschaftszentrum Berlin für Sozialforschung.

Walter, I. (1993). *The Battle of the Systems*. Kiel: Institut für Weltwirtschaft.

——, and Smith, R. C. (2000). *High Finance in the €uro-Zone: Competing in the New European Capital Market*. Financial Times Prentice Hall.

Wenger, E., and Hecker, R. (1995). 'Übernahme- und Abfindungsregeln am deutschen Aktienmarkt—eine kritische Bestandsaufnahme im internationalen Vergleich', *ifo-Studien*, 41: 51–87.

Witt, P. (2001). 'Konsistenz und Wandlungsfähigkeit von Corporate Governance-Systemen', *Zeitschrift für Betriebswirtschaft*, 71 Suppl. 4/2001: 73–97.

Wüstemann, J. (2001). *Ökonomische Theorie gesetzlicher Informationsprinzipien*, Tübingen: Mohr Siebeck.

Zingales, L. (1998). 'Corporate Governance', *The New Palgrave Dictionary of Economics and the Law*. London: MacMillan.

13

Investor Protection and Capital Market Regulation in Germany

ERIC NOWAK

13.1. INTRODUCTION

In a series of highly acclaimed papers, Rafael La Porta, Florencio Lopez-de-Silanes, Andrei Shleifer, and Robert Vishny (LLSV) have shown that differences among countries in legal codes and enforcement of investor protection account for much of the disparity in the size and development of their financial markets (La Porta *et al.* 1997, 1998, 2000). LLSV and others show that indicators of investor protection are associated, among other things, with dispersed ownership structures, higher dividend payout policies, lower private benefits of control, and a lesser tendency to manage earnings. According to their empirical measure of shareholder protection, Germany scores only one out of five possible points on an aggregated index scale, which is less than the shareholder protection score for the United States (5.0) and the United Kingdom (5.0), less than the average score of the forty-nine countries considered (3.0), and less even than the scores for Thailand (2.0), Greece (2.0), or Ecuador (2.0).

While I agree with some of the main conclusions in these articles, I shall argue that this assessment is no longer correct (assuming that it ever was). True, Germany is a civil law country where, until quite recently, shareholder protection has been relatively limited. And consistent with LLSV's argument, German capital markets have been comparatively undeveloped, while, at the same time, the legal protection of creditors has traditionally been strong, leading to the evolution of a relationship-oriented banking system. However, during the past years, Germany has reformed its capital market regulation in ways that now afford much greater shareholder protection. The purpose of this survey is to examine these developments in the German capital market and their effect on changes in corporate governance and investor protection to date. A lot has changed since LLSV published their first article in 1997, and now it is time to re-assess the progress made and also to clarify some anecdotal views about weak shareholder protection in Germany.[1]

---

[1] The original data from which the LLSV measures are constructed go back from 1980 to 1995.

There are several empirical approaches to measuring the relative degree of a country's equity orientation and corporate governance system. Following John Coffee, an analysis of changes in the corporate governance system can be divided into (i) changes in the structure of share ownership, (ii) growth of the stock market, (iii) formal legal changes, and (iv) the emergence of a market for corporate control (Coffee 2001).

Although no one would deny that changes in any one of these categories might affect the others, there is considerable disagreement among academics about which of these kinds of changes are more important, or more 'fundamental' in the sense of *causing* other changes. For example, while LLSV's school of thought holds that law 'matters a lot', another argues that law and regulation are likely to be an outcome or result of the economic system (Easterbrook 1997). What seems clear though is that the formal legal developments—driven by the European Union and designed to meet the international appetite for investor protection—have led to a shift in the foundations of German equity markets (Federal Ministry of Finance and Federal Ministry of Justice 2003).[2]

The remainder of the chapter falls into four sections. After the introduction I shall briefly present some stylized quantitative facts about the development in German equity markets. The second section, which constitutes the main part of the chapter, covers formal legal changes in corporate governance and investor protection that have a profound effect on the German equity markets. In the third section, I discuss the emergence of a German market for corporate control. Finally, I offer some conclusions.

13.2. CHANGES IN THE STRUCTURE OF SHARE OWNERSHIP AND GROWTH OF THE GERMAN STOCK MARKET

The following stylized empirical facts provide a general idea of what is really going on in the German capital market, which used to be (or still is) a non-equity bank-dominated system. It is an irony of history that Germany had an active stock market prior to the First World War, as evidenced by almost 1200 quoted stock companies in comparison to only about 600 stocks listed on the New York Stock Exchange, as well as an active underwriting market with 300 initial public offerings (IPOs) from 1905 to 1914 (Eube 1998; Goetzmann *et al.* 2001). Measured in terms of total market capitalization, the German stock market is now number five in the world, just surpassed by France in 1999.[3] Nevertheless, the market capitalization of the German

---

[2] '80% of the [German] capital market regulations owe their origins to decisions of the European judiciary.'

[3] The four largest markets in the world are, in order of size, the United States, United Kingdom, Japan, and France. The data are provided by the World Federation of Exchanges on www.FIBV.com.

market seems unimpressive when considered in relation to the size of the German economy. Although market cap rose from US$ 392 billion in 1989 to US$1,072 billion in 2001, Germany still lags behind relative to other nations. Market cap as a percentage of GDP in Germany, although it has almost doubled from 30.9 per cent in 1989 to 58.1 per cent in 2001, is still relatively low compared to other stock markets. The European average ratio is 70.7 per cent, and major countries like the United States with 137.1 per cent as well as the United Kingdom with 152.2 per cent have outpaced German stock market growth by far. A slightly different picture emerges when we take a look at listed domestic companies, whose number increased from 609 in January 1989 to 715 in 2002. In the same period, the number of US firms quoted decreased from 6,386 in 1989 to 5,689 in 2002. Nevertheless, Japan (3,431), Spain (2,986), UK (1,890), Australia (1,355), Canada (1,252), and even France or China all had more domestic firms quoted on the public stock market than Germany in 2002. This has not changed much despite the IPO boom of the late 1990s, which began with the privatization of the former state monopoly Deutsche Telekom in November 1996. The Telekom IPO, which was heavily advertised in order to attract small shareholders, was, with 714 million shares issued, the biggest ever flotation of equity securities in Europe. However, the following increase in IPOs—147 from 1980 to 1989 vs. 412 from 1990 to 1999 (still 142 alone in 2000)—did not keep Germany ahead of other stock markets.

The number of shareholders in Germany increased from 3.2 million in 1988 to 5.3 million by the end of 2002 (Deutsches Aktieninstitut 2003). The number of individuals who own investment funds experienced an increase from 2.3 million in 1997 to 8.4 million in 2002. Stock investments as a percentage of total monetary wealth held by private households almost doubled from 5.69 per cent in 1992 to 9.47 per cent in 2001. With an annual increase of 44 per cent equity, mutual funds experienced the biggest growth of all investment vehicles in this period.

Overall, the statistics do not suggest that the German financial system is about to be transformed into a US-style market-based system. It looks more like a gradual evolution towards a market-oriented equity culture, in line with international developments, will occur. This finding is consistent with empirical evidence showing that Germany continues to be a bank-dominated rather than a market-dominated financial system (Schmidt *et al.* 1999; see also Chapter 2).[4] However, this chapter is not about providing evidence of a convergence of the German financial system from a comparative standpoint, but rather aims at showing that there have been several milestone events in recent years which may (although not necessarily) catalyse the development of the German capital market towards the Anglo-American model.

---

[4] Schmidt *et al.* find that during the period 1980–98 the German financial system continued to be bank-dominated, whereas the British system still appears to be market-dominated.

13.3. A CHRONOLOGY OF FORMAL LEGAL CHANGES IN THE GERMAN CAPITAL MARKET

The goal of this section and indeed the main purpose of this chapter is to provide a comprehensive survey of the legal innovations brought about by the German and European reforms between the last decade and the beginning of the millennium. In this section I outline material events and innovations that have pushed the German stock market ahead. The selection of these 'milestones' is necessarily subjective. At first sight, the events and cases may seem to be only loosely connected or even randomly chosen. What is important, however, is to recognize that it is the interplay of developments at the European regulatory level in connection with innovations at the micro level of private organizations that has led to a shift in the institutional structure of the German capital market.

In Germany, capital market law as such did not exist until 1990. Before then, rules and regulations concerning the issuance and trading of securities were to be found in various parts of the law, particularly in stock corporation law, securities exchange law, and banking law.

13.3.1. Act on the Prospectus for Securities Offered for Sale—Prospectus Act (1990)

The Prospectus Act ('Verkaufsprospektgesetz'), released in 1990, is the first legal act that directly addresses the protection of the capital market in Germany as its primary goal (see for an overview Assmann *et al.* 2002).[5] The Prospectus Act in connection with the Sales Prospectus Ordinance ('Verkaufsprospekt-Verordnung') governs the prospectus requirements for securities. It requires the prior publication of a prospectus for all initial public offerings, that is, for all issues that have not been registered for trading on a German stock exchange before. The requirements are not as detailed and far-reaching as those imposed by the SEC under the Securities Act. Baums and Hutter (2002) thus criticize the German law for being too lax as compared to US law and call for a reform. For example, there is no 'plain German' rule, then, there is no prohibition on other publishing and advertising efforts in connection with an offering, and also, the subsequent post-listing duties of the issuer are not covered, once the securities are admitted for trading at a stock exchange. Thus, the scope of the act is somewhat limited. The Prospectus Act also allows some further exceptions from the prospectus requirement, for example, there is no prospectus requirement for private placements yet.

---

[5] It was changed in 1998 and, most recently, due to the introduction of the Takeover Act in 2001, the Fourth Financial Market Promotion Act, and the Law on Integrated Financial Services Supervision in 2002.

Prospectus liability for incorrect or incomplete information is regulated in connection with Section 45 of the Stock Exchange Act. The German liability standard is less strict than that of the Securities Act in the United States.[6] First, prospectus liability is limited to 'intentional acts' and 'gross negligence', both of which are hard to prove in court and can even be waived on the grounds of prior due-diligence. Second, there is no liability for advising lawyers and auditors, but only for 'those responsible for the prospectus', that is, the issuer, incumbent owners, and the underwriter. However, even though the requirements were not as detailed and far-reaching as those imposed by the US SEC, the combination of the requirements with enforceable liability standards was clearly a necessary first step toward increased securities issuance.

13.3.2. First Financial Market Promotion Act (1990)

The second major legal innovation in 1990 was the First Financial Market Promotion Act ('Erstes Finanzmarktförderungsgesetz'—FFG I). FFG I was an aggregation of drafts on several capital market related laws. The following changes, in particular, were important: (i) drafting of investment guidelines ('Investment-Richtlinie-Gesetz'), (ii) removal of some anachronistic taxes, such as the capital transfer tax and the stock exchange turnover tax, (iii) legal widening of business opportunities and investment possibilities for trust companies and mutual funds.

These three changes were only small steps towards a modern securities market law, but they were steps in the right direction. And in fairness to German legislators, much of their attention was focused in those days on Reunification and the political and economic restructuring of the East. But FFG I was only the starting point for a regulatory wave of legal innovations strengthening shareholder protection in Germany and more acts were soon to follow.

13.3.3. Second Financial Market Promotion Act: Securities Trading Act (1994)

The Second Financial Market Promotion Act ('Zweites Finanzmarktförderungsgesetz'—FFG II) can be regarded as *the* watershed event in the legal development of German securities markets. FFG II overhauled German financial law completely and established a regulatory apparatus comparable to that of the United States. Released in July 1994, the act expressed the German government's commitment to establishing international standards in its own

---

[6] This follows also from the fact that in the United States there is both a specific prospectus liability in sections 11 and 12 of the Securities Act (SA), as well as a general prospectus liability to be derived from Rule 10b-5.

securities laws and to ensuring the enforcement of those standards, all with the ultimate aim of promoting the growth of German financial markets (Hopt 1998).

The core element of the Second Financial Market Promotion Act was the Securities Trading Act ('Wertpapierhandelsgesetz'—WpHG), which regulated (i) the establishment of the new Federal Securities Supervisory Office ('Bundesaufsichtsamt für den Wertpapierhandel'—BAWe), (ii) the prohibition of insider trading, (iii) current reporting duties ('Ad-hoc-Publizität'), and (iv) notification of changes in major holdings of voting rights (for firms quoted on the Official Market). The Securities Trading Act is a 'law in action', since it frequently had to be updated owing to necessary changes and problems in its interpretation by both the financial and the legal communities.

13.3.3.1. *Federal securities supervisory office (1995)*

The Federal Securities Supervisory Office was established in Frankfurt am Main on 1 January 1995 to secure the proper functioning of the securities and derivatives markets by pursuing the underlying principles of investor protection, market transparency, and market integrity.[7] Following the adoption on 22 April 2002, of the Law on Integrated Financial Services Supervision ('Gesetz über die integrierte Finanzaufsicht'—FinDAG), the BAWe, together with the former offices for banking supervision ('Bundesaufsichtsamt für das Kreditwesen'—BAKred), and insurance supervision ('Bundesaufsichtsamt für das Versicherungswesen'—BAV) was integrated to form a single state regulator, the new Federal Financial Supervisory Authority ('Bundesanstalt für Finanzdienstleistungsaufsicht'—BaFin). The BaFin, established on 1 May 2002, supervises banks, financial services institutions, and insurance companies across the entire financial market and comprises the key functions of consumer protection and solvency supervision. The BaFin, which is located in Frankfurt and Bonn, is a federal institution governed by public law and is affiliated to the Federal Ministry of Finance.

The Securities Supervision Directorate, relating to the former BAWe, deals with the following tasks: (i) combating and preventing insider dealing, (ii) monitoring compliance with the Section 9 reporting requirements of all transactions in securities and derivatives, (iii) monitoring *ad hoc* disclosure requirements of listed companies, (iv) monitoring the disclosure requirements in the event of changes in holdings of voting rights in officially listed companies, (v) monitoring the Rules of Conduct and the compliance organization of investment services firms, (vi) serving as the depository for prospectuses, (vii) national and international cooperation regarding the supervision of securities trading.

---

[7] Most of the following information as well as the legal text is directly provided by the BaFin through its website www.bafin.de.

13.3.3.2. *Insider trading prohibition (1994)*

One of the central tasks of the BaFin as laid down in the WpHG is the prohibition of insider trading.[8] Prior to its inception in 1 August 1994, there was a voluntary insider code, which was governed only by a self-organizing insider commission under private law. Although most stock companies accepted the code, owing to the lack of enforcement this 'gentleman's agreement' did not seem to impose a credible threat to insiders (Blum 1986).

Under the Securities Trading Act, the BaFin investigates all possible cases of insider trading and monitors the collection and evaluation of all securities and derivatives transactions (which have to be reported according to Section 9 of the WpHG). If an insider case is reported, the BaFin may request information on all securities transactions during the six months prior to the suspected insider trading. Issuers of insider securities[9] must, upon request, disclose to the BaFin all documents and details about events and developments relating to a given case of inside information, including those persons with access to this inside information.

If an insider deal is suspected, the BaFin has to pass the case on to a public prosecutor, who may (or may not) conduct further investigations and criminal prosecution. The lack of enforcement powers on the part of the BaFin/BAWe has long been criticized, and it is cited as the reason why there have been so few insider prosecutions to date. For example, from 1999 to 2001, the BaFin started 145 investigations (against one or more insiders of a firm), and passed on 60 cases to public prosecutors.[10] The prosecutors, from the period 1995–2001, turned 161 out of 177 cases down, settled fourteen with a down payment, and found only two insiders guilty in cases brought to court (BAWe 2001). In 2002, the BaFin started sixty-nine new investigations (sixty-one old cases still pending), of which fifteen were turned down because of lacking evidence, and thirty-three cases were passed on to public prosecutors. Eighty-two investigations are still pending with the prosecutors, who settled thirteen cases with a down payment and turned down cases against thirty-seven insider suspects in 2002. Three cases had a final verdict in 2002 with one insider found guilty in court and two further which received *Strafbefehl* penalties (BaFin 2003).

---

[8] According to Section 13 of the WpHG, *insiders* are 'persons who, due to their function or by any other way, have learned of non-public and price-sensitive information'.

[9] According to Section 12 of the WpHG, securities potentially qualifying as *insider securities* are all those 'securities which are admitted to stock exchange trading or traded on the free market or securities which are admitted to trading on an organized market in the European Economic Area'.

[10] One insider investigation passed on by the BaFin to public prosecutors may lead to more than one judicial verdict against single insiders. Therefore, the 'success' numbers cannot be compared on a one-to-one basis.

13.3.3.3. Ad hoc *Disclosure—Section 15 of the Securities Trading Act (1995)*

Another major breakthrough for investor protection and capital market transparency was the introduction of *ad hoc* disclosure requirements. Since 1 January 1995, in accordance with Section 15 of the WpHG, the issuers of securities admitted to trading on a German stock exchange have been required to publish immediately any corporate information, which (i) constitutes a fact that is not publicly known, (ii) relates to the issuer's sphere of business activity, (iii) because of the effect on the assets, concerns the financial position or the general business activities of the issuer, (iv) is likely to have a significant influence on the stock price of the issuer's securities, or (v) in the case of listed bonds, might impair the issuer's ability to meet his liabilities. The BaFin may on request exempt an issuer from the *ad hoc* disclosure requirement if publication of the information is likely to damage its legitimate interests. If irregularities are discovered, administrative proceedings will be instituted by the BaFin, which has the power to impose fines of up to €1.5 million.

The *ad hoc* disclosure law formally prohibits selective disclosure of material information to particular capital market participants, for example, analysts, portfolio managers, or financial journalists. Thus, a 'Regulation Fair Disclosure', as introduced by the SEC in the United States only very recently in October 2000, has been effective in Germany much earlier.

However, this important innovation has not been entirely successful so far. Even eight years after the introduction of the *ad hoc* disclosure rule, there is still considerable uncertainty among German companies about how to comply with the legal requirements, particularly with respect to what constitutes *material*, that is, price sensitive, information and therefore has to be disclosed. Given this uncertainty, *ad hoc* disclosures have been misused by some issuers as a public relations tool, while many other issuers have not disclosed a single statement. Nevertheless, *ad hoc* disclosure activity of domestic issuers increased sharply, rising from 991 notifications in 1995 to 5057 disclosures in 2000, and falling again to 4605 in 2001 and 3781 in 2002, respectively.

In spite of the problems with enforcement, it seems indisputable that these two aspects of the Securities Act, that is, the *ad hoc* disclosure requirements and the insider trading prohibition, were critically important legal milestones in providing a level of investor protection comparable to that of the US market.

13.3.3.4. *Notification of changes in major holdings of voting rights*

According to Section 21 of the Securities Trading Act, natural and legal persons, who are holding a 5, 10, 25, 50, or 75 per cent share in the capital of a company quoted on the Official Market, are required to notify the BaFin and the company immediately (within seven calendar days) of their holdings of voting rights. The notifying party must state (i) the respective threshold, (ii) the exact size of the percentage of the voting rights, and (iii) the date on which the threshold has been reached, exceeded or fallen below. The notification requirement applies to the voting rights in—and not to shares in the capital of—a company that has its registered office in Germany and whose shares are admitted to official trading on a stock exchange in a Member State of the European Community or other contracting state to the Agreement on the European Economic Area. The BaFin can punish violations of the notification and publication requirements with fines of up to €250,000. In addition, it can suspend the respective voting rights until the notification is made.[11]

13.3.4. Changing the Rules and Regulations of the German Stock Market (1997)

Competitive pressure from financial integration and the rising demand for investments accelerated the rapid modernization and internationalization of the Frankfurt Stock Exchange, founded in 1585 (Baehring 1985). In January 1993, the former mutual Frankfurt Stock Exchange was privatized by its members and became a part of the newly founded Deutsche Börse AG (DBAG). DBAG now operates and administers the largest German stock exchange in Frankfurt. It markets a cutting edge electronic trading system (Xetra), and runs the highly successful joint cross-border derivatives market Eurex (along with the Swiss Exchange), which have both proved successful in attracting capital from overseas investors.[12]

In March 1997, DBAG established the Neuer Markt (NM), a trading segment for innovative growth stocks. NM issuers were supposed to be innovative enterprises, whose activities were expected to generate high turnover and profits in the future. Trading on NM took place in the Regulated Unofficial Market ('Freiverkehr') under private law, but all companies admitted to NM also had to be admitted to the Regulated Market ('Geregelter Markt'). Organized under private law, DBAG formally imposed admission and disclosure requirements for NM stricter even than for the Official Market ('Amtlicher Handel').

The legal and regulatory framework of NM was described in the Rules and Regulations book. The NM Rules and Regulations governed the requirements for admission, the admission process, post-listing duties and sanctions for violations. The intended goal of the NM Rules and Regulations was to ensure that investors were sufficiently informed with the greatest possible transparency. The NM Rules and Regulations imposed far-reaching requirements on prospective issuers pertaining to (i) detailed instructions for the content of the

---

[11] The BaFin also provides a database of all notifications, which is searchable for owners and issuers, and accessible online for everyone interested (www.bafin.de).

[12] Interestingly, owing to political struggles and provincial egoism, the other regional stock exchanges in Germany have not taken comparable steps, the most important of which would be to merge their redundant operating activities.

IPO prospectus, (ii) the publication of annual and quarterly reports in accordance with internationally accepted accounting standards (IAS or US-GAAP), (iii) the underwriting of ordinary shares only with voting rights, (iv) the issuance of a minimum of €5 million and placement of at least 20 per cent of shareholders' equity, (v) a mandatory lock-up provision of 6 months applying to former shareholders and management, and (vi) two designated sponsors guaranteeing that bid and offer quotes ensure sufficient liquidity for trading the shares at all times (without affecting the market price). In theory, the legal framework of the NM Rules was comparable to and, in some respects, even stricter than the admission requirements and post-listing duties under the SEC regime in the US (Shearman and Sterling 2001). In practice, however, the system has been hampered by inconsistent enforcement by DBAG. The NM Rules were purely private agreements between DBAG and its issuers (who were also its customers) and the BAWe did not have a mandate to supervise these (which changed under FFG IV).

Spurred by the high-tech-bubble-driven boost into going public, 342 companies had listed on NM by July 2001. Although a number of other European growth markets opened, for example the Nouveau Marché (Paris), the Nuovo Mercato (Milan), the SWX New Market (Zürich), the Alternative Investment Market (AIM) in London and NASDAQ Europe in Brussels (EASDAQ), they had been significantly less popular with issuers. NM quickly became Europe's biggest exchange for securities of innovative growth companies, gaining a market share in issuance volume and market capitalization of well over 50 per cent by the year 2000. In the end, NM was severely hit by the slump of share prices following the bursting of the bubble and was finally shut down, because of the irreparable loss in investor confidence.

13.3.5. Third Financial Market Promotion Act (1998)

On 1 April 1998, the Third Financial Market Promotion Act ('Drittes Finanzmarktförderungsgesetz'—FFG III) went into effect, bringing about further changes in German corporate and securities trading law. Most of these changes were amendments to prior capital market reforms such as the Securities Trading Act and the Prospectus Act. Some changes within the FFG III represented important legal innovations. The Third Financial Promotion Act objectives as stated in the law were to (i) improve the availability of risk-diversifying equity capital raising for small and medium-sized enterprises, (ii) reduce transaction costs for raising capital on the stock market, (iii) widen the range of futures exchange products for investment companies, (iv) approve pension plan investment funds, which were now allowed to offer new products particularly designed for private pension schemes, and (v) widen the supply of financing capital for non-listed companies. These changes made private equity investments much more attractive and helped prepare the way for a steep increase in German venture capital funding in the 1990s (Feinendegen *et al.* 2001).

13.3.6. Raising of Equity Relief Act (1998)

The Raising of Equity Relief Act ('Kapitalaufnahmeerleichterungsgesetz'—KapAEG) has allowed German stock companies, from February 1998 onwards, to use internationally accepted accounting standards. More precisely, it allows listed group parents to prepare consolidated financial statements that are in accordance with either IAS or US GAAP.

Many companies benefit from this facilitation. Some companies, like those subject to the DBAG segment rules and regulations, are required to use IAS or US GAAP for consolidated financial reporting; others have voluntarily adopted IAS or US GAAP. The most obvious beneficiaries of the KapAEG were those German companies like Daimler or Deutsche Telekom with securities listed on US stock exchanges that were *required* to prepare US GAAP financial statements anyway (Radebaugh *et al.* 1995). In this sense, the KapAEG further encouraged the internationalization of the German equity landscape.

13.3.7. Corporation Control and Transparency Act—KonTraG (1998)

Another legal milestone in 1998 was the Corporation Control and Transparency Act (KonTraG). A number of cases of supervisory board and audit failure in the effective monitoring of German companies gave rise to calls for legal reform of the corporate governance system.[13] The KonTraG, which became effective in May 1998, provided some gradual but very important changes in German corporate governance law as well as new regulations affecting almost every corporate legal institution (for a detailed treatment see Baums 1999). Its primary goals were to improve the monitoring effectiveness of German supervisory boards and corporate disclosure to the investment community.

13.3.7.1. *Management board*
The KonTraG imposes stronger duties on the management board, which has to implement adequate risk management and internal revision systems, capable of foreseeing future danger to the current concern of the firm. Therefore, a detailed outlook on operational risks and potentially dangerous future developments has to be provided in the annual report and presented to the supervisory board. Legal liability of the management board in the event of fraudulent behaviour has been tightened by appropriate measures, open to shareholders who hold shares of at least five per cent of total shares or with a

---

[13] Prominent cases are Metallgesellschaft, Klöckner-Humboldt-Deutz, Schneider, Balsam-Procedo, Bremer Vulkan. Some of them are described by Wenger and Kaserer (1998).

nominal value of €500,000. In order to provide the management with performance-based incentives, the KonTraG also simplifies the use of stock option programs via two means. First, the law liberalizes share buybacks by the company in the open market, and second, it eases seasoned equity issues, thereby facilitating the use of stock options for executive compensation.

13.3.7.2. *Supervisory board*
With respect to strengthening the role of the supervisory board, the law introduces several innovations: (i) the maximum number of supervisory board seats an individual may hold, which is (still) restricted to ten, now takes chairmanships into account twice; (ii) meetings of the supervisory board of quoted stock companies now have to take place at least four times a year and must be stated in the report to shareholders; (iii) the auditor will now be chosen by the supervisory board, must attend the board meetings, and has to deliver his audit report to every board member in advance.

13.3.7.3. *General meeting of shareholders and bank monitoring*
The KonTraG also introduces some amendments to the Stock Corporation Act limiting the role of banks in board representation and proxy voting.[14] It is now the case that banks must rule out potential conflicts of interest by (i) appointing a management board member as compliance person, and by (ii) abstaining from exercising proxy votes in companies where they hold more than five per cent of the shares, (iii) they must consult shareholders of listed companies prior to making use of proxy votes and disclose when bank shareholdings exceed 5 per cent of the voting rights, (iv) banks have to submit alternative proposals on how to exercise the voting rights of their customers, and (v) they have to disclose board memberships of their managers and employees.

13.3.7.4. *One share–one vote*
The Act prohibits deviations from the one share–one vote principle by abolishing and phasing out multiple voting stock, caps on voting rights, as well as maximum voting rights for listed stock. With respect to limiting the effect of interlocking shareholdings, the use of voting rights in the election of supervisory board members of affiliated companies is no longer permitted.

13.3.7.5. *Audit*
Several rules are introduced in the KonTraG to ensure the independence and quality of the financial audit: (i) an auditor is excluded from performing the audit, if more than 30 per cent of his total revenue over the previous 5 years stems from one company; (ii) the same employee of an audit firm may not sign

---

[14] According to Baums (1999) this limitation imposed by the KonTraG is only 'marginal'.

the certificate more than six times in 10 years; (iii) auditor liability has been increased from €250,000 to €4 million for quoted companies; (iv) segmentation and cash flow statements are mandatory for consolidated financial statements.

13.3.8. German Accounting Standards Committee—GASC (1998)

The KonTraG also laid the foundations for the formation and legal acceptance of a privately organized standard setting body, the German Accounting Standards Committee.[15] The German Accounting Standards Committee was established in March 1998, in order to develop proposals for the application of the basic principles of group accounting and to represent Germany in international standard setting bodies, in particular the International Accounting Standards Committee (IASC). The aims of the GASC, as stated in the charter, are (i) the introduction and financing of standardization in accordance with Anglo-American and international practices by means of an independent expert committee, (ii) the development of accounting standards for application in the area of consolidated financial reporting, (iii) the acceleration of international harmonization through cooperation in international and intergovernmental organizations and in cooperation with the IASC and other standards committees, (iv) consultation on the development of legislation at national and intergovernmental level with regard to accounting regulations, (v) the representation of Germany on international standardization committees, and (vi) the promotion of academic accounting research.

In summary, by the end of 1998, the legal and institutional framework for the German capital market was moving toward the goal of meeting international standards for investor protection and corporate governance. However, there was still more to be accomplished and some setbacks to be faced.

13.3.9. Tax Reform: Tax Reduction Act (2000)

In addition to stronger shareholder protection measures, the Tax Reduction Act ('Steuererleichterungsgesetz') of July 2000 resulted in a reduction of corporation tax and a change in the system of taxing corporations and shareholders. Two legal changes have had a direct impact on capital markets. First, concerning the taxation of dividends, the full imputation system was replaced by the so-called half-income system to make cross-border investment within Europe more attractive. Under this system, only half of the distributed profits of a corporation are included in the shareholder's personal income tax base. In return, it is no longer necessary to credit the corporation tax paid by the company against the shareholder's income tax. Second, capital gains from the

---

[15] Charter of the GASC on www.dasc.de.

sale of cross-corporation shareholdings are now generally exempt from tax, in effect from the 2002 tax year. This last change was expected to have a tremendous effect on the sale of stakes and resulting mergers and acquisitions transaction volume (Orr 2001). Particularly banks and other financial institutions announced that they would be selling off many of their huge share stakes in industrial companies, which would supposedly lead to what was termed the 'unbundling of corporate Germany'. However, three years later the sale of equity stakes by German corporations has been only modest, perhaps also because of the depressed stock market situation. Another possible reason why the new tax legislation has not made a huge difference to date may be the fact that it creates a lump sum gain in shareholder value (at the expense of another stakeholder, the tax payer) with no dynamic effect on the sale of shareholdings. The reason being that, in general, the marginal rates that matter for investment decisions, are not affected by this change. However, only the future development of the German M&A market will tell.

13.3.10. Scandals on the Neuer Markt and the Advent of Shareholder Litigation (2001)

The new millennium also witnessed the bursting of the high-tech bubble. A number of scandals involving misleading disclosure practices, insider trading, and, in some cases, outright fraud, have put German companies under pressure from investors, investigators, and the media. In the year 2000 alone, 102 companies were officially criticized for inadequate quarterly reporting. DBAG introduced contractual penalties as a sanctioning mechanism, but some companies refused to publish quarterly reports.[16] Many companies delisted because of bankruptcy or owing to takeovers, while a growing number of issuers decided to move into less regulated market segments.

In response to the scandals and related public criticism, the DBAG announced its intent to tighten disclosure rules. In March 2001, new rules were introduced regulating the disclosure of directors' stock sales and purchases as well as the extension and standardization of quarterly reporting. And in July 2001, the DBAG announced a delisting rule for NM companies comparable to the standards set by NASDAQ. Formally, the legal framework of the NM Rules and Regulations were comparable to or in part even stricter than the admission requirements and post-listing duties under the SEC regime in the United States (Shearman and Sterling 2001). However, due to lacklustre enforcement the rules have not proven to be sufficient to restore investor confidence. As a consequence, DBAG decided to shut down NM and completely reorganized its market segments (see Chapter 5).

---

[16] For example, issuers Porsche AG and Spar AG were even excluded from the MDAX for that reason.

13.3.11. Fourth Financial Market Promotion Act (2002)

Not surprisingly, the combination of the stock market crash with the afore-mentioned scandals has shaken investor sentiment in Germany. As has frequently happened in the United States, the collapse of stock prices has led many small shareholders to seek legal remedies for foolish investments, and several German law firms have begun to specialize in US-style securities litigation (Rützel 2001). Moreover, on 24 September 2001, a German court decided for the first time ever in favour of shareholders in a case of fraudulent disclosure.[17] However, the complexity of the Securities Trading Act (as well as its partially insufficient enforcement by the BAWe) has led to legal uncertainty and harsh criticism.

Partly in response to such problems, the German Ministry of Finance released on 4 September 2001 its long-awaited draft proposal for the Fourth Financial Market Promotion Act ('Viertes Finanzmarktförderungsgesetz'—FFG IV). This act, effective from 1 July 2002, represents another major initiative toward greater investor protection, transparency, and market integrity. FFG IV introduces far-reaching amendments to (i) the Stock Exchange Act, (ii) the Securities Trading Act, (iii) the Investment Companies Act, and (iv) the Banking Act ('Kreditwesengesetz'—KWG). The most important amendments relate to the first two laws and shall be discussed briefly below.

13.3.11.1. *Market and price manipulation*
Market price manipulation is now part of the Securities Trading Act.[18] An intentional false statement about a fact which is significant to the valuation of a security, as well as every other deliberate deceptive measure that influences this valuation, is now punishable as a criminal act (WpHG: § 20a). The proof of significance or materiality of a price change, induced by manipulation, is now the critical determinant for conviction of a criminal act. This small amendment will probably lead to the frequent use of event studies in German courtrooms (Mitchell and Netter 1994). The BaFin now monitors all investigations of manipulation cases in its capacity as a central federal institution (WpHG: § 20b). This new regulation facilitates identification and punishment of market manipulation.

13.3.11.2. *Deregulation of the Stock Exchange Act*
Forwards and futures are newly defined in the law. Furthermore, the stock exchanges are granted flexibility in setting their own regulatory standards and trading mechanisms for their different market segments. This enables, for example, DBAG to place its newly structured market segments under the

---

[17] This decision on the case of the Neuer Markt firm Infomatec was overtaken by a higher court on 1 October 2002, however, and is still waiting for a final verdict.
[18] Before it was part of the Stock Exchange Law ('Börsengesetz'—BörsG: § 88).

federal enforcement regime of the BaFin, which was not possible before in the case of the Neuer Markt and its Rules and Regulations under private law. Investors in these market segments are thus better protected by now.

13.3.11.3. *Mandatory disclosure of Director's Dealings*
Given cases of spectacular share sales particularly by founding shareholders and management members of NM firms, the act intends to limit the possibility of 'cashing out' shortly following an IPO, without the small shareholders taking notice. DBAG, as stated in the NM Rules and Regulations, required all NM issuers to sign and comply with the 'Prohibition on Disposal' and to disclose 'Director's Dealings'. However this private contract between the issuers and DBAG in many cases seems not to have been sufficient (Nowak and Gropp 2002).

An amendment to the Securities Trading Act now requires sell and buy transactions of management and supervisory board members as well as their affiliates to be disclosed (WpHG: § 15a). Insiders of all (not only NM) firms are now legally required to disclose sell transactions above €25,000 immediately to the BaFin and on the internet in order to protect outstanding and less informed shareholders.[19]

13.3.11.4. *Reform of* ad hoc *publicity*
After years of uncertainty about *ad hoc* disclosure requirements and their frequent abuse as a public relations tool, Section 15 of the Securities Trading Act is specified in more detail.

Misuse of *ad hoc* disclosures in the form of misleading announcements will now be punished with fines of up to €1.5 million. Furthermore, details about whether and how mandatory facts must be disclosed, for example, by presenting comparable numbers, are now more precisely specified in the law.

13.3.11.5. *Shareholder litigation*
Of even more importance to shareholders is the newly introduced option to privately sue issuers for making untimely, false, or misleading statements as well as for the non-disclosure of material information (WpHG: § 37b). The Securities Trading Act previously excluded private litigation actions explicitly, and it remains to be seen how these shareholder litigation cases will be handled in reality. Nevertheless, this is a major structural break in the German code law system as well as a movement towards Anglo-American measures of shareholder protection and its importance should not be understated.

FFG IV represents a big step forward in improving the regulatory framework, but it is not the end of the German government's efforts to strengthen investor protection and promote financial markets.

---

[19] Similar to the NM Rule 7.2 on Director's Dealings.

On 25 February 2003, the Federal Government presented a new 10-Point Programme on improving enterprise integrity and investor protection (Federal Ministry of Finance and Federal Ministry of Justice 2003). The elements of the Programme are simultaneously part of the Financial Market Promotion Plan 2006 (FMPP). The issues dealt with in the FMPP are (i) the Investment Law 2003/Investment Tax Law, (ii) hedge funds/alternative investments, (iii) the securitizations market/asset-backed securities, and (iv) FMF elements of the 10-Point Programme (enforcement, direct liability of corporate bodies for incorrect *ad hoc* disclosures, stock exchange reform/supervision legislation, grey capital market, analysts/rating).

13.4. THE EMERGENCE OF A MARKET FOR CORPORATE CONTROL

13.4.1. Developments in Takeover Markets

13.4.1.1. *The slow arrival of hostile takeovers (1988–98)*

Hostile tender offers have been virtually non-existent in Germany until very recently. There are, however, exceptions to this rule, and many observers believe that these were the initial signs of an upcoming market for corporate control in Germany. Three well-known cases of takeover *attempts* in Germany are the merger bid from Pirelli Spa for Continental AG in 1990, the bid by the Flick brothers in 1988 and, later in 1989, of Veba AG for Feldmühle Nobel AG, which was family-owned until then, and also the rather friendly takeover of Hoesch AG by Fried. Krupp AG in 1991. All of these cannot be regarded as hostile takeovers in the narrow sense, meaning they were not successfully closed public tender offers.

The nearest approach to a successful hostile acquisition in Germany was the Thyssen–Krupp merger that finally took place in 1999. Thyssen tried to take over Krupp in the early 90s, but failed then owing to the entrenched ownership structure of Krupp (approximately 50 per cent was owned by a foundation, which in turn was headed by a former Krupp CEO). In March 1997, Hoesch–Krupp (Krupp) made a bid for Thyssen AG in the form of a tender offer to all Thyssen's shareholders at a 25 per cent premium over the prevailing market price. Not surprisingly, the bid provoked an outbreak of public opposition from politicians, union representatives, the media, and employees, as well as the management of the target company (Emmons and Schmid 2001). The leader of the IG Metall union, Klaus Zwickel, accused the Krupp management of using 'wild west' methods, and Chancellor Helmut Kohl urged both parties to find a 'prudent solution' based on careful consideration of their 'social responsibility'.

After several weeks of public opposition, Krupp finally withdrew its formal takeover bid and then began talks about a friendly merger with Thyssen in September 1997. In January 1998, the supervisory boards of both companies approved the merger plan, and in December 1998, the merger was approved in special stockholders' meetings of both companies. Owing to a quirk in US GAAP rules, the merger had to be accounted for as if Thyssen had acquired Krupp, whereas in reality Krupp's management was finally successful in achieving control of the combined company, as reflected in their dominant positions on the executive board.

Another supposedly friendly merger in 1998 was no less remarkable. The cross-border merger between Daimler Benz and Chrysler Corporation created what can be called the first *truly global* company. Many Americans objected to the fact that the resulting business entity was incorporated in Germany and viewed the merger as 'a disaster from day one' (Meredith 2001). The merger had profound implications for *German* capital markets simply by virtue of the fact that it 'injected a substantial element of US-style shareholder activism into the governance of a major German corporation' (Gordon 1999). In effect, the Daimler-Chrysler merger established a new model of cross-border corporate governance, prompting a new series of legal changes intended to support the globalization of German firms.[20]

13.4.1.2. *Hostile takeovers at the gate: the Mannesmann–Vodafone takeover (1999)*

The Vodafone–Mannesmann takeover made history for being the first successful hostile takeover bid via a public tender offer in Germany. In November 1999, the telecom company Vodafone Airtouch placed a bid to acquire the German competitor Mannesmann AG via a hostile tender offer. As in the Krupp–Thyssen case, public opinion in Germany was directed against the takeover. Again, politicians like Chancellor Gerhard Schröder expressed concern about 'certain methods that foreign firms undertake to buy German companies' and criticized that 'hostile takeovers destroy the corporate culture' in Germany. Nevertheless, this time the German capital market and the shareholders of Mannesmann were ready to see the deal done. On February 4, 2000, terms were agreed with the supervisory board of Mannesmann by which the company would become a part of the Vodafone group. The €120 billion transaction is still the biggest merger in history and almost doubled the size of the Vodafone Group. The agreement to acquire Mannesmann received European Commission clearance on 12 April 2000. Besides representing the largest cross-country merger ever, this transaction marked a giant leap forward in establishing the legitimacy of corporate control contests in Germany.

And, in fact, the second successful German hostile takeover was announced shortly afterwards. On 15 October 2001, the management board of FAG Kugelfischer Georg Schäfer AG said it had reached an agreement regarding a public tender offer from competitor INA-Holding Schaeffler KG. After initial

---

[20] One such change was the Raising of Equity Relief Act, described earlier.

opposition to the bid, FAG finally recommended that shareholders accept the offer. Perhaps even more significantly, in this case the takeover was not accompanied by a public outcry by politicians and the media. Thus, it appears that hostile takeovers have finally achieved acceptance as a means of improving corporate governance. This change in attitude was also made possible by important regulatory changes.

13.4.2. Developments in Takeover Regulation (1995–2002)

13.4.2.1. *The voluntary takeover code*

Until recently, there were no mandatory takeover regulations in Germany. In July 1995, a Takeover Code ('Übernahmekodex') was introduced as a voluntary guideline by the Exchange Expert Commission ('Börsensachver-ständigenkommission').[21] Appointed by the Ministry of Finance to advise the Government on capital market and stock exchange matters, the Commission provided a set of (voluntary) rules of conduct for parties involved in public tender offers. The Code was amended in January 1998.

The most important provision of the Code established the bidder's duty to make an offer to all minority shareholders in cases in which the bidder acquires the majority of the voting shares of a stock company. It also stipulated that the mandatory offer price be either the weighted average of the prices of additional purchases after obtaining control or, if no additional securities have been purchased by the acquirer, 'reasonably related' to the highest stock exchange price within the last 3 months.

Although the code appears to have succeeded in reducing control premiums,[22] its acceptance among issuers has been fairly modest. Since June 2000, only 64 per cent of all listed German companies have actually signed the Takeover Code. Notable among those companies that had *not* accepted it were the DAX automobile companies BMW and Volkswagen. For such companies, the only way to gain compliance appears to be mandatory legal action at the European level.

13.4.2.2. *Rejection of the European Takeovers*
Directive Proposal (2001)

After 12 years of discussion and debate, the EC proposal for a uniform policy on cross-border mergers and acquisitions was finally voted down by the European parliament on 4 July 2001. The directive would have banned anti-takeover defences by incumbent management without shareholder approval. Given its own criticism of parts of the proposal, the German

---

[21] Takeover Code adopted by the Exchange Expert Commission at the Federal Ministry of Finance on 14 July 1995.

[22] Support for this argument comes from a study by Hoffmann-Burchardi (1999).

government viewed the failure of the EC measure as a welcome opportunity to formulate a national law.

13.4.2.3. *Introduction of the German Takeover Act (2002)*

Shortly after the rejection of the EC Directive, one week later on 11 July 2001, the German government passed its own Takeover Act ('Wertpapiererwerbs- und Übernahmegesetz'—WpUeG), which took effect on 1 January 2002.

Unlike the voluntary Takeover Code and the EC proposal, the new German act permits anti-takeover devices in the corporate charter ('Vorratsbeschlüsse') and defensive actions by the incumbent management in the event of a hostile tender offer. This has led Jeffrey Gordon to call the Takeover Act an 'Anti-takeover law' (Gordon 2002). But the Takeover Act also makes the minority protection provision of the 1995 voluntary code a legal obligation for the acquirer. Upon reaching a threshold of 30 per cent of the voting stock, an acquiring shareholder must make an unconditional offer for the remaining shares within 4 weeks.

The consequences of this rule for the protection of minority shareholders are not completely clear. Once a controlling majority has been reached, the provision could also be used to 'squeeze out' minority shareholders against their will. For this reason, the Takeover Act also includes a 'squeeze-out rule' which stipulates that upon reaching a threshold of 95 per cent of the voting stock, a shareholder has to offer 'adequate' cash payments to the remaining minority shareholders. However, the fact that the majority shareholder is allowed to determine what constitutes an 'adequate' price means that minority share-holders are still vulnerable.[23]

Thus, while the Takeover Act is certainly an improvement over the old voluntary guideline, the EC proposal would have provided greater protection to minority shareholders. In sum, however, it can be concluded that a German market for corporate control has emerged both in *de jure* conditions and de facto relevance, although the latter is subject to interpretation.

13.5. SUMMARY AND OUTLOOK

Things have changed a lot in Germany since La Porta *et al.* first published their findings on investor protection around the world. During the last decade there have been material developments in German capital markets and investor protection. This chapter has aimed to give an overview on and an analysis of these developments from a US law and finance perspective, focusing thereby on the legal foundations for investor protection and corporate governance. Clearly, a lot of *de jure* convergence is visible today, particularly with respect

---

[23] This has become particularly evident in the recent takeover of Wella by Procter & Gamble, where the holders of ordinary shares have received a 50 per cent premium against the non-voting shares.

Appendix: A Chronology of Formal Legal Changes in the German Capital Market

Year	Legal Innovation	Description
1990	Prospectus Act/ Sales Prospectus Ordinance	First legal act that directly addresses the protection of the capital market in Germany; (i) requires publication of a sales prospectus for all issues that have not been registered for trading on a German stock exchange before (ii) limits liability to intentional acts and gross negligence of 'those responsible for the prospectus'
1990	1st Financial Market Promotion Act	(i) drafting of investment and conduct guidelines for mutual funds (ii) removal of some anachronistic taxes (e.g. capital transfer tax and stock exchange turnover tax) (iii) abolition of some restrictions regarding business areas and investment possibilities of trust companies and mutual funds
1994	2nd Financial Market Promotion Act/Securities Trading Act	Completely overhauls German capital market law. The new Securities Trading Act (i) establishes the Federal Securities Supervisory Office/BAWe (now integrated to the Federal Financial Supervisory Authority/BAFin) (ii) prohibits insider trading (the BAWe/BaFin has to pass cases on to a public prosecutor, whomay (or may not) conduct further investigations and criminal prosecution) (iii) implements current reporting duties ('ad-hoc-disclosure') requiring companies to publish immediately any information that is likely to have a significant influence on the stock price, and prohibiting 'selective disclosure' (iv) requires shareholders of corporations, quoted on the official market, to report changes in major holdings of voting rights within seven days
1995	Voluntary Takeover Code	Voluntary guideline set by an expert commission, amended in 1998, which was only accepted by 65 percent of German issuers (i) establishes a bidder's duty to make an offer to all minority shareholders when he acquires the majority of a company's voting shares (ii) stipulates that mandatory offer price has to be 'reasonably related' to the stock price
1998	3rd Financial Market Promotion Act	(i) reduces transaction costs for raising capital on the stock market in an attempt to simplify capital raising for SMEs (ii) extends the permissible range of futures exchange products that can be purchased by investment companies (iii) approves pension plan investment funds designed for private pension schemes
1998	Raising of Equity Relief Act	Allows listed group parents to prepare exempting consolidated financial statements in accordance with either IAS or US GAAP
1998	Corporation Control and Transparency Act	(i) requires corporations to implement adequate risk management and internal revision systems (ii) allows representative action measures, open to shareholders holding at least five percent of total shares (or >500K EURO) in case of dishonest or fraudulent behaviour of the management board (ii) simplifies the use of stock option programs and liberalizes share buybacks by the company in the open market (iii) now takes chairmanships into account twice when restricting the maximum number of supervisory board seats per person to ten, requires that supervisory boards of quoted stock companies meet at least four times a year, requires supervisory boards to appoint auditors (iv) banks must rule out potential conflicts of interest by appointing a management board member as compliance person and by abstaining from exercising proxy votes in companies where they hold more than five percent of the shares; they must consult shareholders prior to making use of proxy votes and submit alternative proposals on how to exercise the voting rights and they have to disclose board memberships of their managers and employees

Appendix: A (Continued)

Year	Legal Innovation	Description
		(v) prohibits deviations from the one share–one vote principle by abolishing multiple voting stock, caps on voting rights, as well as maximum voting rights for listed stock; the use of voting rights in the election of supervisory board members of affiliated companies is not permitted
		(vi) revenues for auditors per client is restricted to 30% of total revenues and auditor liability is increased to 4 million EURO for quoted companies
		(vii) makes segment reporting and cash flow statements mandatory for consolidated financial statements
		(viii) establishes legal acceptance for a privately organized standard-setting body - the German Accounting Standards Committee
1999	New Insolvency Code*	(i) introduces insolvency plans as the German equivalent to chapter-11—procedures in order to facilitate reorganizations
		(ii) courts may allow debtor to stay in possession of his assets and to present an insolvency plan
		(iii) courts may 'cram down' a dissenting creditor group
2000	Tax Reduction Act	(i) replaces full imputation system where the corporation tax paid by the company had to be credited against the shareholder's income tax by the 'half-income system' in which half of the distributed profits of a corporation will be included in the shareholder's personal income tax base
		(ii) exempts capital gains from the sale of cross-corporation shareholdings from corporate tax base
2002	4th Financial Market Promotion Act	(i) establishes the BAFin as a comprehensive financial services authority
		(ii) Makes market price manipulation punishable as a criminal act, if an intentional false statement about a fact significant for the valuation of a security, as well as every other deliberate deceptive measure that influences this valuation, has been made (monitored by BAFin)
		(iii) stock exchanges are granted flexibility in setting own regulatory standards and trading mechanisms for their different market segments
		(iv) requires sell and buy transactions (above €25,000) of management and supervisory board members as well as their affiliates to be disclosed immediately as 'Directors' Dealings' on the internet
		(v) introduces an option to privately sue issuers for making untimely, false, or misleading statements as well as for non-disclosure of material information (structural break in the German code law system)
		(vi) reforms and specifies ad hoc publicity requirements and punishes their misuse through misleading announcements
2002	Takeover Act	Right after the fall of the EC Directive on July 4, the Government approved its own Takeover Act, that governs public offers to acquire securities of a German stock corporation
		(i) upon reaching a threshold of 30% of the voting stock, a shareholder has to make an unconditional tender offer for the remaining shares within four weeks
		(ii) the offer document must contain enough information to present a true and fair view of all relevant circumstances, the target must publish a reasoned opinion on the offer
		(ii) the consideration (cash or liquid stock) for the stock of the target company must not be less than the weighted average share price of the last three months prior to the offer or any higher price paid by the purchaser (or any affiliated company) in the same period

		(iii) upon reaching a threshold of 95%, a shareholder may 'squeeze out' minority shareholders by offering an appropriate cash payment
		(iv) subject to the approval of the supervisory board or by relying on resolutions passed in advance by a SGM management can take measures to repel a hostile attack
2002	German Corporate Governance Codex*	(i) summarizes current enacted statutory regulations for the management and supervision of German listed companies and thereby aims at making the German CG system understandable to international investors
		(ii) presents standards for good and responsible governance that go beyond legal requirements and obliges corporations to disclose deviations
		(iii) establishes a standing committee that monitors developments and adapts codex annually
2001	Law gov. Registered Shares and Simplification of Voting	(i) facilitates to exchange anonymous bearer share equity for registered shares
		(ii) authorizes electronic notices of meetings and other actions, as well as electronic tabulation of vote counts at AGMs
		(iii) allows web voting (ballots transmitted by remote investors have to be cast by proxy broker physically at the meeting)
2002	Transparency and Disclosure Act*	(i) publicly listed firms must explain whether and to what extent they have adhered to the provisions of the Corporate Governance Codex
		(ii) the management report shall report in writing to the supervisory board on the company's business performance and key strategic measures
		(iii) companies can choose the form and degree of public access to their annual general meeting
		(iv) auditors must report to the supervisory board on any objections they may have
2004	Investment Modernization Law*	(i) obliges corporations to prepare a cash flow statement, a schedule of changes in equity and segment reporting
		(ii) modernizes and reforms supervisory regulation and tax lax concerning the investment industry
		(iii) enables admission of and investing into hedge funds in Germany

* Legal changes in the shaded area are not covered in this chapter.

to legislation (*de lege lata*). Germany in 2003 has a modern and investor-oriented capital market law that is definitely able to meet international standards, and can even cope with the US regulatory framework governed by the SEC (Shearman and Sterling 2001). After the Fourth Financial Market Promotion Act came into effect, the problems to be resolved today are more a matter of credible enforcement (*de lege ferenda*). Thus, an open question remains with respect to whether the shift in the legal foundations will indeed lead to a sustainable German equity culture, in other words, will *de jure* convergence lead to *de facto* convergence? The final answer is left to the future in the eye of the reader.

References

Assmann, H. D., Lenz, J., and Ritz, C. (2002). *Nachtrag zu Assmann/Lenz/Ritz: Verkaufsprospektgesetz, Verkaufsprospekt-Verordnung und Verkaufsprospektgebühren-Verordnung*. Köln: Verlag Dr. Otto Schmidt KG.

Baehring, B. (1985). *Börsen-Zeiten. Frankfurt in vier Jahrhunderten zwischen Antwerpen, Wien, New York und Berlin*. Eds. Vorstand der Frankfurter Wertpapierbörse. Frankfurt: Fritz Knapp.

Baums, T. (1999). 'Il sistema di "corporate governance" in Germania ed i suoi recenti sviluppi', *Rivista delle società*, XLIX: 1 ff.

——, and Hutter, S. (2002). 'Die Information des Kapitalmarkts beim Börsengang (IPO)', *Festschrift für P. Ulmer*. München 2002.

Blum, J. (1986). 'The Regulation of Insider Trading in Germany: Who's Afraid of Self-Restraint?', *Northwestern Journal of International Law & Business*, 7(3): 507–31.

Bundesanstalt für Finanzdienstleistungsaufsicht (2003). *Jahresbericht 2002*.

Bundesaufsichtsamt für den Wertpapierhandel (2002). *Jahresbericht 2001*.

Coffee, J. C. (2001). 'The Rise of Dispersed Ownership', *Yale Law Journal*, 111: 1–82.

Deutsches Aktieninstitut (2003). *DAI-Kurzstudie, 1/2003*.

Easterbrook, F. (1997). 'International Corporate Differences: Markets or Law?', *Journal of Applied Corporate Finance*, 9(4): 23–9.

Emmons, W., and Schmid, F. (2001). 'Takeover Regulation and Corporate Law in Germany from an International Perspective', *Federal Reserve Bank of St. Louis Working Paper*.

Eube, S. (1998). *Der Aktienmarkt in Deutschland vor dem Ersten Weltkrieg*. Frankfurt am Main: Knapp.

Federal Ministry of Finance, and Federal Ministry of Justice (2003). *Benchmark Paper: The Financial Market Promotion Plan 2006*. Berlin.

Feinendegen, S., Hommel, U., and Wright, M. (2001). 'Zum Stand der Beteiligungskapitalfinanzierung in Deutschland', *Finanz Betrieb*, 10.

Goetzmann, W. N., Ibbotson, R. G., and Peng, L. (2001). 'A New Historical Database for the NYSE 1815 to 1925: Performance and Predictability', *Journal of Financial Markets*, 4: 1–32.

Gordon, J. N. (1999). 'Pathways to Corporate Convergence? Two Steps on the Road to Shareholder Capitalism in Germany: Deutsche Telekom and DaimlerChrysler', *Columbia Journal of European Law*, 5 (219 Spring).

Gordon, J. N. (2002). 'An American Perspective on the New German Anti-takeover Law', *Die Aktiengesellschaft*, 12.

Hoffmann-Burchardi, U. (1999). 'Corporate Governance Rules and the Value of Control—A Study of German Dual-class Shares', *FMG Discussion Paper* 315. London School of Economics.

Hopt, K. (1998). 'Company Law in the European Union: Harmonization or Subsidiarity', *Centro di studi e ricerche di diritto comparato e straniero. Saggi, Conferenze e Seminari* 31. Rome.

La Porta, R., Lopez-de-Silanes, F., Shleifer, A., and Vishny, R. (1997). 'Legal Determinants of External Finance', *Journal of Finance*, 52: 1131–50.

——, ——, ——, and —— (1998). 'Law and Finance', *Journal of Political Economy*, 106: 1113–55.

——, ——, ——, and —— (2000). 'Investor Protection and Corporate Governance', *Journal of Financial Economics*, 58: 3–28.

Meredith, R. (2001). 'The Anti-Iacocca', *Forbes Magazine*. 20 August 2001.

Mitchell, M. L., and Netter, J. M. (1994). 'The Role of Financial Economics in Securities Fraud Cases: Applications at the Securities and Exchange Commission', *The Business Lawyer*, 49: 545–90.

Nowak, E., and Gropp, A. (2002). 'Ist der Ablauf der Lock-up-Frist bei Neuemissionen ein kursrelevantes Ereignis? Eine empirische Analyse von Unternehmen des Neuen Marktes', *Schmalenbachs Zeitschrift für betriebswirtschaftliche Forschung*, 54(1): 19–45.

Orr, D. (2001). 'Germany faces the future', *Forbes Global*, 23 July 2001.

Radebaugh, L., Gebhardt, G., and Gray, S. (1995). 'Foreign Stock Exchange Listings: A Case Study of Daimler-Benz', *Journal of International Financial Management and Accounting*, 6(2).

Rützel, S. (2001). 'Der Anlegeranwalt—ein Neues Bankenrisiko?' *Die Bank* 9: 666–9.

Schmidt, R. H., Hackethal, A., and Tyrell, M. (1999). 'Disintermediation and the Role of Banks in Europe: An International Comparison', *Journal of Financial Intermediation*, 8: 36–67.

Shearman and Sterling (2001). 'Does German Capital Markets Law Meet International Standards?', in Deutsche Börse AG (ed.), *Neuer Markt Report: Gateway to European Capital Markets—Key to Growth*. Frankfurt, 53–89.

Wenger, E., and Kaserer, C. (1998). 'The German System of Corporate Governance—A Model Which Should Not Be Imitated', in S. W. Black and M. Moersch (eds.), *Competition and Convergence in Financial Markets: The German and Anglo-American Models*. Amsterdam: North-Holland, 413–59.

14

The Role of Accounting in the German Financial System

CHRISTIAN LEUZ AND JENS WÜSTEMANN

14.1. INTRODUCTION: ACCOUNTING MYTHS

Conventional wisdom has it that financial accounting in Germany is 'uninformative', or at least not as informative as in Anglo-American countries. The main complaints are that German accounting is very conservative, too heavily influenced by tax avoidance strategies, offers too much discretion allowing firms to build large hidden reserves, and lacks detailed disclosures.[1] Although these characterizations may be correct, they generally evaluate German accounting and disclosure from the perspective of outside investors trading in public debt or equity markets and relying on publicly available information. In Germany, however, stock markets are comparatively small, corporate ownership is concentrated, and firms rely heavily on bank loans and other forms of private debt (see Chapters 2, 5, and 6). Moreover, the above characterizations narrowly focus on the financial statements, that is, on elements of the system that publicly disseminate information. They rarely consider institutional arrangements for privately communicating information, such as the extensive German audit report ('Prüfungsbericht'), to which the attribute 'uninformative' certainly does not extend.

A country's accounting and disclosure system is part of its financial system and more generally its institutional infrastructure. Economic theory suggests that, in well-functioning economies, the elements of the institutional infrastructure evolve to fit and reinforce each other. Thus, the accounting system is likely to be geared towards the informational and contracting needs of the key parties in the economy. For this reason, it is important to understand the role of financial accounting in a country's institutional infrastructure and, in particular, its role in corporate governance and capital markets. Thus, a key question in evaluating an accounting system is whether it satisfies the needs of

---

[1] See, for example, Investors Chronicle (1994). 'Whose Bottom Line Is It Anyway?', *Financial Times Business Reports*, 14 January 1994: 64; Evans (1996). 'Brave New Welt: German companies finally become more shareholder-friendly', Barron's, 23 December 1996: 24; Review and Outlook (Editorial) (1997). *Shake it Up*, WSJ: A18.

the economy's main contracting parties and, in the context of financial systems, whether the relevant financing parties are well informed.

Using these questions as guiding principle, this chapter describes the main elements of the German financial accounting and disclosure system. We take a broader view and cover public as well as less-known private informational arrangements, which are integral parts of the German accounting system. We discuss the role of the various elements in the German financial system and analyse how they provide information to the key financing parties. Given the nature of the German financial system, which is often described as an 'insider system', we expect that information asymmetries are primarily resolved via private information channels rather than public disclosure. Thus, the accounting system likely exhibits elements that support insider governance and relationship-based contracting. Our institutional analysis confirms these expectations.

Due to the existence of private information channels, financial statements are less important in terms of monitoring economic performance and assume other roles, such as determining dividends. However, for this reason, arm's length or outside investors relying primarily on public disclosures are not as well informed in the German system as they are in Anglo-American economies. To support this claim, we survey empirical accounting research using German data. We argue that the findings are generally consistent with this hypothesis as well as several other expectations for the German accounting system.

The following section develops hypotheses about the role and properties of accounting in the German financial system. Section 14.3 describes the key elements of the German accounting system and ties them in with the financial system. Section 14.4 reviews empirical accounting research on Germany and discusses to what extent the findings are consistent with our hypotheses and the institutional analysis. The chapter concludes with a brief summary and some suggestions for future research.

14.2. FINANCIAL ACCOUNTING AND THE INSTITUTIONAL FRAMEWORK

In this section, we discuss the link between the accounting system and the institutional framework and, in particular, the financial system. We develop hypotheses about the properties of German accounting based on the idea that, in well-functioning economies, the elements of the institutional infrastructure evolve to fit each other. These hypotheses guide our institutional analysis and empirical survey in subsequent sections.

14.2.1. Accounting and Financial Contracting

Accounting information plays an important role in financial contracting (e.g. Watts and Zimmerman 1986). Financial claims and control rights are often defined in accounting terms. For instance, debt contracts use accounting numbers and financial ratios to specify when a corporate borrower is in default. In determining dividend payments to shareholders, firms frequently refer to past and current accounting earnings. Investors in public equity markets use financial statements to monitor their claims, make investment decisions or exercise their rights at shareholder meetings.

Given this role, it is reasonable to expect that accounting systems evolve such that they facilitate financial transactions and contracting. Moreover, standardizing accounting, either by regulation or private standard setting, is likely to reduce transaction costs. It seems cheaper to provide a common set of measurement rules for all or many contracts, rather than to negotiate a particular set of measurement rules on a contract-by-contract basis (e.g. Ball 2001). To capitalize on this effect, accounting standards are geared towards the informational and contracting needs of the key parties in an economy which are also likely to be the main lobbying parties (McLeay et al. 2000). That is, the accounting system is likely to reflect ownership and governance structures and the financing patterns in a country.

However, the properties of an existing accounting system can also shape financial contracting. A comparison of debt contracting in Germany and the United States provides an illustrative example in this regard (Kübler 1989; Leuz 1996; Leuz et al. 1998; Wüstemann 1996, 1999, 2002a). German accounting has traditionally been governed by 'prudence' and 'creditor protection', that is, measurement rules that are favourable to creditors and limit payouts to shareholders. As a result, German debt contracts generally do not have extensive debt covenants restricting dividends to shareholders; they simply rely on the legal restrictions imposed by the accounting rules. In contrast, US-GAAP is not geared towards debt contracting. Not surprisingly, US debt contracts generally include extensive debt covenants, such as accounting-based payout restrictions, and in some cases even specify modifications of US-GAAP to take into account the needs of debt contracting.

In summary, the accounting system is a subsystem of the financial system interacting with the other subsystems (e.g. equity and credit markets, corporate governance). Ideally, the accounting system is complementary to the other elements of the institutional framework.[2] This fit between the accounting system and a country's institutional infrastructure is likely to result in different accounting systems and informational regimes across countries.

14.2.2. Stylized Institutional Frameworks and the Role of Accounting

We illustrate the link between the accounting system and the other elements of the institutional infrastructure using two stylized financial systems. Following

---

[2] Note, however, that we do not take a stance on the 'bigger' question whether the German system is efficient or not. We simply analyse whether German accounting informs the key parties in the system, taking other elements of the institutional structure as given, whether they are efficient or not.

prior research, we distinguish between an 'arm's length' or 'outsider' system and a 'relationship-based' or 'insider' system (Franks and Mayer 1994; Berglöf 1997; Schmidt and Tyrell 1997; Rajan and Zingales 1998; Allen and Gale 2000; Chapters 2 and 15). The two systems differ in the way they channel capital to investment opportunities, how they ensure a return to investors and, most importantly for our purposes, in the way they reduce information asymmetries between contracting and financing parties.

In an outsider system, firms rely heavily on public debt or equity markets in raising capital. Corporate ownership is dispersed and to a large extent in the hands of consumers that directly or indirectly via mutual funds invest their savings in public debt or equity markets. Investors are at arm's length from firms and do not have privileged access to information. They are protected by explicit contracts and extensive investor rights, which are enforced by the legal system (e.g. La Porta *et al.* 1998). Public debt and equity markets and, in particular, the market for corporate control play a major role in monitoring managers and firms (e.g. Franks and Mayer 1994). Consequently, financial disclosure is crucial as it enables investors to monitor their financial claims and exercise their rights. Disclosure is also important for a well-functioning takeover market. Thus, in an outsider system, information asymmetries between firms and investors are primarily resolved via public disclosure (e.g. Ball *et al.* 2000). The accounting and disclosure system focuses on outside investors ensuring that they are reasonably well informed and, hence, willing to invest in the public debt and equity markets.

In contrast, in a relationship-based system, firms establish close relationships with banks and other financial intermediaries and rely heavily on internal financing, instead of raising capital in public equity or debt markets. Corporate ownership is generally concentrated and characterized by substantial cross holdings. Corporate governance is mainly in the hands of insiders with privileged access to information (e.g. board members). Given the nature of the system, information asymmetries are resolved primarily via private channels rather than public disclosure (e.g. Ball *et al.* 2000). Thus, the key contracting and financing parties are reasonably well informed, while outside investors face a lack of transparency. However, opacity is an important feature of the system because it provides barriers to entry and protects relationships from the threat of competition (e.g. Rajan and Zingales 1998). Opacity effectively grants the financing parties some monopoly power over the firm, which allows insiders to secure sufficient returns and in turn ensures insider financing to firms.

In this system, the role of accounting is not so much to publicly disseminate information, but to facilitate relationship-based financing, for instance, by limiting the claims of outside shareholders to dividends, which protects creditors and promotes internal financing. In essence, as insiders have privileged access to information through their relationships, accounting can take on other roles such as the determination or restriction of payouts. The accounting system is also likely to support private channels of information.

For these reasons, it is important to adopt a broader perspective when evaluating the overall performance of accounting systems. In insider economies, the key elements of the accounting system may not be those that publicly disseminate information (even though they have been the focus of international accounting research). A more complete assessment includes private information channels and contracting roles of accounting.

14.2.3. Implications and Hypotheses for German Accounting

As the previous characterizations were stylized, real financial systems generally do not fit them in all respects. However, the United Kingdom or United States are typically viewed as good examples of an outsider or arm's length system. Germany is often viewed as the prototype of a relationship-based or insider system. The German stock market is quite small in comparison to United States or United Kingdom markets. The primary sources for German firms are internal and bank financing (e.g. pension liabilities, retained earnings, bank loans). Traditionally, firms have a close relationship with a bank, the so-called *Hausbank*. But banks not only play a major role in financing, they also control substantial equity stakes, either directly or indirectly through proxy voting. They are typically represented on the supervisory board ('Aufsichtsrat')—the main instrument of German corporate governance. Ownership is concentrated and many firms are still under the control of families. There are also substantial corporate cross holdings. Corporate governance and control are primarily in the hands of insiders.[3]

Given these features of the German financial system, the key financing parties are expected to have little demand for public information. Their role in the corporate governance provides them with privileged access to private information. We, therefore, expect the key financing parties to be reasonably well informed. Moreover, as much of the information is privately communicated, we expect the German disclosure system to be less developed than in outsider economies, that is, disclosure levels to be relatively low and reported earnings to be less informative about firm performance. Consequently, outside investors are likely to be less informed than the key financing parties.

Traditionally, outside investors have not been at the centre of the German accounting system. Rather, the system is expected to exhibit elements that support insider governance and relationship-based contracting. That is, the system is likely to include institutional arrangements that ensure that the key

---

[3] See Franks and Mayer (1994), Hackethal and Schmidt (2000), Naumann (2000), and several chapters of this book, especially Chapter 5 by Theissen on the role and size of financial markets, Chapter 7 by Elsas and Krahnen on bank–client relationships, Chapter 12 by Schmidt on corporate governance and Chapter 2 by Schmidt and Tyrell on financing patterns, for more detailed characterizations of Germany's financial system.

financing parties privately obtain the necessary information to exercise their control rights. We expect it to assume roles other than the public dissemination of information. Finally, the enforcement of accounting rules is expected to be a function of internal corporate governance rather than of market governance.

14.2.4. Recent Changes in Germany

In recent years, several elements of the German institutional framework have been subject to major reforms such as the 1994 Securities Act or the 1998 Corporate Control and Transparency Act (Section 14.3 of this chapter; Nowak 2001*b*). These reforms suggest that the German financial system is moving towards an arm's-length system.

These changes can be explained in part by the immense financing needs of the German economy created by the reunification in 1990. Shortly after the reunification, Germany's total capital imports started to exceed its total capital exports.[4] That is, after years of exporting capital, Germany became a net capital importer. This change implies that the German economy could no longer rely on the traditional sources of finance. As international capital markets are not relationship-based, German firms had to play by international rules and faced demands for reliable public information. The 1998 Raising of Equity Relief Act, which allowed German firms that are listed on an exchange to furnish internationally accepted accounting standards, could be viewed as a reflection of this demand.[5]

To what extent do these recent trends and reforms alter our preceding predictions for the German accounting system? In principle, they should work against our hypotheses. However, complementarities among the elements of the institutional framework make it unlikely that reforms take hold unless several other elements of the system are changed simultaneously (e.g. Ball 2001; Schmidt and Spindler 2002). But complementarities in the infrastructure also imply that once a sufficient number of changes have been made there are strong economic forces to make the remaining ones.

Thus, although we are sceptical that recent changes substantially alter our predictions based on the traditional features of the German financial system, we consider this possibility in the subsequent institutional analysis and analyse whether recent changes have fundamentally altered the accounting system or

---

[4] See Bundesbank Statistics, EU time series 4628 and 4629 (http://www.bundesbank.de). We estimate a simple time-series model and confirm that net capital flows are significantly negative in the years after the reunification, even after controlling for a time trend and lagged net capital flows.

[5] Even prior to this rule change, certain German firms that heavily relied on arm's length financing, for example, because of non-traditional ownership structures or large financing needs, had strong incentives to commit to more disclosure in order to compensate the information deficits of outside investors and to reduce the associated premium in the cost of capital (e.g. Leuz and Verrecchia 2000).

the financial system's reliance on private information channels and insider governance.

14.3. INSTITUTIONAL ANALYSIS

In this section we describe the key institutional features of the German accounting and disclosure regulation, which are presently subject to marked changes. We identify the relevant accounting and disclosure rules and briefly compare them in their legal quality to US GAAP. Throughout this section it is not our intent to cover accounting and disclosure rules in detail, but rather to analyse their relevant economic characteristics with respect to our hypotheses. More specifically, we summarize the role of German financial accounting in restricting and ensuring payments to owners and in tax accounting. We describe the channels that supply the public debt and equity markets with information. But we also identify and describe important sources of private— as opposed to public—information to key contracting parties, thereby putting unprivileged parties (e.g. outside investors) at an informational disadvantage. The section ends with an outline of German enforcement mechanisms.

14.3.1. The Relevant Rules and Standard Setting Institutions

German accounting regulation in general is codified in the German Commercial Code ('Handelsgesetzbuch'—HGB), which applies to all legal forms of economic undertakings such as corporations, partnerships, and closed corporations. Important accounting principles are directly codified in the German Commercial Code, such as the principle of prudence, the realization principle, or the principle of timeliness. Those principles are of fundamental importance for the system of German Generally Accepted Accounting Principles ('Grundsätze ordnungsmäßiger Buchführung'—German GAAP). The term 'German GAAP' is, nevertheless, broader. It encompasses all legal rules, principles, standards, and norms that have to be applied by a company in the preparation of its financial statements. Unlike, for instance, in the United States these accounting rules govern purposes of corporation law as well as purposes of securities regulation.[6]

German GAAP are a legal concept which means that they are ultimately subject to legislation and jurisdiction. German courts established a long time ago that accounting practice has some relevance in determining sound accounting principles, but that, in case of conflict, accounting would be considered a *normative* rather than a positive issue. In a leading decision, Germany's Federal Tax Court of Appeals ('Bundesfinanzhof') stated as early as 1967 that, even though prevailing accounting practice could be considered

---

[6] See Siegel (1985) for a discussion of differences in state and federal regulation and Wüstemann (1999: 91 ff.) for a comparison with German regulation.

in court, only practice leading to financial statements that are in conformity with the legally intended purpose of the stated accounting rules could become GAAP.[7] The same applies to professional standards, such as accounting recommendations promulgated by the German Institute of Certified Public Accountants ('Institut der Wirtschaftsprüfer in Deutschland e. V.').

From a legal point of view, the accounting principles and standards established in court decisions are part of German GAAP. Put differently, German courts *determine* GAAP, whereas US courts have to decide whether professional accounting standards such as US-GAAP are appropriate under the circumstances (Wüstemann 1999: 9 ff.). In Germany, accounting principles are considered to be legal rules ('Rechtsnormen') and not professional standards ('Fachnormen'). Consequently, and in accordance with the German constitution, the determination of German GAAP is for the most part a matter of 'legal interpretations' (Ordelheide and Pfaff 1994: 85) and does not result from the activities of private standard setting bodies, such as the Financial Accounting Standards Board (FASB) or the International Accounting Standards Board (IASB). The codified accounting principles, which are of a rather general nature, are interpreted and developed further by the courts.

Over the last 40 years, beginning with several leading decisions in the late sixties, courts reached a very high level of technical competence in accounting issues, which manifests itself in important journal articles by federal judges. In interpreting accounting rules, German courts have—in literally thousands of court rulings—established a system of sound accounting principles and detailed standards regarding the recognition and measurement of assets and liabilities (Beisse 1994; Euler 1996; Moxter 1985, 1999, 2003). This system minimizes legal risks and creates what could be called legal security ('Rechtssicherheit')—even in questions of detail.

For these reasons, simply looking into Germany's Commercial Code provides only a rudimentary picture of German GAAP, missing the entire body of accounting case law. This predominance of law in the field of accounting regulation distinguishes the way in which accounting standards are determined in Germany from that, for example, in the United States.

14.3.1.1. Recent trends and their relation to the existing accounting system

Responding to the pressures of multinational corporations a new legislative initiative in 1998 (the 1998 Raising of Equity Relief Act) permitted listed corporations for the first time to apply 'internationally accepted accounting principles' instead of German GAAP for the preparation of group accounts. The intent of the legislation was to improve the ability of German multinationals to raise capital in the global equity markets. The law eliminated the burden of having to prepare two types of financial statements, one for

---

[7] Decision of the Federal Tax Court of Appeals on 31 May 1967 (I 208/63, BFHE 89, 191, 194).

purposes of SEC-filing and one according to the German GAAP. Legislation made clear that both US-standards (US-GAAP) and International Accounting Standards (IAS) are regarded as 'internationally accepted accounting principles', leaving also open the possibility of an acceptance of other national accounting systems. Note, however, that de lege lata only consolidated accounts ('Konzernabschluss') can be prepared in conformity with US-GAAP and IAS: The so-called individual accounts ('Einzelabschluss') are prepared for purposes of corporation law (e.g. distributions) and tax accounting, whereas groups must additionally prepare consolidated accounts for information purposes. Thus, the application of IAS by a German corporation does not have *legal* consequences for its tax payments and distributions to shareholders. However, it is likely to have factual consequences on its distributions to shareholders.

It has to be emphasized that German accounting legislation is already the result of European harmonization efforts. To summarize very briefly, European Directives (particularly the 2nd, 4th, and 7th Council Directive) have harmonized accounting and disclosure in Europe, requiring national governments to transform the Directives into national law. In Germany, this transformation took place with the 1985 Reform Act ('Bilanzrichtlinien-Gesetz'). Despite these harmonization efforts, the Directives left national choices and much discretion in the transformation. Moreover, it is neither historically nor currently clear, how much harmonization and standardization the European Union intends in accounting and disclosure matters (Fresl 2000). Recently, the European Union adopted a Directive stipulating the use of IAS for the consolidated financial statements of all publicly traded companies. The rules will become effective for fiscal years beginning on or after 1 January 2005.[8] Germany is—for the moment—one of the few European countries that accept internationally accepted accounting standards as a real substitute for national accounting standards (and not as a set of additional financial statements).

The legal character of German GAAP implies that only legislation and jurisdiction have, ultimately, the power to decide which accounting standards are to be applied. Nevertheless, the 1998 Corporate Control and Transparency Act established the German Accounting Standards Board (GASB). It is the function of this private standard setting body to advise the Ministry of Justice in matters relating to accounting issues and also to represent Germany in international private standard setting bodies such as the IASB. It also promulgates accounting standards for companies' group accounts which are

---

[8] Article 9 of the Regulation (EC) No 1606/2002 of the European Parliament and of the Council of 19 July 2002 on the application of international accounting standards provides for an exception for 'companies...whose securities are admitted to public trading in a non-member State and which, for that purpose, have been using internationally accepted standards since a financial year that started prior to the publication of this Regulation in the Official Journal of the European Communities'. This article applies, for instance, to corporations that are registered with the SEC and obliged to provide financial statements in conformity with US-GAAP.

presumed to be in conformity with the law, but in principle could be challenged in court because as professional standards they cannot claim the same authority as legal accounting rules. The GASB surely has an important function in the harmonization of international accounting standards with the goal of ultimately arriving at a globally accepted set of accounting standards. However—as in the United States (e.g. Metcalf 1977)—, the formulation of accounting standards by a group of organized users with obvious self-interests in the solution of accounting issues is not unquestioned.

So far, the GASB has issued thirteen German Accounting Standards (GAS), covering mere disclosure issues (e.g. risk reporting, interim financial reporting, cash flow statements, and segment reporting) and questions of recognition (e.g. accounting for investments in joint ventures in consolidated financial statements, non-current intangible assets). Given that the GASB took up its work only in 1998, it is still too early to pass judgment on the issues raised above. Furthermore, it is not quite clear whether there will even be a need for a traditional *national* standard setting body after the incorporation of IAS into European accounting law in 2003.

14.3.1.2. *The purposes of German accounting regulation*

German corporation law binds any distributions to owners to the existence of profits available for distribution in a company's individual accounts. The determination of distributable profits has to be in accordance with German GAAP. These legal rules are a transformation of the legal capital scheme laid down in the 2nd European Directive into German law. However, the link between financial accounting and corporate distributions (e.g. dividends) is much older and constitutes an important element of the German institutional infrastructure.

Ever since the nineteenth century, the connection between the accounting rules and distributions to shareholders has heavily influenced the nature of German accounting numbers. It was argued that if the profits of a company with limited liability are to be available for distribution, then German GAAP have to be interpreted in the light of precisely this purpose (the so-called teleological approach to law). This interpretation implies that the accounting rules must ensure payments to the owners but at the same time must also restrict payouts to the residual claimants. Payout determination ('Ausschüttungsbemessung') is therefore viewed as the primary purpose of the German individual accounts.

As a consequence of this primary purpose, German accounting regulation severely restricts the realization of revenues. For instance, benefits resulting from long-term construction type contracts can be realized only after final inspection and approval of the client—or, in other words, revenues can be realized only if it is as sure as possible that there is no significant remaining risk to the transaction. Also, holding gains from changes in the market value of securities must not be recognized; these gains only show up in the income statement when the securities are actually sold. On the other hand, losses—as a result of the predominant legal principle of prudence—have to be recognized as soon as they arise.

Courts have developed a full scale of jurisprudence for accounting, which very often interprets accounting matters in the light of the underlying legal structure (e.g. using the specific contractual structure to determine the relevant economic benefits and risks). This approach leads to an emphasis on the reliability and the verifiability of accounting numbers. It manifests itself also in a very strict asset–liability approach to the balance sheet: Tangible things as well as legal rights are normally considered to be assets; things that only have a certain economic use are subject to additional recognition criteria. Intangible fixed assets that are self-generated by the company must not be recognized; if they are not self-generated they can be recognized if and only if they stem from reciprocal contracts with a third (independent) party. Deferred charges—which have been characterized as a 'dumping ground for a number of small items' (Kieso and Weygandt 2001: 621) in the United States—must not be included in the balance sheet because they lack the quality of an asset.

Similarly, accounting for liabilities and contingencies under German GAAP can generally be characterized as being more prudent than under US-GAAP or IAS due to the legal concept that profits are available for distributions.[9] However, the prudence principle does not imply that accounting for liabilities and contingencies is completely left to management's discretion. It must be kept in mind that accounting is also subject to court rulings in prior cases, which narrows management's room for accounting choices. The application of the principle of prudence is, therefore, limited from both directions.

German GAAP also govern the determination of income taxes (principle of the authoritativeness of accounting for tax purposes). Income determination for tax purposes as laid down in the Federal Income Taxation Act specifically refers to commercial law (i.e. the HGB). Systematically, however, the reason for this principle was always grounded in the idea that it would be unjust if the treasury demanded tax payments from corporations on a basis larger than that available for distributions to shareholders. Likewise, there would be no reason why taxes to the treasury should be derived from a smaller basis. Thus, it was postulated that, legally, the purposes of accounting for distributions and tax accounting are identical (Döllerer 1971: 1334). However, this conclusion is not equally valid for the consolidated accounts. Distributions and taxes are legally not tied to the consolidated accounts, which have exclusively informational purposes.[10]

In summary, recognition and measurement of assets and liabilities according to German GAAP is characterized by (1) the legal concept of distributable profits, (2) the principle of prudence, (3) the emphasis on objectification

---

[9] Note, however, that the 4th European Directive also says that 'the principle of prudence has to be regarded under all circumstances' (Article 31, translated from the German version).

[10] Of course, legally, the individual accounts have a very important informational function, too.

('Objektivierung')—which often means a focus on the nature of contracts and things, as a counterbalance to this predominant civil law, (4) a substance-over-form approach and, finally, (5) a systematic and principles-based approach to accounting. Although the economic consequences of different modes of standard setting still need to be studied in greater detail, one should not underestimate the advantages of a legalistic concept, which lie in a systematic and principles-based approach and the resulting uniformity of terms across different fields of law.

14.3.2. Information Systems Available to Outside Investors

The fundamentals of German accounting and disclosure requirements are grounded in the regulations of the German Commercial Code and are equally binding for all legal types of firms (for details see Ballwieser 2001). The statutes oblige firms to keep books (HGB: § 238), to draw up an inventory at the end of each financial year (HGB: § 240), and to annually prepare a balance sheet and a profit and loss account (HGB: § 242). Recognition and measurement of all elements of financial statements (assets, liabilities, revenues, and expenses) have to be in accordance with German GAAP (HGB: § 243). As indicated, the statutes and legal rules concerning recognition and measurement are supplemented by the exhaustive case law developed by the courts (predominantly tax courts), commentaries, and the relevant literature of academic scholars (Moxter 2003: 9 ff.).

In addition to these general requirements, all firms organized as corporations have to add notes to the financial statements and, with the exception of small corporations, must prepare a management report.[11] The annual report comprises the balance sheet, the income statement and accompanying notes (HGB: § 264). They constitute a composite whole. The annual report has to give a true and fair view of the corporation's financial position and results of operations. If the application of the relevant accounting and disclosure rules is not sufficient to give a true and fair view, additional information must be given (HGB: § 264). For corporations, specific valuation rules, which are more investor-oriented than those for non-corporations, apply (e.g. duty to reverse asset impairments if their reasons cease to exist, HGB: § 280). The legal rules also prescribe very detailed und uniform formal requirements (layouts) for the presentation of the balance sheet and the profit and loss account (HGB: §§ 266, 275). The contents of the notes to the financial statements include details on the applied accounting policies, the individual positions of the balance sheet and the profit and loss account as well as on specific valuation methods (HGB: § 284). The disclosure rules further require information about specific items that are not in the financial statements, for instance, the total amount of financial commitments that are not included in the balance sheet, a detailed

---

[11] This also applies to companies in other legal forms that are subject to the Public Disclosure Act because of their economic importance ('Publizitätsgesetz').

breakdown of revenues, the number of employees, and the total sum of management's compensation (HGB: § 285). However, the corporation must not disclose facts that endanger national welfare and it may omit some of the required information if they are to the disadvantage of the corporation (HGB: § 286). The management report must include (1) a fair report on the corporation's prospects with particular emphasis on future risks (GAS 5), (2) a statement on material events that happened after the balance sheet date, and (3) a report on research and development activities of the corporation (HGB: § 289). In contrast to the financial statements, the management report presents results and prospects from management's viewpoint, and thereby complements the annual report.[12]

In addition to the annual report for the individual accounts, a corporation that controls subsidiary undertakings has to draw up consolidated (or group) accounts and to provide a consolidated annual report (HGB: § 290).[13] The consolidated annual report comprises the consolidated balance sheet, the consolidated profit and loss account, and accompanying notes (HGB: § 297; for details see Ordelheide 2001). Legal rules, commentaries, literature of academic scholars, and GAS detail consolidation techniques as well as accounting and disclosure requirements. The consolidated report is again supplemented by a management report (HGB: § 315). As mentioned before, the group accounts are neither the basis of dividends nor tax payments; they serve purely informational purposes. Recent amendments to the German Corporation Code ('Aktiengesetz'—AktG) could give grounds for legal action against the management and the supervisory board on the basis of the *consolidated* annual report (AktG: §§ 170, 171).

As an alternative to German GAAP, corporations with publicly traded securities can prepare their consolidated annual reports in conformity with either IAS or US-GAAP (HGB: § 292a). The resulting choice between three different accounting and disclosure regimes for the consolidated annual report, which remains until 2004, is quite unique and may prove as an interesting field for future research in the field of regulatory competition of accounting regimes (e.g. Leuz and Verrecchia 2000; Leuz 2003*a*, *b*). Appendix 14A.1 provides descriptive statistics on the application of the three accounting regimes in Germany.

Although the fundamental accounting and disclosure requirements are set forth in corporate law, there are supplementary information requirements for listed companies, which are laid down in the German securities laws. The most important requirements can be organized along the following lines:

1. *Recent amendments to the basic consolidated financial statements following the 1998 Corporate Control and Transparency Act*: Listed companies have to present a statement of cash flows (GAS 2), segment

[12] It, therefore, can be compared with SEC's MD&A disclosure.

[13] This requirement also applies to companies in other legal forms if they are subject to the Public Disclosure Act because of their economic importance.

reporting (GAS 3), and a statement of changes in equity (GAS 7). These statements form a separate part of the notes (HGB: § 297).

2. *Prospectus*: Corporations issuing shares have to file prospectuses. In these 'information tableaux' (Hommelhoff 2000: 756), financial statements (both annual accounts and group accounts are required) serve only as one of the key pieces of information that shall enable investors to properly evaluate business and prospects of the issuing corporation (Stock Exchange Act ('Börsengesetz'—BörsG): § 30).

3. *Interim financial reporting*: Listed companies are also generally required to publish at least one set of interim financial statements during the financial year. The interim financial statements shall give a true and fair view of the firm's financial position and the results of operations (BörsG: § 40).

4. *Ad hoc disclosure*: German securities law requires issuers to disclose any material new fact that is capable of considerably influencing its share prices (WpHG: § 15).

5. *Disclosure requirement in specific equity market segments*: Under public law, a listing in the 'Segment Prime Standard' of the Frankfurt Stock Exchange requires, as an example, quarterly reports, application of international standards, and ad hoc disclosure in English language (Frankfurt Stock Exchange Regulation ('Börsenordnung'): §§ 62, 63, 66).[14] In addition, the stock exchange may prescribe alternative or supplementary disclosure requirements on the basis of private law. To be listed at the former New Market, for instance, the Frankfurt Stock Exchange required companies to prepare their financial statements in accordance with either US-GAAP or IAS, and to publish quarterly reports.[15]

In summary, the information system available to outside investors has two characteristics: First, at the company law level, the dissemination of information is highly harmonized and integrated for different legal types of economic firms. It gives investors a standardized set of financial information which is not dependent on, for instance, state regulation of corporation law. Second, at the level of securities regulation, diverse reporting requirements prevail. They certainly have important interdependences, but they are not fully integrated.[16] We see this as a possible shortcoming of the information system available to outside investors in Germany. Moreover, the sanctions and liabilities are not dependent on any general type of 'misleading statements' as they are in the

---

[14] See Chapter 5 of this book for details on the various segments of the German stock market.
[15] See Sections 7.1 and 7.2.2 New Market Regulation.
[16] The public disclosure system in German securities regulation (but not company law) somewhat resembles the situation in the United States before the reforms that led to the 'integrated disclosure system' (see Loss and Seligman 1999: 606–627; Wüstemann 2002a: 132 ff.).

United States of America by means of rule 10b-5 and rule 14a-9, which in principle even extends to oral statements by management.

14.3.3. Private Information Systems

According to our hypotheses, the key financing parties in an insider system are less reliant on public information of the type discussed so far because they have access to private information channels. In the following, we examine how German corporate governance allocates informational rights to the key contracting and financing parties permitting and improving their control of management. These informational rights create several private information systems, which all reduce informational asymmetries between ownership and control. They constitute individual and separate 'information regimes' (Hommelhoff 2000: 749).

First, there exists a sophisticated system that confers informational rights on individual shareholders and does not depend on a controlling stake in the company (e.g. HGB: § 325; AktG: § 131). The group of shareholders encompasses—as a result of the Treaty of the European Union and rulings of the European High Court—not only current shareholders but also *potential* shareholders. However, there are certain informational rights that assume a *factual* position as shareholder, and hence cannot be viewed as part of the public information system. For instance, informational rights at the shareholders' general meeting can only be exercised if one is already a shareholder of the company. In addition to the individual rights of *all* shareholders, there are informational rights, which are only attached to those shareholders who are members of the supervisory board. A membership in the supervisory board gives broad access to virtually any value-relevant information of the company. The legal rules explicitly oblige management to furnish this information. Its reporting duties cover, for instance, financing and investment decisions, human resource management, the corporation's profitability and questions of corporate strategy (AktG: § 90).

As another important source of finance, creditors also have important informational rights: Principal creditors may—and very often do indeed—claim a seat in the supervisory board. Creditors are not only entitled but required by German banking law to obtain detailed non-public information about a company's prospects for any credit exceeding 250,000 Euro (KWG: § 18; Chapter 7). Finally, the German *Hausbank* system with its relationship lending ensures detailed cash flow information about all financial transactions handled by the *Hausbank*, thereby giving banks a broad database of historical information, for example, a company's paying habits, to their default risks.

A very important but less known private information channel in the system of German corporate governance is the audit report (Ordelheide and Pfaff 1994; Baetge and Thiele 1998; Schmidt 1998; Ballwieser 2001). Audit reports in German corporation law have to be distinguished from an audit opinion

('Bestätigungsvermerk'). In the audit opinion the auditor briefly expresses whether he regards the company's accounting as conforming to German GAAP, often in a boilerplate fashion. Audit opinions are published in the annual report and are a part of the public disclosure system. In contrast, the audit report has to be submitted only to the managing board of directors and the supervisory board. Recent legislation has made clear that all members of the supervisory board have to be given copies of the audit report. In the past, practice of some firms has been to exclude some board members, especially labour representatives from the report (Schmidt 1998: 750). It is an interesting feature of Germany's system of corporate governance that the audit report is not available for common shareholders, not even at their general meeting. In the first part of the audit report, the auditor has to stress the company's future prospects and especially those factors which threaten its survival. In its main parts, the auditor has to describe and analyse all items on the balance sheet that have a material influence on the firm's financial position. Moreover, the auditor has to evaluate the consequences of all significant accounting choices. This means, for example, explaining the effects of sale-and-lease-back transactions. The auditor also has to pass judgment on accounting choices within the management's discretion (e.g. overly optimistic but legally justifiable estimations of uncertain liabilities). An audit report of a publicly traded DAX 30 company has the size of several hundred pages. Wüstemann (2001) shows in his analysis of the relevant legal rules that an audit report leads to a much broader insight into a firm's financial position and results than publicly available annual reports. For instance, the requirement to analyse the consequences of accounting choices on the firm's financial position exceeds public disclosure requirements. In the notes to the public financial statements, such an analysis is not generally required, even if it was of legitimate interest to outside investors. Wüstemann (2002b) argues that recent legislation has even strengthened these tendencies. The legal evidence indicates a relatively high stability of private information channels in the traditional German corporate governance and suggests rather constant informational asymmetries within the group of shareholders. These recent changes were expressly meant as a reinforcement of the (private) information flows within the firm and to the relevant monitoring parties (Reform Act ('TransPuG') 2002: 18). They were rounded off by measures to increase information flows to outside investors as well (e.g. the requirement to disclose a statement of retained earnings for certain public corporations).

Recent decisions of Germany's Supreme Court may serve as the last piece of institutional evidence on the relative importance of the channels that give insiders in the German financial system privileged information and control rights.[17] In the underlying case, a legal norm was challenged which gives

---

[17] See Decisions of the German Supreme Court from 20 September 1999—1 BvR 636/95 and 1 BvR 168/93.

management the right not to answer any questions concerning the difference between the book value and the fair value of the assets at the shareholders' general meeting (AktG: § 131). Plaintiffs argued that without this information a control of management would not be effective since hidden reserves would distort a fair presentation of the company's financial position, thereby enabling management to draw on the reserves unnoticed and to cover up the firm's true financial position. In its decisions the court pointed out that the legal guarantee of property rights includes the right to obtain information over matters of the company in which one is a shareholder. The right to obtain information is hence a material component of shareholder rights. According to the court ruling, however, management's right to refuse information (AktG: § 131) is the proper restraint of the former: Hidden reserves are viewed as a means to protect against possible risks of insolvency and to secure the corporation against general risks for which there would be no protection otherwise. That is, in the court's view, hidden reserves can be in the interest of the company ('Gesellschaftsinteresse'). The challenged disclosure of hidden reserves would complicate the necessary measures of precaution considerably. The court also pointed out that the existence of hidden reserves could be in the interest of controlling shareholders, for whom entrepreneurial aspects are more important than distributions. Thus, the court ruling explicitly acknowledges the existence of divergent interests of majority and minority shareholders, but it also identifies information and control rights that are only available to majority shareholders, thereby granting them legitimate ways of exerting insider control. This is consistent with our main hypothesis that institutional arrangements are geared towards the main contracting parties.

In summary, our institutional analysis suggests that the key contracting parties in Germany are reasonably well informed once we consider both private and public sources of information. In fact, it seems plausible that they are at least as well informed as investors in an outsider system with extensive public disclosure requirements.[18] It has to be emphasized that the supply of information to controlling insiders and the supervisory board does not have an informal character but follows along legal rules, which ensures that the information flows are—as legally protected interests—enforceable. However, the existence of private information regimes also implies an informational disadvantage of outside investors.

14.3.4. Enforcement of Accounting Rules

Enforcement of accounting and disclosure rules can be achieved either via corporate governance or market regulation. In Germany, enforcement is basically driven by corporate governance. We identify and discuss three main

---

[18] In contrast, securities regulation in the United States stresses the importance of equally distributed disclosure (e.g. Regulation FD).

enforcement mechanisms, which all have been strengthened recently (Reform Act 2002). First, management itself is obliged by law to ensure proper application of accounting standards. The management also has to establish a monitoring system which enables it to detect developments that might endanger the economic survival of the corporation. Second, the supervisory board has to examine the financial statements, supported therein by the audit report and the auditor, either during meetings of the audit committee or in the general meeting of the supervisory board. Finally, it is the purpose of the statutory audit to guarantee that firm's financial statements give a true and fair view of the company's financial position and results. In order to strengthen the auditor's independence, the 1998 Corporate Control and Transparency Act introduced among other rules a rotation of the responsible auditor (but not the audit firm) after 7 years (for listed corporations only). The 1998 Corporate Control and Transparency Act also requires that the supervisory board hires the audit firm. Before the reform, the management board hired the auditors, which raised questions concerning the auditors' independence. The enforcement of either IAS or US-GAAP lies with the auditors, whose legal liability has considerably increased since an amendment of the German Commercial Code (HGB: § 323) enacted by the 1998 Corporate Control and Transparency Act. In addition, auditors and directors can face criminal prosecution for misleading or fraudulent financial statements (HGB: §§ 331, 332). It is also possible to sue for damages in civil courts, but only after a conviction in criminal proceedings.

US-style litigation or SEC-like monitoring does not exist. But recent legislation has at least established certain elements of a market oriented enforcement of accounting standards. For the first time, shareholders in Germany can sue the company on the grounds of misleading statements resulting in losses from irregular share prices (Fourth Financial Market Reform Act 2002 ('Viertes Finanzmarktförderungsgesetz')). In addition, it has been proposed to establish a private enforcement panel, following the British example of the Financial Reporting Review Panel (FRRP). This panel will investigate any complaints from private persons about violations of the accounting standards that materially affect a company's financial position. A possible establishment of a state agency like the SEC was discussed but rejected. Some enforcement is exercised by the monitoring activities of the State Bars of Certified Public Accountants ('Wirtschaftsprüferkammern'), which regularly review published annual reports and which have established a system of peer reviews following the US example (prior to the recent changes induced by the Sarbanes–Oxley Act). Limited enforcement could also result from the registration department of the stock exchanges, for example, the Frankfurt Stock Exchange. Last, but not least, indirect enforcement of accounting rules results from the activities of tax authorities. Since the *individual* accounts are authoritative for tax purposes, enforcement actions by the tax authorities regarding the tax accounts have repercussions for the underlying individual accounts (e.g. questions of recognition of assets, liabilities, revenues, and expenses). Interestingly, this enforcement mechanism is weakened by recent trends towards international accepted accounting standards for the consolidated accounts.

14.4. EMPIRICAL EVIDENCE

In this section, we provide a brief survey of the empirical accounting literature using German data (for earlier reviews Coenenberg *et al.* 1984; Möller and Keller 1999). We review empirical studies on (1) financial statements, (2) other financial disclosures to the capital markets, (3) the role of accounting in contracting and corporate governance, (4) earnings management and enforcement. We organize our review along six hypotheses, which are based on the preceding institutional analysis as well as extant accounting and finance research.

14.4.1. Hypothesis 1 (Price-Earnings-Relations)

The institutional analysis suggests that the key contracting and financing parties in Germany are reasonably well informed. Direct evidence supporting this prediction is likely to be limited since the information is communicated mainly via private channels. However, share prices can provide indirect evidence. If insiders can trade based on privately communicated information, prices should reflect this information in a timely fashion and well before it is incorporated in the accounting numbers and publicly disclosed.[19] Thus, private information transmission in conjunction with insider trading reduces the contemporaneous association of accounting numbers with stock returns (i.e. their value relevance) and increases the interval by which prices lead accounting numbers.[20]

Several empirical studies suggest that, despite voluntarily adopted restrictions, insider trading was fairly widespread in Germany, at least until 1994, when insider trading became illegal (e.g. Seeger 1998). But even thereafter, reporting of insider trades was not required until 2002. The lack of reporting requirements and recent anecdotal evidence question whether insider trading was effectively curbed. We, therefore, expect that the contemporaneous association of earnings and stock returns is lower and that prices lead earnings over longer intervals in Germany than in countries with strictly enforced insider trading provisions.

There are several studies examining the value relevance of earnings and shareholders' equity of German firms. Joos and Lang (1994) find that the value relevance of earnings and book value of equity are comparable in

---

[19] The information is eventually reflected in earnings, for instance, when the cash flows are realized.

[20] See Kothari and Sloan (1992) for the idea of prices leading earnings. Jacobson and Aaker (1993) make a similar argument for Japan and present supporting evidence.

Germany and the United Kingdom using price and 18-month return regressions. Harris *et al.* (1994) compare German and US accounting numbers and report that the value relevance of earnings is comparable, but that shareholders' equity in Germany is significantly less associated with share price than in the United States. In contrast, the results of Alford *et al.* (1993) suggest that German earnings are less value relevant than US (or UK) earnings because (a) they exhibit a significantly lower association with 15-month stock returns and (b) they capture a smaller proportion of the total information impounded in share price using a hedge portfolio approach. Ali and Hwang (2000) report that the value relevance is lower in 'bank-oriented' financial systems, such as the German, than in 'market-oriented' financial systems, such as the United Kingdom or the United States, using several measures of value relevance. Finally, Ball *et al.* (2000) analyse the timeliness of earnings across countries using reverse regressions (i.e. earnings on returns). They show that (a) earnings are significantly more timely in common-law countries, such as the United States, than in code-law countries, such as Germany, and (b) that this finding is primarily driven by the timely recognition of economic losses in earnings, which is suggested to facilitate outsider monitoring.

Studies explicitly comparing the lead–lag structure of stock returns and earnings for Germany and Anglo-American countries do not exist. However, Ali and Hwang (2000) document that the fraction of earnings information incorporated in leading period (as opposed to contemporaneous) returns is greater for bank-oriented countries. This finding is consistent with German returns leading earnings over a longer interval than in the United Kingdom or the United States.

Overall, the evidence is consistent with the hypothesis that German accounting numbers are less value relevant and less timely, in part because prices reflect information privately communicated to key parties. However, the value relevance of earnings and the lead-lag structure with prices are also affected by other factors (e.g. poor accounting quality and earnings management), making it difficult to attribute the results solely to the transmission of information via private channels.[21]

14.4.2. Hypothesis 2 (Announcement Returns)

A further implication of private communication (and insider trading) is that the information content of accounting numbers at the time of their public announcement is low. That is, the stock market reaction to the public announcement is weak because insiders already possess the information contained in the accounting numbers and have traded on it. Based on this logic,

---

[21] Comparative value relevance studies often ascribe their findings to differences in accounting quality. However, differences in information channels are an equally plausible explanation.

we expect the information content of financial statements to be lower in Germany than, for example, in the United States.

There are several event studies examining the information content of various German accounting reports (e.g. Coenenberg and Möller 1979; Keller and Möller 1993). They generally conclude that unexpected realizations of accounting numbers lead to significant stock market reactions around the event date. However, it is difficult to compare these reactions and the implied information content to findings in other countries. The stock market reaction at the announcement is not only a function of how much private information is already impounded in prices. Other factors are likely to differ across countries and may even pull in opposite directions. For instance, *poor* quality of the announced information and *high* quality interim disclosures both reduce the information content of announcements. Thus, it is again difficult to attribute differences in information content solely to the channels of information transmission.

Extant studies, nevertheless, provide several indications that the information content of German accounting numbers *at the time of their public announcement* is relatively low, consistent with our hypothesis. First, early German event studies do not use the press release date, but define preceding ones, such as the supervisory board meeting or the completion of the audit. These event dates are explicitly chosen to address information leakage and insider trading (e.g. Keller and Möller 1992; Seeger 1998). Recent changes in the securities laws (notably WpHG: § 15) that stipulate ad-hoc disclosure of price-relevant information are likely to mitigate these problems (Nowak 2001a). Second, even after these changes in 1995, event studies continue to exhibit relatively low significance levels. Only a small fraction of the market reactions (frequently less than 10 per cent of the sample) are individually significant (Nowak 2001a). These findings are likely to reflect the difficulty of measuring the information content of news announcements in an environment where the key financing parties have private access to information.[22]

14.4.3. Hypothesis 3 (Transparency)

Given that the key contracting parties are less reliant on public information, the level and the quality of financial disclosures of German firms are likely to be low compared to other countries where arm's length investors play a larger role.

Consistent with this hypothesis, several international comparisons document that the level of financial disclosure is low in Germany compared to the United Kingdom or the United States. For instance, the disclosure index developed by Saudagaran and Biddle (1992) ranks Germany only seventh out of eight

---

[22] Another problem is the correct specification of the market's expectations. Even the more recent convention to use analysts' forecasts as a proxy is unlikely to solve the problem as analysts' expectations may not reflect the marginal investor's expectation in insider economies.

countries, whereas the United States is first and the United Kingdom third. Similarly, the CIFAR disclosure index reported in La Porta *et al.* (1998) assigns only rank twenty-five (out of forty-one) to Germany, whereas the United Kingdom and the United States take the places four and eleven, respectively. These studies generally rely on indices of disclosure practice and hence measure both mandatory and voluntary disclosures. Cooke and Wallace (1990) focus specifically on disclosure regulation and find that Germany has fewer mandated disclosures than the United Kingdom or the United States. More recently, La Porta *et al.* (2002) conduct a comprehensive survey of disclosure requirements prior to security offerings in forty-nine countries. Germany ranks only in thirty-ninth place and exhibits lower disclosure requirements than most developed countries. All these findings are consistent with the view that, in Germany, public disclosure plays a minor role in informing the key financing and contracting parties. Interestingly, this view seems to be shared by both firms and regulators.

However, there are also studies suggesting that disclosure levels may not be low for every information type. For instance, Frost and Ramin (1997) report that German firms provide more earnings and sales forecasts than United Kingdom or United States firms.[23] On one hand, this finding is consistent with the low risk of shareholder litigation in Germany. But on the other hand, such disclosures are less likely to be important in the German environment. Consistent with the latter view, Meek and Gray (1989) and Baetge *et al.* (1997) find that forward-looking disclosures in German annual reports are particularly poor. More research is necessary to resolve this apparent contradiction.

14.4.4. Hypothesis 4 (Voluntary Disclosures)

Although the 'typical' German firm is characterized by concentrated ownership and strong reliance on private financing, there are German firms with less traditional capital and ownership structures. As these firms rely more on arm's length financing, they have stronger incentives to communicate information publicly. Economic theory suggests that these firms voluntarily provide additional information and exceed mandatory disclosures. They could also adopt more informative accounting standards or cross list in the United Kingdom or the United States, thereby committing to higher disclosure standards.

Studies using firm-level data reveal considerable cross-sectional variation in the disclosure practice across German firms (e.g. Coenenberg *et al.* 1984, for a survey of earlier studies). The results, which are generally consistent with disclosure theory and evidence in other countries, suggest that external financing needs, dispersed ownership, and foreign listings are among the key

---

[23] Along the same lines, Meek and Gray (1989) compare voluntary disclosures of European firms listed at the London Stock Exchange and find that German firms are particularly forthcoming in their employee disclosures, social and environmental reporting, but not in their financial disclosures.

determinants of voluntary disclosures in Germany. For instance, Leuz (2003*a*) presents evidence that firms trade off capital-market benefits (e.g. external financing) and proprietary costs in deciding whether to disclose segment information. Leuz (2000) analyses the adoption pattern of voluntary cash flow statements that are in line with international practice. He finds that German firms facing pressures in the international capital markets are among the first to voluntarily disclose such statements, followed by firms that are likely to have relatively high benefits in the domestic capital markets.

The latter study also suggests a trend towards improved disclosure. Disclosure index studies conducted at regular intervals confirm that German disclosure practice is steadily improving (Baetge *et al.* 1997). In particular, the number of firms presenting financial statements in accordance with international standards, such as IAS and US GAAP, is rapidly increasing (see also our Appendix). Leuz and Verrecchia (2000) document that German firms voluntarily adopting financial statements in accordance with international standards, such as IAS or US-GAAP, garner substantial capital-market benefits. Although these trends are consistent with Germany's recent movements towards a more capital market oriented financial system, more research is necessary to establish whether these developments are in fact fundamental changes in firms' disclosure policies or whether the documented economic benefits are based on perhaps unwarranted expectations. In this regard, the now closed New Market at the Frankfurt Stock Exchange provides an interesting example (Leuz 2003*b*).

14.4.5. Hypothesis 5 (Dividend Restrictions)

The institutional analysis in Section 14.3 emphasizes the important role of German accounting numbers in determining payouts (e.g. dividends, taxes). In particular, the fact that accounting rules are geared towards restricting dividends to shareholders is likely to be reflected in German debt contracts.

There are few studies that systematically study the use of earnings and other accounting numbers in contracts for German firms. One reason is that there is no disclosure requirement for bonus or debt contracts, which is not surprising given the nature of the German institutional framework.[24] However, there are several studies that provide indirect evidence supporting hypothesis 5. First, Harris *et al.* (1994) find that the dividend payout level is significantly higher in Germany than in the United States. This finding highlights the importance of dividends and payout determination in Germany. Second, Ball *et al.* (2000) report that, in Germany, dividends are timelier than earnings, that is, dividends

---

[24] Schwalbach and Graßhoff (1997) report based on estimates by Kienbaum Consulting that roughly 90 per cent of Germany's top executives receive (variable) incentive packages amounting to about 25–40 per cent of the total compensation. But they do not report how incentive compensation is determined.

incorporate a larger proportion of economic income as measured by the stock return. This finding again emphasizes the special role of dividends in Germany.

More direct evidence on the role of accounting in German debt contracting is provided by a study by Leuz *et al.* (1998). They compare legal and con- tractual dividend restrictions in the United Kingdom, the United States, and Germany and find that contractual restrictions are very rare in Germany and used only in special circumstances. This result is in contrast to the ubiquity of dividends constraints in UK and US debt agreements. However, German corporate law imposes detailed payout restrictions and the accounting rules are geared towards the problem of restricting dividends to shareholders. Survey evidence and the fact that these legal restrictions are similar to the contractual constraints in the United Kingdom and the United States suggest that the existence of relatively strong legal restrictions is responsible for the lack of contractual dividend restrictions in Germany.[25]

Finally, McLeay *et al.* (2000) present indirect evidence of a different sort. They analyse constituent lobbying and its impact on the development of financial reporting regulation in Germany. Studying commentaries on draft accounting legislation, they identify three primary constituencies: (1) industry and banks, (2) auditors, and (3) academic experts. Of the three groups, the first exerts the strongest influence—in particular with respect to disclosure issues. Noteworthy and consistent with the (contracting) role of accounting in the German economy is the absence of financial analysts and arm's length investors in the political process.

14.4.6. Hypothesis 6 (Earnings Management and Enforcement)

Based on the role of reported earnings in the German institutional setting, we conjecture that earnings management is more prevalent in Germany than in outsider economies. First, as the key contracting parties rely less on reported earnings to make investment decisions or monitor firms, there is less demand for earnings that accurately reflect a firm's operating performance (Ball *et al.* 2000; Ball 2001). Second, insiders enjoy higher private control benefits in the German setting than in outsider economies, and hence have a greater need to conceal or obfuscate firm performance to reduce outsider interference (Leuz *et al.* 2003).

There is ample anecdotal evidence of earnings management. German firms are frequently criticized for their 'hidden reserves' used to manipulate earnings (Coenenberg *et al.* 1984; Harris *et al.* 1994: 188). But there are also several empirical studies providing evidence consistent with our hypothesis. For instance, Keller and Möller (1992) compare financial reports of industrials and banks in terms of their information content. They document that the

---

[25] The institutional comparison of legal payout restrictions in the United States and Germany by Wüstemann (1996) further supports this view. He concludes that the US restrictions in state corporation law are relatively weak, which essentially leaves the problem to debt contracting.

reports' information content is considerably lower for banks than industrials. As German banks have more discretion in valuing their assets (e.g. loan loss reserves) than industrials, they view their finding as evidence of substantial earnings management, but it could also reflect the opaque nature of banks. The findings in Ball *et al.* (2000) on the properties of earnings are consistent with the hypothesis that German firms engage in more earnings management than firms in the United States or the United Kingdom. Analysing the degree of flexibility embedded in the accounting standards, d'Arcy (2000) shows that the codified rules grant managers more accounting choices than UK or US standards, which could give rise to more earnings management. However, as explained in Section 14.3, German GAAP are not determined by the codified rules alone, making a comparison difficult.

More directly addressing the hypothesis, Leuz *et al.* (2003) examine the pervasiveness of earnings management across thirty-one countries. Their evidence suggests that the level of earnings management and income smoothing is higher in Germany than in outsider economies like the United Kingdom or the United States. The study also documents that earnings management is negatively associated with outside investor protection and positively associated with private control benefits. Thus, it should not come as a surprise that Germany exhibits relatively high levels of earnings management.

The reliance on insider control and the relatively low demand for public information that accurately reflects firms' operating performance is also reflected in the enforcement of accounting rules. Anecdotal evidence suggests that the level of enforcement in the area of consolidated financial accounting is rather low (e.g. Ordelheide 1998). Recent studies by Glaum and Street (2003) and Gebhardt and Heilmann (2003) show that there is considerable cross-sectional variation in firms' compliance with German and international accounting standards, which is also consistent with low enforcement. Unfortunately, an empirical study that explicitly compares the level of accounting enforcement across countries does not exist.

In summary, we find that the extant literature broadly supports our hypotheses. In many areas, however, more research is necessary to explicitly address these hypotheses and to improve our understanding of the links between accounting, disclosure and the financial system in Germany (and elsewhere).

14.5. CONCLUSION

This chapter analyses the role of financial accounting in the German financial system. We begin our analysis by noting that the widespread characterization of German accounting as rather 'uninformative' stems from an implicit or explicit comparison with accounting systems in outsider economies like the United States and the United Kingdom. We therefore adopt a broader perspective and include public disclosure and private information channels in our institutional analysis of the German accounting system.

Confining the comparison to financial statements and disclosure, outside investors relying primarily on public information seem not as well informed in the German system as they are in the Anglo-American economies. However, the German accounting system exhibits several arrangements that privately communicate information to insiders, notably the supervisory board. Due to these features, the key financing and contracting parties seem reasonably well informed. Thus, the informativeness of the German accounting system depends on which elements of the system and which parties are included in the analysis.

Our survey of extant empirical accounting research generally supports these arguments. The evidence is consistent with the notion that the German accounting system is not geared as much towards arm's length investors as the US or the UK system. It suggests that the level of public disclosure is lower in Germany and that financial statements of German firms are generally less informative than those of UK or US firms. Moreover, stock price reactions to and associations with accounting numbers are consistent with the notion that a substantial amount of information is communicated via private channels. However, there is little research that directly addresses the informedness of arm's length investors in Germany and even less direct evidence on how well insiders are informed. Our conclusions should, therefore, be viewed as hypotheses and as motivation for future research, rather than answers to the questions posed in the introduction.

Areas for future research also arise from recent institutional reforms in Germany and Europe such as the adoption of IAS. We argue that these changes have not yet fundamentally altered the German accounting system and its reliance on private information channels and insider governance. Complementarities among the elements of the institutional framework make it unlikely that reforms take hold unless several other elements of the system are changed simultaneously (e.g. Ball 2001). Although the process towards an outsider system seems to have been set in motion and several elements of the German institutional framework have been reformed, there are still many areas, which are crucial to an outsider system but are largely unchanged (e.g. enforcement of accounting rules and shareholder litigation).

Before these reforms take place, we are sceptical that the recent changes have fundamentally and lastingly altered the German accounting system and its informational properties. Frankfurt's—now closed—New Market provides a case in point. The experience with this stock market segment illustrates the importance of enforcement and that changing the accounting standards is unlikely to be sufficient to ensure high-quality information to outside investors. In fact, recent studies provide evidence that accounting quality is largely determined by firms' reporting incentives, and not the accounting standards *per se* (e.g. Ball and Shivakumar 2002; Ball *et al.* 2003; Leuz 2003*b*; Leuz *et al.* 2003). The idea is that accounting standards necessarily leave discretion and that this discretion is used (or abused) depending on controlling insiders' incentives, which in turn are shaped by corporate governance and institutional factors. These findings suggest that if accounting and disclosure practice is to be improved, the emphasis should not be on reforming accounting standards, but on improving firms' reporting incentives by changing the institutional framework and, in particular, corporate governance. Advancing our understanding of these links is an important area for future research.

Appendix

The data for Tables 14A.1–14A.4 is based on a more comprehensive survey on the frequencies of accounting regimes in Germany. For further information see Fischer *et al.* (2001), Glaum (2001), Kirsch *et al.* (2002), Küting *et al.* (2002), Leuz (2003*b*), and Spanheimer and Koch (2000).

Table 14A.1. *Applied accounting standards of listed companies in Germany as of 1 January 2002*

Market segment	Percentage of companies applying German GAAP (%)	Percentage of companies applying US-GAAP (%)	Percentage of companies applying IAS (IFRS) (%)
DAX 30	13	27	60
DAX 100	39	20	41
M-DAX	51	16	33
NEMAX 50	0	72	28

Note: See Chapter 10 of this book for definitions of market segments.

Table 14A.2. *Number of German multinationals listed outside Germany (selected stock exchanges)*

Year	New York (NYSE and NASDAQ)[a]	London[b]	Tokyo[c]
1995	0	7	8
1998	11	8	8
2000	19	9	6
2002	23	9	5

[a] New York Stock Exchange: Complete list of Non-US companies 2002, http://www.nyse.com/international/international.html, 30.10.2002, 9.00h. Nasdaq: International Companies, http://www.nasdaq.com/asp/NonUsOutput.asp?page = G&previousCount = 0&region = europe, 30.10.2002, 9.00h.
[b] London Stock Exchange: International Companies, http://www.londonstockexchange.com/international/WE/trigger.asp?filter = 3&submitted = &CNS = &iPageNum = 1, 30.10.2002, 9.15h.
[c] Tokyo Stock Exchange: Listed/delisted foreign companies, http://www.tse.or.jp/english/listing/companies/transition.html, 30.10.2002, 9.30h.

Table 14A.3. *Applied accounting standards 1985–2002 in Germany DAX 100*

Year	Percentage of companies applying German GAAP (%)	Percentage of companies applying US-GAAP[a] (%)	Percentage of companies applying IAS[a] (IFRS) (%)
1985	100	0	0
1995	94	1	5
1998	81	6	13
2000	53	17	30
2002	39	20	41

[a] Including reconciliations from German GAAP.

Note: chapter 10 of this book for definitions of market segments.

Table 14A.4. *Legal forms of business enterprises and accounting standards in 2000 (individual accounts)*

	Number of companies applying German GAAP	Number of companies applying US-GAAP	Number of companies applying IAS (IFRS)
Private Ltd. company	446,797	0	0
Corporation	5,526	0	0
Sole proprietorship	2,040,713	0	0
Business partnership	364,967	0	0

Source: Statistisches Bundesamt, Wiesbaden.

References

Alford, A., Jones, J., Leftwich, R., and Zmijewski, M. (1993). 'The Relative Informativeness of Accounting Disclosures in Different Countries', *Journal of Accounting Research*, 31 Suppl.: 183–223.

Ali, A., and Hwang, L. (2000). 'Country-Specific Factors Related to Financial Reporting and the Value Relevance of Accounting Data', *Journal of Accounting Research*, 38: 1–23.

Allen, F., and Gale, D. (2000). *Comparing Financial Systems*. Cambridge: MIT Press.

Baetge, J., and Thiele, S. (1998). 'Disclosure and Auditing as Affecting Corporate Governance', in K. J. Hopt *et al.* (eds.), *Comparative Corporate Governance*. Oxford: Oxford University Press, 719–41.

Baetge, J., Armeloh, K., and Schulze, D. (1997). 'Empirische Befunde über die Qualität der Geschäftsberichterstattung börsennotierter deutscher Kapitalgesellschaften', *Deutsches Steuerrecht*, 35: 212–19.

Ball, R. (2001). 'Infrastructure requirements in the area of accounting and disclosure policy', in R. Litan and R. Herring (eds.), *Brookings-Wharton Papers on Financial Services*. Washington: Brookings Institution Press, 127–69.

Ball, R., Kothari, S., and Robin, A. (2000). 'The effect of international institutional factors on properties of accounting earnings', *Journal of Accounting and Economics*, 29: 1–52.

Ball, R., Robin, A., and Wu, J. (2003). 'Incentives versus Standards: Properties of Accounting Income in Four East Asian Countries, and Implications for Acceptance of IAS', *Journal of Accounting and Economics*, forthcoming.

——, and Shivakumar, L. (2002). 'Earnings Quality in U.K. Private Firms', Working Paper. University of Chicago and London Business School.

Ballwieser, W. (2001). 'Germany—Individual Accounts', in D. Ordelheide and KPMG (eds.), *Transnational Accounting*, 2nd edn. New York: Palgrave, 1217–351.

Beisse, H. (1994). 'Zum neuen Bild des Bilanzrechtssystems', in W. Ballwieser *et al.* (eds.), *Bilanzrecht und Kapitalmarkt: Festschrift zum 65. Geburtstag von Prof. Dr. Dr. h. c. Dr. h. Adolf Moxter*. Düsseldorf: IDW-Verlag: 3–31.

Berglöf, E. (1997). 'A note on the typology of financial systems', in K. J. Hopt and E. Wymeersch (eds.), *Comparative corporate governance: Essays and materials*. Berlin *et al.*: Gruyter: 151–64.

Coenenberg, A., and Möller, H. P. (1979). 'Entscheidungswirkungen von Jahresabschlußinformationen vor und nach der Aktienrechtsreform von 1965', *Betriebswirtschaftliche Forschung und Praxis*, 31: 438–54.

——, ——, and Schmidt, F. (1984). 'Empirical research in financial accounting in Germany, Austria and Switzerland: A review', in A. Hopwood and H. Schreuder (eds.), *European contribution to accounting research–The achievements of the last decade*. Amsterdam: Vu Uitgeverij 61–81.

Cooke, T., and Wallace, R. (1990). 'Financial Disclosure Regulation and Its Environment: A Review and Further Analysis', *Journal of Accounting and Public Policy*, 9: 79–110.

d'Arcy, A. (2000). 'The Degree of Determination of National Accounting Systems—An Empirical Investigation', *Schmalenbach Business Review*, 52: 45–67.

Döllerer, G. (1971). 'Maßgeblichkeitsprinzip der Handelsbilanz in Gefahr', *Betriebs-Berater*, 26: 1333–5.

Euler, R. (1996). *Das System der Grundsätze ordnungsmäßiger Bilanzierung*. Stuttgart: Schäffer-Pöschel.

Fischer, T., Becker, S., and Wenzel, J. (2001). 'Wertorientierte Berichterstattung—Ein empirischer Vergleich der internetbasierten Geschäftsberichte von DAX 30- und Nemax 50-Unternehmen', *Kapitalmarktorientierte Rechnungslegung*, 2: 14–25.

Franks, J., and Mayer, C. (1994). 'Corporate control: A comparison of insider and outsider systems', Working Paper. London Business School.

Fresl, K. D. (2000). *Die Europäisierung des deutschen Bilanzrechts*. Wiesbaden: Gabler.

Frost, C., and Ramin, K. (1997). 'Corporate Financial Disclosure: A Global Assessment', in F. Choi (ed.), *International Accounting and Finance Handbook*, 2nd edn. New York: Wiley, chapter 18.

Gebhardt, G., and Heilmann, A. (2003). 'Compliance with German and International Accounting Standards in Germany: Evidence from Cash Flow Statements', in A. Hopwood et al. (eds.), *Economics and Politics of Accounting*. Oxford: Oxford University Press, forthcoming.

Glaum, M. (2001). 'Die Internationalisierung der deutschen Rechnungslegung', *Kapitalmarktorientierte Rechnungslegung*, 1: 124–34.

——, and Street, D. (2003). 'Compliance with the Disclosure Requirements of Germany's New Market: IAS versus US GAAP', *Journal of International Financial Management and Accounting*, 14: 64–100.

Hackethal, A., and Schmidt, R. H. (2000). 'Finanzsystem und Komplementarität', in H. Francke et al. (eds.), *Finanzmärkte im Umbruch, Beihefte zu Kredit und Kapital*, Heft 15. Berlin: Duncker & Humblot, 53–102.

Harris, T., Lang, M., and Möller, H. (1994). 'The value relevance of German accounting measures: An empirical analysis', *Journal of Accounting Research*, 32: 187–209.

Hommelhoff, P. (2000). 'Anlegerinformationen im Aktien-, Bilanz- und Kapitalmarkt-recht', *Zeitschrift für Unternehmens- und Gesellschaftsrecht*, 29: 748–75.

Jacobson, R., and Aaker, D. (1993). 'Myopic Management Behavior with Efficient, but Imperfect Financial Markets: A Comparison of Information Asymmetries in the US and Japan', *Journal of Accounting and Economics*, 22: 383–406.

Joos, P., and Lang, M. (1994). 'The Effects of Accounting Diversity: Evidence from the European Union', *Journal of Accounting Research*, 32 (Suppl.): 141–68.

Keller, E., and Möller, H. P. (1992). 'Einstufung von Bankbilanzen am Kapitalmarkt infolge von § 26a KWG', *Zeitschrift für Bankrecht und Bankwirtschaft*, 4: 169–83.

Keller, E., and Möller, H. P. (1993). 'Die Auswirkungen der Zwischenberichterstattung auf den Informationswert von Jahresabschlüssen am Kapitalmarkt', in W. Bühler *et al.* (eds.), *Empirische Kapitalmarktforschung, Zeitschrift für betriebswirtschaft-liche Forschung*. Düsseldorf: Handelsblatt, Sonderheft 31: 35–60.

Kieso, D., and Weygandt, J. (2001). *Intermediate Accounting*, 10th edn. New York *et al.*: Wiley.

Kirsch, H.-J., Dohrn, M., and Wirth, J. (2002). 'Rechnungslegungs- und Prüfung-spraxis der DAX-100-Unternehmen—Bestandsaufnahme und Auswirkungen der EU-Verordnung zur Anwendung internationaler Rechnungslegungstandards', *Die Wirt-schaftsprüfung*, 55: 1217–31.

Kothari, S., and Sloan, R. (1992). 'Information in Prices about Future Earnings: Implications for Earnings Response Coefficients', *Journal of Accounting and Eco-nomics*, 21: 143–72.

Kübler, F. (1989). *Unternehmensfinanzierung und Kapitalmarkt*. Köln: Bank-Verl.-GmbH.

Küting, K., Dürr, U., and Zwirner, C. (2002). 'Internationalisierung der Rechnungs-legung in Deutschland—Ausweitung durch die Unternehmen des SMAX ab 2002', *Kapitalmarktorientierte Rechnungslegung*, 2: 1–13.

La Porta, R., Lopez-de-Silanes, F., Schleifer, A., and Vishny, R. (1998). 'Law and Finance', *Journal of Political Economy*, 106 (6): 1113–55.

——, ——, ——, and —— (2002). 'What works in Securities Laws?', Working Paper. Harvard University.

Leuz, C. (1996). *Rechnungslegung und Kreditfinanzierung*. Frankfurt am Main: Lang.

—— (2000). 'The Development of Voluntary Cash Flow Statements in Germany and the Influence of International Reporting Standards', *Schmalenbach Business Review*, 52 (April): 182–207.

—— (2003a). 'Proprietary versus Non-Proprietary Disclosures: Evidence from Germany', in A. Hopwood et al. (eds.), *The Economics and Politics of Accounting: International Essays*. Oxford: Oxford University Press, forthcoming.

—— (2003b). 'IAS versus U.S. GAAP: Information-Asymmetry-Based Evidence from Germany's New Market', *Journal of Accounting Research*, 41: 445–72.

——, and Verrecchia, R. (2000). 'The Economic Consequences of Increased Dis-closure', *Journal of Accounting Research*, 38(Suppl.): 91–124.

Leuz, C., Deller, D., and Stubenrath, M. (1998). 'An International Comparison of Accounting-Based Payout Restrictions in the United States, United Kingdom and Germany', *Accounting and Business Research*, 28 (Spring): 111–29.

——, Nanda, D., and Wysocki, P. (2003). 'Earnings Management and Investor Protection: An International Comparison', *Journal of Financial Economics*, 69: 505–27.

Loss, L., and Seligman, J. (1999). *Securities Regulation, Vol. II*. New York: Aspen Law & Business.

McLeay, S., Ordelheide, D., and Young, S. (2000). 'Constituent lobbying and its impact on the development of financial reporting regulations: evidence from Germany', *Accounting, Organizations and Society*, 25: 79–98.

Meek, G., and Gray, S. (1989). 'Globalization of Stock Markets and Foreign Listing Requirements: Voluntary Disclosures by Continental-European Companies listed on the London Stock Exchange', *Journal of International Business Studies*, (Summer): 315–36.

Metcalf, L. (1977). 'The Accounting Establishment: A Staff Study prepared by the Subcommittee on Reports, Accounting and Management of the Committee on Government Operations (excerpts)', *News Report, Journal of Accountancy*, 143 (March): 7–18.

Möller, H., and Keller, E. (1999). 'Financial Reporting and the Stock Market in Germany', in W. Bühler *et al.* (eds.), *Empirical Research on the German Capital Market*. Heidelberg: Physica: 135–48.

Moxter, A. (1985). 'Das System der handelsrechtlichen Grundsätze ordnungsmäßiger Bilanzierung', in Gerhard Gross (ed.), *Der Wirtschaftsprüfer im Schnittpunkt nationaler und internationaler Entwicklungen: Festschrift zum 60. Geburtstag von Prof. Dr. Klaus v. Wysock*. Düsseldorf: IDW-Verlag, 17–28.

—— (1999). *Bilanzrechtsprechung*, 5th edn. Tübingen: Mohr.

—— (2003). *Grundsätze ordnungsgemäßer Rechnungslegung*. Düsseldorf: IDW-Verlag.

Naumann, K. P. (2000). 'Financial reporting enforcement mechanisms as an element of corporate governance in Germany and reflections on their further development', *The European Accounting Review*, 9: 655–72.

Nowak, E. (2001a). 'Ermittlung der Eignung von Sachverhalten zur erheblichen Kursbeeinflussung bei Ad-hoc Mitteilungen: Eine empirische Untersuchung', *Zeitschrift für Bankrecht und Bankwirtschaft*, 13: 449–524.

—— (2001b). 'Recent developments in German Capital Markets and Corporate Governance', *Journal of Applied Corporate Finance*, 14 (3): 35–48.

Ordelheide, D., and Pfaff, D. (1994). *European Financial Reporting—Germany*. London: Routledge.

—— (1998). 'Wettbewerb der Rechnungslegungssysteme IAS, US-GAAP und HGB— Plädoyer für eine Reform des deutschen Bilanzrechts', in C. Börsig and A. Coenenberg (eds.), *Controlling und Rechnungswesen im internationalen Wettbewerb*. Stuttgart: Schäffer-Poeschel, 15–53.

—— (2001). 'Germany–Group Accounts', in D. Ordelheide and KPMG (eds.), *Transnational Accounting*, 2nd edn. Palgrave: New York, 1353–449.

Rajan, R., and Zingales, L. (1998). 'Financial dependence and growth', *American Economic Review*, 88: 559–87.

Saudagaran, S., and Biddle, G. (1992). 'Financial Disclosure Levels and Foreign Stock Exchange Listing Decisions', *Journal of International Financial Management and Accounting*, 4: 106–48.

Schmidt, P. J. (1998). 'Disclosure and Auditing. A German Perspective', in K. J. Hopt *et al.* (eds.), *Comparative Corporate Governance*. Oxford: Oxford University Press, 743–52.

Schmidt, R. H., and Spindler, G. (2002). 'Complementarity, Path Dependence and Corporate Governance', *International Finance*, 5: 311–33.

——, and Tyrell, M. (1997). 'Financial systems, corporate finance and corporate governance', *European Financial Management*, 3: 333–61.

Schwalbach, J., and Graßhoff, U. (1997). 'Managervergütung und Unternehmenserfolg', *Zeitschrift für Betriebswirtschaft*, 67: 203–17.

Seeger, H. (1998). *Insiderhandel am deutschen Aktienmarkt: eine empirische Untersuchung von Existenz und Erkennbarkeit*. Frankfurt a. M.: Lang.

Siegel, S. (1985). 'A critical examination of state regulation of accounting principles', *Journal of Comparative Business and Capital Market Law*, 7: 317–31.

Spanheimer, J., and Koch, C. (2000). 'Internationale Bilanzierungpraxis in Deutschland—Ergebnisse einer empirischen Untersuchung der Unternehmen des DAX und MDAX sowie des Neuen Marktes', *Die Wirtschaftsprüfung*, 53: 301–9.

Watts, R. L., and Zimmerman, J. L. (1986). *Positive Accounting Theory*. Englewood Cliffs, NJ: Prentice-Hall.

Wüstemann, J. (1996). 'US-GAAP: Modell für das deutsche Bilanzrecht?', *Die Wirtschaftsprüfung*, 49 (11): 421–31.

——(1999). *Generally Accepted Accounting Principles*. Berlin: Duncker & Humblot.

——(2001). 'Mängel bei der Abschlußprüfung: Tatsachenberichte und Analysen aus betriebswirtschaftlicher Sicht', in M. Lutter (ed.), *Der Wirtschaftsprüfer als Element der Corporate Governance*. Düsseldorf: IDW-Verlag.

——(2002a). *Institutionenökonomik und internationale Rechnungslegungsordnungen*. Tübingen: Mohr.

——(2002b). 'Normdurchsetzung in der deutschen Rechnungslegung—Enforcement nach dem Vorbild der USA', *Betriebs-Berater*, 57: 718–25.

Table 14A.3. *Applied accounting standards 1985–2002 in Germany DAX 100*
(group accounts)

Year	Percentage of companies applying German GAAP (%)	Percentage of companies applying US-GAAP[a] (%)	Percentage of companies applying IAS[a] (IFRS) (%)
1985	100	0	0
1995	94	1	5
1998	81	6	13
2000	53	17	30
2002	39	20	41

[a] Including reconciliations from German GAAP.

Note: See chapter 10 of this book for definitions of market segments.

Table 14A.4. *Legal forms of business enterprises and accounting standards*
in 2000 (individual accounts)

	Number of companies applying German GAAP	Number of companies applying US-GAAP	Number of companies applying IAS (IFRS)
Private Ltd. company	446,797	0	0
Corporation	5,526	0	0
Sole proprietorship	2,040,713	0	0
Business partnership	364,967	0	0

Source: Statistisches Bundesamt, Wiesbaden.

References

Alford, A., Jones, J., Leftwich, R., and Zmijewski, M. (1993). 'The Relative Informativeness of Accounting Disclosures in Different Countries', *Journal of Accounting Research*, 31 Suppl.: 183–223.

Ali, A., and Hwang, L. (2000). 'Country-Specific Factors Related to Financial Reporting and the Value Relevance of Accounting Data', *Journal of Accounting Research*, 38: 1–23.

Allen, F., and Gale, D. (2000). *Comparing Financial Systems*. Cambridge: MIT Press.

Baetge, J., and Thiele, S. (1998). 'Disclosure and Auditing as Affecting Corporate Governance', in K. J. Hopt *et al.* (eds.), *Comparative Corporate Governance*. Oxford: Oxford University Press, 719–41.

Baetge, J., Armeloh, K., and Schulze, D. (1997). 'Empirische Befunde über die Qualität der Geschäftsberichterstattung börsennotierter deutscher Kapitalgesellschaften', *Deutsches Steuerrecht*, 35: 212–19.

Ball, R. (2001). 'Infrastructure requirements in the area of accounting and disclosure policy', in R. Litan and R. Herring (eds.), *Brookings-Wharton Papers on Financial Services*. Washington: Brookings Institution Press, 127–69.

Ball, R., Kothari, S., and Robin, A. (2000). 'The effect of international institutional factors on properties of accounting earnings', *Journal of Accounting and Economics*, 29: 1–52.

PART IV

PERSPECTIVES

15

Taking Stock and Looking Ahead: The German Financial System at the Crossroads?

JAN PIETER KRAHNEN AND REINHARD H. SCHMIDT

15.1. WHAT WE WANT TO ACHIEVE IN THIS CHAPTER

It is the purpose of this chapter to draw conclusions concerning possible developments of the German financial system. On the basis of the earlier chapters in this book, we will give a tentative answer to the following questions:

1. What are the major recent changes and developments that are likely to shape the working and the performance of the individual segments of Germany's financial system? Or in more simple terms: What is the current status of the German financial system?
2. Given its current status, is it still appropriate to classify the German financial system as a bank-based system, or is it already a largely market-based system?
3. Are there any reasons to expect that this classification as either bank-based or market-based—or indeed neither of the two—will change in the foreseeable future?

Of course, these questions are closely related since the structure of any financial system is determined to a large extent by the character of its constituent elements. In addition, financial systems are changing over time, and it is tempting to ask whether a given financial system will, after a wave of changes, retain its basic character. The basic character of financial systems is commonly classified by placing it on a scale that ranges from bank-based to market-based. We will follow this tradition in our discussion, largely because Germany is widely seen as the epitome of a bank-based financial system.

Chapter 2 argued that complementarity between its various elements is an important feature of any financial system. The last section of Chapter 2 tried to show that only a few years ago Germany had a largely consistent bank-based financial system, which was clearly different from the capital market-based financial system of Great Britain and the United States. Many developments that have occurred over recent years have strengthened investor protection and transparency and have fostered the growth of capital markets in general. This raises the question to what extent the German financial system may already have transformed into a market-based system.

As the individual chapters in this book demonstrate, the past six years have witnessed more changes in the German financial system than decades before. Nevertheless, if we do not look at its individual parts or elements but rather at the system as a whole, we find these developments difficult to classify. Notably the run-up period to the stock market peak in the spring of 2000 saw an unprecedented increase in capital market activity—and possibly also a stronger capital market orientation of the German financial system—not least in the heads of management and commentators. The following years, however, were characterized by a swinging back of the pendulum. Many of the recent innovations were wiped out again. For instance, the euphoria concerning the growth and the viability of a local venture capital industry and its forceful exit channel, the *Neuer Markt*, simply disappeared. This leads us to the question which is at the centre of this chapter: Has the transition of the German financial system from a bank-based system to a (more) capital market-based system been delayed, stopped or even reversed; or is it inappropriate in the first place to classify the events of the late 1990s as the start of such a transition?

Where can an answer to this question be found? One possible source is provided by the developments in specific parts of the German financial system as they are reported and analysed in Chapters 3–14 of this book. In Section 15.2 we will briefly review them chapter by chapter. This will be an extremely selective review; its sole purpose is to illustrate that in all parts of the financial system change and continuity exist side by side. We hope that the chapters of the book together with this brief summary present a clear picture of the German financial system as it is today.

However, a financial system is more than the sum of its elements or parts. Therefore, as we will show, the enumeration of elements of change leaves open the question whether, taken together, these partial changes have also altered the basic structure of the system. Therefore, we address this question directly in Section 15.3 by discussing three views or interpretations of German financial system development. One view, which we call the 'markets only' view, contends that a capital market-oriented financial system is under almost all circumstances superior in terms of welfare to a bank-based system. It is believed that there has been, and possibly still is, strong economic pressure to make the transition from the outdated bank-based system to the more modern capital market-based system, and that this pressure has recently become stronger and/or that the impediments to its effectiveness have become weaker.

The second view, the 'banks-or-markets' view, also presupposes that there are two distinct types of financial systems, and that only these, and not any hybrid or other type of financial system, can be efficient. While the two types of financial systems can be distinguished, it is not possible to say in general terms that one of the two is simply better than the other.

The third view can be called the 'banks-and-markets' view. It questions the conventional confrontation of bank and market-based systems altogether, and instead suggests that there is—possibly more so now than in the past—room for synergy and welfare improvement to be gained from a synthesis of the two models which previously appeared to be distinctly different. This view suggests that the current turmoil in parts of German financial developments exemplify the labour pains of giving birth to a new type of financial system that combines increased market orientation with the tradition of long-term financial relationships.

15.2. RECENT DEVELOPMENTS AND THE CURRENT STATE OF THE GERMAN FINANCIAL SYSTEM: CONTINUITY AND CHANGE

This section provides a brief and highly selective review of Chapters 3–14 in this book. When they wrote their contributions about parts or elements or segments of the German financial system, the authors of these chapters had various topics, aspects, and *leitmotifs* in mind. After all, this was the task we had set them, and we are grateful that they took up the challenge. Nevertheless, irrespective of the wealth of ideas, facts, and theories reported in the chapters, we single out only one aspect here. We simply ask what the chapters on individual parts of the financial system contribute to answering the question of continuity and change both in the area covered by the respective chapter and in the system as a whole.

A look at *banks and banking structure* in Germany suggests that this is an area in which change is more pronounced than continuity. Andreas Hackethal starts Chapter 3 by quoting a former CEO of Dresdner Bank who, in a recent speech, vividly described the 'cosy world' of German banking as it used to be only 10 years ago, and said that since then 'no stone has been left unturned'. His view is certainly shared by many other experts from the banking world and from academia as well as by politicians. International comparisons also support the assessment that there have been enormous changes in banking, and this strongly suggests that Germany cannot be an exception to this worldwide trend.

However, there is also continuity and stability or even, as it is sometimes called, stagnation. Two traditional features of the German banking system have so far not changed: the relative importance of banks by type (savings banks, cooperative banks, and private banks), and the relative importance of intermediaries and capital markets. The size structure of the German banking industry has also largely remained as it used to be. There is a large—though steadily declining—number of legally independent banking institutions, which comprise some 600 savings banks and close to 2000 cooperative banks.

The remaining share of the private banks is much smaller than in most other industrialized countries. The small share of the four leading (private) banks in almost all areas of banking except investment banking can, therefore, be considered to be a reflection of the strong role of regionally oriented savings and cooperative banks. Equally, the role of banks that are not strictly profit oriented in Germany has not declined in recent years. Indeed, that of the savings banks system may even have increased. As Hackethal argues at the end of his contribution, current developments in European de- and re-regulation can be assumed to work strongly, albeit not overnight, against these traditional features of German banking.

However, the most stunning aspect of continuity is to be observed in the role played by banks in the process of financial intermediation and in their capacity as providers of funding to industry. The example of the United States might be taken as evidence that a worldwide process of disintermediation is under way, driving banks in all advanced industrialized countries out of their traditional roles as collectors of deposits and as providers of liquidity and loans. Hackethal shows that on an aggregate basis this is not the case in Germany, at least in so far as there is no indication that banks are being marginalized. Thus, in contrast to what might have been expected, there is not only change but also a strong dose of continuity in the German banking system. Given the central role which banks play in the German financial system, this can be regarded as an indication, though certainly not more, that continuity might be the prevailing feature of the entire financial system.

It is a general trend that the role of *institutional investors* in financial systems is steadily increasing. Germany is not an exception to this rule, though this trend is not equally strong for the two groups of institutional investors which Raimond Maurer covers in Chapter 4 of this book. In the insurance industry, the more traditional branch, continuity dominates, while the investment industry has experienced considerable growth and also more changes.

During the past decade, the insurance industry in Germany has maintained most of its specific characteristics as far as the legal forms and structures of insurance companies, product design, regulatory regime and industry structure are concerned. One of these characteristics refers to the solvency regulation for life insurance companies. Policy-holders are not protected through equity requirements like in many other countries, but rather through a set of relatively tight restrictions with respect to the allocation of funds. Another peculiarity is that German insurance companies are still permitted, if not even encouraged, to smooth the return which they report and in part also pay out to policy-holders. These two features are intended to make insurers appear and indeed be stable because private life insurance was once introduced in Germany as a substitute for the public pay-as-you go pension system. As such it was meant to provide a comparable capability to absorb intertemporal or intergenerational risk. A further element of continuity is that big German insurance groups typically have sizable portfolios of equity holdings in other big companies. However, the cross-holdings which used to exist within the financial sector have recently been reduced.

The German investment industry has grown more than any other part of the financial sector. In the mid-1990s, a key driver of growth was the increase in the so-called special funds, which investment management companies manage on behalf of other institutions. In the late 1990s, the stock market boom became the driver of this development. As a consequence of this boom and the ensuing bust, the German investment funds are now developing more subtle risk management tools and policies than they used to have in the past. The next challenge for them, and possibly also the next push for further growth, will come from the roll-out of the so-called Riester reform of 2001. This reform of the German pension system aims at supplementing unfunded public pensions by funded private pensions. Contrary to what some observers believed at the time when it was initiated, this reform is not meant to substitute the public pension scheme to an extent which would make the German pension system similar to that of the United States or the United Kingdom. It is rather no more than a—much needed—reform of the existing pension system and does not constitute a fundamental change, which might have induced an equally fundamental transformation of the entire German financial system.

Chapter 5 is dedicated to the German *organized capital markets*. Its author Erik Theissen inquires whether the German stock exchange system still deserves to be called 'in some sense underdeveloped', a widely held view among observers of Germany as 'the archetype of a bank-dominated system'. In order to provide an answer, he surveys stock market development in Germany over the last decade, relating it to the results of a number of recent empirical studies.

Theissen distinguishes three dimensions of inquiry, each referring to a specific economic role of the stock market. The first dimension is that of the stock market as a source of funding for firms and as an outlet for household savings. In this capacity, the organized German capital market is still as 'underdeveloped' after the turn of the millennium as it has been for the last 50 years. The second dimension is that of the organization and the quality of the trading systems, of transaction costs and of liquidity. Here Theissen argues that as a provider of liquidity and an instrument to incorporate information, the German stock exchange system with its duality of floor-trading and the screen-based trading systems IBIS (until 1997) and XETRA (since then) is anything but underdeveloped. The third dimension is that of the ownership and governance system of the German stock exchange. Here, the modernity of the Deutsche Börse AG and the traditional public law structure of the Frankfurter Wertpapierbörse and of the rest of Germany's stock exchange system form an odd alliance.

Thus, the German stock exchange system cannot easily be classified as being either modern or old-fashioned, as much as it is not shaped by either continuity or change. There is a great deal of both. But what does this suggest with respect to the development of the German financial system as a whole? The changes which have occurred concern the trading function of the capital market and not the funding and investment functions. These changes may indicate a step towards a more capital market-based system. But having a well-functioning trading system for secondary markets is not evidently inconsistent with a traditional bank-based system; an underdeveloped secondary market may coincide with a bank-based system, but it is not an essential feature of such a system. If by contrast, the changes had concerned the funding and investment sides rather than the trading side, they might have been a strong indicator of a general change. Such a more fundamental change, however, eventually hinges on a country's general pension policy, for example, the extent to which the current system is replaced by a funded system. It is widely believed that Germany will experience a stepwise transition from today's pure tax financed pay-as-you-go system to a mixed system in which only a base income, comparable to the minimum social security income, will be tax financed, while any surpassing pension claim will rely on private accumulation. This need for funding and accumulation is expected to greatly increase the diversity as well as the volume of investment products, driving capital market growth from the supply side.

In Chapter 6 on *monetary policy transmission* in Germany, Andreas Worms analyses the extent to which monetary impulses, for example, restrictive measures, translate into an adjustment of lending volume by banks. From the point of view of a central bank—the Bundesbank until 2000, the ECB thereafter—a clear understanding of the transmission process is critical for the design of monetary policy measures. The author stresses the importance of properly incorporating the institutional structure of the financial system into the analysis. The structure of the banking system, with its distribution of market shares between the network of savings banks, cooperative banks, and private banks has remained remarkably stable over the past decades. Worms presents new evidence on intra-sector lending that allows him to explain why the credit channel, which is generally believed to be of primary importance in the monetary transmission process, appears to be so weak in Germany. In his empirical survey Worms finds the importance of loans, during the recent past, to be largely unchanged for small and medium firms, while it has decreased for large firms, due to the ongoing securitization process. He also finds that, contrary to experiences in the United States and other economies, in Germany a bank's reaction to monetary impulses is not directly related to the size of the bank. In view of these features of the German financial system, it may not be surprising that earlier studies on the credit channel in Germany have concluded that it does not even exist. Using an enlarged data set and improved methodology, Worms finds that there are strong effects of monetary policy changes on real variables, for example output and prices, and that the overall impact of the credit channel is measurable but small, even for smaller companies. Worms then goes on to show that intra-sector lending activities within the savings bank network and within the cooperative bank network are effectively operating as buffers against unexpected shocks to liquidity. Until now, there has been no indication that any of these dependencies has changed materially since the ECB took over the responsibility for monetary policy, emphasizing the continuity of relationship lending in the financial system.

The intensive relationship between banks and their (corporate) customers, which Ralf Elsas and Jan P. Krahnen discuss in Chapter 7, is often seen as the centrepiece of a bank-based financial system. Whether this characterization holds true for Germany, and if it does, whether *Hausbank*ing is a vice or a virtue has been the subject of much recent debate in the literature. In their chapter on *bank financing and relationship lending*, Elsas and Krahnen investigate the importance of bank lending in the German financial system. Their assessment of the role of relationship lending in Germany up to the present time uncovers both continuity and change. There is continuity in the economic substance of relationship lending, and there is considerable change in its assessment by economists. The authors distinguish between a bank's role in lending and in corporate control. While banks are creditors in the first instance, they are investors in the second, holding equity stakes in corporations, sitting on their boards and/or using proxy votes in the company's general meeting. Accordingly, the exercise of control via these three routes (shareholding, board membership, and proxy voting) is restricted to the class of large, public enterprises. In this top size class of companies, all three routes are used frequently, compared to other countries, but their importance has been steadily declining over the past years. With respect to proxy voting and board representation, several recent studies could not find a significant effect on corporate performance, measured by book to market, or returns on equity. Equity shareholdings by banks, in contrast, have a positive and significant effect. The conclusion, therefore, is that equity holdings tend to be beneficial, while board membership and proxy voting tend to be neutral. This does not lend support to the widely held belief that banks commonly abuse their control stakes.

Turning to the lending business, the authors cite evidence that underscores the important economic role played by relationship lending in the so-called German *Mittelstand*, that is, small and medium-sized enterprises. Given that companies in Germany tend to have multiple lenders, it is necessary to differentiate between the (at most one) *Hausbank*, and the (several) non-*Hausbank*s, and their characteristics. Most importantly, the authors cite evidence demonstrating that *Hausbank*s provide liquidity to companies which have experienced a liquidity shock. The availability of credit from the *Hausbank* appears to be based on this bank's better access to information. The close relationship carries over to distress situations, where *Hausbank*s are more active than others in supporting workouts. The role of banks in corporate distress is a further argument in support of the claim of 'continuity in substance and change in assessment'. While it has been widely believed that German banks, owing to collateralized lending, are not willing to engage in workouts, the authors report results from new and unique data sets that suggest just the opposite. Relying on a pooling of interest, German banks typically coordinate their behaviour well before the onset of any formal bankruptcy proceedings and arrange for a workout. Court intervention is effectively reserved for the hopeless cases—explaining the low workout incidence in the official German bankruptcy statistics. Ironically, this fact has puzzled observers and politicians for more than two decades. What is the source of this high degree of bank involvement in private workouts? The authors point to important features of the German bankruptcy code, which have remained invariant throughout the twentieth century, and which have largely survived the 1999 reform of the Insolvency Code intact. These features strengthen the rights of creditors and facilitate their involvement in pre-bankruptcy settlements.

In Chapter 8 on *initial public offerings and venture capital in Germany*, Stefanie Franzke, Stefanie Grohs, and Christian Laux survey and evaluate the current situation in the area of venture capital financing reporting that the German economy has recently experienced its arguably most spectacular challenge relating to continuity and change, that is, the rise and the fall of the *Neuer Markt*, the newly founded stock market segment for young and innovative firms. The *Neuer Markt* became the epitome of a new stock market culture amidst a traditional, bank-centred financial system, while its closure only a few years later, in early 2003, revived the question of the role of venture capital financing and of going public in Germany. The early success of the *Neuer Markt* demonstrated to the world the potential for change in the German venture capital industry in the form of a large number of IPOs, unheard of for almost a century, a sharp decrease in the average age of firms going public (from 50 years down to 10), moderate IPO costs on an international level, as well as the burgeoning investment boutiques as advisors and underwriters for the IPO process. But there is also considerable continuity, as is convincingly shown by Franzke, Grohs, and Laux. While the mentality of market participants, an often cited argument, appears to be rather elusive, there are underlying business conditions of the SME economy which may explain the widespread reluctance to rush to the capital market. For family businesses, still very prominent among SMEs, going public typically implies foregoing the private benefits associated with complete control. The authors also stress the formative role of banks in the market entry decision of firms. For a long time, banks were the most important source of credit for firms. Furthermore, they were the underwriter in a possible IPO, they owned the exchange and sat in their committees defining entry conditions, and they managed the major investment funds. In a relatively isolated financial market, characteristic for Germany up to the 1990s, it is conceivable that a booming IPO market was simply not in the interests of the banking industry. It is telling that in these times investor protection, an often proclaimed objective of lawmakers, was quite generally interpreted as shielding ordinary investors from business risk, rather than from managerial misconduct and unfair pricing. How far-reaching the changes surrounding the new equity culture really are, remains to be seen. The authors conclude their assessment by pointing to the increasing openness of the German financial market, and the strengthened competition in the investment banking arena.

In Chapter 9, Frank Schmid and Mark Wahrenburg study the social setting and the regulatory framework relating to *mergers and acquisitions in Germany*. Their report conveys a colourful picture, on the one hand, of an economy with a strong tradition of defending incumbent management and majority shareholders against outside investors and, on the other, of a recent revision of the traditional regulatory framework that has drastically altered the opportunities to engineer corporate control changes. Even more than in other areas of financial markets covered in this book, we are left with the impression that the overhaul of the legal framework has copied many features that characterize the Anglo-American financial system, while at the same time leaving some of the more important traditional features intact. Again, we find significant change amidst continuity. Schmid and Wahrenburg emphasize that real change in the M&A business has to be judged by its results, rather than with respect to its legal preconditions. They describe the recent experiences with hostile takeovers in Germany, exemplified by the Thyssen/Krupp and Mannesmann/Vodafone cases. The first case was finally completed in the form of a friendly takeover, following fierce resistance by management, workers, and politicians. Only 2 years later, the second case was completed without interference by the traditional *Deutschland AG*—not least because the legal environment had changed by then.

Schmid and Wahrenburg describe the many recent legal changes affecting the functioning of the M&A market, and explain where continuity prevails, and what its impact will probably be for the M&A industry. Codetermination, proxy voting, and non-voting shares are discussed, and it appears that their impact on M&A has been exaggerated by many observers. They also point to the fact that despite the strong role of banks in corporate finance, there exists an active M&A market among SMEs, which form the most important business segment in Germany. While the legal innovations described in this chapter are too recent to be already borne out in the data, it seems safe to conclude that after a process of adaptation M&A will be more openly practised and more visible than it was only a few years ago.

Karl-Hermann Fischer and Christian Pfeil survey *regulation and competition in German banking* in Chapter 10. As a point of departure, they ask whether the commonly held view, namely that Germany's banking system is stable but not competitive, is justified. Building on recent available evidence, the authors focus their analysis on this alleged trade-off. They observe a remarkable stability with respect to the general competitive structure of the banking industry. There are three segments in the market, that is, the publicly owned banks (notably savings banks and their apex institutions, the *Landesbanks*), the cooperative banks and the private banks. These segments were already in existence when national banking regulation was initiated in 1931, and their respective market shares have remained fairly stable ever since.

Fischer and Pfeil also present a new assessment of concentration in German banks. In retail banking, where they define markets as being local, the authors report fairly high and stable average concentration ratios, with significant variation between the East and the West, and even more importantly between large cities and smaller towns and rural areas. They also demonstrate the economic significance of concentration by indicating a strong impact of concentration ratios on deposit rates. In investment banking, the market operates at the national (or even international) level, and the indices reported here suggest a considerable decrease in concentration. The high degree of concentration notwithstanding, the authors find competition in German banking markets to be high by international standards.

The monetary authority has always played a significant role in the supervisory process in Germany, assisting the supervisory agency in collecting and analysing reported data through their comprehensive branch network. In addition, the authors argue that the monetary authority has for a long time played a decisive role in protecting the deposit franchise of the existing financial institutions by keeping competition from new institutions, new financial instruments, or international competitors at bay. The overall impression is that there is a lot of continuity in this area because the interplay of industrial organization and institutional stability has remained intact to date. However, there seems to be considerable change ahead relating to, among others, the European integration process. These changes have already posed a formidable challenge for publicly owned *Landesbanks*, which have to dispose of their state guarantee in the near future. Moreover, the authors expect more visible changes in the German banking system to emerge once the de facto boundaries between the three segments of the market disappear.

In the two chapters on *corporate governance* by Oliver Rieckers and Gerald Spindler and by Reinhard H. Schmidt, as well as in the chapter on *investor protection* by Eric Nowak change and continuity are obviously topical. There is hardly any element of the German financial system which has changed quite so much. Only a few years ago, the term corporate governance was still largely unknown even to people in touch with the associated facts, rules, and problems. Today, corporate governance is a household word and a field of permanent activity in Germany. Over the last decade, policy-makers have taken measures to improve corporate governance and investor protection. For more than a decade, better corporate governance and more investor protection have become synonymous with the 'promotion of the German financial market' by way of changing the body of corporate and capital market legislation. As Eric Nowak describes in detail, a series of comprehensive laws on the promotion of the financial market ('Finanzmarktförderungsgesetz') as well as several other laws have been prepared, passed and implemented in the last decade. Several high-level commissions have produced reports on German corporate governance, including long lists of required reforms. Besides advocating legal changes, these reports typically argued in favour of self-regulation by the industry, a takeover code, and for a German corporate governance code. The latter was later backed up by law. Taken together, these activities have at least the potential to improve corporate governance in Germany. There can also hardly be any doubt that German investor protection has improved. The highly critical assessment of investor protection in Germany in the widely publicized work of La Porta *et al.* is not applicable today.[1] The series of financial market promotion acts has profoundly changed the legal protection of shareholders in general, and of minority shareholders in particular. Some observers argue that the legal framework defining investor protection in Germany is no longer materially different from the situation in the United Kingdom, for example.

So there is change. However, there is also continuity. As Rieckers and Spindler and Schmidt explain in their chapters, the German corporate governance system has always had very specific features which set it apart from that of the Anglo-American countries. German corporate governance is (de lege lata) not exclusively shareholder-oriented, but rather a stakeholder-oriented system, which reflects, among other things, the importance of bank financing for corporations. The stakeholder orientation has its roots in corporate law and in the de facto distribution of power in publicly held corporations. The board of managing directors is obliged by law to further the interests of several stakeholder groups and not merely those of their shareholders; it is monitored by a supervisory board in which power resides with a coalition of stakeholders, comprising banks, blockholders, employees, and, typically, former top managers. In many cases, the chairman is the former CEO. Genuine shareholders are not part of this coalition. In their survey in Chapter 2, Schmidt and Tyrell argue that the corporate governance system has been aligned with, or complementary to and consistent with, other elements of the traditional German bank-based financial system.

When looking at the developments of the past decade, which clearly strengthened the legal underpinnings of corporate governance in the sense of exposing management to more effective control by the supervisory board, and which strengthened shareholder protection, the question can be asked whether these changes have also altered the traditional logic of the German insider-controlled corporate governance system and possibly even replaced it by a market-based outsider-controlled and shareholders-only-oriented system. The

---

[1] We have tried to be careful with our words here since most lawyers and many economists in Germany regard the characterization of Germany's corporate governance in the La Porta *et al.* (2000) studies as inappropriate not only for today but also for the time span for which these authors claim to have collected data.

answer is negative. Neither the legal nor the de facto distribution of power has changed in a fundamental way. German corporate governance remains pluralistic, stakeholder-oriented and insider-controlled. Even the increased attention awarded to shareholder value might turn out to be more of a management fashion of the 1990s than a lasting orientation, although this is not really likely to be the case. Small shareholders or their representatives have not gained power and influence in supervisory boards of large corporations, and the expectation from early 2000 that Germany would soon develop a functioning market for corporate control, which had been inspired by the successful hostile bid of Vodafone for Mannesmann, has so far not been fulfilled. Eric Nowak adds to this account that some of the legal improvements in the field of investor protection still have to be implemented to become real.

In their Chapter 14 on the *role of accounting* in the German financial system, Christian Leuz and Jens Wüstemann grapple with the widespread belief that the accounting information in Germany is generally poor and of little value for investors and other decision-makers. The authors conclude that this belief is correct if seen from the perspective of outside investors, while it is incorrect if seen from the position of an inside investor as, for instance, a large shareholder or a large creditor. This type of financier typically plays a dominant role in Germany's corporate finance, often holding a seat on the supervisory board. Accounting rules, therefore, appear to be well adapted to the traditional institutional pattern. Board members, large investors, and large creditors receive substantially more information than is publicly available. Furthermore, accounting information may be less stringent simply because the general accounting rules applicable in Germany already constrain management behaviour. Dividend restrictions are a case in point. These restrictions in favour of creditors are specified as bond covenants in the United States, while no such individual stipulation is needed in Germany due to the appropriate general accounting rules.

Leuz and Wüstemann see two sources of change: the desire of large, internationally active companies to be present in the US capital market, and the harmonization of accounting standards across Europe. Both developments leave their mark in the current debate about accounting standards in Germany. Led by the German Accounting Standard Board, a general transition to IAS standards is being prepared, with special attention paid to the major pillars of German accounting rules. These pillars include the constraints on the distribution of corporate funds through the legal definition of profit, the principle of prudence, the valuation on the basis of 'objective' values, and the interpretation of specific accounting rules in the light of general accounting principles.

The authors conclude that the main thrust of change still lies ahead—it will not unfold unless the reporting incentives, that is, the financing patterns and the role of outside financiers in particular, changed substantially.

The chapter on accounting concludes the array of partial views, or views on elements and aspects, of the German financial system. The above summary has stressed the fact that we observe substantial change in the legal underpinnings as well as in business practice in almost every field—driven by a series of recent financial market promotion acts, with a strong impact on corporate governance, investor protection, banking and insurance markets, capital market infrastructure, M&A, and accounting. Notwithstanding these changes, we find the mechanics of the traditional system intact and merely adjusting to the changing environment. These traditional mechanics comprise the predominance of closely held firms, the importance of debt finance, the relevance of relationships on financial markets, the powerful role of other stakeholders, notably employees and creditors in corporate governance, and the reliance on defined benefit pay-as-you-go schemes for the provision of pensions and social security.

Clearly, the changes need time to be borne out by the data, that is, it takes a while before economic agents—enterprises and individuals, but also regulatory bodies—can properly adjust. In the next section we will try to guess where these adjustments are leading us.

15.3. LOOKING AHEAD: A DEBATE BETWEEN THREE POSITIONS

15.3.1. The Need to Look Ahead

In the last section we tried to answer the first of our questions which referred to the current state of the German financial system. As an important part of the answer, we would have liked to find support for a statement such as 'the German financial system has already changed its character' or 'it is in the middle of a transition', hopefully also specifying where the possible transition would lead us. But although the last section clearly supports the general conviction that there have indeed been many changes during the past six years, it does not permit us to make a general statement of the kind we would have liked to find. Some of the developments may be more apparent than real; others seem to be like the swings of a pendulum or the movement of the stock prices during the past half decade; some are changes which may improve the system but leave its basic structure intact, while some contain the seeds of a change towards a more capital market-oriented financial system. Thus, in order to better understand the current situation, we must explicitly address its future development. This is what we aim to do in this section.

However, here we face a difficulty. As the joint authors of this chapter as well as the editors of the book, we have discovered that we disagree on what we should write here. Since different readers will probably also disagree among themselves, and some readers will even find it difficult to adopt a particular position for themselves, we have decided to structure this section in the form of a debate between different positions on the development of the German financial system.

The future of financial systems in general and of the German financial system in particular is an extremely complex topic. We cannot even attempt to do justice to its full complexity here. Therefore, we have decided to present the three positions in a radically stylized way. We supplement our discussion with graphs which are based on the notion of a financial system being either bank-based or capital market-based—or more bank based or more market based—without, however, assuming for all three views that such a classification is indeed meaningful.

For presenting the three views, we will use a set of simple two-dimensional graphs.[2] On the *x*-axis, we show the extent to which a financial system is bank-based or market-based. The value along the *y*-axis shows a measure of welfare to which a financial system may lead, or its 'economic value'. Note that the purpose of these graphs is purely illustrative; we will, therefore, neither try to define the term 'welfare' with any precision nor discuss in detail what constitutes a bank-based and a market-based financial system. We hope that our intuition—and that of our readers—will suffice to imagine a dimension along which financial systems can be located, ranging from purely bank-based at one end of the scale (on the left) to purely market-based at the other (on the right). While the economic basis of the conventional typology and dichotomy of financial systems has been presented in Chapter 2, namely the twin concepts of complementarity and consistency, we want to emphasize here that, in principle, there may be more than two consistent configurations of financial system elements, or types of financial systems. The ordering of financial systems according to their degree of bank or capital market orientation should, of course, not be misunderstood as implying, for instance, that in a bank-based system capital markets are not present, or conversely that a capital-market-based system does not have a role for banks.

15.3.2. The Conventional 'Markets Only' View

To illustrate the use of our graphs and at the same time to introduce the view which we have called the 'markets only' view in the introduction to this chapter, we present Figure 15.1. The value line increases from left to right, which reflects the assumption of a general welfare improvement for all movements from a (more) bank-based to a (more) market-based financial system.

It may be argued that the developments of the late 1990s in Germany and elsewhere lend some credibility to this position. At that time the role of capital

---

[2] A more formal way of characterizing financial systems is presented in Hackethal and Schmidt (2000). The graph used here can be understood as a simplified two-dimensional adaptation of the more complex multidimensional representation, which, however also amounts to distinguishing financial systems by the degree to which they conform to the conventional notion of being bank-based or market-based.

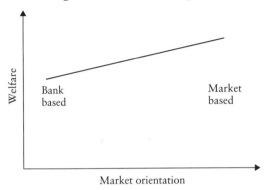

Figure 15.1. *Illustration of the 'markets only' view.*

markets increased greatly in Germany, and the capital market-based financial systems of the United States and the United Kingdom appeared to be extremely attractive models to follow.

Proponents of this view differ with respect to what constitutes the driving forces behind the recent shift towards more capital market orientation. Their suggestions range from technological advances, globalization and liberalization or European integration to the dynamics resulting from an increase in competition. Following Goldsmith (1969) and Rybczynski (1984), it may be assumed that there is a general tendency for financial systems to move 'from left to right', that is, to become more market-oriented over time. However, this in itself does not necessarily imply that more market orientation also means more welfare.

While the normative claim underlying Figure 15.1, as we have drawn it, namely that of a general superiority of a market-based system in welfare terms, is plausible and probably widely shared, not least among German policy-makers (Nawrath 2003), we are not aware of any theoretical or empirical work supporting it. In fact, comparing various welfare proxies in a large sample of countries and over an extended period, Beck and Levine (2000), among others, find no indication that either system is superior. In a similar vein, Allen and Gale (2000) present theoretical arguments to the effect that general welfare comparisons of the type expressed in Figure 15.1 cannot be made.

We accept the empirical and theoretical arguments and also do not advocate the 'markets only' view in a normative sense. Moreover, since we tend to think that efficiency might be a strong driving force behind the development of real-world financial systems, we also do not believe that the German financial system is changing from being (more) bank-based to being (more) capital market-based as a mere reflection of stronger pressure, which might arise from globalization and deregulation, to adopt an economically more efficient financial system.

15.3.3. The 'Banks-*or*-Markets' View—Efficiency at the Extremes (only)

The second position can be summarized as follows. Through the injection of a strong dose of capital market orientation, the previously consistent, bank-based German financial system had become inconsistent towards the end of the last millennium. With the end of the stock market boom, this development came to a standstill. As a consequence, inconsistency remained, and it has started to cause serious problems in various parts of the financial system, especially in the financial sector. This could be the situation which prevails at present. If this really is the situation—a statement which is hard or even impossible to prove, but which one can also not rule out given the current turmoil in the banking and insurance sectors in Germany—then the question arises as to what the future might bring.

As was pointed out in Chapter 2, it is extremely important in economic terms to have a 'good' financial system in place. According to the second view presented here, one standard for calling a financial system 'good' is that its elements are well adjusted to each other. And conversely, inconsistency of the financial system may bring with it serious economic disadvantages.

To a certain extent, the German financial system must get out of its present situation, and this can only happen if consistency is restored in some way. If only financial systems which are either largely bank-based or largely capital market-based can be consistent and able to offer the economic benefits which go together with consistency, then there are only two options. One option would appear to be a return to the bank-based system, and the other one the continuation of the transformation towards a capital market-based system. Nobody can safely say which of the two options would be better if they could be reached in the first place—and we certainly do not claim to know this either. However, this may not even be the choice facing us since in reality both are not equally attainable if it is true that we started from a situation of inconsistency after having had a largely consistent bank-based financial system for a long time.

The transition to a capital market-oriented system may, in fact, not yet have gone very far, but it may already have become irreversible. With sufficient external pressure to adopt a financial system which is consistent, there will be a further strengthening of capital market orientation. The endpoint of such a development would, it is hoped, be a full-blown capital market-based system. In the positive case, which is not unlikely, a fully developed market-based system is not only better than a system which is an inconsistent mixture of two systems, but is also better than the old consistent bank-based system. However, the possibility cannot be ruled out that the capital market-based financial system would be worse. Thus, there is a definite possibility of arriving at a new equilibrium—that is, a consistent financial system in Germany—which may be worse in economic terms than the one from which the system started not too long ago.

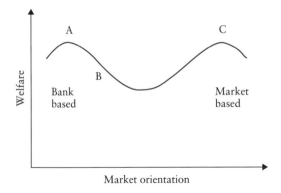

Figure 15.2. *Illustration of the 'banks-or-markets' view.*

Before we describe and differentiate this position in more detail, we want to present it in the form of the non-formal, intuitive graph introduced in the previous section. Figure 15.2 captures the 'banks-or-markets' view.

The graph of the function which relates potential economic benefit, or welfare, to financial sector characteristics has two peaks of about the same height, which represent the two types of financial systems. Both peaks are consistent configurations of financial system elements. The valley between the peaks is deep. This shape of the graph reflects the four assumptions of the position:

1. There are strong complementarities.
2. Consistency is important, or inconsistency can have serious negative effects.
3. There are two, and only two, peaks or types of financial systems.
4. The two consistent systems are indistinguishable with respect to their height or economic value.

Figure 15.2 shows what the proponents of this view would consider as the most important development of the past years.[3] They would argue that only a few years ago the German financial system was at point A, from where it moved in the direction of Point C in the years up to 2000. But the development stopped somewhere between the two peaks, possibly in the valley, and possibly at a point like B, that is, before even reaching the lowest point. As the

---

[3] Two more developments have occurred at the same time. One is that external factors have made the market system relatively more attractive. In Figure 15.2, this could be represented by a (slight) rotation of the graph, lifting its right side and possibly lowering the left side, but without making Point B higher than Point A. The other development is that the real German financial system has moved closer to its potential, that is, from a point 'somewhat' below A to a point closer to A. The individual chapters provide several arguments to support our belief that these developments have indeed occurred.

height of point B suggests, the inconsistency of a system like that of point B can be expected to have serious negative consequences.

However, it is precisely because of inconsistencies that a situation represented by point B is not sustainable. Both consistent points A and C would be improvements over B. Moving to point C would amount to a complete transformation of the German financial system, while moving to point A would require a complete reversal of the developments of the 1990s. However, such a reversal does not seem possible any more today. Thus the only possibility is a full transformation, starting from point B and aiming at point C, even though this may imply first 'wandering through a valley of tears' and then reaching a new peak which may turn out to be higher or lower than that of point A.

We now want to supplement this account of the past and the present and the view of possible future developments with some empirical material. In the second half of the 1990s, the formerly bank-based German financial system started to change and to become more capital market-oriented.

1. Measured along any conceivable scale, the stock market boom had reached its peak in early 2000. However, at that time there was no particular reason to assume that this was indeed a peak and not just a point somewhere on a long upward slope.
2. The two most important German private banks, Deutsche and Dresdner, were involved in serious merger talks that aimed at a transformation of these institutions into an investment bank, while at the same time selling the retail business to a competitor (Allianz, an insurance company).
3. The spectacular control contest between Mannesmann, a German telephone company, and Vodafone, a British rival, produced the first successful hostile takeover among large corporations in Germany, pointing in the direction of a fundamental change of the German corporate governance system.
4. At that time it was even conceivable that a clearly market-oriented takeover regulation would be accepted under pressure from Brussels, which would have nicely complemented the steps that had for some time already improved investor protection in Germany.

However, this process of modernization and transformation was half-hearted and is not yet complete. So far, it has stopped short of altering the legal duties of top managers to act in the sole interests of shareholders. It has not abolished codetermination, and it has left labour laws largely intact. In 2000 the capital market-friendly momentum stopped abruptly. Between March 2000 when it reached its peak, and March 2003, the German stock market has lost more than half of its value and most of its attraction for bankers as well as for the general public; the banking system has not been profoundly transformed; and the expected wave of hostile takeovers has not materialized. Instead of a shareholder-friendly takeover law, the German government introduced one which offered management ample protection, allowing them to take defensive measures in the case of a takeover threat. In fact, today one might even be inclined to think that after a short-lived outburst of modernity, the German financial system simply reverted to the way it used to be before the late 1990s.

In 2000 the development towards capital market orientation could have been expected to continue. If this had been the case, a relatively short transitory phase in which the German financial system was inconsistent, would probably not have mattered a great deal. However, the development until 2000 had made the German financial system lose its former consistency as a bank-based system without providing the benefit of a consistent, and therefore also well functioning capital market-based system. Inconsistency became a medium-term, if not even a long-term phenomenon, and as such it is a serious economic problem. There are many examples of inconsistency which could be cited here. One example is the evident contradiction between the widely held expectation that managers should act in the sole interest of shareholders and the fact that mandatory codetermination has not only remained untouched, but has also hardly been mentioned as something to be reconsidered. Another example is the transformation which the large private German banks have undergone in order to become 'real' investment banks, a burden which they seem to find hard to unload at present.

Extended and profound inconsistency can even lead to a crisis if it affects the basic structure or the functional mechanism of the financial system. And this seems to be the case in Germany. There are presently serious problems in the financial system, especially in the financial sector. We only mention three of them as they present themselves at the time of writing.

1. In order to regain investor confidence, the German Stock Exchange had to abolish its *Neuer Markt*, which had so to speak been the lighthouse of the boom period. In its place, a new market segment was introduced which may be quite similar in terms of substance, but seems to lack the glamour and the public recognition of the former *Neuer Markt*.
2. The cost and profitability problems of almost all big private banks have reached an unprecedented level in early 2003, which is believed by many to affect their lending business in a negative way and which has left its mark on the overall solvency assessment, as is evidenced by several rating downgrades. At the same time, the savings banks were able to expand their roles even further, particularly in the retail and the commercial banking segments. This may well have negative consequences for competition in the dominating regional and local banking markets in Germany.
3. Finally, the traditional de facto assurance of a steady and sufficient credit supply of the banks to their solvent business clients does not seem to hold any more; there are even indications of a credit crunch in Germany (Westermann 2003).

At least for capital market advocates, the transformation of German corporate governance must be a cause of frustration. It does not seem to have led to more outside monitoring of top management. On the contrary, there are now more former CEOs of DAX-30 companies chairing the supervisory board of their 'own' company than ever before. The situation seems to be especially severe in the financial industry. Only recently almost all former CEOs of the big banks and insurance conglomerates have moved to the helm of the supervisory board of the firms they used to manage.

Of course, there is no definite proof that these problems are linked in a causal way to the inconsistencies created by the half-hearted and stalled transformation of the German financial system, and perhaps such proof can never be provided. Seeing it this way implies an assessment, a proposition, perhaps even a speculation, hopefully a well-founded one. It rests on the assumption that complementarity is strong in the financial system and that therefore consistency of the system is very important, perhaps more than the question of whether a country's financial system is bank-based or capital market-based. What this account of the past and the present suggests for the future has already been explained above. What needs to be added are the arguments for our assumption that the events of the past are irreversible.

The external developments of the late 1990s mentioned above might simply make the old system unattainable. For instance, the influence of international investors and international banks cannot be reversed, given the attempts of the European Union to create a level playing field throughout Europe. This may apply with even greater force to the dis-solution, or at least the weakening, of the close ties which used to exist between banks and their business clients and between the various institutions forming the financial sector and for whose functioning long-time acquaintance and trust are extremely important. As has often been reported informally, various big banks have not only competed, but also cooperated. In the case of the near-bankruptcy of a large client the willingness of various banks to mix competition and cooperation is clearly important. The recent insolvency cases of Holzmann and Kirch suggest that this attitude has become more difficult today. All of these recent developments make it unlikely that the old bank-based financial system will be restored without serious alteration. This completes the argument behind the banks-or-markets-view. Its prediction is that the German financial system is likely to become capital market-based in the future, quite irrespective of a possible superiority of a market-based system; and the transition to this possible new equilibrium is going to be quite difficult.[4]

---

[4] The argument is developed in more detail in Schmidt and Spindler (2002).

15.3.4. The 'Banks-*and*-Markets' View—Efficiency between the Poles

The preceding section explored the idea that all efficient financial systems ought to be 'pure' systems, either bank-based or market-based, and that there are welfare losses associated with middle-of-the-road financial system development. In this subsection we develop a contrasting viewpoint, stressing the potential welfare gains from an efficient blending of financial institutions and markets. We call this the 'banks-and-markets' view. This view may not only be descriptively correct, but also be relevant with respect to policy implications for management and regulators in Germany.

The basic hypothesis is that the financial pattern of any economy is a function of its underlying legal infrastructure. Some recent literature has stressed the idea that differences in financial infrastructures are rooted in differences in legal traditions, most prominently those of British common law and French (and German) civil law. While the former develops according to judiciary decisions on a case-by-case basis, the latter is based on a comprehensive codified framework, which is set (and amended) by parliament or other legislative bodies (e.g. La Porta *et al.* 1998; and Beck *et al.* 2002).

While our understanding of financial system comparison has greatly improved due to the studies carried out in this literature, we are not convinced that distinct legal traditions are the clue to comparative financial system analysis. The reason is twofold. First, as Rajan and Zingales (2003) have shown, the evidence presented by the 'legal traditionalists' is consistent in a particular cross section, but it is not stable over time (while legal tradition is stable). To catch a glimpse of Rajan and Zingales' argument, we have compiled Table 15.1 from various tables in their 2003 article.

Table 15.1. *Selected summary statistics of financial market development in the United States and in Germany before and after the World Wars, that is, in 1913, in 1950, and in 1999*

	1913		1950		1999	
	US	Germany	US	Germany	US	Germany
Stock market capitalization over GDP	0.39	0.44	0.33	0.15	1.52	0.67
# of listed companies per million people	4.75	27.96	8.94	13.22	28.88	12.74
Ratio of deposits to GDP	0.33	0.53	0.40	0.15	0.17	0.35

Source: Compiled from Rajan and Zingales (2003: tables 2, 3, and 5).

It shows that the size of stock markets and corporate bond markets relative to GDP has changed dramatically, both in each country over time as well as between countries.

Before the First World War, the stock market capitalization as a percentage of GDP was more important in Germany than in the United States. This relationship reversed after the Second World War, when German market cap was less than half, in relative terms, of that in the United States. Since then, this gap has widened even further. A similar picture emerges when the number of companies listed on a stock exchange is considered, relative to the size of the population. It turns out that not only the relevant figure for Germany was higher than the US figure in 1913 (actually six times as high), but it was also as high as the US figure almost a century later. Over the same period, however, the German figure has more than halved, again reversing the relative numbers between 1913 and 1999. Finally, the ratio of deposits to GDP, as a proxy of the importance of financial intermediation via banks, is hump shaped for the United States (increasing between 1913 and 1950, then falling below the 1913 level), while it is trough shaped in the case of Germany (decreasing between 1913 and 1950, and rising thereafter). The authors conclude from their analysis that the relationship between legal tradition and market development is unstable over time, calling into question the validity of the legal tradition view.

The third view builds on this earlier work and emphasizes the concept of core legal rules, an unorthodox variant of the legal tradition argument. These core rules are clusters of legal attributes (rules, provisions, and practices) with a strong and lasting influence on the opportunity set of investors and creditors. These clusters can, and typically will, differ considerably from country to country, sometimes with no close connection to a particular legal tradition. Core legal rules develop over time, producing different paths. Each financial system (comprising an accounting system, a disclosure policy, a particular set of financial intermediaries, a certain level and a particular efficiency of primary and secondary stock market trading, and so on) will try to adjust optimally to the underlying set of core legal rules.

The relevance of the core legal rules derives from their impact on the decision-making of firms and individuals, shaping conflict resolution *ex post*, and influencing contractual design *ex ante*. There is probably only a small number of these core legal rules at any particular point in time. One core legal rule that has attracted much attention in the literature is investor protection, describing a set of rules which allows people who are not well informed and non-organized to trust products and services in an anonymous market place (see La Porta *et al.* 1998; and Nowak, this volume). A second core legal rule is the bankruptcy code, which has attracted much less attention in the financial economics literature to date (see Elsas and Krahnen in this volume for details). These two core legal rules affect the *ex ante* incentives of market participants. More precisely, both core legal rules exert a strong influence on investment decisions and on financial contracting. Investor protection is fundamental for the development

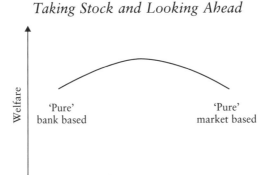

Figure 15.3. *Illustration of the 'banks-and-markets' view.*

of financial markets. A high level of investor protection lowers transaction costs, thereby facilitating direct financial links—debt and equity—between firms and households. Other things being equal, a high degree of investor protection tends to increase the share of market financing relative to intermediary-based financing. The bankruptcy code, in contrast, is formative for the emergence and the functional role of financial intermediaries. A strong bankruptcy code defines the legal rights of all claimholders and their covenants in a clear, easy-to-anticipate way, leaving little room for discretion or renegotiations. A strong code is formative for the emergence of financial intermediaries and for their share in overall corporate and household financing. It reduces the costs of intermediation, limits the costs associated with claim collection and, in the case of corporate distress, it reduces the costs of transfer of control from the owners to the lenders. Ongena and Smith (2000) have found that firms maintain more bank relationships, on average, in countries with inefficient judicial systems and poor enforcement of creditor rights.

Figure 15.3 summarizes this line of thought. In contrast to the view presented in Figure 15.2, there is now a maximum achievable welfare level for any particular set of core legal rules. The welfare line is an efficient frontier, which is reached when all agents and institutions in an economy adjust their choices and contracts optimally to the given set of core legal rules.

Depending on the specific content of the core legal rules, an economy will find itself more or less bank-oriented or market-oriented. The humped shape of the welfare line entails a proposition, namely the belief that a middle-of-the-road system, which efficiently combines arm's length market interaction with long-term relationship interaction, has the potential to reach a higher welfare level than those of 'conventional' bank-based or market-based financial systems. Of course, like the 'banks-or-markets' view, this is also merely a conjecture at this point.

The 'banks-and-markets' view represented in Figure 15.3 is particularly suited for assessing the situation in Germany. Arguably, the reason for this is obvious. Germany has a strong tradition of relationship banking, comprising the lending business (see Elsas and Krahnen in this volume for details on the real effects of relationship lending), the deposit business (see Maurer in this volume on the large and stable share of deposits in total household investment; and Worms in this volume on the loyalty of bank customers, both retail and corporate, to their local financial institution), the investment business (see Maurer in this volume on the dominant role of bank-owned investment vehicles in the funds market), and even the trading of stocks and bonds (see Theissen in this volume for the formative influence of banks on the trading process, and Franzke, *et al.* in this volume for their influence on the retarded IPO-activity). Despite this tradition, the importance of financial markets has risen consistently over the past 10 years. The increase in market orientation is again evident from many areas of finance, notably the growth of the investment fund industry, the reliance on market valuation in management remuneration, the emergence of a corporate bond market, and the widespread participation in the IPO business during the internet boom.

In the remainder of this section we want to explore whether a greater reach of financial markets in Germany will eventually crowd out relationships. Our argument builds on a tentative explanation of the role of relationships and markets in Germany. Why have relationships developed around corporate lending and retail saving, and what drives the widely observed growth of markets in this country? In line with the explanation underlying Figure 15.3, the development of relationships can be traced to a particular design of the German legal infrastructure, namely its strong reliance on creditor protection. In contrast, the inroads made by markets seem to be caused by the widespread loss of confidence in a tax-based, defined benefit pension system. Growing concern over the true value of pension claims has created a sense of uncertainty, and thus induced a demand for individual risk sharing, absent in earlier periods. The challenge we are currently witnessing, therefore, is the encounter of relationship underwriting (i.e. providing insurance and financial smoothing services, using an intermediary's balance sheet) with a fair value orientation (supporting general risk spreading and risk trading on a secondary market). A number of recent innovations suggest that this challenge will eventually be mastered, and will actually strengthen the stability of the financial system as a whole. Let us review the argument in greater detail.

First, what explains the fact that relationships have developed around corporate lending and retail saving? In line with our stylized theory about the formative role of core legal principles, we expect to observe the emergence of long-term relationships between borrowers and lenders if and only if the bankruptcy code provides a safe heaven for private contractual relations. This is exactly what we find in Germany, where creditor rights are almost sacrosanct and courts are not supposed to intervene, or to redefine property rights *ex post* (see Elsas and Krahnen in this volume for details on the German bankruptcy code). The strong role of creditors has allowed long-term implicit relationships to evolve.

Second, what drives the recent growth of markets in the German financial architecture? Again, we give a speculative answer to this phenomenon that has puzzled many observers of the German economy. For a long time, probably since the Great Depression in the early thirties of the last century, and originating even further back from Bismarck's legislation on social security of the 1870s, the country has seen an ever-increasing reliance on organized, comprehensive income smoothing. The most important factors in this context are state pensions, together with an array of institutionalized hedges against the individual hazards of life, like unemployment and disability. Still today, the major portion of a representative German household's wealth consists of the present value of the state pension claim, typically surpassing private pension assets by far. Miegel (1983) estimates the average social security wealth ('Versorgungsvermögen') to account for 55 per cent of net household wealth (50 per cent quantile of households, according to net household wealth), and for 30 per cent with respect to the upper half of the population. These numbers have probably not changed much since then.[5]

The pension formula has been held constant for a long time, since it is considered to be a politically sensitive issue. This formula ties the benefit title to the average income over the last three years of a working life. These years are typically the best paid years in a worker's life, allowing the state pension to remain close to the after-tax income level of these last years (which, by construction, is higher than the average income over the entire working life). The refinancing of these claims is done via a pay-as-you-go system, which typically levies in proportion to income. Currently, these levies are set at 19.5 per cent of gross employment income (2003), up from 18 per cent (1980). Due to the trust placed in this pension system, the accumulation of private pension wealth has remained small over the past 50 years (see Maurer, this volume for details on private savings accumulation in Germany).

However, apart from the incentives for private capital formation, the economy has also lacked the positive externalities emerging from asset allocation choices made by private investors. This is the reason why the stock market in Germany has largely remained the playground of a relatively small social strata, with little interest from the rest of the population in market values and private wealth management. A further consequence of the guaranteed state pension has been the widespread denial of personal risks. In fact, it became an obsession in Germany to establish transfers of all sorts in order to nullify the realization of personal chances and risks. For instance, the pension formula is such that the standard deviation of pension income is considerably smaller than the standard deviation of personal income. Other examples can

---

[5] We thank Holger Stein (2003) for allowing us to draw on his (unpublished) dissertation on social security wealth in Germany.

be found in the fields of unemployment benefits, and health insurance. Only in the 1990s did a serious public debate begin about the stability of the state pension system. With the adverse demographics typical for Western Europe, it is by now widely recognized that the state pension system is under enormous pressure, and will almost surely have to curtail its benefits to some broadly accepted social minimum before long. Today, this development has resulted in risk bearing and risk sharing ranking higher on the public interest agenda in Germany than ever before.

Taken together, these and other developments are starting to force individuals to take personal decisions relating to capital market valuation in general and to portfolio choice in particular. Even if a defined benefit pension may still be the most desired product, in the world of 2003 people have to make appropriate financial choices, that is, they have to select financial instruments that offer the desired properties. And by selecting from a set of alternatives, households as well as financial institutions are forced to recognize the opportunity costs of defined benefit plans. We, therefore, believe that the inroad of markets in the German relationship-cum-smoothing economy is only the beginning of a secular trend, which will foster a much larger capital market than today. This answers our second question about what drives the growth of markets. From this explanation it follows directly that proponents of the third view firmly believe that capital markets will grow much more in the near future. The interesting follow-up question is, whether they will do so at the expense of relationships. This brings us to our third question: What is the cumulative effect of markets and relationships on financing patterns—in particular, do markets crowd out relationships?

Relationships, we argued earlier, could prosper in Germany due to the existence of uncontested creditor rights, a core legal principle. Financial market growth, on the other hand, is strongly enhanced by the expected distress of a tax-based, pay-as-you-go pension system. In line with this latter development, investor protection, another core legal rule, had to be strengthened and has indeed been strengthened over the past few years (see Nowak, this volume). If, at the same time, the strength of creditor rights is maintained, the resulting adjustments in market and banking activities may actually improve welfare. When is this likely to happen?

We see these adjustments already under way. Here are some examples of recent innovations that tilt the system towards market orientation while, at the same time, maintaining its relationship capital. Assuming best practice, these innovations may also improve resource allocation as well as the risk sharing capabilities of the financial system as a whole.

15.3.4.1. *Example 1: credit derivatives and the market for loans*
Over the past years, German banks have started to sell the risks contained in loan portfolios, relying on credit default swaps, and on collateralized debt obligations (CDO). The size of the world credit derivatives market today has

been estimated by the British Bankers Association at US$2 trillion (year end 2002), with an expected growth rate of 40–50 per cent for the next two years. In CDO transactions, claims are structured according to default risk, resulting in several layers that differ with respect to their rating. Typically, there is a large AAA-tranche, a much smaller mezzanine tranche, and a small equity tranche. Tailoring the sizes of these tranches, and allocating them to market participants makes all the difference. Due to the ubiquity of relationship lending in Germany, the size and the allocation of the equity tranche is believed to be of great importance for pricing. The challenge is to design the tranches carefully enough in order not to destroy the positive externalities associated with relationship lending, that is, not to destroy the incentives of the lending institution to collect information, and not to destroy its incentives to engage in workout activities should a company whose loan has been securitized be in trouble one day. These relationship-based considerations also put a limit on the amount of risk that can actually be transferred from the intermediaries to the markets, using these instruments. The same argument explains the type of risk that can be transferred to the market and spread among investors, namely relationship-insensitive risks, such as catastrophe risks and the risk of extreme events, causing simultaneous price changes across markets. This latter category of financial markets risk poses a particular threat to an economy because a concurrent loss of value across different asset classes typically renders intermediaries unable to offer liquidity insurance, or short term letters of credit. If left alone, financial intermediaries will then not be able to provide liquidity insurance even to their relationship borrowers. The only scenario in which *Hausbanks* remain capable of offering short term bridge loans despite a concurrent fall in asset prices is when there is reinsurance provided by a solvent business partner. More specifically, if investors (like mutual funds) take over extreme risks (like the risk resulting from a sudden synchronous movement of asset prices), intermediaries preserve their ability to offer stand-by facilities. Properly engineered, CDOs and CDSs (credit default swaps) will achieve exactly this. They will help to leverage the merits of relationship lending by allowing tail risks (extreme risks) to be shared among a broad investor base. By implication, banks that engage in credit securitization and default swaps will eventually hold more risk per unit of capital rather than less.

An additional advantage of such a development may be an increased stability of financial institutions, and a reduced systemic risk, owing to the exclusion of a particular class of credit risk, namely extreme or tail risk. Note that the risks resulting from catastrophes, or from the co-movement of asset prices across the board, will then be borne by investors in the prime credit segments, that is, the investment grade market for collateralized debt obligations. The evolution of this market has desirable systemic features, as outlined above, which are probably larger in countries where corporation finance relies on relationship lending rather than on arm's length lending.

15.3.4.2. Example 2: fair value accounting of financial instruments
Accounting standards worldwide seem to be converging to the IAS book of rules (see Leuz and Wüstemann, this volume). A cornerstone of these new accounting rules is fair value accounting, a true and fair evaluation of financial assets relying on the assessment of a secondary market. While this valuation principle is easy to apply for instruments that trade on an active secondary market, like stocks and bonds, it is much harder to apply to non-traded assets. Take the corporate loan book as an example. There is typically no secondary market for corporate loans. This is particularly true for relationship loans, since this type of lending involves private information. This information, which is the source of value in the lending relationship, cannot easily be transmitted to third parties in a market place, due to conflicts of interest. Consequently, the market price of a financial asset subject to relationship specificity (like a bank loan in Germany) will not reflect the value of the relationship itself. In fact, the higher the value of private information in a relationship, the bigger the wedge between the value of a claim in a bank's loan book, that is, its primary market price, and its secondary market value. To the extent that relationship lending is an important part of a financial institution's activities, the wedge will actually be proportional to the franchise value of the bank. In a lending relationship, the more value that is added through private information and monitoring, the smaller is this loan's fair market value relative to the expected value on the balance sheet. In other words, if relationship lending matters, fair market values will be downward biased estimates of the expected value of the claims as seen by the lender.

Fair market values tend to understate the value of a relationship loan, whereas they tend to state it correctly in the case of an arm's length loan (like a corporate bond). Since relationship lending plays an important role in Germany (and possibly other countries as well), the introduction of fair value accounting poses a threat to it. The more involved they are in relationship affairs, the higher will be the requirement to write down asset values. It is, therefore, not surprising that financial institutions in countries with this type of system put up a fierce struggle against the introduction of these new accounting principles, as evidenced by the ongoing debate in Germany.

A simple way out, which has already entered the debate, would be to allow financial institutions to carry the difference between the nominal value of a claim and its fair market value as an asset (i.e. to activate the wedge as a special goodwill asset), which would probably make fair value accounting acceptable even to the traditional accounting community. At the same time, it will give the market an observable measure of relationship activities delivered by the intermediaries. In other words, fair value accounting may be an effective instrument for communicating to the market the value of relationship lending. The transparency on relationship goodwill may well facilitate further invest-ment in relationship management, rather than seeing it as a cost factor alone. As in the first example, an intelligent blending of relationships with the pricing transparency produced by markets may well enhance the value of relationships, rather than destroying it.

There are other areas in a financial system that rely on relationships, and will probably be significantly affected by growth in the size and scope of financial markets. An important example is the reinsurance industry, which is of notable weight within the German financial system. We can develop arguments similar to the ones on relationship lending that support the general hypothesis of synergies between relationship underwriting on the balance sheet of an intermediary and fair value pricing and risk spreading on a market.

15.3.5. Summing Up

The above discussion on financial system development in Germany suggests three possible paths. One is that the German financial system is simply undergoing a modernization process, which will ultimately lead to the adoption of a (more) market-oriented and also economically more efficient financial system. For advocates of this view, the current events are to be viewed as regrettable interruptions of a development which in the longer term cannot and should not be stopped.

According to the second view, which we call the 'banks-or-markets' view, the medium to long-term development will be such that the inconsistencies in the financial system which we observe at present will be resolved. In principle, this might lead the German financial system either back to its previous state, namely a largely consistent bank-based system, or to a fully developed market-based system which to a greater extent is indistinguishable from that of the United States and the United Kingdom. *A priori*, it would be impossible to assess which of the two development paths would be more attractive. However, this is only the answer in principle. In fact, it seems that it would not be possible to return to the old system, since the events of the last half decade have destroyed the basis of behavioural patterns and expectations which the traditional system requires for its proper functioning. Therefore, what we can really expect for the future is a transition to a strongly market-based system, even though this system might turn out to be economically less attractive than the bank-based system and even though the social costs of transition might be very high. Half-hearted reforms, as we have witnessed in the past, will not suffice and might only prolong the disadvantages of having a system with grave inconsistencies.

According to the third view, the 'banks-and-markets' view, we can hope for the emergence of a mixed financial system, which is also efficient in economic terms. If done carefully and consciously, that is, if the strengthening of investor rights does not go hand in hand with a weakening of creditor rights, and if the investment in relationships is consistently maintained, then a new division of roles between markets and financial intermediaries is likely to emerge. According to this new division of roles, underwriting is a direct function of agency costs and incomplete contracting, and is intended to bond the intermediary *vis-à-vis* its bondholders and depositors. On the other hand, there are markets ready to take over non-relationship specific risks, such as systematic or systemic risks. Allowing underwriting (on the balance sheet) by intermediaries and market-wide risk sharing to work hand in hand may well contribute to the efficiency and even to the stability of the entire financial system. It will also facilitate the maintenance of long-term relationships in corporate finance and retail business despite the growth of markets for corporate bonds and asset backed securities. The view on the German financial system from a 'banks-and-markets' perspective leads to the more general conclusion that, for the purpose of understanding financial architecture, as well as for system stability assessment, relationships should be combined with markets. Indeed, the significance of relationship underwriting can be combined with a strong development of asset markets. If this is the correct view of the future, this future may seem less worrying than that suggested by the second view—and less sanguine than that suggested by the first view. In any event, the future will come, and we look forward to seeing which of the three views will turn out to be true.

At this point we have come full circle. In the first chapter, laying out the agenda for the book, we wanted to understand the financial architecture of a prototype bank-oriented system. Now, after having looked into various segments of the system, we conclude that its future quality may well depend on the operation of the markets—be it in the form of a market-based or a hybrid system. It seems important that market participants and policy-makers, both in the legislative and in regulatory bodies, develop an understanding of the interrelationships stressed by both the second and the third views. Financial system efficiency and stability depend on consistency, either in the sense of consistency and complementarity or on a consistent formulation of the core legal framework suited to mitigate the inherent tension between relationships and markets. We are convinced that these aspects will play a particularly prominent role in the further development of the German financial system.

References

Allen, F., and Gale, D. (2000). *Comparing Financial Systems*. Cambridge: MIT Press.

Beck, T., and Levine, R. (2000). 'New Firm Formation and Industry Growth: Does Having a Market- or Bank-Based System Matter?', World Bank Working Paper 2383.

——, Demirgüc-Kunt, A., and Levine, R. (2002). 'Law and Finance: Why Does Legal Origin Matter?', NBER Working Paper 9379.

Goldsmith, R. (1969). *Financial Structure and Economic Development*. New Haven: Yale University Press.

Hackethal, A. and Schmidt, R. H. (2000). 'Finanzsystem und Komplementaritaet, *Kredit und Kapital*, Special Issue 15, Neue Finanzielle Arrangements: Markte in Umbruch, 53–102.

La Porta, R., Lopez-de-Silanes, F., Shleifer, A., and Vishny, R. (1998). 'Law and Finance', *Journal of Political Economy*, 106: 1113–55.

——, ——, ——, and —— (2000). 'Investor Protection and Corporate Governance', *Journal of Financial Economics*, 58: 3–28.

Miegel, M. (1983). *Die verkannte Revolution—Band 1: Einkommen und Vermögen der privaten Haushalte*. Stuttgart: Bonn Aktuell.

Nawrath, A. (2003). 'Rahmenbedingungen für den Finanzplatz Deutschland: Ziele und Aufgaben der Politik, insbesondere des Bundesministeriums der Finanzen', Working Paper, Institute for Law and Finance, University of Frankfurt.

Ongena, S., and Smith, D. (2000). 'What determines the number of bank relationships? Cross-country evidence', *Journal of Financial Intermediation*, 9: 26–56.

Rajan, R., and Zingales, L. (2003). 'The Great Reversals: The Politics of Financial Development in the 20th Century', *Journal of Financial Economics*, forthcoming.

Rybczynski, T. (1984). 'Industrial Financial Systems in Europe, U.S. and Japan', *Journal of Economic Behaviour and Organization*, 5: 275–86.

Schmidt, R. H. and Spindler, G. (2002). 'Path Dependence, Complementarity and Corporate Governance', *International Finance*, Vol. 5: 311–33.

Stein, H. (2003). *Vermögen in Deutschland—Anatomie der Vermögensverteilung in der Bundesrepublik Deutschland zwischen 1983 und 1998*. Unpublished doctoral dissertation, University of Frankfurt.

Westermann, F. (2003). 'Zur Kreditklemme: Ein Vergleich zwischen Deutschland und Japan', *ifo-Schnelldienst* 1/2003.

List of Websites

LEGISLATIVE, EXECUTIVE AND JUDICATIVE INSTITUTIONS AND SUPERVISORY UNITS FOR FINANCIAL MARKETS AND FINANCIAL INTERMEDIARIES

German Ministry of Finance
www.bundesfinanzministerium.de

Federal Financial Supervisory Authority
www.bafin.de

Bundesbank
www.bundesbank.de

European Central Bank
www.ecb.int

German Finance Agency
www.deutsche-finanzagentur.de

Federal Cartel Office
www.bundeskartellamt.de

RESEARCH INSTITUTIONS

Center for Financial Studies
www.ifk-cfs.de

Department of Finance at Goethe Universität Frankfurt
www.finance.uni-frankfurt.de

Pension Finance
www.pension-finance.de

Deutsches Aktieninstitut
www.dai.de

IMF (Institute for mid-cap research)
www.ifm-bonn.de

NEWSPAPER

Börsenzeitung
www.boersen-zeitung.com

Financial Times Deutschland
www.ftd.de

Financial Times
www.ft.com

Frankfurter Allgemeine Zeitung
www.faz.de

Handelsblatt
www.handelsblatt.de

GENERAL ECONOMIC DATA

Federal Statistical Office Germany
www.destatis.de

ASSOCIATIONS OF BANKS

Association of German banks (private banks)
www.bankenverband.de

Association of credit co-operatives
www.bvr.de

Association of Savings banks and Landbanks
dsgv:de

Association of public banks
www.voeb.de

ASSOCIATIONS OF NON-BANK FINANCIAL INTERMEDIARIES

Associations of Insurance Firms
www.gdv.de

Associations of Investment Firms and Venture Capital Firms
www.bvi.de

ASSOCIATION OF CREDIT BUREAUS

Association of Creditreform
www.creditreform.de

FINANCIAL MARKETS AND RELATED SERVICES

Deutsche Börse Group
www.deutsche-boerse.com

Eurex
www.eurexchange.com/index.html

Deutsches Aktieninstitut
www.dai.de

Deutsche Gesellschaft für Ad-hoc-Publizität (DGAP)
www.dgap.com

EURO AD HOC
www.euroadhoc.com

The World Federation of Exchanges
www.world-exchanges.org

The International Organization of Securities Commissions
www.iosco.org

ACCOUNTING

Standard setters:
www.iasb.org.uk
www.fasb.org
www.drsc.de

The European Federation of Accountants (FEE)
www.fee.be

German Auditors' Institute
www.idw.de

MERGERS AND ACQUISITIONS

Mergers and Acquisitions
www.mergers-and-acquisitions.de

The Takeover Panel
www.thetakeoverpanel.org.uk

German Corporate Governance Code
www.corporate-governance-code.de

VENTURE CAPITAL

Federal Ministry of Economics and Technology
www.bmwi.de

National Venture Capital Association (NVCA)
www.nvca.org

IMF (Institute for mid-cap research)
www.ifm-bonn.de

Venture Economics
www.ventureeconomics.com

LEGAL INSTITUTIONS AND RELATED SERVICES

German Ministry of Justice
www.bmj.de

German Court of Justice
www.bundesgerichtshof.de

Court of Justice of the European Communities
www.curia.eu.int

EU-Directives
europa.eu.int/comm/internal_market/reporting-company_en.htm

Index